£23 · 50

THE POEMS OF ALEXANDER POPE
VOLUME VI
MINOR POEMS

The Twickenham Edition of the Poems of Alexander Pope

★

GENERAL EDITOR: JOHN BUTT

★

ALEXANDER POPE
Marble Bust by L. F. Roubillac
Shipley Art Gallery, Gateshead-on-Tyne

ALEXANDER POPE

MINOR POEMS

*

Edited by
NORMAN AULT

Completed by
JOHN BUTT

LONDON: METHUEN & CO. LTD
NEW HAVEN: YALE UNIVERSITY PRESS

REPRINTED WITH MINOR CORRECTIONS 1964
REPRINTED 1970
REPRODUCED AND PRINTED IN GREAT BRITAIN BY
REDWOOD PRESS LIMITED
TROWBRIDGE & LONDON
SBN 416 47750 X
1.2

PREFACE

WHEN Norman Ault died in 1950, he had been occupied with this edition of Pope's Minor Poems at intervals for seventeen years. During the whole of this time I had been closely associated with him, and since I knew perhaps more of his intentions than others of his friends, it fell to me to complete his unfinished book. Much of it was ready for the printer; even the introduction was in draft; and I was especially pleased to find a list of those many persons to whom Mr Ault wished to make public acknowledgement of the help they had given him.

But though much was in final form, several problems had been left for further consideration, and several portions needed rewriting after the publication of Mr Ault's last book, *New Light on Pope*. One or two authentic poems have since been discovered, and one or two recent publications have illuminated what had hitherto been dark. Detailed revision was therefore required; but it has not been considered desirable to distinguish the reviser's work from Mr Ault's, since no line can be firmly drawn between revision and the task of a general editor.

The first duty of an editor of Pope's Minor Poems is to determine the canon. Mr Ault brought to this task unrivalled knowledge of eighteenth-century poetical miscellanies, tirelessness in the search for evidence, and acuteness in argument, qualities with which readers of *Pope's Own Miscellany* and *New Light on Pope* are familiar. In those books he made the best case he could for attributing to Pope certain poems of doubtful authorship. He hoped to draw the fire of other students, and to profit, in determining the canon, from their observations; but death prevented him from reconsidering his tentative conclusions. The decision on admitting a poem to the canon has therefore rested with the reviser of his work. I have followed Mr Ault's policy of admitting no poem unless the balance of evidence points to Pope's authorship. But in the reading of evidence we cannot count on general agreement. I have relegated to an appendix a few poems which at one time Mr Ault believed to be canonical; but in each case I have left the evidence to speak for itself, and the reader is therefore at liberty to reinstate poems which

v

I have discarded. Cautiousness in defining the canon is what every editor owes to his author. It is particularly necessary in the editor of a poet who set himself a high standard of correctness. Mr Ault recognized this, and readers may perhaps share the reviser's admiration of the care and patience with which the credentials of the most familiar and long accepted poems have been scrutinized. It is there that Mr Ault showed his most distinguished qualities as an editor.

J. B.

POSTSCRIPT

A reprint of the first edition being required, the opportunity has been taken to make certain minor corrections and additions without altering the original pagination. The discovery of the autograph manuscript of Pope's version of Boethius (p. 73) and of a photograph of the lost autograph of his "Impromptu, to Lady Winchelsea" (p. 120) revealed a few revisions that needed making. A couplet previously overlooked has been recorded on p. 406. Some misapprehensions and errors pointed out by correspondents and by writers in learned journals (to all of whom I am grateful) have been corrected. The arguments of those few scholars who have addressed themselves to canonical questions have not succeeded in convincing me that the apocrypha should be either enlarged or reduced.

J. B.

Edinburgh, 1964

CONTENTS

* On the significance of the asterisk, see Introduction, p. xiii.

1*

* * *

Frontispiece: ALEXANDER POPE. From the Marble Bust by L. F.
Roubillac
   (*Reproduced by kind permission of the Curators, Shipley Art Gallery,*
   Gateshead-on-Tyne)

INTRODUCTION

I

WHEN Pope published the first collected edition of his *Works*
in 1717, he included besides his major poems thirteen shorter
pieces under the heading "Miscellanies on Several Occasions". He
took a similar opportunity of collecting occasional pieces when the
second volume of the *Works* appeared in 1735 and when the octavo
editions were published during the next five years. By this means
he garnered some forty of his shorter poems for official recognition.
Many more had been written, and several of them had been given
a kind of bastard recognition in the miscellanies which Pope edited
from time to time, notably *Poems on Several Occasions* (1717) and the
Pope-Swift *Miscellanies* (1727 and 1732). Pope's first editor, War-
burton, devoted half of his sixth volume to "Miscellaneous Pieces
in Verse", amounting, with the occasional poems published in his
first five volumes, to fifty-three pieces in all. Of these, four had not
previously been printed and five had been published anony-
mously; two more were not by Pope. In attempting to determine
the canon Warburton thus set an example, to be followed by almost
every succeeding editor, of printing newly discovered works from
manuscript, of recognizing Pope's hand in anonymous pieces, and
of adding unwittingly to the apocrypha.

The first steps in determining the canon are not difficult to take.
To those poems which Pope publicly acknowledged by including
them in his *Works* must be added those (such as "A Hymn Written
in Windsor Forest") which he privately acknowledged, those (such
as "Verses in Imitation of Cowley. By a Youth of Thirteen") which
he tacitly acknowledged by attributing them to "the same Hand"
as authentic poems, and those (such as "A Roman Catholick Ver-
sion of the First Psalm") about whose authorship he admitted to
have "equivocated pretty genteely". Another group of unques-
tionably canonical poems is that of which corrected holographs
still survive. Examples of these are "The Court Ballad" and "The
Six Maidens". This is as far as an editor can go with complete
security; and to denote poems in these groups an asterisk is used in
the list of contents.

But though some measure of doubt attaches to the credentials of all other poems, that measure varies from a scruple which the most conservative editor may safely neglect to a weight which only the most rash will overlook. In each instance the decision will rest upon the value of supporting testimony, external evidence drawn from previous attributions and from the occasion of the poem, internal evidence of allusions and of style, and evidence from the nature of the text itself. Thus the existence of a poem in Pope's autograph is not of itself sufficient proof of his authorship, for the manuscript may be no more than his transcription of another poet's work. But if there are corrections in the holograph, these may be taken to imply a draft at which he had been working. Or if a poem in his autograph was attributed to him by his contemporaries (*e.g.*, "Sandys's Ghost" and "The Capon's Tale"), and the attribution is supported by internal evidence, the poem is admitted to the canon, but without the complete assurance which an asterisk implies.

A contemporary attribution is not accepted unless it is supported by other evidence. Though the assertions of such close associates as Warburton and the Earl of Oxford cannot be lightly set aside, they were liable to error, and in at least two instances Warburton was mistaken. Where Warburton's assertion is circumstantial and supported by external and internal evidence, as in "On receiving from the Right Hon. the Lady Frances Shirley a Standish and two Pens", the credentials of the poem are very strong. But even where internal evidence of style alone supports his assertion (as in "Verbatim from Boileau") this is taken as sufficient evidence for admission to the canon.

Stylistic evidence alone has not been used in this edition to attribute a poem to Pope, but it is constantly used in support of other evidence. It has also been used (as in "Dawley Farm") to justify rejecting an attribution where other evidence seems to point to Pope.

The danger of admitting spurious poems cannot therefore be entirely avoided; but it is hoped that a careful scrutiny of the evidence has reduced the apocrypha to at least minimal dimensions.

II

Special attention has also been given in this edition to the chronological arrangement of the poems, the bibliography appended to each piece, its occasion, and the history of its text.

It has long been known that for various reasons (such as Pope's care for correctness and polish, inopportune seasons for publication, second thoughts, and, it may be, simple forgetfulness) there were considerable delays between the writing and printing of many of his poems. But it has not always been recognized how numerous these delayed poems were. Neither has it been noted that the publication of them had its times and seasons: that, in fact, the production of each of his miscellanies brought forth from desk and drawer a fresh batch of old verses, which, after correction and the not infrequent insertion of some topical allusion, was presented to the public anonymously, and without the least hint of date of writing. The same phenomenon of delay is present, though to a lesser degree because they contained fewer new pieces, in the collected *Works* of 1717, and the second volume of 1735, and also in the quite numerous later editions. With all these volumes of the official *Works* the problem is at times not too few dates but too many. Pope had a way of changing his mind from edition to edition about the date of some poems: an outstanding example being the epistle "To Mr Addison Occasioned by his Dialogues on Medals", in dating which he made at different times at least four apparently incompatible statements or implications.

Though these difficulties have hindered, they have not prevented a chronological arrangement of the Minor Poems, in which the titles of the major poems have been inserted in their proper years. It is hoped that such an arrangement will prove valuable to all students of Pope's life and works. Such a chronology will enable the student of his poetry to see both the whole range of his poetical work in perspective, and the development of his style step by step from 1700 to 1744; besides presenting, for the student of his life, an intermittent but progressive record of his activities, thoughts, and feelings. Furthermore, this arrangement not only shows the interconnection between contemporary pieces, but reveals very strikingly Pope's reactions to the various blessings and buffets of fortune —such, for example, as his counter-attacks in the "Battle of the Iliad" in 1715.

The chronological plan has, however, necessitated some dispersion of two or three groups of kindred pieces—an arrangement which Pope not too consistently experimented with from time to time, and one which his editors have since more rigorously perpetuated. Thus the "Epitaphs" and "Epistles" have been allotted to their several years, and two or three of the "Imitations of English Poets" have been withdrawn from the group to appear elsewhere. But for convenience of reference the groups are once again reassembled in the Index under their old titles.

The one significant departure from strictly chronological arrangement is the grouping of verse fragments at the end of each decade. These are for the most part impromptu outbreaks into verse culled from Pope's letters, and would have appeared undeservedly prominent if they had been given separate positions in their true chronological places. They are included for the sake of completeness rather than for any light they may throw on his poetical career.

III

Each considerable poem is followed by a separate bibliography, which terminates with the first inclusion of the piece in a posthumous edition of the poems. These bibliographies also specify the present position of autograph manuscripts and of contemporary transcripts. In those cases, comparatively few, where poems or fragments are grouped together, it has sometimes been found convenient to diverge from the general rule, and either give a collective bibliography at the head of the group, or, more rarely, relegate the bibliographical matter to the footnote accompanying each versicle.

One interesting feature about the publication of Pope's occasional verse may be noted in this place, namely, the necessity for the bibliographer not only to watch the daily calendar but even the round of the clock to determine his first editions. On a number of occasions, two and sometimes three different newspapers published the same poem on the same day; and in these cases the problem of priority, though scarcely a matter of importance, had to be settled by unusual if not unorthodox means—indeed, in one instance, the key was supplied by news of the notorious Jack Sheppard.

IV

The history of the text of each poem (or group of poems) is given in a footnote. Thus, with its accompanying bibliography, each poem is furnished with all the available relevant information about it. The account ceases with Pope's last known revision of the piece, or with its posthumous inclusion in his Works, or with what may be called its candidature for the canon. Incorporated in these histories are the stories of the occasion of the poems concerned, retold whenever possible in the words of the original documents. New light is thrown on many of the pieces, which are, for the greater part, "poems on several occasions", and, unlike the pure lyric, with its universal application and generalized background, are full of topical and personal allusion which often cannot be understood without some knowledge of their setting, characters, and circumstances. Detailed information on these points is supplied as far as possible in footnotes; but nuances of atmosphere and personality which lie beyond the scope of the footnote are more properly found in the introductory note. In that place are also discussed the evidence and arguments on which various poems have in the past been, or are now first, attributed to Pope, as well as reasons for the dates ascribed to the numerous undated pieces.

V

The design of this volume also covers many poems which cannot be included in the canon of Pope's works, but of which some recognition must be taken, namely, (a) poems of doubtful authorship attributed to Pope on indecisive evidence, and (b) poems wrongly attributed to Pope. An annotated list of these will be found in an appendix, together with the texts of doubtful poems most plausibly attributed to Pope but not reasonably accessible in print elsewhere.

VI

The textual origins of Pope's Minor Poems are of unparalleled variety. Some pieces have survived in a single holograph, some in a single contemporary transcript, some (such as "To Mr C.") were first printed many years after his death from a holograph which has since been lost. Some appeared, with or without the poet's consent, in miscellany, magazine, or newspaper. Some (such as "Upon a Girl of Seven Years Old") made a solitary appearance in an edition of his Works or a miscellany edited by him, and were subsequently lost sight of, and some exist only in broadsheet. Some are cut in marble, and one is to be found engraved in stone on the outside wall of a village church.

Of others there are several holographs. Of one ("The Court Ballad") a text must be constructed from an early draft in the poet's hand, a later transcript, and a pirated issue; of another ("Verses on a Grotto") the editor must pick his way through ten contemporary transcripts and seven printed texts. One ("To Mrs M. B. on her Birth-day") exists in five distinct forms, and of many there are revisions to be noted from one authentic edition to another.

Although in the circumstances the choice of text must necessarily differ from poem to poem, it is possible to present a consistent policy covering the great majority of these pieces. Of poems printed in Pope's lifetime, the printed edition chosen for copy-text is the earliest for which it may be confidently asserted that Pope was responsible, whether that edition was a volume of his Works or a miscellany of which he was the editor. The copy-text is therefore not derived from a manuscript, or a newspaper, magazine, or broadsheet text unless no other text is available. In the same way a lapidary inscription is rarely used for copy-text (though the texts of all such inscriptions have been collated and substantial variants noted), since insufficient is known about the degree of control exercised by Pope over the stonemason.

Certain departures from the copy-texts have consistently been made. The use of inverted commas and notes of exclamation has been regularized to prevent the reader's confusion; printer's errors both in letters and in punctuation have been silently corrected; such manuscript contractions as "y^e", "w^t", "w^d", "&" have been expanded; and since lines of verse are numbered throughout, the numeral at the head of a stanza has been omitted. It has been found impracticable to follow the copy-texts in the varied representation of the first word of a poem; the policy has therefore been adopted of using throughout a two-line initial capital followed by small capitals all in roman type, except where the fragmentary nature of a poem made this practice unsuitable. Some licence also has been taken in laying out the titles of poems.

Substantial variants from the poet's last corrected version have been incorporated in the copy-text. These are not always the readings of the octavo editions published by Lintot and Dodsley between 1740 and 1743, or of Warburton's edition of 1751, since neither the booksellers nor Warburton were careful to discover which earlier edition contained Pope's latest corrections.

The text is accompanied by a critical apparatus of variants, selected on the basis explained in Vol. II, p. ix, and Vol. IV, p. viii. These are variants of substance only, and are drawn from manuscript and printed texts which appear to derive from an authoritative source. Thus variants in a transcript made for the Earl of Oxford or in a pirated edition published by Curll may ultimately derive from the poet's manuscript; but the variants in transcripts and reprints of the late eighteenth century would appear to have no authority and have not been recorded.

Thanks are due to many people, strangers as well as friends, for kindnesses, too numerous to mention in detail, received during the preparation of this work: to the Librarians and staffs of the Bodleian and the British Museum Libraries for their ready and unfailing help over many years; to Their Graces the Dukes of Devonshire and Portland, the Earls of Bath and Harrowby, the late E. Riddell-Blount, Esq. of Mapledurham, R. W. Ketton-Cremer, Esq., of Felbrigg Hall, Messrs P. J. Dobell & Son, Messrs W. H. Robinson Ltd, the Libraries of the Royal College of Surgeons and Ushaw College in England, and in the United States, the late Dr A. S. W. Rosenbach, Mr Donald F. Hyde, Mr Roy G. Fitzgerald of Dayton, Ohio, the Libraries of the Universities of Yale and Harvard, and of Wellesley College; the Boston Public Library, the William Andrews Clark Memorial Library, Los Angeles, and the Pierpont Morgan Library, New York, for kindly allowing use to be made of manuscripts or photostats of manuscripts in their possession, particulars of which are given in the separate bibliographies and notes hereafter; for further assistance of various kinds to Mr Desmond Bland, Mr John C. Bryce, Miss Dorothy Coates, Dr Herbert Davis, Mr Giles E. Dawson, Professor Bonamy Dobrée, the Earl of Ilchester, the late Dr Robin Flower, Miss Barbara Flower, Dr H. A. Hammelman, Professor Helen Sard Hughes, Mr

Frank Kermode, Mr C. Long, Professor T. O. Mabbott, Professor Maynard Mack, Mr J. C. Maxwell, Mr Francis Needham, Mr Desmond Neill, Professor George Sherburn, Professor D. Nichol Smith, Professor James R. Sutherland, Mr Francis Thompson, Professor Geoffrey Tillotson, Mr C. H. Wilkinson, Sir Harold Williams, Professor R. Wittkower, Dr C. E. Wright.

LIST OF ABBREVIATIONS

AULT = New Attributions to Pope. By Norman Ault. *Modern Philology*, vol. XXXV, November 1937.

AYRE = Memoirs of the Life and Writings of Alexander Pope, Esq. By William Ayre. 2 vols., 1745.

BIOG. APP. = Biographical Appendix.

CARRUTHERS = The Poetical Works of Pope. Ed. R. Carruthers. 2 vol. edition of 1858 used.

CASE = New Attributions to Pope. By Arthur E. Case. *Modern Philology*, vol. XXXIV, February 1937.

CROKER = Notes by Croker in the Elwin-Courthope edition of Pope's Works.

EC = The Works of Pope. Ed. W. Elwin and W. J. Courthope. 10 vols., 1871–89.

FABER = The Poetical Works of John Gay. Ed. G. C. Faber. 1926.

GEC = The Complete Peerage of Great Britain. By G.E.C. A new edition in progress, by V. Gibbs, H. A. Doubleday, and Lord Howard de Walden. 1910 etc.

GRIFFITH = Alexander Pope. A Bibliography. By R. H. Griffith. 1 vol. in two parts, 1922, 1927.

HERVEY MEMOIRS = Memoirs of the Reign of George II. By John, Lord Hervey. Ed. R. Sedgwick. 3 vols, 1931.

KERBY-MILLER = Memoirs of . . . Martinus Scriblerus. Ed. C. Kerby-Miller. 1950.

MABBOTT = Information kindly given by Professor T. O. Mabbott.

NEW LIGHT = New Light on Pope. By Norman Ault. 1949.

OED = Oxford English Dictionary.

P = Note by Pope; usually followed by dates of the editions in which it was printed.

POM = Pope's Own Miscellany. Ed. Norman Ault. 1935.

POPE'S PROSE = The Prose Works of A. Pope. Ed. Norman Ault. Vol. I, 1936.

RUFFHEAD = The Life of Alexander Pope, Esq. By Owen Ruffhead. 1769.

SHERBURN = The Early Career of A. Pope. By George Sherburn. 1934.

SPENCE = Anecdotes . . . of Books and Men. By Joseph Spence. Ed. S. W. Singer. 1820.

SUFFOLK = Letters to and from Henrietta, Countess of Suffolk. 2 vols., 1824.

WAKEFIELD = Works of A. Pope. Ed. Gilbert Wakefield. 1794. Observations on Pope. By G. Wakefield. 1796.

WALPOLE = Notes on the Poems of Pope, by Horatio, Earl of Oxford, contributed by Sir W. A. Fraser. 1876. Also, Marginal notes from his copies of Warton's *Essay* and *Additions to Pope's Works* (1776), now in the British Museum.

WARBURTON 1751 = Works of A. Pope. Ed. W. Warburton. 9 vols., 1751. First edition of 1751 quoted.

WARD = Poetical Works of A. Pope. Ed. A. W. Ward. 1869. Reprint of 1924 used.

WARTON = Works of A. Pope. Ed. J. Warton. 9 vols., 1797. Edition of 1822 quoted.

WILLIAMS = The Poems of Jonathan Swift. Ed. H. Williams. 3 vols., 1937.

MINOR POEMS

ODE on SOLITUDE.

Happy the man, whose wish and care
    A few paternal acres bound,
Content to breathe his native air,
            In his own ground.

Whose herds with milk, whose fields with bread,   5
Whose flocks supply him with attire,
Whose trees in summer yield him shade,
            In winter fire.

Blest! who can unconcern'dly find
Hours, days, and years slide soft away,   10
In health of body, peace of mind,
            Quiet by day,

Sound sleep by night; study and ease
Together mix'd; sweet recreation,
And innocence, which most does please,   15
            With meditation.

Title Solitude. An Ode. *1717*. Solitude. Sapphick. *1726*.
1–4   Happy the Man, who free from Care,
            The Business and the Noise of Towns,
        Contented breaths his Native Air,
                In his own Grounds: *MS, 1727*.

        How happy he, who free from care,
            The rage of courts, and noise of towns;
        Contented breaths his native air,
                In his own grounds. *1717, 1726*.
10 Hours . . . away,] His years slide silently away, *MS, 1727*.
  soft] swift *1717, 1726*.
13 Sound sleep by] Repose at *MS, 1727*.

Thus let me live, unseen, unknown;
Thus unlamented let me dye;
Steal from the world, and not a stone
        Tell where I lye.   20

17 unseen] unheard *1717, 1726.*

Pope's autograph: Bodleian MS Rawl. letters 90 [17 July 1709].
Poems on Several Occasions. 1717.
Miscellany Poems. Vol. I. 5th Edition. 1726 (and 1727; 6th Edition, 1732).
Miscellanea. In Two Volumes. Vol. I. 1727.
Letters of Mr. Pope ... Vol. I. 1735.
Mr. Pope's Literary Correspondence. Vol. I. 1735 (and 3rd Edition, 1735).
The Works ... Vol. I. With Explanatory Notes and Additions ... 1736.
The Works ... Vol. V. Consisting of Letters. 1737.
The Works ... Vol. V. Containing ... Letters. 2nd Edition. 1737.
The Works ... Vol. I. Part I. 1740 (and 1743).
The Lark. 1740 (and 1742).
The Works ... Vol. IV. Part I. Containing ... Letters. 1742.
A Select Collection of Modern Poems. 1744.
Philomel. Being a Small Collection of Only the Best English Songs. 1744.
A Collection of Moral and Sacred Poems. J. Wesley. Vol. I. 1744.
The London Magazine. April 1744.
The Aviary. [1744].
The Life of Alexander Pope, Esq. 1744.
Memoirs of ... Alexander Pope, Esq. W. Ayre. Vol. I. 1745.
The Thrush. 1749.
The Works. Ed. Warburton. Vols. I and VII. 1751.

This poem was declared by Ruffhead, Pope's biographer, to be "the first fruit now extant of his poetical genius". Pope himself, in the latter part of his life, frequently stated that it was "written at about twelve years old". Although he was always inclined to stress the precocity of his juvenile writings, the first draft may well date from the end of the seventeenth century; for, as early as 1709, when sending a copy in a letter to Henry Cromwell, he said it was "written when I was not twelve years old". Nevertheless, as it was Pope's practice to correct his verses as occasion offered, and as the poem was revised several times subsequently, it is improbable that even the autograph, transcribed nine years after composition and itself showing corrections, represents the earlier text untouched.

In spite of its Horatian quality, no specific poem can be identified as the original, or inspiration, of the *Ode*, whose classical echoes seem to derive from Cowley's translations of a group of Latin poems in his *Essays, in Verse and Prose.* Pope was confessedly an enthusiastic student and imitator of Cowley in his early youth (see *post*, p. 13, for a number of *Imitations of Cowley written by a Youth of thirteen*), and in letters of 1709 and 1723, in two *Spectators* of 1712, and in *Mor. Ess.,*

1 95 (Vol. III 11, p. 22) he was still quoting from these same translations. It is not surprising, therefore, to find many similarities of subject and feeling between them and the *Ode*; and not a few instances of more direct copying (two or three of which are indicated in the footnotes). These resemblances were lessened by subsequent revision (see ll. 9–13*n*.). Pope formally acknowledged his authorship of the *Ode on Solitude* when, in 1736, after its final revision, it was for the first time included in the *Works*.

The text of *1717* has been taken as copy-text, into which subsequent revisions have been incorporated.

1–4. Cf. text and *MS* with Cowley's lines:

> Happy the Man whom bounteous Gods allow
> With his own Hands Paternal Grounds to plough!
> Like the first golden Mortals Happy he
> From Business and the cares of Money free! *Horat. Epodon 2.*

and with Cowley's translation of "Claudian's Old Man of Verona" (*Discourse*, VII):

> Happy the Man, who his whole Time doth bound
> Within th' Enclosure of his little Ground.

9–13. Cf. text and *MS* with Cowley's lines:

> Thus let my life slide silently away
> With Sleep all Night, and Quiet all the Day. *Mart. Lib. 2. Ep. 90.*

17–20. Cf. Cowley's lines:

> Here wrapt in th' Arms of Quiet let me ly, . . .
> Here let my Life, with as much silence slide . . .
> Nor let my homely Death embroidered be
>   With Scutcheon or with Elegie.
> An old Plebean let me Dy . . .   *Seneca, ex Thyeste, Act 2, Chor.*

A
PARAPHRASE

on *Thomas a Kempis*; L. 3, C. 2.

Done by the Author at 12 years old.

S PEAK, Gracious Lord, oh speak; thy Servant hears:
For I'm thy Servant, and I'l still be so:
Speak words of Comfort in my willing Ears;
  And since my Tongue is in thy praises slow,
And since that thine all Rhetorick exceeds;   5
Speak thou in words, but let me speak in deeds!

Nor speak alone, but give me grace to hear
    What thy cælestïal Sweetness does impart;
Let it not stop when entred at the Ear
    But sink, and take deep rooting in my heart.   10
As the parch'd Earth drinks Rain (but grace afford)
With such a Gust will I receive thy word.

Nor with the Israelites shall I desire
    Thy heav'nly word by Moses to receive,
Lest I should die: but Thou who didst inspire   15
    Moses himself, speak thou, that I may live.
Rather with Samuel I beseech with tears
Speak, gracious Lord, oh speak; thy Servant hears.

Moses indeed may say the words but Thou
    Must give the Spirit, and the Life inspire;   20
Our Love to thee his fervent Breath may blow,
    But 'tis thy self alone can give the fire:
Thou without them may'st speak and profit too;
But without thee, what could the Prophets do?

They preach the Doctrine, but thou mak'st us do't;   25
    They teach the Misteries thou dost open lay;
The Trees they water, but thou giv'st the fruit;
    They to Salvation shew the arduous way,
But none but you can give us Strength to walk;
You give the Practise, they but give the Talk.   30

Let them be silent then; and thou alone
    (My God) speak comfort to my ravish'd Ears;
Light of my eyes, my Consolation,
    Speak when thou wilt, for still thy Servant hears.
What-ere thou speak'st, let this be understood;   35
Thy greater Glory, and my greater Good!

Pope's autograph: MS in possession of Messrs W. H. Robinson Ltd, 1938.

The Athenaeum. 15 July 1854.

The Works. Ed. Carruthers. Vol. I. 1858.

Preserved originally among the Caryll Papers (but withheld when the rest were given to the British Museum), the manuscript is an undated fair copy written in Pope's "script hand".

The text follows the autograph in every respect.

Title] The paraphrase is based upon *De Imitatione Christi*, lib. 3, cap. 2, "*Quod veritas intus loquitur sine strepitu verborum*".

Of a LADY *singing to her* LUTE.
[In imitation of Waller.]

Fair charmer cease, nor make your voice's prize
  A heart resign'd the conquest of your eyes:
Well might, alas! that threaten'd vessel fail,
Which winds and lightning both at once assail.
We were too blest with these inchanting lays,   5
Which must be heav'nly when an angel plays;
But killing charms your lover's death contrive,
Lest heav'nly musick should be heard alive.
Orpheus could charm the trees, but thus a tree
Taught by your hand, can charm no less than he;   10
A poet made the silent wood pursue;
This vocal wood had drawn the poet too.

Title Of her singing to a Lute *1717*.

1–2 Fair charmer cease, nor add your tuneful breath
    T' o'ercome the slave your eyes have doom'd to Death *1717*.

7 your] the *1717*.

11 The silent wood, of old, a poet drew *1717*.

Poems on Several Occasions. 1717.

Miscellanea. In Two Volumes. Vol. I. 1727.

Mr. Pope's Literary Correspondence. Vol. II. 1735 (and 2nd Edition, 1735).

The Works . . . Vol. III. Consisting of Fables, Translations, and Imitations. 1736.

The Works . . . Vol. I. Part II. Consisting of Fables, Translations, and Imitations. 1741 (and 1745).

The Works. Ed. Warburton. Vol. II. 1751.

Though formerly known as one of the *Imitations of English Poets*, first collected under that title in *Works*, Vol. III, 1736, this poem was originally published without Pope's name in a miscellany for which he was responsible (see below). It stood in a group of six pieces entitled *Verses in imitation of Waller. By a Youth of thirteen*, which should mean that, whatever alteration it may subsequently have undergone, it was composed in 1701.

The copy-text adopted is *1717*, into which the final revisions of *1727* have been incorporated.

11f. Cf. MS of *Pastoral* ii:

> Had You then liv'd, when he the Forests drew,
> The Trees and *Orpheus* both had follow'd You.

and Waller earlier had written in *Of a Tree cut in Paper*, ll. 13–14:

> Orpheus could make the Forest dance, but you
> Can make the Motion and the Forest too.

Verses in imitation of WALLER. *By a Youth of thirteen.*

Poems on Several Occasions. 1717.

The London Mercury. October 1924.

Pope's Own Miscellany. Ed. N. Ault. 1935.

This group of "Verses", which originally included the preceding poem, was first published in a miscellany believed to have been compiled by Pope, whose part therein is set out in the introduction to the reprint entitled, *Pope's Own Miscellany*. As Pope later included in his *Works* one of the six pieces which in 1717 he said were written by a youth of thirteen, the remaining five may be accepted as authentic, even though he never acknowledged or reprinted them. With no separate existence, they all have the same bibliography, and are therefore treated here as a group. Though the imitations have cadences in plenty recalling Waller's music, there are no poems in parallel and very few duplicated phrases, identifiable likenesses being almost wholly limited to titles and subjects.

The text of all five pieces follows *1717* in every respect.

I.

Of the Lady who could not sleep in a stormy Night.

As gods sometimes descend from heav'n and deign
  On earth a while with mortals to remain,
So gentle sleep from *Serenissa* flies,
To dwell at last upon her lover's eyes.
That god's indulgence can she justly crave,   5
Who flies the tyrant to relieve the slave?
Or should those eyes alone that rest enjoy,
Which in all others they themselves destroy?
Let her whom fear denies repose to take,
Think for her love what crowds of wretches wake.   10
So us'd to sighs, so long inur'd to tears,
Are winds and tempests dreadful to her ears?
Jove with a nod may bid the world to rest,
But *Serenissa* must becalm the breast.

3f. Cf. Waller's *Of the Lady who can Sleep when she pleases*, ll. 1–2:
          No wonder Sleep from careful Lovers flies,
          To bathe himself in Sacharissa's Eyes.

II.

Of her Picture.

THE nymph her graces here express'd may find,
  And by this picture learn to dress her mind;
For here no frowns make tender love afraid,
Soft looks of mercy grace the flatt'ring shade,
And, while we gaze, the gracious form appears   5
T'approve our passion and forbid our fears.
Narcissus here a different fate had prov'd,
Whose bright resemblance by himself was lov'd;
Had he but once this fairer shade descry'd,
Not for his own, but hers, the youth had dy'd.   10

III.

Of her Sickness.

AH *Serenissa*, from our arms
    Did you for death's preserve your charms;
From us that serv'd so long in vain,
Shall heav'n so soon the prize obtain?
Sickness, its courtship, makes the fair   5
As pale as her own lovers are.
    Sure you, the goddess we adore,
Who all cœlestial seem'd before,
While vows and service nothing gain'd,
Which, were you woman, had obtain'd;   10
At last in pity, for our sake,
Descend an human form to take,
And by this sickness chuse to tell
You are not now invincible.

IV.

Of her walking in a Garden after a
Shower.

SEE how the sun in dusky skies
    Veils his fair glories, while he spies
Th' unclouded lustre of her eyes!
    Her bashful beauties once descry'd,
The vanquish'd roses lose their pride,   5
And in their buds their blushes hide.
    Myrtles have lost their balmy smell,
And drooping lillies seem to tell
How much her sweets their own excel.
    See! She retires: Nor can we say   10
If light breaks out or goes away,
For *Sol*'s is now the only ray.

Lo how their heads the lillies rear,
And with fresh sweets perfume the air,
When their bright rival is not there.   15

Again grown proud, the spreading rose
Its bloomy beauties does disclose,
And to the skies its incense throws.

Her glorious charms eclipse the day;
Nature itself is only gay,   20
When *Serenissa* is away.

Like, yet unlike these flow'rs am I;
I languish when her charms draw nigh,
But if she disappears, I dye.

V.

Of her Sighing.

WHEN love would strike th' offending fair,
This incense bribes the god to spare;
And *Cytheræa* now does prize
No sweets but *Serenissa*'s sighs.
The yielding nymph by these confest,   5
Encourag'd lovers seek her breast:
So spicy gales at once betray
Th' *Arabian* coast, and waft us on our way.

7f. Cf. Waller, *The Night-Piece*, ll. 39–42:

So we th' Arabian coast do know
At distance, when the spices blow;
By the rich odour taught to steer,
Though neither day nor stars appear.

WEEPING.

[In imitation of COWLEY.]

WHILE *Celia*'s tears make sorrow bright,
 Proud grief sits swelling in her eyes:
The sun (next those the fairest light)
 Thus from the ocean first did rise.
And thus thro' mists we see the sun,   5
Which else we durst not gaze upon.

These silver drops, like morning dew,
 Foretell the fervour of the day;
So from one cloud soft show'rs we view,
 And blasting lightnings burst away.   10
The stars that fall from *Celia*'s eye,
Declare our doom in drawing nigh.

The baby, in that sunny sphere
 So like a *Phaëton* appears,
That heav'n, the threaten'd world to spare, 15
 Thought fit to drown him in her tears:
Else might th' ambitious nymph aspire,
To set, like him, heav'n too on fire.

1f.   How lovely sorrow seems, how bright!
     Drest in the glories of her eyes *1717*.
4 ocean] waters *1717*.
5 see] view *1717*.
7–12   As the soft dews of morning skies
     Foretell the noon's increasing beams;
   So these mild drops from *Celia*'s eyes
     But threaten more destructive flames.
   From the same cloud we thus descry
   The showr's descend, and lightnings fly. *1717*.
17f.   'Twas else th' ambitious *Celia*'s aim,
   Those eyes shou'd set the world on flame. *1717*.

Poems on Several Occasions. 1717.
The Works . . . Vol. III. Consisting of Fables, Translations, and Imitations. 1736.
The Works . . . Vol. I. Part II. Consisting of Fables, Translations, and Imitations.
1741 (and 1745).
The Works. Ed. Warburton. Vol. II. 1751.

This poem, the first of a group of three anonymous imitations of Cowley "By
a Youth of thirteen" when first published in 1717, was revised by Pope in 1736
and reprinted as one of his *Imitations of English Poets*. It has thus a separate
bibliographical history, and is therefore here separated from the following group
(see introductory note below).

The copy-text adopted is *1717*, into which the final revisions of *1736* have been
incorporated.

Verses in imitation of COWLEY. *By a Youth of thirteen.*

Poems on Several Occasions. 1717.
The London Mercury. October 1924.
Pope's Own Miscellany. Ed. N. Ault. 1935.

As with the preceding group of imitations of Waller, this smaller group is
identified as Pope's because it likewise originally included a poem which he later
incorporated in his *Works*. In this case the acknowledged poem is *Weeping*, which
immediately precedes these other Verses. For the circumstances of the discovery
and reprinting of these poems, see *P.O.M.* Pope's imitations of Cowley, as of
Waller, were designed to be in the manner of the master rather than para-
phrases of particular poems or echoes of his diction.

The text of these two poems follows *1717* in every respect.

I.

Presenting a Lark.

Go tuneful bird, forbear to soar,
    And the bright sun admire no more;
Go bask in *Serenissa*'s eyes,
And turn a bird of paradise.

In those fair beams thy wings display,   5
Take shorter journies to the day,
And at an humbler pitch prefer
Thy musick to an angel's ear.

Nor, tho' her slave, thy lot deplore;
The god of love himself's no more: 10
Ev'n him to constancy she brings,
And clips, like thine, his wav'ring wings.

She gains from us, as now from thee,
Our songs by our captivity;
But happier you attention gain,   15
While wretched lovers sing in vain.

13f. Cf. *Pastorals: Summer*, ll. 45–7.
　　Oh! were I made by some transforming pow'r
　　The captive bird that sings within thy bow'r!
　　Then might my voice thy list'ning ears employ.

II.

The River.

HAIL sacred spring, whose fruitful stream
　　Fattens the flocks, and cloaths the plain;
The melancholy poets theme,
　　And solace of the thirsty swain.

Thou fly'st, like time, with eager haste;   5
　　Behind thy self thou still dost stay;
Thy stream, like his, is never past,
　　And yet is ever on the way.

While mankind boasts superior sight,
　　With eyes erect the heav'ns to see;   10
The starry eyes of heav'n delight
　　To gaze upon themselves in thee.

A second sun thou dost present,
 And bring new heav'ns before our eyes;
We view a milder firmament,   15
 And pleas'd, look downward to the skies.

Thy streams were once th' impartial test
 Of untaught nature's humble pride,
When by thy glass the nymphs were drest,
 In flow'rs, the honours of thy side.   20

Of thee they drank, till blushing fruit
 Was ravisht from the tender vine;
And man, like thee, was impollute,
 Till mischief learn'd to mix with wine.

7f. Cf. Pope's *Thoughts on Various Subjects*, XL, *1741*: "The Vanity of human life is like a River, constantly passing away, and yet constantly coming on."

To the AUTHOR *of a* POEM, *intitled,* SUCCESSIO.

Begone ye Criticks, and restrain your Spite,
 Codrus writes on, and will for ever write;
The heaviest Muse the swiftest Course has gone,
As Clocks run fastest when most Lead is on.
What tho' no Bees around your Cradle flew, 5
Nor on your Lips distill'd their golden Dew?
Yet have we oft discover'd in their stead,
A Swarm of Drones, that buzz'd about your Head.
When you, like *Orpheus*, strike the warbling Lyre,
Attentive Blocks stand round you, and admire. 10

Title] *After* SUCCESSIO, *1726 reads:* In Imitation of the late E. of D.

Wit, past thro' thee, no longer is the same,
As Meat digested takes a diff'rent Name;
But Sense must sure thy safest Plunder be,
Since no Reprizals can be made on thee.
Thus thou may'st Rise, and in thy daring Flight   15
(Tho' ne'er so weighty) reach a wondrous height;
So, forc'd from Engines, Lead it self can fly,
And pondrous Slugs move nimbly thro' the Sky.
Sure *Bavius* copy'd *Mævius* to the full,
And *Chærilus* taught *Codrus* to be dull;   20
Therefore, dear Friend, at my Advice give o'er
This needless Labour, and contend no more,
To prove a dull *Succession* to be true,
Since 'tis enough we find it so in You.

Miscellaneous Poems and Translations. 1712 (and 2nd Edition, 1714; 3rd Edition, 1720; 4th Edition, 1722).

Miscellany Poems. Vol. I. By Mr. Pope. 5th Edition, 1726 (reprinted 1727; and 6th Edition, 1732).

The Works . . . To which are added, I. Cooper's-Hill . . . Dublin. 1727.

The Works. Ed. Roscoe. Vol. II. 1824.

This poem, Pope's earliest satire, was attributed to him on first publication and was also included in a large group of his pieces labelled "By Mr. Pope" in Lintot's *Miscellany* in 1720. Nevertheless it was not printed in any edition of his *Works* until 1824. Pope claimed that it was "writ at Fourteen Years old [*i.e.* in 1702] and soon after printed" (*Dunciad* A, 1 177n.). That is not to say the existing version dates from 1702 or that "soon after printed" is to be taken too literally; because Pope, on his own showing, revised the text before printing it, and he latterly became lax about dates. Looking back from middle age, 1712 may have seemed nearer to 1702 than it did in his youth. More inexplicable is the connection between this satire and Wycherley's imperfect *Panegyrick on Dulness,* which was first seen by Pope, so he says, in 1705, corrected by him in manuscript in 1707, but not published until 1728–9 (Wycherley's *Posthumous Works,* 1728–9, and Pope's *Letters,* 1735, etc.); for Pope's satire, as printed in 1712, contains a line (l. 4) which he admits deleting from Wycherley's original manuscript of *Dulness* in 1707, when he substituted four lines in its place (see pp. 55f.). Accepting 1702 as the date of composition (whatever changes were wrought later), previous editors have noted that the person addressed by Pope as the *Author of . . . Successio* was Elkanah Settle, whose poem in praise of the Hanoverian succession, entitled *Eusebia Triumphans,* was published in that year. In 1712 Pope stated that this and the following poem were written in imitation of the style of "Two Persons of

Quality", and in 1726 he announced that the style imitated here was that of the Earl of D[orset]. But when the group of *Imitations of English Poets* was formed in 1736, this poem was not included.

The text follows that of *1712*. Except in the title, there are no verbal variants.

2. *Codrus*] A Latin poet, *temp.* Domitian, whose poverty became proverbial, here used to indicate Elkanah Settle. See *Dunciad* A, II 136*n*.

4. Originally a line in Wycherley's *Panegyrick on Dulness*, deleted by Pope from the manuscript in 1707, and inserted here in 1712. (See l. 17*n*.)

11f. Used again by Pope in *The Second Satire of Donne Versifyed*, 33f.:

> Sense, past thro' him, no longer is the same,
> For food digested takes another name.

17f. Pope inserted these lines later in the *Dunciad* A, I 177–80, with a revision of l. 4:

> As, forc'd from wind-guns, lead itself can fly,
> And pond'rous slugs cut swiftly thro' the sky;
> As clocks to weight their nimble motion owe,
> The wheels above urg'd by the load below.

19. *Bavius . . . Mævius*] Two stupid and malevolent poets of the Augustan age.

20. *Chærilus*] Pope had met Chærilus, who was patronized by Alexander the Great, in Horace, *Ars Poetica*, 357 and *Ep.* II I 233. He is there represented as a type of blundering poet who occasionally writes a good line. It need not be supposed that Pope was glancing at a contemporary.

On SILENCE.

[In imitation of the Earl of ROCHESTER.]

SILENCE! Coœval with Eternity;
   Thou wert e'er Nature's self began to be,
'Twas one vast Nothing, All, and All slept fast in thee.

Thine was the Sway, e'er Heav'n was form'd or Earth,
   E'er fruitful *Thought* conceiv'd Creation's Birth,   5
Or Midwife *Word* gave Aid, and spoke the Infant forth.

Then various Elements against thee join'd,
   In one more various Animal combin'd,
And fram'd the clam'rous Race of busie Human-kind.

2 Nature's self] Nature first *1712–32*.

The tongue mov'd gently first, and Speech was low,   10
'Till wrangling *Science* taught it Noise and Show,
And wicked *Wit* arose, thy most abusive Foe.

But Rebel Wit deserts thee oft in vain;
Lost in the Maze of Words, he turns again,
And seeks a surer State, and courts thy gentle Reign.   15

Afflicted *Sense* thou kindly dost set free,
Oppress'd with Argumental Tyranny,
And routed *Reason* finds a safe Retreat in thee.

With thee in private modest *Dulness* lies,
And in thy Bosom lurks in *Thought*'s Disguise;   20
Thou Varnisher of *Fools*, and Cheat of all the *Wise*.

Yet thy Indulgence is by both confest;
Folly by thee lies sleeping in the Breast,
And 'tis in thee at last that *Wisdom* seeks for Rest.

Silence, the Knave's Repute, the Whore's good Name,   25
The only Honour of the wishing Dame;
Thy very want of Tongue makes thee a kind of Fame.

But could'st thou seize some Tongues that now are free,
How Church and State should be oblig'd to thee!
At Senate, and at Bar, how welcome would'st thou be!   30

Yet *Speech*, ev'n there, submissively withdraws
From *Rights* of *Subjects*, and the *Poor Man's Cause*;
Then pompous *Silence* reigns, and stills the noisie Laws.

15 gentle] gentler *1712–32*.
29 should] wou'd *1712–32*.

Past Services of Friends, good Deeds of Foes,
  What Fav'rites gain, and what the Nation owes,   35
Fly the forgetful World, and in thy Arms repose.

The Country Wit, Religion of the Town,
  The Courtier's Learning, Policy o' th' Gown,
Are best by thee express'd, and shine in thee alone.

The Parson's Cant, the Lawyer's Sophistry,   40
  Lord's Quibble, Critick's Jest; all end in thee,
All rest in Peace at last, and sleep eternally.

35 the Nation] th' Exchequer *1712–32*.

Miscellaneous Poems and Translations. 1712 (1714, 1720, 1722; *Miscellany Poems*,
1726, 1727, 1732).
  The Works of Mr. Alexander Pope. 1717.
  The Works . . . Dublin. 1718.
  The Works . . . (Printed by T. J.) 1718 (and 1720).
  The Works . . . *To which are added, I. Cooper's-Hill* . . . Dublin. 1727.
  The Works . . . *Vol. III. Consisting of Fables, Translations, and Imitations*. 1736.
  The Works . . . *Vol. I. Part II. Consisting of Fables, Translations, and Imitations*
1741 (and 1745).
  The Works. Ed. Warburton. Vol. II. 1751.
  The early date of this poem has been consistently asserted. When first published
in 1712, it and the preceding poem (p. 16) were together entitled: "Two Copies
of Verses, Written Some Years since in Imitation of the Style of Two Persons of
Quality". In 1736 Pope included it in the *Imitations of English Poets: Done by the
Author in his Youth*, which he explained in the "Advertisement" were done early,
"some of them at fourteen or fifteen Years old", and in a footnote the next year
declared it was "done at fourteen years old" as an "imitation of the Earl of
Rochester's poem on Nothing". A recently discovered autograph manuscript
(see p. 463) shows that the poem was much revised before it reached the stage
of print.
  The copy-text adopted is that of *1712*, into which the final revisions of *1736*
have been incorporated.

2*

LINES from *ALCANDER*
and the EARLY POEMS.

Miscellanies. The Last Volume. 1727 (and subsequent editions).
The Works . . . In Prose. Vol. II. 1741.
The Works. Ed. Warburton. Vol. VI. 1751.
Anecdotes . . . of Books and Men. J. Spence (Singer's Edition). 1820.

Among the vanished works of Pope's youth is an "Epic Poem", *Alcander* (sometimes referred to as the epic on Deucalion), begun, he told Spence (*Anecdotes*, p. 276f.) a little after the age of twelve. "I wrote four books toward it . . . and had the copy by me, till I burnt it, by the advice of the Bishop of Rochester. . . I endeavoured, (said he, smiling), in this poem, to collect all the beauties of the great epic writers into one piece: there was Milton's style in one part, and Cowley's in another; here the style of Spenser imitated, and there of Statius; here Homer and Virgil, and there Ovid and Claudian." A little earlier Pope stated that *Alcander* was "writ at fifteen years old" (*Letters*, 1737). All that is left of these four books (which amounted to some four thousand lines) is a handful of couplets, two of "which I have since inserted in some of my other poems, without any alteration". The two mentioned to Spence are given below (II,III), with another (I) recalled at the same time. At another time he said to Spence (*Anecdotes*, pp. 316f.), "I remember two lines I wrote, when I was a boy, that were very faulty this way [*i.e.* in sacrificing musical quality to an effect of speed]. 'Twas on something that I was to describe as passing away as quick as thought"—whereupon followed No. IV.

Warton in a footnote to *The Art of Sinking* says, "Mr. Spence informed me that this passage [No. V], and many other ridiculous ones, in this treatise, were quoted from our poet's own early pieces, particularly his epic poem, called Alcander" (*Works*, VI 207, 1797); and immediately following No. V, in *1741*, is a couplet on "the same lady", No. VI. Warton again is the authority for No. VII: "These five lines are quoted from his own youthful poems; as indeed are most of those marked *Anonymous*" (*op. cit.*, p. 222). Similarly, Ruffhead, deriving from Warburton, when speaking of *Alcander*, said that Pope "took a pleasure in laughing at the childish extravagances in this poem. . . Some of these . . . are pleasantly produced for examples in the art of *sinking in poetry*, under the title of verses by an Anonymous" (*Life*, p. 27, 1769). It appears, therefore, that the remaining pieces thus designated in *1741* (Nos. VIII–XI) are likewise for the most part, if not all, from Pope's early poems. Five other pieces, without subscription or mark of any kind, are also interspersed throughout the *Art of Sinking*, these also are probably Pope's (see *post*, p. 413); and for the final group of illustrations which seem to have been written still later, see p. 288.

The text of Nos. I–IV follows Spence, 1820; and of Nos. V–XII, follows the *Miscellanies* (1727).

I.

Shields, helms, and swords all jangle as they hang,
And sound formidinous with angry clang.

II.

Whose honours with increase of ages grow;
As streams roll down enlarging as they flow.

III.

As man's meanders to the vital spring
Roll all their tides, then back their circles bring.

IV.

So swift,—this moment here, the next 'tis gone,
So imperceptible the motion.

V.

On a lady's drinking the Bath-waters.

She drinks! She drinks! Behold the matchless Dame!
To her 'tis Water, but to us 'tis Flame:
Thus Fire is Water, Water Fire, by turns,
And the same Stream at once both cools and burns.

VI.

The same lady goes into the Bath.

Venus beheld her, 'midst her Crowd of Slaves,
And thought *Herself* just risen from the Waves.

VII.
The Metonymy.

Lac'd in her *Cosins* new appear'd the Bride,
A *Bubble-boy* and *Tompion* at her Side,
And with an Air divine her *Colmar* ply'd.
Then oh! she cries, what Slaves I round me see?
Here a bright *Redcoat*, there a smart *Toupee*.

4 Then] And *1727*; But *Misc. 1736*.

VIII.
An Eye-witness of things never yet beheld by Man.

Thus have I *seen*, in *Araby* the blest,
A *Phœnix* couch'd upon her Fun'ral Nest.

IX.
How inimitably circumstantial is this [description] *of a War-Horse!*

His Eye-Balls burn, he wounds the smoking Plain,
And knots of scarlet Ribbond deck *his* Mane.

X.
The Hyperbole.
Of a Scene of Misery.

Behold a Scene of Misery and Woe!
Here *Argus* soon might weep himself quite blind,
Ev'n tho' he had *Briareus'* hundred Hands
To wipe those hundred Eyes ——

XI.

The Periphrasis
A Country Prospect.

I'd call them Mountains, but can't call them so,
For fear to wrong them with a Name too low;
While the fair Vales beneath so humbly lie,
That even humble seems a Term too high.

II. Incorporated in *Ess. on C.*, ll. 191–2.

III. Incorporated in *Dunciad* A, III 47–8.

V. From *The Art of Sinking*, chap. VII.

VI. From the same.

VII. The Inversion of Causes for Effects, of Inventors for Inventions, *&c.*
[P. *1727–41*]. From chap. X.
    1. *Cosins*] Stays, called after the famous maker of that day.
    2. *Bubble-boy*] Tweezer-case.   *Tompion*] Watch, from the name of Thomas
Tompion, a celebrated watchmaker, *temp.* Queen Anne.
    3. *Colmar*] Fan (from Colmar, Alsace?).
    5. *Toupee*] A sort of periwig. "All Words in use in this present Year 1727" [P.
1727–41].

VIII. From chap. V.

IX. From chap. VIII.

X. From chap. XI. This looks like a jest on Montrose's famous lines:

Upon the Death of Charles the First

Great God, and Just, could I but rate
My griefs, and thy too rigid fate,
I'd weep the world to such a strain
As it should deluge once again.
But since thy loud-tongued blood demands supplies
More from Briareus' hands, than Argus' eyes,
I'll sing thy obsequies with trumpet sounds,
And write thy epitaph with blood and wounds.

XI. From chap. XI.

Polyphemus and Acis

[written about 1702; published December 1749; vol. I, pp. 363–73]

Pastorals

[written before 1706; published 2 May 1709; vol. I, pp. 57–95]

January and May; or The Merchant's Tale: from Chaucer

[written before 1706; published 2 May 1709; vol. II, pp. 13–54]

The Wife of Bath Her Prologue, From Chaucer

[written before 1706, see vol. II, p. 5n.; published 29 December 1713, vol. II, pp. 55–78]

An Epistle to Henry Cromwell, *Esq;*

DEAR Mr. Cromwell,

MAY it please ye!
Sit still a Moment; pray be easy—
Faith 'tis not five; no Play's begun;
No Game at *Ombre* lost or won.
Read something of a diff'rent Nature,   5
Than *Ev'ning Post*, or *Observator*;
And pardon me a little Fooling,
—Just while your Coffee stands a Cooling.

Since your Acquaintance with one *Brocas*,
Who needs will back the Muses Cock-horse,   10
I know you dread all those who write,
And both with Mouth and Hand recite;
Who slow, and leisurely rehearse,

As loath t' enrich you with their Verse;
Just as a Still, with Simples in it,   15
Betwixt each Drop stays half a Minute.
(That Simile is not my own,
But lawfully belongs to *Donne*)
(You see how well I can contrive a
Interpolatio Furtiva)   20
To *Brocas*'s Lays no more you listen
Than to the wicked Works of *Whiston*;
In vain he strains to reach your Ear,
With what it wisely, will not hear:
You bless the Powers who made that Organ   25
Deaf to the Voice of such a *Gorgon*,
(For so one sure may call that Head,
Which does not Look, but Read Men dead.)

    I hope, you think me none of those
Who shew their Parts as *Pentlow* does,   30
I but lug out to one or two
Such Friends, if such there are, as you,
Such, who read *Heinsius* and *Masson*,
And as you please their Doom to pass on,
(Who are to me both *Smith* and *Johnson*)   35
So seize them Flames, or take them *Tonson*.

    But, Sir, from *Brocas*, *Fouler*, me,
In vain you think to 'scape Rhyme-free,
When was it known one Bard did follow
Whig Maxims, and abjure *Apollo*?   40
Sooner shall Major-General cease
To talk of War, and live in Peace;
Yourself for Goose reject Crow Quill,
And for plain *Spanish* quit *Brasil*;
Sooner shall *Rowe* lampoon the UNION   45

34 Their Doom to pass on] *all texts, however, read* to pass their Doom.

Tydcombe take Oaths on the Communion;
The *Granvilles* write their Name plain *Greenfield*,
Nay, Mr. *Wycherly* see *Binfield*.

I'm told, you think to take a Step some
Ten Miles from Town, t' a Place call'd *Epsom*,   50
To treat those Nymphs like yours of *Drury*,
With—I protest, and I'll assure ye;—
But tho' from Flame to Flame you wander,
Beware; your Heart's no *Salamander*!
But burnt so long, may soon turn Tinder,   } 55
And so be fir'd by any Cinder-
(Wench, I'd have said did Rhyme not hinder) }
Shou'd it so prove, yet who'd admire?
'Tis known, a Cook-maid roasted *Prior*,
Lardella fir'd a famous Author,   } 60
And for a Butcher's well-fed Daughter
Great *D—s* roar'd, like Ox at Slaughter. }

(Now, if you're weary of my Style,
Take out your Box of right *Brasil*,
First lay this Paper under, then,   65
Snuff just three Times, and read again.)

I had to see you some Intent
But for a curst Impediment,
Which spoils full many a good Design,
That is to say, the Want of Coin.   70
For which, I had resolv'd almost,
To raise *Tiberius Gracchus* Ghost;
To get, by once more murd'ring *Caius*,
As much as did *Septimuleius*;
But who so dear will buy the Lead,   75
That lies within a Poet's Head,
As that which in the Hero's Pate
Deserv'd of Gold an equal Weight?

Sir, you're so stiff in your Opinion,
I wish you do not turn *Socinian*;   80
Or prove Reviver of a Schism,
By modern Wits call'd *Quixotism*.
What mov'd you, pray, without compelling,
Like *Trojan* true, to draw for *Hellen*:
Quarrel with *Dryden* for a Strumpet,   85
(For so she was, as e'er show'd Rump yet,
Tho' I confess, she had much Grace,
Especially about the Face.)
Virgil, when call'd *Pasiphae Virgo*
(You say) he'd more good Breeding; *Ergo*—   90
Well argu'd, Faith! Your Point you urge
As home, as ever did *Panurge*:
And one may say of *Dryden* too,
(As once you said of you know who)
He had some Fancy, and cou'd write;   95
Was very learn'd, but not polite—
However from my Soul I judge
He ne'er (good Man) bore *Hellen* Grudge,
But lov'd her full as well it may be,
As e'er he did his own dear Lady.   100
You have no Cause to take Offence, Sir,
Z—ds, you're as sour as *Cato Censor*!
Ten times more like him, I profess,
Than I'm like *Aristophanes*.

To end with News—the best I know,   105
Is, I've been well a Week, or so.
The Season of green Pease is fled,
And Artichoaks reign in their Stead.
Th' Allies to bomb *Toulon* prepare;
G—d save the pretty Lady's there!   110
One of our Dogs is dead and gone,
And I, unhappy! left alone.

> If you have any Consolation
> T'administer on this Occasion,
> Send it, I pray, by the next Post,   115
> Before my Sorrow be quite lost.
>   The twelfth or thirteenth Day of *July*,
>   But which, I cannot tell you truly.

Miscellanea. In Two Volumes. Vol. I. 1727.
Mr. Pope's Literary Correspondence. Vol. II. 1735 (and 2nd Edition, 1735).
A Supplement to the Works ... 1757.
Additions to the Works of Alexander Pope, Esq. Vol. I. 1776.
The Works. Ed. Dyce. Vol. II. 1831.

The autograph of this letter, which was never published by Pope in his correspondence, disappeared between the date of Curll's purchase of Pope's letters to Cromwell from Mrs Thomas (Cromwell's old mistress) and their deposit in the Bodleian. Curll's two texts (*1727, 1735*) are thus the only contemporary sources extant—in which connection, it is reassuring to know that Curll's texts are generally satisfactory; for instance, in the second rhymed letter to Cromwell (p. 39), the autograph of which has survived, there is, apart from one obvious misprint, no verbal difference from the MS. There can be no doubt of Pope's authorship, for he tacitly admitted it insomuch that he never excepted this rhymed letter from his complaints that Curll had obtained his letters by underhand means and printed them without his knowledge or consent. Moreover the epistle itself is too full of personal allusion to be other than genuine. Pope concluded the letter with the day and the month, but omitted the year, in which it was written; but this (1707) is established by the allusion to the preparations for the bombardment of Toulon (see G. M. Trevelyan, *England under Queen Anne: Ramilies*, pp. 305ff.).
    The text is that of *1727*.

9. *Brocas*] Commonly call'd Beau *Brocas* [Curll, *1735*]. Little is known about this man; he is also mentioned in a letter from Pulteney to George Berkeley "Brocas, Marriot, and all the water-poets are now here," in Bath (10 November 1735; *Suffolk Corr.*, II 146). See also *A Farewell*, p. 131).

15–18. Cf. Donne's *Fourth Satire*, 94–5: ". . . and as a Still which stayes / A Sembrief, 'twixt each drop",—and Pope's imitation (Vol. IV, p. 35, ll. 126–7):
    He hears; and as a Still, with Simples in it,
    Between each Drop it gives, stays half a Minute;
Pope used the same image again in *The Guardian*, No. 92 (*Prose*, I 127).

22. *Whiston*] 1667–1752. Succeeded to Sir Isaac Newton's professorship at Cambridge, 1701. His Boyle lectures (1707) were suspected of heterodoxy.

30. *Pentlow*] A Gamester remarkable for his *Virile* Parts, which he us'd to be fond of Shewing [Curll, *1735*].

33. *Heinsius and Masson*] Heinsius was a Dutch and Masson a French critic.

35. *Smith and Johnson*] Bays's two Friends in the *Rehearsal* [Curll, *1735*].

37. *Fouler*] Nothing is known of this poet.

40. An allusion to the Whig maxim of abjuring the Pretender [Sherburn].

44. *Spanish . . . Brasil*] Two kinds of snuff; see below, ll. 64–6.

45. *Rowe*] See Biog. App., Vol. IV. The great measure of the Union had just been passed, and Rowe was a candidate for office [Croker].

46. *Tydcombe*] Lieutenant-General John Tidcombe (1642–1713), a member of the Kit-Cat club and an acquaintance of Pope's.

48. . . . *Binfield*] Refers to Wycherley's reluctance to make visits to the country. Pope wrote to Cromwell (1 November 1708): "Nothing could allure Mr. Wycherley to our forest."

55f. *Cinder-Wench*] See p. 265, l. 2*n*.

59. *Cook-maid*] One of Mr. Prior's Does was of that Vocation [Curll, *1735*].

60. *Lardella . . . Author*] Lardella is a character in the *Rehearsal*; and Elwin suggests that the famous author was Dryden [EC, vi 6.;].

62. *D—s*] Dennis [Curll, *1735*]; see Biog. App., Vols. IV, V.

72. Pope was possibly meditating a tragedy on the Gracchi.

73–8. An allusion to the story that Septimuleius, who cut off the head of Caius Gracchus, and was rewarded with its weight in gold, fraudulently filled the skull with lead [Croker].

83f. He was to use the rhyme again in *Mor. Ess.*, II 193f.

100. *his own dear Lady*] Mr. *Dryden* married Lady *Elizabeth Howard* [Curll, *1735*]. His marriage is presumed to have been unhappy.

109. See introductory note.

Sapho to Phaon

["written first in 1707"; published March 1712; vol. 1, pp. 391–404]

The Episode of Sarpedon
The Arrival of Ulysses in Ithaca

[written about 1707–8; published 2 May 1709, 29 Dec. 1713; vol. 1, pp. 447–74]

ODE for MUSICK.
on
St. *CECILIA*'s Day.

DESCEND ye Nine! descend and sing;
   The breathing Instruments inspire,
Wake into Voice each silent String,
   And sweep the sounding Lyre!

In a sadly-pleasing Strain   5
Let the warbling Lute complain:
   Let the loud Trumpet sound,
   Till the Roofs all around
   The shrill Ecchos rebound:
  While in more lengthen'd Notes and slow,   10
The deep, majestick, solemn Organs blow.
   Hark! the Numbers, soft and clear,
   Gently steal upon the Ear;
   Now louder, and yet louder rise,
   And fill with spreading Sounds the Skies;   15
Exulting in Triumph now swell the bold Notes,
In broken Air, trembling, the wild Musick floats;
   Till, by degrees, remote and small,
    The Strains decay,
    And melt away   20
   In a dying, dying Fall.

By Musick, Minds an equal Temper know,
  Nor swell too high, nor sink too low.
If in the Breast tumultuous Joys arise,
Music her soft, assuasive Voice applies;   25
   Or when the Soul is press'd with Cares
   Exalts her in enlivening Airs.
Warriors she fires with animated Sounds;
Pours Balm into the bleeding *Lover*'s Wounds:
   Melancholy lifts her Head;   30

7 *om. 1730.*
8f. *Lines transposed to 15–17 below, 1730.*
10 While in more] In more *1730.*
14 Now louder, they sound, *1730.*
15–17 *omm.; ll. 8f. being substituted, 1730.*
26 press'd] sunk *1730.*   27 in] with *1730.*
28 with animated] by sprightly *1730.*
29 bleeding] *om. 1730.*   30–3 *omm. 1730.*
30 *Melancholy*] At Musick, *Melancholy 1713–14.*

   Morpheus rowzes from his Bed;
    Sloath unfolds her Arms and wakes;
    List'ning *Envy* drops her Snakes;
  Intestine War no more our *Passions* wage,
  And giddy *Factions* hear away their Rage.   35

  But when our Country's Cause provokes to Arms,
  How martial Musick every Bosom warms!
  So when the first bold Vessel dar'd the Seas,
  High on the Stern the *Thracian* rais'd his Strain,
    While *Argo* saw her kindred Trees   40
    Descend from *Pelion* to the Main.
   Transported Demi-Gods stood round,
   And Men grew Heroes at the Sound,
    Enflam'd with Glory's Charms:
   Each Chief his sevenfold Shield display'd, 45

31 *Morpheus*] Dull *Morpheus 1713–14.*
32 *Sloath* from its Lethargy awakes, *1713–14.*
33 List'ning] And list'ning *1713–14.*
34 Passions no more the Soul engage, *1730.*
35 And] Ev'n *1713–32.* giddy] om. *1730.*
 Following line 35, 1730 prints an additional stanza, not found else-
 where :

   Amphion thus bade wild Dissention cease,
   And soften'd Mortals learn'd the Arts of Peace.
    Amphion taught contending Kings,
     From various Discords to create
     The Musick of a well-tun'd State,
    Nor slack nor strain the tender Strings;
     Those useful Touches to impart
     That strike the Subjects answ'ring Heart;
   And the soft, silent Harmony, that springs
   From Sacred Union and consent of Things.

38f.   When the first Vessel dar'd the Seas,
     The *Thracian* rais'd his Strain, *1730.*
40 While] And *1730.*

And half unsheath'd the shining Blade;
And Seas, and Rocks, and Skies rebound
    To Arms, to Arms, to Arms!

But when thro' all th' Infernal Bounds
Which flaming *Phlegeton* surrounds,   50
Love, strong as Death, the Poet led
To the pale Nations of the Dead,
What Sounds were heard,
What Scenes appear'd,
    O'er all the dreary Coasts!   55
      Dreadful Gleams,
      Dismal screams,
      Fires that glow,
      Shrieks of Woe,
      Sullen Moans,   60
      Hollow Groans,
    And Cries of tortur'd Ghosts.
But hark! he strikes the golden Lyre;
And see! the tortur'd Ghosts respire,
    See shady Forms advance!   65
Thy stone, O *Sysiphus*, stands still;
Ixion rests upon his Wheel,
    And the pale Spectres dance!
The Furies sink upon their Iron Beds,
And Snakes uncurl'd hang list'ning round their Heads.   70

51–56   Sad *Orpheus* sought his Consort lost;
    Th' Inexorable Gates were barr'd,
  And nought was seen, and nought was heard
      Around the dreary Coast,
      But dreadful Gleams, *1713–32*.
  1730 follows 1713 except for Th' Inexorable *read* The Adamantine.
66f. *omm. 1730.*

By the Streams that ever flow,
By the fragrant Winds that blow
   O'er th' *Elysian* Flowers,
By those happy Souls who dwell
In Yellow Meads of *Asphodel*,   75
   Or *Amaranthine* Bowers:
By the Heroe's armed Shades,
Glitt'ring thro' the gloomy Glades,
By the Youths that dy'd for Love,
Wandring in the Myrtle Grove,   80
Restore, restore *Eurydice* to Life;
Oh take the Husband, or return the Wife!

He sung, and Hell consented
   To hear the Poet's Pray'r;
Stern *Proserpine* relented,   85
   And gave him back the Fair.
   Thus Song could prevail
   O'er Death and o'er Hell,
A Conquest how hard and how glorious?
   Tho' Fate had fast bound her   90
   With *Styx* nine times round her,
Yet Musick and Love were Victorious.

But soon, too soon, the Lover turns his Eyes:
Again she falls, again she dies, she dies!
How wilt thou now the fatal Sisters move?   95
No Crime was thine, if 'tis no Crime to love.
   Now under hanging Mountains,
   Beside the Falls of Fountains,
   Or where *Hebrus* wanders,
   Rolling in *Mæanders*,   100
     All alone,
     Unheard, unknown,

92 *1730 ends with this line.*

      He makes his Moan;
        And calls her Ghost
    For ever, ever, ever lost!   105
    Now with Furies surrounded,
    Despairing, confounded,
    He trembles, he glows,
    Amidst *Rhodope*'s Snows:
See, wild as the Winds, o'er the Desart he flies;   110
Hark! *Hæmus* resounds with the *Bacchanals*' Cries—
      —Ah see, he dies!
Yet ev'n in Death *Eurydice* he sung,
Eurydice still trembled on his Tongue,
      Eurydice the Woods,   115
      Eurydice the Floods,
Eurydice the Rocks, and hollow Mountains rung.

      Musick the fiercest Grief can charm,
      And Fate's severest Rage disarm:
      Musick can soften Pain to Ease,   120
      And make Despair and Madness please:
      Our Joys below it can improve,
      And antedate the Bliss above.
        This the divine *Cecilia* found,
And to her Maker's Praise confin'd the Sound.   125
When the full Organ joins the tuneful Quire,
    Th' Immortal Pow'rs incline their Ear;
Born on the swelling Notes our Souls aspire,
While solemn Airs improve the sacred Fire;
    And Angels lean from Heav'n to hear!   130
Of *Orpheus* now no more let Poets tell,
To bright *Cecilia* greater Pow'r is giv'n;
    His Numbers rais'd a Shade from Hell,
    Hers lift the Soul to Heav'n.

118 Grief] Griefs *1713–32*.
127 Th'] The *1713–14*.

Ode for Musick. 1713 (and later editions).

Miscellaneous Poems and Translations. 2nd Edition. 1714 (and 1720, 1722; and *Miscellany Poems*, 1726, 1727, 1732).

An Essay on Criticism. Written by Mr. Pope. 5th Edition. 1716.

The Works of Mr. Alexander Pope. 1717.

The Works . . . Dublin. 1718.

The Works . . . (Printed by T. J.) 1718 (and 1720).

The Works . . . *To which are added, I. Cooper's-Hill* . . . Dublin. 1727.

Quæstiones, una cum Carminibus, in Magnis Comitiis Cantabrigiæ Celebratis 1730. 1730.

The Works . . . *Vol. I. With Explanatory Notes and Additions* . . . 1736 (both variants).

A Miscellany of Lyric Poems. 1740.

The Works . . . *Vol. I. Part I.* 1740 (and 1743).

Carmen Cl. Alexandri Pope In S. Cæciliam Latine Reditum A Christophero Smart. 1743 (and 1746).

A Select Collection of Modern Poems. 1744.

The Works. Ed. Warburton. Vol. I. 1751.

The *Ode for Musick* was published by Lintot as a folio pamphlet of twelve pages on 16 July 1713, the half-title reading, "Mr. Pope's Ode on St. Cecilia's Day"; and a week later (23 July) Pope received £15 from Lintot in payment for it. The date of composition is less easily determined. In the 1736 edition of *The Works* . . . *Vol. I*, Pope dated the poem 1708, and about the same time said to Spence (p. 158): "Many people would like my Ode on Music better, if Dryden had not written on that subject. It was at the request of Mr. Steele that I wrote mine; and not with any thought of rivalling that great man, whose memory I do and always have reverenced." As there is nothing to show that Pope and Steele knew each other before 1711—about which time their mutual friend John Caryll is generally supposed to have made them acquainted—it is difficult to reconcile Pope's statement to Spence with his forthright dating of the Ode, although in two lines of his rhymed letter to Cromwell (25 April 1708) he seems to be quoting from it (see ll. 75–8 above, also p. 40). On 26 July 1711 Steele wrote to Pope desiring "to know whether you are at leisure to help Mr. Clayton [a musical composer of the time] . . . to some words for music against winter", and, the following week, Pope wrote to Caryll (2 August) saying, "I have two letters from Mr. Steele . . . to persuade me to write a musicall Interlude to be sett next winter by Clayton. . . . The desire I have to gratifye Mr. Steele has made me consent to his request." To these should be added an unprinted letter from Pope to Steele dated 6 December 1712, formerly among the Blenheim MSS and sold at Messrs Sotheby's on 1 July 1920, in which (according to their catalogue) he tells Steele "to do what he pleases with a paper he has written" and "speaks of the Ode left with Steele last winter". Whatever the "paper" may have been (and the *Temple of Fame* has been conjectured), it is quite certain that "last winter" was the winter of 1711–12, against which time Pope had promised Steele to write "some words for music". Seeing, therefore, that there is no other known "ode" of Pope's to which he could be referring at that time in that way, it is probable that the poem to which he refers in this letter, and therefore in the others, was the *Ode for Musick*.

The Ode seems to have been one of two poems (the other being *Windsor Forest*) which were set up in type for inclusion in the first edition of "Lintot's Miscellany" and then withdrawn just before it went to press. It is practically certain that Pope was the concealed editor of the miscellany and, for some reason, probably political, he and Lintot agreed that a separate publication in folio of *Windsor Forest* would be more advantageous at a later date. As, however, the poem occupied more than one sheet, the rest of the second sheet containing the *Ode for Musick* was withdrawn likewise. This would explain why the miscellany, when published on 20 May 1712, had a gap of thirty-two missing pages in the pagination where two complete sheets (with signatures Y and Z) had been removed; and how, in the second edition (which in the main was a re-issue of the unsold sheets of the first) the gap no longer exists, having been filled by the restoration of these two poems to their original—if temporary—place in the volume. In the meantime the two poems—after the longer had received some additions—had been published separately in folio, *Windsor Forest* on 7 March 1712/13, and the *Ode* on 16 July. (See further "Pope and the Miscellanies" by N. Ault; *Nineteenth Century and After*, November 1934, CXVII, pp. 566–70.)

It would therefore seem that, on receiving Steele's request, Pope looked through his unpublished work, sketches, rough drafts, and unpublished pieces, and found, revised, or re-wrote an old ode of his which had originally been roughed out in 1708.

St Cecilia's Day (22 November) had been observed as an annual festival by musicians in London since 1683 (similar festivals being held at Oxford and a few other places), and many poets were called on to provide the odes, songs, or hymns which were set to music for performance on that day. Among the poets who thus wrote for the festival are Oldham, Dryden (twice), Addison (twice), Yalden, Shadwell, Congreve, and Hughes—all before Pope. The custom was falling into disuse by about 1708, though sporadic attempts were later made to revive it. Thus Pope's *Ode* was probably never set to music by Clayton, nor performed on St Cecilia's Day, for no such setting seems either to have survived or to have been anywhere recorded. In 1730, however, Pope rewrote it for Dr Greene, whose musical setting was performed at "Publick Commencement" at Cambridge on 6 July of that year. The *Ode* in its original form was set to music still later by W. Walond, and performed at Oxford in 1758.

The first edition (*1713*) has been adopted as copy-text and emended in the light of later revisions. Collations are also given from the version revised for Dr Greene's setting (*1730*).

130. Cf. *Temple of Fame*, 375: "Ev'n list'ning Angels lean'd from Heaven to hear."

EPIGRAM.
Occasion'd by
Ozell's Translation of *Boileau's Lutrin.*

Printed for *E. Sanger,* and recommended by Mr. *Rowe,* in which
Mr. *Wycherley's* POEMS printed in 1704, were reflected on.

O ZELL, at *Sanger's* Call, invok'd his Muse, ⎫
      For who to sing for *Sanger* could refuse? ⎬
His Numbers such, as *Sanger's* self might use. ⎭
Reviving *Perault,* murd'ring *Boileau,* he
Slander'd the Ancients first, then *Wycherley*;   5
Not that it much that Author's Anger rais'd,
For those were slander'd most whom *Ozell* prais'd:
Nor had the toothless Satyr caus'd complaining,
Had not sage *Rowe* pronounc'd it *Entertaining.*
How great, how just, the Judgment of that Writer! 10
Who the *Plain-dealer* damns, and prints the *Biter.*

Title] MS has no title in Pope's hand; Curll (1727) added a title: "The
    Translator".
6 Which yet not much that Old Bard's Anger rais'd, *MS, 1727.*
7 For] Since *MS, 1727.*
8 toothless Satyr] gentle Satire *MS, 1727.*
10 great, how just,] great must be *MS, 1727.*

Pope's autograph: Bodleian MS Rawl. letters 90.
Miscellanea. In Two Volumes. Vol. I. 1727.
The Posthumous Works of William Wycherley, Esq. Vol. II. 1729.
Mr. Pope's Literary Correspondence. Vol. II. 1735 (and 2nd Edition, 1735).
A Supplement to the Works . . . 1757.
Additions to the Works of Alexander Pope, Esq. Vol. I. 1776.
The Works. Ed. Warton. Vol. II. 1797.

On 1 June 1708, John Ozell published his translation of Boileau's *Lutrin.* In his
description of the mock battle in Canto v, where the combatants arm themselves
for the fray with "ammunition books", he wrote:

> One with vindictive Hand light Durfey shakes;
> Another, Wycherley more weighty, takes.

The offensiveness of the allusion derives from the fact that Wycherley's *Miscellany*

Poems, which had been rather pretentiously published four years earlier in unusually large folio (a copy in the Bodleian measures 14 by 9 inches and contains nearly 500 pages), had been something of a failure in spite of his renown as a playwright. To make matters worse, Rowe, in his appreciative foreword to Ozell's *Lutrin*, spoke of the translator's "mustering up a Set of English Authors of equal Degree and like kind of Dulness with those mention'd by M. Boileau"; and said that he found "The Satyr upon our own Countrymen . . . very just and entertaining"—a remark which elicited a verbal echo from Pope. For Pope himself was at that time actually engaged in selecting, correcting, and revising Wycherley's poems, published and unpublished; and, impelled to champion his friend, he wrote and sent him an epigram on the subject, to which the old man replied on 13 November 1708: "I thank you for the Friendship as well as the Wit of your Epigram, which I cou'd praise more were it less to my own Praise."

This epigram was never acknowledged by Pope, presumably because of its attack on Rowe with whom Pope later became friendly. It was not published until long after Rowe's death, when Curll printed it as Pope's in *Miscellanea*. More than twenty years later, Pope was still resentful of Ozell's treatment of Wycherley; for he not only included the epigram anonymously in the second volume of *The Posthumous Works*, but in another footnote in the same volume alluded again to Ozell's poor version of the *Lutrin*, and again stated that "it reflected upon Mr. Wycherley by name" (see *post*, p. 60).

The text is that of *1729* (Pope's only printed text), with collations from the autograph (*MS*) and the first printed edition.

Title: *Boileau*] 1636–1711. His *Lutrin*, of which cantos i–iv were published in 1674, created a new kind of burlesque in French literature.

1. *Ozell*] See Biog. App., Vol. V.   *Sanger*] Egbert Sanger, book-seller, served his apprenticeship with Jacob Tonson, followed Lintot in occupation of the shop at the Middle-Temple-Gate, 1707–12.

4. *Reviving Perault*] *Characters . . . of the Greatest Men . . . in France . . . By Monsieur Perrault . . . Render'd into English, by J. Ozell.* Two vols. Printed for Bernard Lintott. 1704–5.

5. *Wycherley*] See introductory note.

9. *Rowe . . . Entertaining . . . how just*] In the foreword to Ozell's *Lutrin* Rowe had praised the translation in these words. See introductory note.

11. *Plain-dealer . . . Biter*] Wycherley wrote the former play (and was himself sometimes so designated) and Rowe the later, and inferior, play. This line was used again the following year in the MS *Conclusion to The Bill of Fare* (see p. 59, l. 14).

LETTER to *CROMWELL*.

April ye 25. 1708.

Sir,

T HIS Letter greets you from the Shades;
(Not those which thin, unbody'd Shadows fill,
 That glide along th' Elysian Glades,
Or skim the flow'ry Meads of *Asphodill*:)
But those, in which a Learned Author said,   5
 Strong Drink was drunk, and Gambolls play'd,
And two substantial Meals a day were made.
 The Business of it is t' express,
 From me and from my Holiness,
 To you and to your Gentleness,   10
How much I wish you Health and Happiness;
And much good News, and little Spleen as may be;
 A hearty Stomach, and sound Lady;
And ev'ry Day a double Dose of Coffee,
To make you look as sage as any Sophy.   15

[*The letter is continued "in plain prose" for a space, only to resume verse
with—*]

If Wit or Critick blame the tender Swain,
Who stil'd the gentle Damsels in his Strain
The Nymphs of *Drury*, not of *Drury*-Lane;
Be this his Answer, and most just Excuse—
'Far be it, Sirs, from my more civill Muse,   20
'Those Loving Ladies rudely to traduce.
'Allyes and Lanes are Terms too vile and base,
'And give Idea's of a narrow Pass;
'But the well-worn Paths of the Nymphs of Drury
'Are large and wide; *Tydcomb* and I assure ye. 25

[*After a further section in prose, the letter concludes thus—*]

To *Baker* first my Service, pray;
  To *Tydcomb* eke,
  And Mr. *Cheek*;
Last to *yourself* my best Respects I pay,
And so remain, for ever and for ay,   30
           Sir,
        Yʳ Affectionate, humble Servᵗ:
           A. Pope.

Pope's autograph: Bodleian MS Rawl. letters 90.
Miscellanea. In Two Volumes. Vol. I. 1727.
The Female Dunciad. 1728 (middle section only).
Mr. Pope's Literary Correspondence. Vol. II. 1735 (and 2nd Edition, 1735).
A Supplement to the Works ... 1757.
Additions to the Works of Alexander Pope, Esq. Vol. II. 1776.
A Supplementary Volume to the Works of Alexander Pope, Esq. 1807 (omits middle section).

The second rhymed letter to Cromwell, unlike the earlier epistle (p. 24), has two long lapses into prose which are here omitted.

The text follows that of the autograph in every respect.

2–4. Cf. these lines with *Ode for Music*, ll. 73–8, which Pope claimed to have written the same year, especially "In the yellow meads of Asphodel" (see p. 35).

16. *the tender Swain*] *i.e.* Pope himself. The whole passage refers back to his previous letter in rhyme (see p. 26, l. 51).

18. *Drury-Lane*] Notorious as the abode of loose women.

25. *Tydcomb*] See p. 29.

26. *Baker*] Possibly Thomas Baker, the dramatist (fl. 1700–09).

An Essay on Criticism

[written 1709; published 15 May 1711; vol. 1, pp. 233–326]

IMITATIONS

OF

ENGLISH POETS.

The *Imitations of English Poets* was a relatively late grouping of poems admittedly written at different times, and, for the most part, published separately over a period of twenty-four years. They were first collected under this title in 1736, when nine were published in the third volume of the *Works*, a tenth being added in 1741. An "Advertisement" to "Vol. III" declared that the pieces in this group were written early, "some of them at fourteen or fifteen Years old", and that there should be no mistake Pope also stated in the group title, "Done by the Author in his Youth". For the six pieces which were not—or cannot be—more precisely dated, the statement "in his Youth" is taken to mean "written before he was twenty one years old", and they are therefore dated "before 1709". Of the remainder, Pope elsewhere declared that two were written at thirteen (*i.e.* in 1701, see pp. 8, 13), and one at fourteen (*i.e.* 1702, see p. 19), and the last of them, the Swift imitation, is for other reasons dated *circa* 1713 (see p. 111).

I.

CHAUCER.

Women ben full of Ragerie,
Yet swinken nat sans Secresie.
Thilke moral shall ye understond,
From Schole-boy's Tale of fayre *Irelond*:
Which to the Fennes hath him betake,   5
To filch the gray Ducke fro the Lake.
Right then, there passen by the Way,
His Aunt, and eke her Daughters tway:
Ducke in his Trowzes hath he hent,
Not to be spied of Ladies gent.   10

Title A Tale of Chaucer. Lately found in an old Manuscript. *1727.*
1–4   Women, tho' nat sans Leacherie,
                Ne swinken but with Secrecie:
                This in our Tale is plain y-fond,
                Of Clerk, that wonneth in *Irelond*: *1727.*

"But ho! our Nephew," (crieth one,)
"Ho!" quoth another, "Cozen *John*!"
And stoppen, and lough, and callen out,—
This sely Clerk full low doth lout:
They asken that, and talken this,   15
"Lo here is *Coz*, and here is *Miss*."
But, as he glozeth with Speeches soote,
The Ducke sore tickleth his Erse Roote:
Fore-piece and Buttons all-to-brest,
Forth thrust a white Neck, and red Crest.   20
Te-he cry'd Ladies; Clerke nought spake:
Miss star'd; and gray Ducke crieth *Quaake*.
"O Moder, Moder," (quoth the Daughter,)
"Be thilke same Thing Maids longen a'ter?
"Bette is to pyne on Coals and Chalke,   25
"Then trust on Mon, whose yerde can *talke*."

Miscellanies. The Last Volume. 1727 (and later editions).

The Works . . . Vol. III. Consisting of Fables, Translations, and Imitations. 1736.

The Works . . . Vol. I. Part II. Consisting of Fables, Translations, and Imitations.
1741.

Miscellanies. The Fourth Volume. Consisting of Verses . . . 1742 (and later editions).

The Works. Ed. Warburton. Vol. II. 1751.

First printed anonymously in 1727 [1728] as *A Tale of Chaucer. Lately found in an
old Manuscript*, this poem was not acknowledged until 1736 when Pope included
it as the opening piece in his newly formed group of *Imitations of English Poets*. For
date, see introductory note above.

The copy-text (*1727*) has been emended to incorporate the final revisions of
1736.

II.

SPENSER.

The ALLEY.

IN ev'ry Town, where *Thamis* rolls his Tyde,
    A narrow Pass there is, with Houses low;
Where ever and anon, the Stream is ey'd,
And many a Boat soft sliding to and fro.
There oft' are heard the Notes of Infant Woe,   5
The short thick Sob, loud Scream, and shriller Squawl:
How can ye, Mothers, vex your Children so?
Some play, some eat, some cack against the Wall,
And as they crouchen low, for Bread and Butter call.

And on the broken Pavement here and there,   10
Doth many a stinking Sprat and Herring lie;
A Brandy and Tobacco Shop is near,
And Hens, and Dogs, and Hogs are feeding by;
And here a Sailor's Jacket hangs to dry:
At ev'ry Door are Sun-burnt Matrons seen,   15
Mending old Nets to catch the scaly Fry;
Now singing shrill, and scolding eft between,
Scolds answer foul-mouth'd Scolds; bad Neighbourhood
        I ween.

The snappish Cur, (the Passengers annoy)
Close at my Heel with yelping Treble flies;   20
The whimp'ring Girl, and hoarser-screaming Boy,
Join to the yelping Treble shrilling Cries;
The scolding Quean to louder Notes doth rise,
And her full Pipes those shrilling Cries confound:
To her full Pipes the grunting Hog replies;   25
The grunting Hogs alarm the Neighbours round,

Title The Alley. An Imitation of Spenser. *1727.*

3

And Curs, Girls, Boys, and Scolds, in the deep Base are
    drown'd.

Hard by a Sty, beneath a Roof of Thatch,
Dwelt *Obloquy*, who in her early Days
Baskets of Fish at *Billingsgate* did watch,   30
Cod, Whiting, Oyster, Mackrel, Sprat, or Plaice:
There learn'd she Speech from Tongues that never cease.
Slander beside her, like a Magpye, chatters,
With *Envy*, (spitting Cat,) dread Foe to Peace:
Like a curs'd Cur, *Malice* before her clatters,   35
And vexing ev'ry Wight, tears Cloaths and all to Tatters.

Her Dugs were mark'd by ev'ry Collier's Hand,
Her Mouth was black as Bull-Dogs at the Stall:
She scratched, bit, and spar'd ne Lace ne Band,
And Bitch and Rogue her Answer was to all;   40
Nay, e'en the Parts of Shame by Name would call:
Yea when she passed by or Lane or Nook,
Would greet the Man who turn'd him to the Wall,
And by his Hand obscene the Porter took,
Nor ever did askance like modest Virgin look.   45

Such place hath *Deptford*, Navy-building Town,
Woolwich and *Wapping*, smelling strong of Pitch;
Such *Lambeth*, Envy of each Band and Gown,
And *Twick'nam* such, which fairer Scenes enrich,
Grots, Statues, Urns, and *Jo—n*'s *Dog* and *Bitch*:   50
Ne Village is without, on either side,
All up the silver *Thames*, or all a down;
Ne *Richmond*'s self, from whose tall Front are ey'd
Vales, Spires, meandring Streams, and *Windsor*'s tow'ry Pride.

39 ne Lace ne Band] nor Lace and Band *1727*.
40 to all] at all *1727*.   42 Yea when she] Whene'er she *1727*.
53 are ey'd] is ey'd *1727*.

Miscellanies. The Last Volume. 1727 (and later editions).
The Works . . . Vol. III. Consisting of Fables, Translations, and Imitations. 1736.
The Works . . . With Explanatory Notes and Additions . . . Vol. I. 1736.
The Works . . . Vol. I. Part II. Consisting of Fables, Translations, and Imitations.
1741.
Miscellanies. The Fourth Volume. Consisting of Verses . . . 1742 (and later editions).
The Works. Ed. Warburton. Vol. II. 1751.

About the time of the anonymous publication of this poem in 1727–8, Spence
made the following note of a remark of Pope's (p. 23): "The Alley, in imitation of
Spenser, was written by Mr. Pope, with a line or two of Mr. Gay's in it"—but as
he was not curious enough to make further inquiry, which lines Gay contributed
will probably never be known. The poem was not publicly acknowledged until
the 1736 edition of The Works . . . Vol. III, when it was placed second in the group
of Imitations of English Poets. Done by the Author in his Youth. It is therefore dated
"before 1709" (see introductory note, p. 41), though ll. 49f. perhaps suggest a
late revision.

The copy-text (1727) has been emended to incorporate the final revisions of
1736.

50. Jo—n's Dog and Bitch] James Johnston (1655–1737), one-time Secretary of
State for Scotland, and responsible for the inquiry into the Glencoe massacre; in
retirement he was a near neighbour of Pope's at Twickenham, and displayed on
his garden wall "two miserable little leaden figures of a dog and a bitch" (re-
discovered by Croker in the last century) which apparently moved Pope to
mirth.

III.

WALLER.

On a FAN *of the Author's design,*
in which was painted the story of
CEPHALUS *and* PROCRIS *with*
the Motto, AURA VENI.

COME, gentle Air! th' *Æolian* Shepherd said,
  While *Procris* panted in the secret shade;
Come, gentle Air, the fairer *Delia* cries,
While at her feet her swain expiring lies.
Lo the glad gales o'er all her beauties stray,   5
Breathe on her lips, and in her bosom play!
In *Delia's* hand this toy is fatal found,

Nor could that fabled dart more surely wound:
Both gifts destructive to the givers prove;
Alike both lovers fall by those they love. 10
Yet guiltless too this bright destroyer lives,
At random wounds, nor knows the wound she gives:
She views the story with attentive eyes,
And pities *Procris*, while her lover dies.

8 could] did *1712*.   12 wound] wounds *1712*.

The Spectator. No. 527. 4 November 1712.
The Works of Mr. Alexander Pope. 1717.
The Works . . . Dublin. 1718.
The Works . . . (Printed by T. J.) 1718 (and 1720).
Miscellaneous Poems and Translations. 3rd Edition. 1720 (and all later editions
to *Miscellany Poems*, 6th Edition, 1732).
The Works . . . To which are added, I. Cooper's-Hill . . . Dublin. 1727.
A Collection of Epigrams. 1727 (and 2nd Edition, 1735).
The Works . . . Vol. I. Part II. Consisting of Fables, Translations, and Imitations
1741 (and 1745).
The London Magazine. June 1741.
Joe Miller's Jests. 5th Edition. 1742 (and later editions).
The Works. Ed. Warburton. Vol. II. 1751.

This poem was first printed in *The Spectator*, preceded by the following letter,
undoubtedly from Pope's hand (see *The Prose Works*, I xxxv):

Mr. SPECTATOR,

YOU will oblige a languishing Lover if you will please to print the en-
closed Verses in your next Paper. If you remember the *Metamorphosis*, you
know *Procris*, the fond Wife of *Cephalus*, is said to have made her Husband, who
delighted in the Sports of the Wood, a Present of an unerring Javelin. In Pro-
cess of Time he was so much in the Forest, that his Lady suspected he was pur-
suing some Nymph, under the Pretence of following a Chace more innocent.
Under this Suspicion she hid herself among the Trees to observe his Motions.
While she lay concealed, her Husband, tired with the Labour of Hunting,
came within her Hearing. As he was fainting with Heat, he cry'd out *Aura veni*;
Oh charming Air approach.

The unfortunate Wife taking the word *Air* to be the Name of a Woman,
began to move among the Bushes, and the Husband believing it a Deer, threw
his Javelin and kill'd her. This History painted on a Fan, which I presented to
a Lady, gave Occasion to my growing poetical.

The poem was not associated with Waller's name until 1741, when it was at last

included in the *Imitations of English Poets*. As these were stated to have been
"Done by the Author in his Youth", the poem is dated, like most of the others,
"before 1709" (see introductory note, p. 41).

No revisions were made after *1717*, which has been chosen for copy-text.

IV.
COWLEY.
The GARDEN.

FAIN would my Muse the flow'ry Treasures sing,
   And humble glories of the youthful Spring;
Where opening *Roses* breathing sweets diffuse,
And soft *Carnations* show'r their balmy dews;
Where *Lillies* smile in virgin robes of white,   5
The thin Undress of superficial Light,
And vary'd *Tulips* show so dazling gay,
Blushing in bright diversities of day.
Each painted flouret in the lake below
Surveys its beauties, whence its beauties grow;   10
And pale *Narcissus* on the bank, in vain
Transformed, gazes on himself again.
Here aged trees Cathedral walks compose,
And mount the Hill in venerable rows:
There the green Infants in their beds are laid,   15
The Garden's Hope, and its expected shade.
Here *Orange*-trees with blooms and pendants shine,
And vernal honours to their autumn join;
Exceed their promise in the ripen'd store,
Yet in the rising blossom promise more.   20
There in bright drops the crystal Fountains play,
By *Laurels* shielded from the piercing Day:
Where *Daphne*, now a tree as once a maid,
Still from *Apollo* vindicates her shade,
Still turns her beauties from th' invading beam,   25
Nor seeks in vain for succour to the Stream.

The stream at once preserves her virgin leaves,
At once a shelter from her boughs receives,
Where *Summer*'s beauty midst of *Winter* stays,
And *Winter*'s Coolness spite of *Summer*'s rays.   30

The Works . . . *Vol. III. Consisting of Fables, Translations, and Imitations.* 1736.
The Works . . . *Vol. I, Part II. Consisting of Fables, Translations, and Imitations.*
1741 (and 1745).
The Works. Ed. Warburton. Vol. II. 1751.
The Garden was printed for the first time in 1736, when it appeared among the
Imitations of English Poets. Done by the Author in his Youth. Pope apparently had this
poem in mind about 1730 (possibly with a view to including it in the *Miscellanies*);
for one of its lines (8) is worked into *Mor. Ess.*, IV (1731), l. 84, and Spence reports
him as expatiating on the possiblity of obtaining cathedral-like effects by planting
trees in rows (*Anecdotes*, 1728–30, p. 12), an idea also touched on in the poem.
The poem is dated "before 1709" for reasons stated in the general introductory
note (p. 41).
    The text follows that of *1736*. There are no variants.
    8. Cf. *Mor. Ess.*, IV 84.

V.

E. of DORSET.

i. ARTIMESIA.

T HO' *Artimesia* talks, by Fits,
        Of Councils, Classicks, Fathers, Wits;
    Reads *Malbranche*, *Boyle*, and *Locke*:
Yet in some Things methinks she fails,
'Twere well if she would pare her Nails,   5
    And wear a cleaner Smock.

Haughty and huge as *High-Dutch* Bride,
Such Nastiness and so much Pride
    Are odly join'd by Fate:
On her large Squab you find her spread,   10
Like a fat Corpse upon a Bed,
    That lies and stinks in State.

She wears no Colours (sign of Grace)
On any Part except her Face;
   All white and black beside: 15
Dauntless her Look, her Gesture proud,
Her Voice theatrically loud,
   And masculine her Stride.

So have I seen, in black and white
A prating Thing, a Magpy height,   20
   Majestically stalk;
A stately, worthless Animal,
That plies the Tongue, and wags the Tail,
   All Flutter, Pride, and Talk.

ii. PHRYNE.

PHRYNE had Talents for Mankind,
   Open she was, and unconfin'd,
   Like some free Port of Trade:
Merchants unloaded here their Freight,
And Agents from each foreign State,   5
   Here first their Entry made.

Her Learning and good Breeding such,
Whether th' *Italian* or the *Dutch*,
   Spaniard or *French* came to her;
To all obliging she'd appear: 10
'Twas *Si Signior*, 'twas *Yaw Mynheer*,
   'Twas *S'il vous plaist, Monsieur*.

1 for] to oblige *MS.*   3 Like] As *MS.*
4 unloaded] unladed *MS.*   5 Agents] Envoys *MS.*
6 Entry] Entrys *MS.*   8 Whether] Whither *MS.*
9 *Spaniard*] *Spaniards 1736–51.*   11 'twas *Yaw*] & Yaw *MS.*
12 'Twas] & *MS.*

Obscure by Birth, renown'd by Crimes,
Still changing Names, Religions, Climes,
    At length she turns a Bride: 15
In Di'monds, Pearls, and rich Brocades,
She shines the first of batter'd Jades,
    And flutters in her Pride.

So have I known those Insects fair,
(Which curious *Germans* hold so rare,)   20
    Still vary Shapes and Dyes;
Still gain new Titles with new Forms;
First Grubs obscene, then wriggling Worms,
    Then painted Butterflies.

13–15 *MS reads:*

    Now all her various States worn out
    The Town in Coach & 6 about
    She does in Triumph ride

16 Pearls] silks *MS.*
19 known those Insects] seen an Insect *MS.*
21–4 *MS reads:*

    full often change its name
    And varying still in State & form
    From Grub Obscene, & wriggling Worm
    It Butterfly became.

Lady M. W. Montagu's autograph: Harrowby MS Sandon. [*Phryne* only.]
Miscellanies. The Last Volume. 1727 (and later editions).
The Works . . . Vol. III. Consisting of Fables, Translations, and Imitations. 1736.
The Works . . . With Explanatory Notes and Additions . . . Vol. I. 1736.
A Collection of Epigrams. Vol. II. 1737.
The Works . . . Vol. I. Part II. Consisting of Fables, Translations, and Imitations. 1741 (and 1745).
Miscellanies. The Fourth Volume. Consisting of Verses . . . 1742 (and later editions).
The Works. Ed. Warburton. Vol. II. 1751.
    Entitled simply *Artimesia*, and *Phryne*, with no mention of Dorset, or of Imitations, when first published in 1727–8, these two poems appear in the *Works* (1736) as imitations of the Earl of Dorset in the group called *Imitations of English Poets.* Pope apparently forgot to include his earlier imitation of Dorset (see p. 17) in this group of similar imitations "Done by the Author in his Youth". For reasons

stated in the introductory note (p. 41) these pieces are dated "before 1709".

It is unnecessary to search, with earlier commentators, for prototypes of these two type-characters.

The text of both pieces follows that of *1727* with collations from Lady Mary's transcript (*MS*) of *Phryne*. The single verbal variant in a later printed text is probably not authentic.

(*i*) 3. Nicole Malebranche (1638–1715), French philosopher. His *Recherche de la Vérité* (1674) had been translated into English in 1694. Robert Boyle (1627–91) the author of numerous books on chemistry, physics, and philosophy. John Locke (1632–1704). *An Essay concerning Humane Understanding* (1690) had reached a seventh edition by 1716.

10. *Squab*] A sofa or couch.

(*ii*) *Phryne*] *Grk.* φρύνη, a toad. The nickname of several Athenian courtesans.

ARGUS.

WHEN wise *Ulysses*, from his native coast
Long kept by wars, and long by tempests tost,
Arriv'd at last, poor, old, disguis'd, alone,
To all his friends, and ev'n his Queen, unknown,
Chang'd as he was, with age, and toils, and cares,   5
Furrow'd his rev'rend face, and white his hairs,
In his own Palace forc'd to ask his bread,
Scorn'd by those slaves his former bounty fed
Forgot of all his own domestic crew;
The faithful Dog alone his rightful Master knew!   10
Unfed, unhous'd, neglected, on the clay,
Like an old servant now cashier'd, he lay;
Touch'd with resentment of ungrateful Man,
And longing to behold his ancient Lord again.
Him when he saw—he rose, and crawl'd to meet,   15

10 The faithful] His faithful *MS, 1727, US, GM*; alone *omm. MS, 1727, US, GM*.
12 *Following this line MS, 1727, US, GM read:*
        And tho' ev'n then expiring on the Plain,

3*

('Twas all he cou'd) and fawn'd, and lick'd his feet,
Seiz'd with dumb joy—then falling by his side,
Own'd his returning Lord, look'd up, and dy'd!

16 lick'd] kiss'd *MS, 1727, US, GM, 1735, 1742, 1751.*

Pope's autograph: Bodleian MS Rawl. letters 90.
Miscellanea. In Two Volumes. Vol. I. 1727.
The Universal Spectator. 4 January 1735.
The Gentleman's Magazine. January 1735.
The London Magazine. January 1735.
Letters of Mr. Pope . . . Vol. I. 1735.
Mr. Pope's Literary Correspondence. Vol. I. 1735 (and 3rd Edition, 1735).
Letters of . . . Pope ["Works . . . In Prose". Vol. I.]. 1737.
The Works . . . Vol. V. Consisting of Letters. 1737 (and 2nd Edition, 1737).
The Works . . . Vol. IV. Part I. Containing . . . Letters. 1742.
Joe Miller's Jests. 5th Edition. 1742 (and some later editions).
The Works . . . Volume VII. Containing . . . Letters. Ed. Warburton. 1751.
A Collection of Select Epigrams. J. Hackett. 1757.
Colley Cibber's Jests. 1761.
The Works. Ed. Dyce. Vol. II. 1831.

These lines were sent to Henry Cromwell in a letter dated 19 October 1709. After speaking of his own dog and mentioning others, Pope continues: "Homer's Account of Ulysses's dog Argus, is the most pathetic imaginable, . . . and an excellent Proof of the Old Bard's Good nature. Ulysses had left him at Ithaca when he embarkd for Troy, & found him on his return after 20 years, (wch by the way is not unnatural, as some Criticks have said, since I remember ye Dam of my Dog who was 22 years old when she dy'd: May the Omen of Longevity prove fortunate to her Successour!) You shall have it in Verse—". Unlike the fragments of Homer which he attempted in English verse from time to time, Pope did not inset this in the great work: no more than two separate couplets and a single line were amended and transferred to it, the piece as a whole being condensed too much for inclusion in a full-scale translation of the *Odyssey*.

The text follows that of *Letters 1735*, with the incorporation of one correction from the final text of *1737*, overlooked in the last edition of Pope's lifetime, and by Warburton. Collations are given from the first four texts mentioned above (*MS, 1727, US, GM*).

10. This line reappeared in *Od.* XVII 345, thus: "*Argus*, the Dog, his ancient master knew."

11–12. This couplet reappeared thus:
            Now left to man's ingratitude he lay,
            Un-hous'd, neglected, in the publick way; (356–7).

15–16. And this couplet took this form:
            He knew his Lord; he knew, and strove to meet,
            In vain he strove, to crawl, and kiss his feet; (360–1).

LINES
On Dulness

THUS Dulness, the safe Opiate of the Mind,
   The last kind Refuge weary Wit can find,
Fit for all Stations and in each content
Is satisfy'd, secure, and innocent:
No Pains it takes, and no Offence it gives,   5
Un-fear'd, un-hated, un-disturb'd it lives.
—And if each writing Author's best pretence,
Be but to teach the Ignorant more Sense;
Then Dulness was the Cause they wrote before,
As 'tis at last the Cause they write no more;   10
So Wit, which most to scorn it does pretend,
With Dulness first began, in Dulness last must end.

Title Verses omitted in the Panegyrick on Dulness. Vol. I. Page 12.
   1729.
3 each] all *1729.*

> *The Posthumous Works of William Wycherley, Esq.* Vol. II. 1729.
> *Letters of Mr. Pope . . . Vol. I.* 1735.
> *Mr. Pope's Literary Correspondence.* Vol. I. 1735 (and 3rd Edition, 1735).
> *The Works . . . Vol. V. Consisting of Letters.* 1737.
> *The Works . . . Vol. V. Containing . . . Letters. 2nd Edition.* 1737.
> *The Works . . . Vol. IV. Part I. Containing . . . Letters.* 1742.
> *The Works . . . Vol. VII. Containing . . . Letters.* Ed. Warburton. 1751.

Pope on his own confession made considerable additions to Wycherley's
poems in manuscript between the years 1706 and 1710 (see p. 54). Only one
passage, however, the lines "On Dulness", has any bibliographical history; for
which reason it is convenient here to separate it from the others.

    Writing to Wycherley (20 November 1707) Pope describes what alterations he
has made in *A Panegyrick on Dulness*: "The fourth Part I have wholly added, as a
Climax which sums up all the *praise, advantage,* and *happiness* of Dulness in a few
words, and strengthens them by the opposition of the *disgrace, disadvantage,* and
unhappiness of Wit, with which it concludes." To this statement in the *Posthumous
Works*, Vol. II, he appended a footnote in which he printed the first six of these
twelve lines on Dulness, saying they were omitted "in the present Edition"—*i.e.
The Posthumous Works of William Wycherley, Esq.*, Vol. I, 1728, which had been
edited by Theobald. Pope also printed separately these twelve lines in the section

of "Miscellaneous Poems" in the same Vol. II, with the explanatory title: "Verses Omitted in the Panegyrick on Dulness. Vol. I. Page 12". The twelve lines reappear once more in *Letters . . . Vol. I.*, 1735, but all subsequent editions of the Letters include only the first six.

The text follows that of *1729*, but incorporates a single correction from *1735*.

LINES
Added to *WYCHERLEY*'s Poems.

The Posthumous Works of William Wycherley, Esq. Vol. I. 1728; and Vol. II. 1729.

There is much evidence in their correspondence between 1706 and 1710 to show that when Pope was requested to correct Wycherley's poems, he was also encouraged to make what additions he thought fit. Some of the passages he added were pointed out by Pope himself in footnotes to the *Letters* from 1735 onwards (such as the lines "On Dulness" on the preceding page, and the "Similitudes of the Byass of a Bowl, and the Weights of a Clock" on the following page). But Pope had made explicit statements about these additions several years earlier, in Wycherley's *Posthumous Works*, Vol. II, of which he was the anonymous editor, and which, it is thought, he suppressed soon after publication. In an address "To the Reader" Pope explains (in the third person) how the volume came into being, touching on the *Letters* briefly and talking at length about the poems and "the History of their Correction". Next comes "The Contents Of Vol. I." which begins with the note: "N.B. What Pieces have a Star prefix'd, were touch'd upon by Mr. Pope, as appears by the Manuscripts in the Harley Library and others" (there are nineteen stars in all). It is by means of these asterisks and Pope's comments in the reprinted "Contents" of Vol. I, that it has been possible to ascertain and reprint for the first time as Pope's work several pieces of some length and importance written about 1709. Most of the poems distinguished by the asterisk have no further indication either of the extent or position of Pope's additions; in consequence only those sections or passages which are specifically designated as Pope's additions have been included below. They are here grouped together for convenience sake under the date of the last one.

The text in every case is that of the original printing: Nos. I to III following *1728* and No. IV following *1729*.

I.

SIMILITUDES.

(a)

Of the Byass of a Bowl.

THE Poize of Dulness to the heavy Skull,
Is like the Leaden Byass to the Bowl,
Which, as more pond'rous, makes its Aim more true,
And guides it surer to the Mark in view;
The more it seems to go about, to come   5
The nearer to its End, or Purpose, home.

(b)

Of the Weights of a Clock.

So Clocks to Lead their nimble Motions owe,
The Springs above urg'd by the Weight below;
The pond'rous Ballance keeps its Poize the same,
Actuates, maintains, and rules the moving Frame.

Inserted in *A Panegyrick of Dulness*. In his letter to Wycherley dated 20 November 1707, after saying he is "sending you the fair Copy of the *Poem* on *Dulness*" by a friend who is going to London, Pope goes on to describe "the method of the Copy I send you... The Poem is now divided into four Parts... The Second Part contains the *advantages* of Dulness; 1st, In Business; and 2dly, at Court, where the Similitudes of the Byass of a Bowl, and the Weights of a Clock ... illustrate the advantages of Dulness, tho' introduced before in a place where there was no mention made of them; (which was your only objection to my adding them.)"

(a) *Of the Byass of a Bowl.*] Pope used this simile again in *Dunciad* A, 1 147–50:
                Dulness! . . .
                  . . . of business the directing soul,
                To human heads like byass to the bowl,
                Which as more pond'rous makes their aim more true,
                Obliquely wadling to the mark in view.

(b) *Of the Weights of a Clock.*] Pope used the first two lines in *Dunciad* A, 1 179–80:
                As clocks to weight their nimble motion owe,
                The wheels above urg'd by the load below.

Pope, in *Posthumous Works*, Vol. II, said, instead of these four lines Wycherley originally wrote:

As clocks run fastest when most lead is on.

See note to *Successio*, l. 4 (p. 17).

II.

SIMILITUDES.

Thus *either Men in private useless Ease*
    Lose a dull Length of undeserving Days;
Or waste, for others Use, their restless Years
In busie Tumults, and in publick Cares,
And run precipitant, with Noise and Strife,   5
Into the vast Abyss of future Life;
Or others Ease and theirs alike destroy,
Their own Destruction by their Industry.
So Waters putrifie with Rest, and lose
At once their Motion, Sweetness, and their Use;   10
Or haste in headlong Torrents to the Main,
To lose themselves by what shou'd them maintain,
And in th' impetuous Course themselves the sooner drain:
Neglect their Native Channel, Neighb'ring Coast,
Abroad in foreign Service to be lost;   15
Or else their Streams, when hinder'd in their Course,
Quite o'er the Banks to their own Ruin force.

    The Stream of Life shou'd more securely flow
In constant Motion, nor too swift nor slow,
And neither swell too high, nor sink too low;   20
Not always glide thro' gloomy Vales, and rove
('Midst Flocks and Shepherds) in the silent Grove;
But more diffusive in its wand'ring Race;
Serve peopled Towns, and stately Cities grace;
Around in sweet Meanders wildly range,   25
Kept fresh by Motion, and unchang'd by Change.

Inserted in *The Various Mix'd Life*. Among Pope's letters published in *1735* is one to Steele, dated 18 June *1712*, but printed anonymously in *The Spectator* on 16 June *1712* (see *The Prose Works*, I, p. xxxiv). The letter, inspired by Steele's move into the country, discusses the different effects on man of town and country life, with comparisons drawn from streams flowing or stagnant; to which in *1735* Pope added a footnote: "The foregoing similitudes our author had put into verse some years before, and inserted into Mr. Wycherley's poem on Mixed Life. We find him apparently in the versification of them as they are since printed in Wycherley's Posthumous Works, 8vo. page 3 and 4." Further, in *1729* Pope prefixed an asterisk to the title of this poem to indicate that he had worked on it (see introductory note, p. 54). The "similitudes" properly begin with "So Waters putrifie . . ." (l. 9); but as that is in the middle of a paragraph, and as the previous eight lines state the argument, it is possible that Pope wrote the first part of the paragraph also. It is therefore printed here in italic. The prose parallels in the letter follow.

1–8. Cf. "Moralists and philosophers . . . run . . . into extremes, in commending entirely either solitude or public life. In the former, men for the most part grow useless by too much rest, and in the latter are destroyed by too much precipitation".

9–17. Cf. "—as waters, lying still, putrefy and are good for nothing; and running violently on, do but the more mischief in their passage to others, and are swallowed up and lost the sooner themselves."

18–26. Cf. "Those, indeed, who can be useful to all states should be like gentle streams, that not only glide through lonely valleys and forests amidst the flocks and the shepherds, but visit populous towns in their course, and are at once of ornament and service to them."

III.

LINES

On Solitude and Retirement.

Honour *and Wealth, the Joys we seek, deny*
    By their Encrease, and their Variety;
And more confound our Choice than satisfie:
Officious, bold Disturbances they grow,
That interrupt our Peace, and work our Woe: 5
Make Life a Scene of Pain, and constant Toil,
And all our Days in fresh Pursuits embroil.

But if to Solitude we turn our Eyes,
To View a thousand real Blessings rise;
Pleasures sincere, and unallay'd with Pain,   10
An easie Purchase, but an ample Gain!
There Censure, Envy, Malice, Scorn, or Hate,
Cannot affect Us in our tranquil State:
Those Cankers that on busie Honour prey,
And all their Spight on active Pomp display.   15

Alone, remov'd from Grandeur and from Strife,
And ev'ry Curse that loads a publick Life,
In Safety, Innocence, and full Repose,
Man the true Worth of his Creation knows.
Luxurious Nature's Wealth in Thought surveys,   20
And meditates her Charms, and sings her Praise.
To him, with humble Privacy content,
Life is, in Courts, and gawdy Pride, mis-spent.
To him, the Rural Cottage does afford
What he prefers to the *Patrician* Board: 25
Such wholsome Foods as Nature's Wants supply,
And ne'er reproach him with his Luxury.
He traverses the blooming verdant Mead,
Nor envies those that on rich Carpets tread.
Basks in the Sun, then to the Shades retires,   30
And takes a Shelter from his pointed Fires.
Wak'd by the Morning-Cock, unseals his Eyes,
And sees the Rusticks to their Labours rise;
And in the Ev'ning, when those Labours cease,
Beholds them cheary eat the Bread of Peace: 35
Sees no foul Discords at their Banquets bred,
Nor Emulations, nor Disgusts succeed:
But all is quiet, jocund, and serene,
A Type of Paradise, the Rural Scene!

Inserted in *For Solitude and Retirement against the Publick, Active Life*. This title in the "Contents" has an asterisk prefixed, signifying that Pope had worked on the poem; and has appended to it the following note: "Very much disagrees with

Mr. Wycherley's Original. It is presumed the pages 135, 136, are not to be pro-
duced in his Papers" (p. 135 contains the above ll. 1–19 and p. 136, ll. 20–39).
It is possible that Pope's interpolation begins with the fresh paragraph at l. 8, and
not at the top of p. 135 with l. 1, which is *not* the beginning of a paragraph
—for which reason ll. 1–7 are printed here in italic. Among Pope's letters to
Wycherley is one dated 29 November 1707, in which he informs the old man
which of his poems he is going to revise next—"I will go next upon the Poems of
Solitude, on the *public* and on the *mixt Life*," [etc., etc.].

IV.
CONCLUSION
of
The Bill of Fare.

Aт *length the Board, in loose disjointed Chat,*
    Descanted, some on this Thing, some on that;
Some, over each Orac'lous Glass, fore-doom
The Fate of Realms, and Conquests yet to come;
What Lawrels *Marlbro'* next shall reap, decree,   5
And swifter than *His* Arms, give *Victory*:
At the next Bottle, all their Schemes they cease,
Content at last to leave the World in Peace.
'Till having drown'd their Reason, they think fit
Railing at Men of Sense, to show their Wit;   10
Compare De Foe'*s Burlesque with* Dryden'*s Satyr,*
And Butler *with the* Lutrin'*s dull Translator,*
Decry'd each past, to raise each present Writer,
Damn'd the *Plain-dealer*, and admir'd the *Biter*.

    These Censures o'er, to different Subjects next,   15
'Till rallying all, the Feast became the Text;
So to mine Host, the greatest Jest, they past,
And the Fool Treater grew the Treat at last.
Thus having eaten, drunk, laught, at his Cost,   ⎫
To the next Day's Repentance, as they boast,   ⎬   20
They left their senseless, treating, drunken Host. ⎭

Soft be his Slumbers! But may this suffice
Our Friends the Wits and Poets to advise,
(Tho' Dinners oft they want and Suppers too)
Rather to starve, as they are us'd to do,   25
Than dine with Fools, that on their Guests will force
Mixt Wine, mixt Company, and mixt Discourse:
Since not much Wine, much Company, much Food, ⎫
Make Entertainments please us as they shou'd;   ⎬
But 'tis of each, the *Little*, and the *Good*.   ⎭ 30

Pope's responsibility for these lines emerges from the following facts. Wycher-
ley's poem, lacking this *Conclusion*, was printed by Theobald in *The Posthumous
Works*, Vol. I, 1728. When Pope published "Vol. II" in 1729, he added an asterisk
to the title of the poem to indicate that he had "touch'd upon it" (see introduc-
tory note, p. 54), and a note saying "The Conclusion of this wanting"; and
then, elsewhere in the volume, he printed these lines separately with the explana-
tory title: *Conclusion Added in the Year 1709 to the Poem call'd The Bill of Fare*. More-
over, in his youth when correcting Wycherley's poems he wrote (29 November
1707): "I will go next upon the Poems on *Solitude*, ... *The Bill of Fare*," [etc.].
Comparison of l. 14 and Pope's footnote (below) with the last lines of his Epi-
gram on Ozell's *Lutrin* (see *ante*, p. 37) shows the same hand and animus in them
all. The half-dozen lines which he has taken over more or less untouched from
Wycherley's (*1728*) conclusion are printed in italics.

12. *The Lutrin's dull Translator*] Ozell, who had just at that Time made a poor
Version of *Boileau's Lutrin*, and in it reflected upon Mr. *Wycherley* by Name [P.
1729].

14. *Plain-dealer...Biter*.] See p. 37, l. 11n.

The Fable of Vertumnus and Pomona
[written about 1709; published 1712; vol. I, pp. 375–82]

The First Book of Statius his Thebais
[written about 1709; published 20 May 1712; vol. I, pp. 405–46]

The Fable of Dryope
[written about 1709; published 3 June 1717; vol. I, pp. 383–90]

RONDEAU.

You know where you did despise
 (T'other day) my little eyes,
Little legs, and little thighs,
And some things of little size,
                     You know where.   5

You, 'tis true, have fine black eyes,
Taper legs, and tempting thighs,
Yet what more than all we prize
Is a thing of little size,
                     You know where.   10

Title Rondeau.] A Rondeau to Phillis. *TS.*
4 things of] things else of *TS.*
6 black] blew *TS.*
8 Yet] But *TS.*

Pope's autograph: Bodleian MS Rawl. letters 90.
Caryll transcript: BM MS Add. 28618.
Mist's Weekly Journal. 26 February 1726.
Miscellanea. In Two Volumes. Vol. I. 1727.
The Female Dunciad. 1728.
Mr. Pope's Literary Correspondence. Vol. I. 1735 (and 3rd Edition, 1735).
Letters of Mr. Pope . . . Vol. I. 1735.
The Works . . . Vol. V. Consisting of Letters. 1737.
The Works . . . Vol. V. Containing . . . Letters. 2nd Edition. 1737.
The Works . . . Vol. IV. Part I. Containing . . . Letters. 1742.
The Works . . . Vol. VII. Containing . . . Letters. Ed. Warburton. 1751.

This rondeau is now included in the Poetical Works for the first time. Pope sent it to Cromwell in a letter dated "June ye 24th 1710" without comment as to its source. Cromwell replied: "You have refined upon Voiture, whose *Où vous savez* is much inferior to your *You know where.*" See *Œuvres de Monsieur de Voiture* (1665), Poësies, p. 72. In the following year Pope sent the same piece, slightly revised, to Caryll, at his request, and it is from this second autograph that the Caryll transcript was made.

Pope seems to have lost sight of his revision; but since he was content to print the earlier version in his *Letters* without change, that is the text which has been chosen for this edition. Variants from the Caryll transcript are given in the apparatus.

EPISTLE
TO
Miss BLOUNT,
With the Works of *VOITURE*.

IN these gay Thoughts the Loves and Graces shine,
   And all the Writer lives in ev'ry Line;
His easie Art may happy Nature seem,
Trifles themselves are Elegant in him.
Sure to charm all was his peculiar Fate,   5
Who without Flatt'ry pleas'd the Fair and Great;
Still with Esteem no less convers'd than read;
With Wit well-natur'd, and with Books well-bred;
His Heart, his Mistress and his Friend did share;
His Time, the Muse, the Witty, and the Fair.   10
Thus wisely careless, innocently gay,
Chearful, he play'd the Trifle, Life, away,
'Till Fate scarce felt his gentle Breath supprest,
As smiling Infants sport themselves to Rest:
Ev'n Rival Wits did *Voiture*'s Death deplore,   15
And the Gay mourn'd who never mourn'd before;
The truest Hearts for *Voiture* heav'd with Sighs;
Voiture was wept by all the brightest Eyes;
The *Smiles* and *Loves* had dy'd in *Voiture*'s Death,
But that for ever in his Lines they breath.   20
    Let the strict Life of graver Mortals be
A long, exact, and serious Comedy,
In ev'ry Scene some Moral let it teach,
And, if it can, at once both Please and Preach:
Let mine, an innocent gay Farce appear,   25

13 'Till Death scarce felt did o'er his Pleasures creep, *1712–15.*
   Fate] death *1717–26.*
14 Rest:] Sleep. *1712–26.*
15 Death] Fate *1712–26.*
25 an innocent] like *Voiture*'s, a *1712–26.*

And more Diverting still than Regular,
Have Humour, Wit, a native Ease and Grace;
Tho' not too strictly bound to Time and Place:
Criticks in Wit, or Life, are hard to please,
Few write to those, and none can live to these.   30
    Too much *your Sex* is by their Forms confin'd,
Severe to all, but most to Womankind;
Custom, grown blind with Age, must be your Guide
Your Pleasure is a Vice, but not your Pride;
By nature yielding, stubborn but for Fame;   35
Made Slaves by Honour, and made Fools by Shame.
Marriage may all those petty Tyrants chace,
But sets up One, a greater, in their Place;
Well might you wish for Change, by those accurst,
But the last Tyrant ever proves the worst.   40
Still in Constraint your suff'ring Sex remains,
Or bound in formal, or in real Chains;
Whole Years neglected for some Months ador'd,
The fawning Servant turns a haughty Lord;
Ah quit not the free Innocence of Life!   45
For the dull Glory of a virtuous Wife!
Nor let false Shows, or empty Titles please:
Aim not at Joy, but rest content with Ease.
    The Gods, to curse *Pamela* with her Pray'rs,
Gave the gilt Coach and dappled *Flanders* Mares,   50
The shining Robes, rich Jewels, Beds of State,
And to compleat her Bliss, a Fool for Mate.
She glares in *Balls*, *Front-boxes*, and the *Ring*,
A vain, unquiet, glitt'ring, wretched Thing!
Pride, Pomp, and State but reach her outward Part,
She sighs, and is no *Dutchess* at her Heart.   56
    But, Madam, if the Fates withstand, and you
Are destin'd *Hymen*'s willing Victim too,
Trust not too much your now resistless Charms,
Those, Age or Sickness, soon or late, disarms;   60

28 Tho' . . . to] No matter for the Rules of *1712–26*.

Good Humour only teaches Charms to last,
Still makes new Conquests, and maintains the past:
Love, rais'd on Beauty, will like That decay,
Our Hearts may bear its slender Chain a Day,
As flow'ry Bands in Wantonness are worn;   65
A Morning's Pleasure, and at Evening torn:
This binds in Ties more easie, yet more strong,
The willing Heart, and only holds it long.

    Thus *Voiture*'s early Care still shone the same,
And *Monthausier* was only chang'd in Name: 70
By this, ev'n now they live, ev'n now they charm,
Their Wit still sparkling and their Flames still warm.

    Now crown'd with Myrtle, on th' *Elysian* Coast,
Amid those Lovers, joys his gentle Ghost,
Pleas'd while with Smiles his happy Lines you view,
And finds a fairer *Ramboüillet* in you.   76
The brightest Eyes of *France* inspir'd his Muse,
The brightest Eyes of *Britain* now peruse,
And dead as living, 'tis our Author's Pride,
Still to charm those who charm the World beside.   80

74 Amid] Amidst *1712–22*.

Miscellaneous Poems and Translations. By Several Hands. 1712, 1714, 1720, 1722; and *Miscellany Poems,* 1726, 1727, 1732.
  The Works Of . . . Monsieur Voiture. 1715 (and 1725, 1736).
  The Works of Mr. Alexander Pope. 1717.
  The Works . . . Dublin. 1718.
  The Works . . . (Printed by T. J.) 1718 (and 1720).
  A Miscellaneous Collection of Poems. T. M. 1721.
  The Works . . . To which are added, I. Cooper's-Hill. [etc.]. 1727.
  Ethic Epistles, to Henry St. John L. Bolingbroke. Written in the Year 1732. 1735.
  The Works of Alexander Pope, Esq; Vol. II. 1735.
  The Works . . . Vol. II. Containing his Epistles and Satires. 8vo., 1735 (and 1736).
  The Works . . . Vol. II. Containing his Epistles, &c. 1739 (both editions).
  The Works . . . Vol. II. Part I. Containing his Epistles, &c. 1740 (and 1743).
  The Works. Ed. Warburton. Vol. VI. 1751.
  This poem presents two related problems (fully discussed in *New Light*, pp. 49–56) of date of composition and of address. It was published in Lintot's miscellany on 20 May 1712, with the title *To a Young Lady, with the Works of Voiture,* which

was altered in *1735* to read *To Miss Blount, with the Works of Voiture*, and was then stated to have been "Written at 17 years old" (*i.e.*, in 1705). Other evidence points to a date four or five years later. Pope seems to anticipate some of the lines in a letter to Cromwell (29 August 1709; see ll. 21–8*n.*); and Cromwell discusses and quotes from the poem in a letter to Pope (5 December 1710) thus: "Your poem shows you to be, what you say of Voiture, *with books well bred*". This may mean that, though the poem was drafted in 1705, it was not completed till 1710.

It cannot be confidently associated at this stage with either Teresa or Martha Blount. The evidence of Pope's first acquaintance with the sisters (set out in *New Light*, pp. 52–3) is conflicting, but points to the year 1711. But if, as seems probable, the poem was written to an imaginary lady, there can be no doubt that when addressed to "Miss Blount" in *1735* the compliment was intended for Martha.

The copy-text of *1712* has been emended in the light of the final revisions of *1735*.

Title: *Miss Blount*] See introductory note.

Voiture] Vincent de Voiture (1598–1648), French poet and letter-writer. A selection of his letters, translated by Dryden and Dennis, was published in 1696 and reprinted in 1700.

21–8. Cf. "Life for the most part [is] like an old play... As for myself, I would not have my life a very regular play. Let it be a good merry farce a G—d's name, and a fig for the critical unities!" (Pope to Cromwell, 29 August 1709.)

49. *Pamela*] For the use and pronunciation of the name see *Rev. of Eng. Stud.*, xxv (1949), 325–30.

53. *The Ring*] Where the carriages of fashionable society drove in Hyde Park. See Vol. II, p. 375f.

69. *Voiture's early care*] Madamoiselle Paulet [P. *1712–51*]. "She was the Daughter of Charles Paulet, Secretary of the King's Bed-Chamber... She was call'd the Lyoness, on account of her high Spirit, and yellow Hair." (*Works Of... Voiture*, 1715).

70. *Monthausier*] Julie Lucine d'Angennes, duchesse de Montausier (1607–71) eldest daughter of the Marquise de Rambouillet, known as "La princesse Julie"; married the duc de Montausier, 1645; correspondence about her between Montausier, Chapelain, and Voiture who was especially devoted to her.

76. *Rambouillet*] See preceding note.

On the Statue of CLEOPATRA, made into a Fountain by LEO the Tenth. Translated from the Latin of Count CASTIGLIONE.

CLEOPATRA *speaks.*

WHOE'RE thou art whom this fair statue charms,
  These curling aspicks, and these wounded arms,
Who view'st these eyes for ever fixt in death,
Think not unwilling I resign'd my breath.
What, shou'd a *Queen*, so long the boast of fame,   5
Have stoop'd to serve an haughty *Roman* dame?
Shou'd I have liv'd, in *Cæsar*'s triumph born,
To grace his conquests and his pomp adorn?
I, whom the blest *Ægyptian* climate bore
To the soft joys of *Nile*'s delightful shore.   10
Whom prostrate Kings beheld unrival'd shine,
And the wide *East* ador'd with rites divine!
Deny'd to reign, I stood resolv'd to die,
Such charms has death when join'd with liberty.
Let future times of *Cleopatra* tell,   15
Howe're she liv'd none ever dy'd so well.
No chains I felt, but went a glorious ghost,
Free, and a Princess, to the *Stygian* coast.
Th' eluded victor, envious of my fate,
Vex'd with vain rage, and impotently great,   20
To *Jove*'s high Capitol ignobly led
The mournful image of a Princess dead.
Yet not content with this to feast his eyes,
Lest kinder time shou'd hide our miseries,
Lest the last age our fortunes shou'd not know,   25
This breathing stone immortaliz'd my woe:
This with the noblest force of sculpture grac'd,
In *Rome*'s proud *Forum* young *Octavius* plac'd,
And in the midst of that majestic band

Of Gods and heroes, made a Woman stand;   30
But in the rock my flowing tears supprest,
Those tears, which only cou'd have have eas'd my breast.
Not that I'd ask a single drop to mourn
A fate so glorious, and so nobly born,
(Not death it self from me cou'd force a tear,   35
Or teach the soul of *Cleopatra* fear)
But for my *Antony*—to whom these eyes
Give all his rites, and all his obsequies!
To his dear ashes and his honour'd shade,
My tears eternal tribute shou'd be paid: 40
My tears the want of off'rings had supply'd;
But these, ev'n these, remorseless *Rome* deny'd!

   But thou great *Leo!* in whose *golden* days
Revive the honours of *Rome*'s ancient praise;
If Heav'n, to pity human woes inclin'd,   45
Has sent thee down in mercy to mankind,
And boundless pow'r with boundless virtue join'd;
If all the Gods entrust thee to bestow
With bounteous hands their blessings here below;
Let not a suppliant Queen entreat in vain,   50
The only wretch beneath thy happy reign!
Sure just and modest this request appears,
Nor is it much to give me back my tears;
Release my eyes, and let them freely flow;
'Tis all the comfort fate has left me now!   55
The haughty *Niobe* whose impious pride
Scorn'd Heaven it self, and durst the Gods deride,
Still, tho' a rock, can thus relieve her woe,
And tears eternal from the marble flow.
No guilt of mine the rage of Heav'n cou'd move;   60
I knew no crime, if 'tis no crime to love.
Then as a lover give me leave to weep;
Lull'd by these fountains the distrest may sleep;
And while the Dogstar burns the thirsty field,
These to the birds refreshing streams may yield;   65

The birds shall sport amidst the bending sprays,
And fill the shade with never ceasing lays;
New greens shall spring, new flow'rs around me grow,
And on each tree the golden apples glow;
Here, where the fragrant Orange groves arise,   70
Whose shining scene with rich *Hesperia* vies.

Poems on Several Occasions. 1717.
Pope's Own Miscellany. Ed. N. Ault. 1935.
This is the first of a group of four anonymous pieces all "by the same hand"; and the cumulative effect of the evidence for the whole group makes an overwhelming case for Pope's authorship. Pope's editorship of the *1717* collection (see p. 8) is the basis, as the numerous remarkable parallels of his acknowledged work is the main edifice, of proof. Only the more striking of these doubles can be given in the footnotes, but while many of these repeat earlier passages, others ante-date Pope's recognized use of them. Corroboration of Pope's authorship is supplied by the third poem of the group which he once tacitly acknowledged (see p. 72). The poem is tentatively dated not later than 1710. See further *P.O.M.*, pp. xl ff.

Pope probably met Castiglione's poem in Atterbury's ΑΝΘΟΛΟΓΙΑ, *seu Selecta Quædam Poemata Italorum qui Latine scripserunt* (1684), p. 215, whence he transferred it in 1740 to his own *Selecta Poemata Italorum*.

The text follows that of *1717* in every respect.

Title] Baldessare Castiglione (1478–1529), Italian diplomat, is best known by his treatise on courtesy, *Libro del Cortegiano* (1528), translated into English by Sir Thomas Hoby (1561).

17f. Cf. *Iliad*, xxiv, 948f.
> This felt no Chains, but went a glorious Ghost
> Free, and a Hero, to the *Stygian* Coast.

20–21. Cf. *Prologue to Cato*, 29:
> Ignobly vain and impotently great.

26. Cf. *Od.*, xvii 237:
> In sculptur'd stone immortaliz'd their care.

43f. Cf. *Ess. on C.*, 697ff.
> But see! each Muse, in *Leo*'s Golden Days,
> Starts from her Trance, and trims her wither'd Bays!
> *Rome*'s ancient Genius . . .

43. *Leo*] Pope Leo X, whose tenure of office lasted 1513–21.

47. Cf. *Temple of Fame*, 166:
> With boundless Pow'r unbounded Virtue join'd.

61. Cf. *Ode for Musick*, 96:
> No Crime was thine, if 'tis no Crime to love;

Unfortunate Lady, 6:
    Is it, in heav'n, a crime to love too well?
Eloisa to Abelard, 68:
    Too soon they taught me 'twas no sin to love.
64. Cf. *Pastoral : Summer*. 21:
    The sultry *Sirius* burns the thirsty Plains.

PSALM XCI.

HE who beneath thy shelt'ring wing resides,
  Whom thy hand leads, and whom thy glory guides
To Heav'n familiar his bold vows shall send,
And fearless say to God—*Thou* art my friend!
'Tis Thou shalt save him from insidious wrongs, 5
And the sharp arrows of censorious tongues.
When gath'ring tempests swell the raging main,
When thunder roars, and lightning blasts the plain,
Amidst the wrack of nature undismay'd,
Safe shall he lye, and hope beneath thy shade. 10
By day no perils shall the just affright,
No dismal dreams or groaning ghosts by night.
His God shall guard him in the fighting field,
And o'er his breast extend his saving shield:
The whistling darts shall turn their points away, 15
And fires around him innocently play.
Thousands on ev'ry side shall yield their breath;
And twice ten thousand bite the ground in death;
While he, serene in thought, shall calm survey
The sinners fall, and bless the vengeful day! 20
  Heav'n is thy hope: thy refuge fix'd above;
No harms can reach thee, and no force shall move.
I see protecting Myriads round thee fly,
And all the bright *Militia* of the sky.
These in thy dangers timely aid shall bring, 25
Raise in their arms, and waft thee on their wing,
These shall perform th' almighty orders given,

Direct each step, and smooth the path to Heaven.
Thou on the fiery Basilisk shalt tread,
And fearless crush the swelling Aspick's head,   30
Rouze the huge Dragon, with a spurn, from rest,
And fix thy foot upon the Lion's crest.
Lo *I*, his *God!* in all his toils am near:
I see him ever, and will ever hear:
When he the rage of sinners shall sustain,   35
I share his griefs, and feel my self his pain:
When foes conspiring rise against his rest,
I'll stretch my arm, and snatch him to my breast.
Him will I heap with honours, and with praise,
And glutt with full satiety of days;   40
Him with my glories crown; and when he dies,
To him reveal my joys, and open all my skies.

Poems on Several Occasions. 1717.
Pope's Own Miscellany. Ed. N. Ault. 1935.

"By the same Hand" as the preceding poem, *Psalm XCI* was first ascribed to
Pope and first reprinted in *P.O.M.*, in which the evidence for the ascription is
stated. Striking echoes and anticipations of his acknowledged verse are again
present, the more significant of them being recorded in the footnotes. The attri-
bution is supported by the imagery of ll. 29–30, which is derived, like the imagery
of *Messiah*, not from the Authorised Version, the Book of Common Prayer, or
Sternhold and Hopkins, but from the Douai Version with which Pope as a
Roman Catholic would be familiar.

Pope, writing to Cromwell (10 April 1710) says: "I had written to you sooner,
but that I made some scruple of sending profane things to you in Holy Week.
Besides, our family would have been scandalised to see me write, who take it for
granted that I write nothing but ungodly verses." Of the few religious poems
known to be Pope's none can be dated 1710; if, therefore, his hint meant anything
at all, the particular poem on which he was, or had just been, engaged is not
improbably *Psalm XCI*, or the lines *From Boetius* (p. 73)—; indeed, both may
have been written during that particular Holy Week. The poem is tentatively
dated not later than 1710.

The text is that of *1717* in every respect.

8. Cf. *Statius*, 525:

While thunder roars and lightning round him flies.

13f. Cf *Il.*, XI 333–4:

Defends him breathless on the sanguine field,
And o'er the body spreads his ample shield.

15–16. Cf. *Il.*, IV 632–3:

> Might Darts be bid to turn their Points away,
> And Swords around him innocently play.

Wakefield thought that in "And with their forky tongues shall innocently play" (*Messiah*, 84), Pope had borrowed from Dryden's *Palamon and Arcite*: "And troops of lions innocently play." *Psalm XCI*, however, was probably written before *Messiah*, and in that context "innocently play" looks like an unconscious memory of Dryden's phrase.

23f. Later Pope re-wrote these lines for *The Rape of the Lock*, I 41–2:

> Know then, unnumber'd Spirits round thee fly,
> The light *Militia* of the lower Sky.

29f. Cf. Douai Version, V 13:

> Upon the aspe, and the basilicus thou shalt walke.

40f. *Il.*, XXII 549:

> To melt in full Satiety of Grief.

STANZA'S.

From the french of *MALHERBE*.

At length, my soul! thy fruitless hopes give o'er,
  Believe, believe the treach'rous world no more.
Shallow, yet swift, the stream of fortune flows,
Which some rude wind will always discompose;
As children birds, so men their bliss pursue,   5
Still out of reach, tho' ever in their view.

In vain, for all that empty greatness brings,
We lose our lives amidst the courts of kings,
And suffer scorn, and bend the supple knee;
The monarch dies—one moment's turn destroys   10
Long future prospects, and short present joys:
Oh unperforming, false mortality!

All is but *dust*, when once their breath is fled;
The fierce, the pompous majesty lyes dead!
The world no longer trembles at their pow'r!   15

4 Which] While *1726*.

Ev'n in those tombs where their proud names survive,
Where still in breathing brass they seem to live,
Th' impartial worms that very *dust* devour.

The lofty styles of happy, glorious great,
The Lords of fortune, Arbiters of fate,   20
And Gods of war, lye lost within the grave!
Their mighty minions then come tumbling down,
They lose their flatt'rers as they lose their crown,
Forgot of ev'ry friend, and ev'ry slave!

Poems on Several Occasions. 1717.

Miscellany Poems. Vol. I. By Mr. Pope. The Fifth Edition. 1726 (reprinted 1727; also *The Sixth Edition.* 1732).

A Collection of Moral and Sacred Poems. J. Wesley. Vol. I. 1744.

Pope's Own Miscellany. Ed. N. Ault. 1935.

A Treasury of Unfamiliar Lyrics. Ed. N. Ault. 1938.

The third of the group of four poems by the same hand published anonymously by Pope in *P.O.M.* (see *ante*, p. 68) differs from the other three in that he once implicitly acknowledged his authorship. He inserted it in the fifth edition of *Miscellany Poems,* 1726 (his last edition of that collection, see *New Light,* p. 36), where it appears as the twenty-fourth poem in a group of twenty-seven, all otherwise and elsewhere acknowledged. Yet he afterwards neglected the poem, and it was never incorporated in the official *Works.* Pope's knowledge of Malherbe's poems is shown in his letters to Walsh (22 October 1706) and Cromwell (7 May 1709); and Spence reports him (*Anecdotes,* p. 10) as saying that Malherbe was the second poet of the French. Taking all things into account, not omitting the remarkable couplet which Pope later inserted in the *Characters of Women,* there cannot be much doubt about the authenticity of this poem—and if of this, then of the three accompanying pieces also. The poem is tentatively dated not later than 1710.

The text follows that of *1717,* with collations from *Miscellany Poems (1726).*

Title: *Malherbe*] François de Malherbe (1555–1628); French poet, and re-former of lyric poetry; established rules of versification. This is a translation of his "Paraphrase du Psaume CXLV" first published in *Recueil des plus beaux vers,* 1627.

5f. Cf. *Mor. Ess.,* II 231f:

> Pleasures the sex, as children Birds, pursue,
> Still out of reach, yet never out of view.

17. *breathing brass*] Cf. *Cleopatra,* 26: "breathing stone"; *Ep. to Jervas,* 55: "breathing paint".

From *BOETIUS, de cons. Philos.*

O qui perpetua mundum ratione gubernas.

O THOU, whose all-creating hands sustain
    The radiant Heav'ns, and Earth, and ambient main!
Eternal Reason! whose presiding soul
Informs great nature and directs the whole!
Who wert, e're time his rapid race begun,   5
And bad'st the years in long procession run:
Who fix't thy self amidst the rowling frame,
Gav'st all things to be chang'd, yet ever art the same!
Oh teach the mind t' ætherial heights to rise,
And view familiar, in its native skies,   10
The source of good; thy splendor to descry,
And on thy self, undazled, fix her eye.
Oh quicken this dull mass of mortal clay;
Shine through the soul, and drive its clouds away!
For thou art Light. In thee the righteous find   15
Calm rest, and soft serenity of mind;
Thee they regard alone; to thee they tend;
At once our great original and end,
At once our means, our end, our guide, our way,
Our utmost bound, and our eternal stay!   20

  1 Thou who did'st form, and form'd dost still sustain *MS.*
  9 heights] Height *MS.*
10 its] her *MS.*
12 undazled . . . eye] fix her undazzl'd Eye! *MS.*
13 Oh quicken] Enliven *MS.*   this] the *MS.*
17 they . . . they] we . . . we *MS.*
19 our means, our end] our Strength, our Aid *MS.*

Pope's autograph: Brotherton Library, Leeds University.
Poems on Several Occasions. 1717.
Pope's Own Miscellany. Ed. N. Ault. 1935.
    This is the last of the four anonymous poems "by the same hand" which Pope
grouped together towards the end of his *1717* miscellany, and which were attri-

buted to him in *P.O.M.* (see *ante*, p. 8). Pope's autograph fair copy was found
with an autograph draft by Sir William Trumbull of the same passage from
Boethius in the Trumbull papers formerly owned by the Marquess of Down-
shire and sold by Sotheby & Co, 30 July 1963. The cataloguer (item 577)
plausibly suggests that Pope undertook the translation at Trumbull's request,
"and possibly as an exercise in composition with the retired statesman". The
piece is tentatively dated not later than 1710.

The text follows that of *1717*.

Title] A translation of *De Consolatione Philosophiæ*, lib. 3, metrum 9, the work of
a sixth-century Roman philosopher. It has been translated into English by King
Alfred, Chaucer, and Queen Elizabeth.

3-4, 7-8. Cf *Ess. on Man*, I 267-70:

> All are but parts of one stupendous whole,
> Whose body Nature is, and God the soul;
> That, chang'd thro' all, and yet in all the same,
> Great in the earth, as in th' æthereal frame.

6. Cf. *Il.*, VI 302: "He bids the train in long procession go."

COUPLETS & VERSICLES
1708-1710

[See *ante*, p. xvi]

Pope's autograph: Bodleian MS Rawl. letters 90. [No. III.]
Miscellanea. In Two Volumes. 1727. [No. III.]
The Posthumous Works of William Wycherley, Esq. Vol. II. 1729. [No. II.]
Mr. Pope's Literary Correspondence. Vol. I. 1735 (and 3rd Edition, 1735).
[Nos. I-III.]
Letters of Mr. Pope . . . Vol. I. 1735. [Nos. I-III.]
Letters of . . . Pope ["Works . . . In Prose". Vol. I]. 1737. [No. II.]
The Works . . . Vol. V. Consisting of Letters. 1737. [Nos. I, II.]
The Works . . . Vol. V. Containing . . . Letters. 2nd Edition. 1737. [Nos. I, II.]
The Works . . . Vol. IV. Part I. Containing . . . Letters. 1742. [Nos. I, II.]
The Works. Vol. VII. Containing . . . Letters. Ed. Warburton. 1751. [Nos. I,
II.]
A Supplement to the Works . . . 1757. [No. III.]
Additions to the Works . . . 1776. [No. III.]

Scattered amongst Pope's letters and prose works are numerous short pieces of
verse, some complete in themselves and of an epigrammatic cast, others scraps of
translation, or descriptive or illustrative passages, but all of so diverse a character

as to have little in common save their author, and a certain whimsical or playful quality which is perceptible perhaps in most. For convenience of reference and space, these disjecta membra are collected together at intervals of ten years, the later groups covering the periods 1711–20 (p. 228), 1721–30 (p. 306), and 1731–40 (p. 390); and each gathering being preceded by a bibliography common to that particular group.

I.
EPIGRAM.
On Poets.

Damnation follows Death in other Men,
But your damn'd Poet lives and writes agen.

Title] *No title originally.* (*See below.*)

II.
EPIGRAM.
On Authors and Booksellers.

What Authors lose, their Booksellers have won,
So Pimps grow rich, while Gallants are undone.

Title] *No title originally.* (*See below.*)

III.
LINES.
i.

Fatis agimur, cedite fatis!
Which, in our Tongue, as I translate, is,
Fate rules us: then to Fate give way!
—Now, dreadful Critic! tell me pray,
What have you against this to say?

4

ii.

My *Pylades*! what *Juv'nal* says, no Jest is;
Scriptus & in tergo, nec dum finitus Orestes.

I. On 10 May 1708, Pope wrote to Cromwell expatiating on renown, contemporary and posthumous. He begins with these words: "You talk of fame and glory . . ." and ends with this epigram which he introduces thus: "If ever I seek for immortality here, may I be damn'd, for there's not so much danger in a Poet's being damn'd." The epigram follows, of which Pope thought well enough to "save it" in his *Prologue, Design'd for Mr. Durfey's last Play*, where it exactly reappears as the third and fourth lines (see *post*, p. 101).

The text follows that of *Letters, 1735*.

II. The occasion of this epigram was the publication by Jacob Tonson of *Poetical Miscellanies: The Sixth Part . . . By the most Eminent Hands*, 1709, in which Pope made his first appearance in print as a poet with his *Pastorals, January and May*, and a translation of the *Episode of Sarpedon* from the *Iliad*. In a letter to Wycherley (20 May 1709) Pope makes fun of the "Eminent Hands", and ends thus: "*Jacob* creates Poets, as Kings sometimes do Knights, not for their honour, but for money. Certainly he ought to be esteem'd a worker of Miracles, who is grown rich by Poetry." After which the couplet follows and concludes the letter.

The text follows that of *1729*, later editions showing no verbal change.

III. These two scraps of verse occur in Pope's letter of 12 October 1710 to Cromwell.

(*i*) The first is introduced thus: "I will only observe that these four lines [which had been earlier quoted from Persius] are as elegant & musicall as any in Persius, not excepting those 6 or 7 wch Mr Dryden quotes as ye only such in all that Author.—I cou'd be heartily glad to repeat the Satisfaction describd in them, but alas!" Whereupon follow the lines.

(*ii*) The second scrap concludes the letter, and is Pope's whimsical apology for its length. "He compares it to what Juvenal says of Codrus's tragedy of Orestes, which from its prolixity was written, contrary to the ancient custom, upon the back of the parchment as well as the front" (EC, VI 105). Juv. *Sat*. 1 6.

The text of both pieces follows the autograph.

HYMN of St. *FRANCIS XAVIER*.

THOU art my God, sole object of my love;
  Not for the hope of endless joys above;
Not for the fear of endless pains below,
Which they who love thee not must undergo.

For me, and such as me, thou deign'st to bear   5
An ignominious cross, the nails, the spear:
A thorny crown transpierc'd thy sacred brow,
While bloody sweats from ev'ry member flow.

For me in tortures thou resign'd'st thy breath,
Embrac'd me on the cross, and sav'd me by thy death. 10
And can these suff'rings fail my heart to move?
What but thyself can now deserve my love?

Such as then was, and is, thy love to me,
Such is, and shall be still, my love to thee—
To thee, Redeemer! mercy's sacred spring!   15
My God, my Father, Maker, and my King!

2 hope] hopes *TS.*   3 Not . . . fear] Nor . . . fears *TS.*
4 they] those *TS.*
9 resign'd'st] resign'st *1854, TS.*
16 my Father, Maker] my maker, Father *TS.*

Contemporary transcript: Ushaw College MS.
The Gentleman's Magazine. October 1791.
The European Magazine. September 1803.
The Works. Ed. Carruthers. Vol. IV. 1854.
The poem was thus introduced on its first printing in *The Gentleman's Magazine*:

                                                    Baltimore.
  Mr. Urban
  The perusal of a small book lately printed by you has revived an intention
. . . of communicating to the publick an original composition of the celebrated
Mr. Pope, with which I became acquainted near forty years ago. I was a stu-
dent at that time in a foreign college, and had the happiness of conversing often
with a most respectable clergyman of the name of Brown, who died some time

after, aged about ninety. This venerable man had lived in England, as domestic chaplain in the family of the Mr. Caryl to whom Pope inscribes the Rape of the Lock, . . . and at whose house he spent much of his time in the early and gay part of his life.

I was informed by Mr. Brown, that, seeing the Poet often amuse the family with verses of gallantry, he took the liberty one day of requesting him to change the subject of his compositions, and to devote his talents to the translating of the Latin hymn, or *rythmus*, which I find in the 227th page of "A Collection of Prayers and Hymns" lately printed. The hymn begins with these words, *O Deus! ego amo te*, &c. and was composed by the famous missionary, Francis Xavier, . . . Mr. Pope appeared to receive his proposition with indifference, but the next morning, when he came down to breakfast, he handed Mr. Brown a paper, with the following lines, of which I took a copy, and have since retained them in my memory. Many other students in the same college have been long in possession of them. . . Senex.

Carruthers, however, prints from a MS: "in the handwriting of Mr. Fermor, of Tusmore, the last of the name", who has prefaced the verses with this statement:

The following translation was made at the desire of the Rev. Mr. Brown, chaplain to Mr. Caryl, of Lady-Holt, a Roman Catholic gentleman, on Mr. Pope . . . making a visit there, who being requested by Mr. Brown to translate the following hymn or *rythmus*, composed by St. Francis Xavier, Apostle to the Indies, on the morning after produced what follows.

The attribution arriving thus by different channels is probably correct, and as Pope, writing to Caryll on 19 July 1711, sends his "most humble service" to various friends ending with "and Mr. Brown", the year 1711, the only definite date in the Pope-Brown connection, is taken as the approximate date of composition.

Though the 1854 version has no stanza division or abbreviated words, it is verbally identical—except for the variant, or misprint, noted, with the *1791* text here reprinted. Variants are quoted from the Ushaw transcript (*TS*), entitled "An Act of divine love to J.C. crucified, from S. Francis Zavier". The inscription on the verso reads "Translated by Alex. Pope, when on a visit at Lady Holt's in Sussex (Mr. Caryls) at the request of F^r Brown the Chaplain".

Title: *St. Francis Xavier*] The famous Jesuit missionary (1506–52), whose labours in the East, united with his eminent sanctity of life, procured him the title of "Apostle of the Indies".

LINES

FROM

The Critical Specimen.

I.
A SIMILE.

So on *Mæotis'* Marsh, (where Reeds and Rushes
Hide the deceitful Ground, whose waving Heads
Oft' bend to *Auster's* blasts, or *Boreas'* Rage,
The Haunt of the voracious *Stork* or *Bittern*,
Where, or the *Crane*, Foe to *Pygmæan* Race,   5
Or Ravenous *Corm'rants* shake their flabby Wings,
And from soak'd Plumes disperse a briny Show'r,
Or spread their feather'd Sails against the Beams,
Or, of the Rising or *Meridian* Sun)
A baneful *Hunch-back'd Toad*, with look Maligne,   10
Glares on some Traveller's unwary steps,
Whether by Chance, or by Misfortune led
To tread those dark unwholsome, misty Fens,
Rage strait Collects his Venom all at once,
And swells his bloated Corps to largest size.   15

II.
A RHAPSODY.

Fly Pegasæan *Steed, thy Rider bear,*
    To breath the Sweets of pure Parnassian *Air,*
Aloft I'm swiftly born, methinks I rise,
And with my Head Sublime *can reach the Sky.*
Large Gulps of Aganippe's *streams I'll draw,*   5
And give to Modern Writers Classic *Law;*
In Grecian Buskins *Tragedy shall Mourn,*
And to its Ancient *Mirth the* Comic Sock *return.*

The Critical Specimen. 1711.
Prose Works. Ed. N. Ault. Vol. I. 1936.

The Critical Specimen is an anonymous reply to Dennis's virulent attack on Pope, entitled *Reflections Critical and Satyrical upon a late Rhapsody call'd, An Essay upon Criticism*, 1711. When the pamphlet was reprinted in the *Prose Works*, evidence was adduced (pp. xi–xviii) to prove that it was written by Pope himself. In brief, the pamphlet fills a gap in the Pope-Dennis quarrel, being the reply to Dennis's *Reflections*, many passages of which it incorporates and reflects back again in disparagement of their author. Secondly, it exactly follows Pope's ideas of the conduct of literary warfare as laid down by him in a letter to Caryll (19 November 1712), and elsewhere. Thirdly, there are parallels between *The Critical Specimen* and Pope's works. This evidence, together with the difficulty of naming any other writer at that time who would have been concerned enough about the attack on Pope to take up cudgels on his behalf, points convincingly to his authorship. There are, in addition, several points of similarity between *The Critical Specimen* and another attack on Dennis, *The Narrative of Dr. Robert Norris*, 1713, which Pope repudiated in early life, and acknowledged more than once in later life, and which a consensus of opinion now gives to him. Pope's authorship of *The Critical Specimen* is thus so very probable that the two fragments of verse contained in it must be included among his poetical works.

The first of these pieces, *A Simile*, was satirically included as a fragment, too beautiful to lose, of a projected epic poem on the life of Dennis the Critic; and was intended to ridicule his trick of "frowning and swelling with Anger and Resentment, as ready to burst with Passion". Dennis in his attack had likened Pope to "a hunch-back'd Toad"; and here in this *Simile* the compliment is returned full measure, with a note drawing attention to the fact that the simile was Dennis's originally.

The second piece, *A Rhapsody*, occurs in a specimen chapter of a mock life of Dennis, where it is said to have been uttered by him several times when astride his hobby-horse as a small boy.

The text of both pieces follows that of *1711* in every respect.

I. 1. *Mæotis*] Mæotis Palus, or Sea of Azov, north of the Euxine or Black Sea.

10. The Author has been very just in the Application of this Simile, though he has not dealt so ingeniously with Mankind as to own that he took the Hint from Mr. Dennis's Critical and Satyrical Reflections. vid. Crit. and Sat. Reflections [*1711*].

II. 1. The Author has made the Critick Speak his Rhapsody in Rhime, which seems to deviate from his Character, but this, in my Opinion, wants no Excuse, since it was before he had taken the Bells off his Hobby-Horse [*1711*].

4. *Sublimi feriam Sydera Vertice*. vid. Hor. [*1711*]. The reference is to *Hor. Od.*, I i 36.

5. *Aganippe*] A fountain at the foot of Mount Helicon, sacred to the Muses, and believed to inspire those who drank of it.

EPITAPH.

On *JOHN* Lord *CARYLL*.

A MANLY Form; a bold, yet modest mind;
  Sincere, tho' prudent; constant, yet resign'd;
Honour unchang'd; a Principle profest;
Fix'd to one side, but mod'rate to the rest;
An honest Courtier, and a Patriot too;   5
Just to his Prince, and to his Country true:
All these were join'd in one, yet fail'd to save ⎫
The Wise, the Learn'd, the Virtuous, and the Brave; ⎬
Lost, like the common Plunder of the Grave! ⎭

    Ye Few, whom better Genius does inspire,   10
Exalted Souls, inform'd with purer Fire!
Go now, learn all vast Science can impart;
Go fathom Nature, take the Heights of Art!
Rise higher yet: learn ev'n yourselves to know;
Nay, to yourselves alone that knowledge owe.   15
Then, when you seem above mankind to soar,
Look on this marble, and be vain no more!

The Athenæum. 15 July 1854.

The Works. Ed. Elwin and Courthope, Correspondence. Vol. I. 1871.

When Dilke printed this epitaph in *The Athenaeum*, he recorded neither the source nor the owners of the document and omitted to describe it in any way. Since it has not been possible to locate the original papers, Dilke's words must serve as preface. "It is . . . a fact that though Pope did not know 'Mr. Secretary' [Caryll], he wrote an epitaph on him, in recognition of his Catholic zeal and Jacobite sufferings, and, no doubt, still more out of compliment to the nephew [*i.e.* Pope's friend, John Caryll] . . . he subsequently made other use of this same epitaph—made the first six lines serve to introduce his Whig friend Trumbull; and the remainder was re-cast, and appears as a flourish about Bridgewater in 'The Epistle to Jervas'." (See pp. 169 and 160.) Although this never became an official epitaph, and has survived only in manuscript, there can be little doubt about its authenticity—for Pope's characteristically thrifty habits of composition further testify to his authorship. Caryll, who withdrew to France in 1689 and became Secretary of State to the exiled dynasty, died in 1711.

The text follows that of *1854*.

1–6. Used again, after some revision, in the epitaph on Trumbull (see p. 169).

11, and 16–17. Cf. *Ep. to Mr. Jervas*, ll. 50, 53–4 (see p. 157).
12–15. Cf. *Essay on Man*, II 19–30.

The Balance of *Europe*.

N OW *Europe*'s balanc'd, neither Side prevails,
   For nothing's left in either of the Scales.

Title] *TS adds :* An Epigram.
1 neither] and no *TS*.

Caryll transcript: BM MS Add. 28618.
Miscellanies. The Last Volume. 1727 (and later editions).
A Collection of Epigrams. Vol. II. 1737.
A Supplement to Dr. Swift's and Mr. Pope's Works. Dublin. 1739.
Miscellanies. The Fourth Volume. Consisting of Verses. 1742 (and later editions).
The Nut-Cracker. F. Foot. 1751.
The Festoon. 1766 (and later editions).
The Christmas Treat. 1767.
The Works. Ed. Roscoe. Vol. VI. 1824.
This comment on the state of affairs in Europe in 1711 appears at the end of
Caryll's transcript of Pope's letter of 19 July 1711. Pope later included the epi-
gram but, like his other contributions, without his name, in *Miscellanies, The Last
Volume*.
The text follows that of *1727* with collations from the transcript (*TS*).

VERSES
To be prefix'd before
BERNARD LINTOT's
New MISCELLANY.

S OME *Colinæus* praise, some *Bleau*,
   Others account 'em but so so;
Some *Plantin* to the rest prefer,

Title] Verses design'd to be prefix'd to Mr. Lintott's Miscellany.
1712–22.   2 'em] them *1712–22.*   3 *Plantin*] *Stephens 1712–22.*

And some esteem *Old-Elzevir*;
Others with *Aldus* would besot us;   5
I, for my part, admire *Lintottus*.——
His Character's beyond Compare,
Like his own Person, large and fair.
They print their Names in Letters small,
But LINTOT stands in Capital: 10
Author and he, with equal Grace,
Appear, and stare you in the Face:
Stephens prints *Heathen Greek*, 'tis said,
Which some can't construe, some can't read:
But all that comes from *Lintot*'s Hand   15
Ev'n *Ra*——*son* might understand.
Oft in an *Aldus*, or a *Plantin*,
A Page is blotted, or Leaf wanting:
Of *Lintot*'s Books this can't be said,
All fair, and not so much as read.   20
Their Copy cost 'em not a Penny
To *Homer*, *Virgil*, or to any;
They ne'er gave *Sixpence* for *two Lines*,
To them, their Heirs, or their Assigns:
But *Lintot* is at vast Expence,   25
And pays prodigious dear for — Sense.
Their Books are useful but to few,
A Scholar, or a Wit or two:
Lintot's for gen'ral Use are fit;
For some Folks read, but all Folks sh—.   30

4 *Old-*] old *1712-22*.
7f. *omm. 1712-22, which read:*
          Those printed unknown Tongues, 'tis said,
          Which some can't construe, most can't read;
          What *Lintott* offers to your Hand,
          Even *R*—— may understand:
13–16 *introduced earlier in 1712-22; see preceding note.*
21–6 *omm. 1712-22.*

4*

Miscellaneous Poems and Translations. By Several Hands. 1712 (and 2nd Edition, 1714; 3rd Edition, 1720; 4th Edition, 1722).

The Catholick Poet; or, Protestant Barnaby's Sorrowful Lamentation. 1716.

Pope's Miscellany. 1717.

Court Poems In Two Parts Compleat. 1719.

Court Poems. In Two Parts. By Mr. Pope, &c. 1726.

Miscellanea. In Two Volumes. Vol. I. 1727. [1726.]

Miscellanies. The Last Volume. 1727 [1728] (and later editions).

Mr. Pope's Literary Correspondence. Vol. II. 1735 (and 2nd Edition, 1735).

A Supplement to Dr. Swift's and Mr. Pope's Works. Dublin. 1739.

Miscellanies. The Fourth Volume. 1742 (and later editions).

The History of John Bull. [1750?]

A Supplement to the Works . . . 1757.

Additions to the Works of Alexander Pope, Esq. Vol. I. 1776.

Some six months before this poem was published, Pope wrote to Cromwell (12 November 1711) for a copy of a poem just written by Gay, addressed to Lintot the printer; and, on 21 December, after acknowledging it, went on to say: "His Verses to *Lintot* have put a Whim into my head, which you are like to be troubled wth in the opposite page. Take it as you find it, ye ⟨Diversion⟩ Production of half an hour t'other morning." To which remark Elwin (EC, VI 130) adds a footnote identifying the "Production" with the poem under discussion. Unfortunately, "the opposite page" is missing from the Bodleian autographs of Pope's letters to Cromwell. Five months later the piece was printed anonymously in the miscellany it satirizes, where it was preceded by Gay's *On a Miscellany of Poems. To Bernard Lintott*, likewise anonymous. Their inclusion together in this miscellany was due to Pope himself, who is believed to have been its editor (see N. Ault, "Pope and the Miscellanies", *Nineteenth Century*, 1934, pp. 566–73). Pope revised the poem at some date between its final inclusion in Lintot's miscellany (fourth edition) in 1722 and the appearance of the expanded version in 1726, when Curll contrived to publish it, and attributed it to Pope in *Miscellanea* (dated 1727, published 14 July 1726). Later still, Pope himself included the revised version anonymously in *Miscellanies. The Last Volume*.

The text follows that of Pope's last revision (*1727*) with collations from its first printing (*1712*).

1. *Colinæus*] Simon de Colines (Simon Colinaeus). French printer of Greek and Latin books, at work between 1520 and 1546; successor of Henri Estienne (see Stephens below).

Bleau] Willem Janszoon Blaeu (1571–1638), and his son Jan Blaeu (d.1679), Printers, at Amsterdam, of maps and books on geography.

3. *Plantin*] Christophe Plantin (1514–89). A Belgian printer of Latin and Greek classics, and a polyglot Bible in folio.

4. *Old-Elzevir*] Louis Elzevier (1540–1617). Born at Louvain, established at Leyden in 1580. Printer of Latin classics chiefly. (Several later Elzeviers: Bonaventura (1583–1652); Ludvig (1604–70), and Daniel (1628?–80).)

5. *Aldus*] Aldus Manutius (c. 1450–1515). Venice. Italian printer of Greek and Latin classics (editio princeps of Aristotle).

6. *Lintottus*] Facetious reference to Bernard Lintott (see Biog. App., Vol. IV).

13. *Stephens*] Estienne, Robert (1503–59), and Henri (1528–98). French printers of Greek and Latin classics at Paris; Robert best known for the Bible in Latin and Hebrew and New Testament in Greek; and Henri for a Thesaurus Graecae Linguae.

16. *Ra—son*] Thomas Rawlinson (1681–1725), barrister and bibliophile; collected books, pictures, and manuscripts, the last-named now preserved in the Bodleian; portrayed by Addison as "Tom Folio" (*Tatler*, no. 158, 13 April 1710).

29f. Pope makes the same lamentable joke in his epigram on Cibber's praise of Nash (see p. 360).

VERSES

Occasion'd by an &c. *at the End of Mr.* D'URFY's *Name in the Title to one of his Plays.*

J OVE call'd before him t'other Day
  The *Vowels, U, O, I, E, A,*
  All *Dipthongs,* and all *Consonants,*
Either of *England* or of *France;*
And all that were, or wish'd to be,   5
Rank'd in the Name of *Tom D'Urfy.*

Title] *MSS read:* Verses Occasion'd by Mr Thomas D'Urfey's adding a Flourish at the End of His Name which was taken for an &ca. *MS 2 omits* Thomas. *1726 reads* Verses Occasioned by Mr. *Durfy*'s adding an &c. at the End of his Name.

3 And discontented Consonants. *MSS, 1726.*

4 Either] Whether *MSS.*

5–6   That beggd with Letters to supply
                    Thy Name De Urfey or D'Urfey. *MSS;*
                    That seem'd to fill the Name unworthy
                    Of fam'd *Tom Durfy,* or *De Urfe. 1726.*

Fierce in this Cause, the *Letters* spoke all,
Liquids grew rough, and *Mutes* turn'd vocal:
Those four proud Syllables alone
Were silent, which by Fates Decree   10
Chim'd in so smoothly, one by one,
To the sweet Name of *Tom D'Urfy.*

N, by whom Names subsist, declar'd,
To have no Place in this was hard:
And *Q* maintain'd 'twas but his Due   15
Still to keep Company with *U*;
So hop'd to stand no less than he
In the great Name of *Tom D'Urfy.*

E shew'd, a *Comma* ne'er could claim
A Place in any *British* Name;   20
Yet making here a perfect Botch,
Thrusts your poor Vowell from his Notch:
Hiatus mî valde deflendus!
From which good *Jupiter* defend us!
Sooner I'd quit my Part in thee,   25
Than be no Part in *Tom D'Urfy.*

P protested, puff'd, and swore,
He'd not be serv'd so like a Beast;

7 this Cause] the Cause *1726*.   9 four proud] happy *MSS*.
10 by Fates Decree] kind Fate thought worthy *1726*.
11 Chim'd in] To run *1726*.
12 To form the Name of Tom: D'Urfey *MSS*; In the great Name
    of *Thomas Durfy. 1726*.
17 no less than] as well as *1726*.
22 Vowell] Vowells *MS, 1*.   23 *mî*] mihi *1726*.
25 Sooner I'd ... my] Sooner we'd ... our *MSS*; Who'd sooner ...
    our *1726*.
26 in ... *D'Urfy*] of ... D'Urfey *MS, 2, 3*; of ... *Durfy 1726*.
28 not be serv'd] ne'er be us'd *MSS*; ne'er be serv'd *1726*.

He was a Piece of Emperor,
And made up half a Pope at least.   30
C vow'd, he'd frankly have releas'd
His double Share in *Cæsar Caius*,
For only one in *Tom Durfeius*.

    I, Consonant and Vowel too,
To *Jupiter* did humbly sue,   35
That of his Grace he would proclaim
Durfeius his true *Latin* Name;
For tho' without them both, 'twas clear,
Himself could ne'er be *Jupiter*;
Yet they'd resign that Post so high,   40
To be the Genitive, *Durfei*.

    B and *L* swore Bl— and W—s
X and *Z* cry'd, P—x and Z—s
G swore, by G—d, it ne'er should be;
And *W* would not lose, not he,   45
An *English Letter*'s Property,
In the great Name of *Tom Durfy*.

    In short, the rest were all in Fray,
From *Christcross* to *Et cætera*.
They, tho' but Standers-by too, mutter'd;   50

---

31 *C* vow'd] *C* cried *MSS.*
36 he would proclaim] he'd make a Patent *1726.*
37 *Durfeius* his] D'urfeius the *MSS.* To turn the Name into good
    Latin: *1726.*
38 them both, 'twas clear] their help 'twas clear *MSS*; them ('twas
    most clear) *1726.*
42–7 *1726 transposes this stanza to follow l. 26.*
44 ne'er should] shou'd not *MSS, 1726.*
45 would not lose] wou'd lose *MS, 1, 2*; wou'dn't lose *1726.*
50 They (tho' meer Standers by) too mutter'd *MSS*; Ev'n they
    (meer Standers by) too mutter'd; *1726.*

Dipthongs, and Tripthongs, swore and stutter'd,
That none had so much Right to be
Part of the Name of stuttering *T*—
T— *Tom*—a—as—*De*—*Dur*—fe—fy.

Then *Jove* thus spake: With Care and Pain   55
We form'd this Name, renown'd in Rhyme;
Not thine, Immortal *Neufgermain*!
Cost studious *Cabalists* more Time.
Yet now, as then, you all declare,
Far hence to *Egypt* you'll repair,   60
And turn strange Hieroglyphicks there;
Rather than Letters longer be,
Unless i' th' Name of *Tom D'Urfy*.

Were you all pleas'd, yet what I pray,
To foreign Letters cou'd I say?   65
What if the *Hebrew* next should aim
To turn quite backward *D'Urfy*'s Name?
Should the *Greek* quarrel too, by *Styx*, I
Cou'd ne'er bring in *Psi* and *Xi*;
Omicron and *Omega* from us   70
Wou'd each hope to be *O* in *Thomas*;
And all th' ambitious Vowels vie,
No less than *Pythagorick Y*,
To have a Place in *Tom D'Urfy*.

51 Dipthongs, and Tripthongs] Diphthong & Triphthong *MSS*.
54 T— To— To—mas—De—De—D'Urfey *MSS*; *T*— *Tom*—a—
     Ass D— Dur—f—fy *1726*.
55 thus spake: With] spake thus with *1726*.
58 *MSS read:* Cost our high thought more care and time
     Cabalists] Providence *1726*.   60 Far] From *MS 1, 2, 1726*.
62 Letters, you swear, no more you'l be *MSS*.
63 Unless i' th'] Except ith' *MSS*.
65 foreign] other *MSS, 1726*.   66 aim] claim *MSS, 1726*.
67 backward *D'Urfy*'s] backwards Durfy's *MSS, 1726*.

Then, well-belov'd and trusty Letters!   75
Cons'nants! and Vowels, (much their betters,)
WE, willing to repair this Breach,
And, all that in us lies, please each;
Et cæt'ra to our Aid must call,
Et cæt'ra represents ye all: 80
Et cæt'ra therefore, we decree,
Henceforth for ever join'd shall be
To the great Name of *Tom Durfy*.

76 (much their betters,)] too (their Betters) *MS, 2, 3*; too, their
    Betters! *MS, 1, 1726.*
79 must call] will call *1726.*
80 ye] you *MSS.*
82 Henceforth for ever] For ever henceforth *MSS, 1726.*

Contemporary transcripts: Welbeck Abbey, Harley Papers; Longleat, Port-
land Papers, XIII; and BM MS Harl. 7316.
    Miscellanea. In Two Volumes. Vol. I. 1727. [1726.]
    Miscellanies. The Last Volume. 1727 [1728] (and later editions).
    The Works of Monsieur Voiture. Vol. I. 3rd Edition, 1736.
    A Supplement to Dr. Swift's and Mr. Pope's Works. Dublin. 1739.
    Miscellanies. The Fourth Volume. Consisting of Verses. 1742 (and later editions).
    The History of John Bull. [1750?]
    The Works. Ed. Carruthers. New Edition. Vol. II. 1858.
    The Songs of Thomas D'Urfey. C. L. Day. 1933.
This is one of the best authenticated of Pope's attributed pieces. Lord Oxford
wrote to Pope on 26 October 1724 reminding him that he had forgotten to send
him "The copy of verses upon Durfey". To which Pope replied on 12 December:
"In the melancholy and hurry I have been, I had forgot to send the verses on
Durfey. Here they are as much corrected as they deserve, that is, but little." This
is the only poem "on Durfey" to be found in the various collections of Lord
Oxford's papers, a copy appearing in each of the Harleian collections at Welbeck,
Longleat, and the British Museum, and in all of them superscribed "by Mr.
Pope". The poem is also similarly attributed in each of the two copies of the
Pope-Swift *Miscellanies. The Last Volume*, now at Welbeck, which belonged to
Lord Oxford's wife and daughter; and is marked with an asterisk in *Miscellanies*
(1742) to indicate that it was *not* written by Swift. Lastly Curll, who was the first
to print these verses, also named Pope as their author. Though final proof is lack-
ing, Pope's authorship is thus morally certain.
    The occasion and date present more difficulties. None of Durfey's available
title-pages displays that absurd "&c" which suggests that the printer cancelled

the erring title-page with very little delay. Other evidence suggests that it was a comparatively early composition. (1) Durfey's dramatic activity, which began as early as 1676, ceased with the production of *The Modern Prophets* (1709), and as subsequent editions of his plays between 1709 and 1724 seem to be limited to a reprint of *A Fond Husband* (1711), and of *The Richmond Heiress* (1718), (whose titles are all correct), it follows that the only other opportunities for the mis-printed "&c" to appear on the title-page of a Durfey play must have occurred before 1712. (2) As Pope's letter shows, when the poem came to be sent to Oxford, Pope found that it needed correction, which suggests that it dated from an earlier period. (3) By far the greater number of Pope's pieces published by Curll in the first volume of his *Miscellanea* date from 1707 to 1711, that is from the period of the poet's close friendship and correspondence with Henry Cromwell (whose cast mistress sold these manuscripts of Pope to Curll, presumably in 1726). It is clear, moreover, that the copy of the poem followed by Curll was the early uncorrected version. (4) The poem is extremely unlike Pope's maturer manner—the work he was doing in 1726; while, on the other hand, late in 1711 he was in fact writing a banter on Lintot (p. 82) comparable in subject, treatment, and style, with this on Durfey; and, during the preceding year, is known to have been reading, quot-ing, and imitating Voiture (see pp. 61, 62), which probably accounts, in part at least, for this piece seemingly inspired by two poems of Voiture, *Plainte des con-sonnes qui n'ont pas l'honneur d'entrer au nom de Neuf-germain*, and *Response faite par l'autheur à la precedente plainte, sous le nom de Jupiter* (see Pope's note to l. 57). The poem is therefore tentatively dated "before 1712". The apparatus shows three distinct stages of development, the first represented by Curll's text of 1726; the second by the Welbeck (1), Longleat (2), and Harley (3) MSS which apparently incorporate the corrections made for Lord Oxford in 1724; the final text being established by the further revisions appearing in the 1728 *Miscellanies*, from which the present text is printed.

Title: *D'Urfy*] See Biog. App., Vol. V.

Plays] This Accident happen'd by Mr. *D'Urfy*'s having made a Florish there, which the Printer mistook for a *&c*. [P. *1727*]. See introductory note.

49. *Christcross*] The figure of a cross formerly placed in front of the alphabet in hornbooks [*OED*].

57. *Neufgermain*] A Poet, who used to make Verses ending with the last Syl-lables of the Names of those Persons he praised: Which *Voiture* turn'd against him in a Poem of the same kind. [P. *1727*]. Voiture's skit upon Louis de Neufgermain's manner is entitled *Vers à la mode de Neuf-Germain, à Monsieur d'Avaux, les lettres du nom finissans les vers*.

Messiah: A Sacred Eclogue, compos'd of several Passages of Isaiah the Prophet.

Written in Imitation of Virgil's Pollio.

[written 1712; published 14 May 1712; vol. I, pp. 109–22]

The Rape of the Locke. An Heroi-Comical Poem

[2 Canto version; published 20 May 1712; vol. II, pp. 125–37]

The Temple of Fame

[written before November 1712, see vol. II, p. 243; published
1 February 1714–15; vol. II, pp. 249–89]

Adriani morientis ad Animam.

I.
Translated: *Ah fleeting Spirit . . .*

II.
Imitated: *Vital Spark . . .*

The story of the Hadrian pieces begins with *The Spectator*, no. 532, of 10 November 1712, which prints a letter from Pope discussing "the famous Verses which the Emperor *Adrian* spoke on his Death-bed", of which he gives a prose paraphrase.

Next comes an undated letter to Caryll, referring to the *Spectator* letter and continuing the discussion (subsequently printed by Pope as a letter to Steele, dated 29 November 1712). Then on 12 June 1713, towards the end of a letter to Caryll,

Pope transcribes three anonymous poems, namely, (a) his translation of *Adriani morientis* . . . ; and (b) his adaptation, *Christiani morientis* . . . ; these two pieces being preceded by Prior's translation of Hadrian's lines; and he concludes by asking Caryll's "opinion of these verses, & which are best written. They are of three different hands." (Seeing that (a), besides containing phrases from Pope's prose paraphrase in the *Spectator*, was repeatedly printed and implicitly acknowledged by him from *1735* onwards, and that (b) was explicitly acknowledged from *1736* onwards, the concluding sentence was probably no more than a temporary expedient to obtain an unbiased opinion.) Nothing more is known of the poems until 1730, when they appear in print for the first time, together and anonymously, in Lewis's Miscellany—presumably with Pope's permission, to judge from a hitherto unpublished letter (see p. 315) which he wrote to Wesley concerning another of his poems about to be published in that miscellany. Then in 1735 Pope printed (or caused to be printed) in his Correspondence the *Spectator* letter above mentioned as a personal letter to Steele, dated 7 November 1712, with his translation (a) *Adriani morientis* . . . appended as though it originally belonged to that letter. The following year, the adaptation (b) *Christiani morientis* . . . was included in *The Works . . . Vol. I. With . . . Additions . . .* 1736, and the year after, 1737, he printed two letters: the first from Steele (4 December 1712) asking him to put "the Emperor Adrian's *Animula vagula* . . . into two or three stanzas for music"; and the second, his reply to Steele (undated, and thought to be apocryphal) as follows:

> I do not send you word I will do, but have already done the thing you desired of me. You have it, as Cowley calls it, just warm from the brain. It came to me the first moment I waked this morning. Yet you will see, it was not so absolutely inspiration, but that I had in my head not only the verses of Adrian, but the fine fragment of Sappho, &c.

Whereupon followed *The Dying Christian to his Soul* in its *revised* version. This same year, 1737, also saw Pope omitting the short translation, *Adriani morientis* . . . , at the end of the Spectator-Steele letter in the quarto edition of the *Letters*; and saw it later again reinstated in *The Works . . . Vol. V. . . . Second Edition*, with the remarkable note—for which Pope almost certainly was responsible—that "the Author seems to have but a mean opinion of these verses, having suppressed them in his Edition." Mean opinion or not, the translation, *Adriani morientis* . . . , remains practically as it was first written in 1712, whereas the adaptation, *Christiani morientis* . . . , was, for two-thirds of it, rewritten at some date between 1730 and 1736. See further *New Light*, pp. 60–7.

The text of *Adriani morientis* . . . is that of *1730* as amended (l. 7) in *1735*.

The text of *The Dying Christian* follows the final revision of *1736*, with collations from the transcript (*TS*) and the first printing (*1730*).

I.

Adriani morientis ad Animam,

OR,

The Heathen to his departing Soul.

Aн fleeting Spirit! wand'ring Fire,
    That long hast warm'd my tender Breast,
Must thou no more this Frame inspire?
    No more a pleasing, chearful Guest?

Whither, ah whither art thou flying!   5
    To what dark, undiscover'd Shore?
Thou seem'st all trembling, shivr'ing, dying,
    And Wit and Humour are no more!

7 shiv'ring] fainting *1730.*

Caryll transcript: MB MS Add. 28618.
Miscellaneous Poems, By Several Hands. D. Lewis. 1730.
Mr. Pope's Literary Correspondence. I. 1735 (and 3rd Edition, 1735).
Letters of Mr. Pope . . . Vol. I. 1735.
The Works . . . Vol. V. Containing . . . Letters. 2nd Edition. 1737.
The Works . . . Vol. VI. Containing . . . Letters. 1737.
The Works . . . Vol. IV. Part I. Containing . . . Letters. 1742.
A Collection of Moral and Sacred Poems. J. Wesley. Vol. II. 1744.
The Works . . . Volume VII. Containing . . . Letters. Ed. Warburton. 1751.
The Works. Ed. Carruthers. Vol. II. 1853.
Title] The original lines are attributed to the Emperor Hadrian by Aelius Spartianus in his *De Vita Hadriani,* §xxv. See *Scriptores Hist. August.,* ed. D. Magie (1922), 178.

II.
The Dying Christian to his Soul,
ODE.

VITAL spark of heav'nly flame!
　　Quit, oh quit this mortal frame:
Trembling, hoping, ling'ring, flying,
Oh the pain, the bliss of dying!
Cease, fond Nature, cease thy strife,　　　　　5
And let me languish into life.

Hark! they whisper; Angels say,
Sister Spirit, come away.
What is this absorbs me quite?
Steals my senses, shuts my sight,　　　　　10
Drowns my spirits, draws my breath?
Tell me, my Soul, can this be Death?

The world recedes; it disappears!
Heav'n opens on my eyes! my ears
　　With sounds seraphic ring:　　　　　15
Lend, lend your wings! I mount! I fly!
O Grave! where is thy Victory?
　　O Death! where is thy Sting?

Title] Xani morientis ad Animam *MS*.
2 Dost thou quit this mortal Frame? *MS, 1730.*
6 And let me] Let me *MS, 1730.*
7–18 *Second and third stanzas in 1730 read:*
　　　　My swimming Eyes are sick of Light,
　　　　The lessening World forsakes my Sight,
　　　　A Damp creeps cold o'er every Part,
　　　　Nor moves my Pulse, nor heaves my Heart,　　　　10
　　　　The hov'ring Soul is on the Wing;
　　　　Where, mighty Death! Oh where's thy Sting?

> I hear around soft Musick play,
> And Angels beckon me away!
> Calm, as forgiven Hermites rest,   15
> I'll sleep, or Infants at the Breast,
> 'Till the last Trumpet rend the Ground;
> Then wake with Transport at the Sound!

The foregoing is also the MS text, except that for l. 17 the MS reads:

> Till the Trumpet rends the Ground;

and, in l. 18, for Transport *reads* pleasure.

Caryll transcript: BM MS Add. 28618.
Miscellaneous Poems. By Several Hands. D. Lewis. 1730.
The Dying Christian to his Soul . . . Adapted for three Voices, and the Piano Forte.
[1736?]
The Works . . . Vol. I. With Explanatory Notes and Additions. 1736.
The Works . . . Vol. V. Containing . . . Letters. 2nd Edition. 1737.
The Works . . . Vol. VI. Containing . . . Letters. 1737.
The Works . . . Vol. I. Part I. 1740 (and 1743).
The Works . . . Vol. IV. Part I. Containing . . . Letters. 1742.
A Select Collection of Modern Poems. 1744.
A Collection of Moral and Sacred Poems. J. Wesley. Vol. II. 1744.
The Art of Poetry Made easy. 1746.
The Universal Magazine. November 1748.
The Magazine of Magazines. October 1750.
The Edinburgh Entertainer. 1750.
The Works. Ed. Warburton. Vol. I and Vol. VII. 1751.
3–4. Cf. T. Flatman's *A Thought of Death*, l. 3f.

> Fainting, gasping, trembling, crying,
> Panting, groaning, speechless, dying.

7–18. The "fine fragment of Sappho" which Pope admits to imitating (see
above, p. 92) is Fragment 2, φαίνεταί μοι κῆνος ἴσος θέοισιν, rendered familiar
by Boileau's version in his translation of Longinus (*Traité du Sublime*, chap. VIII).
7–8. Cf. Flatman, op. cit. ll. 12–13:

> Methinks I hear some Gentle Spirit say,
> Be not fearful, come away!

17–18. Cf. I Corinthians, xv 55.

Windsor Forest

[written 1704–13, see vol. I, pp. 125–31; published 7 March 1712–13; vol. I,
pp. 145–94]

PROLOGUE
TO
Mr. *ADDISON*'s Tragedy
OF
CATO.

To wake the soul by tender strokes of art,
  To raise the genius, and to mend the heart;
To make mankind, in conscious virtue bold,
Live o'er each scene, and be what they behold:
For this the Tragic Muse first trod the stage,   5
Commanding tears to stream thro' ev'ry age;
Tyrants no more their savage nature kept,
And foes to virtue wonder'd how they wept.
Our author shuns by vulgar springs to move,
The hero's glory, or the virgin's love;   10
In pitying love we but our weakness show,
And wild ambition well deserves its woe.
Here tears shall flow from a more gen'rous cause,
Such tears, as Patriots shed for dying Laws:
He bids your breasts with ancient ardour rise,   15
And calls forth *Roman* drops from *British* eyes.
Virtue confess'd in human shape he draws,
What *Plato* thought, and godlike *Cato* was:
No common object to your sight displays,
But what with pleasure heav'n itself surveys;   20
A brave man struggling in the storms of fate,
And greatly falling with a falling state!
While *Cato* gives his little senate laws,
What bosom beats not in his Country's cause?
Who sees him act, but envies ev'ry deed?   25
Who hears him groan, and does not wish to bleed?
Ev'n when proud *Cæsar* 'midst triumphal cars,
The spoils of nations, and the pomp of wars,
Ignobly vain and impotently great,

Show'd *Rome* her *Cato*'s figure drawn in state;   30
As her dead Father's rev'rend image past,
The pomp was darken'd, and the day o'ercast,
The triumph ceas'd—Tears gush'd from ev'ry eye;
The World's great Victor pass'd unheeded by;
Her last good man dejected *Rome* ador'd,   35
And honour'd *Cæsar*'s less than *Cato*'s sword.
   Britons attend: Be worth like this approv'd,
And show, you have the virtue to be mov'd.
With honest scorn the first fam'd *Cato* view'd
Rome learning arts from *Greece*, whom she subdu'd;   40
Our scene precariously subsists too long
On *French* translation, and *Italian* song.
Dare to have sense your selves; assert the stage,
Be justly warm'd with your own native rage.
Such Plays alone should please a *British* ear,   45
As *Cato*'s self had not disdain'd to hear.

41 Our] Your *1751*.
45 please] win *1751*.

The Guardian, No. 33. 18 April 1713.
Cato. A Tragedy . . . By Mr. Addison. 1713 (27 April and later editions).
The Works of Mr. Alexander Pope. 1717.
The Works . . . Dublin. 1718.
The Works . . . (Printed by T. J.) 1718 (and 1720).
Miscellaneous Poems and Translations. 3rd Edition 1720 (and 4th Edition, 1722).
Miscellany Poems. Vol. I. 5th Edition. 1726 (and 1727; and 6th Edition, 1732).
The Works of the Right Honourable Joseph Addison, Esq; Vol. I. 1721.
The Works of Mr. Alexander Pope. To which are added, I. Cooper's-Hill. [etc.]. 1727.
The Works . . . Vol. I. With Explanatory Notes and Additions . . . 1736.
The Works . . . Vol. I. Part I. 1740 (and 1743).
Cupid Triumphant . . . With several other Poems. [1747.]
The Works. Ed. Warburton. Vol. I. 1751.

The *Prologue to Cato* was presumably written early in 1713. In February of that year Pope wrote to Caryll (*Corr.* 1 173) saying he had lately had the entertainment of reading Addison's tragedy, and had wept over it. He also foretold its success as a play. A later letter to Caryll (30 April) describes the excitement and concern of the first night (14 April), which occasion both Whig and Tory parties alike endeavoured to convert into a political event. He also tells how Addison and, one suspects, Pope himself, "sweat'd behind yᵉ scenes", for, besides the general applause, "the Prologue-Writer . . . was clapp'd into a stanch Whig sore against his will, at allmost ev'ry two lines." The play had an unprecedented success, in which the prologue (spoken by the actor, Wilks) shared. Indeed, Pope reports to Caryll that "the Prologue & Epilogue are cry'd about the streetts by the Common Hawkers", but no copy of this broadside seems to have survived. Further light on the popularity of the play will be found in the following epigram and its introductory note. This was the first occasion on which Pope wrote for the theatre.

Works (*1717*), the first text for which Pope was responsible, has been chosen for copy-text, with which all subsequent texts of Pope's lifetime are in verbal agreement.

20. This alludes to a famous passage of Seneca which Mr. Addison afterwards used as a motto to his play, when it was printed [Warburton, *1751*]. *Dialogi*, De Providentia, II 9: Ecce Spectaculum dignum ad quod respiciat intentus operi suo deus, ecce par deo dignum, uir fortis cum fortuna mala compositus, utique si et prouocauit. Non uideo, inquam, quid habeat in terris Juppiter pulchrius, si conuertere animum uelit, quam ut spectet Catonem iam partibus non semel fractis stantem nihilo minus inter ruinas publicas rectum.

21f. Wakefield compares Ovid, *Her. Ep.*, III 106: Qui bene pro patria cum patriaque iacent.

23. Two years later Pope applied this line satirically to Addison himself and the Buttonians. *Atticus*, 25 (see p. 143).

37. *Britons attend*] Mr. Pope had written it *arise*, in the spirit of Poetry and Liberty; but Mr. Addison frighten'd at so *daring an expression*, which, he thought, squinted at rebellion, would have it alter'd, in the spirit of Prose and Politics, to *attend* [Warburton].

41–6. *Prologue to Sophonisba*, 1730 (see p. 310), in which the same theme is treated at greater length.

45. *please*] "win" was substituted in *1751* to avoid the homophone with "plays". This looks like Warburton's work, for if Pope had been offended by the pun, he might have removed it at an earlier stage.

46. *As Cato's self*] This alludes to the famous story of his going into the Theatre, and immediately coming out again [Warburton, *1751*]. See *Martial*, Lib. I, Epigr. I.

On a LADY who P—st
at the TRAGEDY of *CATO*;
Occasion'd by an
EPIGRAM on a LADY who wept at it.

WHILE maudlin Whigs deplor'd their *Cato*'s Fate,
  Still with dry Eyes the Tory *Celia* sate,
But while her Pride forbids her Tears to flow,
The gushing Waters find a Vent below:
Tho' secret, yet with copious Grief she mourns,   5
Like twenty River-Gods with all their Urns.
Let others screw their Hypocritick Face,
She shews her Grief in a sincerer Place;
There Nature reigns, and Passion void of Art,
For that Road leads directly to the Heart.   10

Title Upon a Tory Lady who happen'd to open her Floodgates at
  the Tragedy of Cato. An Epigram. *1713*; Epigram on a Lady
  who shed her Water at seeing the Tragedy of Cato. *1714*; On a
  Lady that Pist herself at Cato *TS*.
1 While ... deplor'd] Whilst ... deplore *1713, 1714*. their] yor *TS*.
3 But while ... forbids ... Tears] But tho' ... forbad ... Eyes
  1713, 1714. Although ... forbade ... Tears *TS*.
4 find] found *1713, 1714, TS*.
5 Grief] Streams *1713, 1714, TS*.
7 their] a *1713, 1714, TS*.
9 There] Here *1713, 1714*.   10 that] this *1713, 1714*.

Contemporary transcript: BM Harley MS 7316 f.109^b.
  The Poetical Entertainer: Consisting of Epigrams, Satyrs, Dialogues, &c. . . . Numb.
V. *1713* [published 18 February 1714 (*Post-Boy*)].
  Poems on Several Occasions. By Nicholas Rowe. 3rd Edition, 1714.
  The Poetical Works of Nicholas Rowe. 1715 (and later editions).
  The Elzevir Miscellany. 2nd Edition. 1715.
  A Collection of Historical and State Poems . . . Being the Fifth Volume of Miscellanies.
By the Author of the London Spy. 1717.
  A Miscellaneous Collection of Poems. Vol. I. 1721.
  A Collection of Epigrams. 1727 (and 1735).

Miscellanies. The Last Volume. 1727 (and later editions).

The St. James's Miscellany. [1729?]

Female Inconstancy Display'd. 1732 (and 2nd Edition, 1732).

A Supplement to Dr. Swift's and Mr. Pope's Works. Dublin. 1739.

Miscellanies. The Fourth Volume. Consisting of Verses . . . 1742 (and later editions).

Joe Miller's Jests. 5th Edition, 1742 (and later editions).

The Sports of the Muses. Vol. II. 1752.

A Collection of Select Epigrams. J. Hackett. 1757.

The authorship of this epigram is not definitely established. A month after its first publication, Burnet wrote to Duckett, 18 March 1713: "That copy of Verses of a Lady bepissing her self at Cato, was written by Pope & Rowe both in Ridicule of those that cryed at Cato" (BM MS Add. 36772). Shortly afterwards the piece was included (by Curll) in the third edition of the *Poems* of Nicholas Rowe (1714), among whose works it has since been usually printed. Later it appeared in Pope and Swift's *Miscellanies. The Last Volume* (1727), where it is marked "By Mr. Pope" in both the Harley-annotated copies at Welbeck Abbey. This volume of *Miscellanies*, though dated 1727, was published on 7 March 1728, and on 3 April 1728, a writer in *The Daily Journal* accused the "authors" of *Miscellanies* of plagiarism "in publickly taking to themselves an *Epigram* of the late Mr. Rowe's, singly upon the Merit of putting one low and foolish Word into the Title of that *Epigram*." Later still, but still within Pope's life-time, *Joe Miller's Jests*, 1742 (and later editions) gave the epigram to Pope; but the majority of printed and manuscript copies of the poem within that period are anonymous. On its first printing, and frequently afterwards, the piece was accompanied by a Latin "imitation" which suggests that perhaps Pope did one version and Rowe the other. The weight of the evidence would seem to imply that Pope was involved in the matter. It is probably significant that he included it in *Miscellanies* (in which nothing of Rowe's is known to have appeared, and where, in 1742, this piece is marked as *not* by Swift) with an altered title, and a text incorporating revisions which have never appeared in Rowe's works either before or after his death. A not improbable solution is that Pope wrote the original English lines, and that it was by Rowe they were "Thus turn'd into Latin".

The text follows that of *Miscellanies* (*1727*) with collations from the first printing (*1714*), which agrees with that in Rowe's *Poems* and the Harleian transcript (*TS*).

Title: *Occasion'd by an Epigram*] Perhaps Eusden's "To a Lady, That wept at the hearing Cato read", published in Steele's *Miscellanies*, 1714, although it can in no way be termed an epigram. No other alternative has been noted.

PROLOGUE,

Design'd for

Mr. Durfy's last Play.

GROWN old in Rhyme, 'twere barbarous to discard
   Your persevering, unexhausted Bard:
Damnation follows Death in other Men,
But your damn'd Poet lives and writes again.
Th' advent'rous Lover is successful still,   5
Who strives to please the Fair *against her Will:*
Be kind, and make him in his Wishes easy,
Who in your own *Despite* has strove to please ye.
He scorn'd to borrow from the Wits of yore;
But ever writ, as none e'er writ before.   10
You modern Wits, should each Man bring his Claim,
Have desperate Debentures on your Fame;
And little wou'd be left you, I'm afraid,
If all your Debts to *Greece* and *Rome* were paid.
From his deep Fund our Author largely draws;   15
Nor sinks his Credit lower than it was.
Tho' Plays for Honour in old Time he made,
'Tis now for better Reasons——to be paid.
Believe him, he has known the World too long,
And seen the Death of much Immortal Song.   20
He says, poor Poets lost, while Players won,
As Pimps grow rich, while Gallants are undone.
Tho' *Tom* the Poet writ with Ease and Pleasure,
The Comick *Tom* abounds in other Treasure.
Fame is at best an unperforming Cheat;   25
But 'tis substantial Happiness to *eat*—
Let Ease, his last Request, be of your giving,
Nor force him to be damn'd, to get his Living.

Title Prologue, Design'd for Mr. *D*—'s last Play. Written by several
hands. *1714.*   19 him, he has] him, Sirs, h' has *1714–27.*

Poetical Miscellanies . . . Publish'd by Mr. Steele. 1714 (both issues, and 1726; and 2nd Edition, 1727).

Miscellanies. The Last Volume. 1727 (and later editions).

A Supplement to Dr. Swift's and Mr. Pope's Works. Dublin. 1739.

Miscellanies. The Fourth Volume. 1742 (and later editions).

The History of John Bull. [1750?]

The Works. Ed. Roscoe. Vol. VI. 1824.

This poem was never acknowledged by Pope. On its first publication in Steele's miscellany (29 December 1713, and also in the later editions) the Prologue is stated to have been "Written by several Hands." Steele should have been in a position to know the facts, for, besides being Pope's friend, it was in his paper, *The Guardian* of 28 May and 15 June 1713, that a benefit performance of one of D'Urfey's old plays, *A Fond Husband: or The Plotting Sisters*, was advertised and recommended. The earlier notice was written by Addison, who seems to have initiated, if not organized, the "Benefit". The later notice, which appeared on the day of the performance and is said to be by Steele, urged D'Urfey's merits as an old writer, and his deserts and needs as an old man in the slightly patronizing tone which Addison had adopted. Pope also was writing for *The Guardian* at that time; his letter to Caryll (23 June 1713) points out that Addison wrote the paper "on Tom Durfey" (28 May), and mentions another paper (10 June) from his own pen. It is probable therefore, in spite of the ambiguity of the word "last" in the title, that the Prologue, which was published some six months later, was written for this benefit performance. Not so certain are the identities of the "several hands" —if indeed that was not a fiction taken over from the actual performance. Steele and Addison may have made suggestions and set the tone of good-humoured condescension which pervades the *Guardian*'s recommendations and the Prologue alike; but as the prevailing note of witty equivocation and veiled banter is characteristic of Pope, and as several of the lines are undoubtedly his, his hand would appear to have "held the pen" throughout. [Thus far Mr Ault. An interesting case is made for Steele's authorship in *The Occasional Verse of Richard Steele*, ed. R. Blanchard (1952), pp. 103–6.]

Apart from one correction of *1742*, the text is that of *Miscellanies (1727)*. Collations are given from its first printing *(1714)*.

3–4. This couplet appears in a letter to Cromwell, 10 May 1708 (see *ante*, p. 75).

21–2. A slightly different version of this couplet is found in a letter to Wycherley, 20 May 1709, see *ante*, p. 75.

THE
GARDENS of *ALCINOUS*.
From the SEVENTH BOOK of
HOMER's *ODYSSES*.

CLOSE to the gates a spacious garden lies,
    From storms defended, and inclement skies:
Four acres was th' allotted space of ground,
Fenc'd with a green enclosure all around.
Tall thriving trees confess'd the fruitful mold;   5
The red'ning apple ripens here to gold,
Here the blue fig with luscious juice o'erflows,
With deeper red the full pomegranate glows,
The branch here bends beneath the weighty pear,
And verdant olives flourish round the year.   10
The balmy spirit of the western gale
Eternal breathes on fruits untaught to fail:
Each dropping pear a following pear supplies,
On apples apples, figs on figs arise:
The same mild season gives the blooms to blow,   15
The buds to harden, and the fruits to grow.
    Here order'd vines in equal ranks appear
With all th' united labours of the year,
Some to unload the fertile branches run,
Some dry the black'ning clusters in the sun,   20
Others to tread the liquid harvest join,
The groaning presses foam with floods of wine.
Here are the vines in early flow'r descry'd, ⎫
Here grapes discolour'd on the sunny side,   ⎬
And there in autumn's richest purple dy'd. ⎭ 25
    Beds of all various herbs, for ever green,
In beauteous order terminate the scene.
    Two plenteous fountains the whole prospect ⎫
        crown'd;   ⎬
This thro' the gardens leads its streams around, ⎪
Visits each plant, and waters all the ground: ⎭ 30

While that in pipes beneath the palace flows,
And thence its current on the town bestows;
To various use their various streams they bring,
The People one, and one supplies the King.

The Guardian, No. 173. 29 September 1713 (and later editions).
Poetical Miscellanies . . . By the best Hands. Publish'd by Mr. Steele. 1714 (and 1726; and 2nd Edition, 1727).
The Works of Mr. Alexander Pope. 1717.
The Works . . . Dublin. 1718.
The Works . . . (Printed by T. J.) 1718 (and 1720).
The Odyssey of Homer . . . Vol. II. 1725 (and later editions).
The Works of Mr. Alexander Pope. To which are added, I. Cooper's-Hill. [etc.]. 1727.
The Gardens of Alcinous had a separate existence for some twelve years following its first appearance in the well-known *Guardian* essay on Gardens, where it was introduced in the following words:

. . . The Pieces I am speaking of are *Virgil*'s Account of the Garden of the old *Corycian*, and *Homer*'s of that of *Alcinous*. The first of these is already known to the *English* Reader, by the excellent Versions of Mr. *Dryden* and Mr. *Addison*. The other having never been attempted in our Language with any Elegance, and being the most beautiful Plan of this sort that can be imagined, I shall here present the Reader with a Translation of it.

The *Works* (*1717*) has been chosen for copy-text, since it is the first for which Pope was certainly responsible. The *Guardian* text (from which *1714* was set up) and that included in the *Odyssey*, Vol. II (*1725*) are in verbal agreement.

Title: Seventh Book.] Lines 142–75, in Pope's translation.

TWO OR THREE;

OR

A Receipt to make a Cuckold.

Two or *Three* Visits, and *Two* or *Three* Bows,
   Two or *Three* civil Things, *Two* or *Three* Vows,
Two or *Three* Kisses, with *Two* or *Three* Sighs,
Two or *Three* Jesus's—and let me dyes—
Two or *Three* Squeezes, and *Two* or *Three* Towses,   5
With *Two* or *Three* thousand Pound lost at their Houses,
Can never fail Cuckolding *Two* or *Three* Spouses.

Title] *1713 reads:* Epigram upon Two or Three. *1714 reads:*
   Receipt to make a Cuckold.
1 and] with *TS*; *om. 1713.*
3 with] and *TS, 1726*; *om. 1713.*
5 and] *om. 1713.*
6 thousand] hundred *TS, 1713.* Pound] pounds *TS, 1713, 1726.*

Caryll transcript: BM MS Add. 28618.
Miscellaneous Poems and Translations. 2nd Edition. 1714. [1713.]
Poems and Translations. By Several Hands. 1714.
Original Poems and Translations. By Several Hands. 2nd Edition. 1714 (and 1719).
Miscellany Poems. Vol. I. 1726 (and 1727).
Miscellanies. The Last Volume. 1727 [1728] (and later editions).
A Supplement to Dr. Swift's and Mr. Pope's Works. Dublin. 1739.
Miscellanies. The Fourth Volume. Consisting of Verses . . . 1742 (and later editions).
The Works. Ed. Elwin and Courthope, Correspondence. Vol. I. 1871.

After its first anonymous publication by Pope on 3 December 1713, in the
second edition of Lintot's miscellany, and its quick suppression (as described in
the introductory note to the following poem, p. 106), this epigram was neglected
by its author for thirteen years. But not long after its appearance in print, a manu-
script copy fell into the hands of Curll and Oldmixon, who included it, with the
ascription "By Mr. Pope", in a miscellany they were on the point of producing,
and apologized for it in the Preface as follows: "I know but of one *Poem* that has
crept into it [*i.e.* the miscellany], which I would have had kept still in *Manuscript*.
'Tis a very little One and will be easily slipt over in so great a Number of Others
that seem intended for the Press; which certainly that never was. Thus much was
due to Justice, considering the Company it is in." Their volume was published
probably not later than June 1714, and there can be little doubt that this offence
against Pope stands near, if not at, the very beginning of his life-long quarrel with
Curll and of his persistent animosity to Oldmixon. Caryll apparently made some
inquiry about it, for on 19 November 1714, Pope wrote in reply: "The Thing
they have been pleas'd to call a Receipt to make a Cuckold, is only six lines, w^{ch}
were stolen from me, as follows:" whereupon he transcribed this seven-line epi-
gram for Caryll's amusement. Thus, although he never publicly acknowledged
it or included it in his *Works*, his authorship of it is beyond question. It is now
included in his poetical works for the first time.

   The copy-text of *1713* has been amended in the light of later revisions. Colla-
tions are given from the transcript (*TS*) and *Miscellany Poems* (*1726*).

   4. *Jesus's and let me dyes*] Fashionable ejaculations: cr. "*Jesu! Jesu!*" *Donne IV*,
257 (Vol. IV, 47), and "But let me die", *Epil. to Jane Shore*, 11 (see *post*, p. 113).

UPON A
Girl of Seven Years old.

WIT's Queen, (if what the Poets sing be true)
    And Beauty's Goddess Childhood never knew,
Pallas they say Sprung from the Head of *Jove*,
Full grown, and from the Sea the Queen of Love;
But had they, Miss, your Wit and Beauty seen,   5
Venus and *Pallas* both had Children been.
They, from the Sweetness of that Radiant Look,
A Copy of young *Venus* might have took:
And from those pretty Things you speak have told,
How *Pallas* talk'd when she was Seven Years old.   10

Miscellaneous Poems and Translations . . . The Second Edition. 1714.
    This anonymous epigram was first attributed to Pope by simple assertion in the
Catalogue of the Lefferts's Collection in 1910, and on that statement alone has
been given a place in Griffith. No other reference to the poem seems to have sur-
vived, and the lines themselves have apparently never been reprinted hitherto.
Nevertheless, there is a case for Pope's authorship, which, though not perhaps
overwhelming, does at least account for several curious and otherwise inexplic-
able facts connected with its publication. Pope was the concealed editor of
Lintot's miscellany, in the successive editions of which he included an ever
increasing number of his poems with or without his name (see *ante*, p. 84). As
editor, therefore, he was responsible for the inclusion of this epigram (its one and
only appearance in print) in the second edition. This edition was a re-issue of the
unsold sheets of the first edition (1712) with four or five additional poems by
Pope inserted. Three of the new pieces are *Windsor Forest*, *Ode for Musick*, and *An
Essay on Criticism*, which are present in all copies; but besides these three poems,
some copies also contain an extra leaf (with duplicate page numbers 321*, 322*),
having on each side of it an anonymous epigram, one of which, *A Receipt to make a
Cuckold*, Pope privately acknowledged later but never included in his works (see
p. 105); and the other is the poem under discussion. It would seem probable,
therefore, that this remaining poem was similarly an unacknowledged editorial
contribution; and that its absence from most copies (together with its fellow epi-
gram) is due to Pope's second thoughts, which led him, after a few copies had been
sold, to cancel that leaf in the remaining stock in order to suppress, not this in-
offensive *Girl of Seven*, but the rather improper epigram on cuckolds on the other
side. This is suggested, first, by the presence of a stub (conjugate with the bastard
title-page of *Windsor Forest*) in those copies which do not contain the two epigrams,
and secondly, by the deprecatory tone of his private acknowledgement to Caryll

—together with his persistent public rejection—of the cuckold epigram. The *Girl of Seven* having thus been fortuitously suppressed, Pope apparently lost interest in it; so that, after a brief and restricted existence, it was left, like so many of his fugitive pieces now first collected in the present volume, unacknowledged and unreprinted.

The text follows that of *1714* in every respect.

7. *They*] *i.e.*, the poets.

The Rape of the Lock
An Heroi-Comical Poem. In Five Cantos

[published 4 March 1713/14; vol. II, pp. 139–212]

To BELINDA
on the
RAPE OF THE LOCK.

PLEAS'D in these lines, *Belinda*, you may view
How things are priz'd, which once belong'd to you:
If on some meaner head this Lock had grown,
The nymph despis'd, the Rape had been unknown.
But what concerns the valiant and the fair,   5
The Muse asserts as her peculiar care.
Thus *Helens* Rape and *Menelaus*' wrong
Became the Subject of great *Homer*'s song;
And, lost in ancient times, the golden fleece
Was rais'd to fame by all the wits of *Greece*.   10
   Had fate decreed, propitious to your pray'rs,
To give their utmost date to all your hairs;
This Lock, of which late ages now shall tell,
Had dropt like fruit, neglected, when it fell.

11–14 *1769 omits this paragraph, and instead of it reads*:
     But yet if some, with Malice more than Wit,

Nature to your undoing arms mankind   15
With strength of body, artifice of mind;
But gives your feeble sex, made up of fears,
No guard but virtue, no redress but tears.
Yet custom (seldom to your favour gain'd)
Absolves the virgin when by force constrain'd.   20
Thus *Lucrece* lives unblemish'd in her fame,
A bright example of young *Tarquin*'s shame.
Such praise is yours—and such shall you possess,
Your virtue equal, tho' your loss be less.
Then smile Belinda at reproachful tongues,   25
Still warm our hearts, and still inspire our songs.
But would your charms to distant times extend,
Let *Jervas* paint them, and let *Pope* commend.
Who censure most, more precious hairs would lose,
To have the *Rape* recorded by his Muse.   30

Will needs misconstrue what the Poet writ;
Deem it but Scandal which the jealous raise,
To blast his Fame, and to detract your Praise.
Too bright your Form, and too renown'd his Song,
Not to draw Envy from the baser throng.
Whose minds, I know not by what awkward fate,
Like eyes a-squint, look every way but straight.

28 *Jervas*] Kneller *1769*.
29f. *omm. 1769*.

Poems on Several Occasions. 1717.
The Life of Alexander Pope, Esq. By O. Ruffhead. 1769.
Pope's Own Miscellany. Ed. N. Ault. 1935.
   The first version of *The Rape of the Lock* having caused some gossip (see Vol. II,
pp.89–94) which apparently affected the good name of its heroine, Belinda (Mrs
Arabella Fermor), Pope took steps to prevent a recurrence of the nuisance when
the full and completed version was ready for the press. As he tells Caryll in a letter
of 9 January 1713/14, he submitted to Miss Fermor two alternative introductory
pieces in manuscript for her to choose from: one a dedication to her in her real
name, which he wrote "upon great deliberation" and claimed to have "managed
... so nicely y^t it can neither hurt ye Lady, nor ye Author"; and the other, "A Pre-
face which salv'd the Lady's honour, without affixing her name". The lady chose

the "dedication" which consequently accompanied the complete edition pub-
lished on 2 March 1713/14. If my contention is correct, this poem is the rejected
"Preface". It was presumably put on one side in accordance with Pope's thrifty
habit, and published anonymously in the miscellany he edited in 1717 (see
p. 8). The evidence for Pope's authorship is stated in detail in *P.O.M.*, pp. lxxi-
lxxvii; a few points, however, may be touched on here. Pope said that his "pre-
face" was intended to accompany *The Rape of the Lock*; this poem, *To Belinda*, as
its opening lines show, was designed with the same intention, but it was thrust
into the miscellany exactly as were a number of Pope's old unpublished, un-
ascribed pieces which, on his own confession, had been written years earlier. *To
Belinda* was obviously written before *The Rape* was published, or it would have
had no meaning; it must therefore have been written about the time Pope wrote
his "Preface"; and as it was meant to accompany *The Rape*, it must have been in
his hands about the same time. But as nothing is known of two rejected prefaces,
it is only reasonable to suppose that Pope's and this are one and the same. More-
over, *To Belinda* exactly answers Pope's description of his "Preface": it is con-
cerned to salve the lady's honour and acquit her of the least breath of scandal
without mentioning her name. There are also several passages parallel to Pope's
work contained in *To Belinda*, examples of which are given in footnotes to the
text. From a survey of the whole evidence it would appear that the poem is
almost certainly authentic. It was included in Ruffhead's *Life* (pp. 131ff.) as an
unprinted, anonymous piece; but the text appears to be an earlier version, per-
haps the version designed for publication in 1714.

The text follows that of *1717* with collations from *1769*.

1. Cf. *Epistle to Miss Blount with... Voiture*, 75:
            Pleas'd while with Smiles his happy Lines you view.

these lines] i.e., in *The Rape of the Lock*.

6. *peculiar care*] Pope was peculiarly fond of this phrase. He uses it, among other
places, in *January and May*, 466; *Statius*, 406; *Iliad*, I 494 and xv 260; *Odyssey*,
XIII 258; and *Essay on Man*, I 111 (in the first edition) and IV 135. It was, however,
not unknown a little earlier, Mrs Singer and Tickell each using it once in
Poetical Miscellanies, Part VI, 1709.

16. var. Cf. *Rape*, v 143f. "Not all the Tresses . . . Shall draw such Envy . . ."
15f. Cf. *Iliad*, VII 350-1:
            Whom Heav'n adorns, superior to thy Kind,
            With Strength of Body, and with Worth of Mind.

        Iliad, IX 73-4:
                    . . . in whom the Gods have join'd
            Such Strength of Body with such Force of Mind.

24. Cf. *Iliad*, IV 459:
            Our Valour equal, tho' our Fury less.

27f. A striking parallel of idea, in which Pope and Jervas are similarly men-
tioned, concludes the *Epistle to Mr. Jervas* (see p. 158). This poem, which begins
with the writer's wish that the fame of their conjoint names might last to distant
ages, subsequently mentions several ladies the last of whom is this same Belinda,

and, referring to them, declares (ll. 69–70, 77–8) of Jervas and Pope that their

> . . . kindred arts shall in their praise conspire,
> One dip the pencil, and one string the lyre . . .
> Alas! how little from the grave we claim?
> Thou but preserv'st a Face and I a Name.

28. *Jervas*.] Charles Jervas (1675?–1739), portrait painter and translator of Don Quixote. His house in Cleveland Court, St James's, was Pope's London residence from 1713 for several years, and there Pope took lessons in painting from him in 1713–14.

The Happy Life
OF A
COUNTRY PARSON.

Parson, these Things in thy possessing
Are better than the Bishop's Blessing.
A *Wife* that makes Conserves; a *Steed*
That carries double when there's need:
October, store, and best *Virginia*,   5
Tythe-Pig, and mortuary *Guinea*:
Gazettes sent Gratis down, and frank'd,
For which thy Patron's weekly thank'd:
A large Concordance, (bound long since,)
Sermons to *Charles* the First, when Prince;   10
A Chronicle of antient standing;
A *Chrysostom* to smooth thy Band in:
The *Polygott*—three Parts,—my *Text*,
Howbeit,—likewise—now to my next,
Lo here the *Septuagint*,—and *Paul*,   15
To *sum the whole*,—the *Close of all*.

Between title and first line MS reads:
    Vitam quae faciunt beatiorem &c. [Martial, x. 47. 1.]
4 when] if *MS.*   5 and] the *MS.*
13 The *Polygott—three Parts*] Three Parts—the Polyglott *MS.*

> He that has these, may pass his Life,
> Drink with the 'Squire, and kiss his Wife;
> On Sundays preach, and eat, his Fill;
> And fast on Fridays, if he will;   20
> Toast Church and Queen, explain the News,
> Talk with Church-Wardens about Pews,
> Pray heartily for some new Gift,
> And shake his Head at Doctor *S*——*t*.

Pope's autograph: Longleat, Portland Papers, XIII.

Miscellanies. The Last Volume. 1727 (and later editions).

The Works . . . Vol. III. Consisting of Fables, Translations, and Imitations. 1736.

The Works . . . With Explanatory Notes and Additions . . . Vol. I. 1736.

The Works . . . Vol. I. Part II. Consisting of Fables, Translations, and Imitations. 1741 (and 1745).

Miscellanies. The Fourth Volume. Consisting of Verses . . . 1742 (and later editions).

The Agreeable Companion. 1745.

The Works. Ed. Warburton. Vol. II. 1751.

On its first publication this poem, which was then anonymous, was entitled *The Happy Life of a Country Parson. In Imitation of Martial.* In 1736, however, when he included it in his "Vol. III", Pope called it an imitation of Swift, placing it last in the new-formed group of *Imitations of English Poets. Done by the Author in his Youth.* Judged by tone and detail, it was almost certainly written after Pope and Swift had become friends, most probably in 1713 (or, possibly, in 1712—the question largely depending on the date of an undated letter from Pope to Gay. See Sherburn, p. 75, and *Prose Works,* I, pp. xxxviff.). And because of line 21, the poem must also have been written before Queen Anne's death in 1714. This imitation is therefore tentatively dated *circa* 1713.

The text is that of *1727,* with collations from the autograph (*MS*). There were no subsequent verbal variants.

5. *October*] *i.e.,* ale brewed in October.

6. *Tythe-Pig*] A pig due to the parson in payment of tithe.

mortuary Guinea] A customary gift formerly claimed by the incumbent of a parish from the estate of a deceased parishioner.

7. *frank'd*] Superscribed with a privileged signature, *e.g.,* of a Member of Parliament, and so free from postage dues.

12f. *Chrysostom*] No doubt Sir Henry Savile's great edition in eight volumes, 1610–13.

13. *Polyglot*] Brian Walton's *Biblia Sacra Polyglotta,* "the great triumph in oriental studies by English scholars of the period", was published in six volumes in 1657.

THE

THREE *gentle* SHEPHERDS.

O F *gentle Philips* will I ever sing,
    With *gentle Philips* shall the Vallies ring.
My Numbers too for ever will I vary,
With *gentle Budgell*, and with *gentle Carey*.
Or if in ranging of the Names I judge ill,   5
With *gentle Carey* and with *gentle Budgell*.
Oh! may all *gentle* Bards together place ye,
Men of good Hearts, and Men of Delicacy.
May *Satire* ne'er befool ye, or beknave ye,
And from all Wits that have a Knack Gad save ye.   10

Miscellanea. The Second Volume. 1727 [1726].
A Supplement to the Works of Alexander Pope, Esq. 1757.
Additions to the Works of Alexander Pope, Esq. Vol. I. 1776.
The Works. Ed. Warton. Vol. II. 1797.

This piece, which Pope neither published nor acknowledged, was only once printed in his lifetime. It has, nevertheless, been included in the canon without comment or qualification by the principal editors of Pope's *Works* from Warton to Elwin and Courthope, solely—it would seem—on the word of Curll, the piratical bookseller. But although no point of contact with Pope has been established, internal evidence suggests that Curll's attribution was correct. The "Three Shepherds" themselves were among the earliest of Pope's bêtes noires, and time and again he "reflected upon them by name" both singly and jointly; there is, moreover, no evidence that any other poet either harboured a grudge against this particular trio or ever attacked all three of them. Pope's grievance against the "Gentle Shepherds" almost certainly originated in their close association with Addison: for they were not only prominent members of his "Little Senate" and contributors to both *The Spectator* and *The Guardian*, but were among his "chief companions", and presumably therefore (like all good Buttonians) sharers and backers of the great man's reiterated praise of Philips's *Pastorals* and preference of them to those of Pope. Because the epigram refers only to the "pastoral" activities of the three men, and not to the greater grievance of their advocacy of Tickell's rival translation of *The Iliad*, sponsored by Addison (see pp. 144, 145), it would seem to have been written not long after Pope's famous *Guardian* essay comparing his and Philips's *Pastorals*; and is therefore tentatively dated *circa* 1713. The fact that neither Budgell nor Walter Carey (both writers of verse as well as prose) is now known to have produced anything of a bucolic character, does not rule out the probability that Pope knew them each to have written one or more of the numerous anonymous pastoral poems which are to be found in the news-sheets and miscellanies of the period.

   The text follows that of the first printing in every respect.
   1. *Philips*] Ambrose Philips, see Biog. App., Vols. IV, V.
   4. *Budgell*] Eustace Budgell, see Biog. App., Vols. IV, V.
   Carey] Walter Carey, see p. 141.
   9. Perhaps an allusion to Pope's *Guardian* essay, No. 40, on Pastorals; see introductory note above.

The Second Satire of Dr. Donne

[written about 1713; vol. IV, pp. 132–44]

EPILOGUE
TO
JANE SHORE.
Design'd for Mrs. OLDFIELD.

PRODIGIOUS this! the Frail one of our Play
From her own sex should mercy find to day!
You might have held the pretty head aside,
Peep'd in your fans, been serious, thus, and cry'd,
The Play may pass—but that strange creature, *Shore*,   5
I can't—indeed now—I so hate a whore—
Just as a blockhead rubs his thoughtless skull,
And thanks his stars he was not born a fool;
So from a sister sinner you shall hear,
"How strangely you expose your self, my dear!"   10
But let me die, all raillery apart,
Our sex are still forgiving at their heart;
And did not wicked custom so contrive,
We'd be the best, good-natur'd things alive.

   There are, 'tis true, who tell another tale,   15
That virtuous ladies envy while they rail;

Such rage without betrays the fire within;
In some close corner of the soul, they sin:
Still hoarding up, most scandalously nice,
Amidst their virtues, a reserve of vice.   20
The godly dame who fleshly failings damns,
Scolds with her maid, or with her chaplain crams.
Wou'd you enjoy soft nights and solid dinners?
Faith, gallants, board with saints, and bed with sinners.

    Well, if our author in the Wife offends,   25
He has a Husband that will make amends.
He draws him gentle, tender, and forgiving,
And sure such kind good creatures may be living.
In days of old they pardon'd breach of vows,
Stern *Cato*'s self was no relentless spouse: 30
Plu—Plutarch, what's his name that writes his life?
Tells us, that *Cato* dearly lov'd his wife:
Yet if a friend a night, or so, should need her,
He'd recommend her, as a special breeder.
To lend a wife, few here would scruple make,   35
But pray which of you all would take her back?
Tho' with the Stoick chief our stage may ring,
The Stoick husband was the glorious thing.
The man had courage, was a sage, 'tis true,
And lov'd his country—but what's that to you?   40
Those strange examples ne'er were made to fit ye,
But the kind cuckold might instruct the City:
There, many an honest man may copy *Cato*,
Who ne'er saw naked Sword, or look'd in *Plato*.

    If, after all, you think it a disgrace,   45
That *Edward*'s Miss thus perks it in your face,
To see a piece of failing flesh and blood,
In all the rest so impudently good:
Faith, let the modest matrons of the town,
Come here in crowds, and stare the strumpet down.   50

The Works of Mr. Alexander Pope. 1717.

Miscellaneous Poems and Translations. 3rd Edition, 1720 (4th Edition, 1722; and Miscellany Poems, 5th Edition, 1726, 1727; and 6th Edition, 1732).

The Works . . . Dublin. 1718.

The Works . . . (Printed by T. I.) 1718 (and 1720).

The Works . . . To which are added, I. Cooper's-Hill. [etc.]. 1727.

The Works . . . Vol. I. With Explanatory Notes. 1736.

The Works . . . Vol. I. Part I. 1740 (and 1743).

Cupid Triumphant . . . With several other Poems. [1747.]

The Works. Ed. Warburton. Vol. I. 1751.

This piece may be dated by the first performance of Rowe's *Jane Shore* on 2 February 1713. For an explanation of the circumstances, in which the epilogue was neither spoken in the theatre nor printed with the play, yet was seemingly advertised by Pope as a rejected work, see *New Light*, pp. 133–8.

The text follows that of *1717*. There are no verbal variants.

Title: *Mrs. Oldfield*] See Biog. App., Vol. IV.

11. *But let me die*] A fashionable ejaculation, cf. *Two or Three*, l. 4 (p. 104).

18. An echo of "In some close corner of my brain", in an anonymous "Ode" (l. 20) in *A Poetical Rhapsody*, 1602, variously ascribed to Donne and Hoskins. Cf. also: "This heart . . . shall never want a corner at your service; where . . . your idea lies as warm and as close as any idea in Christendom" (Pope to Lady M. W. Montagu [1716]).

31–4. See Plutarch's life of Cato the Younger, §xxv.

37. When first published in 1717, this line would have been read as a reference to Addison's *Cato*, since no one was then likely to reflect that *Cato* was produced ten weeks later than *Jane Shore*. This may indicate later revision.

46. *Edward's Miss*] Jane Shore was Edward IV's mistress.

VERSES
in the
SCRIBLERIAN MANNER.

In the winter of 1713–14 Pope and his friends formed themselves into a society to which they gave the name of the "Scriblerus Club". Besides Pope, who seems to have been the prime mover, the more or less regular members were Swift, Gay, Arbuthnot, and Parnell. At their meetings, often held in Arbuthnot's rooms, they discussed and in some measure drafted schemes for books which were to be corporate works. Thus the *Memoirs of Martin Scriblerus* came to be projected, material began to be collected for the *Art of Sinking* (see p. 288), a proposal for *The*

Works of the Unlearned was talked over, and *Gulliver's Travels* and even the *Dunciad* owe not a little to the discussions of the club. For a full discussion, see *Memoirs*, ed. C. Kerby-Miller (1950). Among the more frequent visitors to the club in the spring of 1714 was Robert Harley, Earl of Oxford, to whom invitations in rhyme were often sent in the names of the members. In these also Pope was probably the moving spirit, and, to judge from the pieces in the Longleat manuscripts (Nos. I–IV and the late 1718 invitation) he most frequently held the pen. From various indications, including the signatures and internal evidence, it appears that the Scriblerian Verses are all—except No. II—the result of two or more hands in collaboration, Pope's occurring most frequently. A further example from Pope's autograph, dated 1718, will be found on page 196.

I.

Tho the Dean has run from us in manner uncivil;
  The Doctor, and He that's nam'd next to the Devil,
With Gay, who Petition'd you once on a time,
And Parnell, that would, if he had but a Rhyme.
(That Gay the poor Sec: and that arch Chaplain Parnell,   5
As Spiritual one, as the other is Carnal),
Forgetting their Interest, now humbly sollicit
You'd at present do nothing but give us a Visit.

	A. Pope.	
That all this true is	T. Parnell	10
Witness E. Lewis.	Jo: Arḅuthnot	
	J. Gay.	

This invitation is in Pope's autograph, and is printed in Kerby-Miller (p. 357), where Oxford's reply will also be found. The four signatures are in the different members' handwriting, the Lewis couplet being in still another (probably Lewis's) hand. The document is dated June 1714 by Lord Oxford. (Text from Portland Papers, XIII.)

2. *The Doctor*] Arbuthnot, see Biog. App., Vol. IV.

He] Pope added an asterisk to "He", and wrote in the margin "Poᴅe".

5. *the poor Sec.*] Gay had been secretary to the Duchess of Monmouth, but resigned his post the same month as this invitation was written.

10–11. *E. Lewis*] See Biog. App., Vol. IV.

II.

MY Lord, forsake your Politick Utopians,
    To sup, like Jove, with blameless Ethiopians
                                                    Pope.

This couplet is in Pope's autograph, and in the MS is followed by four others each in the hand of its author and signed respectively "Dean", "Parnell", "Doctor", "Gay". It is found in Portland Papers, XIII, from which the text is taken; and is printed in Williams (I 187) and Kerby-Miller (p. 353).

2. *Jove . . . Ethiopians*.] Pope was at this time translating the first books of the *Iliad*. See I 554, 556–7:

> The sire of gods, and all th' æthereal train . . .
> Now mix with mortals, nor disdain to grace
> The feast of Æthiopia's blameless race.

III.

THE Doctor and Dean, Pope, Parnell and Gay
    In manner submissive most humbly do pray,
That your Lordship would once let your Cares all alone
And Climb the dark Stairs to your Friends who have none:
To your Friends who at least have no Cares but to please you
To a good honest Junta that never will teaze you.   6

From the Doctor's Chamber
past eight.

Although this is in Swift's handwriting it purports to be the voice of the club, and probably was the result of corporate suggestion. It is addressed "To the Lord High Treasurer", and dated by Lord Oxford "Marc: 20: 1713/14". The text is taken from Portland Papers, XIII. Previously printed in EC (VIII 225*n*.), Williams (I 185), and Kerby-Miller (p. 351).

6. *Junta*] The formidable combination of Whig Lords, Halifax, Wharton, Somers, Sunderland.

7. *the Doctor's Chamber*] The room in the palace occupied by Arbuthnot as physician to the Queen.

IV.

A pox of all Senders
   For any Pretenders
Who tell us these troublesome stories,
   In their dull hum-drum key
   Of Arma Virumque   5
Hannoniae qui primus ab oris.

   A fig too for H——r
   Who prates like his Grand mere
And all his old Friends would rebuke
   In spite of the Carle   10
   Give us but our Earle,
And the Devil may take their Duke.

   Then come and take part in
   The Memoirs of Martin,
Lay by your White Staff and gray Habit,   15
   For trust us, friend Mortimer
   Should you live years forty more
Haec olim meminisse juvabit.

              by order of yᵉ Club
                  A. Pope
                  J. Gay
                  J. Swift
                  J. Arbuthnot
                  T. Parnel

1 of] on *1766*.   6 Hannoniae] Hanoniæ *1766*.
7 *1766 reads:* A pox too on Hanmer,
8 Grand mere] gran-mere *1766*.
12 And the] The *1766*.   15 by] down *1766*.
18 *1766 ends with this line.*

This transcript, possibly in Gay's hand, implies by its signatures a multiple authorship. It is the only one of the Longleat invitations to have been printed in the eighteenth century, and is found in Swift's *Letters* (ed. Hawkesworth), Vol. I, 1766, also in Williams (p. 186) and Kerby-Miller (p. 354), who tentatively dates it 14 April 1714 on the evidence of l. 7 and of Oxford's reply. The text follows the transcript (Portland Papers, XIII), with collations from the printed text (*1766*).

6. *Hannoniae*] The duchy of Hainault, the scene of Marlborough's campaigns. The duke's return about this time was expected; he arrived in England on 2 August 1714 [Hawkesworth, Williams]. Kerby-Miller, however, sees in this play on the opening lines of the *Æneid* a reference to current excitement over rumours that the Pretender was arming to invade England with the Duke of Lorraine's help. But though attractive, this explanation does not show how Oxford could be expected to interpret "Hannoniae" as "Lorraine".

7. *H—r*] Hanmer, Sir Thomas (1677–1746). Chief of Hanoverian Tories; refused office from Lord Oxford, 1713; Speaker 1714–15.

12. *Duke*] The choice lies between Marlborough and Argyle (see p. 215).

14. *Martin*] Martinus Scriblerus (see introductory note).

16. *Mortimer*] Robert Harley, Earl of Oxford and Mortimer.

18. *Æneid*, I 203. Kerby-Miller notes that the promise that one day it would "please him to remember these things" was fulfilled: see p. 241.

V.

L ET not the whigs our tory club rebuke;
  Give us our earl, the devil take their duke.
Quaedam quae attinent ad Scriblerum,
Want your assistance now to clear 'em.
  One day it will be no disgrace,   5
  In scribbler to have had a place.
Come then, my lord, and take your part in
The important history of *Martin*.

This invitation, tentatively dated 1 April 1714 by Kerby-Miller, is not found among the Longleat MSS but was printed in 1766 by Hawkesworth (who says it was chiefly written by the Dean) from whose edition of Swift's *Letters*, I, the text is taken. Reprints in Williams (p. 186) and Kerby-Miller (p. 352).

2. *earl . . . duke*] References to Lord Oxford and the Duke of Argyle, "who, because of his opposition to the ministry, was deprived of his command in the Horse Guards by the Queen on April 1" [Kerby-Miller].

VI.

How foolish Men on Expeditions goe!
  Unweeting Wantons of their wetting Woe!
For drizling Damps descend adown the Plain
And seem a thicker Dew, or thinner Rain;
Yet Dew or Rain may wett us to the Shift,   5
We'll not be slow to visit Dr. Swift.

This rhyme, though not an invitation, is appended because it was written in the same vein and year. It is taken exactly from the autograph of Pope's letter to Dr Arbuthnot, dated 11 July 1714, now preserved in the Royal College of Surgeons. It is introduced, and explained, in these words: "That I may not conclude this Letter without some Verses, take the following Epigram wch Dr Parnelle & I composed as we rode toward the Dean in the Mist of ye Morning, & is after the Scriblerian Manner." It was printed in EC (VII 471).

IMPROMPTU,
To Lady WINCHELSEA.

Occasion'd by four Satyrical Verses on Women-Wits, in the RAPE of the LOCK.

In vain you boast Poetick Dames of yore,
  And cite those Sapphoes wee admire no more;
Fate doom'd the fall of ev'ry female Wit,
But doom'd it then when first Ardelia writ.
Of all examples by the world confest,
I knew Ardelia could not quote the best,
Who, like her Mistresse on Britannia's Throne,
Fights and subdues in quarrells not her own.
  To write their Praise you but in vain essay,
Ev'n while you write, you take that praise away,
Light to the Stars the Sun does thus restore,
But shines himselfe till they are seen no more.

Title To Lady Winchelsea occasioned by four verses in the Rape of
   the Lock. By Mr. Pope. *MS, TS, 1741.*
 1 Dames] Names *TS, 1741, 1742.*
 12 But] And *TS, 1741.*

Pope's autograph: facsimile in the catalogue of the Anderson Auction
Company, New York, 9–10 December 1909.

Contemporary transcript: BM MS Add. 4457.
A General Dictionary. P. Bayle. Vol. X. 1741.
Miscellanies. The Fourth Volume. 1742 (and later editions).
The London Magazine. September 1747.
The Works. Ed. Roscoe. Vol. VI. 1824.

The date of this amiable quarrel remains in some uncertainty. Although
Pope's poem was not published until 1741, the allusion in the seventh line to
Queen Anne shows that it must have been written before her death on 1 August
1714. And his letter to Caryll of 15 December 1713, in which he speaks of
having dined with Lady Winchilsea, shows that he must have been seeing her
at the time that he was finishing the additions to the *Rape of the Lock* (published
2 March 1714). It is probable therefore that the *Impromptu* dates from the first
half of 1714. The "four lines" which occasioned the dispute seem to have been
correctly identified by Ward with a part of the invocation of the goddess *Spleen*
(canto IV, ll. 59–62):

> Parent of Vapors and of Female Wit,
> Who give th' *Hysteric* or *Poetic* Fit,
> On various Tempers act by various ways,
> Make some take Physick, others scribble Plays.

Such lines might easily have struck the Countess as a personal quiz, seeing that
The Spleen was her best-known poem, and that she had also written two plays. But
she good-humouredly took up the quarrel on behalf of women authors, and not of
herself, and justified their writing by citing "Poetick Dames of yore". The manu-
script of her reply was used by Pope for transcribing his version of *Iliad* Bk XIII and
is preserved in the British Museum (MS Add. 4807, ff. 209, 210). It bears correc-
tions in Pope's hand, made for his 1717 Miscellany and reads, uncorrected, as
follows:

> Disarm'd, with so Genteel an Air,
>   The Contest I giue ore,
> Yett, Alexander! have a care,
>   And shock the sex no more.
> We rule the World, our Lives whole Race,
>   Men but assume that Right,
> First slaves to ev'ry tempting Face,
>   Then, Martyrs to our spight.

You, of one Orpheus, sure have read,
   Who wou'd, like you, have Writt,
Had He in London Town been bred,
   And Pollish'd, to his Wit;
But He, poor soul, thought all was Well,
   And great shou'd be his Fame,
When he had left his Wife in Hell,
   And Birds, and Beasts cou'd tame.
Yett, ventring then with scoffing Rimes
   The Women to Incense,
Resenting Heroines, of those Times
   Soon punished his Offence.
And as through Hebrus, rowl'd his scull,
   And Harpe besmear'd with Blood,
They, clashing, as the Waves grew full,
   Still harmonis'd the Flood.
But You, our Follies, gently treat,
   And spinn so fine the Thread,
You need not fear his awkward Fate;
   The *Lock* wo'n't cost the *Head*.
Our Admiration, you Command,
   For all that's gone before;
What, next we look for, at your Hand
   Can only raise itt more.
Yett sooth the Ladies, I advise,
   As me, to Pride you've wrought;
We're born to wit, but to be wise
   By admonitions taught.

Although Pope printed his corrected version of this *Answer* to his *Impromptu* (see *P.O.M.*, p. 79), he kept the *Impromptu* itself unpublished for twenty-five years; and then, after it had appeared with the *Answer* in Bayle's *Dictionary* in 1741, only included it anonymously in *Miscellanies*, 1742. This text seems inferior to the autograph (a fair copy) in two particulars where it differs in substance: *Names* for *Dames* (l. 1), and the failure to mark a fresh paragraph at l. 9. The title of the poem, however, seems to have been reconsidered for the 1742 text and is adopted here in preference to the manuscript, whose text is otherwise followed with expansion of abbreviations. Collations are given from the transcript (*TS*) and the first printing (*1741*), and *Miscellanies* (*1742*).

   4. *Ardelia*] The name under which the Countess occasionally wrote, and by which she later became known; *e.g.* Swift's poem: "Apollo Outwitted. To the Honourable Mrs. Finch, under her Name of Ardelia".

   7. *her Mistresse*] Queen Anne.

To *EUSTACE BUDGELL*, Esq.
On his Translation of the Characters of
THEOPHRASTUS.

'TIS rumour'd, *Budgell* on a time
   Writing a Sonnet, cou'd not rhime;
Was he discouragd? no such matter;
He'd write in Prose—To the *Spectator*.
There too Invention faild of late: 5
What then? Gad damn him, he'd Translate,
Not Verse, to that he had a Pique—
From *French*? He scornd it; no, from *Greek*.
He'd do't; and ne'r stand Shill—I Shall—I,
Ay, and inscribe to *Charles* Lord *Halli*——   10
Our *Gallo-Grecian* at the last
Has kept his word, Here's *Teophraste*.
How e're be not too vain, Friend *Budgell*!
Men of Ill Hearts, you know, will judge ill.
Some flatly say, the Book's as ill done,   15
As if by *Boyer*, or by *Gildon*;
Others opine you only chose ill,
And that this Piece was meant for *Ozell*.
For me, I think (in spite of Blunders)
You may, with *Addison*, do wonders.   20
But faith I fear, some Folks beside
These *smart, new Characters* supplyd.
The *honest Fellow out at Heels*
Pray between Friends, was not that *Steel*'s?
The *Rustic Lout* so like a Brute,   25
Was *Philips*'s beyond Dispute.
And the *fond Fop* so clean contrary,
Tis plain, tis very plain, was *Cary*.
Howe're, the *Coxcomb*'s thy own Merit,
That thou hast done, with *Life* and *Spirit*.   30

Pope's autograph: Chatsworth MS 143.69.

Budgell's translation of *The Moral Characters of Theophrastus* was dedicated to the Earl of Halifax and published by Tonson in May 1714 (*Daily Courant*, 25 May 1714). It reached a third edition in 1718.

Pope's poem exists in a single undated manuscript, and has not hitherto been printed. It appears to have been aimed at Addison's "little Senate" at Button's Coffee House, and to have been inspired by "the battle of the Iliads". It may be ascribed with confidence to 1714.

1. *Budgell*] 1686–1737. A writer of miscellaneous prose and verse. See Biog. App., Vols. IV and V.

4. Budgell contributed some thirty papers to *The Spectator*.

16. Abel Boyer (1667–1729), newswriter and compiler of a French-English dictionary: see Biog. App., Vol. V. Charles Gildon (1665–1724), critic and dramatist (see Biog. App., Vol. V): in *A New Rehearsal* (April 1714), Gildon had ridiculed the claims of "Sawney Dapper" to a knowledge of Greek and to a capacity for translating Homer.

18. John Ozell (d. 1743), a voluminous translator, whose version of Boileau's *Lutrin* had occasioned Pope's Epigram (p. 37). See Biog. App., Vol. V.

20. Addison was Budgell's cousin and had helped him, as Pope told Spence (p. 257), to write the successful epilogue to Philips's *The Distrest Mother* (1712).

22–30. There are no characters so entitled in Budgell's translation.

25ff. Ambrose Philips and Walter Carey had already been associated by Pope in *The Three Gentle Shepherds* (p. 112).

EPISTLE

To Miss BLOUNT, on her leaving
the Town, after the CORONATION.

As some fond virgin, whom her mother's care
   Drags from the town to wholsom country air,
Just when she learns to roll a melting eye,
And hear a spark, yet think no danger nigh;
From the dear man unwilling she must sever,   5
Yet takes one kiss before she parts for ever:
Thus from the world fair *Zephalinda* flew,
Saw others happy, and with sighs withdrew;
Not that their pleasures caus'd her discontent,

She sigh'd not that They stay'd, but that She went.   10
   She went, to plain-work, and to purling brooks,
Old-fashion'd halls, dull aunts, and croaking rooks,
She went from Op'ra, park, assembly, play,
To morning walks, and pray'rs three hours a day;
To pass her time 'twixt reading and Bohea,   15
To muse, and spill her solitary Tea,
Or o'er cold coffee trifle with the spoon,
Count the slow clock, and dine exact at noon;
Divert her eyes with pictures in the fire,
Hum half a tune, tell stories to the squire;   20
Up to her godly garret after sev'n,
There starve and pray, for that's the way to heav'n.
   Some Squire, perhaps, you take delight to rack;
Whose game is Whisk, whose treat a toast in sack,
Who visits with a gun, presents you birds,   25
Then gives a smacking buss, and cries—No words!
Or with his hound comes hollowing from the stable,
Makes love with nods, and knees beneath a table;
Whose laughs are hearty, tho' his jests are coarse,
And loves you best of all things—but his horse.   30
   In some fair evening, on your elbow laid,
You dream of triumphs in the rural shade;
In pensive thought recall the fancy'd scene,
See Coronations rise on ev'ry green;
Before you pass th' imaginary sights   35
Of Lords, and Earls, and Dukes, and garter'd Knights;
While the spread Fan o'ershades your closing eyes;
Then give one flirt, and all the vision flies.
Thus vanish sceptres, coronets, and balls,
And leave you in lone woods, or empty walls.   40
   So when your slave, at some dear, idle time,
(Not plagu'd with headachs, or the want of rhime)
Stands in the streets, abstracted from the crew,
And while he seems to study, thinks of you:
Just when his fancy points your sprightly eyes,   45

Or sees the blush of soft *Parthenia* rise,
Gay pats my shoulder, and you vanish quite;
Streets, chairs, and coxcombs rush upon my sight;
Vext to be still in town, I knit my brow,
Look sow'r, and hum a tune—as you may now.   50

46 soft *Parthenia*] *Parthenissa 1717–32.*
47 *Gay*] *G—y 1717–32.*   50 tune] *song 1717–35.*

Contemporary transcript: BM MS Stowe 970.
The Works of Mr. Alexander Pope. 1717.
Miscellaneous Poems and Translations. By several Hands. 3rd Edition. 1720 (and later editions, 1722, 1727–7, 1732).
The Works . . . Dublin. 1718.
The Works . . . (Printed by T. J.) 1718 (and 1720).
The Works . . . To which are added, I. Cooper's-Hill. [etc.]. 1727.
The Works . . . Vol. II. 1735.
The Works . . . Vol. II. Containing his Epistles and Satires. 1735 (and 1736).
Ethic Epistles, to Henry St. John L. Bolingbroke. Written in the Year 1732. 1735.
The Works . . . Vol. II. Containing his Epistles, &c. 1739 (both editions).
The Works . . . Vol. II. Part I. Containing his Epistles, &c. 1740 (and 1743).
Memoirs of . . . Alexander Pope, Esq. W. Ayre. Vol. II. 1745.
The Works. Ed. Warburton. Vol. VI. 1751.

This epistle has always followed the epistle, *To a Young Lady, with the Works of Voiture*, in the *Works*, where it has always been entitled, *To the same, On her leaving the Town after the Coronation.* Consequently it has been similarly involved in the problem of the identity of the "Young Lady" (see p. 65). Thus, when, in 1735, Pope changed the title of the first epistle from "To a Young Lady . . ." to "To Miss Blount . . .", meaning thereby not the quarrelsome and estranged Teresa, but his life-long friend, Martha, general opinion seems to have decided that this epistle was addressed to Martha Blount also. That Pope was quite willing this opinion should be generally held is certain, if only because he did nothing to change it, but continued to use the equivocal "Miss Blount" in the title; and this opinion, in spite of some editors, has persisted ever since. Nevertheless, the poem was originally addressed to Teresa, as is shown not only by Ruffhead, who in the *Life* states that Teresa is actually named in the manuscript (see l. 7n.), but by Pope himself, who in the course of a letter to Martha in 1714 speaks of her unfailing good humour, and says "That Face must needs be irresistible, which was adorned with Smiles even when it could not see the Coronation." Therefore, as the whole point of the poem lies in the effect the coronation had on the "Young Lady" who saw it, the poem cannot have been written to Martha, who did not see it. The coronation was that of George I. An alleged conclusion of the epistle, said to have been written by Pope but not printed in his lifetime, is printed in "Couplets and Versicles, 1711–1720" below.

The copy-text of *1717* has been emended in the light of later revisions of *1735* and *1739*.

Title.] *1739–43* add a footnote continuation: "Of King George the first, 1715". It should be [20 October] 1714; Pope's memory after nearly thirty years betrayed him.

7. *Zephalinda*] The name assumed by Teresa Blount in a lengthy correspondence with a Mr H. More of Fawley Hall, who wrote under the name of Alexis: see J. T. Hillhouse, "Teresa Blount and 'Alexis'", *Mod. Lang. Notes* (1925), xl 88ff. Ruffhead said that in "the original copy" this line read: "So fair *Teresa* gave the town a view," (*Life*, p. 405*n*.). And Carruthers has this note: "In the original: 'Thus from the world the fair Teresa flew'." which would seem to be an intermediate correction between the first and final forms.

24. *Whisk*] Whist.

46. var. *Parthenissa*] Martha Blount is thus spoken of by Lord Chesterfield (Suffolk, II 114).

To a LADY *with the*
Temple of Fame.

WHAT's Fame with Men, by Custom of the Nation,
Is call'd in Women only Reputation:
About them both why keep we such a pother?
Part you with one, and I'll renounce the other.

1 with] in *MS*.   3 keep] make *MS*.
4 If you'l but give up one, I'll give up tother *MS*.

Pope's autograph: MS in possession of Messrs W. H. Robinson Ltd, 1953.
Miscellanies. The Third Volume. 1732 (and later editions).
A Collection of Epigrams. Vol. II. 1737.
The Works . . . Vol. V. Consisting of Letters. 1737 (and 2nd Edition, 1737).
A Supplement to Dr. Swift's and Mr. Pope's Works. Dublin. 1739.
Miscellanies. The Fourth Volume. 1742 (and later editions).
The Works . . . Vol. IV. Part I. Containing . . . Letters. 1742.
The Works . . . Volume VII. Containing . . . Letters. Ed. Warburton. 1751.
A Collection of Select Epigrams. J. Hackett. 1757.
Biographia Britannica. Vol. V. 1760.
The Life of Alexander Pope, Esq. O. Ruffhead. 1769.
Select Epigrams. Vol. I. 1797.
The Works. Ed. Roscoe. Vol. VI. 1824.

Pope concludes an undated letter to an anonymous lady: "Now I talk of fame, I send you my *Temple of Fame*, which is just come out; but my sentiments about it you will see better by this Epigram:" whereupon, in those editions which print the whole letter, these four lines follow. Roscoe said that the letter was addressed "to Martha Blount", without stating his evidence. But though the original autograph has not been found among the Blount papers at Mapledurham, his assertion may be correct, for the epigram is to be seen written in Pope's hand on the verso of the title page of Martha Blount's copy of *The Temple of Fame*. The *Temple of Fame* was published on 1 February 1715; the epigram would therefore appear to have been written within a few days of that date. The piece was erroneously ascribed to Swift in the two collections of Epigrams, 1757 and 1797.

The text follows that of *1732*, there being no verbal variants in the printed versions. Collations are given from the *MS*.

A Farewell to LONDON.

In the Year 1715.

DEAR, damn'd, distracting Town, farewell!
    Thy Fools no more I'll teize:
This Year in Peace, ye Critics, dwell,
    Ye Harlots, sleep at Ease!

Soft *B– – –* and rough *C– – –s*, adieu!   5
    Earl *Warwick* make your Moan,
The lively *H– – – –k* and you
    May knock up Whores alone.

To drink and droll be *Rowe* allow'd
    Till the third watchman toll;   10
Let *Jervase* gratis paint, and *Frowd*
    Save Three-pence, and his Soul.

Title] *MSS read:* Farewell to London. 1714. *1775 reads as above but with the same mistake of date, 1714; 1776 corrects this to 1715 (see introductory note).*
6 *Warwick*] *W– – –k Welbeck MS.*

Farewell *Arbuthnot*'s Raillery
　　On every learned Sot;
And *Garth*, the best good Christian he,   15
　　Altho' he knows it not.

Lintot, farewell! thy Bard must go;
　　Farewell, unhappy *Tonson*!
Heaven gives thee for thy Loss of *Rowe*,
　　Lean *Philips*, and fat *Johnson*.   20

Why should I stay? Both Parties rage;
　　My vixen Mistress squalls;
The Wits in envious Feuds engage;
　　And *Homer* (damn him!) calls.

The Love of Arts lies cold and dead   25
　　In *Hallifax*'s Urn;
And not one Muse of all he fed,
　　Has yet the Grace to mourn.

My Friends, by Turns, my Friends confound,
　　Betray, and are betray'd: 30
Poor *Y––r*'s sold for Fifty Pound,
　　And *B––––ll* is a Jade.

Why make I Friendships with the Great,
　　When I no Favour seek?
Or follow Girls Seven Hours in Eight?—   35
　　I need but once a Week.

Still idle, with a busy Air,
　　Deep Whimsies to contrive;
The gayest Valetudinaire,
　　Most thinking Rake alive.   40

31 Pound] *in the MSS*; Pounds *1775, 1776.*

Solicitous for others Ends,
   Tho' fond of dear Repose;
Careless or drowsy with my Friends,
   And frolick with my Foes.

Laborious Lobster-nights, farewell!   45
   For sober, studious Days;
And *Burlington*'s delicious Meal,
   For Sallads, Tarts, and Pease!

Adieu to all but *Gay* alone,
   Whose Soul, sincere and free,   50
Loves all Mankind, but flatters none,
   And so may starve with me.

Contemporary transcripts: Welbeck Abbey, Harley Papers; and BM MS Harl. 7316, ff. 193^b–194^a.

   The St. James's Chronicle. 14–16 September 1775.
   The Edinburgh Magazine and Review. October 1775.
   Additions to the Works of Alexander Pope, Esq. Vol. I. 1776.
   The Annual Register . . . For the Year 1775. 1776.
   The Muse's Mirrour. Vol. I. 1778.
   The Poems of Pope, Vol. I. (in Johnson's *English Poets*). 1779.

   A Farewell was written probably about the end of May 1715; that is between 19 May, the date of Lord Halifax's death (referred to in the poem) and 12 June, when the poem was mentioned in Jervas's letter to Pope, as follows: "Gay had a Copy of the Farewell with yr Injunctions. No other extant. Ld Harvey had the Homer & Letter . . . I hear nothing of the Sermon—The Generality will take it for the Deanes and that will hurt neither you nor him." There can be no doubt that the "Farewell" is the present poem, and little doubt that the dearth of "copies" referred to by Jervas explains in great measure why the piece escaped the hands of "Curll and his resemblers", and remained unpublished till 1775. The restrictions and secrecy which attended its circulation among Pope's friends are also shown, on the one hand, in the fewness of the surviving MSS, three only having been recorded (one of which cannot be traced since the eighteenth century); and, on the other, in the Welbeck copy itself, which is anonymous, and which has been endorsed in Edward Harley's hand, "Mr. P— private". Since 1775, when it began to be known to the public, the poem has everywhere been accepted as genuine, and with good reason—for it is typical Pope, full of characteristic allusion. Nevertheless, it remains an attributed piece, for no acknowledgement of his authorship of it—or even any reference to it—by Pope has yet been recorded.

   The occasion of the poem was his departure for Binfield about the end of May, after some five busy months in London, during which, in addition to the social events mentioned in the poem, he had contrived to publish not only *The Key to the Lock* about 25 April, but also, it would seem, the "Sermon" (referred to by Jervas) on *The Dignity, Use and Abuse of Glass-Bottles* on 24 May (see *Prose Works*, I 1936, pp. lxxvff.), besides carrying out his main task of seeing the first volume of his *Iliad* through the press for publication on 4 June, and all this, while enduring the nervous strain of persistent newspaper attacks on himself and his translation. Small wonder if his expressed delight at leaving the dear, damn'd, distracting Town was not wholly feigned; although at Binfield he had immediately to set to work on the next instalment of Homer.

Except for one word, the text follows that of the first printing in 1775. Collations are given from the Harley and Welbeck transcripts (*MSS*), and *Additions to . . . Pope* (*1776*).

5. *B – – –*] Identity uncertain; Brocas, and, more probably, Bethel, have been conjectured; see Biog. App., Vol. IV, and p. 28.

C – – – s] Generally, but not certainly, identified as Craggs the younger. See Biog. App., Vol. IV.

6. *Warwick*] Son-in-law to Addison.

7. *H – – – – k*] Doubtless Edward Richard, Viscount Hinchinbroke.

9. *Rowe*] Pope's letter to Caryll (20 September 1713) mentions Rowe's "vivacity and gaiety of disposition"; and Pope once told Spence that "he would laugh all day long." See Biog. App., Vol. IV.

11. *Jervase*] See p. 110. Philip Frowde (d. 1738), poet and friend of Swift, had suffered from his father's improvidence. *Journal to Stella*, 11 November 1711.

15. *Garth*] On Garth's death Pope wrote to Jervas (12 December 1718): "if ever there was a good christian without knowing himself to be so, it was Dr. Garth." See Biog. App., Vol. IV.

17. *Lintot*] Pope's bookseller, who had undertaken to publish the *Iliad*, the first volume of which was due in a few days' time. See Biog. App., Vol. IV.

18. *Tonson*] 1656?–1736. The leading publisher of his generation.

19. *Loss of Rowe*] i.e. when King George I made him one of the land surveyors of the port of London [*1776* note].

20. *Philips.*] Ambrose Philips, Pope's perennial butt; see Biog. App., Vol. IV. The "gift" was, perhaps, Philips's projected Miscellany (see p. 138, l. 5*n.*).

Johnson] He may be . . . said to have fallen a victim to the rotundity of his parts [*1776* note]. See Biog. App., Vol. V.

24. *Homer . . . calls.*] See conclusion of introductory note above.

26. *Hallifax*] Charles Montagu, Earl of Halifax (1661–1715). Politician, poet, and patron of poets; of whom Pope had written in the Preface to the *Iliad* (published within three weeks of Halifax's death): "it is hard to say whether the Advancement of the Polite Arts is more owing to his Generosity or his Example" (*Prose Works*, I 254).

31. *Y – – r*] Mrs. Elizabeth Younger (1699?–1762), actress, performed in *The What d'ye call it*, named among Pope's friends in Gay's *Welcome from Greece*; sister of Mrs Bicknell (see below).

32. *B – – – – ll*] Mrs M. Bicknell (1695?–1723), actress, sister of Mrs Younger (see above); performed in *The What d'ye call it* and *Three Hours after Marriage*; named by Gay amongst Pope's friends in the *Welcome from Greece*.

47. *Burlington*] Cf. "I am to pass three or four days in high luxury, with some company, at my Lord Burlington's" (Pope to M. Blount, 1716).

FOUR POEMS
from
A KEY to the LOCK.

A Key to the Lock . . . By Esdras Barnivelt, Apoth. The Second Edition. To which are added commendatory . . . Verses. 1715 (both issues, and later editions).

The Prose Works of Alexander Pope. Ed. N. Ault. Vol. I. 1936.

For the occasion and story of these four poems see *Prose Works*, I, lxxiiiff., lxxxviff. For some months previously, repeated attacks had been made on Pope's forthcoming translation of Homer by various enemies, chief among whom were Thomas Burnet and Philip Horneck (see Biog. App., Vols. IV and V), the editors respectively of two journals, *The Grumbler* and *The High German Doctor*, in which their attacks were published. On 25 April 1715 (according to an advertisement in *The Flying-Post*), Pope had published his pseudonymous pamphlet, *A Key to the Lock*, which had been written the previous year; this was a burlesque exposure by one "Esdras Barnivelt, Apothecary" of the supposed Romish and Jacobite propaganda concealed in *The Rape of the Lock*. On 31 May, the second edition of the *Key* was published "with some Congratulatory Poems" (as the advertisements called them) which he had recently written under the pen-names, and in caricature, of "The Grumbler", "High German Doctor", and others, and which were addressed to Barnivelt (*i.e.* Pope himself) for "proving beyond all Contradiction, the dangerous Tendency of a late Poem, entitul'd, *The Rape of the Lock*, to Government and Religion". Pope received from Lintot, the publisher, the sum of £12 10s. for *A Key to the Lock* on "31 April" (see Griffith, I 39); but there is no record of any additional payment for these poems. Doubtless all the reward he desired was the opportunity they provided of paying off old, and new, scores, including his first public intimation to Addison and Tickell that their part in the rather discreditable business of the rival translation of the *Iliad* had not gone unnoticed (see p. 145, and *Prose Works*, I, p. lxxiv).

The text of all four pieces follows that of the first printing.

I.

To my much Honoured and Esteemed Friend, Mr. E. Barnivelt, *Author of the* Key to the Lock. *An* Anagram *and* Acrostick. *By* N. Castleton, *A Well-willer to the Coalition of Parties.*

BARNIVELT.
Anagram,

UN BAREL IT.

B arrels conceal the Liquor they contain,
A nd Sculls are but the Barrels of the Brain.
R ipe Politicks the Nation's Barrel fill,
N one can like thee its Fermentation still.
I ngenious Writer, lest thy Barrel split,   5
V nbarrel thy just Sense, and broach thy Wit.
E xtract from *Tory* Barrels all *French* Juice, ⎫
L et not the *Whigs Geneva*'s Stumm infuse,   ⎬
T hen shall thy Barrel be of gen'ral Use.   ⎭

N. CASTLETON.

Title: *E. Barnivelt*] See introductory note.

N. Castleton] An obscure writer, whose penchant for "the Mixture of Inconsistent Metaphors" and "the running of Metaphors into tedious Allegories" was ridiculed in the *Spectator* (17 September 1714), to which he replied with a pamphlet entitled: "*Several Preparatory Instances of Mr. Castleton's way of Writing Produc'd against the intricate Representation Of Him in the . . . Spectator,* 1715. With this pamphlet were two others with consecutive page numbers, and probably published simultaneously, namely, *An Essay towards a Coalition of Parties in Great Britain,* 1715 (which was published 18 January 1714–15, and was mainly an attack on *A Tale of A Tub* and its author), and *An Explanatory Supplement* to it—both markedly anti-Catholic, both consequential and absurd, and both signed "Nath¹. Castleton". Nathaniel, having thus attacked both Pope's religion and his friend, became fair game for the poet, who took this opportunity of caricaturing his trick of overworking his metaphors and his obsession with Swift's *Tub*.

II.
To the Ingenious Mr. E. BARNIVELT.

HAIL, dear Collegiate, Fellow-Operator,
    Censor of Tories, President of Satyr,
Whose fragrant Wit revives, as one may say,
The stupid World, like *Assa fetida*.
How safe must be the King upon his Throne,   5
When *Barnivelt* no Faction lets alone.
Of secret Jesuits swift shall be the Doom,
Thy Pestle braining all the Sons of *Rome*.
Before thy Pen vanish the Nation's Ills,
As all Diseases fly before thy Pills.   10
Such Sheets as these, whate'er be the Disaster,
Well spread with Sense, shall be the Nation's Plaister.

HIGH GERMAN DOCTOR.

1. *Collegiate, Fellow-Operator*] "Barnivelt" was supposed to be an apothecary.
13. *High German Doctor*] Philip Horneck's pseudonym, taken from the title of his paper, which was scurrilously anti-Catholic. (See introductory note.)

III.
To my Ingenious Friend, the Author of the Key to the Lock.

THO' many a Wit from time to time has rose
    T' *inform* the World of what *it better knows*,
Yet 'tis a Praise that few their own can call,
To tell Men things they never *knew at all*.
This was reserv'd, Great *Barnivelt*, for Thee,   5
To save this Land from dangerous Mystery.
But thou too gently hast laid on thy Satyr;
What awes the World is Envy and ill Nature.
Can Popish Writings do the Nations good?
Each Drop of Ink demands a Drop of Blood.   10

A Papist wear the Lawrel! is it fit?
O *Button!* summon all thy Sons of Wit!
Join in the common Cause e'er 'tis too late;
Rack your Inventions some, and some *in time* translate.
If all this fail, let Faggot, Cart, and Rope,   15
Revenge our Wits and Statesmen on a *Pope*.

The GRUMBLER.

1–2. This couplet is a stroke at Burnet who in his best-known pamphlet, *The Necessity of Impeaching the Late Ministry*, 1715, wrote: "Give me Leave, my Lord, for once to inform your Lordship of Things which you are much better acquainted with than my self, . . ." (p. 8). This bull of Burnet's became a joke of the Town, and several of the replies to his pamphlet make play with it.

6. *dangerous Mystery*] i.e. the supposed Romish propaganda concealed in *The Rape of the Lock.*

12. *Button*] Daniel Button, the manager of the coffee-house where Addison held his court. Pope wrote to Mrs Marriot (19 July [1712?]): "I should summon a council of all the witts at Button's Coffee-house . . ."

13. *the common Cause*] i.e. the decrying, or suppression, of Pope's *Iliad*.

14. *your Inventions*] Doubless an allusion to *Homerides*, written by Burnet and Ducket attacking Pope's *Iliad*, published 7 March; also, probably, to *Æsop at the Bear-Garden*, published two days earlier attacking *The Temple of Fame*, with an inserted leaf ridiculing the forthcoming *Iliad*.

14. *in time translate*] A jeer at the shifts resorted to by the people responsible for the rival translation of the *Iliad* (Tickell and Addison in chief) to synchronize their publication with Pope's.

17. *The Grumbler*] Burnet's pseudonym, taken from the title of his paper. (See introductory note.)

IV.

To the most Learned Pharmacopolitan, and Excellent Politician, Mr. ESDRAS BARNIVELT.

By Sir JAMES BAKER, Knt.

THE *Spaniard* hides his Ponyard in his Cloke,
    The Papist masques his Treason in a Joke;
But ev'n as Coughs thy *Spanish* Liquorish heals,
So thy deep Knowledge dark Designs reveals.

Oh had I been Ambassador created,   5
Thy Works in *Spanish* shou'd have been translated,
Thy Politicks should ope the Eyes of *Spain*,
And, like true *Sevil* Snuff, awake the Brain.
Go on, Great Wit, contemn thy Foe's Bravado,
In thy defence I'll draw *Toledo*'s Spado.   10
Knighthoods on those have been conferr'd of late,
Who save our Eyesight, or wou'd save our State,
Unenvy'd Titles grace our mighty Names,
The learn'd Sir *William*, or the deep Sir *James*.
Still may those Honours be as justly dealt,   15
And thou be stil'd Sir *Esdras Barnivelt*.

JAMES BAKER, Knt.

Ascription: *Sir James Baker, Knt.*] This pseudonym was used again by Pope, so
it seems, in the following year, in the single-sheet skit called *God's Revenge against
Punning* (see *Prose Works*, I cxff.); but the original Baker whose name he took still
eludes convincing identification. At least he is *not* the bookseller, J. Baker, who
published with Curll from time to time, and so might have given similar offence
to Pope; for that Baker was undoubtedly John. But there seems to have been a
James Baker who had to do with the publication of the *St James's Journal* and the
Whitehall Evening Journal, and who was probably alluded to in a letter in *Gulliveri-
ana*, 1728, addressed "To Sir James Baker, Knight, Chief Journalist of Great
Britain" (p. 10). But why, so early as 1715 and 1716, Pope should be ridiculing
him, if he it was, is unknown.

14. *Sir William*] Sir William Read (d. 1715). An itinerant quack doctor,
originally a tailor; knighted in 1705 for curing soldiers and sailors of blindness for
nothing; later became oculist to Queen Anne, and very wealthy.

The Iliad of Homer

[Books I–IV; published 6 June 1715; vol. VII]

CHARACTERS

The year 1715, which saw the publication of the first volume of Pope's *Iliad*, saw also the development of a concerted attack upon him (see N. Ault, "Pope and Addison", *Review of English Studies*, 1941, XVII 428–51, and *Prose Works*, I lxxivff. where his counter-attacks were first described). Further evidence of his reactions to this persecution is also to be seen in sketches of various personalities, which, though not published until some years later, almost certainly date from this period. Such are the poems, *Macer*, *Umbra*, and *Atticus*, here placed together under the group title, "Characters"—a heading used by Pope himself to describe one of them.

I.
MACER.

WHEN simple *Macer*, now of high Renown,
   First sought a Poet's Fortune in the Town:
'Twas all th' Ambition his great Soul could feel,
To wear red Stockings, and to dine with *St——*
Some Ends of Verse his Betters might afford,   5
And gave the harmless Fellow a good Word.
Set up with these, he ventur'd on the Town,
And in a borrow'd Play, out-did poor *Cr——n.*
There he stopt short, nor since has writ a tittle,
But has the Wit to make the most of little: 10
Like stunted hide-bound Trees, that just have got
Sufficient Sap, at once to bear and rot.
Now he begs Verse, and what he gets commends,
Not of the Wits his Foes, but Fools his Friends.

Title Macer.] A Short History of Am— Ph—s. *MS*; Macer: A
    Character. *1727.*
  1 simple *Macer*] Am— Ph—s *MS.*
  3 great Soul] high soul *MS, 1727, 1738.*
  4 *St*—] *Steel MS, 1727, 1738.*
  5 Ends] end *MS.* might] did *MS.*
  8 *Cr—n*] *Crown MS, 1727, 1738.*
  10 But has the Wit] Just Wit enough *MS.*

So some coarse Country Wench, almost decay'd,   15
Trudges to Town, and first turns Chambermaid;
Aukward and supple, each Devoir to pay,
She flatters her good Lady twice a Day;
Thought wond'rous honest, tho' of mean Degree,
And strangely lik'd for her *Simplicity*:   20
In a translated Suit, then tries the Town,
With borrow'd Pins, and Patches not her own;
But just endur'd the Winter she began,
And in four Months, a batter'd Harridan.
Now nothing's left, but wither'd, pale, and shrunk,   25
To bawd for others, and go Shares with Punk.

Contemporary transcript: Welbeck Abbey, Harley Papers.
Miscellanies. The Last Volume. 1727 [1728] (and later editions).
The Works . . . Vol. I. Dublin. 1736.
The Works . . . Vol. II. Part II. Containing . . . Pieces . . . 1738.
The Works . . . Vol. II. Containing his Epistles, &c. 1739 (both variants).
Miscellanies. The Fourth Volume. Consisting of Verses. 1742 (and later editions).
The Works. Ed. Warburton. Vol. VI. 1751.

Macer has, since Bowles's edition, been accepted as a caricature of Ambrose Philips (see Biog. App., Vols. IV, V), whose name had been deduced from hints in the poem, as shown below; but this conjecture is now confirmed by the discovery that the poem is entitled, *A Short History of Am— Ph—s*, in Lord Oxford's transcript at Welbeck. And as, in this transcript, the first line also reads, "When Am— Ph—s now of high renown", this version in all probability preserves the original text, before it was—like so many of its companion pieces—unearthed and revised for publication in *Miscellanies*.

A point of particular interest in this poem, unnoticed by the poet's biographers, is his ridicule of Philips, in text and footnote, for doing exactly what Pope himself had done (or caused to be done) when compiling *Miscellaneous Poems and Translations. By several Hands*, 1712, namely, advertising for contributors to a projected miscellany (ll. 13–14). Pope's collection was, as previously shown (p. 36), the first miscellany to be anonymously edited by him (its second edition was in fact advertised by Lintot as *Mr. Pope's Collection of Miscellany Poems*). Some seven months before its publication announcements began to appear in *The General Post* from 10 October 1711, onwards, stating that "A New Miscellany of Poems . . . by Mr. Pope . . . Mr. Butler and Mr. Smith . . . and other Great Men" was in preparation, and contributions to it were solicited in the following words: "Those who have excellent Copies by them, may command a Place in this Miscellany, if sent before the 1st of November, to B. Lintott at the Cross Keys in Fleet-street."

The date, 1715, now attributed to *Macer* is derived from two facts: (*a*) that all

the allusions in it except one refer to events earlier than 1715; the exception
(which forms the climax of the poem) being the concluding reference to Philips's
advertisement of 8 January 1714/15; and (b) that the line "*Now* he begs verse..."
at the climax of the poem, shows that it must have been written about the time of
the advertisement to which it refers. This date is further supported by the pro-
vocations Pope received from Philips in 1714, of which glimpses are caught in his
correspondence; by the improbability that Pope, on the eve of his grand attack
on the Dunces (1728), would have bothered to write short poems like these detail-
ing old non-topical affairs and offences of his early career; and lastly, by his
avowed search for—and revision of—his *old* pieces in 1727 for inclusion in *Mis-
cellanies.*

The copy-text of *1727* has been corrected in the light of *Miscellanies* (*1742*), and
collations are given from the Welbeck transcript (*MS*).

1. *Macer*] Lat. *macer*, meagre; cf. *A Farewell to London*, l. 20, "Lean *Philips*".

2. Probably in 1708, after the termination of Philips's fellowship at St John's,
Cambridge. Tonson was then preparing the sixth volume of *Poetical Miscellanies*
(Pope to Wycherley, 13 May 1708), in which Philips's *Pastorals* formed the
opening, as Pope's *Pastorals* the closing, feature.

4. *red Stockings*] Pope mentions Philips's stockings again in *A Further Account Of
the...Condition of Mr. Edmund Curll*, 1716, where he describes him as "a Pindarick
Writer in Red Stockings".

dine with St—] Cf. Steele to Swift (8 October 1709): "Mr. Philips dined with me
yesterday: he is still a shepherd, and walks very lonely through this unthinking
crowd in London."

5f. Possibly an allusion to the praise lavished by Addison and others on
Philips's "pilfer'd Pastorals" in the *Spectator* and *Guardian*, and so largely withheld
from Pope's; and to the translations from Sappho in the *Spectator*, in which
Addison is said to have assisted.

8. *a borrow'd Play*] i.e., *The Distrest Mother*, 1712, taken from Racine's *Andro-
maque*. The anonymous *Andromache* (1675) was revised by Crowne.

Cr—*n*] John Crowne (d. 1703?), dramatist; notorious for his borrowed plays in
the latter half of the previous century.

13. *begs Verse*] He requested by publick Advertisements, the Aid of the
Ingenious, to make up a Miscellany in 1713 [P. *1727–42*]. On 8 January 1714/15,
Philips advertised in *The London Gazette* (and probably elsewhere): "There is now
preparing for the Press, a Collection of Original Poems and Translations by the
most eminent Hands, to be Published by Mr. Philips. Such Gentlemen therefore
who are willing to appear in this Miscellany, are desired to communicate the
same, directed to Jacob Tonson Bookseller in the Strand." The project came to
nothing.

20. *Simplicity*] An allusion to the laboured simplicity of Philips's *Pastorals*,
which Pope had ridiculed earlier in *Guardian*, No. 40.

21. *a translated Suit*] Probably a fling at the *Persian Tales*, translated by Philips
and published by Tonson in 1714. Cf. pp. 176, 284.

6

II.
UMBRA.

C LOSE to the best known Author, *Umbra* sits,
The constant Index to all *Button*'s Wits.
Who's here? cries *Umbra:* "Only *Johnson*"—*Oh!*
Your Slave, and *exit*; but returns with *Rowe*,
Dear Rowe, *lets sit and talk of Tragedies:*   5
Not long, *Pope* enters, and to *Pope* he flies.
Then up comes *Steele*; he turns upon his *Heel*,
And in a Moment fastens upon *Steele*.
But cries as soon, *Dear* Dick, *I must be gone,*
For, if I know his Tread, here's Addison.   10
Says *Addison* to *Steele*, 'Tis Time to go.
Pope to the Closet steps aside with *Rowe*.
Poor *Umbra*, left in this abandon'd Pickle,
E'en sits him down, and writes to honest *T—*.
        Fool! 'tis in vain from Wit to Wit to roam;   15
Know, Sense, like Charity, *begins at Home.*

Miscellanies. The Last Volume. 1727 [1728] (and later editions).
Miscellanies. The Fourth Volume. Consisting of Verses . . . 1742 (and later editions).
A Supplement to Dr. Swift's and Mr. Pope's Works. Dublin. 1739.
The Works. Ed. Roscoe. Vol. VI. 1824.

Pope never acknowledged this poem, nor is it at all sure that he ever alluded to
it. For although, after this piece had been published, he introduced the name,
Umbra, in other poems (*e.g. Mor. Ess.*, I 59; *Donne Sat.*, IV 177; *Ess. on Man*, IV
278), it would appear to have been used rather as a generic term for a social
parasite, than as a reference to any individual, much less the person sketched in
this "Character". Moreover, this poem seems only once to have been associated
with Pope's name in the eighteenth century, when the nameless author of *Charac-
ters of the Times* (1728), accused him of having written it. Nevertheless, although
on the known facts *Umbra* must be regarded as no more than an attributed poem,
its provenance, its general resemblance to Pope's style, and its characteristic allu-
sions, together confirm in great measure the generally accepted attribution. Its
precise date of composition is uncertain, though obviously much earlier than
1728, the year of publication. It must post-date 1712, when Button opened his
coffee-house under Addison's patronage, and ante-date Rowe's death in 1718.
As it appears to have been written after Pope had become a celebrity, and before
Addison's marriage to the Countess of Warwick had made his visits to Button's

less a matter of course, that is, between 1714 and 1716; and as it seems to be associated with Pope's other "Characters", *Macer* and *Atticus*, in *Miscellanies*, where they together form a group, this poem like them is tentatively dated 1715. Mr R. G. Sawyer, however, argues for a date at least a year earlier, since Umbra would not need to "write" (l. 14) to Tickell after midsummer 1714, when he left Oxford and became Addison's secretary.

The character eludes authentic identification. Walter Carey, Ambrose Philips, Charles Johnson, and James Moore Smythe have each had their advocates. But Moore Smythe was only about thirteen years old in 1715; Johnson, already figuring in the poem, could not "shadow" himself; and the enmity existing between Philips and Pope would certainly have prevented Philips "flying" to his persecutor's side, besides which, Addison's friendship for Philips would similarly have prevented the older man cutting him in the manner described in the poem. There remains Walter Carey (asserted to be Pope's victim in the above-mentioned *Characters of the Times*) who may have had a strange weakness for the society of men of letters, and yet somehow have managed to offend them. But in *To Eustace Budgell, Esq.* (p. 123), Pope had characterized Carey as a Fop. Umbra is less a Fop than a Coxcomb, a character Pope applies in the same poem to Budgell. In view of this, Budgell may seem a more probable identification.

The text is that of *1727*. There are no verbal variants.

Title] Possibly intended as a character of Walter Carey (1686–1757), an Oxford wit. Subsequently M.P., Helston 1722–7, Dartmouth 1727–57; Warden of the Mint, 1725; Clerk in Extraordinary to the Privy Council, 1727; Clerk in Ordinary, 1729. He served as secretary to the Duke of Dorset, when Lord Lieutenant of Ireland, and is mentioned severely by Swift in *The Legion Club*, ll. 103–6. For Budgell see Biog. App., Vol. IV.

2. *Button's Wits*] The habitual Whig frequenters of Button's coffee-house, often mentioned thus in a slightly derogatory manner by Pope because of the unflagging animosity shown by many of them towards him: cf. *To Mr. John Moore*, l. 39: "Ev'n Button's Wits to Worms shall turn". Rowe and Steele, however, were his personal friends.

3. *Johnson*] See Biog. App., Vol. V.

14. *T—*] Tickell. If the epithet "honest" occurred in the original version it was probably used sarcastically, in allusion to his rival translation of the *Iliad*, and all the "underhand dealing" connected with it. But about 1734 Pope spoke of Tickell to Spence without innuendo, as "a very fair worthy man" (*Anecdotes*, p. 148).

III.
ATTICUS.

Quod Te Roma legit, Rumpitur Invidia!

I<small>F</small> meagre Gildon draws his venal quill,
I wish the Man a Dinner, and sit still;
If D——s rhymes, and raves in furious Fret,
I'll answer D——s, when I am in debt:
Hunger, not Malice, makes such Authors print,   5
And who'l wage War with Bedlam or the Mint?
But were there One whom better Stars conspire
To bless, whom Titan touch'd with purer Fire,
Who born with Talents, bred in Arts to please,
Was form'd to write, converse, and live, with ease: 10
Should such a man, too fond to rule alone,

Title ATTICUS] *Customary title only, taken from Ep. to Arbuthnot.
TS and 1722 omit title. 1723 reads:* Verses Occasioned by Mr.
Tickell's Translation of the First Iliad of Homer. *MS reads:*
Fragment.
Motto Quod . . . Invidia.] In TS only, all other texts omit.
  1 meagre] meaner *TS, 1727.* Gildon] Gil—n *1722.* venal] meaner
    1723. 1–4 *1723 reverses the order of these two couplets.*
  2 Man] Wretch *1727.* sit] stand *TS.*
3–4 D—s] Dennis *TS, 1723, 1727;* Den—s *1722.*
  3 rhymes] rails *TS, 1722;* writes *1723, 1727.* raves] rails *1723,
    1727.* Fret] Pet *TS, 1722, 1723, 1727.*
  4 I am in] he's out of *TS.*
  5 'Tis Hunger and not Malice makes them Print *TS, 1722, 1727.*
5f. *1723 omits couplet.*   6 who'l] who'd *TS, 1722, 1727.*
  7 But were . . . whom] But should . . . whose *1723.*
8ff. *TS, 1722, 1723, 1727 read:*
    To form a Bard, and [or *1722*] raise his [a *1723*] Genius higher;
    Blest with each Talent, and each Art to please
    And Born to Write [Live *1723*], Converse and live [Write *1723*]
        at [with *1722, 1723, 1727*] Ease;
 11 man, too fond] One, too fond *TS;* One, resolv'd *1723;* be fond
    1727. rule] Reign *TS, 1722, 1723, 1727.*

Bear, like the Turk, no Brother near the Throne;
View him with scornful, yet with jealous eyes,
And hate, for Arts that caus'd himself to rise;
Damn with faint praise, assent with civil Leer,   15
And without sneering, teach the rest to sneer;
Or pleas'd to wound, and yet afraid to strike,
Just hint a Fault, and hesitate Dislike;
Alike reserv'd to blame or to commend,
A tim'rous Foe and a suspitious Friend: 20
Fearing ev'n Fools, by Flatterers besieg'd;
And so obliging, that he ne'r oblig'd:
Who when two Wits on rival themes contest,
Approves them both, but likes the worst the best:
Like Cato, gives his little Senate Laws,   25
And sits attentive to his own Applause;
While Fops and Templars ev'ry Sentence raise,
And wonder with a foolish Face of Praise:
What pity, Heav'n! if such a Man there be?
Who would not weep, if A——n were He?   30

12 near] on *TS*; to *1722*.
13 scornful . . . jealous] Jealous . . . Scornful *TS, 1723*.
14 And hate . . . that] Hate him . . . that *1723*; And hate . . . which
   TS, 1722.
17f. *1723 transposes couplet to follow l. 22.*
17 Or pleas'd] Willing *TS, 1722, 1723*; Wishing *1727*. and] but
   TS.
18 hint a] *1723 misprints* hit the. a Fault] Affront *1722*.
19 blame or to] Censure, or *TS*.
23f. *This couplet was omitted later in the expanded version.*
24 them both, but] of each, but *1722*; of Both, but *1723*; of Both,
   yet *TS*; of Each, yet *1727*.
25 gives] give *1723*.
27 While Fops] Whilst Wits *1722, 1727*; While Wits *TS, 1723*.
29 What pity, Heav'n! . . . Man] Who but must Grieve, . . . Man
   1722; Who but must Grieve . . . One *TS*; Who would not laugh,
   . . . Man *1723, 1727*.
30 A—n] Ad—n *1722*; Addison *TS, 1727*.

Contemporary transcripts: Welbeck Abbey, Harley Papers; BM MSS Harl. 7316, and Add. 34,109.

Pope's autograph: Longleat, Portland Papers, XIII.

The St James's Journal. 15 December 1722.

Cythereia: Or, New Poems Upon Love and Intrigue. 1723.

Court Poems. in Two Parts. 1726.

Miscellanea. In Two Volumes. Vol. I. 1727. [1726.]

Mr. Pope's Literary Correspondence. Vol. IV. 2nd Edition. 1736.

[For the longer version of "Atticus", see *post*, p. 283.]

For a full account of Pope's relations with Addison and for the evidence on which the following summary is based, see *New Light*, pp. 101-27.

This poem, provoked by the "Battle of the Iliad", was originally sketched out about the time of the publication of the rival translation in the summer of 1715, but, on second thoughts, put on one side. On some fresh offence of Addison's (whether real or falsely reported by Lord Warwick, may never be known), Pope sent him "the first sketch" with a covering letter, by way of warning, on some date before 7 May 1716; from which time to his death on 17 June 1719, "about three years after", Addison used Pope "very civilly". And Pope, for his part, not only met his quondam enemy half way and withheld the "Character" from publication, but, probably in the latter part of 1717, actually wrote the panegyric on him in the *Epistle to Mr. Addison* (see p. 202). Three and a half years after Addison's death and some two years after the epistle to him had been printed, this Character appeared anonymously in a newspaper, where it seems to have aroused no attention. Whether Pope had any hand in its publication is not known. But for some months previously the poem was being handed about in manuscript, which shows that it could have fallen into the hands of its first printer without its author's knowledge or consent; and also explains how the piratical Curll—who was certainly responsible for the next three reprints of it, and who was the first to reveal its author's name—could have obtained his copy. In 1727 Pope expanded the Character to more than double its original length (by additions not materially affecting the Addison portrait), and in 1734 incorporated it, after further revision, in the *Epistle to Dr. Arbuthnot*, where it occupies lines 151-214 (see Vol. IV).

The text is that of Pope's autograph which apparently enshrines his last revision of the short version, with collations from the Welbeck transcript (*TS*; probably the earliest extant), first and second printings (*1722*), and (*1723*). Harley 7316 is in verbal agreement with the autograph. No printed text before its expansion in *Miscellanies* (*1727*) has Pope's authority, so far as is known. (For the long version see *post*, p. 283.)

1-3. *Gildon . . . Dennis*] Charles Gildon, and John Dennis (see Biog. App., Vols. IV, V).

6. *the Mint*] A sanctuary for insolvent debtors in Southwark (see Vol. IV, 14*n*.).

11f. This idea, the jealousy of Eastern kings, had probably been associated with Addison in Pope's mind for some time. For Addison introduced his criticism of the *Ess. on C.* (*Spectator*, 20 December 1711) with a quotation from Denham ending:

> . . . Eastern Kings, who, to secure their reign
> Must have their brothers, sons, and kindred slain;

and then began by saying that Pope was not entirely free from jealousy of this nature. Pope now returns the compliment. Moreover, in a letter to Craggs (15 July 1715) he said of Addison: "We have it seems a great Turk in poetry, who can never bear a brother on the throne."

15. *Damn . . . praise*] An echo of the Prologue to Wycherley's *Plain-Dealer*, 1677: "And, with faint Praises, one another Damn."

22. *so obliging*] In the letter to Craggs above mentioned, speaking of Addison and himself, Pope wrote: "We are each of us so civil and obliging, that neither thinks he is obliged."

23f. A reference to Tickell's rival translation of the *Iliad*, Bk. I, which was published, with Addison's complicity and approval, within three or four days of Pope's. Gay wrote to Pope, 8 July 1715: ". . . and Mr. A. says, that your translation and Tickell's are both very well done, but that the latter has more of Homer."

25. A satirical repetition of a line in Pope's Prologue to Addison's *Cato*, 1713: "While Cato gives his little Senate laws"; the "little Senate" being the Whig frequenters of Button's coffee-house, to whom he also refers as "the little senate of Cato" in the letter to Craggs above noted. Instances of Addison's "rule" can be found in Burnet's letters to Duckett (ed. D. Nichol Smith, 1914) between February 1715 and June 1716.

27. *Fops and Templars*] A probable allusion to Thomas Burnet, one of Pope's enemies, who entered the Middle Temple in 1709 and was called to the bar early in 1715; a frequenter of Button's, and a subservient follower of Addison (see previous note and Biog. App., Vol. IV).

30. *Addison*] When this Character came to be included in the *Epistle to Arbuthnot*, Pope changed this name to Atticus.

THE UNIVERSAL PRAYER.

DEO OPT. MAX.

FATHER of All! in every Age,
   In every Clime ador'd,
By Saint, by Savage, and by Sage,
   Jehovah, Jove, or Lord!

Title A Hymn. *MS 1*; A Prayer to God. 1715. *MS 2*.
3 by Christian Saint, by Heathen sage *MS 1*; By . . . or *MS 3*.

Thou Great First Cause, least understood!   5
    Who all my Sense confin'd
To know but this,—that Thou art Good,
    And that my self am blind:

Yet gave me, in this dark Estate,
    To see the Good from Ill;   10
And binding Nature fast in Fate,
    Left free the Human Will.

What Conscience dictates to be done,
    Or warns me not to doe,
This, teach me more than Hell to shun,   15
    That, more than Heav'n pursue.

What Blessings thy free Bounty gives,
    Let me not cast away;
For God is pay'd when Man receives,
    T' enjoy, is to obey.   20

5 Thou . . . Cause] O First of Things! *MS 1.*
6 all] hast *MSS 1 and 2*; last *MS 3.*   8 And that] And I *1738a.*
9–12 *MSS 1 and 3 preserve this stanza, 1 instead of st. 3, 3 in addition:*
    Who all dost see & [who *MS 3*] all dost know
    And all dost Love the best
    bidst Fortune rule yᵉ World below
    And Conscience guide yᵉ Breast
9 gave me] gav'st us *MS 2.*
10 see] know *MSS 2 and 3.*
12 free the Human] Conscience free, and *MS 2, and 1738ab.* Left]
   Left'st *MS 2.*
13–16 *For this stanza, MS 1 reads:*
    Wᵗever Conscience thinks not well
    Wᵗere it bids me do
    That let me shun ev'n more than Hell
    This more than Heaven persu
17 Blessings] pleasures *MSS 1 and 3.*   19 God] Heav'n *MS 1.*

Yet not to Earth's contracted Span,
    Thy Goodness let me bound;
Or think Thee Lord alone of Man,
    When thousand Worlds are round.

Let not this weak, unknowing hand   25
    Presume Thy Bolts to throw,
And deal Damnation round the land,
    On each I judge thy Foe.

If I am right, oh teach my heart
    Still in the right to stay;   30
If I am wrong, Thy Grace impart
    To find that better Way.

20 *Following this line, MSS 1 and 3 have the suppressed stanza which*
   reads :   Can Sins of Moments claim yᵉ Rod
           of Everlasting Fires?
           Can those be Sins wᵗʰ [Crimes to *MS 3*] Natures God
           Wᶜʰ Natures selfe inspires?
  For other versions of the suppressed stanza, see introductory note below.
21 Yet not] But if *MSS 1 and 3*; But not *MS 2.*
22 Omnipotence I bound *MS 1*; Omnipotence we bound *MS 3.*
23 Or] Nor *MS 2.*   24 Whole Systems flaming round *MS 3.*
25 Let not] If ere *MSS 1 and 3.*
26 Presume] Presumes *MS 3.*
27 And] Or *MS 2.* Damnation] Destruction *MS 3.*
28 thy] my *MS 1.*
29–32 *MS 3 omits this stanza and reads :*
           If I condemn one Sect or part
             Of those that seek thy Face;
           If Charity within this Heart
             Holds not the highest Place!
  MSS 1 and 2 transpose to follow l. 40, and read as follows : 29 oh
  reach my heart] thy grace impart *MSS, 1738ab.*
30 stay] *word partly obliterated in MS 2.*
31 Thy Grace impart] Oh reach my heart *MSS, 1738ab.*
32 To find that] To know yᵉ *MS 1.*

6*

Save me alike from foolish Pride,
　　Or impious Discontent,
At ought thy Wisdom has deny'd,   35
　　Or ought thy Goodness lent.

Teach me to feel another's Woe;
　　To hide the Fault I see;
That Mercy I to others show,
　　That Mercy show to me.   40

Mean tho' I am, not wholly so
　　Since quicken'd by thy Breath,
O lead me wheresoe'er I go,
　　Thro' this day's Life, or Death:

This day, be Bread and Peace my Lot;   45
　　All else beneath the Sun,
Thou know'st if best bestow'd, or not;
　　And let Thy Will be done.

To Thee, whose Temple is all Space,
　　Whose Altar, Earth, Sea, Skies;   50
One Chorus let all Being raise!
　　All Nature's Incence rise!

33–6 *For this stanza MS 1 reads:*
　　　　If 'ere my foolish breast knew Pride
　　　　for ought that thou hast given
　　　　If 'ere the Wretched I deny'd
　　　　Do thou deny me Heaven
　　So too MS 3, with Or other's wants with Scorn deride *for l. 35.*
37f.　　　　As from my little I bestow
　　　　Wⁿ I the needy see *MS 1.*
37 Teach me to] But if I *MS 3.*   38 To hide] Or hide *MS 3.*
39 As I to others mercy show, *MS 2.*
41–52 *MS 1 omits the last three stanzas.*
41 tho'] as *MS 2.*   49–52 *MS 2 omits the last stanza.*

Lady M. W. Montagu's autograph: Harrowby MS, Sandon.

Contemporary transcripts: Hooke (Chicago University), Lort (*Thraliana*, ed. K. C. Balderston, 1942, pp. 405ff.).

The Universal Prayer. By the Author of the Essay on Man. 1738 (22 June).

The Universal Prayer . . . 1738 (8vo. edition).

The Works . . . Vol. II. Part II. Containing . . . Pieces . . . written since the former Volumes. 1738 (published 1739).

The Works . . . Vol. II. Containing his Epistles, &c. 1739.

The Works . . . Vol. II. Part I. Containing his Epistle, &c. 1740 (and 1743).

The Gentleman's Magazine. November 1741.

An Essay on Man . . . With Notes by William Warburton. 1745.

An Essay on Man. In Four Epistles. 1745.

An Essay on Man . . . With Notes by Mr. Warburton. 1746.

The Scots Magazine. December 1747.

An Essay on Man . . . With the . . . Notes of Mr. Warburton. 1748.

An Essay on Man . . . With Notes by William Warburton. 1749.

An Essay on Criticism. With Notes by Mr. Warburton. 1751.

The Works. Ed. Warburton. Vol. III. 1751.

Though Warburton declared that *The Universal Prayer* was composed as a pendant to the *Essay on Man*, it is now known (see Sherburn, p. 61) that the *Prayer* was written nearly twenty years before the *Essay*. In a letter to Ralph Allen, Pope wrote: ". . . I've sent you the Hymn, a little alterd, & enlargd in one necessary point of doctrine, viz: yᵉ third stanza, which I think reconciles Freedom & Necessity; & is at least a Comment on some Verses in my Essay on Man which have been mis-construed. Mʳ Hooke transcribed this Copy, without having one himself; as I believe no man has, since I gave it twenty years ago, in its first state, to the Duke of Shrewsbury . . ."

The transcribed poem accompanying this letter is headed *A Prayer to God. 1715*. The letter itself is dated 8 September, and as the year 1736 is indicated by internal evidence, the Duke would have received his copy in 1716, that is, in the year following the composition of the piece. The Duke's copy seems to have vanished; and "Mr Hooke's" transcript, containing twelve stanzas, was admittedly taken from a text "alterd" from "its first state". It is probable, therefore, that Lady Mary Wortley Montagu's autograph copy, transcribed about 1740 and hitherto unrecorded, most nearly represents the text as it was originally written in 1715, since (i) it does not follow any of the printed texts, although it was copied out by her *after* the poem had become easily accessible in three or four different editions; (ii) it is entitled simply *A Hymn*, which is what (in the above letter) Pope calls the poem in "its first state"; whereas (iii) the "alterd" version which he sent Allen was entitled *A Prayer to God*, and the published version was always called by its title *The Universal Prayer*; (iv) Pope and Lady Mary were intimate friends at or about the time the Hymn was originally written, and were also in the habit of exchanging poems with each other in manuscript; whereas (v) they had long been completely estranged when the poem came to be rewritten and published; (vi) Lady Mary's version not only preserves the text of the third stanza *before* it was "alterd . . . in one necessary point of doctrine", but also alone retains the "licentious" stanza which is said to have figured in the "Original Manuscript" (see below), and which was later suppressed.

A version of the suppressed stanza with possibly later readings was recorded by Mrs Thrale in *Thraliana* (ed. K. C. Balderston, 1947, p. 252): "Mr Lort told me once that he had seen Pope's universal Prayer in the Original Manuscript; and that the Stanza was there—

> Can Sins of Moments claim the Rod
>   Of everlasting Fires:
> Or that offend 'gainst Nature's God
>   Which Nature's Self inspires?"

With the early date of the poem established, Warburton's note to *The Universal Prayer*, which originally ran:

> *Universal Prayer*.] Concerning this poem, it may be proper to observe, that some passages, in the preceding *Essay*, having been unjustly suspected of a tendency towards Fate and *Naturalism*, the author composed this Prayer as the sum of all, to shew that his system was founded in *free-will*, and terminated in piety: That the first cause was as well the Lord and Governor of the Universe as the Creator of it; and that, by submission to his will (the great principle inforced throughout the *Essay*) was not meant the suffering ourselves to be carried along with a blind determination; but a religious acquiescence, and confidence full of *Hope* and Immortality. To give all this the greater weight and reality, the poet chose for his model the LORD's PRAYER, which, of all others, best deserves the title prefixed to this Paraphrase.

should be corrected accordingly, and instead of "the author composed this Prayer" should read "the author altered and enlarged this Prayer . . ."

The first edition *1738a* has been taken as copy-text and emended in the light of subsequent revisions; collations are recorded from Lady Mary's transcript (*MS 1*), "Mr. Hooke's" transcript (*MS 2*), the Lort transcript (*MS 3*), and the octavo editions listed above, up to Pope's last revision of 1740.

20. var. Dr Johnson observed (*Life of Johnson*, ed. Hill-Powell, III 346, 527) that the thought of the suppressed stanza was borrowed from Guarini. See *Chorus II from Brutus* (p. 153), ll. 9ff. and *n.*, where the same passage is alluded to.

Two CHORUS's to the Tragedy of *BRUTUS*.

I.
Chorus of *Athenians*.

Strophe 1.

YE shades, where sacred truth is sought;
  Groves, where immortal Sages taught;
Where heav'nly visions *Plato* fir'd,
And *Epicurus* lay inspir'd!
In vain your guiltless laurels stood,   5
Unspotted long with human blood.
War, horrid war, your thoughtful walks invades,
And steel now glitters in the Muses shades.

Antistrophe 1.

Oh heav'n-born sisters! source of art!
Who charm the sense, or mend the heart;   10
Who lead fair Virtue's train along,
Moral *Truth*, and mystic *Song!*
To what new clime, what distant sky
Forsaken, friendless, shall ye fly?
Say, will ye bless the bleak *Atlantic* shore?   15
Or bid the furious *Gaul* be rude no more?

Strophe 2.

When *Athens* sinks by fates unjust,
When wild *Barbarians* spurn her dust;
Perhaps ev'n *Britain*'s utmost shore

Title] *1717 adds, after Brutus*, not yet publick.
Chorus of Athenians.] First Chorus. Of Athenian Philosophers.
   Written at the Command of his Grace, by Mr. Pope. *1723*.
Strophe, and Antistrophe] *om. 1723, stanzas being numbered* I–IV.
4 And *Epicurus*] And godlike *Zeno 1717, 1723*.

Shall cease to blush with stranger's gore,   20
See arts her savage sons controul,
And *Athens* rising near the pole!
'Till some new Tyrant lifts his purple hand,
And civil madness tears them from the land.

Antistrophe 2.

Ye Gods! what justice rules the ball?   25
Freedom and Arts together fall;
Fools grant whate'er ambition craves,
And men, once ignorant, are slaves.
Oh curs'd effects of civil hate,
In every age, in every state!   30
Still, when the lust of tyrant pow'r succeeds,
Some *Athens* perishes, some *Tully* bleeds.

II.
Chorus of Youths and Virgins.

Semichorus.

O H tyrant Love! hast thou possest
  The prudent, learn'd, and virtuous breast?
Wisdom and wit in vain reclaim,
And arts but soften us to feel thy flame.
 Love, soft intruder, enters here,   5
 But entring learns to be sincere.
 Marcus with blushes owns he loves,
 And *Brutus* tenderly reproves.

22 And] An *1717, 1723, 1736.*
32 perishes, some] perishes, or some *1722.*
II. Chorus . . . Virgins.] *1723 reads:* Second Chorus. Of Athenian
 Youths and Virgins. By Mr. Pope.
Semichorus.] *Youths. 1723.*
5f. *omm. 1723.*   7 *Marcus*] *Varius 1723.*

Why, virtue, doest thou blame desire,
　　Which nature has imprest?   10
Why, nature, dost thou soonest fire
　　The mild and gen'rous breast?

Chorus.

Love's purer flames the Gods approve;
The Gods, and *Brutus* bend to love:
Brutus for absent *Portia* sighs,   15
And sterner *Cassius* melts at *Junia*'s eyes.
　　What is loose love? a transient gust,
　　Spent in a sudden storm of lust,
　　A vapour fed from wild desire,
　　A wandring, self-consuming fire.   20
　　　　But *Hymen*'s kinder flames unite;
　　　　And burn for ever one;
　　　　Chaste as cold *Cynthia*'s virgin light,
　　　　Productive as the Sun.

Semichorus.

Oh source of ev'ry social tye,   25
United wish, and mutual joy!
What various joys on one attend,
As son, as father, brother, husband, friend!
　　Whether his hoary sire he spies,
　　While thousand grateful thoughts arise;   30
　　Or meets his spouse's fonder eye;
　　Or views his smiling progeny;

Chorus.] *Virgins. 1723.*
17–20 *Instead of these four lines, 1723 reads:*
　　　　What is loose Love? A wand'ring Fire,
　　　　A transient Fit of fond Desire.
21 kinder flames] flames like stars *1717, 1723.*
Semichorus.] *Youths. 1723.*
25f. *omm. 1723.*   28 brother,] *om. 1723.*
30 While] And finds a *1723.*

What tender passions take their turns,
 What home-felt raptures move!
His heart now melts, now leaps, now burns,   35
 With rev'rence, hope, and love.

Chorus.

Hence guilty joys, distastes, surmizes,
Hence false tears, deceits, disguises,
Dangers, doubts, delays, surprizes;
 Fires that scorch, yet dare not shine: 40
Purest love's unwasting treasure,
Constant faith, fair hope, long leisure,
Days of ease, and nights of pleasure;
 Sacred *Hymen!* these are thine.

Chorus.] *Chorus of Both. 1723.*
38 Hence false tears,] False oaths, false tears, *1717, 1723.*

The Works of Mr. Alexander Pope. 1717.
The Works . . . Dublin. 1718.
The Works . . . (Printed by T. J.) 1718 (and 1720).
Miscellaneous Poems and Translations. 3rd Edition, 1720 (4th Edition, 1722;
Miscellany Poems, 5th Edition, 1726 and 1727, and 6th Edition, 1732).
[*Four Choruses.* 1723.]
The Works of John Sheffield . . . Duke of Buckingham. 1723 (and later editions).
The Hive. 1724 (and later editions). [The Second Chorus only.]
The Works . . . To which are added, I. Cooper's-Hill. [etc.]. 1727.
The Works . . . Vol. I. With Explanatory Notes. 1736 (both variants).
The Works . . . Vol. I. Part I. 1740 (and 1743).
The Works. Ed. Warburton. Vol. I. 1751.
The Duke of Buckingham, who endeavoured to improve on Shakespeare's
Julius Caesar by splitting it up into two tragedies (called *Brutus* and *Julius Caesar*
respectively) and making other alterations, had the further inspiration of insert-
ing lyrical choruses between the acts. Two of these choruses were "Written at the
Command of his Grace, by Mr. Pope". Seeing that Pope did not include them
with the two other choruses to Brutus, written by Buckingham himself, in "Lin-
tot's Miscellany" in 1712, or in 1714, it is probable they were not then in exis-
tence, but were written between the latter date and 1716, in which year Pope was
assembling these and other pieces for publication in the *Works* (1717). These two
pieces are therefore tentatively dated "before 1716". The old Duke, John Shef-
field, died in 1722, and Pope undertook to collect and edit his friend's works.

These he published on 24 January 1722/3 (not without trouble from several quarters) in a sumptuous edition, in which these two "Choruses to Brutus" appeared in their proper places in the tragedy for the first time. But although *Brutus* seems never to have been either printed separately, or acted, in Pope's day, his two choruses, together with the Duke's, all alike set to music by Bononcini, are stated by the Duchess, in an autograph note in a music manuscript, to have been "performed on my son the Duke of Buckingham's Birthday Jan. the 10th, 1723" at Buckingham House (see Sotheby's Catalogue of the sale of the P.M. Pittar library, 4–7 November 1918). At this performance copies of the words appear to have been distributed to the audience. Two copies are known to survive, one in the Duke of Portland's library, one in Mr Cottrell-Dormer's. The Welbeck copy, which seems to have belonged to the second Earl of Oxford, contains a manuscript note: "This paper was given me in the Salon at Buckingham House on the 11th of Jan 1722/3 being the Duks Birth Day, where the Dutches Caus'd this Entertainment to be Performed with great Magnifisence and Order ye Musick being composed by Sig^r Bononcine sung ye best by ye best Voices M^rs A: Robinson & others & ye best Instruments of all sorts."

The copy-text of *1717* has been amended in the light of later revisions, made in 1723, 1736, and 1740. The texts of *1723* and the Four Choruses (1722/3) are verbally identical.

Title] Altered from Shakespear by the Duke of Buckingham, at whose desire these two Choruses were composed to supply as many wanting in his play. They were set many years afterwards by the famous Bononcini, and performed at Buckingham-house. [P. *1740–51*]. For the performance, see above.

I. 4. *And Epicurus*] The fact that the earlier reading was "And godlike Zeno" seems to dispose of Warburton's theory that Pope deliberately chose the names of Plato and Epicurus to correspond with the philosophical views of Brutus and Cassius.

II. 9. *Why, Virtue*, &c] In allusion to that famous conceit of Guarini, *Se il peccare è si dolce*, etc. [Warburton, *1751*]. *Il Pastor Fido*, III iv 14ff., which reads:

> O fortunate voi fere selvagge,
> A cui l'alma Natura
> Non die' legge in amar, se non d'amore:
> Legge umana inumana,
> Che dai per pena dell' amar la morte:
> Se'l peccar' è si dolce,
> E'l non peccar si necessario; o troppo
> Imperfetta natura
> Che repugni alla legge:
> O troppo dura legge,
> Che la natura offendi.

Cf. *Univ. Prayer*, p. 150, suppressed stanza.

EPISTLE
TO
Mr. JERVAS,
With *Dryden*'s Translation of *Fresnoy*'s *Art* of *Painting*.

THIS verse be thine, my friend, nor thou refuse
  This, from no venal or ungrateful Muse.
Whether thy hand strike out some free design,
Where life awakes, and dawns at ev'ry line;
Or blend in beauteous tints the colour'd mass,   5
And from the canvas call the mimic face:
Read these instructive leaves, in which conspire
Fresnoy's close art, and *Dryden*'s native fire:
And reading wish, like theirs, our fate and fame,
So mix'd our studies, and so join'd our name,   10
Like them to shine thro' long succeeding age,
So just thy skill, so regular my rage.

    Smit with the love of Sister-arts we came,
And met congenial, mingling flame with flame;
Like friendly colours found them both unite,   15
And each from each contract new strength and light.
How oft' in pleasing tasks we wear the day,
While summer suns roll unperceiv'd away?
How oft' our slowly-growing works impart,
While images reflect from art to art?   20
How oft' review; each finding like a friend
Something to blame, and something to commend?
What flatt'ring scenes our wand'ring fancy wrought,
Rome's pompous glories rising to our thought!

Title To Mr. Jervas, with Fresnoy's Art of Painting, Translated
    by Mr. Dryden. *1716-32.* Epistle IV. To Mr. Jervas, . . .
    Dryden. *1735.*
15 them both] our Arts *1716, 1717*; our Hearts *1720-35.*

Together o'er the *Alps* methinks we fly,   25
Fir'd with ideas of fair *Italy*.
With thee, on *Raphael*'s Monument I mourn,
Or wait inspiring dreams at *Maro*'s Urn:
With thee repose, where *Tully* once was laid,
Or seek some ruin's formidable shade;   30
While fancy brings the vanish'd piles to view,
And builds imaginary *Rome* a-new.
Here thy well-study'd Marbles fix our eye;
A fading Fresco here demands a sigh:
Each heav'nly piece unweary'd we compare,   35
Match *Raphael*'s grace, with thy lov'd *Guido*'s air,
Caracci's strength, *Correggio*'s softer line,
Paulo's free stroke, and *Titian*'s warmth divine.
    How finish'd with illustrious toil appears
This small, well-polish'd gem, the work of years!   40
Yet still how faint by precept is exprest
The living image in the Painter's breast?
Thence endless streams of fair ideas flow,
Strike in the sketch, or in the picture glow;
Thence beauty, waking all her forms, supplies   45
An Angel's sweetness, or *Bridgewater*'s eyes.
    Muse! at that name thy sacred sorrows shed,
Those tears eternal, that embalm the dead:
Call round her tomb each object of desire,
Each purer frame inform'd with purer fire: 50
Bid her be all that chears or softens life,
The tender sister, daughter, friend and wife;
Bid her be all that makes mankind adore;
Then view this marble, and be vain no more!
    Yet still her charms in breathing paint engage;   55
Her modest cheek shall warm a future age.
Beauty, frail flow'r that ev'ry season fears,
Blooms in thy colours for a thousand years.
Thus *Churchill's* race shall other hearts surprize,

And other Beauties envy *Worsley*'s eyes,   60
Each pleasing *Blount* shall endless smiles bestow,
And soft *Belinda*'s blush for ever glow.
    Oh lasting as those colours may they shine,
Free as thy stroke, yet faultless as thy line!
New graces yearly, like thy works, display;   65
Soft without weakness, without glaring gay;
Led by some rule, that guides, but not constrains;
And finish'd more thro' happiness than pains!
The kindred arts shall in their praise conspire,
One dip the pencil, and one string the lyre.   70
Yet should the Graces all thy figures place,
And breathe an air divine on ev'ry face;
Yet should the Muses bid my numbers roll,
Strong as their charms, and gentle as their soul;
With *Zeuxis*' *Helen* thy *Bridgewater* vie,   75
And these be sung 'till *Granville*'s *Myra* die;
Alas! how little from the grave we claim?
Thou but preserv'st a Face and I a Name.

60 *Worsley*'s] *Wortley*'s *1716–32.*
78 Face] Form *1716–22.*

The Art of Painting : By C. A. Du Fresnoy . . . 2nd Edition, 1716.
The Works of Mr. Alexander Pope. 1717.
The Works . . . Dublin. 1718.
The Works . . . (Printed by T. J.) 1718 (and 1720).
Miscellaneous Poems and Translations, By several Hands. 3rd Edition, 1720 [and later editions 1722, 1726–7, 1732].
The Works . . . To which are added, I. Cooper's-Hill. [etc.]. 1727.
The Works of Alexander Pope, Esq. Vol. II. 1735.
The Works . . . Vol. II. Containing his Epistles and Satires. 1735 (and 1736).
Ethic Epistles, to Henry St. John L. Bolingbroke. Written in the Year 1732. 1735.
The Works . . . Vol. II. Containing his Epistles, &c. 1739 (both editions).
The Works . . . Vol. II. Part I. Containing his Epistles, &c. 1740 (and 1743).
The Works. Ed. Warburton. Vol. VI. 1751.

    This poem was published on 20 March 1716. What appears to be a first draft is preserved in the Homer MSS (Addit. MS 4807, f. 128b) on the back of part of *Iliad*, Bk IX, and is printed in *New Light*, pp. 72–3. The substitution of Lady Bridgewater's name for Lady Berkeley's in the draft of what is now l. 46 led EC to suppose that the draft was made before Lady Bridgewater's death on 22 March 1714. But this view is tenable only on the assumption that when Pope took a sheet of paper for drafting *Iliad* IX, he abandoned what was at this time his usual practice of picking up what lay ready to hand and chose some long-discarded sheet. The draft of Book VIII on ff. 108, 116, and 120 was written on the backs of letters written in June and July 1715, and the draft of Book IX on f. 129 was written on the back of a letter of 2 October. It is therefore highly probable that the draft of this *Epistle* was written in the autumn of 1715. This does not conflict with Pope's statement that the poem "was written some years before" the epistles to Craggs, Oxford, and Arbuthnot—the date of the remaining epistle there mentioned is problematic (see p. 205)—and the mis-dating of publication by a single year in the same statement is easily attributable to a lapse of memory.

The copy-text is that of *Works* 1717, which has been amended in the light of later revisions.

Title: *Mr. Jervas*] See p. 110.

Fresnoy] Charles Alphonse Dufresnoy (1611–65), painter and poet, formerly pupil of Perrier and Vouet; in Italy 1632–56, where he largely abandoned painting for poetry; chief work *De arte graphica*, published posthumously in 1668 by his friend Mignard the painter, and translated by Dryden, 1695.

1. This Epistle, and the two following, were written some years before the rest, and originally printed in *1717* [P. *1735–51*].

17f. Wakefield compares Ovid, *Pont.*, x 10. 37:

> sæpe dies sermone minor fuit; inque loquendum
> tarda per æstivos defuit hora dies.

20. Cf. *Epistle to Addison*, l. 52, "And Art reflected images to Art."

21f. For rhyme and phrasing, cf. *Atticus* (p. 143), ll. 19f.

33. *thy well-study'd Marbles*] Perhaps in reference to Jervas's studies in Italy, where he had been sent at Dr George Clarke's expense. See H. Walpole, *Anecdotes of Painting*, ed. R. N. Wornum (1888), II 271.

36ff. These judgements appear to have been in part derived from Du Fresnoy. "Raphael . . . above all, . . . possessed the graces in so advantageous a manner, that he has never since been equalled by any other", *The Judgment of Du Fresnoy, on the Works of the principal and best Painters of the two last Ages* (Dryden, *Works*, ed. W. Scott, 1808, XVII 491); "the laborious and diligent Annibal Caracci", *The Art of Painting* (*op. cit.*, XVII 389); "Corregio . . . his pencil was both easy and delightful . . . he painted with . . . great sweetness", *Judgment*, pp. 494–5; "Paulo Veronese was wonderfully graceful in his airs of women, with . . . incredible vivacity and ease", *ibid.*, p. 494; "Georgione . . . first began to make choice of glowing . . . colours, the perfection and entire harmony of which were afterwards to be found in Titian's pictures . . . [Titian's] painting is wonderfully glowing, sweet, and delicate", *ibid.*, pp. 492–3. Guido is praised for his "gracefulness and beauty" in execution (*ibid.*, p. 497.)

40. *the work of years*] *Fresnoy* employ'd about twenty years in finishing this Poem [P. *1717–51*].

46. *Bridgewater*] Elizabeth, Countess of Bridgewater, was the third of the four

beautiful daughters of the Duke of Marlborough, who are together alluded to in line 59 as "Churchill's race" (the others being Henrietta, Countess of Godolphin, Anne, Countess of Sunderland, and Mary, Duchess of Montagu). Lady Bridgewater, reputed to have been the most beautiful of them, died of smallpox on 22 March 1714. Jervas affected to be in love with her, hence "thy Bridgewater" in line 75.

50, 53–4. These lines had been foreshadowed in the epitaph on John Lord Caryll (p. 81):

> Exalted Souls, inform'd with purer Fire (l. 11)
> Then, when you seem above mankind to soar,
> Look on this marble, and be vain no more! (ll. 16–17).

59. *Churchill's race*] The four daughters of the Duke of Marlborough (see l. 46.)

60. *Worsley's eyes*] Wife of Sir Robert Worsley, Bart., to whom Swift wrote on 19 April 1730 saying that when he saw her last, three years previously, "Your eyes dazzled me as much as when I first met them, which, considering myself, is a greater compliment than you are aware of. . ." Nevertheless, in the early versions it was Lady Mary Wortley Montagu whose eyes Pope praised (as he did in another couplet a few months later, see *post*, p. 236), and whose name, after his quarrel with her, he changed to Worsley by the alteration of one letter.

61. *Blount*] Martha and Teresa Blount.

62. *Belinda*] Arabella Fermor, the heroine of *The Rape of the Lock*. See Vol. II, pp. 371–5.

67f. For this doctrine cf. *Ess. on C.*, ll. 141–55.

75. *thy Bridgewater*] See l. 46n.

76. *Granville's Myra*] George Granville, Lord Lansdowne (see Biog. App. Vol. IV) who in his poems frequently celebrated the Countess of Newburgh under the name of Myra.

77f. Cf. *To Belinda*, l. 27f. (see p. 108).

The Iliad of Homer, Vol. II

[Books v–viii; published 22 March 1715/6; vol. vii]

To Mr. JOHN MOORE,
Author of the Celebrated Worm-Powder.

How much, egregious *Moor*, are we
　　Deceiv'd by Shews and Forms!
Whate'er we think, whate'er we see,
　　All Humankind are Worms.

Man is a very Worm by Birth,　　　　　　　5
　　Vile Reptile, weak, and vain!
A while he crawls upon the Earth,
　　Then shrinks to Earth again.

That Woman is a Worm we find,
　　E'er since our Grandame's Evil;　　　　10
She first convers'd with her own Kind,
　　That antient Worm, the Devil.

The Learn'd themselves we Book-Worms name;
　　The Blockhead is a Slow-worm;
The Nymph whose Tail is all on Flame　　　15
　　Is aptly term'd a Glow-worm:

The Fops are painted Butterflies,
　　That flutter for a Day;

Title] *TS2 omits; 1716 reads:* To the Ingenious Mr. Moore, Author
　　of the Celebrated Worm-Powder.
　4 Humankind] Humane Race *TSS*; Human Race *1716*.
　6 Proud Reptile, vile *TS2, 1716*; Vile Reptile, Proud *TS1, 3*.
10 Grandame's] Gran'ams *TS2, 1716*.
12-13 *Between these lines TSS1, 3 and 1716 have a stanza which reads:*
　　　　　But whether Man, or He, God knows,
　　　　　　　Fæcundified her Belly,
　　　　　With that pure Stuff from whence we rose,
　　　　　　　The Genial *Vermicelli*.

First from a Worm they take their Rise,
    And in a Worm decay: 20

The Flatterer an Earwig grows;
    Thus Worms suit all Conditions;
Misers are Muckworms, Silk-worms Beaus,
    And Death-watches Physicians.

That Statesmen have the Worm, is seen   25
    By all their winding Play;
Their Conscience is a Worm within,
    That gnaws them Night and Day.

Ah *Moore!* thy Skill were well employ'd,
    And greater Gain would rise,   30
If thou could'st make the Courtier void
    The Worm that never dies!

O learned Friend of *Abchurch-Lane,*
    Who sett'st our Entrails free!
Vain is thy Art, thy Powder vain,   35
    Since Worms shall eat ev'n thee.

Our Fate thou only can'st adjourn
    Some few short Years, no more!
Ev'n *Button*'s Wits to Worms shall turn,
    Who Maggots were before.   40

19 take] took *TS2, 1716.*   20 And] Then *TS2, 1716.*
22 Thus] Some *TSS, 1716.*   25 the Worm] a Worm *TSS, 1716.*
34 Powder] Powders *TS1.*
37 Thou only can'st our Fates [fate *TS1*] adjourn *TSS, 1716.*

Contemporary transcripts: Congleton Papers (in Gay's hand) *TS1*; Welbeck
Abbey, Harley Papers *TS2*; Brotherton Library, Leeds University *TS3.*
    To the Ingenious Mr. Moore, Author of the Celebrated Worm-Powder. By Mr. Pope.
1716. [Two issues, with, and without, date and imprint. Also 2nd Ed. 1716.]
    The London Post. 28 April–5 May 1716.
    The Weekly Journal. 5 May 1716. *State Poems.* 1716.

Court Poems. Dublin. 1716.
Pope's Miscellany. 1717 (and 2nd Edition, 1717).
Court Poems. Part II. 1717.
The Ladies Miscellany. 1718.
Love's Invention. 1718 (and 2nd Edition, 1718).
Court Poems In Two Parts Compleat. 1719.
A Miscellaneous Collection of Poems, Songs and Epigrams. T. M. 1721.
The Hive. 1724 (and later editions).
Court Poems. In Two Parts. By Mr. Pope, &c. 1726.
The Altar of Love. 1727 (and 3rd Edition, 1731).
Miscellanea. The Second Volume. 1727.
Miscellanies. The Last Volume. 1727 (and later editions).
The Musical Miscellany. Vol. II. 1729.
The Merry Musician. Vol. III. [1731.]
A Miscellany on Taste. 1732.
The Choice. [Vol. I.] 2nd Edition, 1732.
The Vocal Miscellany. [Vol. I.] 2nd Edition, 1734 (and 3rd Edition, 1738).
Mr. Pope's Literary Correspondence. Vol. II. 1735 (and 2nd Edition, 1735).
A Supplement to Dr. Swift's and Mr. Pope's Works. Dublin. 1739.
The Merry Companion. 2nd Edition. 1742.
Miscellanies. The Fourth Volume. Consisting of Verses . . . 1742 (and later editions).
The Aviary. [1744.]
The Goldfinch. 1748.
The Charmer. 1749.
The Thrush. 1749.
The History of John Bull. [1750?]
Vocal Melody. 1751.
The Works. Ed. Warburton. Vol. VI. 1751.

"This Day is publish'd, The Worms, a Satyr; written by Mr. Pope. Printed for E. Curl . . . Price Two Pence"—this advertisement which *The Post Boy* displayed on 1 May 1716, announced probably the most popular poem (at least in his own day) that Pope is supposed to have written.

Although he never included the piece in his *Works,* and always withheld his name from it when printing it in *Miscellanies;* and although Horace Walpole (according to EC) was of the opinion that Dodington wrote it, there can be little doubt that Curll's original attribution was correct. For besides the fact that the general voice of the public chimes with the particular testimony of Warburton, Pope's literary executor, and the Welbeck copies of *Miscellanies,* in giving it to him, there are likenesses between this and Pope's other ballads to make conviction doubly sure. Originally issued with eleven stanzas, many reprints, including the one in *Miscellanies* (which must have passed through Pope's hands), have only ten, the original fourth stanza having been omitted.

It is not known whether Pope ever intended to publish the satire. Its publication, like that of the *First Psalm* (see p. 164) two months later, was contrived by Curll in revenge for the emetic episode; and in turn helped to provoke Pope to further retaliation (for an account of the Pope-Curll quarrel, see *Prose Works*, I, pp. xciv–cix). And if Pope complained (as he did to Swift on 20 June 1716) of Curll's malpractices in printing verses that were never meant for publication, Curll might have replied (as he says he did) that "they should not be wrote; for if they were they would be printed"—in which he went, for once, nearer to the root of the matter than did Swift, who replied: "the frolics of merry hours . . . should not be left to the mercy of our best friends, until Curll and his resemblers are hanged."

The text is that of *Miscellanies* (*1727*) with collations from the transcripts (*TSS*) —of which *TS3* credits Pope with the authorship, the others remaining silent.

Title: *John Moore*] Moore's advertisements are familiar to readers of contemporary newspapers. He died in 1737.

17–19. Cf. *Phryne*, 23–4: "First grubs obscene, then wriggling Worms, Then painted Butterflies."

33. *Abchurch-Lane*] Moore's shop was at the Pestle and Mortar in Abchurch Lane.

39. *Button's Wits*] The Whig frequenters of Button's coffee-house.

A Roman Catholick VERSION
OF THE
FIRST PSALM,
For the Use of a YOUNG LADY

THE Maid is Blest that will not hear
    Of Masquerading Tricks,
Nor lends to Wanton Songs an Ear,
    Nor Sighs for Coach and Six.

To Please her shall her Husband strive   5
    With all his Main and Might,
And in her Love shall Exercise
    Himself both Day and Night.

She shall bring forth most Pleasant Fruit,
    He Flourish still and Stand,   10
Ev'n so all Things shall prosper well,
    That this Maid takes in Hand.

No wicked Whores shall have such Luck
    Who follow their own Wills,
But Purg'd shall be to Skin and Bone,   15
    With *Mercury* and *Pills*.

For why? the Pure and Cleanly Maids
    Shall All, good Husbands gain:
But filthy and uncleanly Jades
    Shall Rot in *Drury-Lane*.   20

A Roman Catholick Version of the First Psalm, For the Use of a Young Lady. By Mr. Pope. 1716.

    The Flying-Post. (No. 3827) 12–14 July 1716.

    Pope's Miscellany. 1717 (and 2nd Edition, 1717).

    Court Poems. Part II. 1717.

    The Ladies Miscellany. 1718.

    Court Poems In Two Parts Compleat. 1719.

    Court Poems. In Two Parts. By Mr. Pope, &c. 1726.

    Miscellanea. The Second Volume. 1727.

    The Female Dunciad. 1728.

    A Miscellany on Taste. 1732.

    Mr. Pope's Literary Correspondence. Vol. II. 1735 (and 2nd Edition, 1735; also Vol. VI. 2nd Edition, 1736).

    A New Catechism for the Fine Ladies . . . 1740.

    A Supplement to the Works. 1757.

    Additions to the Works of Alexander Pope, Esq. Vol. I. 1776.

This burlesque of Sternhold's version of Psalm 1 was never openly acknowledged by Pope. For the circumstances of its piratical publication by Curll and its subsequent history see *New Light*, pp. 156–62, and *Rev. of Eng. Stud.*, XVIII (1942), pp. 441–7.

    The text follows that of the first edition.

  1. *The Maid is Blest . . .*] Compare *The Whole Book of the Psalms, Collected into English Metre, By Thomas Sternhold, John Hopkins, And Others. 1716.*

PSALM I.

The man is blest that hath not lent
    to wicked men his ear:
Nor led his life as sinners do
    nor sat in scorners chair.

But in the law of God the Lord
    doth set his whole delight:
And in the same doth exercise
    himself both day and night.

He shall be like a tree that is
   planted the Rivers nigh:
Which in due season bringeth forth
   its fruit abundantly.

Whose leaf shall never fade nor fall
   but flourishing shall stand:
Even so all things shall prosper well
   that this man takes in hand.

As for ungodly men, with them
   it shall be nothing so:
But as the chaff which by the wind
   is driven to and fro,

Therefore the wicked man shall not
   in judgment stand upright:
Nor in assembly of the just
   shall sinners come in sight.

For why? the way of godly men
   unto the Lord is known:
Whereas the way of wicked men
   shall quite be overthrown.

20. *Drury-Lane.*] Notorious as the haunt of prostitutes in Pope's day; see p. 39,
and *Ep. to Arbuthnot*, l. 41.

IMITATION OF *MARTIAL*,
Book 10, Epig. 23.
Jam numerat placido felix Antonius ævo, &c.

At length my Friend (while Time, with still career,
   Wafts on his gentle wing his eightieth year)
Sees his past days safe out of fortune's pow'r,
Nor dreads approaching fate's uncertain hour;
Reviews his life, and in the strict survey
Finds not one moment he cou'd wish away,
Pleas'd with the series of each happy day.
Such, such a man extends his life's short space,

            5

And from the goal again renews the race;
For he lives twice, who can at once employ   10
The present well, and ev'n the past enjoy.

Title] *1717 reads:* Sent to Sir Philip Meadows on his Birth-Day, by
  Sir William Trumbull. In Imitation of Martial, Book 10, Epig.
  23. *1737* and *1742* have no title, *the footnote being headed with the Latin
  line only.*

1 f. *In place of these two lines,* 1717 *reads:*
          Now blest *Antonius*, free from hopes and fears,
          Has truly liv'd the space of seventy years,
          In prudent ease; still chearful, still resign'd;
          In health of body, and in peace of mind:

3 Sees his] He sees *1717.*

Poems on Several Occasions. 1717.
Letters of . . . Pope ["Works . . . In Prose". Vol. I]. 1737.
The Works . . . Vol. IV. Containing . . . Letters. 1737.
Mr. Pope's Literary Correspondence. Vol. V. 1737.
The Works . . . Vol. V. Containing . . . Letters. 2nd Edition, 1737.
The Works . . . Vol. IV. Part I. Containing . . . Letters. 1742.
A Collection of Moral and Sacred Poems. J. Wesley. Vol. I. 1744.
The Works. Ed. Warburton. Vol. VII. Letters. 1751.
The Works. Ed. Carruthers. Vol. II. 1858.

This Imitation was first published anonymously, together with the poem im-
mediately following it, in a miscellany of which Pope was the concealed editor
(see *ante*, p. 8). It was eventually acknowledged twenty years later by the unob-
trusive insertion in his correspondence as a footnote to a letter from Trumbull.
Between the first and second printing of the poem, Pope completely changed the
character of its opening lines. Thus, as with other pieces (for example, see p. 193),
he either forgot, or did not care, when he added the revised version as a pendant
to a letter dated 19 January 1715/16, that this connection might in years to come
mislead the unsuspecting reader into thinking it earlier than the *1717* version;
whereas the revision was probably made shortly before its publication in 1737.
Trumbull's letter to Pope, to which these lines were appended, says that he had
sent "your imitation of Martial's epigram on Antonius Primus" as a birthday
greeting to a friend; and it was to identify this "imitation" that, in *1735*, the foot-
note quoted the first line of the Latin original only, and, in *1737*, printed the
corrected Imitation for the first time.

   The revisions of *1737* have been incorporated into the copy-text (*1717*).

   1 f. The echo of the first lines of Milton's sonnet on his twenty-third birthday is
also heard in *Imit. Hor.*, *Ep.* ii ii 76, which was probably drafted shortly after this
revision. See Vol. IV, p. 170n.

8–11. Cf. Cowley, *Several Discourses*, "xi Of My Self":
> Thus would I double my Life's fading Space;
> For he that runs it well, runs twice his Race.

Written over a Study;
out of MAYNARD.

In English for Sir W. TRUMBULL.

T IR'D with vain hopes, and with complaints as vain,
   Of anxious love's alternate joy and pain,
Inconstant fortune's favour and her hate,
And unperforming friendships of the great;
Here both contented and resign'd, I lye;   5
Here learn to live; nor wish, nor fear to die.

Poems on Several Occasions. 1717.
The London Mercury. October 1924.
Pope's Own Miscellany. Ed. N. Ault. 1935.

The case for Pope's authorship of these lines may be summarized thus: (1) the connection, as shown in the title, with Pope's old friend Trumbull; (2) the juxtaposition of this piece with another Trumbull poem which Pope himself acknowledged later (p. 167); and (3) that this juxtaposition was due to Pope's action as the concealed editor of the miscellany (see *ante*, p. 8). To these might be added stylistic likenesses between the two Trumbull poems; a parallel passage; and the possible genesis of the piece in a letter from Trumbull to Pope (19 January 1716), in which he confesses having sent the preceding poem written by Pope, as his birthday greeting to a friend; and then hints that Pope should supply him with other pieces which he could pass off as his own. Pope's printing two Trumbull poems for the first time and together looks as though he had been so far amenable as to send him these lines for his study. In *1717* the lines are preceded by the French original:

> Las d'esperer, & de me plaindre
> De l'amour, des grands, & du sort,
> C'est icy que j'attens la mort,
> Sans la desirer, ni la craindre.

The text follows that of the first printing in every respect.

Title: *Maynard*] François Maynard (1582–1646), French poet, disciple of Malherbe (see p. 72); one of the founders of the Academie Française. The verses above his study door were written in Toulouse towards the end of his life.

4. *unperforming friendships*] Pope, writing to Caryll Junior (8 November 1712), talks of "our nominal, unperforming friends"; and he uses the same word, unperforming, in at least two other poems. Dryden and Watts had used the word before him, but it was still very uncommon when Pope was writing.

EPITAPH.
On Sir WILLIAM TRUMBULL.

One of the Principal Secretaries of State to King William III, *who having resigned his Place, died in his Retirement at* Easthamsted *in* Berkshire, 1716.

A PLEASING form, a firm, yet cautious mind,
　　Sincere, tho' prudent, constant, yet resign'd;
Honour unchang'd, a principle profest,
Fix'd to one side, but mod'rate to the rest;
An honest Courtier, yet a Patriot too,　　　　　　5
Just to his Prince, yet to his Country true;
Fill'd with the sense of age, the fire of youth;
A scorn of wrangling, yet a zeal for truth;
A gen'rous faith, from superstition free,
A love to peace, and hate of tyranny;　　　　　　10
Such this man was; who now, from earth remov'd,
At length enjoys that liberty he lov'd.

5 yet] and *1717–32*.

The Works of Mr. Alexander Pope. 1717.
The Works . . . Dublin. 1718.
The Works . . . (Printed by T. J.) 1718 (and 1720).
Miscellaneous Poems and Translations. 3rd Edition, 1720 (and all later editions down to Miscellany Poems, 6th Edition, 1732).
The Works . . . To which are added, I. Cooper's-Hill. [etc.]. 1727.
The Works of Mr. Alexander Pope. Volume II. 1735.
The Works of Alexander Pope, Esq. Vol. II. 1735.
The Works . . . Vol. II. Containing his Epistles and Satires. 1735 (and 1736).
Ethic Epistles, Satires, &c. . . . Written by Mr. Pope. 1735.
Ethic Epistles, to Henry St. John L. Bolingbroke. Written in the Year 1732. 1735.

Mr. Pope's Literary Correspondence. Vol. V. 1737.
The Works . . . Vol. II. Containing his Epistles. &c. 1739 (both editions).
The Works . . . Vol. II. Part I. Containing his Epistles, &c. 1740 (and 1743).
A Collection of Moral and Sacred Poems. Vol. I. J. Wesley. 1744.
The Works. Ed. Warburton. Vol. VI. 1751.

On its first publication, Pope printed this epitaph without the name of its sub-ject; possibly because his friends, the Carylls, would recognize its first six lines as having already been used by him in an epitaph on their relative, John, Lord Caryll, who had died in 1711 (see *ante*, p. 81). He may have thought it would seem to them less of a misappropriation of those lines if they were made part of an ideal, or imaginary, epitaph, than if pressed into the service of a second deceased. Whatever the reason, the ideal character of the epitaph was retained for nearly twenty years, for Trumbull's name was not connected with it until 1735; nor was the epitaph inscribed upon Trumbull's monument in Easthampstead church.

The text follows that of *1717*, but incorporates the revision of l. 5 first made in *1735*.

Title] Sir William Trumbull (1639–1716) had had a long public career as lawyer and diplomat, before being appointed Secretary of State in 1695. Pope told Spence (p. 194) that "it was while I lived in the Forest, that I got so well acquainted with Sir William Trumbull, who loved very much to read and talk of the classics in his retirement. We used to take a ride out together, three or four days in the week, and at last, almost every day."

11f. This couplet is put to fresh use in the *Epitaph on Mr. Rowe* (see p. 400).

SANDYS's GHOST:
Or A Proper New BALLAD on the New
OVID's *METAMORPHOSIS*:

As it was intended to be
Translated by Persons of Quality.

Yᴇ Lords and Commons, Men of Wit
     And Pleasure about Town;
Read this, e'er you translate one Bit
     Of Books of high Renown.

Title] *MS reads:* Sandys' Ghost: A proper new Ballad on T—n's
     Ovid, to be translated by Persons of Quality.
3 e'er you] ere ye *MS.*

Beware of *Latin* Authors all!   5
　　Nor think your Verses Sterling,
Tho' with a Golden Pen you scrawl,
　　And scribble in a *Berlin*:

For not the Desk with silver Nails,
　　Nor *Bureau* of Expence,   10
Nor Standish well japan'd, avails
　　To writing of good Sense.

Hear how a Ghost in dead of Night,
　　With saucer Eyes of Fire,
In woful wise did sore affright   15
　　A Wit and courtly 'Squire.

Rare Imp of *Phœbus*, hopeful Youth!
　　Like Puppy tame that uses
To fetch and carry, in his Mouth,
　　The Works of all the Muses.   20

Ah! why did he write Poetry,
　　That hereto was so civil;
And sell his Soul for Vanity,
　　To Rhyming and the Devil?

A Desk he had of curious Work,   25
　　With glitt'ring Studs about;
Within the same did *Sandys* lurk,
　　Tho' *Ovid* lay without.

7 you] ye *MS*.　　8 And] Or *MS*.
10 Nor *Bureau* of] Nor Box of fair *MS*.
11 *MS reads:* Nor Nightgown without Sleeves, avails
13 in] at *MS*.
16 *MS reads:* S—m M—x, Esquire!
17 *MS reads:* Apollo's Imp, right hopeful Youth;
18 Like] Court *MS*.　　26 *MS reads:* Inlayed all about;

Now as he scratch'd to fetch up Thought,
 Forth popp'd the *Sprite* so thin;   30
And from the Key-Hole bolted out,
 All upright as a Pin,

With Whiskers, Band, and Pantaloon,
 And Ruff compos'd most duly;
This 'Squire he dropp'd his Pen full soon, 35
 While as the Light burnt bluely.

Ho! Master *Sam*, quoth *Sandys*' Sprite,
 Write on, nor let me scare ye;
Forsooth, if Rhymes fall in not right,
 To *Budgel* seek, or *Carey*.   40

I hear the Beat of *Jacob*'s Drums,
 Poor *Ovid* finds no Quarter!
See first the merry *P*—— comes
 In haste, without his Garter.

Then Lords and Lordings, 'Squires and Knights,
 Wits, Witlings, Prigs, and Peers;   46
Garth at *St James*'s, and at *White*'s,
 Beats up for Volunteers.

31 from] at *MS.*
32 Pin,] *is the reading of 1727; 1742 reads:* Pin.
33 Whiskers] whisker *MS.*
37 *Sam*] — *1727*
38 ye] you *MS.*
39 Rhymes] rhyme *MS.*
40 *Budgel . . . Carey*] B—ll . . . C—y *1727. MS reads:* You may be
 helped by C—ew.
41 *Jacob*'s] *Tonson*'s *MS.*
43 *MS reads:* See, see, ye great New—le comes,
45 Then] Next *MS.*
47 *Garth*] G—th *MS, 1727.*

What *Fenton* will not do, nor *Gay*,
    Nor *Congreve*, *Rowe*, nor *Stanyan*,   50
Tom B—n—t or *Tom D'Urfy* may,
    John Dunton, *Steel*, or any one.

If Justice *Philip*'s costive Head
    Some frigid Rhymes disburses;
They shall like *Persian* Tales be read,   55
    And glad both Babes and Nurses.

Let *W–rw—k*'s Muse with *Ash—t* join,
    And *Ozel*'s with Lord *Hervey*'s:
Tickell and *Addison* combine,
    And *P—pe* translate with *Jervis*.   60

L—— himself, that lively Lord
    Who bows to ev'ry Lady,
Shall join with *F——* in one Accord,
    And be like *Tate* and *Brady*.

Ye *Ladies* too draw forth your Pen,   65
    I pray where can the Hurt lie?
Since you have Brains as well as Men,
    As witness Lady *W—l–y*.

49 *Fenton*] *Congreve MS.*   50 *Congreve*] *Fenton MS.*
51 *B–n–t*] *Burnet MS.*   52 *Steel*] *St— MS, 1727.*
53 *Philip*'s] *Ph—'s 1727.*   54 Rhymes] *lines MS.*
57 *W–rw—k*'s] *Warwick's MS*; *Ash—t*] *Ashurst MS.*
58 *Ozel*'s] *Loisell MS*; *L'O—ls 1727.* Hervey's] *H–v–'s 1727.*
59 *Tickell* and *Addison*] *T—ll* and *Ad—n 1727.*
60 *Jervis*] *J—s MS, J–v–s 1727.*   61–4 *Stanza omitted in MS.*
68–9 *Between these lines MS has a stanza, never before printed, which*
   reads: In your French Dictionaries look,
            Ye Fair ones that are able!
        For tho ye seldome write a book,
            Ye all can tell a Fable.

Now, *Tonson*, list thy Forces all,
　　Review them, and tell Noses;　　　　　　　　　70
For to poor *Ovid* shall befal
　　A strange *Metamorphosis*.

A *Metamorphosis* more strange
　　Than all his Books can vapour;
"To what, (quoth 'Squire) shall *Ovid* change?"
　　Quoth *Sandys*: *To Waste-Paper*.　　　　　　76

73 *Metamorphosis*] Metamorpho-sis *MS*.
75 'Squire] Sam *MS*.
76 *Sandys*] Sand's *MS*; *To*] *Into MS, 1727*.

Pope's autograph: Longleat, Portland Papers, xiii.
Contemporary transcript, BM MS Harl. 7316.
Miscellanies. The Last Volume. 1727 (and later editions).
A Supplement to Dr. Swift's and Mr. Pope's Works. Dublin. 1739.
Miscellanies. The Fourth Volume. 1742 (and later editions).
The History of John Bull. [1750?]
The Works. Ed. Roscoe. Vol. VI. 1824.
Although Pope never publicly acknowledged this ballad, his autograph copy, unknown to previous editors, together with much internal evidence, may be taken to justify its presence in the canon. The occasion of the ballad is clearly stated in the title, but the date of composition is less apparent. There were two rival translations of *Ovid's Metamorphoses* projected at the same time, in each of which Pope is represented: the one sponsored by Garth and published by Tonson, the other put out by Curll who employed Sewell under certain restrictions to act as editor. Both works are dated 1717, but while Curll stole a march on Tonson and produced his volumes as early as 27 October 1716 (*The Post Boy*), Tonson did not publish his until 4 July 1717 (*The Post-Man*); and it is with the Garth-Tonson collection that the ballad is concerned. Its composition therefore must have been earlier than July 1717; and, seeing that Pope shows little knowledge of the names of his fellow translators—mentioning several persons as contributors who did not contribute, and at least four (in lines 49–50) as having refused to write for Garth, who in fact did write—it is practically certain that the ballad was written in the early days of the project, for which reason it is tentatively assigned to the winter of 1716–17, although the allusion to Philips's poems about children and the mention of Lord Hervey show that Pope revised the poem shortly before its first publication in *Miscellanies*.
　　The text is that of *1727*, except that names as printed in *1742* are given instead of dashes. Collations are provided from the autograph (*MS*).

Title: *Sandys*] George Sandys (1578–1644) poet; published a translation of Ovid's *Metamorphoses*, 1621–6, versified the Psalms, 1636; and wrote other sacred verse. In the MS title, "T—n" is of course Jacob Tonson, the publisher (see note to l. 41 below).

8. *scribble in a Berlin*] A Berlin was a four-wheeled covered carriage with a hooded seat behind. This is probably a stroke at Blackmore (see Biog. App., Vol. IV) with whom Pope was at enmity from the spring of 1716 onwards. In Pope's letter to Burlington (1716?) he reports Lintot's account of facile writers: "And there's Sir Richard in that rumbling old chariot of his, between Fleet-ditch and St. Giles's pound, shall make you half a Job." Blackmore's *Paraphrase on the Book of Job* was published in 1700, soon after which Dryden satirized him as one who "Writes to the rumbling of his coach's wheels" (Prologue to the *Pilgrim*).

11. *Standish*] inkstand.

16. *'Squire*] The MS makes it evident that Samuel Molyneux was thus alluded to; see also "Master Sam" in l. 37.

18ff. For the image cf. *Ep. to Arbuthnot*, 225f.

37. *Master Sam*] MS version of l. 16 shows it was Samuel Molyneux, the astronomer (see p. 264), *not* Samuel Garth.

40. *Budgel*] See Biog. App., Vols. IV, V.

Carey] Walter Carey, see p. 141.

41. *Jacob*] Jacob Tonson the publisher, who is drumming up volunteers for the translation of Ovid (see l. 48 and note below).

43. *P—*] Pelham, Thomas, Duke of Newcastle, as is shown by the MS reading. See Biog. App., Vol. IV.

47. *Garth*] Sir Samuel Garth, the editor of this translation (see Biog. App., Vol. IV).

St. James's . . . White's] The former was a well-known coffee-house, a favourite resort of politicians; the latter a chocolate-house in St James's Street notorious as a gaming house (see Vol. IV, p. 135).

48. Cf. "Drums are daily Beating up for Volunteers by reason a great many Foot Guards have lately been discharged . . ." *The Original Weekly Journal*, 22–29 December 1716.

49–50. *Fenton . . . Rowe*] The fact that, together with Stanyan, four of these five friends of Pope *did* contribute to the *Metamorphoses*, suggests that this ballad was written at the time when Garth was asking for "volunteers", probably in 1716.

50. *Stanyan*] There were two brothers, Temple (d. 1752), author and politician, who contributed to Book XII of the *Metamorphoses*, appointed by Addison Under Secretary of State 1717, and Abraham (d. 1752), diplomatist and author; both probably friends of Pope.

51. *B—t . . . D'Urfy*] For Burnet and D'Urfey, see Biog. App., Vols. IV, V.

52. *John Dunton*] Eccentric bookseller and satirist (1659–1733), mentioned in *Dunciad* (see Biog. App., Vol. V).

Steel] In the MS and all editions prior to *1742* the allusion was simply to "*St—*";

the case for identifying *St—* with Steele is well argued by Robert Hopkins in *Notes and Queries* (February, 1964), pp. 53–5.

53. *Philip's*] Ambrose Philips.

55. *Persian Tales*] See *ante*, p. 139. The allusion to "Babes and Nurses" in the next line must be a late revision, as the reference is to Philips's "Namby Pamby" poems which were not written until 1725.

57. *W–rw–k*] Earl of Warwick (see p. 131).

Ash—t] Dr. Ashurst of whom little is known.

58. *Ozell*] John Ozell (see Biog. App., Vol. V).

Lord Hervey] This is probably another of Pope's late revisions, for this Lord Hervey was so styled only after the death of his elder brother in 1723. One of the contributors, however, was a Stephen Hervey who translated a portion of Book IX.

59. *Tickell and Addison*] This is another public reference to their complicity in the rival translation of the *Iliad*.

60. *Jervis*] Pope at this time was translating the *Iliad*, and his friend Charles Jervas the painter later translated *Don Quixote*.

61. *L—*] Lansdowne has hitherto been conjectured; but the reference is almost certainly to Richard Lumley, second Earl of Scarbrough (1688?–1740). He was described in Pope's day as having "all the gallantry of the [camp] and the politeness of the [court]" (see Biog. App., Vol. IV, p. 369).

63. *F—*] Probably Philip Frowde (see p. 131).

64. *Tate and Brady*] The rather pedestrian versifiers of the Psalms, 1696. Nahum Tate (1652–1715), poet and dramatist, created poet laureat in 1692; best known by his Christmas hymn "While shepherds watched . . ." Nicholas Brady (1659–1726) divine and poet, chaplain to William III, Mary, and Anne.

68. *W—l–y*] Lady Mary Wortley Montagu. See Biog. App., Vol. IV.

EPIGRAM.
On the Toasts of the Kit-Cat Club,
Anno 1716.

WHENCE deathless *Kit-Cat* took its Name,
    Few Criticks can unriddle;
Some say from *Pastry Cook* it came,
    And some from *Cat* and *Fiddle*.
From no trim Beau's its Name it boasts,   5
    Gray Statesman, or green Wits;
But from this Pell-mell-Pack of Toasts,
    Of old *Cats* and young *Kits*.

Miscellanies. The Third Volume. 1732 (and later editions).
A Collection of Epigrams. Vol. II. 1737.
A Supplement to Dr. Swift's and Mr. Pope's Works. Dublin. 1739.
Miscellanies. The Fourth Volume. 1742 (and later editions).
A Collection of Select Epigrams. J. Hackett. 1757.
The Works. Ed. Roscoe. Vol. VI. 1824.

Anonymous on its first publication in 1732, this piece was marked with an asterisk in the 1742 edition of *Miscellanies* (which Pope helped to prepare) to indicate that it was not by Swift. The case for Pope's authorship is broadly stated in the introductory note to the poems from the 1732 *Miscellanies* (see p. 345). He was interested in the Kit-Cat Club, knew many of its members (Steele, Congreve, Garth, Pulteney, and Addison amongst them), and as late as 1730 gave Spence a long description of it with considerable detail (*Anecdotes*, p. 337f.).

The text is that of *1732*.

Title: *Kit-Cat Club*] A famous Whig club, c. 1695–c. 1717, which first met in a tavern near Temple Bar and later at the house of its secretary, Jacob Tonson, at Barn Elms (see R. J. Allen, *The Clubs of Augustan London*, 1933, pp. 35–54).

3. *Pastry Cook*] The club is supposed to have derived its name from Christopher Katt, a pastry-cook, who kept the house where they dined.

4. *Cat and Fiddle*] Ned Ward in his *History of Clubs* derives the name from that of one Christopher who lived at the sign of the Cat and Fiddle.

PROLOGUE
TO THE
Three Hours after Marriage.

AUTHORS are judg'd by strange capricious Rules,
    The Great Ones are thought mad, the Small Ones Fools:
Yet sure the Best are most severely fated,
For Fools are only laugh'd at, Wits are hated.
Blockheads with Reason Men of Sense abhor;   5
But Fool 'gainst Fool, is barb'rous Civil War.
Why on all Authors then should Criticks fall?
Since some have writ, and shewn no Wit at all.
Condemn a Play of theirs, and they evade it,
Cry, damn not us, but damn the *French* who made it,   10
By running Goods, these graceless Owlers gain,
Theirs are the Rules of *France*, the Plots of *Spain*:
But Wit, like Wine, from happier Climates brought,
Dash'd by these Rogues, turns *English* common Draught:
They pall *Moliere*'s and *Lopez* sprightly strain,   15
And teach dull *Harlequins* to grin in vain.
How shall our Author hope a gentler Fate,
Who dares most impudently—not translate.
It had been civil in these ticklish Times,
To fetch his Fools and Knaves from foreign Climes;   20
Spaniard and *French* abuse to the World's End,
But spare old *England*, lest you hurt a Friend.
If any Fool is by our Satyr bit,
Let him hiss loud, to show you all—he's hit.
Poets make Characters, as *Salesmen* Cloaths,   25
We take no Measure of your Fops and Beaus;
But here all Sizes and all Shapes you meet,
And fit your selves—like Chaps in *Monmouth-Street*.
    Gallants look here, this *Fool's-Cap has an Air—

10 who] that *1717, 1727*.   17 gentler] gentle *1717, 1727*.
27 you] ye *1717, 1727*.

Goodly and smart,—with Ears of *Issachar*.   30
Let no One Fool engross it, or confine:
A common Blessing! now 'tis yours, now mine.
But Poets in all Ages, had the Care
To keep this Cap, for such as will, to wear;
Our Author has it now, for ev'ry Wit   35
Of Course resign'd it to the next that writ:
And thus upon the Stage 'tis fairly †thrown,
Let him that takes it, wear it as his own.

31 Fool] Man *1717*.

Three Hours after Marriage. A Comedy. 1717.
Miscellanies. The Last Volume. 1727 (and later editions).
Miscellanies In Prose and Verse. The Third Volume. 2nd Edition. Dublin. 1733.
A Supplement to Dr. Swift's and Mr. Pope's Works. Dublin. 1739.
Miscellanies. The Fourth Volume. Consisting of Verses . . . 1742 (and later editions).
The Works. Ed. Roscoe. Vol. VI. 1824.

In the "Advertisement" prefixed to the published play, *Three Hours after Marriage*, and signed "John Gay", the writer concludes his remarks by acknowledging "the Assistance I have receiv'd in this Piece from two of my Friends; who . . . will not allow me the honour of having their names join'd with mine." That the collaborating friends were Pope and Arbuthnot was however no secret even before production, and soon afterwards became widely known.

The method and details of the collaboration are uncertain, though widely speculated on at the time. A broadside entitled *The Drury-Lane Monster*, which was published on 22 January 1716/17, while the play was still running, apportions the contributions thus—to Pope the "Bawdy and Blasphemy, Hand in Hand joining"; to Gay the "Conundrums and Puns and Quibbles Elastick", while "the third and chief Parent", Dr Arbuthnot, could be seen in "the low Wit" and "false terms of Art" (that is, of science). The only genuine clue, however, is found in an undated letter from Gay to Pope, in Ayre's *Memoirs*, 1744, in which he writes:

> *Dear Pope*, Too late I see, and confess myself mistaken, in Relation to the Comedy, yet I do not think had I follow'd your Advice, and only introduc'd the *Mummy*, that the Absence of the *Crocodile* had sav'd it. . . . as to your Apprehension that this may do us future Injury, do not think it; the Doctor has a more valuable Name than can be hurt by any Thing of this Nature, and yours is doubly safe; I will (if any Shame there be) take it all to myself, as indeed I ought, the Motion being first mine, and never heartily approv'd of by you.

There is therefore no extrinsic evidence to connect Pope in particular with the prologue. Nevertheless, because of its anticipation of a couplet later used in the *Dunciad*, and the circumstances of its production, it is practically certain that

Pope had some part in this prologue, and it is perhaps worth noting also that some slight revision of the text was made, presumably by Pope, after the death of his two collaborators. The bibliographical list above mentions only texts of the prologue reprinted separately from the play. The whole play (with the prologue) was included in *A Supplement to . . . Pope*, 1757; *Additions to . . . Pope*, Vol. II, 1776; Bowles' edition of the *Works*, Vol. X, 1806; and *A Supplementary Volume to . . . Pope*, 1807; it also appears in most editions of the works of Gay—whose latest editor includes the prologue as Gay's without comment (G. C. Faber, p. 362).

The copy-text of *1717* has been amended in the light of the corrections of *Miscellanies (1742)*.

5-6. Cf *Dunciad* A, III 169-70 (Vol. V, 167 and *n.*):

> Blockheads with reason wicked wits abhor;
> But fool with fool is barb'rous civil war.

11. *Owlers*] Smugglers, whose exploits were much in the papers about this time.

15. *Lopez*] Lopez de Vega (1562-1635), the famous Spanish dramatist.

17-22. The same criticism is made in the prologue to *Cato* (see p. 97), ll. 42-6.

28. *Chaps*] Chapmen, cheap salesmen.

Monmouth-Street] The famous second-hand clothes market.

29. **Fool's-Cap*] *Shews a Cap with Ears. [Stage direction, *1717-42*].

30. *Ears of Issachar*] Donkey's ears. (See *Genesis*, XLIX 14: Issachar is a strong ass crouching down.)

37. *fairly* †*thrown*] †Flings down the Cap and *Exit*. [Stage direction, *1717-42*].

THE
COURT BALLAD.

To the Tune of "*To all you Ladies now at Land*," &c.

To one fair Lady out of court
    And two fair Ladies in
Who think the Turk and Pope a sport
    And Wit and Love no Sin,
Come these soft lines, with nothing Stiff in   5
To B——n L——ll and G—n
        With a fa.

Title] The Ladys invitation to Leicester Fields *L*; The Challenge. A Court Ballad *1735. No title in S*.

3 the] both *S, L*.   4 Wit and Love] Love and Wit *S*.

What passes in the dark third row
   And what behind the Scene,
Couches and crippled Chairs I know,   10
   And Garrets hung with green;
I know the Swing of sinful Hack,
Where many a Damsel cries oh lack.
         With a fa.

Then why to court should I repair   15
   Where's such ado with Townsend.
To hear each mortal stamp and swear
   And ev'ry speech in Z—nds end,
To hear 'em rail at honest Sunderland
And rashly blame the realm of Blunderland.   20
         With a fa.

Alas, like Shutz I cannot pun
   Like C—n court the Germans
Tell P—g how slim she's grown
   Like M—s run to sermons,   25
To court ambitious men may roam,
But I and M—o' stay at home.
         With a fa.

5 these soft lines] these lines *L*.
6 To Balindine, Lapell, and Griffin *L*; To B–ll–ne, Le–p–lle, and
   G–ff–n *1717*; To Bellenden, Lepell, and Griffin *1735*.
10 Couches] Coaches *1717a*.
13 Where many Damsels cry alack *1717–35*.
16 Where's] There's *L*. Townsend] T—d *S*.
17 swear] stare *L*.   18 in] with *L*, *1717*, *1735*.
19 'em] you *S*; them *L*. Sunderland] S—d *S*.
20 and scorn the Government of Blunderland *S*; and rashly scorn
   the realm of Blunderland *L*.
22 Shutz] Schuts *L*; S—z *1717*.
23 C—n] Clayton *L*; C–t–n *1717*; Grafton *1735*.
24 P—g] Buckenburg *L*; P–k–n–g *1717*; Pickenburg *1735*.
   slim] thin *S*, *L*.   25 M—s] R— *S*; Meadows *L*, *1717–35*.

In truth by what I can discern,
   Of Courtiers from you Three,   30
Some Wit you have and more may learn,
   From Court than Gay or me,
Perhaps in time you'll leave High Diet,
And Sup with us on Mirth or Quiet,
                With a fa.   35

In Leister fields, in house full nigh,
   With door all painted green,
Where Ribbans wave upon the tye,
   (A Milliner's I ween)
There may you meet us, three to three,   40
For Gay can well make two of me.
                With a fa.

But shou'd you catch the Prudish itch,
   And each become a coward,
Bring sometimes with you Lady R——   45
   And sometimes Mistress H—d,
For Virgins, to keep chaste, must go
Abroad with such as are not so.
                With a fa.

29–35 *om. S.*   30 from] 'twixt *1717–35.*

32 Court] Courts *L.*   33 in time] at last *L.*

34 Mirth or Quiet] Mirth on Quiet *L*; Mirth and Quiet *1717*; Milk and Quiet *1735.*

36 In Leister fields, in house not high *S*; At *Leicester-Fields* a House full high *1717–35.*

39 A Milliner I mean *1717–35.*

41 can] may *S.*

45 Lady R—] Lady Ritch *L, 1735*; Mistress *R—h 1717a*; Lady *R—h 1717b.*

46 H—d] Howard *L, 1717–35.*

48 such as] those that *S, L.*

And thus fair Maids, my ballad ends,   50
    God send the K. safe landing,
And make all honest ladies friends,
    To Armies that are Standing.
Preserve the Limits of these nations,
And take off Ladies Limitations.   55
           With a fa.

50 thus . . . my] so . . . our *S, L.*   51 K.] King *L. 1717–35.*
52 make] keep *S.* honest] loyal *S, L.*
54 Preserve] God keep *S, L.*
55 And] But *S, L.*

Pope's autograph: BM MS Stowe 973, ff. 52–3.
Contemporary transcript: BM MS Lansd. 852, f. 204[b]–205[a].
The Court Ballad. By Mr. Pope. To the Tune of, To all you Ladies now at Land, &c.
[1717] (and "The Second Edition, Corrected", n.d.).
The Parson's Daughter . . . To which are added, Epigrams, and the Court Ballad, By Mr. Pope. 1717.
Pope's Miscellany. The Second Part. 1717.
Court Poems In Two Parts Compleat. 1719.
The Female Dunciad. 1728.
Mr. Pope's Literary Correspondence. Vol. III. 1735.
A Supplement to the Works . . . 1757.
Additions to the Works of Alexander Pope, Esq. Vol. I. 1776.
The Works. Ed. Warton. Vol. II. 1797.

This poem was never acknowledged by Pope, but the survival of an early draft in his hand removes all doubt of authenticity. It was written between 12 December 1716 and 18 January 1717 (see ll. 16*n.*, 51*n.*) and published on 31 January (*The Post-Man*) as a folio half-sheet by R. Burleigh, whom Curll often used as a screen. See further, p. 187.

Pope's final text cannot be established with confidence. He may have connived at Curll's publication; but he can scarcely have corrected proofs, for there are obvious misreadings of manuscript in ll. 10 and 39. Furthermore he is unlikely to have approved inferior readings in ll. 13, 34, and 36. On the other hand readings in ll. 48, 50, 52, and 54 are slight improvements which may well be credited to the author, and suggest that Curll's text was not a memorial transcript but an imperfect copy of a corrected autograph. It has been decided in the circumstances to present an eclectic text based upon Pope's autograph (*S*) as copy-text, with collations from Lansdowne 852 (*L*), which represents a later stage in composition, the first and second ballad printings (*1717a, b*), and *Literary Correspondence* (*1735*).

3. *The Turk*] Ulric, the little Turk [*Curll, 1735*], who belonged to George I, according to Horace Walpole.

6. Ladies in waiting to Princess Caroline. There were two Misses Bellenden, daughters of the second Lord Bellenden: Margaret, mentioned by Gay in *Mr. Pope's Welcome from Greece*, v ix, as "the tallest of the land", and Mary, described in the following line as "soft and fair as down". Mary, who married Col. John Campbell about 1720 and died in 1736, was in Hervey's opinion "the most agreeable, the most insinuating, and the most likeable woman of her time" (*Memoirs*, p. 41); see also *Suffolk*, 1 56-7. Mary Lepell (1700-68) was almost equally admired. She married Lord Hervey in 1720; see *Memoirs*, pp. xvi-xvii, *Suffolk*, 1 181. Of Miss Griffin nothing is known.

8-13. Though the full meaning of this stanza is obscure, there is seemingly some allusion to dalliance at the theatre (in the dark third row of the boxes, and in the green room) and in hackney coaches.

16. An allusion to the dismissal of Charles, Viscount Townshend (1674-1738) from the office of Secretary of State on 12 December 1716.

19. Charles Spencer, Earl of Sunderland (1674-1722) had helped to turn Townshend out of office.

20. *Blunderland*] Ireland [*1717, 1735*].

22. Seemingly an allusion to Augustus Schutz, equerry to the Prince of Wales (see Biog. App., Vol. IV), or, in view of ll. 23 to 25, to a lady of his family. There is no MS or printed support for Miss D. M. Stuart's reading, "Schatz", *i.e.* the nickname of Mary Lepell (*Suffolk*, 1 325).

23-5. Mrs Clayton, Lady Bucquenbourg, Miss Meadows, ladies of the court. Mrs Clayton (subsequently Lady Sundon, d. 1742) had great influence with the Princess of Wales. Her *Memoirs* were published in 1847. See Hervey, *Memoirs*, 166-8. For Lady Bucquenbourg, see p. 465; for Miss Meadows, see p. 343.

27. *M—o*] The Duke of Marlborough had a paralytic stroke and fell into senile decay in 1716.

36. *Leister fields*] Now Leicester Square, where the Prince of Wales lived.

38. *tye*] Perhaps *OED*, sense 4, "the stuffed case forming a mattress or pillow".

41. Gay was accustomed to make fun of his fatness (cf. *Mr. Pope's Welcome from Greece*, ll. 133-4), and Pope of his diminutive size (*Prose Works*, 1 xxxiff.). Cf. the playfully affectionate coupling of Pope's name with Gay's in *A Farewell to London* (p. 130), ll. 49-52.

45. Lady Rich, wife of Field-Marshal Sir Robert Rich.

46. Mrs Howard, Countess of Suffolk, mistress of George II, and friend of Swift.

51. The *London Gazette* reported that "His Majesty landed at Margate" on 18 January 1716-17, on his return from Hanover.

53. A frequent subject of political controversy, see Vol. IV, p. 11*n.*; but a *double entendre* is evident.

EPIGRAMS,
Occasion'd by
An Invitation to Court.

I.

In the *Lines* that you sent, are the *Muses* and *Graces*;
You have the *Nine* in your *Wit*, and *Three* in your *Faces*.

Title] *MS reads:* Epigrams into the Bargain.
1 Lines] Song *MS.*
2 You have] You've *MS, 1735.* and *Three*] and the Three *MS.*

II.

They may talk of the *Goddesses* in *Ida* Vales,
But *you* show your *Wit*, whereas *they* show'd their *Tails*.

1 talk of the *Goddesses*] tell of three Goddesses *MS.*

III.

You *B—n—ne, G—ff—n*, and little *La P—ll*,
By G—d you all lie like the D—l in Hell;
To say that at Court there's a Dearth of all Wit,
And send what *A—le*, would he *write*, might have writ.

1 *MS reads:* You Balandine, Griffin, ... Lapell; *1735 reads:* You
   Bellenden, Griffin, ... Lepell,
2 G—d] G— *1735.* D—l] Divel *MS.*
3 Dearth] Death *MS.*
4 *A—le*] Argyle *1735*; Argile *MS.*

IV.

Adam had fallen twice, if for an apple
The D—l had brought him *B—n—ne* and *La P—ll.*

2 D—l] Dev'l *MS. B–n–ne* and *La P–ll*] Balandine and Lapell
MS; Bellenden and Lepell *1735.*

V.

On Sunday at Six, in the Street that's call'd *Gerrard,*
You may meet the *Two Champions* who are no Lord *S—d.*

1 *Gerrard*] Gerards *MS.*
2 the] your *MS. S—d*] Sherrards *MS*; Sh—rd *1735.*

VI.

They say *A*—'s a Wit, for what?
For writing? no,—for writing not.

1 *A*—'s] A—ll's *1735.*
This line has also been variously printed: You say A—'s a wit, for
what? *1776.* A— they say has wit, for what? *1727.* A—e, they
say, has wit, for what? *1742.* Argyll, they say, has Wit, for what?
1745. Arthur, they say, has wit; for what? *1766, 1767.*

Contemporary transcript: BM MS Lansd. 852 [Nos. I–v].
*The Parson's Daughter. A Tale . . . To which are added, Epigrams, and the Court
Ballad, By Mr. Pope.* 1717. [Nos. I–VI.]
Pope's Miscellany. The Second Part. 1717. [Nos. I–VI.]
Court Poems In Two Parts Compleat. 1719. [Nos. I–VI.]
A Collection of Epigrams. 1727. [No. VI only.]
Mr. Pope's Literary Correspondence. Vol. III. 1735. [Nos. I–VI.]
The Flowers of Parnassus . . . For the Year M.DCC.XXXVII. 1737. [No. VI only.]
Joe Miller's Jests. 5th Edition, 1742 (and later editions). [No. VI only.]
A Supplement to the Works . . . 1757. [Nos. I–VI.]
The Festoon. 1766 (and later editions). [No. VI only.]

The Christmas Treat. 1767. [No. VI only.]
Additions to the Works of Alexander Pope, Esq. Vol. I. 1776. [Nos. I–VI.]
The Poems of Pope. Vol. I (in Johnson's *English Poets*). 1779. [No. I only.]

These epigrams were originally published on 21 February 1716/17, in *The Parson's Daughter. A Tale. For the Use of pretty Girls with small Fortunes . . . To which are added, Epigrams, and the Court Ballad, By Mr. Pope. From correct Copies*—a title so calculatedly ambiguous that no one can say with certainty what is or is not ascribed to Pope. Exactly three weeks previously, *The Court Ballad* had been published alone, with his name, unquestionably on Curll's responsibility (see *ante*, p. 183); and it is practically certain that the same predatory bookseller was behind this publication also. For although the book purports to have been "Printed for J. Harris", the name disappears from subsequent issues or editions of this book in favour of Curll's more usual screen [Mrs.] R. Burleigh, the nominal publisher of *The Court Ballad* itself. Moreover, Curll advertised *The Parson's Daughter* in his own lists, and, from 8 August 1717 onwards for many years, was printing these *Epigrams* in miscellanies, in which the attribution to Pope varies from the implication of the above-quoted title-page, to the definite statement, "Pieces by Mr. Pope" in the *Literary Correspondence* of 1735. That the epigrams were intended to form a pendant to the ballad by the same hand is suggested by the fact that, in the manuscript, as well as on their first appearance in print (which coincided with the ballad's first publication in book form), the epigrams follow immediately on *The Court Ballad*; and, indeed, in the manuscript are entitled *Epigrams, into the Bargain*. Further corroboration is found in the advertisements of the book which announced them as "Court Epigrams, and the Court Ballad"; in the names of the ladies who are addressed in both, the Misses Bellenden, Griffin, and Lepell; and lastly in the occasion which seems to have inspired ballad and epigrams alike— for the latter are stated in their title to have been "Occasion'd by an Invitation to Court", while the former is largely taken up with the writer's excuses for not going there. For these reasons, and because the same kind of wit, skirting ever and again the edge of impropriety with the gayest irresponsibility, which characterizes all these pieces alike, is likewise typical of Pope's work in this genre, it appears probable not only that the *Ballad* and the *Epigrams* are by the same hand, but also that the hand is Pope's.

The six epigrams have not always been reprinted together; the first was included in *The Poems of Pope* in "Johnson's Edition", 1779 and 1790, and in those of Anderson (1795), Chalmers (1810), and Lupton (1867); and the last has appeared alone several times with as many variants, one of which (that in *Joe Miller's Jests*, 5th Edition, 1742, and some later editions, and also in *The Nut-Cracker*, 1751) was ascribed to Gay.

The text is that of the first printing, with collations from the transcript of Nos. I–V (*MS*), and *Mr. Pope's Literary Correspondence* (*1735*).

I. 2. *Three*] The three Graces being the Misses Bellenden, Griffin, and Lepell (see Epigram III).

II. 1. *the Goddesses*] A reference to the judgement of Paris.

III. For the three ladies addressed in this epigram, the Misses Bellenden, Griffin, and Lepell, see p. 184.

4. *A—le*] John Campbell, second Duke of Argyle. (See Biog. App., Vol. IV.)

IV. 2. *B—n—ne and La P–ll*] See note above.

V. The two champions may be Gay and Pope. (See *Court Ballad*, ll. 40–1.) The allusion to "Lord *S—d*" awaits explanation.

VI. 1. *A—*] Probably Argyle, see Epigram III above; but what he might have written or failed to write is not clear.

Occasion'd by some VERSES *of his Grace* *The Duke of* BUCKINGHAM.

M USE, 'tis enough: at length thy labour ends,
And thou shalt live; for *Buckingham* commends.
Let crowds of criticks now my verse assail,
Let *D—s* write, and nameless numbers rail:
This more than pays whole years of thankless pain;   5
Time, health, and fortune, are not lost in vain.
Sheffield approves, consenting *Phœbus* bends,
And I and Malice from this hour are friends.

4 *D—s*] Dennis *1751*.

> *The Works of Mr. Alexander Pope.* 1717.
> *The Works* . . . Dublin. 1718.
> *The Works* . . . (Printed by T. J.) 1718 (and 1720).
> *The Works of John Sheffield, . . . Duke of Buckingham.* Vol. I. 1723.
> *The Works of Mr. Alexander Pope. To which are added, I. Cooper's-Hill* . . . Dublin. 1727.
> *A General Dictionary.* P. Bayle. Vol. IX. 1739.
> *The Works.* Ed. Warburton. Vol. VI. 1751.

The poem which occasioned these lines was the Duke of Buckingham's commendatory verses "On Mr. Pope and his Poems", which Pope placed in the forefront of *The Works*, 1717, and for which he returned thanks in this poem at the other end of the volume. *The Iliad*, the third volume of which was apparently published on the same day as *The Works*, had been especially singled out for praise by the Duke ("so wonderful, sublime a thing, As the great *Iliad*"), and it is implicitly alluded to in the fifth line of this reply. Though its financial success cannot have been entirely foreseen in 1717, it, at least, must be excepted from those labours of Pope's muse which he found so unremunerative (see l. 6n.).

The text follows that of *1717* (with which *1723* is in verbal agreement), with a collation from Warburton's edition (*1751*).

Title: *Buckingham*] John Sheffield, Duke of Buckingham, see Biog. App., Vol. IV.

4. *D—s*] Warburton prints "Dennis", an obviously correct identification. Dennis had attacked most of Pope's poems as they came out, and only a few months previously had published his adverse *Remarks upon Mr. Pope's Translation of Homer*, 1717.

6. *fortune . . . lost*] Although Pope had received from Lintot not very princely sums for his various poems (£22 for *The Rape*; £32 5s. for *Windsor Forest*; £15 for *Ode for Musick*, and so on), at least he lost no fortune over *The Iliad*, the *profits* of which amounted to between £5,000 and £6,000 (EC, v 156).

The Iliad of Homer. Vol. III

[Books IX–XII; published June 1717; vol. VII]

VERSES
Sent to Mrs. T. B. with his Works.
By an Author.

THIS Book, which, like its Author, You
    By the bare Outside only knew,
(Whatever was in either Good,
Not look'd in, or, not understood)
Comes, as the Writer did too long,   5
To be about you, right or wrong;
Neglected on your Chair to lie,
Nor raise a Thought, nor draw an Eye;
In peevish Fits to have you say,
See there! you're always in my Way!   10
Or, if your Slave you think to bless,
I like this Colour, I profess!

> *That Red is charming all will hold,*
> *I ever lov'd it—next to Gold.*

> Can Book, or Man, more Praise obtain?   15
> What more could *G—ge* or *S—te* gain?

> Sillier than *G–ld–n* cou'dst thou be,
> Nay, did all *J–c–b* breath in thee,
> She keeps thee, Book! I'll lay my Head,
> What? throw away a *Fool in Red*:   20
> No, trust the Sex's sacred Rule;
> The gaudy Dress will save the Fool.

17 *G—ld–n*] Gildon *MS.*
18 all *J–c–b*] James Baker *MS.*
19 She keeps . . . I'll lay] She'l keep . . . I lay *MS.*

The Grove; Or, A Collection of Original Poems, Translations, &c. 1721.
A Miscellany of Original Poems . . . Collected . . . by Mr. Theobald. 1732.
Contemporary transcript: BM MS Harl. 7316. [Lines 17–22 only.]
The St. James's Chronicle. 5–7 October 1775. [Lines 17–22 only.]
Additions to the Works of Alexander Pope, Esq. Vol. I. 1776. [Lines 17–22 only.]
Notes and Queries. Sixth Series. Vol. III. 11 June 1881.

Pope was one of the original subscribers to *The Grove*, in which this poem appears, taking as many as four copies in "Royal Paper", one of which may be the copy in the Blount collection at Mapledurham. Ostensibly he had no connection with it. If, however, he was an anonymous contributor, his taking four copies would be more intelligible. It is not surprising, therefore, to find that apart from these "Verses" the collection contains another piece probably from his hand: *In behalf of Mr. Southerne. To the Duke of Argyle*, which was found "in his own Hand-Writing" as long ago as 1745 (see *post*, p. 214). Moreover, these two pieces attributed to Pope are printed next to each other in the miscellany, thus possibly showing there was some connection between them in the editor's mind.

The Mapledurham copy of *The Works of Mr. Alexander Pope*, 1717, admirably suits the description of the book mentioned in the poem: it is inscribed in the owner's hand, "Teresa Maria Blount given by the Author", and is bound, *not* in the normal brown calf covers of the period, but in a rich red morocco with gold tooling. As with the "Works", so with the lady to whom it was presented. "Mrs. T. B." of the poem is the very double of Mistress Teresa Blount as revealed in Pope's letters: in her dislike of reading—"you, who read nothing", Pope once wrote to her in 1714 when comparing Martha's interest in books with her lack of it (which he did on more than one occasion); in her love of outside show—"let her put on new gowns to be the gaze of fools" (1716); in her want of sentiment and sympathy—"Since you prefer three hundred pound [cf. l. 14] to two true lovers" (1718). Furthermore, the "Author" and Pope are seen to have much in common, such as their dislike of Gildon and Giles Jacob, and ridicule of James Baker, not to mention one or two rather unusual parallels (see below)—all of which, together with the preceding evidence, make a case for Pope's authorship not lightly to be dismissed.

The last six lines, the address to the book, are also found in a contemporary manuscript, with the title, "Wrote in Mr. Gay's Works, Presented to a Lady the Book finely Bound. To the Book.", and later appeared in print with much the same title in 1775, and, in the following year, in *Additions to . . . Pope*. This excerpt could be quoted by anyone about any gorgeously bound volume; and its appearance may possibly mean no more than that. Nevertheless it contains one interesting variant in the substitution of "James Baker" for "all Jacob"—which, as Baker was a frequent butt of Pope's about 1715-17 (see *ante*, pp. 135, 136), may have been the original reading.

On the whole, the odds would appear to be in favour of Pope's authorship. On that assumption, the poem was probably written in 1717, with "James Baker" as the original reading in line 18, and the correction to "Jacob" probably made after the publication in 1720 of the *Poetical Register* (which, because of its inadequate treatment of Gay, allowing him no "Life", but only "Works", roused Pope's anger on behalf of his friend); and the appearance of these "Verses" in print in 1721, not improbably marked a stage in the growing estrangement between Pope and Teresa Blount, which is significantly shown in the total cessation of their correspondence from that date onwards. See further *New Light*, pp. 163-71.

The text is that of *1721*, with collations from the Harleian transcript (*MS*).

Title: *Mrs. T. B.*] Probably Mistress Teresa Blount, see introductory note above.

11. *Or, if your Slave*] Pope had already addressed Teresa Blount, and her alone, in this style: "So when your Slave . . ." (*Epistle to Miss Blount . . . Coronation*, see *ante*, p. 125) in the *Works* which presumably accompanied this poem.

16. *G—ge or S—te*] Perhaps "George or Senate"; Brooke [*N & Q*, above] conjectures the romantic figure of Count Gage, and Southcote, the priest who was once instrumental in saving Pope's life.

17. *G—ld—n*] Charles Gildon, see Biog. App., Vols. IV and V.

18. *did all J—c—b breathe in thee*] This use of "breathe" is characteristic of Pope; cf. "And all thy god-like Father breathes in thee" (*Iliad*, v 163); "And all Arabia breathes from yonder Box" (*Rape*, 1 134); "in his lines they breathe" (*Ep. to Miss Blount . . . Voiture*, 20).

J—c—b] Giles Jacob (1686-1744). Compiler of *The Poetical Register*, 1720, and a number of law-books, 1714-30. Advertised during March-April 1718 for contributions to the former, saying, "Those who have not yet sent [memoirs relating to their descent, and particulars of their works], are desir'd to transmit what Accounts they intend in a Fortnight's Time at the farthest." He later accused

Pope of having written, or added to, or otherwise made his own, the praise of him-
self in his "Life" in *The Poetical Register*, thereby achieving a niche in the *Dunciad*
(see Vol. V). The present allusion to him was probably due to the scant courtesy
shown to Gay in the same volume (see introductory note, above).

Eloisa to Abelard

[published 3 June 1717; vol. ii, pp. 317–49]

Elegy To the Memory of an Unfortunate Lady

[published 3 June 1717; vol. ii, pp. 361–8]

The PRAYER of *BRUTUS*.

G ODDESS of Woods, tremendous in the chace,
  To Mountain-wolves and all the Savage race,
Wide o'er th' aerial Vault extends thy sway,
And o'er th' infernal Regions void of day,
On thy third Reign look down; disclose our Fate,   5
In what new Nation shall we fix our Seat?
When shall we next thy hallow'd Altars raise,
And Quires of Virgins celebrate thy praise?

2 Mountain-wolves] Mountain Bores *1718*.
3 th' aerial Vault] th' Æthereal Walks *1718*.
4 Regions] Mansions *1718*.
5 *Reign* . . . disclose] Realm . . . unfold *1718*.
6 And say what Region is our destin'd Seat? *1718*.
7 When . . . hallow'd Altars] Where . . . lasting Temples *1718*.

The British History . . . By Aaron Thompson. 1718.
Letters of . . . Pope. ["Works . . . In Prose".] 1737. [Published 19 May.]
Mr. Pope's Literary Correspondence. Vol. V. 1737. [Published 17 June.]
A Supplement to the Works . . . 1757.
Additions to the Works . . . Vol. II. 1776.
The Works. Ed. Dyce. Vol. II. (Aldine Edition). 1831.

In a letter to Edward Blount, dated "Sept. 8 1717", Pope wrote: "I have been lately reading Jeffery of Monmouth . . . in the translation of a clergyman in my neighbourhood. He wanted my help to versify the prayer of Brutus, made when he was much in our circumstances, enquiring in what land to set up his seat, and worship like his fathers"—whereupon he transcribes the *Prayer*, the original Latin of which runs as follows:

> *Diva potens nemorum, terror silvestribus apris;*
> *Cui licet anfractus ire per ethereos,*
> *Infernasque domos; terrestria iura resolve,*
> *Et dic quas terras nos habitare velis?*
> *Dic certam sedem qua te venerabor in aevum,*
> *Qua tibi virgineis templa dicabo choris?*

The only two texts published with Pope's authority are not alike, and there is some difficulty about priority; for though the *1718* version was the first to be published, the *1737* version purports to have been written in 1717. It has been pointed out that *1718* is closer than *1737* to the Latin, and is therefore the revised text. Yet it is unlike Pope to fail to revise a piece before reprinting it, if both need and opportunity are present; indeed, he revised for this same volume of *Letters* the only two other poems in it of more than six lines which had been previously printed; and, as with the *Prayer*, retained the original dates of the letters containing them (see *ante*, pp. 52, 167).

Pope's introduction to Geoffrey of Monmouth by Thompson ultimately resulted in a design of writing an epic poem in blank verse to be entitled *Brutus*, of which only the prose "plan" described by Ruffhead (*Life*, 410–24), and one fragment of blank verse of eight complete lines seem to have survived (see *post*, p. 404).

As first printed in Thompson's *British History*, this prayer was followed, after an interval of prose, by Diana's answer, of which piece Pope has been suggested as the author, but, in the absence of evidence, without much probability (see *post*, p. 421).

The text follows that of the *Works In Prose*, 1737, with collations from the first printing (*1718*).

5. *On Thy third Reign look down*] The italics are Pope's, probably introduced to indicate a quotation, for Pope is here following Milton's "On thy third reign the earth look now," *History of Britain*, ed. Bohn, 1877, v 171 (G. Sherburn, *Manly Anniversary Studies*, 1923, p. 175).

A HYMN
Written in *WINDSOR* Forest.

All hail! once pleasing, once inspiring Shade,
  Scene of my youthful Loves, and happier hours!
Where the kind Muses met me as I stray'd,
  And gently pressd my hand, and said, Be Ours!—
Take all thou e're shalt have, a constant Muse: 5
  At Court thou may'st be lik'd, but nothing gain;
Stocks thou may'st buy and sell, but always lose;
  And love the brightest eyes, but love in vain!

Pope's autograph: Mapledurham MSS.
The Works. Ed. Dyce. Vol. II (Aldine Edition). 1831.
In a letter to the Misses Blount, dated 13 September 1717, and describing his journey to Oxford, Pope tells of his visit to the haunts of his youth in Windsor Forest on his way: "I arrived at Mr Dancastles on Tuesday-noon, . . . & past the rest of the day in those Woods where I have so often enjoyd—an author & a Book; and begot such Sons upon the Muses, as I hope will live to see their father what he never was yet, an old and a good Man. I made a Hymn as I past thro' these Groves; it ended with a deep Sigh, which I will not tell you the meaning of."—whereupon follow these lines.
  The text is that of the autograph.
  A Hymn] Title taken from Pope's letter, see introductory note.
  1. *once pleasing*] Autograph correction; originally *ye pleasing.*
  4. *And . . . hand*] Autograph correction; originally *And took me by the hand.*

The Iliad of Homer. Vol. IV
[Books XIII–XVI; published 28 June 1718; vol. VIII]

LINES to Lord *BATHURST*.

A WOOD? quoth Lewis; and with that,
  He laughd, and shook his Sides so fat:
His tongue (with Eye that markd his cunning)
Thus fell a reas'ning, not a running.
    Woods are (not to be too prolix)   5
Collective Bodies of strait Sticks.
It is, my Lord, a meer Conundrum
To call things Woods, for what grows und'r 'em.
For Shrubs, when nothing else at top is,
Can only constitute a Coppice.   10
But if you will not take my word,
See Anno quart. of Edward, third.
And that they're Coppice calld, when dock'd,
Witness Ann. prim. of Henry Oct.
    If this a Wood you will maintain   15
Meerly because it is no Plain;
Holland (for all that I can see)
Might e'en as well be termd the Sea;
And *C—by* be fair harangu'd
An honest Man, because not hang'd.   20

Pope's autograph: Boston Public Library, Mass.

The Correspondence of Thomas Gray and the Rev. Norton Nicholls. Ed. Mitford. 1843.

The Works. Ed. Carruthers. Vol. IV. 1854.

Lifted out of their context, as they usually have been, these lines lose much of their fun. They are found in a high-spirited letter to Lord Bathurst, dated "London, July 5th", in which Pope banters him on his wood at Oakley, which at that date, 1718, apparently had not long been planted. The lines are thus introduced:

My Lord,—To say a word in praise either of your Wood or you, would be alike impertinent, each being, in its kind, the finest thing I know, & the most agreeable. I can only tell you very honestly, (without a word of the high Timber of the one, or the high Qualities of the other) that I thought it ye best company I ever knew, & the best Place to enjoy it in. I came hither but this day.... Mr. Gay is as zealously carry'd to the Bower by ye force of Imagination, as ever Don Quixote was to an Enchanted Castle. The Wood is to him the

Cave of Montesinos: He has already planted it with Myrtles . . . & there wants nothing but a Christal Rivulet to purl thro the Shades, which might be large enough to allay Mr. Lewis's great Thirst after water. But my Lord, I beg you to be comforted. Gay promises, that whatever may be said by yᵉ Prose-men, of this age, Posterity shall believe there was water in Okely wood; And (to speak boldly) wood also.

The "Lines" follow in this place, at the end of which Pope continues: "The rest of Mr. Lewis's Arguments I have forgotten, for as I am determin'd to live in the Wood, I am likewise resolvd to hear no reasons agˢᵗ it." For the sequel, see Vol. IV, p. 183.

The text follows that of the autograph, and is now printed correctly for the first time.

Title: *Lord Bathurst*] See Biog. App., Vol. IV.

1. *Lewis*] See Biog. App., Vol. IV.

10, 12. The same device was to be used in *Imit. Hor.*, *Sat.* II i 147f. (Vol. IV, p. 19). In that instance the references to the Statutes can be authenticated, but not in this.

19. *C—by*] Thomas, Earl Coningsby, see p. 298.

VERSES
in the
SCRIBLERIAN MANNER.
To the Rᵗ· Honᵇˡᵉ· the Earl of *OXFORD*.

O**NE*** that should be a Saint,
　　and one* that's a Sinner,
And one* that pays reckning
　　but ne'r eats a Dinner,
In short Pope and Gay (as　　　　　　　　　　5
　　you'l see in the margin)
Who saw you in Tower, and since
　　your enlarging,
And Parnell who saw you not since
　　you did treat him,　　　　　　　　　　　10
Will venture it now—you have
　　no Stick to beat him—

Since these for your Jury, good
and true men, vous-avez;
Pray grant Us Admittance,   15
and shut out Miles Davies.

Pope's autograph: Longleat, Portland Papers, XIII.

Memoirs of . . . Martinus Scriblerus. Ed. Kerby-Miller. 1950.

This last example of the "Scriblerian Manner" has been recovered in Pope's autograph from among the Longleat MSS. The verses are headed: "To the R^{t.} Honble. The Earl of Oxford. Tuesday, 5. a clock."; and the paper is endorsed in Oxford's hand: "Verses Mr Pope Mr Parnel Mr Gay July 8: 1718. M^r E: Blunt came with them." In the same volume at Longleat, there is also a contemporary transcript of the verses in another hand, headed: "Verses sent to Ld Oxford from the Ship Tavern by Mr Pope Mr Parnell & Mr Gay. July: 8: 1718." Other specimens of verses in this manner are included earlier (see *ante*, p. 116ff.), to which the reader is referred for some account of their designation.

The text follows the autograph in every respect.

4. *n'er eats a Dinner*] For reasons of chronic ill health Pope was frequently obliged to be very abstemious.

5. *Gay*] See Biog. App., Vol. IV.

7. *in Tower*] Oxford was committed to the Tower on 9 July 1715 and kept there in confinement until 1 July 1717.

9. *Parnell*] See Biog. App., Vol. IV.

16. *Miles Davies*] Bibliographer (1662–1719?); ordained priest at Rome, 1688, recanted 1705; published *Athenae Britannicae*, 7 vols., 1715–16, " a kind of bibliographical, biographical and critical work"; is said to have hawked his works from door to door. There is a letter in French from him to Lord Oxford with a Latin ode in the Harleian MSS; and Oxford possessed some of his books.

THREE EPITAPHS
On *JOHN HEWET* and *SARAH DREW*.

I.

WHEN Eastern lovers feed the fun'ral fire,
On the same pile the faithful fair expire;
Here pitying heav'n that virtue mutual found,
And blasted both, that it might neither wound.

2 the] their *MS.*

Hearts so sincere th' Almighty saw well pleas'd,   5
Sent his own lightning, and the Victims seiz'd.

Pope's autograph: Letter to Martha Blount, 6 August 1718, in Mapledurham MSS.

Pope's autograph: Letter to Lady M. W. Montagu, 1 September 1718, in the Pierpont Morgan Library, New York.

Letters of . . . Pope ["Works . . . In Prose. Vol. I"]. 1737.

The Works . . . Vol. VI. Containing . . . Letters. 1737 (and 2nd Edition, 1737).

The Works . . . Vol. IV. Part II. Containing . . . Letters. 1742.

Memoirs of . . . Alexander Pope, Esq; Vol. II. W. Ayre. 1745.

The Works. Volume VIII. Being . . . Letters. Ed. Warburton. 1751.

On 31 July 1718 two village lovers were killed in each other's arms by lightning in the harvest fields of Stanton Harcourt. Pope, who was staying there at the time, was deeply impressed (see *New Light*, pp. 329–33). He wrote several letters describing the incident, as well as three epitaphs on the lovers.

The first of the epitaphs to be composed was that of six lines, printed above, about which Pope wrote to Martha Blount (6 August): "I have prevailed on my Lord Harcourt to erect a little Monument over them, of plain Stone, and have writ the following Epitaph which is to be engravd on it. 'When Eastern lovers...'" and he similarly claimed authorship of these lines in his letter to Lady Mary W. Montagu (1 September). In the meantime, however, Gay wrote a similarly descriptive letter to Fortescue (9 August) in which he says: "My Lord Harcourt, at Mr. Pope's and my request, has caused a stone to be plac'd over them, upon condition that we should furnish the Epitaph, which is as follows; 'When Eastern lovers . . .' [epitaph quoted in full]. But my Lord is apprehensive the country people will not understand this, and Mr. Pope says he will make one with something of scripture in it, and with as little poetry as Hopkins and Sternhold" (the versifiers of the Psalms). This statement of Gay's might look as though he was in part responsible for the first epitaph; but in view of Pope's two affirmations of his authorship mentioned above, and the further facts that Pope included this letter of Gay's among his own in the 1737 volume, and so knew all about it; that Gay does not actually claim any part in the epitaph; and lastly, that it exists in Pope's own autographs, it is extremely probable that it was entirely Pope's own work. But whoever wrote it, it was discarded in favour of the "godly" epitaph which was written shortly afterwards (see *post*, p. 199).

The text is that of the first printing, with a collation from the letter to Lady Mary (*MS*); there are no other verbal variants, except misprints.

II.

EPITAPH

On *JOHN HEWET* and *SARAH DREW*.

In the Churchyard at *Stanton Harcourt*.

NEAR THIS PLACE LIE THE BODIES OF
JOHN HEWET AND SARAH DREW
AN INDUSTRIOUS YOUNG MAN, AND
VIRTUOUS MAIDEN OF THIS PARISH;
CONTRACTED IN MARRIAGE
WHO BEING WITH MANY OTHERS AT HARVEST
WORK, WERE BOTH IN AN INSTANT KILLED
BY LIGHTNING ON THE LAST DAY OF JULY
1718.

THINK not by rigorous judgment seiz'd,
 A pair so faithful could expire;
Victims so pure Heav'n saw well pleas'd
 And snatch'd them in Cœlestial fire.

Live well and fear no sudden fate;
 When God calls Virtue to the grave,
Alike tis Justice, soon or late,
 Mercy alike to kill or save.

Virtue unmov'd can hear the Call,
And face the Flash that melts the Ball.   10

2 Two hearts like these could e'er expire *TS 1*.
4–5 *Between these two lines, TS 1 and TS 2 have this couplet deleted on
  Atterbury's advice:*
    Their Souls on Wings of Lightning fly
    So soard Eliah to the Sky.
5 and] *The text has an ampersand here.*
7 Justice] Mercy *TS 3*.
9f. *omm. TS 3*.
10 the Flash that] that flash which *TS 2*.

Pope's autograph: Letter to Lady M. W. Montagu, 1 September 1718 (Pierpont Morgan Library, New York).

Contemporary transcript: Letter to John Caryll, 3 September 1718 (BM MS Add. 28618).

Contemporary transcript: Letter to Bishop Atterbury, 3 September 1718 (Longleat MSS, Portland Papers, xiii).

Contemporary transcripts: BM MS Harl. 7316, Stowe 972.

The lapidary inscription at Stanton Harcourt.

The White-hall Evening-Post. No. 3. 20–23 September 1718.

The Weekly Packet, with The Price Courant. 20–27 September 1718.

The Weekly Packet. 4–11 October 1718.

Court Poems In Two Parts Compleat. 1719.

A Miscellaneous Collection of Poems. T. M. Dublin. 1721.

Court Poems. In Two Parts. By Mr. Pope, &c. 1726.

The Flying-Post. 4–7 June 1726.

Miscellanea. The Second Volume. 1727. [1726.]

Sepulchrorum Inscriptiones. Vol. I. 1727.

Mr. Pope's Literary Correspondence. Vol. II. 1735 (and 2nd Edition, 1735; and Vol. IV, 2nd Edition, 1736).

The Whitehall Evening Post. 24–26 May 1737.

The London Magazine. June 1737.

The Works. Volume VIII. Being . . . Letters. Ed. Warburton. 1751.

On its first publication in *The White-hall Evening-Post* (No. 3), this epitaph was prefaced by the following letter:

Chipping Norton, Sept. 21. 1718.

Sir,—Stanton Harcourt being in this Country, and Mr. Pope being here when the Accident happen'd, he wrote the enclosed Epitaph; which being on a remarkable Occasion and new, I send you for your new Paper.

"Near this Place lie the Bodies of John Hewett and Mary Drew, an industrious young Man, and virtuous Maiden of this Parish, who being at Harvest-work (with several others) were in one Instant killed by Lightning, the last Day of July 1718. Think not by rig'rous Judgment seiz'd . . ." [epitaph quoted, ten lines].

Pope submitted the first version of twelve lines to Bishop Atterbury on 3 September, for his "opinion both as to the doctrine and to the poetry"; and followed his advice so far as to delete a couplet after l. 4 before it was inscribed on the memorial tablet on the outside wall of the church.

The text follows that of the inscription (with which Pope's autograph, the Harley transcript, and the first printed version agree), with collations from transcripts from the letters to Caryll (*TS 1*) to Atterbury (*TS 2*), and the Stowe transcript (*TS 3*)

III.

EPITAPH

On the *Stanton-Harcourt* Lovers.

HERE lye two poor Lovers, who had the mishap
Tho very chaste people, to die of a Clap.

Pope's autograph: Mapledurham MSS.

For the context of this epitaph in a letter to Teresa Blount, see *New Light*, p. 333.
Although Pope does not directly say he wrote it, the epitaph itself and the way
he introduces it are together so characteristic of him as to admit of very little
doubt of his authorship. Yet as Gay also was staying at Stanton-Harcourt at the
time, his possible complicity in the matter cannot perhaps be entirely ruled out.

The text is that of the autograph.

ANSWER to Mrs. *HOWE*.

WHAT is PRUDERY?
                                    'Tis a Beldam,
Seen with Wit and Beauty seldom.
'Tis a fear that starts at shadows.
'Tis, (no, 'tisn't) like Miss *Meadows*.
'Tis a Virgin hard of Feature,   5
Old, and void of all good-nature;
Lean and fretful; would seem wise;
Yet plays the fool before she dies.
'Tis an ugly envious Shrew,
That rails at dear *Lepell* and You.   10

1 What is] What's *1718*.
10 You.] *How*. *1718*.

The Weekly Packet. 11–18 October 1718.
Court Poems In Two Parts Compleat. 1719.
A Miscellaneous Collection of Poems. T. M. Vol. II. 1721.
Court Poems. In Two Parts. By Mr. Pope, &c. 1726.

Miscellanea. The Second Volume. 1727.

Miscellaneous Poems, By Several Hands. J. Ralph. 1729.

Mr. Pope's Literary Correspondence. Vol. II. 1735 (and 2nd Edition, 1735).

Memoirs of . . . Alexander Pope, Esq. W. Ayre. Vol. II. 1745.

The Works. Ed. Warburton. Vol. VI. 1751.

When first published, the title, or introduction, of this poem (which sufficiently explains its occasion) ran as follows: "*Mrs. Lepell, and Mrs. How, two Maids of Honour to the Princess, ask'd Mr. Pope what Prudery is. (He making Use of that Expression in Conversation.) His Answer.*" In *Court Poems* the title became: *Mr. Pope upon being ask'd what Prudery was, Writ the following Lines.* In spite of this association of Pope's name with the piece from its first appearance, Pope himself never acknowledged it, nor did he include it anonymously (like so many other pieces of his) in any edition of his miscellanies. There is therefore no documentary certainty, though much probability, of Pope's authorship.

The text follows the *1751* version of the poem, with collations from its first printing, hitherto unknown (*1718*).

Title: *Mrs. Howe*] Sophia, daughter of General Emanuel Howe, maid of honour to the Princess of Wales. She died (1726) "with a blemished reputation, and a broken heart" (*Suffolk*, I 35, where two of her letters are printed, illustrative of her giddy behaviour).

4. *Miss Meadows*] See p. 343.

10. *Lepell*] See p. 184.

To Mr. *ADDISON*,

Occasioned by his Dialogues on MEDALS.

SEE the wild Waste of all-devouring years!
  How Rome her own sad Sepulchre appears,
With nodding arches, broken temples spread!
The very Tombs now vanish'd like their dead!
Imperial wonders rais'd on Nations spoil'd,   5
Where mix'd with Slaves the groaning Martyr toil'd;
Huge Theatres, that now unpeopled Woods,

Title Verses occasioned by Mr. Addison's Treatise of Medals
   1720, 1721, 1726; Epistle V. To Mr. Addison, Occasioned by
   his Dialogues on Medals *1735*.

5–10 *add. 1726–51*.

Now drain'd a distant country of her Floods;
Fanes, which admiring Gods with pride survey,
Statues of Men, scarce less alive than they;   10
Some felt the silent stroke of mould'ring age,
Some hostile fury, some religious rage;
Barbarian blindness, Christian zeal conspire,
And Papal piety, and Gothic fire.
Perhaps, by its own ruins sav'd from flame,   15
Some bury'd marble half preserves a name;
That Name the learn'd with fierce disputes pursue,
And give to Titus old Vespasian's due.
    Ambition sigh'd; She found it vain to trust
The faithless Column and the crumbling Bust;   20
Huge moles, whose shadow stretch'd from shore to shore,
Their ruins ruin'd, and their place no more!
Convinc'd, she now contracts her vast design,
And all her Triumphs shrink into a Coin:
A narrow orb each crouded conquest keeps,   25
Beneath her Palm here sad Judæa weeps,
Here scantier limits the proud Arch confine,
And scarce are seen the prostrate Nile or Rhine,
A small Euphrates thro' the piece is roll'd,
And little Eagles wave their wings in gold.   30
    The Medal, faithful to its charge of fame,
Thro' climes and ages bears each form and name:
In one short view subjected to your eye
Gods, Emp'rors, Heroes, Sages, Beauties, lie.
With sharpen'd sight pale Antiquaries pore,   35
Th' inscription value, but the rust adore;
This the blue varnish, that the green endears,
The sacred rust of twice ten hundred years!
To gain Pescennius one employs his schemes,

22 ruin'd] perish'd *1720–35ab, 1751.*
27 Here] Now *1720–35abc, 1751.*
28 or] and *1720–26.*
33 your] our *1720–39, 1751.*

8

One grasps a Cecrops in ecstatic dreams;   40
Poor Vadius, long with learned spleen devour'd,
Can taste no pleasure since his Shield was scour'd;
And Curio, restless by the Fair-one's side,
Sighs for an Otho, and neglects his bride.
  Theirs is the Vanity, the Learning thine: 45
Touch'd by thy hand, again Rome's glories shine,
Her Gods, and god-like Heroes rise to view,
And all her faded garlands bloom a-new.
Nor blush, these studies thy regard engage;
These pleas'd the Fathers of poetic rage;   50
The verse and sculpture bore an equal part,
And Art reflected images to Art.
  Oh when shall Britain, conscious of her claim,
Stand emulous of Greek and Roman fame?
In living medals see her wars enroll'd,   55
And vanquish'd realms supply recording gold?
Here, rising bold, the Patriot's honest face;
There Warriors frowning in historic brass:
Then future ages with delight shall see
How Plato's, Bacon's, Newton's looks agree;   60
Or in fair series laurell'd Bards be shown,
A Virgil there, and here an Addison.
Then shall thy CRAGS (and let me call him mine)
On the cast ore, another Pollio, shine;
With aspect open, shall erect his head,   65
And round the orb in lasting notes be read,
"Statesman, yet friend to Truth! of soul sincere,
"In action faithful, and in honour clear;
"Who broke no promise, serv'd no private end,
"Who gain'd no title, and who lost no friend,   70
"Ennobled by himself, by all approv'd,
"And prais'd, unenvy'd, by the Muse he lov'd."

67 of] in *1720-26*.

The Works of Mr. Alexander Pope. (Printed by T. J.) 1720.
The Works of the Right Honourable Joseph Addison, Esq. Vol. I. 1721.
Miscellaneous Poems and Translations. 4th Edition, 1722.
Miscellany Poems. 5th Edition, 1726 (and 1727, and 6th Edition, 1732).
Dialogues Upon the Usefulness of Ancient Medals . . . 1726.
The Works of Mr. Alexander Pope. To which are added, I. Cooper's-Hill . . .
Dublin. 1727.
The Works of Mr. Alexander Pope. Volume II. 1735 (folio and quarto).
The Works of Alexander Pope, Esq; Vol. II. 1735 (octavo).
The Works . . . Vol. II. Containing his Epistles and Satires. 1735 (and 1736).
Ethic Epistles, Satires, &c. . . . Written by Mr. Pope. 1735.
Ethic Epistles, to Henry St. John L. Bolingbroke. Written in the Year 1732. 1735.
The Works . . . Vol. II. Containing his Epistles, &c. 1739 (both editions).
The Works . . . Vol. II. Part I. Containing his Epistles, &c. 1740 (and 1743).
The Works. Ed. Warburton. Vol. III. 1751.

The date of composition of this poem is discussed at length in *New Light*,
pp. 119–24. Pope made several statements about it which are difficult to recon-
cile. In an appendix to *The Dunciad Variorum* (Vol. V, p. 236), he said that the
poem was written after the publication of his *Works* in 1717; yet in a note to the
poem appended to the octavo edition of his *Works* (1735), he stated that it was
"written in 1715, at which time Mr. Addison intended to publish his Book of
Medals", to which he added in 1739 ". . . but not printed till Mr. Tickell's Edi-
tion of his works in 1720, at which time the Verses on Mr. Craggs which concluded
this Epistle were added." A further indication of date is provided by Pope's note
(*1735*) to the *Epistle to Jervas*, which is there said to have been written "some years
before the rest", *i.e.* before the Epistles to Addison, Craggs, Oxford, and Arbuth-
not. Since the *Epistle to Jervas* was probably written in 1715 (see p. 159), "some
years" suggests that the *Epistle to Addison* was written later than 1716.

The strained relations of Pope and Addison in 1715 make it seem unlikely that
Pope was then engaged in addressing a complimentary epistle to him. But since
ll. 1–44 are not epistolary in kind and are not entirely derived from Addison's
writings on medals, they (except ll. 5–10, which were added in *1726*) may have
been sketched as a poem on classical antiquities as early as 1715. Relations be-
tween the two writers improved after Addison had seen what is now called the
character of Atticus in May 1716; but *Sandys's Ghost*, written in the winter of
1716–17 (see p. 173), suggests that Pope was still too sore to think of compliments.
Yet the terms in which Addison is addressed imply that ll. 45–62 were written
after Pope had read Addison's *Dialogues* and before his death on 17 June 1719.
It is possible that Craggs or Tickell showed Pope the *Dialogues* when Addison was
dead and then connived at the publication of an epistle which Addison had never
seen; but from what is known of their characters, this is unlikely. A more confi-
dent conclusion could be reached if it were certainly known whether Addison
ever meditated a separate publication of his work.

The concluding lines in celebration of Craggs would seem to have been written
shortly after Addison's death, when Pope learned that Addison had bequeathed

to Craggs the edition of his works then in preparation, and when he assumed that it was in this book that his *Epistle* would first appear. The lines were undoubtedly written before Craggs's death on 16 February 1720/21 since they were printed with the rest of the *Epistle* in some copies of a (possibly) pirated edition of Pope's *Works* in 1720. Pope was to use them again for Craggs's epitaph in 1727 (see p. 281). [After the above was in print, Mr R. G. Sawyer reminded me that Addison intended to publish his *Dialogues* in 1713 (R. E. Tickell, *Thomas Tickell and the Eighteenth Century Poets*, 1931, p. 74). I now incline to think that Pope's poem, except ll. 5–10, 63–72, was drafted in 1713 and revised in 1719 before publication.]

The *Epistle* was enlarged for publication in *Miscellany Poems* 1726 by the addition of ll. 5–10. Slight revisions were made in each of the following editions of Pope's *Works*: folio *1735a*, both octavos *1735cd*, and octavo *1740*. Warburton appears to have reverted to the folio text for his edition of 1751, and he therefore failed to record the later revisions in ll. 22, 27, and 33. In this he has hitherto been followed by subsequent editors.

It is not certain that Pope supervised the production of any text earlier than that of the *1735* folio. That text, after correction in the light of later revisions, has therefore been made the basis of the present text. [But see p. 465.]

For a numismatist's view of the poem, see Thomas O. Mabbott in *Explicator*, x 2 (November 1951).

Title: *To Mr. Addison*] For Pope's note on this poem, see introductory note.

2. *Rome . . . Sepulchre*] Warton misquotes from St Jerome, *Epist.* 130 5: "Urbs tua, quondam orbis caput, Romani populi sepulchrum est."

7f. *Huge Theatres . . . Floods*] i.e. Woods unpeopled of wild beasts to provide for the Roman spectacles, and a countryside drained of water for the mimic naval combats, in amphitheatre or naumachia [EC]. These lines are perhaps a conscious echo of Addison's *Letter from Italy*: "An amphitheatre . . . That on its public shows unpeopled Rome" (l. 75); and "Eridanus . . . that . . . the . . . Alps of half their moisture drains" (l. 28).

18. Mabbott points out that whereas on an incomplete inscription Titus and Vespasian might be indistinguishable since their names were the same, on coins the portrait of a young or old man determines the matter even if the inscription is mutilated.

23. Cf. *Essay on Criticism*, 136.

26ff. Descriptions of coins commemorating conquests of various Cæsars; 26, Coins of Vespasian and Titus show a seated figure of Judea mourning under a palm tree; 27, Triumphal arches appear on the coins of Domitian and Trajan; 28f., some of Hadrian's coins show the Nile, those of Domitian the Rhine, those of Trajan the Euphrates, all figured as river gods prostrate (or recumbent), generally at the feet of the victor; 30, the Roman eagle appears on the coins of several emperors. Addison mentions only the "Judea Capta" (*Works*, 1721, 1520).

33f. Cf. Addison (*ibid.*, 438), "A cabinet of Medals is a collection of pictures in miniature . . . You here see the *Alexanders, Cæsars, Pompeys, Trajans*, and the whole catalogue of Heroes."

35. *sharpen'd*] i.e., by the use of magnifying glasses.

36. *the rust adore*] Cf. *Martinus Scriblerus*, chap. III: "Behold this Rust, . . . this beautiful Varnish of Time,—this venerable Verdure of so many Ages—"; and Addison (*ibid.*, p. 436), "These Gentlemen, says he, value themselves upon being critics in Rust"; also Juvenal, XIII 147–9.

37. *blue . . . green*] The differently coloured patina on bronze coins, blue being a copper sulphate, green a copper carbonate.

39. *Pescennius*] Coins of the pretender Pescennius Niger are the rarest any ordinary collector hopes to possess [Mabbott]. Cf. *Dunciad*, IV 370; Addison, p. 436.

40. Mabbott sees an allusion to Cecrops who killed the emperor Gallienus; if genuine coins were found, it would prove he assumed the purple, which though not recorded is a fit subject for a numismatist's dreams. But Pope's note to *Dunciad*, IV 363, suggests he had in mind a counterfeit of a coin of Cecrops, first king of Athens (of whom no coins exist), imposed upon a noble collector.

41f. The story of the scouring of Woodward's supposedly antique shield is told at greater length in *Martinus Scriblerus*, chap. III (ed. C. Kerby-Miller, 1950, pp. 102–4, 206).

44. Coins of Otho are the rarest in the popular series of the twelve Cæsars [Mabbott]. Cf. *Dunciad*, IV 369; Addison, p. 436.

51f. Cf. *Ep. to Jervas*, l. 20: "While Images reflect from Art to Art", and Addison: "I think there is a great affinity between Coins and Poetry . . ."; "When . . . I confront a Medal with a Verse, I only shew you the same design executed by different hands . . ." (*ibid.*, 446, 448).

53–6. "A compliment to one of Mr. Addison's papers in the *Spectator* on this subject" [Warburton]; *Guardian* (No. 96, 1 July 1713).

57–62. Also alluded to in the *Dialogues*: "You see on Medals not only . . . Emperors, Kings, Consuls . . . and the like characters of importance but . . . the Poets . . ."

62. *A Virgil . . . Addison.*] Cf. Tickell's *To Mr. Addison on . . . his Rosamond*, l. 44: "Which gain'd a Virgil, and an Addison." [Warton.]

64. *Pollio*] Asinius Pollio, friend of Virgil, to whom he addressed his Fourth Eclogue.

67–72. For Pope's later use of these six lines as an Epitaph on Craggs, see introductory note above, and p. 281.

72. *unenvy'd*] It was not likely that men acting in so different spheres as were those of Mr. Craggs and Mr. Pope, should have their friendship disturbed by Envy. We must suppose then that some circumstances in the friendship of Mr. Pope and Mr. Addison are hinted at in this place. [Warburton.]

EPITAPH
Intended for Mr. *ROWE*.
In *Westminster-Abbey*.

THY reliques, *Rowe*, to this fair urn we trust,
And sacred, place by *Dryden*'s awful dust:
Beneath a rude and nameless stone he lies,
To which thy tomb shall guide inquiring eyes.
Peace to thy gentle shade, and endless Rest!   5
Blest in thy genius, in thy love too blest!
One grateful woman to thy fame supplies
What a whole thankless land to his denies.

Title] *Harl. MS reads:* Verses designed for Mr. Rowes Monument by
Mr. Pope, at the request of Mr. Rowes Widow. (*Welbeck MS
reads only* "Epitaph"). *1720 reads:* Epitaph Design'd for Mr.
Rowe in Westminster-Abbey. By Mr. Pope. To the Memory of
Nicholas Rowe Esq; his Wife erected this Monument.
1–4   To Rowes dear Reliques be this Marble just
              Laid Sacred here, by Dryden's awful Dust,
              And let it guide the Worlds enquiring Eies
              To find that Speechless Stone where Dryden lies.
       Harl. MS.
1 urn] shrine *1720–35ab*; tomb *1735cd*.
4 tomb] urn *1735cd*.   7 supplies] supply'd *1720–26*.
8 denies] deny'd *1720–26*.

Contemporary transcripts: BM MS Harl. 7316; and Welbeck Abbey, Harley
Papers.
  Miscellaneous Poems and Translations. 3rd Edition, 1720 (and all later editions
down to *Miscellany Poems*, 6th Edition, 1732).
  The Works . . . To which are added, I. Cooper's-Hill. [etc.]. 1727.
  A Collection of Epigrams. 1727 (and 2nd Edition, 1735).
  The Miscellaneous Works of Nicholas Rowe, Esq. 1733.
  The Works of Mr. Alexander Pope. Volume II. 1735 (folio and quarto).
  The Weekly Oracle. 3 May 1735.
  The Works of Alexander Pope, Esq. Vol. II. 1735 (octavo).
  The Works . . . Vol. II. Containing his Epistles and Satires. 1735 (and 1736).
  Ethic Epistles, Satires, &c. . . . Written by Mr. Pope. 1735.

Ethic Epistles, to Henry St. John L. Bolingbroke. Written in the Year 1732. 1735.
A General Dictionary. P. Bayle. Vol. VIII. 1739.
The Works . . . Vol. II. Containing his Epistles, &c. 1739 (both editions).
The Works . . . Vol. II. Part I. Containing his Epistles, &c. 1740 (and 1743).
Joe Miller's Jests. 5th Edition, 1742 (and later editions).
The Works. Ed. Warburton. Vol. VI. 1751.

"I have not neglected my devoirs to Mr. Rowe; I am writing this very day his Epitaph for Westminster-Abby"—thus Pope in a letter to Jervas, dated 12 December 1718. The version he then composed, which has probably survived only in the Harleian MS, was soon afterwards revised, and except for two or three slight verbal changes, its first printed text of *1720* has remained the official version of the canon. In 1743, however, a widely different version appeared, which included a four-line pendant on Rowe's daughter (see *post*, p. 400, and *New Light*, pp. 146–55).

The text is that of *1720*—with which the Welbeck transcript agrees—corrected in the light of the final revision of *1739*.

3. *a rude and nameless stone*] The Tomb of Mr. *Dryden* was erected [soon after this *1726*] upon this hint by the Duke of *Buckingham*; to which was originally intended this Epitaph . . . [see the epitaph, p. 237] Which the author since chang'd into the plain Inscription now [on the Tomb *1726*] upon it, being only the name of that Great [Man, in this manner *1726*] Poet,

DRYDEN.
Natus Aug. 9. 1631.
Mortuus Maij 1. 1701.
Johannes Sheffield, Dux Buckinghamiensis, fecit.   [P. *1726–51*.]

EPISTLE
TO
James Craggs, Esq;
SECRETARY OF STATE.

A SOUL as full of Worth, as void of Pride,
  Which nothing seeks to show, or needs to hide,
Which nor to Guilt, nor Fear, its Caution owes,
And boasts a Warmth that from no Passion flows;
A Face untaught to feign! a judging Eye,   5
That darts severe upon a rising Lye,
And strikes a blush thro' frontless Flattery.

All this thou wert; and being this before,
Know, Kings and Fortune cannot make thee more.
Then scorn to gain a Friend by servile ways,   10
Nor wish to lose a Foe these Virtues raise;
But candid, free, sincere, as you began,
Proceed—a Minister, but still a Man;
Be not (exalted to whate'er degree)
Asham'd of any Friend, not ev'n of Me.   15
The Patriot's plain, but untrod path pursue;
If not, 'tis I must be asham'd of You.

The Works of Alexander Pope, Esq. Vol. II. 1735.
The Works . . . Vol. II. Containing his Epistles and Satires. 1735 (and 1736).
Ethic Epistles, to Henry St. John L. Bolingbroke. Written in the Year 1732. 1735.
The Works . . . Vol. II. Containing his Epistles, &c. 1739 (both editions).
The Works . . . Vol. II. Part I. Containing his Epistles, &c. 1740 (and 1743).
A Collection of Moral and Sacred Poems. J. Wesley. Vol. I. 1744.
The Works. Ed. Warburton. Vol. VI. 1751.

Line 13 of this Epistle, read in conjunction with the title, suggests that the poem was written when Craggs succeeded Addison as Secretary of State in March 1718, though he had been appointed Secretary at War in the previous year. If this is correct, the footnote appended to the title in *1739*—"In the Year 1720"—may be interpreted, not as the date of the poem, but as Pope's declaration that, though Craggs was involved in the South Sea scandal which burst in 1720, his view of Craggs's character remained unaltered.

When at last the epistle was published in 1735, it appeared not in the handsome folio and quarto editions of the *Works* but in the small octavos. Since it is the least attractive of the *Epistles to Several Persons*, Pope's seeming reluctance to publish it may be attributed to aesthetic considerations.

The text is that of *1735*, which however presents no verbal differences from the later editions.

Title: *Secretary of State*] To these words Pope appended a footnote from *1739* onwards: "In the Year 1720".

13. *a Minister*] Craggs first became a Minister in 1717; see introductory note.

14–17. Compare these lines with *A Dialogue* which follows.

A DIALOGUE.

Pope.   SINCE my old Friend is grown so great,
         As to be Minister of State,
         I'm told (but 'tis not true I hope)
         That *Craggs* will be asham'd of *Pope.*

Craggs. Alas! if I am such a Creature,   5
         To grow the worse for growing greater;
         Why Faith, in Spite of all my Brags,
         'Tis *Pope* must be asham'd of *Craggs.*

Contemporary transcripts: Longleat, Portland Papers, XIX; and BM MS
Harl. 7316.
  The St. James's Chronicle. 21–23 September 1775.
  The Scots Magazine. September 1775.
  Additions to the Works of Alexander Pope, Esq. Vol. I. 1776.
  The Poems of Pope. (Johnson's *English Poets*), Vol. I. 1779 (and Vol. II, 1790).
  This piece is another version, in anticipation or echo, of the last four lines of the
Epistle to James Craggs, Esq. (see previous page); but as it purports to commemor-
ate his recent elevation "to be Minister of State", it would appear to have been
written in 1717 or 1718, as shown in the notes. The attribution is probable, but by
no means certain.
  The text is that of the first printing, which is in verbal agreement with the
Harley and Longleat transcripts.
  2. *Minister of State*] See p. 210.
  4 and 8. Cf. last four lines of the *Ep. to Craggs* (p. 210).

On Lady MARY WORTLEY MONTAGU's
Portrait.

THE play full smiles around the dimpled mouth
    That happy air of Majesty and Youth.
So would I draw (but oh, 'tis vain to try
My narrow Genius does the power deny)
The Equal Lustre of the Heavenly mind   5

8*

Where every grace with every Virtue's join'd
Learning not vain, and wisdom not severe
With Greatness easy, and with wit sincere.
With Just Description shew the Soul Divine
And the whole Princesse in my work should shine.   10

The Works of . . . Lady Mary Wortley Montagu. J. Dallaway. Vol. I. 1803.
The Works. Ed. Bowles. Vol. II. 1806.
From Pope's correspondence with Lady Mary it is known that he arranged
with Kneller to paint her portrait in 1719, and these lines are said to have been
written extempore on its completion. Why they were not printed in the poet's
lifetime may be explained by the quarrel which soon after arose between him and
Lady Mary; for while, on his part, the publication of such a glowing tribute was
not to be thought of after their estrangement, Lady Mary herself was probably
too proud to publish what would have been a telling rejoinder to his attacks on
herself. Nevertheless, she kept Pope's autograph undestroyed, and thus at length
it came into Dallaway's hands, who included in his book a facsimile of it but made
an error of transcription which has been perpetuated by Pope's editors.
    The text follows the facsimile of Pope's autograph in every respect, except in
the use of "y^e" for "the" and of the ampersand.
    Title.] The facsimile (1803) shows no title; Dallaway's heading is *On Lady
M. W. Montagu's Portrait.* Since Bowles's reprint the usual title has read: *Extem-
poraneous Lines on the Picture of Lady Mary W. Montagu, by Kneller.*
    2. *Youth*] Dallaway mistranscribed this word and printed *truth* instead, an
error perpetuated by every reprint hitherto.
    9. *Soul*] Bowles misprinted *work* instead of *Soul*, in which he has since been
followed by most editors.

TO

Sir GODFREY KNELLER,

On his painting for me the Statues of Apollo,
Venus, *and* Hercules.

WHAT God, what Genius did the Pencil move
        When KNELLER painted These?
Twas Friendship—warm as *Phœbus*, kind as Love,
    And strong as *Hercules*.

George Vertue's transcript: Walpole Society, xx. 122.

Poetical Miscellanies . . . Published by Sir Richard Steele. 2nd Edition. 1727.

A Collection of Select Epigrams. J. Hackett. 1757.

Anecdotes of Painting. H. Walpole. Vol. III. 1763 (and later editions).

Additions to the Works of Alexander Pope, Esq. Vol. I. 1776.

The Poems of Pope. Vol. II (in Johnson's *English Poets*, New Edition). 1790.

The occasion of these lines is sufficiently explained in the title Pope gave them on their only appearance in his lifetime. The paintings were to adorn his staircase at Twickenham (EC, IV 453*n*.); and "Pope paid for them with these lines" (H. Walpole, *Anecdotes*, III. 1763, 112). Pope thought well enough of the pictures to mention them in his will, hoping "That my lord Bathurst will find a place for the three statues of the Hercules of Furnese, the Venus of Medicis, and the Apollo in chiaro oscuro, done by Kneller" (*Works*, IX 1751). The date presents some difficulty. Vertue dates the verses "not long before" Kneller's death (1723), but other evidence points to a few years earlier. Pope appears to have moved from Chiswick to Twickenham towards the end of 1718 (letter to Broome, 31 December 1718), and, during the next two years, as his correspondence shows, was much taken up with alterations and improvements to his house and garden. And this would seem to be the most likely time for the adornment of the staircase. In an undated letter from Kneller to Pope, preserved amongst the *Iliad* manuscripts, Kneller wrote: "Dear Friend,—I find them Picturs are so very fresh, being painted in three Collers, and aught to be near a fier, severall days, for as they are, it is impracticable to put them were you intend 'em, it would be pitty, they shou'd take dust." The reference to "three collers" does not necessarily contradict the statement that the paintings were in chiaroscuro, for Kneller is obviously here using the word "colours" for "pigments"; and there is no limit to the number of pigments that may be used when painting in "light and shade". There can be little doubt that these were the pictures of the three statues. That being so, and because the lines from the *Iliad* on the back of Kneller's letter are about half-way though Book XXIV (ll. 515–42); because most of the letters similarly made use of by Pope in this part of the manuscript are dated 1719; and, lastly, because the whole translation, complete with indexes and notes, was published by 12 May 1720, the poem is dated 1719, as the nearest approximation possible.

The text is that of *1727*, the only authoritative text.

In behalf of Mr. SOUTHERNE.
To the Duke of ARGYLE.

EPIGRAM.

A RGYLE his Praise, when *Southerne* wrote,
    First struck out this, and then that Thought; }
Said *this* was Flatt'ry, *that* a Fault.
    How shall your Bard contrive?

My Lord, consider what you do,   5
He'll lose his Pains and Verses too; }
For if these Praises fit not You,
    They'll fit no Man alive.

Title] 1745 has no title, but reads: The following Lines were lately found amongst Mr. Pope's Papers in his own Hand-Writing.
     1721 and MS read as given except that MS has Tom *instead of* Mr.
4 your] our *MSS; the 1721.*
8 fit] serve *MSS, 1721.*

Contemporary transcripts: Longleat, Portland Papers, xviii; and BM MS Harl. 7316.
    The Grove; Or, A Collection of Original Poems, Translations, &c. 1721.
    A Collection of Epigrams. 1727 (and 2nd Edition, 1735).
    A Miscellany of Original Poems . . . Collected . . . by Mr. Theobald. 1732.
    The General Advertiser. 26 October 1745.
    The Sports of the Muses. Vol. II. 1752.
    A Collection of Select Epigrams. J. Hackett. 1757.
    Joe Miller's Jests. 12th Edition [1757?] (and later editions).
    The Festoon. 1766 (and later editions).
    The Christmas Treat. 1767.
    The St. James's Chronicle. 21-23 September 1775.
    The Scots Magazine. September, 1775.
    Additions to the Works of Alexander Pope, Esq. Vol. I. 1776.
    The European Magazine. September 1799.
    The Edinburgh Magazine. October 1799.
    This poem was first attributed to Pope in the year following his death, in a version which claims to have been set up from "his own Hand-Writing". That statement has, at least, the support of a text that was not taken from the earlier printed version, for it contains two readings which, being improvements of it, suggest

revision. The attribution is probable. Pope was on friendly terms with the Duke from about 1716 onwards, dining and staying with him from time to time; and, earlier in this same year, had (possibly) addressed another poetical compliment to him, as he did later (see pp. 422, 380); besides having alluded to him in friendly epigrams as early as 1717 (p. 185)—none of which pieces was ever included by Pope in his works. The epigram is very like Pope's work in this manner with its deftly turned compliment; and in addition contains one of his characteristic rhymes. Of Pope's friendship with Southerne also, there is ample proof (see *post*, p. 398). He could thus have learnt the inner history of Southerne's compliment from either duke or dramatist. The date is fixed by the acting and printing, in the latter half of December 1719, of Southerne's tragedy, the dedication of which was evidently the inspiration of the epigram (see below).

The text is that of the first ascription (*1745*), with collations from the *MSS* and the first printed version (*1721*).

Title: *Southerne*] See Biog. App., Vol. IV.

Duke of Argyle] See Biog. App., Vol. IV.

1. *his Praise*] Southerne's last tragedy *The Spartan Dame* (acted 11 December 1719) is dedicated "To His Grace the Duke of Argyle and Greenwich, &c." in the rather laudatory language usual at that period.

Lines from *ACIS and GALATEA*.

I.

AIR.

THE Flocks shall leave the Mountains,
    The Woods the Turtle-Dove,
The Nymphs forsake the Fountains
    Ere I forsake my Love.

Not Showers to Larks so pleasing,
    Nor Sunshine to the Bee;
Nor Sleep to Toil so easing
    As these dear Smiles to me.

2 Woods] Floods *MS*, *1732*.
3 Fountains] fountain *MS*.
7 Nor] Not *MS*; No *1732*.

II.
CHORUS

WRETCHED Lovers, Fate has past
   This sad Decree, no Joy shall last.
Wretched Lovers, quit your Dream,
Behold the Monster, *Polypheme*.
See what ample Strides he takes,   5
The Mountain nods, the Forest shakes,
The Waves run frighted to the Shores.
Hark! how the thund'ring Giant roars.

Handel's autograph: BM King's Music MSS.

Acis and Galatea: An English Pastoral Opera . . . Set . . . By Mr. Handel. 1732.

Acis and Galatea A Mask As it was Originally Compos'd . . . by Mr. Handel. [c. 1740?]

   The Masque of Acis and Galatea. The Musick by Mr. Handell. 1742. [Omits No. II.]

   Thesaurus Musicus. [1743] (and Vol. I [1745]). [No. I only.]

   Clio and Euterpe. Vol. I. [1758.] [No. I only.]

   Acis and Galatea, A Serenata . . . The Musick composed by Mr. Handel. 1764.

   The Words of Such Pieces As are . . . performed by The Academy of Ancient Music. 1761 (and 2nd Edition, 1768).

   Bell's Edition. The Poetical Works of John Gay. Vol. I. 1777.

Although neither Gay's editors nor his biographers have been able to quote any contemporary attribution of *Acis and Galatea* to him, they have very generally accepted his authorship of the words ever since the masque was first included among Gay's works in 1777. All the early editions were anonymous, only Handel's name as the composer appearing on their title-pages and in the advertisements of its early performances. The earliest connection of Gay's name with the libretto makes it an affair of collaboration; for the Preface of *Omnipotence A Sacred Oratorio,* 1774, states that *Acis and Galatea* was translated from the Italian "by Mr. Pope, Dr. Arbuthnot, and Mr. Gay". Pope and Gay were old collaborators; and it seems certain that the propitious conjunction of at least Gay and Pope and Handel frequently occurred at Lord Burlington's house at Chiswick during the years 1716–18 (see foreword to *Haman and Mordecai, post,* p. 433). Handel is generally supposed to have composed the music for *Acis and Galatea* about 1718–20, when he was Kappelmeister to the Duke of Chandos at Cannons (where the masque was first performed, according to *The Daily Post,* 2 May 1732), the most probable date being 1719. The extent of Pope's contribution to the book is unknown, the only pieces for which any real evidence exists being an "Air" and a "Chorus". That they unmistakably derive from Pope is shown in the notes; but whether Pope remodelled these pieces for Gay, or Gay adapted his friend's lines, it is impossible to say; though Pope's repetition of a phrase or two from his *Iliad* in *Haman and Mordecai* as well as in *Acis and Galatea* may seem to indicate his responsibility.

The text of the "Air" follows that of *1742* (which probably embodies the earliest form of the masque), with collations from Handel's autograph (*MS*) and the first printed version (*1732*); the text of the "Chorus" (which does not appear in the *1742* edition) follows that of *1732* with collations from the *MS*.

I. Cf. Pope's *Autumn*:

> Not bubling Fountains to the thirsty Swain,
> Not balmy Sleep to Lab'rers faint with Pain,
> Not Show'rs to Larks, nor Sunshine to the Bee,
> Are half so charming as thy Sight to me. (ll. 43–6.)

II. Cf. Pope's *Iliad*, 1718 (XIII 27–33):

> At Jove incens'd, with Grief and Fury stung,
> Prone down the rocky Steep he rush'd along.
> Fierce as he past, the lofty Mountains nod,
> The Forests shake! Earth trembled as he trod,
> And felt the footsteps of th' immortal God.
> From Realm to Realm three ample strides he took
> And at the fourth the distant Aegae shook.

also *Haman and Mordecai* (see *post*, p. 429), ll. 141f. and *Iliad* (XX 74–80).

The Iliad of Homer. Vols. V, VI

[Books XVII–XXIV; published 12 May 1720; vol. VIII]

DUKE *upon* DUKE.

An excellent new Ballad. *To the Tune of* Chevy Chase.

T o Lordings proud I tune my Lay,
    Who feast in Bower or Hall:
Though Dukes they be, to Dukes I say,
    That Pride will have a Fall.

1 Lay] Song *1720*.   3 to Dukes I say,] yet Dukes shall see *1720*.

Now, that this same it is right sooth,
   Full plainly doth appear,
From what befel *John* Duke of *Guise*,
   And *Nic.* of *Lancastere*.   5

When *Richard Cœur de Lyon* reign'd,
   (Which means a Lion's Heart)
Like him his Barons rag'd and roar'd,   10
   Each play'd a Lion's Part.

A Word and Blow was then enough,
   (Such Honour did them prick)
If you but turn'd your Cheek, a Cuff,   15
   And if your A—se, a Kick.

Look in their Face, they tweak'd your Nose,
   At ev'ry Turn fell to 't;
Come near, they trod upon your Toes;
   They fought from Head to Foot.   20

Of these, the Duke of *Lancastere*
   Stood Paramount in Pride;
He kick'd, and cuff'd, and tweak'd, and trod
   His Foes, and Friends beside.

Firm on his Front his Beaver sate,   25
   So broad, it hid his Chin;
For why? he deem'd no Man his Mate,
   And fear'd to tan his Skin.

With *Spanish* Wool he dy'd his Cheek,
   With Essence oil'd his Hair;   30
No Vixen Civet-Cat so sweet,
   Nor could so scratch and tear.

27 deem'd] thought *1720*.
31 so] more *1720*.
32 Nor could so] Nor more could *1720*.

Right tall he made himself to show,
    Though made full short by G—d:
And when all other Dukes did bow,   35
    This Duke did only nod.

Yet courteous, blithe, and debonair,
    To *Guise*'s Duke was he;
Was never such a loving Pair,
    How could they disagree?   40

Oh, thus it was. He lov'd him dear,
    And cast how to requite him:
And having no Friend left but this,
    He deem'd it meet to fight him.

Forthwith he drench'd his desp'rate Quill;   45
    And thus he did indite:
"This Eve at Whisk ourself will play,
    "Sir Duke! be here to Night."

Ah no, ah no, the guileless *Guise*
    Demurely did reply, ·   50
I cannot go, nor yet can stand,
    So sore the Gout have I.

The Duke in Wrath call'd for his Steeds,
    And fiercely drove them on;
Lord! Lord! how rattl'd then thy Stones,   55
    Oh Kingly *Kensington*!

All in a Trice he rush'd on *Guise*,
    Thrust out his Lady dear,
He tweak'd his Nose, trod on his Toes,
    And smote him on the Ear.   60

39 Was never] Never was *1720*.
40 How could] Why did *1720*.
57 he rush'd on *Guise*] on *Guise* he rush'd *1720*.

But mark, how 'midst of Victory,
    Fate plays her old Dog Trick!
Up leap'd Duke *John*, and knock'd him down,
    And so down fell Duke *Nic*.

Alas, oh *Nic*! Oh *Nic*. alas!   65
    Right did thy Gossip call thee:
As who should say, alas the Day,
    When *John* of *Guise* shall maul thee.

For on thee did he clap his Chair,
    And on that Chair did sit;   70
And look'd, as if he meant therein
    To do—what was not fit.

Up didst thou look, oh woeful Duke!
    Thy Mouth yet durst not ope,
Certes for fear, of finding there   75
    A T—d instead of Trope.

"Lye there, thou Caitiff vile! quoth *Guise*,
    "No *Sheet* is here to save thee:
"The Casement it is shut likewise;
    "Beneath my Feet I have thee.   80

"If thou hast ought to speak, speak out."
    Then *Lancaster* did cry,
"Know'st thou not me, nor yet thy self?
    "Who thou, and whom am I?

"Know'st thou not me, who (God be prais'd)   85
    "Have brawl'd, and quarrel'd more,
"Than all the Line of *Lancastere*
    "That battl'd heretofore?

62 plays her] shews an *1720*.
81 speak, speak out.] say, now speak. *1720*.
84 and whom] and who *1720*.   86 brawl'd] bawl'd *1720*.

"In Senates fam'd for many a Speech,
    "And (what some awe must give ye,   90
"Tho' laid thus low beneath thy breech,)
    "Still of the Council Privy.

"Still of the *Dutchy* Chancellor,
    "*Durante Life* I have it;
"And turn, as now thou dost on me,   95
    "Mine A—e on them that gave it."

But now the Servants they rush'd in;
    And Duke *Nic.* up leap'd he:
I will not cope against such odds,
    But, *Guise*! I'll fight with thee: 100

To-morrow with thee will I fight
    Under the Greenwood Tree;
"No, not to-morrow, but to night
    "(Quoth *Guise*) I'll fight with thee."

And now the Sun declining low   105
    Bestreak'd with Blood the Skies;
When, with his Sword at Saddle Bow,
    Rode forth the valiant *Guise*;

Full gently praunch'd he o'er the Lawn;
    Oft' roll'd his Eyes around,   110
And from the Stirrup stretch'd, to find
    Who was not to be found.

Long brandish'd he the Blade in Air,
    Long look'd the Field all o'er:
At length he spy'd the Merry-men brown,   115
    And eke the Coach and four.

 96 Mine ... them] My ... those *1720*.
109 praunch'd] praunc'd *1720*. o'er] on *1720*.
110 Eyes] Eye *1720*.   111 the] his *1720*.   113 the] his *1720*.

From out the Boot bold *Nicholas*
   Did wave his Wand so white,
As pointing out the gloomy Glade
   Wherein he meant to fight.   120

All in that dreadful Hour, so calm
   Was *Lancastere* to see,
As if he meant to take the Air,
   Or only take a Fee.

And so he did—for to *New Court*   125
   His rowling Wheels did run:
Not that he shunn'd the doubtful Strife,
   But *Bus'ness* must be done.

Back in the Dark, by *Brompton* Park,
   He turn'd up through the Gore;
So slunk to *Cambden* House so high,   130
   All in his Coach and four.

Mean while Duke *Guise* did fret and fume,
   A Sight it was to see;
Benumm'd beneath the Evening Dew,   135
   Under the Greenwood Tree.

Then, wet and weary, home he far'd,
   Sore mutt'ring all the way,
"The Day I meet him, *Nic.* shall rue
   "The Cudgel of that Day.   140

118 Wand] Hand *1720*.
120 Wherein] Whereat *1720*.
126 rowling . . . did] trowling . . . they *1720*.
131 *Cambden*] Campden *1720*.
133 Duke *Guise*] the *Guise 1720*.
139 him, *Nic.*] *Nic.* he *1720*.

"Mean Time on every Pissing-Post
    "Paste we this Recreant's Name,
"So that each Pisser-by shall read,
    "And piss against the same.

Now God preserve our gracious King!   145
    And grant, his Nobles all
May learn this Lesson from Duke *Nic*.
    That *Pride will have a Fall*.

Duke upon Duke. An Excellent New Play-house Ballad. Set to Musick by Mr. Holde-combe. 1720. [Folio pamphlet, 6 pp., musical setting.]

An Excellent Old Ballad, called Pride will have a Fall. [1720.] [Single sheet broad-side, with illustration, n.d., doubtless the "Grub-street Copy".]

Duke up [on Duke.] *An Excellent* [. . .] *Ballad. Set to Musick by Mr. Holdecombe* [1720?] [Single sheet, printed both sides, musical setting, n.d., torn.]

Duke upon Duke . . . 1723. [Folio pamphlet, 6 pp., musical setting.]

The Hive. 1724 (and later editions).

The Choice. [Vol. I.] 2nd Edition, 1732.

The Vocal Miscellany. [Vol. I.] 2nd Edition, 1734 (and 3rd Edition, 1738).

Miscellanies. The Fourth Volume. Consisting of Verses . . . 1742 (and later editions).

Philomel . . . *a Small Collection of Only the Best English Songs.* 1744.

The Goldfinch. 1748.

The Sports of the Muses. Vol. I. 1752.

The Poems of Gay in Johnson's *English Poets*: 1779 (and 1790).

New Light on Pope, by N. Ault. 1949.

This appears to be "the ballad on Lechmere and Guise", a "good part" of which is ascribed to Pope by Spence on Pope's authority (*Anecdotes*, p. 285), though when transcribing this note for Warburton (BM Egerton MS 1960, f. 4ʳ) Spence called the ballad "the Duke & No Duke". Nothing is known of the quarrel herein recorded. It is not mentioned by Sir John Guise in his additions to the *Memoirs of the Family of Guise* (ed. G. Davies, Camden Soc., 3rd Ser., XXVIII 132–57). Sir John (*c.* 1677–1732) was M.P. for Gloucestershire 1705–10 and for Marlow 1722–7. His sister was married to Pope's friend, Edward Blount. The other disputant, Lechmere, Chancellor of the Duchy of Lancaster, was notori-ously so overbearing in manner, hot-tempered, and violent, as to be a fair target for ridicule. In *The Hive* the poem is said to have been "Written in the Year 1719", but no corroborative evidence of this statement has been found; the piece is therefore dated by the year of publication. See further *New Light*, pp. 186–94.

The text is that of *1742*, the only text whose publication Pope undoubtedly supervised, with collations from the first printing (*1720*).

7. *John Duke of Guise*] Sir John Guise, third Baronet of Elmore (d. 1732), play-

fully called Duke after Dryden's *The Duke of Guise*, 1683 (see introductory note).

8. *Nic. of Lancastere*] Nicholas Lechmere (1675–1727), collaborator of Steele in *The Crisis*, 1714; solicitor-general, 1714–18; privy councillor, 1718; attorney-general, 1718–20; created Baron, 1721; chancellor of the Duchy of Lancaster, 1717–27 (hence the jocular title "Duke of Lancastere" of l. 21); was described in his nephew's diary as "of a temper violent, proud, and impracticable".

29. *Spanish wool*] Wool treated with a dye, used as a cosmetic: "we are indebted to Spanish wool for many of our masculine ruddy complexions". 1755 (*OED*).

47. *Whisk*] The old name of the card game whist.

66. *Gossip call thee*] *i.e.* God-parent christened thee.

76. *Trope*] Lechmere was esteemed as an orator (see below, l. 89).

92. *Council Privy*] Lechmere was made Privy Councillor in 1718.

94. *Durante Life*] Nicholas Lechmere constituted by Patent, Chancellor of the Duchy of Lancaster for Life. (*Historical Register*, II.)

117–18. *Boot . . . Wand*] The boot was the part of the coach where the attendants sat; the wand being a rod of white wood, a sign of office carried erect by an officer of the Court of Justice.

124. *a Fee*] *i.e.* as Attorney-General.

130. *Gore*] Kensington Gore.

131. *Cambden House*] Campden House, Campden Hill, where Lechmere lived.

An Inscription upon a PUNCH-BOWL, in the South-Sea Year for a Club, chas'd with Jupiter placing Callista in the Skies & Europa with the Bull.

COME, fill the South-Sea Goblet full;
    The Gods shall of our Stock take care:
Europa pleas'd accepts the *Bull*,
    And Jove with Joy puts off the *Bear*.

Birch transcript: BM 685. e. 1.
Supplemental Volume to the Works of . . . Pope. [Edited by R. W. Didbin.] 1825.
The Works. Ed. Dyce. Vol. II. 1831.

The attribution of these lines to Pope derives solely from a transcript in Thomas Birch's autograph on the fly-leaf of a copy of the first volume of Warburton's edition of Pope, now in the British Museum, where it is accompanied by the following statement in the same hand: "This Epigram of Mr. Pope was com-

municated by the Rev^d Dr. Warburton to Tho. Birch." (Also there is pasted in
the same volume a second transcript of the inscription in the same hand.) The
occasion of the epigram is not recorded, but it is dated by a reference to the
"South-Sea Year", 1720. The epigram must remain an attributed piece, though
the probability of Pope's authorship is high.

The text is that of Birch's autograph, which agrees with the pasted-in transcript
except for a trifling difference in punctuation and title.

3–4. *Bull . . . Bear.*] *OED* shows that these familiar Stock Exchange terms had
obtained a wide currency by 1720.

To Mr. *GAY*,

Who wrote him a congratulatory Letter on the finishing his House.

A H friend, 'tis true—this truth you lovers know—
   In vain my structures rise, my gardens grow,
In vain fair Thames reflects the double scenes
Of hanging mountains, and of sloping greens:
Joy lives not here; to happier seats it flies,   5
And only dwells where WORTLEY casts her eyes.

What are the gay parterre, the chequer'd shade,
The morning bower, the ev'ning colonade,
But soft recesses of uneasy minds,
To sigh unheard in, to the passing winds?   10

7 the gay parterre] the falling Rills *1737*, *1744*, *1769*; these noon-
tide bowers *1763*. the chequer'd shade] the pendant Shades
1737, *1744*, *1769*; and solemn shades *1763*.
8 The morning bower] The morning Bow'rs *1737*, *1744*, *1769*;
Those gliding streams *1763*. the ev'ning colonade] the Even-
ing Collonades *1737*, *1744*, *1769*; and evening colonades
1763.
9 of uneasy minds] for th' uneasy Mind *1737*, *1744*, *1763*, *1769*.
10 unheard in, to] unseen into *1737*. winds] Wind *1737*, *1744*,
1763, *1769*.

So the struck deer in some sequester'd part
Lies down to die, the arrow at his heart;
There, stretch'd unseen in coverts hid from day,
Bleeds drop by drop, and pants his life away.

11 So...deer] So...doe *1737*; Lo!...deer *1769*.
12 at his] in her *1737*; in his *1744, 1769*; near his *1763*.
13 *1737, 1744, 1763 and 1769 read:* There hid in Shades, and wast-
ing Day by Day, *except that 1763 reads* pining *for* wasting.
14 *1737 reads:* Inly she bleeds, and pants her Soul away. *1744 and
1769 read the same but with* he ... his *instead of* she ... her. *1763
reads:* Inly he bleeds, and melts his soul away. (cf. line from the
Odyssey, below.)

The Works of ... Lady Mary Wortley Montagu. Vol. III. 1803.
The Works. Ed. Bowles. Vol. II. 1806.

[LINES 7–14 only. "What are the falling Rills..."]
The Whitehall Evening Post. 19–22 March 1737.
The London Magazine. March 1737.
The Norfolk Poetical Miscellany. Vol. II. 1744.
The Scots Magazine. January 1754.
The St. James's Magazine. March 1763.
The Poetical Calendar. December 1763.
Letters ... to a Lady. 1769.
The New Foundling Hospital for Wit. Part IV. 1771.
Additions to the Works of Alexander Pope, Esq. Vol. I. 1776.
The Poems of Pope. Vol. I, in Johnson's *English Poets.* 1779.

In a letter dated "Twickenham, 1720", Lady Mary Wortley Montagu writes
to her sister, the Countess of Mar, at Paris: "I see sometimes Mr. Congreve, and
very seldom Mr. Pope, who continues to embellish his house at Twickenham. He
has made a subterranean grotto... I here send you some verses addressed to Mr.
Gay, who wrote him a congratulatory letter on the finishing his house. I stifled
them here, and I beg they may die the same death at Paris, and never go further
than your closet—" whereupon follows the poem. Not long afterwards, Pope and
Lady Mary quarrelled bitterly; and as Pope and his friends would no longer be
inclined to print poetical bouquets to Lady Mary; and as she herself would pub-
lish no compliments from Pope (she effectually "stifled" for some eighty years at
least one other tribute from him, see page 212), the poem as a whole did not
appear in print until the following century.

In the meantime Pope read an anonymous "Imitation of Shakespeare" called
A Fit of the Spleen. Thinking it was written by Mrs Judith Cowper, with whom he
had just begun a correspondence, he wrote to her (5 November 1722) saying

amongst other things: "I can scarce wish the verses yours at the expence of your thinking that way, so early"; going on to point out that it was time enough to seek retirement, "the *pis-aller* of mankind", when one is out of love with everything else. Whereupon he continues: "Would you have me describe my solitude and grotto to you? what if, after a long and painted description of them in verse (which the writer I have just been speaking of [*i.e.* the author of *A Fit of the Spleen*] could better make . . .) what if it ended thus?

> What are the falling rills . . . [eight lines quoted, ll. 7–14].

If these lines want poetry, they do not want sense. God Almighty long preserve you from a feeling of them!" (The poem was in fact written by the Rev. Benjamin Ibbot.)

These same eight lines appeared in print for the first time in *The Whitehall Evening Post* of 19–22 March 1737, appended to the following letter:

> *SIR*,—The following little Piece was writ by a Clergyman. . . You will ob-serve, the last *Eight Lines* are said to be *finish'd by Mr. Pope*; but I think, They are rather Sentiments arising from reading the foregoing, than design'd as a Part of the Poem itself. . . I am, Sir, Your constant Reader, A. Z.

> A FIT *of the* SPLEEN.
> In Imitation of SHAKESPEAR. . . .

A motto of three lines from *The Rape of the Lock* follows, and then the blank verse poem of forty-one lines; after which come the words "Finish'd by Mr. Pope" and this fragment of eight lines. Publication was probably due to some member of the Cowper family since the accidental connection of this fragment with the anony-mous Imitation of Shakespear could hardly have been known outside the Cowper circle; besides which they are the only people (except Lady Mary) who are known to have possessed at that time a copy of the verses.

The text is that of *1803*; with collations of the last eight lines from the first printing (*1737*), the Miscellany (*1744*), the "Arbour" lines (*1763*) and the Cowper letter (*1769*).

Title: Taken from Lady Mary's letter (see introductory note).

6. *Wortley*] Lady Mary Wortley Montagu (see introductory note, and Biog. App., Vol. IV) whose eyes Pope mentions elsewhere (see pp. 160, 236).

14. Cf. "And inly bleeds, and silent wastes away." *Odyssey*, XIII, 434.

COUPLETS & VERSICLES
1711–1720

[See *ante*, p. 74.]

Pope's autographs: Bodleian MS Rawl. letters 90 [Nos. I, II]; Mapledurham MSS [No. IV]; BM MS Add. 4807 [No. IX]; Pierpont Morgan Library, New York [No. XIX].

Caryll transcript: BM MS Add. 28618 [Nos. III, V, XII].

Contemporary transcripts: Longleat, Portland Papers, XX [No. X]; BM MS Harl. 7316 [No. X].

The Temple of Fame. 1715 (and 2nd Edition, 1715). [No. VII.]

A Full and True Account of a . . . Revenge by Poison on the Body of Mr. Edmund Curll, Bookseller. [1716.] [No. X.]

The Iliad Of Homer, Translated by Mr. Pope. Vol. V. 1720 (and later editions). [No. V.]

Miscellanea. In Two Volumes. 1727. [Nos. I, II.]

Miscellanies. The Second Volume. 1727 (and later editions). [No. X.]

The Female Dunciad. 1728. [No. II.]

Mr. Pope's Literary Correspondence. Vol. I. 1735 (and 3rd Edition, 1735). [No. III.]

Mr. Pope's Literary Correspondence. Vol. III. 1735 (and 2nd Edition, 1735). [Nos. I, II.]

Letters of Mr. Pope . . . Vol. I. 1735 (all issues). [No. III.]

Letters of . . Pope ["Works . . . In Prose". Vol. I.] 1737. [No. III.]

The Works . . . Vol. V. Containing . . . Letters. 2nd Edition. 1737. [No. III.]

The Works . . . Vol. VI. Containing . . . Letters. 1737. [No. III.]

The Works . . . In Prose. Vol. II. 1741. [No. X.]

Miscellanies. The Second Volume. 1742 (and later editions). [No. X.]

The Works . . . Vol. IV. Part I. Containing . . . Letters. 1742. [No. III.]

Memoirs of . . . Pope. W. Ayre. 1745. [No. II.]

The Works. Ed. Warburton. 1751. Vol. VI [No. X]; Vol. VII [No. III].

A Supplement to the Works . . . 1757. [Nos. I, II.]

The St. James's Chronicle. 10–12 August 1775. [No. VI.]

Additions to the Works . . . 1776. [Nos. I, II, VI, IX.]

The Muses Mirror. Vol. I. 1778. [No. VI.]

The Works. Ed. Warton. 1797. [Nos. VI, XI.]

A Supplementary Volume to the Works . . . 1807. [No. I.]

The Works. Ed. Carruthers. Vol. II. 1858.

The Works. Ed. Elwin and Courthope. Vol. VI. 1871. [Nos. V, XII.]

The Works. [1876.] [No. VI.]

I.

LINES

On Coffee.

As long as Moco's happy Tree shall grow,
　While Berries crackle, or while Mills shall go;
While smoking Streams from Silver Spouts shall glide,
Or China's Earth receive the sable Tyde;
While Coffee shall to British Nymphs be dear;　　　　5
While fragrant Steams the bended Head shall chear;
Or grateful Bitters shall delight the Tast;
So long her Honour, Name, and Praise shall last!

1 Moco's] *First written* India's, *then crossed out and* Moco's *written above.*
3 glide] *First written* flow *then altered to* glide.

In the summer of 1711, Cromwell spent a fortnight with the Popes at Binfield. After he had left, Pope sent him a letter (15 July) in which these lines on coffee appear with the following introduction: "All you saw in this Country charge me to assure y^u of their humble Service, & the Ladies in particular... The Trophy you bore away from one of 'em, in y^r Snuffbox, will doubtless preserve her Memory, and be a Testimony of your admiration, for ever."

The text is that of the autograph (the printed texts of *1727* and *1735* being in verbal agreement). A year later several of these lines reappear in *The Rape of the Locke*, I 90, 93–4, and 114 (see Vol. II, p. 130), thus:

2–4. Cf.　　The Berries crackle, and the Mill turns round; ...
　　　　　　From silver Spouts the grateful Liquors glide,
　　　　　　And *China*'s Earth receives the smoking Tyde.
6. Cf.　　As o'er the fragrant Steams she bends her Head.
8. *her Honour*] This refers to one of the ladies of Pope's circle (see letter above quoted).

II.

LINES.

On Writing a Tragedy.

TELL me, by all the melting joys of Love,
   By the warm Transports and entrancing Languors,
By the soft Fannings of the wafting Sheets,
By the dear Tremblings of the Bed of Bliss;
By all these tender Adjurations tell me,   5
—Am I not fit to write a Tragedy?

These lines are found in a high-spirited reply (21 December 1711) to Crom-well's suggestion that he should write a tragedy, in which, after playfully raving about "Two of the finest faces in the Universe" (those of Martha and Teresa Blount), he hyperbolically declaims: "How gladly wou'd I give all I am worth, that is to say, my *Pastorals* for *one* of their *Maidenheads*, & my *Essay* for the other? I wou'd lay out all my *Poetry* in *Love*; an *Original* for a Lady, & a *Trans-lation* for a *Waiting Maid*! And now (since you find what a blessed disposition I am in)—". The "Lines" hereupon follow; after which he asks: "And wou'd not these Lines sound admirably in the Mouth of *Wilks*, especially if he humourd each period with his Leg, & stamp'd with just alacrity at the Cadences?"

The text follows that of the autograph (with which those of *1727* and *1735* verbally agree).

III.

COUPLET.

JOVE was alike to *Latian* and to *Phrygian*,
   For you well know, that Wit's of no Religion.

1 *Latian*] Trojan *MS.*

This couplet appears in a letter to Caryll (25 June 1711), in which Pope discusses Dennis's attack on him in the recently published *Reflections Critical and Satyrical upon a late Rhapsody call'd, An Essay upon Criticism*. In the course of his letter Pope complains: "But sure this is ye first time that a Wit was attack'd for his Religion, as you'll find I'm most zealously in this Treatise. And you know, Sir, what alarms I have had from the opposite side on this very account. . . 'Tis however, my happiness that you, Sir, are impartial." The couplet follows.

The text is that of *1735*, with a collation from the transcript (*MS*).

IV.

INSCRIPTION.

Martha Blount; A: P:

EACH pretty Carecter with pleasing Smart
   Deepens the dear Idea in my heart.

2 the] Your *crossed out*, the *written above*.

Written in Pope's autograph in the copy of *Miscellaneous Poems and Translations*, 1712, at Mapledurham, given by him to Martha Blount, as mentioned in his letter to her dated 25 May 1712 (see *New Light*, p. 54).
   1. *Each . . . Carecter*] *i.e.* Carect, or Character; meaning each letter in her name —not improbably in conjunction with his own initials which follow her name in the inscription, as shown above.

V.

A WINTER PIECE.

As when the freezing blasts of Boreas blow,
   And scatter ore the Fields the driving Snow,
From dusky Clowds the fleecy Winter flyes,
Whose dazling Lustre whitens all the Skies.

1 freezing] piercing *1720*.

Found in a letter from Pope to Caryll, dated 21 December 1712, and transcribed by the recipient (BM MS Add. 28618). After complaining about the severe winter, Pope continues: "To fill this Paper . . . I shall here putt togeather severall beautyfull Winter pieces of the Poets, wch have occurrd to my Memory on this Occasion." Among the seven pieces cited in Latin or English verse are four anonymous lines in English from the *Iliad*, which seem not to have been recognized hitherto; but which actually reappeared with little variation nearly eight years later in his translation (Book xix, ll. 380–3).
   The text follows that of the transcript (except in the substitution of "the" for "y^e"), with a collation from the first printing (*1720*).

VI.

LINES suppressed at the End of the Epistle—
To Miss BLOUNT, *on leaving the Town, &c.*

IN this strange Town a different Course we take,
  Refine ourselves to Spirit, for your Sake.
For Want of you, we spend our random Wit on
The first we find with Needham, Brooks, or Briton.
Hackney'd in Sin, we beat about the Town,   5
And like sure Spaniels, at first Scent lie down.
Were Virtue's self in Silks,—faith keep away!
Or Virtue's Virtue scarce would last a Day.

Thus, Madam, most Men talk, and some Men do:
The rest is told you in a Line or two.   10
Some strangely wonder you're not fond to marry—
A double Jest still pleases sweet Sir Harry—
Small-Pox is rife, and *Gay* in dreadful fear—
The good Priests whisper—Where's the Chevalier?
Much in your Absence B—'s Heart endures,   15
And if poor *Pope* is cl–pt, the Fault is yours.

The existence of these lines, which Pope is said to have omitted at the end of the epistle "To a Young Lady, on leaving the Town after the Coronation", was first noted by Ruffhead (p. 405), who, remarking that he had in his hand "the original copy" of the poem, went on to say: "It must be added, that in the original there are sixteen additional lines, which immediately follow the last line of the printed copy. In these the poet humorously describes the manner in which the *beau Esprits* spent their time in town. But on reflection he thought proper to suppress these lines." They were first printed in *The St. James's Chronicle* of 10–12 August 1775, with an introductory letter as follows:

Sir, The enclosed Lines were transcribed from the Original, in the Hand-writing of Mr. Pope. They were added after the present Conclusion of his Address to Miss M. B. on her leaving Town. "As some fond Virgin, &c." I heartily wish I could apologize for their Licentiousness as easily as I can prove their Authenticity. I am, Sir, Your most humble Servant. G. R.

EC (III 223) reports a MS copy of them "among Warburton's papers", the copyist being "R. G." (cf. G. R. above) who had written at the end "Copia vera". [A persuasive case has been made by R. N. Maud, "Some Lines from Pope" (*Rev. of Eng. Stud.*, n.s., IX (1958), 146–50) for detaching these "Lines" from the "Coronation" poem, with whose tone and fiction they seem incompatible, and associating them with poems describing a different milieu, such as "A Farewell to London" (p. 128) and "The Court Ballad" (p. 180).]

The above text follows the first printing, *1775*.

4. 〔M〕other Needham kept a brothel (see Vol. IV, Biog. App.). Nothing is known of Brooks and Briton.

12. "Sir Harry" has not been identified.

VII.

LINES FROM *HORACE III. iv.*

WHILE yet a Child, I chanc'd to stray,
　　And in a Desart sleeping lay;
The savage Race withdrew, nor dar'd
To touch the Muses future Bard:
But *Cytheræa*'s gentle Dove　　　　　　　　5
　　Myrtles and *Bays* around me spread,
　　　And crown'd your Infant Poet's Head,
Sacred to *Musick* and to *Love*.

Reprinted from footnote to *The Temple of Fame* (1715), ll. 222ff. See Vol. II, p. 273.

VIII.

EPITAPH

On P.P. *Clerk of the Parish,*

said to be written by himself.

O READER, if that thou canst read,
　　Look down upon this Stone;
Do all we can, Death is a Man
　　That never spareth none.

Appended to a skit on Bishop Burnet's *History of My Own Time*, entitled "Memoirs of P. P. Clerk of this Parish". It first appeared anonymously in *Miscellanies. The Second Volume*, 1727, but dates from a much earlier period. In the "Testimonies of Authors" (see *Dunciad* A, Vol. V, p. 34) Pope implied that it was written at Lord Harcourt's seat in Oxfordshire before Burnet's death in 1715. And as Pope had stayed with the Harcourts previous to his visit to Stanton Harcourt in 1718, there is no reason to suppose his memory had played him false. It is probable that this "Tract" was planned, if not begun, at some meeting of the "Scriblerus Club" in 1714–15 (see *ante*, p. 115). This may seem to be supported by Pope's statement, when reprinting it in his *Works . . . In Prose. Vol. II*, 1741, to the effect that Gay "had some hand" in its composition; although he did not mention Gay's name when he ascribed it to himself in the *Miscellanies. The Second Volume*, 1742. But whatever its origins, after so many years Pope would certainly have revised it—or recast it if needs be—before publishing it in 1727.

The text is that of *1727*, which is in verbal agreement with *1742*.

IX.
COUPLETS ON WIT.

i.

BUT our Great Turks in wit must reign alone
And ill can bear a Brother on the Throne.

Title] MS omits.
2 a Brother] no living *written above in MS.* on] near *written above.*

ii.

Wit is like faith by such warm Fools profest
Who to be savd by one, must damn the rest.

1 Wit like religion is with spleen profest; Wit has its Bigotts, who can bear no jest; Wit like religion by such Fools profest *MS variants.*

iii.

Some who grow dull religious strait commence
And gain in morals what they lose in sence.

iv.

Wits starve as useless to a Common weal
While Fools have places purely for their Zeal.

v.

Now wits gain praise by copying other wits
As one Hog lives on what another sh——.

vi.

Woud you your writings to some Palates fit
Purge all your verses from the sin of wit
For authors now are so conceited grown
They praise no works but what are like their own

Preserved in the *Homer MSS* on the versos of rough drafts of lines from his translation of the *Iliad* (Book VIII). Echoes or anticipations of at least four of them are found later or earlier in different works of his—for which reason the appearance of the first of them embedded in the "Atticus" lines is of less significance than has been suggested (for a discussion of this couplet and its parallels, see *ante*, p. 144). This page of manuscript was first published, with the caption: "Lines copied from Mr. *Pope*'s Hand-writing, on a Scrap of Paper", in *Additions to the Works of Alexander Pope, Esq;* Vol. I. 1776, which also included some deleted or incomplete lines omitted from the present volume.

i.] For earlier and later parallels, see *ante*, p. 144.

ii.] Cf. *Ess. on C.*, ll. 396–7:
> Thus Wit, like Faith, by each man is apply'd
> To one small sect, and all are damn'd beside.

v.] Pope used "this filthy Simile" again in *Ep. to Sat.*, II 171 ff. (see Vol. IV, p. 323).

vi. 3–4. *For authors . . . own.*] Cf. Epigram: "On *James Moore Smythe*" (p. 300).

9

X.
LINES ON *CURLL*.

So when Curll's Stomach the strong Drench o'ercame,
   (Infus'd in Vengeance of insulted Fame)
Th' Avenger sees, with a delighted Eye,
His long Jaws open, and his Colour fly;
And while his Guts the keen Emeticks urge,   5
Smiles on the Vomit, and enjoys the Purge.

These lines, a parody of Addison's famous simile of the avenging angel in
The Campaign, ll. 287ff., have survived only on the original title-page of Pope's
*A Full and True Account of a Horrid and Barbarous Revenge by Poison on the Body of
Mr. Edmund Curll, Bookseller* (1716), and are now for the first time reprinted and
included in his poems. The event they celebrate occurred early in the quarrel
between Pope and Curll, and was provoked by Curll, who, having previously
irritated Pope by the piratical publication of some of his verse, now offended
Lady Mary W. Montagu in like manner. Pope resolved to revenge her by
tricking Curll into drinking an emetic, and then wrote a ridiculous report of
the episode in this pamphlet. See *Prose Works*, Vol. I, pp. xciv–cix.

The text follows that of the first edition, *1716*.

XI.
IMITATION OF *TIBULLUS*.
(Lib. i. Eleg. iv.)

Here stopt by hasty Death, Alexis lies,
   Who crost half Europe, led by Wortley's eyes!

Found in a letter (10 November 1716) written to Lady Mary W. Montagu
when she was travelling across Europe to Constantinople. After talking of
following her, Pope proceeds: "But if my Fate be such, that this Body of mine
(which is as ill-matched to my Mind as any wife to her husband) be left behind
in the journey, let the Epitaph of Tibullus be set over it.

        Hic jacet immiti consumptus morte Tibullus,
          Messalam, terra, dum sequitur que, mari."

Whereupon the above imitation in English follows.

The text is that of Pope's autograph in the Pierpont Morgan Library, New
York.

XII.
LINES ON MR. *HATTON*'s CLOCKS.

Fʀᴏᴍ hour to hour melodiously they chime
With silver sounds, and sweetly tune out time.

Found in a letter from Pope to Caryll, dated 18 February 1718, transcribed by the latter (BM MS Add. 28618). It is introduced in these words: "I am lately fallen acquainted with Mr. Hatton . . . yᵉ greatest manager of Time in yᵉ Universe. This Measurer of Moments, to whom Hours is literally precious because they get him money, is not only yᵉ most ingenious, but also yᵉ most civil person I ever met with. . . I believe his very Clocks speak in a softer tone than those of others; to say they strike is too boisterous a word. No,"—Whereupon follows the couplet. The fame of Hatton the clock-maker seems to have survived only in Pope's letter, which further states that he had married the daughter of Peter My (or Mee), and flourished in Duke Street near Lincoln's Inn Fields.

The text is that of the transcript.

2. *silver sounds*] Cf. *The Rape of the Lock*, I 18.

EPITAPH
Designed for Mr. *DRYDEN*'s Monument.

Tʜɪs *SHEFFIELD* rais'd. The sacred Dust below
Was *DRYDEN* once: The rest who does not know?

Title] *Supplied from MS.*
2 *DRYDEN*] Drydens *MS.*

Lord Oxford's transcript: Welbeck Abbey; and another contemporary transcript: BM MS Harl. 7316.

Miscellany Poems. Vol. I. By Mr. Pope. 5th Edition, 1726 (and 1727; and 6th Edition, 1732).

The Works of Mr. Alexander Pope. Vol. II. 1735 (folio and quarto).

The Works of Alexander Pope, Esq; Vol. II. 1735 (octavo).

Ethic Epistles, Satires, &c. . . . Written by Mr. Pope. 1735.

Ethic Epistles, to Henry St. John L. Bolingbroke. Written in the Year 1732. 1735.

The Works . . . Vol. II. Containing his Epistles and Satires. 1735 (and 1736).

A General Dictionary. P. Bayle. Vol. VIII. 1739.

The Works . . . Vol. II. Containing his Epistles, &c. 1739 (both editions).

The Works . . . Vol. II. Part I. Containing his Epistles, &c. 1740 (and 1743).
The Works. Ed. Warburton. Vol. VI. 1751.

On Rowe's burial in Westminster Abbey, he was placed beside Dryden's tomb which had no memorial beyond "a rude and nameless stone". Pope's "hint" in his epitaph on Rowe (see *ante*, p. 209), that this was scandalous caused the Duke of Buckingham to erect a monument to Dryden, for which Pope wrote this couplet. Later Pope changed his mind, and composed "the plain inscription now upon it, being only the name of that great Poet".

The epitaph, hitherto printed only in a footnote to the epitaph on Rowe, is here printed for the first time as a separate entity, with the title given it in Lord Oxford's transcript.

The text is that of *1726*, with a collation from Lord Oxford's transcript (*MS*). There are no variants in subsequent editions.

2. *silver sounds*] Cf. *The Rape of the Lock*, ii. 18.

EPISTLE.

TO

ROBERT Earl of *OXFORD*,
and Earl MORTIMER.

S UCH were the Notes, thy once-lov'd Poet sung,
'Till Death untimely stop'd his tuneful Tongue.
Oh just beheld, and lost! admir'd, and mourn'd!
With softest Manners, gentlest Arts, adorn'd!
Blest in each Science, blest in ev'ry Strain!　　5
Dear to the Muse, to HARLEY dear——in vain!
For him, thou oft hast bid the World attend,
Fond to forget the Statesman in the Friend;
For *Swift* and him, despis'd the Farce of State,
The sober Follies of the Wise and Great;　　10
Dextrous, the craving, fawning Crowd to quit,

Title] *MS and 1722 read:* To the Right Honourable, Robert, Earl of Oxford and Earl Mortimer.
2 'Till] When *MS*.

And pleas'd to 'scape from Flattery to Wit.
      Absent or dead, still let a Friend be dear,
(A Sigh the Absent claims, the Dead a Tear)
Recall those Nights that clos'd thy toilsom Days,   15
Still hear thy *Parnell* in his living Lays:
Who careless, now, of Int'rest, Fame, or Fate,
Perhaps forgets that OXFORD e'er was Great;
Or deeming meanest what we greatest call,
Beholds thee glorious only in thy Fall.   20
      And sure if ought below the Seats Divine
Can touch Immortals, 'tis a Soul like thine:
A Soul supreme, in each hard Instance try'd,
Above all Pain, all Passion, and all Pride,
The Rage of Pow'r, the Blast of publick Breath,   25
The Lust of Lucre, and the Dread of Death.
      In vain to Desarts thy Retreat is made;
The Muse attends thee to the silent Shade:
'Tis hers, the brave Man's latest Steps to trace,
Re-judge his Acts, and dignify Disgrace.   30
When Int'rest calls off all her sneaking Train,

12 to 'scape] escape *MS, 1735.*
13 still let a] let either *MS.*
15 Still think on those gay Nights of toilsome Days, *MS.*
21 And] Yet *MS.*
24 Passion,] Anger, *MS, 1722–7.*
28 the silent] thy silent *1743.*
      Fame, and the Muse, pursue thee to the Shade. *MS.*
29 hers] theirs *MS.*
31–40 *MS concludes thus:*
      Wait, to the Scaffold, or the silent Cell,
      When the last lingring Friend has bid farewell.
      Tho' Int'rest calls off all her sneaking Train,
      Tho' next the Servile drop thee, next the Vain,
      Tho' distanc't one by one th' Oblig'd desert,
      And ev'n the Grateful are but last to part;
      My Muse attending strews thy path with Bays,

And all th' Oblig'd desert, and all the Vain;
She waits, or to the Scaffold, or the Cell,
When the last ling'ring Friend has bid farewel.
Ev'n now she shades thy Evening Walk with Bays,   35
(No Hireling she, no Prostitute to Praise)
Ev'n now, observant of the parting Ray,
Eyes the calm Sun-set of thy Various Day,
Thro' Fortune's Cloud One truly Great can see,
Nor fears to tell, that MORTIMER is He.   40

(A Virgin Muse, not prostitute to praise).
She still with pleasure eyes thy Evening Ray,
The calmer Sunsett of thy Various Day;
One truly Great thro' Fortune's Cloud can see,
And dares to tell, that Mortimer is He.

32 And all] When all *1722–35.*
40 *1722 adds at foot: Sept. 25. 1721. A. POPE.*

Pope's autograph: Longleat, Portland Papers, XIII.
Contemporary transcript: BM MS Harl. 7316; Bodl. Rawl. MSS Poet. 153.
Poems on Several Occasions. Written by Dr. Thomas Parnell . . . And Published by Mr. Pope. 1722 (and later editions).
Miscellaneous Poems and Translations. 4th Edition, 1722.
Miscellany Poems. 5th Edition, 1726 (and 1727; 6th Edition, 1732).
The Works . . . To which are added, I. Cooper's-Hill . . . Dublin, 1727.
The Works of Mr. Alexander Pope. Volume II. 1735 (folio and quarto).
The Works of Alexander Pope, Esq; Vol. II. 1735 (octavo).
The Works . . . Vol. II. Containing his Epistles and Satires. 1735 (and 1736).
Ethic Epistles, Satires, &c. . . . Written by Mr. Pope. 1735.
Ethic Epistles, to Henry St. John L. Bolingbroke. Written in the Year 1732. 1735.
The Works . . . Vol. II. Containing his Epistles, &c. 1739 (both editions).
The Works . . . Vol. II. Part I. Containing his Epistles, &c. 1740 (and 1743).
A Collection of Moral and Sacred Poems. J. Wesley. Vol. I. 1744.
The Works. Ed. Warburton. Vol. VI. 1751.

Parnell died in October 1718, bequeathing to Pope, "almost with his dying Breath", the publication of his poems. A note to the *Iliad*, dated 25 March 1720 (printed in G. Tillotson, "Pope's 'Epistle to Harley' ", *Pope and his Contemporaries: Essays presented to George Sherburn*, 1949), suggests that the book would soon be ready. But it was not until 25 September 1721 that the first draft of this poem was written to serve as a dedication, and not until a month later that Pope wrote to the Earl of Oxford for permission to dedicate:

From my Ld Harley's in Dover Street.
Octob^r 21, 1721.

My Lord,

Your Lordship may be surpriz'd at the liberty I take in writing to you; tho you will allow me always to remember, that you once permitted me that honour, in conjunction with some others who better deserv'd it. Yet I hope, you will not wonder I am still desirous to have you think me your gratefull & faithful Servant; but I own I have an Ambition yet farther, to have Others think me so; which is ye Occasion I give your Lordship the trouble of this. Poor Parnell, before he dyed, left me ye charge of publishing these few Remains of his: I have a strong Desire to make them, their Author, and their Publisher, more considerable, by addressing & dedicating 'em All, to You. There is a pleasure in bearing Testimony to Truth; and a Vanity perhaps, which at least is as excusable as any Vanity can be. I beg you My Lord, to allow me to gratify it, in prefixing this paper of honest Verses to ye Book. I send the Book itself, wch I dare say you'l receive more Satisfaction in perusing, than you can from any thing written upon ye Subject of yourself. Therfore I am a good deal in doubt, whether you will care for such an addition to it? I'll only say for it, that tis ye only Dedication I ever writ, & shall be, whether you permit it or not: For I will not bow the knee to a Less Man than my Lord Oxford, & I expect to see no Greater in my Time.

After all, if y^r Lordship will tell my Lord Harley that I must not do this, you may depend upon a total Suppression of these Verses (the only Copy whereof I send you) But you never shall suppress that Great, sincere, & entire, Admiration & Respect, with wch I am always My Lord, Your most faithful, most obedient; & most humble Servant

A. Pope.

To Pope's letter Oxford replied:

Bramton Castle, Nov. 6, 1721.

I received your packet, which could not but give me great pleasure, to see you preserve an old friend in your memory; for it must needs be very agreeable to be remember'd by those we highly value. But then how much shame did it cause me, when I read your very fine verses inclos'd? My mind reproach'd me how far short I came of what your great friendship and delicate pen would partially describe me. You ask my consent to publish it: to what streights does this reduce me? I look back indeed to those evenings I have usefully and pleasantly spent, with Mr. Pope, Mr. Parnel, Dean Swift, the Doctor, &c. I should be glad the world knew You admitted me to your friendship: And since your affection is too hard for your judgment, I am contented to let the world know how well Mr. Pope can write upon a barren subject. I return you an exact Copy of the verses, that I may keep the Original, as a testimony of the only Error you have been guilty of. I hope very speedily to embrace you in London, and to assure you of the particular esteem and friendship wherewith I am Your, &c.

Oxford.

The original manuscripts of both the dedication and Pope's covering letter are preserved at Longleat, the former being endorsed in Oxford's hand: "Alexander Pope Esqʳ / His dedication. / Original. / 1721" and the latter: "From Alex. Pope Esqr. / Octoʳ: 21: 1721 / With His verses." The dedication later became an "Epistle", and its humble origin as mere "preliminary matter" was largely buried out of sight in Pope's explanatory footnote to the title.

The copy-text adopted is that of *1722*, into which later revisions have been incorporated. Collations are given from the autograph (*MS*), and printed editions.

Title: This Epistle was sent to the Earl of Oxford with Dr. Parnelle's Poems published by our Author, after the said Earl's Imprisonment in the Tower and Retreat into the Country, in the year, 1721. [P. *1740–51*.] See Biog. App., Harley, Parnell (Vol. IV).

3. See Virgil, *Æn.*, vi 87of., and parallels cited by Tillotson, *op. cit.*

9–15. Referring to the meetings of the Scriblerus Club, also recalled in Oxford's letter above.

23–6. Cf. Swift, *Drapier's Letters* (ed. Davis, 1935, p. 127), where Oxford is described as "the greatest, the wisest, and the most uncorrupt Minister, I ever conversed with".

27. *Desarts*] i.e., his family seat at Brampton-Bryan in Herefordshire.

31. The force of the image will not be appreciated unless it is recognized that "sneak" and "snake" were homophones at this time.

EPITAPH

On the Honble SIMON HARCOURT,

Only Son of the Lord Chancellor HARCOURT: *at the Church of* STANTON-HARCOURT *in* Oxfordshire, *1720.*

To this sad Shrine, who'er thou art, draw near,
  Here lies the Friend most lov'd, the Son most dear:
Who ne'er knew Joy, but Friendship might divide,
  Or gave his Father grief, but when he dy'd.

How vain is Reason, Eloquence how weak,   5
  If *Pope* must tell what *HARCOURT* cannot speak?
Oh let thy once-lov'd Friend inscribe thy Stone,
  And with a Father's Sorrows mix his own!

2 If ever Friend, if ever Son were dear! *MS, H*; . . . was dear! *S–H, 1726*; . . . Son . . . Friend were dear; *1724a, A.* lov'd] wept *1724b, 1730.*

3 Here lies the Youth who ne'r his Friend deny'd; *MS, S–H, H, A, 1724a, 1726.*

4 Or] Nor *1724b.* 6 If] When *MS, 1724a, b, H.*

7 Oh let] Let then *MS, 1724a, A.* Yet let *1724b, 1730.*

8 Sorrows] Sorrow *1730.*

9f. *1724b* has this additional couplet:

> Ah, no! 'tis vain to strive—It will not be.
> No Grief, that can be told, is felt for THEE.

Pope's autograph: Longleat, Portland Papers, XIII.
The Inscription in Stanton Harcourt Church, Oxon. [1724.]
Contemporary transcripts: BM MSS Harl. 7316, Add. 28101.
The London Journal. 17 October 1724.
The St. James's Evening Post. 15–17 October 1724.
The Whitehall Evening-Post. 15–17 October 1724.
The Plain Dealer. 13 November 1724.
Miscellany Poems. Vol. I. 5th Edition, 1726 (and 1727; 6th Edition, 1732).
The Works . . . To which are added, I. Cooper's-Hill . . . Dublin, 1727.
A Collection of Epigrams. 1727 (and Vol. I, 2nd Edition, 1735).
Miscellaneous Poems, By Several Hands. D. Lewis. 1730.
The Works of Mr. Alexander Pope. Volume II. 1735 (folio and quarto).
The Works of Alexander Pope, Esq; Vol. II. 1735 (octavo).
Ethic Epistles, Satires, &c. . . . Written by Mr. Pope. 1735.
Ethic Epistles, to Henry St. John L. Bolingbroke. Written in the Year 1732. 1735.
The Works . . . Vol. II. Containing his Epistles and Satires. 1735 (and 1736).
The Weekly Oracle. 8 November 1735.
Mr. Pope's Literary Correspondence. Vol. V. 1737.
The Works . . . Vol. II. Containing his Epistles, &c. 1739 (both editions).
The Works . . . Vol. II. Part I. Containing his Epistles, &c. 1740 (and 1743).
Joe Miller's Jests. 5th Edition. 1742 (and later editions).
The Agreeable Companion. 1745.
The Works. Ed. Warburton. Vol. VI. 1751.

Jack Sheppard's escape from Newgate gaol early on Friday morning, 16 October 1724 establishes priority of publication between three copies of this epitaph issued the following day. *The London Journal*, a weekly paper, printed the previous Saturday's news, but gave only a line and a half to the first news of Sheppard's exploit; whereas both the other papers contain news of the current Saturday, and devote much space to Sheppard, the *St. James's* giving him twenty-three lines, and the *Whitehall* twenty-eight plus a further four lines of the latest news of his doings. From which it appears that *The London Journal* was issued some hours before the other two, and thus contained the first printing of the epitaph.

9*

The Honourable Simon Harcourt died in France in the summer of 1720, and his body was brought home and buried in the church of Stanton-Harcourt. Two years later Pope submitted a draft of the epitaph to Lord Harcourt. His reply, dated 6 December (printed in the Pope correspondence) contains some slight criticism of the piece, in apology for which he goes on to say "When once your epitaph is set up there can be no alteration of it." He forgot Pope's craze for "correctness". By 1726 only two lines stand as they stood when cut in stone; the rest have been corrected, some of them two or three times.

The copy-text chosen is that of *1726*, the first for which Pope was certainly responsible. Later substantive variants have been incorporated. Collations are given from Pope's autograph (*MS*), the inscription at Stanton-Harcourt (*S-H*), the first printed version in *The London Journal* (*1724a*), the ten-line version in *The Plain Dealer* (*1724b*), the transcripts in the Harleian (*H*), and Additional (*A*) MSS, and the printed versions of *1726* and *1730*.

3. var. "I doubt whether the word, *deny'd*, in the third line, will justly admit of that construction which it ought to bear (*viz.*) renounced, deserted, *&c.*" Harcourt to Pope, *New Letters of Mr. Alexander Pope*, 1737, pp. 93–4.

6. The Harleian scribe reports that Harcourt "insisted that Mr Pope's own name should be in the Verses". Harcourt objected to what seems to have been the first MS version of the line, "Harcourt stands dumb, and Pope is forc'd to speak". "I can't perfectly . . . reconcile my self to the first part of that line," he wrote to Pope (*op. cit.*); "and the word *forc'd* (which was my own . . .) seems to carry too doubtful a construction for an Epitaph."

To Mrs. M. B. on her Birth-day.

OH be thou blest with all that Heav'n can send,
    Long Health, long Youth, long Pleasure, and a Friend:
Not with those Toys the female world admire,

Title Written, June yᵉ 15th. On Your Birth-Day. *1723. MS.* The Wish; to a Young Lady on her Birth-Day. *1724.* The Wish. Sent to Mrs. M. B. on her Birth-Day, June 15. *1726; S reads* A Wish. To Mrs. M. B. Sent on Her Birth-Day June 15. [*1728*]. To a Lady, on her Birth-Day, 1723. *1769.*

1–4 *omm. L, 1735.*

2 Health] Life *1724, 1769.* Youth] Health *1724.*

3 female world] Woman-World *MS, S, 1724, 1769*; Female Race [*1728*].

Riches that vex, and Vanities that tire.
With added years if Life bring nothing new,   5
But like a Sieve let ev'ry blessing thro',
Some joy still lost, as each vain year runs o'er,
And all we gain, some sad Reflection more;
Is that a Birth-day? 'tis alas! too clear,
'Tis but the Fun'ral of the former year.   10
  Let Joy or Ease, let Affluence or Content,
And the gay Conscience of a life well spent,
Calm ev'ry thought, inspirit ev'ry Grace,
Glow in thy heart, and smile upon thy face.
Let day improve on day, and year on year,   15
Without a Pain, a Trouble, or a Fear;
Till Death unfelt that tender frame destroy,
In some soft Dream, or Extasy of joy:

5–10 *MS, S, 1724, 1726 and 1769 omit.* [*1728*] *reads*:
  Not as the World its pretty Slaves rewards,
  A Youth of Frolicks, an Old-Age of Cards;
  Fair to no Purpose, artful to no End,
  Young without Lovers, old without a Friend;
  A Fop their Passion, but their Prize a Sot;
  Alive, ridiculous; and dead, forgot!
 5 years] Days *L*. bring] give *L, 1735.*
 6 blessing] Pleasure *L, 1735.*
 8 sad Reflection] pensive Notion *L.*
 9 that] this *L, 1735*. 'tis alas! too] ah! tis sadly *L.*
11–20 *omm. L, 1735.* 11 or ... or] and ... and *1724.*
12 gay] glad *MS, 1724.*
13 inspirit] and spirit *1724.*
14 smile upon] sparkle in *1724.*
16 Pain] Sigh *1724.* Fear] Tear *1724.*
17 *MS, S, 1769 read*: And ah! since Death must that dear Frame
 destroy, *1724 reads*: And, oh! when Death shall that fair Face
 destroy, *1726 reads*: And ah! since Death must that lov'd frame
 destroy,
18 *MS, S, 1726 read*: Die by a sudden Extacy of Joy!
 1724 and 1769 read: Die by some sudden Extasy of Joy.

Peaceful sleep out the Sabbath of the Tomb,
And wake to Raptures in a Life to come.   20

19 In some soft Dream may thy mild Soul remove, *MS, 1724, 1769*:
    Or let thy soul in some soft dream remove, *1726*.
    Let the mild soul in some soft dream remove, *S*.
20 And be thy latest Gasp a Sigh of Love. *MS, S, 1724, 1726, 1769*.

(*a*) text; 14 lines, beginning "Oh be thou blest".

Pope's autographs: (i) Morgan Library Book 4239, 1723; (ii) Mapledurham
MSS 4, 1723; (iii) Arthur A. Houghton, Jr., 1723; (iv) Longleat, Portland
Papers, XIII, 1725; (v) BM MS Stowe 964, 1725.
Contemporary transcripts: BM MS Harl. 7316; BM MS Add. 28101.
The British Journal. 14 November 1724.
The Whitehall Evening-Post. 12–14 November 1724.
Miscellany Poems. Vol. I. 5th Edition, 1726.
The Christian Poet. 1735.
Letters of the late Alexander Pope, Esq. To a Lady . . . 1769.

(*b*) text; 20 lines, containing six lines used by Moore Smythe.

The Rival Modes. A Comedy. By James Moore Smythe. 1727. [Six lines only.]
Miscellanies. The Last Volume. 1727 (published 8 March 1728), and later
editions.
The Works . . . With Explanatory Notes and Additions. Vol. I. Dublin. 1736.
Miscellanies. The Fourth Volume. Consisting of Verses . . . 1742 (and later editions).

(*c*) text; 10 lines beginning "With added days".

Contemp. transcripts: Longleat, Portland Papers, XVIII; BM MS Harl. 7316.
The St. James's Chronicle. 28–30 September 1775.
Additions to the Works of Alexander Pope, Esq. Vol. I, 1776.

(*d*) text; 6 lines, beginning "With added days".

Letters of Mr. Pope, and Several Eminent Persons. 1735.
Mr. Pope's Literary Correspondence. Vol. I. 1735 (and 3rd Edition, 1735).
Letters of Mr. Alexander Pope. ("Works . . . In Prose".) 1737.
The Works . . . Vol. VI. Containing . . . Letters. 1737 (and 2nd Edition, 1737).
The Works . . . Vol. IV. Part II. Containing . . . Letters. 1742.
The Works. Ed. Warburton. Vol. VII. 1751.

(*e*) text; 20 lines, beginning "Oh be thou blest".

*The Works . . . Vol. II. Part II. Containing . . . Pieces . . . Written since the former
Volumes*. 1738.
A Choice Collection of Poetry. 1738.
The Works . . . Vol. II. Containing his Epistles, &c. 1739.
The Gentleman's Magazine. June 1739.

The Works . . . Vol. II. Part I. Containing his Epistles, &c. 1740 (and 1743).

The Works. Ed. Warburton. Vol. VI. 1751.

This note summarizes the full account of the history of these lines given in *New Light*, pp. 195–206. But see p. 465.

The original version (text *a*) was written on 15 June 1723 and sent as a birthday greeting to Martha Blount at Mapledurham, where the earliest autograph MS is still preserved. Pope subsequently made several corrected transcripts, one of which was sent to Judith Cowper and was eventually published with his letters to her in 1769. Another transcript reached the editor of the *British Journal*, where it appeared on 14 November 1724, a few hours ahead of an identical copy in the *Whitehall Evening-Post*. The authorized version of the "*a*" text was published in *Miscellany Poems*, 1726, the fifth edition of Pope's first miscellany.

A new version (text *b*) was printed in *Miscellanies. The Last Volume*, embodying a radically altered conclusion which contained six lines already used by James Moore Smythe in his play *The Rival Modes*, 1727. This version continued to appear in successive editions of the Pope-Swift *Miscellanies* at a time when the poem was undergoing further changes; while the six lines used by Moore Smythe were transferred to the second *Moral Essay*, 1735.

In the meantime Pope had written some verses (text *c*), probably in reflection upon his birthday, 21 May 1724.

The transcript in the Portland papers reads as follows:

On a Late Birth Day. 1724.

With added Days, if Life bring nothing new,
But, like a Sieve, let ev'ry Pleasure thro';
Some Joy still lost, as each vain Year runs o'er,
And all we gain, some pensive Notion more!
Is this a Birth-Day? ah! 'tis sadly clear,
'Tis but the Fun'ral of the former Year.
If there's no Hope, with kind, tho' fainter ray
To gild the Evening of our future Day;
If ev'ry Page of Life's long Volume tell
The same dull Story—Mordaunt! thou did'st well.

They were never printed in his lifetime; but a corrected version of the first six lines (text *d*) was transcribed in a letter to Gay written after Congreve's death in January 1729, published with his *Letters* in 1735, and subsequently embodied in a new version of Martha Blount's birthday verses (text *e*). This final revision was probably made shortly before its appearance in the *Works* 1738.

The text follows that of Pope's last revision in *The Works . . . Vol. II. Part II*, 1738, with which Warburton (*1751*) agrees; and collations are given of the earlier versions, viz. (*a*) text: the Mapledurham manuscript (*MS*), the Stowe manuscript (*S*), *The British Journal* (*1724*), *Letters* (*1769*); (*b*) text: *Miscellanies. The Last Volume* [*1728*]; and (*c*) text: the "reflection" on his own birthday in the Longleat transcript (*L*) and in *Letters* (*1735*).

The Odyssey of Homer. Vols. I, II, III

[Books I–XIV; published April 1725; vols. IX, X]

INSCRIPTION.

NYMPH of the Grot, these sacred Springs I keep,
   And to the Murmur of these Waters sleep;
Ah spare my Slumbers, gently tread the Cave!
And drink in silence, or in silence lave!

3 Ah spare my Slumbers,] Whoe'er thou art, ah *1735 all edd.*
4 And drink] Ah bathe *1735 all edd.*

Inscription in the Grotto at Stourhead, Wiltshire.
Mr. Pope's Literary Correspondence. Vol. I. 1735 (and 3rd Edition, 1735).
Letters of Mr. Pope . . . Vol. I. 1735.
Letters of . . . Pope ["Works . . . In Prose", Vol. I.] 1737.
The Works . . . Vol. VI. Containing . . . Letters. 1737 (and 2nd Edition, 1737).
The Works . . . Vol. IV. Part II. Containing . . . Letters. 1742.
Memoirs of . . . Alexander Pope, Esq. W. Ayre. Vol. II. 1745.
The Works. Volume VIII. Being . . . Letters. Ed. Warburton. 1751.
Biographia Britannica. Vol. V. 1760.
The Festoon. 1766 (and later editions).
The Christmas Treat. 1767.
The Life of Alexander Pope, Esq. O. Ruffhead. 1769.
   When writing to Edward Blount on 2 June 1725, Pope concluded a description
of his grotto at Twickenham, in which he talked of its "little dripping murmur,
and the aquatic idea of the whole place", with these words: "It wants nothing to
compleat it but a good statue with an inscription, like that beautiful antique one
which you know I am so fond of,

> *Hujus Nympha loci, sacri custodia fontis*
>   *Dormio, dum blandæ sentio murmur aquæ.*
> *Parce meum, quisquis tangis cava marmora, somnum*
>   *Rumpere, sive bibas, sive lavare, tace.*"

After which followed the lines given above. How soon after 1725 these lines were
inscribed in the grotto at Stourhead is not known; but as early as 1766 they
appeared without the Latin original in *The Festoon* with the following title: *Under
the Statue of a Water-Nymph at Stourhead, Somersetshire: By Mr. Pope. From the Latin.*

The house at Stourhead is the family seat of the Hoares who were bankers in Pope's time; and as he had some—and Gay and Swift many—business dealings with them, it is possible that these lines were obtained more or less directly from Pope at quite an early date. The inscription omits all punctuation, but otherwise agrees with the text here printed, which incorporates the corrections of *1737* into the copy-text of *1735*.

The Latin inscription, whose antiquity is doubtful, enjoyed much popularity, and is said to exist in such widely separated places as Rome, the banks of the Danube, and county Durham. Where Pope met it is uncertain, but he might have found it (as Dr H. W. Garrod informs me) in Grævius, *Thesauros Antiquitatum Romanorum*, XII 859; J. B. Ferretius, *Musæ Lapidariæ Antiquorum in Marmoribus Carmina* (1672), p. 108; D. Humphreys, *Antiquity Explained by the Learned Father Montfaucon* (1721), I 243; and in several anthologies. See P. Burman, *Anthologia Veterum Latinorum Epigrammatum et Poematum* (1759), Lib. I, Ep. LXXXI, p. 62; O. Kurz, "Huius Nympha Loci", *Journal of Warburg Inst.*, XVI (1953), 171–7.

EPITAPH

On Lady *KNELLER.*

ONE day I mean to Fill Sir Godfry's tomb,
    If for my body all this Church has room.
Down with more Monuments! More room! (she cryd)
For I am very large, and very wide.

Pope's autograph: MS in possession of Mr D. F. Hyde, New York.
The Correspondence of Sir Thomas Hanmer, Bart. 1838.
The Works. Ed. Elwin and Courthope. "Correspondence", Vol. X. 1886.

This epitaph is found in the second of four letters written in 1725 by Pope to Lord Strafford protesting against Lady Kneller's proposal to erect in the church at Twickenham "a vast three-hundred-pound pile", or, in other words, a large sculptured memorial of Sir Godfrey, with effigies of him and herself, in "ye best place in ye church to be seen at a distance". But a wall tablet already stood there commemorating Pope's father, and Pope, who had promised Kneller to write his epitaph (see *post*, p. 312), was, as the correspondence shows, disturbed at this project. The letter, dated 6 July, introduces the epitaph thus: "—Since I am got into another page, I will fill it with an Epitaph, wch over & above my promise to Sr G. may serve for my Lady's: & justly celebrates her pious Design of making as Large a figure on ye Tomb as Sr G. himself."

The text follows that of the autograph.

1. *Sir Godfry*] See Biog. App., Vol. IV, Kneller.

On a certain Lady at Court.

I KNOW the thing that's most uncommon;
    (Envy be silent and attend!)
I know a Reasonable Woman,
    Handsome and witty, yet a Friend.

Not warp'd by Passion, aw'd by Rumour,   5
    Not grave thro' Pride, or gay thro' Folly,
An equal Mixture of good Humour,
    And sensible soft Melancholy.

"Has she no Faults then (Envy says) Sir?"
    Yes she has one, I must aver: 10
When all the World conspires to praise her,
    The Woman's deaf, and does not hear.

Title On Mrs Howard by Mr Pope *MS.*
  1 the] a *MS.*
  5 *MS reads:* Not led by custome, mov'd by Rumour,
  6 or gay] nor gay *MS.*   9 Sir] *omitted in MS.*
  11 to praise her] her praise *MS.*
  12 The Woman's] Alas she's *MS.*

Contemporary transcripts: Longleat, Portland Papers, xviii; and BM MS
Harl. 7316.
  Miscellanies. The Third Volume. 1732 (and later editions).
  *Miscellanies In Prose and Verse. The Third Volume. To which are added Several
Poems* . . . 2nd Edition. Dublin. 1733.
  A Supplement to Dr. Swift's and Mr. Pope's Works. 1739.
  Miscellanies. The Fourth Volume. Consisting of Verses . . . 1742 (and later editions).
  The Works. Ed. Warburton. Vol. VI. 1751.
  Nameless in all the printed texts, the "certain Lady" of the title was identified
(with no evidence adduced) by Warton as Mrs Howard, afterwards Countess of
Suffolk. Corroboration of his statement has recently been found in Lord Oxford's
papers—the Longleat and British Museum transcripts of the poem being both
entitled: *On Mrs. Howard by Mr. Pope.* Mrs Howard had long been a friend of
Pope's when he wrote a letter to Swift (dated 14 September 1725), in which the
germ of the poem seems to be contained. He is endeavouring to persuade Swift to
pay a visit to England, and, after speaking of other inducements, continues: "I

can also help you to a lady who is as deaf, though not so old as yourself; you will be pleased with one another . . . though you do not hear one another . . . What you will most wonder at is, she is considerable at court, yet no party woman, and lives in court, yet would be easy, and make you easy." To which Swift replies (29 September): "The lady whom you describe to live at court, to be deaf and no party woman, I take to be mythology . . ." Pope never acknowledged this trifle; but the witness of the two contemporary transcripts, together with Warburton's attribution, can leave little doubt of his authorship. The date is more uncertain, but, in view of the letter above quoted, the year 1725 is tentatively adopted.

The text follows that of *1732*, with collations from the Longleat and Harley transcripts (*MS*).

Title: *a certain Lady*] See introductory note, also Vol. III 11, p. 63.

LINES
On SWIFT's Ancestors.

JONATHAN Swift
    Had the gift,
      By fatherige, motherige,
And by brotherige,
To come from Gutherige,   5
But now is spoil'd clean,
And an Irish Dean.
In this church he has put
A stone of two foot;
With a cup and a can, Sir,   10
In respect to his grandsire;
So Ireland change thy tone,
And cry, O hone! O hone!
For England hath its own.

The Works of Jonathan Swift . . . Ed. Scott. Vol. I. The Memoirs. 1814 (and 1824).

The Poetical Works of Alexander Pope. Ed. Carruthers. Vol. IV. 1854.

The occasion of this *jeu d'esprit* is best told in the words of Sir Walter Scott:

Swift put up a plain monument to his grandfather, and also presented a cup to the church of Goodrich, or Gotheridge. He sent a penciled elevation of the

monument, (a simple tablet,) to Mrs Howard, who returned it with the follow-
ing lines, inscribed on the drawing by Pope. The paper . . . is indorsed in
Swift's hand, "Model of a monument for my grandfather, with Mr. Pope's
roguery." [The lines follow.] The lines, originally written in pencil by Pope,
are traced over in ink by Dr Lyons, as a memorandum bears. It occurred
amongst Dr Lyons' manuscripts.

The monument, a plain slab under the altar, bears these words:

Here lyeth the body of M. Thomas Swift who dyed the second day of May
1658 aged 62 years & tenne moneths who was vicar of Goodridge 34 years.

The cup, or chalice, is still treasured in the church, but is now used only at festi-
vals; it has two inscriptions, the more interesting of which reads:

Tho : Swift hujus Eccles. Vica^r notus in historijs ob ea quæ fecit et passus est pro Car^o 1mo
ex hoc Calice ægrotantibus propinavit. Eundem calicē Ionat^h Swift. S T D Decan. Eccles.
S^{ti} Pat^r Dublⁿ. Thomæ ex filio nepos huic Eccles. in perpetuum dedicat 1726.

While there cannot be much doubt about the authenticity of this little piece,
yet, as Pope neither published nor owned it, and as the original document has
vanished, it must remain an attributed poem, the date of which—if Pope had
anything to do with it—was approximately that of the occasion it celebrates. In
the spring of 1726, after an absence of twelve years, Swift had come to England
on a visit of some months to Pope and his friends; and he is generally supposed on
his way to London to have broken his journey at Goodrich to deposit there his
grandfather's chalice, and arrange for the erection of the monument.

The text is that of *1814*—of which there were two issues: one with the spelling
brotheridge and *Gutheridge,* and one having *brotherige* and *Gutherige,* which is here
followed. The title is supplied by the editor.

The Odyssey of Homer. Vols. IV, V

[Books xv–xxiv; published June 1726; vol. x]

Receipt to make SOUP.
For the Use of Dean SWIFT.

TAKE a knuckle of Veal
  (You may buy it, or steal,
In a few peices cut it,
In a Stewing pan put it.
Salt, pepper and mace   5
Must season this knuckle,
Then what's join'd to a place,
With other Herbs muckle;
That which killed King Will,
And what never stands still,   10
Some sprigs of that bed
Where Children are bred,
Which much you will mend, if
Both Spinage and Endive,
And Lettuce and Beet,   15
With Marygold meet;
Put no water at all;
For it maketh things small:
Which, lest it should happen,
A close cover clap on;   20

Title] *The full heading reads:* Postscript. Just arrived from Twicken-
  ham (as I am assured) Mr. Pope's Receipt to make Soup. For
  the Use of Dean Swift. *MS reads:* A Receipt to make a Soop,
  from Mr Pope to Dean Swift in Irel^d. *The Broadside reads:* A
  Receipt to make a Soop. By Mr. Pope to D—n S—t. *1766 has no
  title, but the introductory sentence speaks of it as a* "receipt for stewing
  veal" [*see below*].
 3 a few] small *BS*; a few *A*.
 4 Stewing pan] Stewing-Pan *BS*; a Stew Pan *A*.
 12 Where] Whence *A*.
 13 Which...will] This...will *MS*; This...may *A*.
 16 With] And *BS*. Marygold] Marigolds *A*.   18 For it] That *BS*.

Put this pot of Wood's mettle
In a hot boiling kettle,
And there let it be,
(Mark the Doctrine I teach)
About——let me see,——   25
Thrice as long as you preach.
So skimming the fat off,
Say Grace, with your hat off
O then, with what rapture
Will it fill Dean and Chapter!   30

21 this] your *MS, BS;* in *A.*
22 In a] That's a *A.* hot boiling] boiling hot *A.*
27 So] Then *BS.*   29 O] And *A.*

Gay's autograph (?): BM MS Add. 4804-6.
Contemporary transcripts: Longleat, Portland Papers, xvii and xviii; BM
MS Harl. 7316; The Pierpont Morgan Library MS, New York; H. Williams
MS; BM MSS Add. 4456, 21544, 34109, and 32463; Sotheby Cat. 13 May 1963,
Lot 238.
  A Receipt To make a Soop. By Mr. Pope to D—n S—t. [Broadside, n.d.]
  Atterburyana. 1727. [Published 5 January 1727, *W.E.P.*]
  The Altar of Love. 1727. [Published 1 April 1727, *E.P.*] (and 3rd Ed., 1731.)
  The Weekly Journal. 30 September 1727.
  Mr. Pope's Literary Correspondence. Vol. II. 1735 (and 2nd Edition, 1735).
  A Choice Collection of Poetry. J. Yarrow. 1738.
  The Gentleman's Magazine. June 1760.
  Letters, written by Jonathan Swift . . . Vol. II. Edited by T. Wilkes. 1766.
Swift's visit to England in the summer of 1726—the first for twelve years—
caused much rejoicing and junketting among his old friends, in particular Pope
and Gay, who were his chief hosts. Shortly after Swift's return to Ireland in
August, Pope, as the correspondence of the group shows, met with an accident.
One night in early September, the coach in which Bolingbroke was sending him
home overturned while crossing a stream, and he was rescued from drowning in
it only at the cost of severe cuts sustained in his right hand when one of the foot-
men "pulled him out through the window". As the news of the accident spread,
Pope's friends gathered round, and despite the absence of Swift, Twickenham
again became the centre of much hospitality. One day, a dish of stewed veal was
prepared according to a recipe from Pulteney's cook, Monsieur Devaux, which
was greatly "approved of at one of our Twickenham entertainments". It was
probably on this occasion that Pope suggested sending Swift a composite letter,
in the production of which he was joined by Gay, Bolingbroke, Mrs Howard, and

Pulteney. Pope's own contribution to this letter (which was called the "Cheddar letter" by Bolingbroke, because, as an old note explains, a cheese of that name is made from the contributions of several dairies) was a rhymed version of the recipe. Since Gay tells Swift how at this time he was helping Pope as "his Emanuensis, which you know is no idle Charge"; and since Swift, addressing Gay in his answer (15 October) to the Cheddar letter, says: "The last part of your part relates to my Twickenham host; therefore I shall answer it to him," which seems to prove that Gay had written for his temporarily incapacitated friend. This explains why a poem which practically all contemporary reference gives to Pope is found in Gay's autograph and was subsequently attributed to Gay. See further *New Light*, pp. 225–31.

The text follows that of Gay's transcript, with collations from *Atterburyana* (*A*), Lady Margaret Harley's transcript (*MS*), the undated broadside (*BS*), and the "Cheddar" version (*1766*).

Title] *1766* has the following footnote: "This is supposed to be the receipt of Mr. Pulteney's cook, mentioned in the preceding [but missing] part of this letter, versified."

7. Vulg. Salary [Gay].

9. Suppos'd Sorrell [Gay]. The supposed name of King William III's horse which indirectly caused his death by stumbling.

10. This is by Dr Bentley thought to be Time or Thyme [Gay]. Pope's antipathy to Richard Bentley, the critic, is well known (see Biog. App., Vol. IV). This is yet another gibe at his method of annotation.

11f. Parsley. *Vide* Chamberlaine [Gay]. Presumably Hugh Chamberlen the younger (1664–1728), a fashionable London man-midwife, like his father and grandfather before him. The fable is still told to inquisitive children, in some parts of the country, that they were born in their mother's parsley bed.

21. *Wood's mettle*] Of this composition [*i.e. The Drapier Letters*] see the Works of the copper farthing Dean [Gay].

26. *Thrice . . . preach*] Which we suppose to be near four hours [Gay].

Presentation Verses to Nathaniel Pigott

T HE Muse this one Verse to learn'd Pigot addresses,
    In whose Heart, like his Writings, was never found flaw;
Whom Pope prov'd his Friend in his two chief distresses,
    Once in danger of Death, once in danger of Law.

                                    Sept. 23. 1726.

Title] *Supplied by the editor.*

Pope's autograph: Harvard College Library.
Harvard Library Bulletin, January 1948.

This quatrain was written by Pope in a copy of his translation of the *Odyssey* (1726) presented to Nathaniel Pigott and now in the Harvard College Library. It is printed here with the kind permission of the librarian. Pigott (1661–1737), a Barrister at Law, lived at Whitton near Twickenham, and it was evidently to his house that Pope was carried after the accident in which his coach was upset when crossing the river Crane on a dark night in September 1726 (see G. Sherburn, "An Accident in 1726", *Harvard Library Bulletin*, Jan. 1948, pp. 121–3).

2. Pigott's principal work, *A Treatise of Common Recoveries*, was not published till 1739.

3f. These lines are echoed at the end of a letter to Caryll (February 1729/30), where Pope writes: "You will give my hearty services to Mr. Pigott when you know I rank him as one of my best friends, for he once in a manner saved my life, and has always taken care to keep me out of law." To what legal service Pope referred is not known.

The CAPON'S TALE:

To a LADY *who father'd her Lampoons upon her Acquaintance.*

I N *Yorkshire* dwelt a sober Yeoman,
  Whose Wife, a clean, pains-taking Woman,
Fed num'rous Poultry in her Pens,
And saw her Cocks well serve her Hens.

A Hen she had, whose tuneful Clocks   5
Drew after her a Train of Cocks:
With Eyes so piercing, yet so pleasant,
You would have sworn this Hen a Pheasant.
All the plum'd Beau-monde round her gathers;

Title To a Lady . . . Acquaintance] To Lady Mary Wortley. *MS.*
1 *MS reads:* There liv'd in Wales a goodly Yeoman,
9f. *MS reverses the order of these two lines.*
9 All] While *MS.*

Lord! what a Brustling up of Feathers!   10
Morning from Noon there was no knowing,
There was such Flutt'ring, Chuckling, Crowing:
Each forward Bird must thrust his head in,
And not a Cock but would be treading.

    Yet tender was this Hen so fair,   15
And hatch'd more Chicks than she could rear.

    Our prudent Dame bethought her then
Of some Dry-Nurse to save her Hen;
She made a Capon drunk: In fine
He eat the Sops, she sipp'd the Wine: 20
His Rump well pluck'd with Nettles stings,
And claps the Brood beneath his Wings.

    The feather'd Dupe awakes content,
O'erjoy'd to see what God had sent.
Thinks he's the Hen, clocks, keeps a Pother,   25
A foolish Foster-Father-Mother.

    Such, Lady *Mary*, are your Tricks;
But since you hatch, pray own your Chicks:
You should be better skill'd in Nocks,
Nor like your Capons, serve your Cocks.   30

13 must] will *MS*.
18 save her] serve for *MS*.
19 drunk: In fine] drunk in fine, *MS*.
20 sipp'd] drank *MS*.
27–30 *Instead of these lines the MS concludes thus:*
        Such, Lady Mary, are your Tricks,
        To make us Capons own your Chicks.
        Hatch on, fair Lady! make dispatch,
        Our Tails may smart for what you hatch.
        The Simile yet one thing shocks,
        We're not two Capons but two Cocks.

Pope's autograph: Pierpont Morgan Library, New York.

Miscellanies. The Last Volume. 1727 (and later editions).

A Supplement to Dr. Swift's and Mr. Pope's Works. Dublin. 1739.

Miscellanies. The Fourth Volume. Consisting of Verses. 1742 (and later editions).

Although Pope himself never acknowledged *The Capon's Tale*, and although it has never been attributed to him by his editors, the discovery of his autograph copy with its sub-title "To Lady Mary Wortley", is suggestive of his authorship. Corroborative evidence of this attribution is not entirely lacking. For instance, the poem seems never to have been printed in Pope's lifetime except by his own act and consent; for it is found only in the successive issues of his and Swift's *Miscellanies*, which he edited, and which he made the repository of many of his anonymous pieces. Further, in the later editions of that collection the poem is distinguished with an asterisk to signify it was not by Swift. And finally, in the two copies of "The Last Volume" which Pope's friend, Lord Oxford, gave to his wife and daughter, the poem is marked (presumably on information supplied by him) "By Mr. Pope". Swift has occasionally been suggested as the author of the piece, but with no reason advanced. Nevertheless, in the last six lines of the autograph version, Pope was unquestionably speaking for another as well as himself. Thus, although Pope undoubtedly held the pen and had a known grievance against Lady Mary, it is not impossible that Swift had some hand in the poem; he was at least staying with Pope at Twickenham in the summers of 1726 and 1727, the two most probable dates of composition.

The occasion of the satire is unknown (see *New Light*, pp. 246f.). But whatever it was, the poem was evidently written after Pope and Lady Mary had become antagonized. And if, as appears, it was written with Swift's complicity (whether active, or—more probably—passive), the date of composition must be that of one of those two visits to England, with the chances in favour of 1726, the year of his longer and more felicitous residence with Pope at Twickenham. The piece is therefore tentatively dated 1726.

The text is that of its first printing (which agrees verbally with the last in Pope's lifetime, *1742*), with collations from the autograph (*MS*).

Title: *To a Lady*] Lady Mary Wortley Montagu. See introductory note, and Biog. App., Vol. IV.

THE
DISCOVERY:
OR,
The SQUIRE *turn'd* FERRET.
An Excellent New
BALLAD.

To the Tune of *High Boys! up go we*; *Chevy Chase*; Or what you please.

MOST true it is, I dare to say,
  E'er since the Days of *Eve*,
The weakest Woman sometimes may
  The wisest Man deceive.

For *D——nt* circumspect, sedate,   5
  A *Machiavel* by Trade,
Arriv'd Express, with News of Weight,
  And thus, at Court, he said.

At *Godliman*, hard by the *Bull*,
  A Woman, long thought barren,   10
Bears *Rabbits*,—Gad! so plentiful,
  You'd take her for a Warren.

These Eyes, quoth He, beheld them clear:
  What, do ye doubt my View?
Behold this Narrative that's here;   15
  Why, Zounds! and Blood! 'tis true!

Some said that *D—gl—s* sent should be,
  Some talk'd of *W—lk—r's* Merit,
But most held, in this Midwifery,
  No Doctor like a FERRET.   20

But *M–l–n–x*, who heard this told,
  (Right wary He and wise)
Cry'd sagely, 'Tis not safe, I hold,
  To trust to *D——nt's* Eyes.

A Vow to God He then did make   25
    He would himself go down,
St. A–d–re too, the Scale to take
    Of that *Phænomenon*.

He order'd then his Coach and Four;
    (The Coach was quickly got 'em)   30
Resolv'd this *Secret* to explore,
    And search it to the *Bottom*.

At *Godliman* they now arrive,
    For Haste they made exceeding;
As Courtiers should, whene'er they strive   35
    To be inform'd of Breeding.

The good Wife to the Surgeon sent,
    And said to him, Good Neighbour,
'Tis pity that two Squires so Gent—
    Should come and lose their Labour.   40

The Surgeon with a *Rabbit* came,
    And first in Pieces cut it;
Then slyly thrust it up *that same*,
    As far as Man could put it.

(Ye *Guildford* Inn-keepers take heed   45
    You dress not such a *Rabbit*,
Ye Poult'rers eke, destroy the Breed,
    'Tis so unsav'ry a-Bit.)

But hold! says *Molly*, first let's try,
    Now that her Legs are ope,   50
If ought within we may descry
    By Help of Telescope.

The Instrument himself did make,
　　He rais'd and level'd right,
But all about was so opake,　　　　　　55
　　It could not aid his Sight.

On Tiptoe then the Squire he stood,
　　(But first He gave Her Money)
Then reach'd as high as e'er He cou'd,
　　And cry'd, I feel a CONY.　　　　　60

Is it alive? *St. A–d–re* cry'd;
　　It is; I feel it stir.
Is it full grown? The Squire reply'd,
　　It is; see here's the FUR.

And now two Legs *St. A–d–re* got,　　65
　　And then came two Legs more;
Now fell the Head to *Molly*'s Lot,
　　And so the Work was o'er.

The Woman, thus being brought to Bed,
　　Said, to reward your Pains,　　　70
St. A–nd–re shall dissect the Head,
　　And thou shalt have the Brains.

He lap'd it in a Linnen Rag,
　　Then thank'd Her for Her Kindness;
And cram'd it in the Velvet Bag　　　75
　　That serves his R—l H——

That Bag—which *Jenny*, wanton Slut,
　　First brought to foul Disgrace;
Stealing the Papers thence she put
　　Veal-Cutlets in their Place.　　　80

O! happy would it be, I ween,
   Could they these *Rabbits* smother;
Molly had ne'er a Midwife been,
   Nor she a shameful Mother.

Why has the Proverb falsly said   85
   Better two Heads than one;
Could *Molly* hide this *Rabbit*'s Head,
   He still might shew his own.

FINIS

Contemporary transcripts: BM MS Lansd. 852 and Bodleian 8° E. 128 Linc.
The Discovery: or, The Squire turn'd Ferret. An Excellent New Ballad. To the Tune of High Boys! up go we ... 1727 (published 20 December 1726); also *The Second Edition,* 1727 (published 24 December 1726).
   The British Journal. No. 224. 7 January 1727.
   The 'Squire turn'd Ferret. An excellent new Ballad. 1727 (published 26 January 1727).
   The Honey-Suckle; Consisting of Original Poems. Vol. I. 1734.
   The story of Mary Toft (or Tofts) of Godalming, who was said to have given birth from time to time to a (variously specified) number of rabbits, began to appear in the newspapers towards the end of November 1726. *The Whitehall Evening-Post* of 26 November printed an "Extract of Letter from Mr. John Howard, Surgeon and Man-Midwife at Guildford, to a near Relation ... dated 22 November 1726," in which he reported the delivery of the seventeenth rabbit, and then went on to say that "last Tuesday" [15 November] Mr St André, his Majesty's Anatomist, who had been present and had assisted Howard, was "satisfied in the Truth of the wondrous Delivery: As was Mr. Molineaux, Secretary to the Prince, who was also here... On Sunday [20 November] I had Mr. Ahlers, Surgeon to the King's Household ... he took Part of the sixteenth Rabbit from her; ..." The affair created the greatest excitement. Not only doctors were interested, but "Great Numbers of the Nobility have been to see her" (*London Journal,* 3 December). Almost everyone who had to do with the inquiry, and many who had not, rushed into print, defending themselves or attacking each other for their credulity or incredulity, while the ribald gave a loose to their astonishing imaginations with pen and pencil in broadside, squib, and picture. Nor did the excitement speedily die down. For although the woman confessed to the fraud on 7 December, and was "ordered to be prosecuted ... for being a vile Cheat and Imposter" on 13 December (*The St. James's Evening Post,* 13 December); and although a sixteen-line recantation by Howard appeared in *The Whitehall Evening-Post* of 17 December, the spate of publications, serious and comic, continued well into 1727; and among them, on 20 December 1726, appeared an

anonymous pamphlet of eight pages folio, entitled *The Discovery*, and post-dated 1727.

Pope informed Spence a year or two before his death that "the ballad on the rabbit-woman [was written] by him and Mr. Pulteney" (*Anecdotes*, p. 285); but the piece itself seems hitherto to have escaped recognition. His interest in the affair had awakened early, and had preceded the flood of pamphlets; and on 5 December, before it was known that the woman had confessed the cheat, he was writing to Caryll: "I want to know w^ht faith you have in ye miracle at Guildford; not doubting but as you past thro' that Town, you went as a Philosopher to in-vestigate, if not as a Curious Anatomist to inspect, that wonderfull Phenomenon. All London is now upon this occasion as it generally is upon all others, Devided into Factions about it." Only two or three months previously St André himself had been attending Pope for an accident to his hand, about which Dr Arbuthnot also was being consulted. As he was still in great pain from it as late as December, it is not impossible that he had obtained medical opinion on the Toft affair as well as his hand—and if from St André, more than one opinion, for the surgeon pub-licly renounced his previous belief on 8 December.

Search has revealed only two poems on the affair which might be regarded as ballads, the first in time being *The Discovery* above-mentioned, which is called a ballad in its title and is of the true ballad form often used by Pope; the second is a piece called *St. A–d–e's Miscarriage*, which, written in a free and easy anapaestic measure with a "Derry down, down" burden quite unlike any known verse of Pope's, implies that it is a ballad in its last line. And of these two ballads the only serious claimant for Pope's hand is *The Discovery*. It was written and published at the height of the excitement, when Pope himself was interested in the subject, and was actually writing about it—if the contemporary attribution of another "un-known" poem to him may be believed. This is a rhymed epistle to Dr Arbuthnot (see *post*, p. 444), which in the MS is entitled "P— to A—t, with a Song. 19 Dec. 1726". It is not unlikely, therefore, seeing that *The Discovery* was published on the following day (20 December), that the "Song" which Pope was sending with his epistle to Arbuthnot was an advance copy of the morrow's ballad. On the other hand *St. A–d–e's Miscarriage* was not published until 2 February 1727, at which time there is nothing to suggest that Pope was still interested in the affair; besides which it would have been quite out of character for Pope to have lagged behind the event so much as this. Another fact pointing to *The Discovery* rather than the *Miscarriage*, is that Pope spoke of "*the* ballad on the rabbit-woman", as though no other would be known to his hearer, Spence, who, in his turn, thought exactly the same about his future readers, or he would surely have explained which ballad he meant. For *The Discovery* ran to at least three editions, was widely known, and has survived in several forms—in pamphlet, newspaper, and printed miscellany, besides MS copies; in marked contrast to the *Miscarriage*, which has survived only in two transcripts in collections of Mary Toft material in the Bodleian. This, at least, could not have been "*the* ballad" of the period. Furthermore, the *Miscar-riage* was not included in Lord Oxford's manuscript miscellany in which both *The Discovery* and the epistle to Arbuthnot are to be found; and lastly, Pope's surgeon, St André, is let off very lightly in *The Discovery*, whereas in the *Miscarriage* he is made to bear the brunt of the ridicule.

Whatever Pulteney's contribution to the ballad may have been, it is probable, to judge from *Duke upon Duke* (see p. 217), that Pope held the pen.

The text follows that of the first edition of the pamphlet, with collations from the Oxford transcript in Lansd. 852 (*MS*).

Title] In the MS the title ends with the following motto:

> *Heu me! per Urbem (nam pudet tanti mali)*
> *Fabula quanta fui!*   Hor.

5. *D—nt*] "Mr. Davenant", who wrote the first account (4 November 1726) seen by St André, of Mary Toft's being "lately delivered of five Rabbets".

9. *Godliman*] Godalming, near Guildford.

17. *D–gl–s*] James Douglas (1675–1742) Physician and Obstetrist, Physician to Queen Caroline, present at Mary Toft's confession, and wrote a pamphlet on the affair (see Biog. App., Vol. V). Pope mentions "his soft, obstetric hand" (*Dunciad* IV 394).

18. *W–lk–r*] Perhaps Dr Middleton Walker, "an eminent Man-midwife", who died 11 November 1732 (*Gent. Mag.*, II 1082).

21. *M–i–n–x*] Samuel Molyneux (1689–1728). Astronomer, experimented in the construction of telescopes; was Secretary to the Prince of Wales; accompanied St André on his visit to Mary Toft (see introductory note).

27. *St. A–d–re*] Nathaniel St André (1680–1776). Surgeon and Anatomist to the King.

49. *Molly*] *i.e.* Molyneux (see above).

76. *R—l H—*] His Royal Highness, the Prince of Wales, to whom Molyneux was secretary.

77–80. It is not known to what incident this stanza alludes.

EPIGRAM, *in a Maid of Honour's* Prayer-Book.

WHEN *Israel's* Daughters mourn'd their past Offences,
    They dealt in *Sackcloth*, and turn'd *Cynder-Wenches*:
But *Richmond's* Fair-ones never spoil their Locks,
    They use white Powder, and wear Holland-Smocks.
O comely Church! where Females find *clean Linen*   5
    As decent to *repent* in, as to *sin* in.

Title] *1727 reads:* Epigram 1726.

3 But . . . never] The Richmond-Fair-ones ne'er will *1727.*

  Locks] Looks *1727.*

5 comely] beauteous *1727.*   find] think *1727.*

Miscellanea. In Two Volumes. Vol. I. 1727. [Published 14 July 1726.]

A Collection of Epigrams. 1727. [Published 25 November 1726] (and 2nd Edition, 1735).

Miscellanies. The Last Volume. 1727. [Published 8 March 1728] (and later editions).

A Supplement to Dr. Swift's and Mr. Pope's Works. Dublin. 1739.

Miscellanies. The Fourth Volume. Consisting of Verses . . . 1742 (and later editions).

The Merry Medley. [1750?]

The Sports of the Muses. Vol. II. 1752.

A Collection of Select Epigrams. J. Hackett. 1757.

The Festoon. 1766 (and later editions).

The Christmas Treat. 1767.

This epigram is ascribed to Pope on the authority, ultimately, of Edward Harley, Earl of Oxford, whose wife and daughter presumably acted on it when they marked the piece "By Mr. Pope" in the copies of *Miscellanies. The Last Volume* which Oxford gave them, and which are still preserved at Welbeck Abbey. Pope's long intimacy with the Harleys must give their attribution definite importance; and that Oxford had special knowledge in this instance would seem to be suggested by the fact that in his day the epigram was always printed anonymously—as it has been ever since. Nor is the attribution intrinsically improbable: the poem is in Pope's manner, and as, in the 1742 edition of their *Miscellanies*, the poem is marked with an asterisk to denote it was *not* by Swift, and as it has never been claimed either by or for Gay or Arbuthnot, Pope is unquestionably the most probable choice of the four contributors-in-chief. One other point suggesting his authorship is the alteration made in the title of the piece; for it was almost certainly he, who, as editor of the *Miscellanies*, changed it from *Epigram 1726*—which is what Curll had called it—to *Epigram, In a Maid of Honour's Prayer-Book*, which was first used in Pope's collection, and for which there is no authority in the epigram itself. The date of the piece was apparently stated in its first title, but the occasion has eluded much search.

The text follows that of *Miscellanies* 1727/8, with collations from the first printing in *Miscellanea*, 1727.

2. *Cynder-Wenches*] A female whose occupation it is to rake cinders from among ashes, *OED*. Cf. rhymed letter to Cromwell, p. 26, and Gay, *Trivia*, II 131: "In the black form of cinder-wench she came."

3. *Richmond's Fair-ones*] The maids of honour at the court of the Prince and Princess of Wales.

5. *Linen*] For other allusions to women's under-linen, clean or dirty, see *Artimesia*, 6 (p. 48); *Mor. Ess.*, II 24; *Imit. Hor.*, *Ep.* I 164.

Verses on *GULLIVER's TRAVELS.*

Contemporary transcript: Welbeck Abbey, Harley Papers. [No. II.]

Travels into Several Remote Nations of the World . . . By Lemuel Gulliver . . . To which are prefix'd Several Copies of Verses . . . never before printed. Vol. I. The Second Edition. 1727. [Nos. I–IV, published 4 May (*The Post-Boy*). Re-issued with No. v a little later.]

Several Copies of Verses On Occasion of Mr. Gulliver's Travels. Never before Printed. 1727. [Nos. I–IV, published 6 May (*The St. James's Evening-Post*). Re-issued with No. v a little later.]

Poems Occasion'd by Reading the Travels of Captain Lemuel Gulliver. Dublin. 1727 [Nos. I–IV.]

Miscellanies. The Last Volume. 1727. [Nos. I, II, IV, published 8 March 1728] (and later editions).

Travels into several Remote Nations of the World . . . By Lemuel Gulliver . . . Vol. I. 1731. [Nos. I–V.]

The Works of J. S.[wift] *. . . Volume III.* Dublin. 1735. [Nos. I, II, IV.] (Also Vol. III. Dublin. 1738, and some later editions of Swift's *Works*.)

Miscellanies. The Fourth Volume. Consisting of Verses. 1742. [Nos. I, II, IV] (and later editions).

The Poetical Works of John Gay. ("Bell's Edition"), 1777. [Nos. I, II, IV. The same three poems appear also in some later editions of Gay's works.]

The Works. Ed. Roscoe. Vol. VI. 1824. [Nos. I–IV.]

The earliest known allusion to the "Gulliver" poems is found in a letter from Pope to Swift, written about 18 February 1727 (Ball, III 380n.), as follows: "You received, I hope, some commendatory verses from a horse [see No. III below] and a Lilliputian [No. I] to Gulliver; and an heroic Epistle of Mrs. Gulliver [No. IV]. The bookseller would fain have printed them before the second edition of the book [*Gulliver's Travels*], but I would not permit it without your approbation: nor do I much like them. You see how much like a poet I write. . ." Of Swift's reply nothing has survived; but that he consented to their inclusion in his book is inferred from their presence in the forefront of the "Second Edition". This book, and *Several Copies of Verses on Occasion of Mr. Gulliver's Travels* contain, not three poems as might have been expected from Pope's letter, but in some copies four, and in others five, and all alike anonymous. The same four poems appear in all copies of both issues (and always in the same order as in the present volume), while the fifth piece, *The Words of the King of Brobdingnag*, invariably consists of a gummed insertion of two leaves printed from the same setting of type (except for an alteration of page numbers and catchword). It would seem, therefore, that subsequent to Pope's letter to Swift, two further additions were made to the "commendatory verses"; namely, the pieces entitled *The Lamentation of Glumdalclitch*, which was written in time to be set up with those named by Pope, amongst which it is placed second in both issues; and *The Words of the King,* which was not set up in type until after both issues of the *Verses* had been printed and published.

There can be no reasonable doubt that Pope wrote at least the three poems he sent to Swift because, although he nowhere acknowledged them, his words to Swift are an implicit confession of authorship; and two of them contain matter which can be paralleled elsewhere in his poems. Such parallels are present to a still greater degree in the fifth poem, *The Words of the King*, which, in addition, contain other characteristic mannerisms of Pope's. Rival ascriptions of these poems to Gay and others, discussed in *New Light* (pp. 237–41), may be dismissed, and a working hypothesis that covers all the known facts attempted.

It appears then that Pope, who had not seen *Gulliver's Travels* before its publication on 28 October 1726 ("Upon my word I never saw it, till printed."— Letter to Caryll, December 1726), was so much excited on reading it that he wrote three poems on various characters in it, and sent them to Swift in February, with the suggestion (no matter whose it was originally) that they should appear in the forefront of the second edition of the book. And when Swift fell in with the idea, Pope, possibly with Gay at his elbow (they had often worked together before), proceeded to draft the first sketch of yet another Gulliver poem, *The Lamentation*, a copy of which presently reached Lord Oxford, probably by Gay's instrumentality and not impossibly in his autograph; for in Pope and Gay's earlier collaborations Gay often acted as secretary; indeed, only a few months previously, after Pope's accident, Gay had been for a time his amanuensis (see *ante*, p. 255). In this way, Lord Oxford could have obtained his copy of the poem, and himself corrected its errors of transcription. It would also seem to be about this time that Gay wrote his *Answer* to Pope's *Lilliputian Ode*, which Pope apparently did not like well enough to use. Thus, sooner or later, Lord Oxford, or his ladies, knowing or hearing that Gay had been occupied on poems about *Gulliver's Travels*, came to assume that *The Lamentation* and one or both of its companion pieces in *Miscellanies* were his likewise, and marked them in their copies accordingly. Finally, shortly after the four "commendatory verses" had been published both "single" and "prefixt", Pope was moved to write the fifth poem, *The Words of the King*, which was at once set up in type, printed by itself on a quarter sheet, and inserted in the unsold copies of both issues of the *Verses*. For a more sceptical review of the evidence, suggesting that the poems are of composite authorship, see G. Sherburn, "the 'Copies of Verses' about Gulliver", *Texas Studies in Literature and Language*, III (1961), 3–7.

The text of Nos. I, II, and IV is that of *1742*, with collations from the first printing (*1727a*) and *Miscellanies* (*1727b*), and also, for No. II, from the Oxford transcript (*TS*). The text of Nos. III and V is that of the first printing only, there being no later authentic variants. The original paragraphs have for the sake of uniformity been retained for all five pieces.

10

I.

To QUINBUS FLESTRIN, *the* Man-Mountain.

A Lilliputian Ode.

IN Amaze
    Lost, I gaze!
Can our Eyes
Reach thy Size?
May my Lays   5
Swell with Praise
Worthy thee!
Worthy me!
Muse inspire,
All thy Fire!   10
Bards of old
Of him told,
When they said
Atlas Head
Propt the Skies: 15
See! and believe your Eyes!

    See him stride
Vallies wide:
Over Woods,
Over Floods.   20
When he treads,
Mountains Heads
Groan and shake;
Armies quake,
Lest his Spurn   25
Overturn
Man and Steed:

Title] *The first printing (1727a) reads :* To Quinbus Flestrin the Man-
Mountain. An Ode. By Titty Tit, Esq; Poet Laureat to his
Majesty of Lilliput. Translated into English.

Troops take Heed!
Left and Right,
Speed your Flight!　　　　　　30
Lest an Host
Beneath his Foot be lost.

Turn'd aside
From his Hide,
Safe from Wound　　　　　　35
Darts rebound.
From his Nose
Clouds he blows;
When he speaks,
Thunder breaks!　　　　　　40
When he eats,
Famine threats;
When he drinks,
Neptune shrinks!
Nigh thy Ear,　　　　　　45
In Mid Air,
On thy Hand
Let me stand,
So shall I,
Lofty Poet! touch the Sky.　　　　　　50

Title: *Quinbus Flestrin*] The Lilliputians' name for Gulliver.

17–24. *See him stride* . . .] There are interesting similarities of image and diction
in three other descriptions by Pope of a giant or god tramping over mountain and
forest (see *ante*, p. 217).

II.

The Lamentation of GLUMDALCLITCH, *for the Loss of* GRILDRIG.

A Pastoral.

SOON as *Glumdalclitch* mist her pleasing Care,
 She wept, she blubber'd, and she tore her Hair.
No *British* Miss sincerer Grief has known,
Her Squirrel missing, or her Sparrow flown.
She furl'd her Sampler, and hawl'd in her Thread,   5
And stuck her Needle into *Grildrig*'s Bed;
Then spread her Hands, and with a Bounce let fall
Her Baby, like the Giant in *Guild-hall*.
In Peals of Thunder now she roars, and now
She gently whimpers like a lowing Cow.   10
Yet lovely in her Sorrow still appears:
Her Locks dishevell'd, and her Flood of Tears
Seem like the lofty Barn of some rich Swain,
When from the Thatch drips fast a Show'r of Rain.

    In vain she search'd each Cranny of the House,   15
Each gaping Chink impervious to a Mouse.
"Was it for this (she cry'd) with daily Care
"Within thy Reach I set the Vinegar?
"And fill'd the Cruet with the Acid Tide,
"While Pepper-Water-Worms thy Bait supply'd;   20
"Where twin'd the Silver Eel around thy Hook,
"And all the little Monsters of the Brook.
"Sure in that Lake he dropt—My *Grilly*'s drown'd"—
She dragg'd the Cruet, but no *Grildrig* found.

Title] *TS reads:* Glumdalcliths Lamentation a Pastoral.
 4 her Sparrow] the sparrow *TS.*
 9 In] Like *TS.*   18 thy Reach] the reach *TS.*
22 And all] With all *TS.*
23 Sure . . . dropt—] He's dropt into the Lake, *TS.*

      "Vain is thy Courage, *Grilly*, vain thy Boast;   25
    "But little Creatures enterprise the most.
    "Trembling, I've seen thee dare the Kitten's Paw;
    "Nay, mix with Children, as they play'd at Taw;
    "Nor fear the Marbles, as they bounding flew:
    "Marbles to them, but rolling Rocks to you.   30

28 mix] mix'd *TS.*   29 fear the] fear'd their *TS.*
30 Rocks] *first written* stones, *corrected to* rocks *by Lord Oxford. TS.*
   Following l. 30 the transcript runs as follows to l. 70:

       Why did I not suspect Hippina's Muff,
       And search the shag of Thighatira's Ruff.
       These filthy Sluts, their Jordans ne'er abscond
       To them a piss-pot, but to thee a pond.
       Art thou in Spider's web, entangled hung?
       Or by some Flea with mortal venom stung?
       Dost thou bewilder'd wander all alone
       In the green Thicket of a Mossy stone?
       Or tumbl'd from the Toadstool's slippery round
       Perhaps all Maim'd lye grovelling on the ground?
       Or happier bosom'd in the Folded Rose,
       Or sunk within the peaches down repose?
       Or in a Bean-shell venture from the shore
       And brush the dangerous deep with strawy Oar?
       Within the Kingcup now his limbs are spread
       Or in the golden Cowslip's velvet head.
       O shew me, Flora, midst those sweets the Flower
       Where sleeps my Grildrig, in the fragrant Bower.
       Why did I trust him with that giddy Youth?
       None from a page can ever learn the truth.
       Perhaps neglected, on the dang'rous strand
       The swelling Billows bore him from the Land,
       Or vers'd in Courts, that money-loving Boy
       To some Lord's daughter sold the living Toy.
       Or rent him Limb from Limb in cruel play
       As children tear the wings of flys away.
       From place to place or'e Brodignack I'll roam
       And never will return, or bring him home.
       But none hath eyes to trace the passing wind,

"Why did I trust thee with that giddy Youth?
"Who from a *Page* can ever learn the Truth?
"Vers'd in Court Tricks, that Money-loving Boy
"To some Lord's Daughter sold the living Toy;
"Or rent him Limb from Limb in cruel Play,   35
"As Children tear the Wings of Flies away:
"From Place to Place o'er *Brobdingnag* I'll roam,
"And never will return, or bring thee home.
"But who hath Eyes to trace the passing Wind,
"How then thy fairy Footsteps can I find?   40
"Dost thou bewilder'd wander all alone,
"In the green Thicket of a Mossy Stone,
"Or tumbled from the Toadstool's slipp'ry Round,
"Perhaps all maim'd, lie grov'ling on the Ground?

How shall I then his Fairy footsteps find?
But all I fear thy little fancy roves
Of little Females and of little loves
Thy Pigmy Island and thy tiny Spouse
And the babes play-things that adorn thy house.
Doors, windows, chimneys and the spacious rooms
Equal in size, to Cells of honey-combs.
Dost thou for these now Float upon the Main?
Shall I ne'er bear thy self and house again?
And shall I set thee on my hand no more,
And see thee leap the lines and traverse o'er
My spacious palm in Stature scarce a Span
Mimick the Actions of a Real Man?
Shall I ne'er see thee turn my watches key
As Seamen at a Capstain Anchors weigh?
Or laugh to see thee walk with cautious tread,
A dish of Tea like Milk-pail on thy head.
Or mow from racy plumbs the savo'ry blew,
And swill in Acorn cups the morning dew,
Or gulp the yelks of Ants delicious eggs,
Or at the Glow-worm warm thy frozen legs?
Or chase the mite that bore thy cheese away,
And keep the rolling maggot at a bay.

"Dost thou, inbosom'd in the lovely Rose,   45
"Or sunk within the Peach's Down, repose?
"Within the King-Cup if thy Limbs are spread,
"Or in the golden Cowslip's Velvet Head;
"O show me, *Flora*, 'midst those Sweets, the Flow'r
"Where sleeps my *Grildrig* in his fragrant Bow'r!   50
    "But ah! I fear thy little Fancy roves
"On little Females, and on little Loves;
"Thy Pigmy Children, and thy tiny Spouse,
"The Baby Play-things that adorn thy House,
"Doors, Windows, Chimnies, and the spacious Rooms,
"Equal in Size to Cells of Honeycombs.   56
"Hast thou for these now ventur'd from the Shore,
"Thy Bark a Bean-shell, and a Straw thy Oar?
"Or in thy Box, now bounding on the Main?
"Shall I ne'er bear thy self and House again?   60
"And shall I set thee on my Hand no more,
"To see thee leap the Lines, and traverse o'er
"My spacious Palm? Of Stature scarce a Span,
"Mimick the Actions of a real Man?
"No more behold thee turn my Watches Key,   65
"As Seamen at a Capstern Anchors weigh?
"How wert thou wont to walk with cautious Tread,
"A Dish of Tea like Milk-Pail on thy Head?
"How chase the Mite that bore thy Cheese away,
"And keep the rolling Maggot at a Bay?"   70

    She said, but broken Accents stopt her Voice,
Soft as the Speaking Trumpet's mellow Noise:
She sobb'd a Storm, and wip'd her flowing Eyes,
Which seem'd like two broad Suns in misty Skies:
O squander not thy Grief, those Tears command   75
To weep upon our Cod in *Newfound-land*:

50 his] the *1727a*.
71 said] spoke *TS, 1727a*.
76 our] Fresh *TS*.

The plenteous Pickle shall preserve the Fish,
And *Europe* taste thy Sorrows in a Dish.

78 a Dish] her dish *TS, 1727a and b.*

11. *Yet...appears*] Cf. "How lovely sorrow seems", *Weeping*, 1.

21. *the Silver Eel*] Cf. *Windsor Forest*, 143, 341.

23. *Sure in that Lake ...*] This adverbial use of "Sure" is characteristic of Pope,
but not at all of Gay.

38. *And...home*] *i.e.* "I'll either bring him home, or will never return".

41–2. *wander... Mossy Stone*] Cf. *Dunciad* B, IV 450: "May wander in a wilder-
ness of Moss".

55f. *spacious Rooms ... Honeycombs*] Cf. V. *The Words of the King*, 29: "Thus
Honey-combs seem Palaces to Bees".

III.

To

Mr. LEMUEL GULLIVER,

The Grateful ADDRESS *of the Unhappy*
HOUYHNHNMS, *now in Slavery and*
Bondage in England.

To thee, we Wretches of the *Houyhnhnm* Band,
Condemn'd to labour in a barb'rous Land,
Return our Thanks. Accept our humble Lays,
And let each grateful *Houyhnhnm* neigh thy Praise.

O happy *Yahoo*, purg'd from human Crimes,   5
By thy sweet Sojourn in those virtuous Climes,
Where reign our Sires! There, to thy Countrey's Shame,
Reason, you found, and Virtue were the same.
Their Precepts raz'd the Prejudice of Youth,
And even a *Yahoo* learn'd the Love of Truth.   10

Art thou the first who did the Coast explore;
Did never *Yahoo* tread that Ground before?
Yes, Thousands. But in Pity to their Kind,

Or sway'd by Envy, or through Pride of Mind,
They hid their Knowledge of a nobler Race,   15
Which own'd, would all their Sires and Sons disgrace.

    You, like the *Samian*, visit Lands unknown,
And by their wiser Morals mend your own.
Thus *Orpheus* travell'd to reform his Kind,
Came back, and tam'd the Brutes he left behind.   20

    You went, you saw, you heard: With Virtue fraught,
Then spread those Morals which the *Houyhnhnms* taught.
Our Labours here must touch thy gen'rous Heart,
To see us strain before the Coach and Cart;
Compell'd to run each knavish Jockey's Heat!   25
Subservient to *New-market*'s annual cheat!
With what Reluctance do we Lawyers bear,
To fleece their Countrey Clients twice a Year?
Or manag'd in your Schools, for Fops to ride,
How foam, how fret beneath a Load of Pride!   30
Yes, we are slaves—but yet, by Reason's Force,
Have learnt to bear Misfortune, like a Horse.

    O would the Stars, to ease my Bonds, ordain,
That gentle *Gulliver* might guide my Rein!
Safe would I bear him to his Journey's End,   35
For 'tis a Pleasure to support a Friend.
But if my Life be doom'd to serve the Bad,
O! may'st thou never want an easy Pad!

                          Houyhnhnm.

8. For phrasing, cf. *Ess. on C.*, l. 135, "Nature and *Homer* were, he found, the same."

9. *the Prejudice of Youth*] Pope used this phrase again in *Epil. to Sat.*, 1 63.

17. *the Samian*] Pythagoras, the Greek philosopher, born at Samos, visited Egypt and many other countries to acquire knowledge.

10*

IV.
MARY GULLIVER *to Captain*
LEMUEL GULLIVER.

ARGUMENT. *The Captain, some Time after his Return, being re-*
tired to Mr. Sympson's *in the Country, Mrs.* Gulliver, *apprehending*
from his late Behaviour some Estrangement of his Affections, writes him
the following expostulating, soothing, and tenderly-complaining Epistle.

WELCOME, thrice welcome to thy native Place!
——What, touch me not? what, shun a Wife's Embrace?
Have I for this thy tedious Absence born,
And wak'd and wish'd whole Nights for thy Return?
In five long Years I took no second Spouse;   5
What *Redriff* Wife so long hath kept her Vows?
Your Eyes, your Nose, Inconstancy betray;
Your Nose you stop, your Eyes you turn away.
'Tis said, that thou shouldst cleave unto thy Wife;
Once *thou* didst cleave, and *I* could cleave for Life.   10
Hear and relent! hark, how thy Children moan;
Be kind at least to these, they are thy own:
Behold, and count them all; secure to find
The honest Number that you left behind.
See how they pat thee with their pretty Paws: 15
Why start you? are they Snakes? or have they Claws?
Thy Christian Seed, our mutual Flesh and Bone:
Be kind at least to these, they are thy own.

    Biddel, like thee, might farthest *India* rove;
He chang'd his Country, but retain'd his Love.   20
There's Captain *Pennel*, absent half his Life,
Comes back, and is the kinder to his Wife.
Yet *Pennell*'s Wife is brown, compar'd to me;
And Mistress *Biddel* sure is Fifty three.

13 Behold,] Be bold, *1727b*.   21 *Pennel*] Pannell *1727a a and b n.*
23 *Pennell*'s] Pannell's *1727a and b.*

Not touch me! never Neighbour call'd me Slut!   25
Was *Flimnap*'s Dame more sweet in *Lilliput*?
I've no red Hair to breathe an odious Fume;
At least thy Consort's cleaner than thy *Groom*.
Why then that dirty Stable-boy thy Care?
What mean those Visits to the *Sorrel Mare*?   30
Say, by what Witchcraft, or what Dæmon led,
Preferr'st thou *Litter* to the Marriage Bed?

Some say the Dev'l himself is in that *Mare*:
If so, our *Dean* shall drive him forth by Pray'r.
Some think you mad, some think you are possest   35
That *Bedlam* and clean Straw will suit you best:
Vain Means, alas, this Frenzy to appease!
That *Straw*, that *Straw* would heighten the Disease.

My Bed, (the Scene of all our former Joys,
Witness two lovely Girls, two lovely Boys)   40
Alone I press; in Dreams I call my Dear,
I stretch my Hand, no *Gulliver* is there!
I wake, I rise, and shiv'ring with the Frost,
Search all the House; my *Gulliver* is lost!
Forth in the Street I rush with frantick Cries: 45
The Windows open; all the Neighbours rise:
Where sleeps my Gulliver? *O tell me where?*
The Neighbours answer, *With the Sorrel Mare.*

At early Morn, I to the Market haste,
(Studious in ev'ry Thing to please thy Taste)   50
A curious *Fowl* and *Sparagrass* I chose,
(For I remember you were fond of those,)
Three Shillings cost the first, the last sev'n Groats;
Sullen you turn from both, and call for *Oats*.

36 will] would *1727a and b.*
52 remember] remember'd *1727a.*
54 turn . . . call] turn'd . . . call'd *1727a.*

Others bring Goods and Treasure to their Houses,   55
Something to deck their pretty Babes and Spouses;
My *only* Token was a Cup like Horn,
That's made of nothing but a Lady's *Corn*.
'Tis not for that I grieve; no, 'tis to see
The *Groom* and *Sorrel Mare* preferr'd to me!   60

These, for some Moments when you deign to quit,
And (at due distance) sweet Discourse admit,
'Tis all my Pleasure thy past Toil to know,
For pleas'd Remembrance builds Delight on Woe.
At ev'ry Danger pants thy Consort's Breast,   65
And gaping Infants squawle to hear the rest.
How did I tremble, when by thousands bound,
I saw thee stretch'd on *Lilliputian* Ground;
When scaling Armies climb'd up ev'ry Part,
Each Step they trod, I felt upon my Heart.   70
But when thy Torrent quench'd the dreadful Blaze,
King, Queen and Nation, staring with Amaze,
Full in my View how all my Husband came,
And what extinguish'd theirs, encreas'd my Flame.
Those *Spectacles*, ordain'd thine Eyes to save,   75
Were once my Present; *Love* that Armour gave.
How did I mourn at *Bolgolam*'s Decree!
For when he sign'd thy Death, he sentenc'd me.

When folks might see thee all the Country round
For Six-pence, I'd have giv'n a thousand Pound.   80
Lord! when the *Giant-Babe* that Head of thine
Got in his Mouth, my Heart was up in mine!
When in the *Marrow-Bone* I see thee ramm'd;
Or on the House-top by the *Monkey* cramm'd;
The Piteous Images renew my Pain,   85
And all thy Dangers I weep o'er again!
But on the *Maiden*'s *Nipple* when you rid,

59 no,] O, *1727a*.

Pray Heav'n, 'twas all a wanton Maiden did!
Glumdalclitch too!—with thee I mourn her Case.
Heav'n guard the gentle Girl from all Disgrace!   90
O may the King that one Neglect forgive,
And pardon her the Fault by which I live!
Was there no other Way to set him free?
My Life, alas! I fear prov'd Death to Thee!

O teach me, Dear, new Words to speak my Flame;   95
Teach me to wooe thee by thy best-lov'd Name!
Whether the Style of *Grildrig* please thee most,
So call'd on *Brobdingnag*'s stupendous Coast,
When on the Monarch's ample Hand you sate,
And hollow'd in his Ear Intrigues of State: 100
Or *Quinbus Flestrin* more Endearment brings,
When like a Mountain you look'd down on Kings:
If Ducal *Nardac*, *Lilliputian* Peer,
Or *Glumglum*'s humbler Title sooth thy Ear:
Nay, wou'd kind *Jove* my Organs so dispose,   105
To hymn harmonious *Houyhnhnm* thro' the Nose,
I'd call thee *Houyhnhnm*, that high sounding Name,
Thy Children's Noses all should twang the same.
So might I find my loving Spouse of course
Endu'd with all the *Virtues* of a *Horse*.   110

11–13. *thy Children . . . Behold, and count them*] Cf. *Dunciad* A, III 121f., written about the same time: "her progeny . . . Behold, and count them."

19ff. *Biddel, etc.*] Names of the Sea Captains mention'd in *Gulliver*'s Travels. [P. *1742*, also *1727b*.]

39–45. *My Bed . . . frantick Cries*] Pope had previously described a similar scene at least twice, with much the same images and phraseology: cf. *Eloisa to Abelard*, 233–48; and *Sapho to Phaon*, 145–60.

62. *at due distance*] Cf. *Ess. on C.*, 174: "Due distance reconciles . . ."

73. *Full in my View how all . . .*] Cf. *Eloisa to Abelard*, 127: "Full in my view set all . . ."

97–104. For phrasing cf. *Dunciad* A, I 17–22; see p. 307.

102. *look'd down on Kings*] The attitude of contempt for Kings is highly characteristic of Pope, and is so often repeated (*e.g. Imit. Hor.*, *Ep.* I i 106, 186, II i 417, *Imit. Donne*, IV 187) that Hawkins Browne made it the climax of his parody, *A Pipe of Tobacco*, 1735: "Come . . . let me taste Thee, unexcis'd by Kings."

V.

The WORDS of the
KING OF BROBDINGNAG,

As he held Captain GULLIVER *between his*
Finger and Thumb for the Inspection of
the Sages and Learned Men of the Court.

IN Miniature see *Nature*'s Power appear;
  Which wings the Sun-born Insects of the Air,
Which frames the Harvest-bug, too small for Sight,
And forms the Bones and Muscles of the Mite!
Here view him stretch'd. The Microscope explains,   5
That the Blood, circling, flows in human Veins;
See, in the Tube he pants, and sprawling lies,
Stretches his little Hands, and rolls his Eyes!

    Smit with his Countrey's Love, I've heard him prate
Of Laws and Manners in his Pigmy State.   10
By Travel, generous Souls enlarge the Mind,
Which home-bred Prepossession had confin'd;
Yet will he boast of many Regions known,
But still, with partial Love, extol his own.
He talks of Senates, and of Courtly Tribes,   15
Admires their Ardour, but forgets their Bribes;
Of hireling Lawyers tells the just Decrees,
Applauds their Eloquence, but sinks their Fees.
Yet who his Countrey's partial Love can blame?
'Tis sure some Virtue to conceal its Shame.   20

    The World's the native City of the Wise;
He sees his *Britain* with a Mother's Eyes;
Softens Defects, and heightens all its Charms,
Calls it the Seat of Empire, Arts and Arms!
Fond of his Hillock Isle, his narrow Mind   25
Thinks Worth, Wit, Learning, to that Spot confin'd;
Thus Ants, who for a Grain employ their Cares,

Think all the Business of the Earth is theirs.
Thus Honey-combs seem Palaces to Bees;
And Mites imagine all the World a Cheese.   30

When Pride in such contemptuous Beings lies,
In Beetles, Britons, Bugs and Butterflies,
Shall we, like Reptiles, glory in Conceit?
Humility's the Virtue of the Great.

9. *Smit...prate*] Cf. *Dunciad* A, II 350: "And smit with love of Poesy and Prate", written about this time; also *Ep. to Jervas*, 13: "Smit with the love of Sister Arts". Pope was curiously fond of this Miltonicism (see *P.O.M.*, p. lxxxi).

20. *'Tis sure*] Cf. *Eloisa to Abelard*, 190, " 'Tis sure the hardest science to forget!" Pope's fondness for the adverbial "sure" has been commented on earlier (see p. 274).

27. *employ their Cares*] Cf. *Ess. on C.*, 500: "our Cares employ"; and *Mor. Ess.*, IV 1: "his Cares employ".

29. *Honey-combs seem Palaces*] Cf. *Lamentation of Glumdalclitch*, ll. 55f.

32. Pope frequently compiled similar lists of incongruities, *e.g. Rape of the Lock*, I 138, IV 120.

EPITAPH
On *JAMES CRAGGS*, Esq.;
In *Westminster-Abbey*.

JACOBUS CRAGGS
REGI MAGNÆ BRITANNIÆ A SECRETIS
ET CONSILIIS SANCTIORIBUS,
PRINCIPIS PARITER AC POPULI AMOR & DELICIÆ:
VIXIT TITULIS ET INVIDIA MAJOR,
ANNOS HEU PAUCOS, XXXV.
OB. FEB. XVI. M DCC XX.

STATESMAN, yet Friend to Truth! of Soul sincere,
In Action faithful, and in Honour clear!

Title] *1727* omits the Latin inscription.
1 *of*] in *1727*, TS.

Who broke no promise, serv'd no private end,
Who gain'd no Title, and who lost no Friend,
Ennobled by Himself, by All approv'd,   5
Prais'd, wept, and honour'd, by the Muse he lov'd.

3 serv'd] sought *TS*.
6 Prais'd ... honour'd] And prais'd unenvy'd *TS*.

Monumental inscription: Westminster Abbey.
Contemporary transcript: BM MS Add. 26877.
Some Memoirs of the Life of Lewis Maximilian Mahomet. 1727 (published
25 February).
The Altar of Love. Consisting of Poems ... By the most eminent Hands. 1727 (pub-
lished 1 April) (and later editions).
The Evening Journal. 14 December 1727.
The St. James's Evening Post. 14–16 December 1727.
The British Journal. 16 December 1727.
The London Journal. 16 December 1727.
*The Works ... Vol. II. Part II. Containing ... Pieces ... written since the former
Volumes.* 1738.
The Works ... Vol. II. Containing his Epistles, &c. 1739 (both editions).
The Works ... Vol. II. Part I. Containing his Epistles, &c. 1740 (and 1743).
Memoirs of ... Alexander Pope, Esq. W. Ayre. Vol. II. 1745.
The Works. Ed. Warburton. Vol. VI. 1751.
In their original form, these lines first appeared as an imaginary inscription at
the end of *Verses occasion'd by Mr. Addison's Treatise of Medals*, which is now known
to have been published in 1720 (see *ante*, p. 206). Since Craggs did not die until
16 February 1721, they cannot have been composed *in memoriam*. Thus their early
history and bibliography belong to the *Epistle to Addison* and will be found in the
introductory matter to that poem.
     The "Epitaph" as such first appeared in *Some Memoirs ... of Lewis Maximilian
Mahomet*, 1727, with this heading:

Postscript. The following Verses upon the Monument just erected to the
Memory of Secretary Craggs in *Westminster* Abbey, might with much more
Justice be applied to Mr. Mehmet (the *first*, and *five last* Words excepted) than
to the *Person* the Poet has thus fulsomely flattered.

But nine months later, on 24 November 1727, Pope wrote to John Knight
(Craggs's brother-in-law) about the monument, saying: "At last I have seen the
statue up ... The inscription on the urn is not done yet, though they [promised] it
two months ago ..." Then, after another three weeks, at least four newspapers
announce: "There is now opened at the West-End of Westminster-Abbey, a fine
white Marble Monument of the late Mr. Secretary Craggs, on which are

inscribed these beautiful Lines, which Mr. Pope wrote upon Mr. Addison's *Treatise of Medals:* . . ." and print the 1720 version, but *not* the revised lines of the inscribed epitaph.

A parody of these lines, in which every statement is reversed, appeared within Pope's lifetime in *The Foundling Hospital for Wit*, 1 1743, as an "Epitaph upon the Political Memory" of Pulteney, "who died to Fame on July 15, 1743"; the first line of which reads: "P—y, no Friend to Truth! in Fraud sincere."

The text follows that of *1738*, with collations from the first separate printing (*1727*)—with which *The Altar of Love* agrees verbally—and from the transcript (*TS*).

Fragment of a SATIRE.

IF meagre *Gildon* draws his venal Quill,
  I wish the Man a Dinner, and sit still.
If dreadful *Dennis* raves in furious Fret,
I'll answer *Dennis* when I am in Debt.
'Tis Hunger, and not Malice, makes them print,   5
And who'll wage War with *Bedlam* or the *Mint?*
    Should some more sober Criticks come abroad,
If wrong, I smile; if right, I kiss the Rod.
Pains, Reading, Study, are their just Pretence,
And all they want is Spirit, Taste, and Sense.   10
Commas and *Points* they set exactly right;
And 'twere a Sin to rob them of their *Mite*.
Yet ne'er one Sprig of Laurel grac'd those Ribbalds,
From slashing *B—y* down to pidling *Tibbalds:*
Who thinks he *reads* when he but *scans* and *spells*,   15
A Word-catcher, that lives on Syllables.
Yet ev'n this Creature may some Notice claim,
Wrapt round and sanctify'd with *Shakespear*'s Name;

3f. *Dennis*] *D—s 1727.*
12 *Following this line, 1727 reads:*
      In future Ages how their Fame will spread,
      For routing *Triplets*, and restoring *ed.*
14 slashing *B—y*] sanguine *Sew— 1727*; *Tibbalds*] *T—s 1727.*

Pretty, in Amber to observe the forms
Of Hairs, or Straws, or Dirt, or Grubs, or Worms: 20
The *Thing*, we know, is neither rich nor rare,
But wonder how the Devil it got there.
　　Are others angry? I excuse them too,
Well may they rage; I give them *but* their Due.
Each Man's true Merit 'tis not hard to find;   25
But each Man's secret Standard in his Mind,
That casting Weight, Pride adds to Emptiness;
This, who can *gratify*? For who can *guess*?
The Wretch whom pilfer'd Pastorals renown,
Who turns a *Persian* Tale for half a Crown,   30
Just writes to make his Barrenness appear,
And strains, from hard bound Brains, six Lines a Year;
In Sense still wanting, tho' he lives on Theft,
Steals much, spends little, yet has nothing left:
Johnson, who now to Sense, now Nonsense leaning,   35
Means not, but blunders round about a Meaning;
And he, whose Fustian's so sublimely bad,
It is not Poetry, but Prose run mad:
Should modest Satire bid all these *translate*,
And own that nine such Poets make a *Tate*;   40
How would they fume, and stamp, and roar, and chafe!
How would they swear, not *Congreve*'s self was safe!
　　Peace to all such! but were there one, whose Fires
Apollo kindled, and fair *Fame* inspires,
Blest with each Talent, and each Art to please,   45
And born to write, converse, and live with ease;
Should such a Man, too fond to rule alone,
Bear, like the *Turk*, no Brother near the Throne;
View him with scornful, yet with fearful eyes,
And hate for Arts that caus'd himself to rise;   50
Damn with faint Praise, assent with civil Leer,
And without sneering, teach the rest to sneer;

24 give] gave *1727*.   35 *Johnson*] *Jo—n 1727*.
40 *Tate*] *T—te 1727*.

Wishing to wound, and yet afraid to strike,
Just hint a Fault, and hesitate Dislike;
Alike reserv'd to blame, or to commend,   55
A tim'rous Foe, and a suspicious Friend,
Dreading ev'n Fools, by Flatterers besieg'd,
And so obliging that he ne'er oblig'd:
Who, if two Wits on rival Themes contest,
Approves of each, but likes the worst the best;   60
Like *Cato* gives his *little Senate* Laws,
And sits attentive to his own Applause;
While Wits and Templars ev'ry Sentence raise,
And wonder with a foolish Face of Praise.
What Pity, Heav'n! if such a Man there be.   65
Who would not weep, if *A—n* were he?

Miscellanies. The Last Volume. 1727 [1728] (and later editions).
The Grub-street Journal. 16 December 1731.
Faithful Memoirs of the Grubstreet Society. 1732.
A General Dictionary. P. Bayle. Vol. I. 1734. [The last 24 ll. only.]
Memoirs of the Society of Grub-street. 1737.
A Supplement to Dr. Swift's and Mr. Pope's Works. Dublin. 1739.
Miscellanies. The Fourth Volume. 1742.
The Life of Alexander Pope, Esq. 1744. [The last 24 ll. only.]
Memoirs of . . . Alexander Pope. W. Ayre. 1745. [The last 24 ll. only.]
Also incorporated in *An Epistle from Mr. Pope to Dr. Arbuthnot.* 1734 (and all
later editions).

For the early history of these lines see p. 144. The expansion of the original
poem of thirty lines to more than twice that length gave Pope opportunity to pay
off a few old scores. So that instead of a Character of Addison introduced by a
six-line quiz at Gildon and Dennis merely, half a dozen names now serve as a pre-
liminary whet to the principal subject. Although Pope never acknowledged these
lines before their incorporation in the *Epistle to Arbuthnot*, 1734 (see Vol. IV), on
his first publication of them in *Miscellanies*, 1727 (for he is not known to have had
any hand in the printing of the earlier shorter version), he and Swift apologize in
the Preface to "The First Volume" for this attack on Addison, in the following
words: "In regard to two Persons only, we wish our Raillery, though ever so
tender, or Resentment, though ever so just, had not been indulged. We speak of
Sir *John Vanbrugh*, . . . and of Mr. *Addison*, whose Name deserves all Respect from
every Lover of Learning."

The copy-text (*Miscellanies*, 1727) has been corrected in the light of *1742* to
form the text here printed.

1–6. For notes on these lines, see *ante*, p. 144, and Vol. IV, pp. 107–11.

14. *slashing B—y*] Richard Bentley. See *Imit. Hor., Ep.* ii i 104*n.* and Biog. App., Vol. IV. The earlier reading, "sanguine Sew—", was an allusion to George Sewell (died 1726), a hack writer, who had published an extra volume, the seventh, to Pope's six-volume edition of Shakespeare, containing his non-dramatic works.

29–30. *The Wretch . . . Crown*] Ambrose Philips (see Biog. App., Vol. IV), of whose "pilfer'd Pastorals" Pope wrote that the "whole third Pastoral is an Instance how well he hath studied the fifth of *Virgil*, and how judiciously reduced *Virgil*'s Thoughts to the Standard of Pastoral; as his Contention of *Colin Clout* and the *Nightingale* [*i.e.* the fifth Pastoral] shows with what Exactness he hath imitated *Strada*" (*Guardian*, No. 40). The *Persian Tales*, translated and published by Philips in 1714, were an old butt of Pope's (see *ante*, p. 176).

35. *Johnson*] Author of the *Victim*, and Cobler of *Preston* [P. *1727–42*]. Charles Johnson, the dramatist (see Biog. App., Vol. V), whose dishonourable mention here was probably earned by his attack on Gay's *Three Hours after Marriage*, in which Pope and Arbuthnot had so large a share (see *ante*, p. 179). This attack had been made in the Prologue to his tragedy *The Sultaness*, 1717, in which he ridicules their farce as "Long-labour'd Nonsense of their own inventing", and ends:

> Such Wags have been, who boldly durst adventure
> To Club a Farce by Tripartite-Indenture:
> But, let them share their Dividend of Praise,
> And their own *Fools-Cap* wear, instead of Bays.

The "Fools-Cap" had figured at the end of Pope's Prologue (see *ante*, p. 178).

38. Verse of Dr. *Ev[ans]*. [P. *1727–42*.]

43–66. For notes on these lines, see *ante*, p. 144.

SYLVIA,

A FRAGMENT

SYLVIA my Heart in wond'rous wise alarm'd,
Aw'd without Sense, and without Beauty charm'd,
But some odd Graces and fine Flights she had,
Was just not ugly, and was just not mad;
Her Tongue still run, on credit from her Eyes,   5
More pert than witty, more a Wit than wise.
Good Nature, she declar'd it, was her Scorn,
Tho' 'twas by that alone she could be born.

Affronting all, yet fond of a good Name,
A Fool to Pleasure, yet a Slave to Fame;   10
Now coy and studious in no Point to fall,
Now all agog for *D—y* at a Ball:
Now deep in *Taylor* and the *Book of Martyrs*,
Now drinking Citron with his *Gr—* and *Ch—*

Men, some to Business, some to Pleasure take.   15
But ev'ry Woman's in her Soul a Rake.
Frail, fev'rish Sex! their Fit now chills, now burns;
Atheism and Superstition rule by Turns;
And the meer Heathen in her carnal Part,
Is still a sad good Christian at her Heart.   20

10 yet] and *1727*.
12 *Following this line, 1727 inserts a couplet:*
           Now with a modest Matron's careful Air,
           Now her Fore Buttocks to the Navel bare.
   [The last line of which reappears in *Dunciad*, ii, 1728 (see Vol. V,
   p. 120), and *Sober Advice*, 1734 (see Vol. IV, p. 79.]

Miscellanies. The Last Volume. 1727 (and later editions).
A Supplement to Dr. Swift's and Mr. Pope's Works. Dublin. 1739.
Miscellanies. The Fourth Volume. Consisting of Verses . . . 1742 (and later editions).
The Works. Ed. Roscoe. Vol. VI. 1824.
This sketch, first printed anonymously in 1727–8 as a single "character", was
incorporated in 1735 in the *Epistle to a Lady. Of the Characters of Women*, where,
with much revision and a little additional matter, it was divided into three
pieces, namely, the characters of Calypso and Narcissa, and a moral reflection on
women (see Vol. III II). Mr Bateson claims (Vol. III II, p. 54n.) that the original
Sylvia was meant for the Duchess of Hamilton, "a lively disreputable woman of
the world", who was well known to Pope, Swift, and Gay, by the last of whom she
was called, in 1720, "the cheerful Duchess". And as Horace Walpole and Warton
also agree that at least the "Narcissa" portion was "designed for her", the identi-
fication may be correct, though the sketch more resembles a caricature than a
portrait.
   There is no internal evidence of the date of composition, and the poem is
therefore assigned to 1727, the nominal year of its publication.
   The copy-text (*Miscellanies*, 1727) has been corrected in the light of *1742* to
form the text here printed.

1-6. In the *Epistle to a Lady* (45-50) these lines run thus:

> 'Twas thus Calypso once each heart alarm'd,
> Aw'd without Virtue, without Beauty charm'd;
> Her Tongue bewitch'd as odly as her Eyes,
> Less Wit than Mimic, more a Wit than wise:
> Strange graces still, and stranger flights she had,
> Was just not ugly, and was just not mad.

7-14, 17-20. In the character of Narcissa (*ibid.*, 59-68) these lines read:

> Why then declare Good-nature is her scorn,
> When 'tis by that alone she can be born?
> Why pique all mortals, yet affect a name?
> A fool to Pleasure, yet a slave to Fame:
> Now deep in Taylor and the Book of Martyrs,
> Now drinking citron with his Grace and Chartres.
> Now Conscience chills her, and now Passion burns:
> And Atheism and Religion take their turns;
> A very Heathen in the carnal part,
> Yet still a sad, good Christian at her heart.

12. *D—y*] Not yet identified.

13. *Taylor, and the Book of Martyrs*] Two popular books of devotion, Jeremy Taylor's *Holy Living and Holy Dying*, and John Foxe's martyrology.

14. *his Gr— and C—*] Philip, Duke of Wharton and Francis Charteris, for whom see Vol. III II, pp. 30*n.*, 85*n.* and Biog. App., Vol. IV.

15-16. This couplet reappeared in *Ep. to a Lady*, ll. 215-16, thus:

> Men, some to Bus'ness, some to Pleasure take;
> But ev'ry Woman is at heart a Rake.

LINES FROM *The Art of Sinking*.

Who knocks at the Door?

For whom thus rudely pleads my loud-tongu'd Gate,
That he may enter?——

Shut the Door.

The wooden Guardian of our Privacy
Quick on its Axle turn.——

Bring my Cloaths.

Bring me what Nature, Taylor to the *Bear*,
To *Man* himself deny'd: She gave me Cold,
But would not give me Cloaths.———

Light the Fire.

Bring forth some Remnant of *Promethean* theft,
Quick to expand th' inclement Air congeal'd
By *Boreas*'s rude breath.———

Snuff the Candle.

Yon Luminary Amputation needs,
Thus shall you save its half-extinguish'd Life.

Uncork the Bottle, and chip the Bread.

Apply thine Engine to the spungy Door,
Set *Bacchus* from his glassy Prison free,
And strip white *Ceres* of her nut-brown Coat.

Miscellanies. The Last Volume. 1727 (and subsequent editions).
The Works . . . In Prose. Vol. II. 1741 (all variants).
The Works. Ed. Warburton. Vol. VI. 1751.
Pope concludes the ludicrous poetical illustrations of his *Art of Sinking* with a page of eight quotations, of which two are ascribed—one to Theobald, and the other to "Temp." (i.e., *The Tempest*)—the remainder having no ascription. Although Pope apparently admitted to various people that most of the examples signed "Anon." were taken from his youthful poems (see *ante*, p. 20), nothing is known for certain of the authorship of the unsigned pieces. Five of them have been tentatively attributed to Pope (see *post*, p. 414); and it is at least probable that these six were his also. There is evidence to show that the treatise was being compiled as early as 1714 (see p. 292), and indeed most of the poetical illustrations are drawn from works published before that date; but the treatise itself is stated (in *1741*) to have been "Written in the Year 1727". These six examples from chap. XII of the "Cumbrous" and "Buskin" styles of writing have all the appearance of having been concocted specially for the comic illustration of those styles. After an amusing description of the two styles, Pope thus introduces these examples of them: "Will not every true lover of the Profound be delighted to behold the most vulgar and low actions of life exalted in the following manner?"
The text follows that of *1727*.

VERSES

To be placed under the Picture of
England's *Arch-Poet: Containing*
a compleat Catalogue of his Works.

SEE who ne'er was or will be half read!
    Who first sung *Arthur*, then sung *Alfred*,
Prais'd great *Eliza* in God's anger,
Till all true *Englishmen* cry'd, hang her!
Made *William*'s Virtues wipe the bare A——   5
And hang'd up *Marlborough* in *Arras*:

    Then hiss'd from Earth, grew Heav'nly quite;
Made ev'ry Reader curse the *Light*;
Maul'd human *Wit* in one thick Satyr,
Next in three Books, sunk human *Nature*,   10
Un-did *Creation* at a Jerk,
And of *Redemption* made damn'd Work.

    Then took his Muse at once, and dipt her
Full in the middle of the Scripture.
What Wonders there the Man grown old, did!   15
Sternhold himself he *out-Sternholded*,
Made *David* seem so mad and freakish,
All thought him just what thought King *Achiz*.
No Mortal read his *Salomon*,
But judg'd *Roboam* his own Son.   20
Moses he serv'd as *Moses Pharaoh*,
And *Deborah*, as She *Sise-rah*:
Made *Jeremy* full sore to cry,
And *Job* himself curse God and die.

    What Punishment all this must follow?   25
Shall *Arthur* use him like King *Tollo*,

15 did!] did? *1732.*

Shall *David* as *Uriah* slay him,
Or dext'rous *Deb'rah Sisera*-him?
Or shall *Eliza* lay a Plot,
To treat him like her Sister *Scot*,   30
Shall *William* dub his better End,
Or *Marlb'rough* serve him like a Friend?
No, none of these—Heav'n spare his Life!
But send him, honest *Job*, thy *Wife*.

31 *Comma supplied from 1742.*

Miscellanies. The Third Volume. 1732 (and later editions).
A Supplement to Dr. Swift's and Mr. Pope's Works. Dublin. 1739.
Miscellanies. The Fourth Volume. Consisting of Verses . . . 1742 (and later editions).
Gay's *Poetical Works*, in Bell's edition of the British Poets, 1773–7 (and sub-
sequently in a number of similar collections).

This poem was first attributed to Pope by the present writer in "Pope and
England's Arch-Poet", *RES*, xix (1943), pp. 376–86, and in *New Light*, pp. 248–
58, to which the reader is referred for full details. The main points of the argument
are as follows. The poem, an attack on Sir Richard Blackmore, was first published
anonymously by Pope in the 1732 volume of his and Swift's *Miscellanies*, which he
edited. When it was reprinted in the "Four Volumes" edition of 1742—with the
preparation of which Pope also had much to do (see *post*, p. 346)—the poem was
marked as *not* by Swift; and it remained unclaimed and unattributed until 1773,
when it was included without evidence in Bell's edition of the poets, amongst the
works of John Gay. Faber excluded it from Gay's canon both for lack of evidence
and because it was not in Gay's manner. Dr Sherburn's more recent reassertion
of Gay's authorship (p. 167), on the strength of a phrase in Pope's letter to Jervas
(14 November 1716), overlooks the internal evidence which proves that *Verses*
cannot have been written before 1723, the date of Blackmore's last poem, *Alfred*.
The poem to which Pope referred in 1716 is unquestionably Gay's *Journey to
Exeter*, then recently published, which attacks Blackmore in its last paragraph.
Similarly unconvincing is the suggestion that Arbuthnot was the author, put
forward by Mr Faber on the ground that Arbuthnot once made a small joke
against Blackmore in a letter to Swift (11 December 1718). There is no evidence
of a quarrel between the two doctors of the bitterness which the poem postulates,
and of which it could hardly be the sole expression.

The case for Pope's authorship of the *Verses* attacking Blackmore begins with
the general arguments advanced in the introductory note to *Poems from Miscel-
lanies, 1732* (p. 345). In addition to them there is the witness of opportunity (as
seen in his editorship of the volume), motive, occasion, and character, besides a
certain amount of internal evidence touching both matter and style. A long-
standing quarrel existed between Pope and Blackmore. As early as 1711, Pope,

resenting Blackmore's abuse of Dryden, had attacked him in *An Essay on Criticism*, l. 463: "New Blackmores and new Milbournes must arise", subsequently in the famous "Emetic" lampoon on Curll (then Blackmore's publisher), 1716; and later that year in a second lampoon, in which the baiting of Blackmore assumes almost the proportions of a major theme (see *Prose Works*, I c–ci). The whole quarrel finally boiled over when Blackmore, in a second volume of *Essays* (26 March 1717) railed against "the godless author [who] has burlesqu'd the First Psalm of David in so obscene and profane a manner". Pope, who had not meant the skit for publication (see p. 165), never forgot or forgave him.

In the meantime, Arbuthnot wrote to Swift (June 1714) that "Pope has been collecting high flights of poetry . . . they are to be solemn nonsense"—doubtless this was the beginning of *The Art of Sinking*, which Pope completed and published in 1728. This work creates Sir Richard "father of the Bathos, and indeed the Homer of it", and uses his epics to illustrate various ridiculous literary lapses. A few weeks later came the *Dunciad*, in which Blackmore's "endless line" is squinted at in Book I, while in Book II, besides two other scoffing references to him, he is given, at the close of the "braying match", ten searing lines all to himself, ending thus:

> All hail him victor in both gifts of Song,
> Who sings so *loudly*, and who sings so *long*.

To the last line just quoted, Pope later added a lengthy footnote, which is virtually a prose counterpart of *Verses*, and insists on the number of "Books" in each of Blackmore's epics as do the footnotes to *Verses*. It runs as follows:

A just character of Sir Richard Blackmore, Kt. . . . whose indefatigable Muse produced no less than six Epic poems: Prince and King Arthur, 20 Books; Eliza 10; Alfred 12; The Redeemer 6: besides Job in folio, the whole Book of Psalms, The Creation, 7 Books, Nature of Man, 3 Books, and many more. 'Tis in this sense he is stiled afterwards, the *Everlasting Blackmore*. . .

And when to all this are added Pope's sneers at him in at least four of the *Imitations of Horace*, and one or two other allusions elsewhere, it is obvious that the *Verses* fits more neatly and convincingly into the Pope-Blackmore feud than into any other contemporary setting. Lastly, in 1732 Blackmore had been dead three years; and though Pope may have been content to publish one of his old pieces on the old theme, it does not follow that he would have included such untopical matter from anyone outside what may be called the "Miscellanies" circle, and all the others within it have already been eliminated.

The poem itself looks like another of Pope's high-spirited, "unofficial" effusions now collected for the first time in the present volume. For besides being cast in a favourite metre (cf. especially the *Epistle to Cromwell*, p. 24), it has the old impolite words found in so many of them, as well as the characteristic acrobatic rhymes. It will be noted that one of his frequent butts, Thomas Sternhold, the Elizabethan versifier of the Psalms (see *ante*, p. 165) reappears here, and that the joke about the use of Blackmore's works for toilet purposes was an old one with Pope.

The cumulative effect of this evidence may carry at least justification for the inclusion of *Verses On England's Arch-Poet* amongst the attributed pieces in the Pope canon. The poem was obviously written between 1723, the date of Sir Richard's last poem, *Alfred*, and 1729, the year of his death; it is therefore provisionally dated 1727, the year in which Pope quoted him so extensively in *The Art of Sinking*.

The text follows that of the first printing.

Title: *England's Arch-Poet*] Sir Richard Blackmore (c. 1660–1729). See Biog. App., Vol. IV.

2. *Arthur*] Two Heroick Poems in Folio, twenty Books [P. *1732*]; *i.e. Prince Arthur*, 1695, and *King Arthur*, 1697.

Alfred] Heroick Poem in twelve Books [P. *1732*]; published 1723.

3. *Eliza*] Heroick Poem in Folio, ten Books [P. *1732*]; published 1705.

5. *Williams' Virtues*] William III is excessively praised in *The Kit-Cats. A Poem*. 1708.

6. *Marlborough . . . Arras*] Instructions to *Vanderbank* a Tapestry-Weaver [P. *1732*]; published 1709.

8. *Light*] Hymn to the *Light* [P. *1732*]; published 1703.

9. *Wit*] Satyr against *Wit* [P. *1732*]; published 1700.

10. *Nature*] Of the *Nature* of Man [P. *1732*]; published 1711.

11. *Creation*] *Creation*, a Poem in seven Books [P. *1732*]; published 1712.

12. *Redemption*] The *Redeemer*, another Heroick Poem in six Books [P. *1732*]; *i.e. Redemption. A Divine Poem . . . To which is added A Hymn to Christ the Redeemer*. 1722.

16. *Sternhold*] The Elizabethan versifier of the Psalms, often derided by Pope.

17. *David*] Translation of all the *Psalms* [P. *1732*]; published 1721.

18. *Achiz*] 1 Samuel xxi, 12ff.: "And David . . . was sore afraid of Achish . . . and feigned himself mad . . . and scrabbled on the doors of the gate . . . Then said Achish . . . Lo, ye see the man is mad . . ."

19. *Salomon*] *Canticles* and *Ecclesiast* [P. *1732*]; published 1700.

21. *Moses . . . Deborah*] Paraphrase of the Canticles of *Moses* and *Deborah*, &c. [P. *1732*]; published 1700.

23. *Jeremy*] The *Lamentations* [P. *1732*].

24. *Job*] The whole Book of *Job*, a Poem in Folio [P. *1732*]; published 1700.

30. *Sister Scot*] Mary, Queen of Scots.

31. *better End*] Kick him on the Breech, not Knight him on the Shoulder [P. *1732*]. Blackmore was knighted in 1697.

The Dunciad.
An Heroic Poem. In Three Books

[published May 1728; vol. v]

To the Right Honourable the Earl of
OXFORD.

Upon a piece of News in MIST, that the Rev. Mr W.
refus'd to write against Mr Pope because his best
Patron had a Friendship for the said P.

W ESLEY, if Wesley 'tis they mean,
     They say, on Pope would fall
Would his best Patron let his Pen
     Discharge his inward Gall.

What Patron this, a doubt must be   5
     Which none but you can clear,
Or Father Francis cross the sea,
     Or else Earl Edward here.

That both were good must be confest,
     And much to both he owes;   10
But which to Him will be the best
     The Lord of Oxford knows.

The Gentleman's Magazine. July 1809.
Literary Anecdotes of the Eighteenth Century. J. Nichols. Vol. IX. 1815.
The Works. Ed. Carruthers. Vol. IV. 1854.

These lines were first published in what was claimed to be a facsimile of Pope's
autograph in the *Gentleman's Magazine*.

The "piece of News in Mist" appeared in *Mist's Weekly Journal* on 8 June 1728
as an epistle purporting to defend Pope from the attacks which followed the pub-
lication of the *Dunciad* in the previous month. As the epistle bears the initials of
James Moore Smythe who, only two months earlier, had been publicly charged
with plagiarism from Pope (possibly by Pope himself); and as it closely resembles
a list of "Resolutions" in Pope's second lampoon on Curll (see *A Further Account
. . . in Prose Works*, I 281–3), it is possible that Pope was responsible for it. The
relevant portion reads as follows:

Ordered, That a Committee of Secrecy be appointed to draw up a *Report*
against the said *Pope.* And that Mr. *M.* Mr. *A. H.* Mr. *W.* Mr. *D.* and the Rev.
Mr. *W.* do prepare and bring in the same.

Mr. *A. H.* petition'd to be excus'd, on Account of some Business he hath to
do in *Muscovy*.

The Rev. Mr. *W.* did the same, on Account of an ancient Friendship between his *best Patron* and the *Pope.* [The initials probably stand for M[orrice], A[aron] H[ill], W[ard], D[ennis], and Rev. Mr W[esley], in that order.]

In the first three issues of the *Dunciad* (see Vol. V) which appeared within a week of the original publication on 18 May, Pope's gibe at those authors whose works are valued for beauties not their own, ends by instancing the names of "*W—y, W—s,* and *Bl—*" (A, I 126*n.*); but in the fourth issue (called "The Second Edition", and published on 25 May, according to *The Country Journal*), these allusions are changed to "*W—s, Q—s,* and *Bl—*"; and from this time onwards "*W—y*" vanished from the poem. The identity of *W—y* was settled by Pope in a note on the line in the *Dunciad Variorum,* 1729, in which he said that *W—y,* mentioned in earlier editions, was a person "eminent for good life", who "writ the Life of Christ in verse". *W—y* was in fact the Rev. Samuel Wesley, the author of *The Life of our Blessed Lord . . . In Ten Books . . . With Sixty Copper-Plates,* 1693; *The History of The New Testament . . . adorn'd with CLII Sculptures,* 1701; and *The History of The Old Testament . . . With One Hundred and Eighty Sculptures,* 1704. Wesley's son, Samuel, was at this time on friendly terms with Pope's intimate friends, Oxford and Atterbury, and was probably known to Pope also—as he certainly was a month or two later, according to a letter from Pope to Oxford dated "August 1728".

It would therefore seem that, immediately on the publication of the *Dunciad,* Samuel Wesley the younger, incensed at the reference to his father's works, complained to Pope, either directly or through his "best patron". It appears, too, that Pope was both complaisant enough to withdraw the allusion within nine days of its appearance, and amused enough to have written these lines to Oxford on the affair—if not also to have initiated, or abetted, the publication of the "piece of news in Mist".

The text follows that of the original facsimile.

1. *Wesley*] Rev. Samuel Wesley the younger (see introductory note).

7. *Father Francis*] Francis Atterbury, the exiled bishop of Rochester.

8. *Earl Edward*] Edward Harley, second Earl of Oxford.

EPITAPH.

On G ——.

WELL then, poor *G——* lies under ground!
　　So there's an end of honest *Jack.*
So little Justice here he found,
　　'Tis ten to one he'll ne'er come back.

Contemporary transcripts: BM MS Harl. 7316, and Longleat, Portland Papers, xx.

Miscellanies. The Third Volume. 1732 (and later editions).

A Supplement to Dr. Swift's and Mr. Pope's Works. Dublin. 1739.

Miscellanies. The Fourth Volume. Consisting of Verses. 1742 (and later editions).

Select and Remarkable Epitaphs. J. Hackett. Vol. I. 1757.

A Select Collection of Epitaphs. 1759.

The Christmas Treat. 1767.

A New Select Collection of Epitaphs. T. Webb. Vol. II. 1775.

The St. James's Chronicle. 21–23 September 1775.

The London Magazine. September 1775.

The Edinburgh Magazine and Review. October 1775.

Additions to the Works of Alexander Pope, Esq. Vol. I. 1776.

The Poems of Pope. Vol. II (in Johnson's *English Poets*). 1779.

This "attributed" epitaph was first published anonymously in the 1732 volume of *Miscellanies*, marked as *not* by Swift in the 1742 edition (see *post*, p. 346), and printed for the first time with Pope's name in the *St. James's Chronicle*. Arguments for Pope's authorship will be found in the introductory note to *Poems from Miscellanies. The Third Volume. 1732* (see *post*, p. 345); and further witness is the contemporary transcript in the Harleian MSS, the title of which reads: *Mr. Gay's Epitaph by Mr. Pope*. The same author and subject are again corroborated by internal evidence; for "honest Jack" of the second line is paralleled a number of times in Pope's letters, it being probably his favourite epithet for Gay, whose honesty and integrity he never tires of praising.

Consequent on the success of *The Beggar's Opera* in February 1728, Gay wrote a "Second Part", *Polly*, the performance of which was banned for political reasons by the Lord Chamberlain on 12 December 1728. The "book", however, was published early in 1729; and Gay's friends at Court thereupon became so solicitous for its success, that the chief of them, the Duchess of Queensberry, was actually "forbid the Court", and, on quitting it, took the Duke with her. Gay about the same time was deprived of his apartments in Whitehall; and Arbuthnot, describing the affair to Swift, said that Gay "has got several [of his partisans] turned out of their places", and that other great ladies were in danger. Early in March, Gay, writing to Pope, remarked that, as a result of it all, he had "no continuing city here. I begin to look upon myself as one already dead, and desire ... that you will ... see these words put upon [my grave-stone]:

> Life's a jest, and all things show it,
> I thought so once, but now I know it,

with what more you may think proper." Pope's response, it is practically certain, was this mock epitaph on Gay's "court" death; for Gay appears to refer directly to the words: "Well then, poor G— lies under ground!" when, writing to Swift (18 March) he says: "Mr. Pope tells me that I am dead, and that this obnoxiousness is the reward of my inoffensiveness in my former life."

This epitaph, then, contrary to general supposition, was neither a heartless

jest on his friend's death—Gay did not die till two months after its publication—
nor the least offence to him while still alive, but only a comment on contemporary
life.

The text follows that of the first printed edition.

EPITAPHS
From the Latin on the Count of Mirandula.

Joannes jacet hic Mirandula—cætera norunt
Et Tagus & Ganges—forsan & Antipodes.

I.
Lord *CONINGSBY*'s Epitaph.

HERE lies Lord Coningsby—be civil,
   The rest God knows—so does the Devil.

1 civil,] *1820 supplies comma, MSS omit.*
2 knows—so does] knows, perhaps *1820.*

II.
Applied to *F. C.*

HERE *Francis Ch—s* lies—Be civil!
   The rest God knows—perhaps the Devil.

Title] 1732 quotes the original Latin inscription (see introductory note),
followed by the words "Applied to F.C."

Contemporary transcripts: Longleat, Portland Papers, **xx**, and BM MS Harl.
7316. [No. I.]
   Miscellanies. The Third Volume. 1732 (and later editions). [No. II.]
   A Supplement to Dr. Swift's and Mr. Pope's Works. Dublin. 1739. [No. II.]
   Miscellanies. The Fourth Volume. Consisting of Verses . . . 1742 (and later editions).
[No. II.]
   The History of John Bull. [1750?] [No. II.]

Select and Remarkable Epitaphs. J. Hackett. Vol. I. 1757. [No. II.]
A Select Collection of Epitaphs. 1759. [No. II.]
A Christmas Treat. 1767. [No. II.]
The St. James's Chronicle. 21–23 September 1775. [No. I.]
Additions to the Works of Alexander Pope, Esq. Vol. I. 1776. [No. I.]
The Poems of Pope. Vol. II (in Johnson's *English Poets*). 1779. [No. I.]
Anecdotes . . . of Books and Men. J. Spence. 1820. [No. I.]
The Works. Ed. Roscoe. Vol. VI. 1824. [No. II.]

"You know I love short inscriptions, and that may be the reason why I like the epitaph on the Count of Mirandula so well. Some time ago I made a parody of it for a man of very opposite character. . ." Thus Spence (p. 165) reports Pope's remarks introducing the Coningsby epitaph. (Giovanni Pico della Mirandola—whose epitaph is given above—was the famous Italian philosopher and scholar, born 1463, who died at thirty-one, one of the most learned persons of his time.) As the conversation dates from 1734–6; as Pope's "some time ago" agrees with the date of Coningsby's death, 30 April 1729, and as Pope's squibs were usually topical (or why make them?), the parody may be assigned to 1729 without any hesitation. Another (but anonymous) version of the epitaph appeared in the "Third" volume of *Miscellanies* (published 4 October 1732), in which the notorious Francis Chartres—who had died earlier that year—was substituted for Coningsby.

The text of No. I follows the two contemporary manuscripts, with collations from Spence (*1820*). The text of No. II follows the first printing of it (*1732*).

I. 1. *Coningsby*] Thomas Lord Coningsby (1656?–1729). A Whig peer, once suspected of peculation; was forward in the impeachment of Pope's friend, Lord Oxford, 1715. "Pope's dislike of him was probably chiefly due to his invectives against the Roman Catholics."—EC, III 158.

II. 1. *Ch—s*] Chartres, or Charteris, Francis. See Biog. App., Vol. IV.

EPIGRAMS
from
THE DUNCIAD.
1729–1730.

Pope's autograph: Longleat, Portland Papers, XIII. [No. VI.]
Contemporary transcripts: *ibid.* Vol. XIX [No. VII]; and BM MS Add. 32096 [No. VII].
The Dunciad, Variorum. 1729 (published 10 April). [No. I.]
The Flying-Post: or, The Weekly Medley. 12 April 1729. [Nos. II, III.]
The Evening Post. 26–28 June 1729. [No. IV.]

The Dunciad . . . The Second Edition, with some Additional Notes. 1729 (published 24 November). [Nos. I–VI.]

A Collection of Pieces . . . publish'd on Occasion of the Dunciad . . . By Mr. Savage. 1732. [Nos. I–VII.]

The Works of Mr. Alexander Pope. Volume II. 1735 (folio and quarto). [Nos. I–VII.]

The Dunciad. An Heroic Poem. To Dr. Jonathan Swift. 1736. [Nos. I–IV, VI, VII.]

A Collection of Epigrams. Vol. II. 1737. [Nos. I–VII.]

The Works . . . Vol. III. Part II. Containing the Dunciad . . . 1741. [Nos. I–IV, VII.]

A Letter from Mr. Cibber to Mr. Pope. 1742. [No. VII.]

The Dunciad, In Four Books. 1743 (4to; published 29 October). [Nos. II, VII.]

The Works . . . Vol. III. Part I. Containing the Dunciad. 1743. [Nos. II, VII, XII.]

Memoirs of . . . Alexander Pope, Esq: . . . By William Ayre. 1745. [No. II.]

The Works . . . Vol. V. Containing the Dunciad. Ed. Warburton. 1751. [Nos. I–V, VII.]

The Nut-Cracker. F. Foot. 1751. [Nos. III, IV, VI, VII.]

A Collection of Select Epigrams. Mr. Hackett. 1757. [Nos. II, III, VII.]

The Festoon. R. Graves. 1766. [Nos. II–VI in all editions; No. VII in all except 1st Edition.]

The Christmas Treat. 1767. [Nos. II–VII.]

A Select Collection of Epigrams. T. C. Rickman. 1796. [No. VII.]

Select Epigrams. Vol. II. 1797. [Nos. II, III, VII.]

Scattered through the "Remarks" in different issues of the *Dunciad*, from the so-called "Second Edition" onwards, are upwards of a dozen anonymous epigrams of eight lines or less, some of which, and almost certainly the majority, were written by Pope himself. Three of them and a part of a fourth are still extant in his autograph; another was included by him elsewhere in his *Works*; and others were attributed to him by Warburton, Cibber, and Savage. In addition, there are four longer pieces likewise anonymous (see Vol. V), one of which is a poem of sixteen lines asserted by Dr Johnson to have been written by David Lewis; two others of twelve lines each, on Pope and the Dunces, improbably (but not impossibly) by Pope; and a ten-line epigram addressed to Welsted, which, though it may well have been written by Pope, must for want of evidence be regarded as apocryphal (see Vol. V, p. 138). The difficulties of attribution may seem to be further complicated by Pope's letter to Dr Sheridan (12 October 1728) in which after describing the forthcoming edition of *The Dunciad, Variorum*, he added: "Some very good epigrams on the gentlemen of the *Dunciad* have been sent me from Oxford, and others of the London authors"; for it has been conjectured that some of those epigrams may have found place in the notes to the *Dunciad*. Nevertheless what evidence there is suggests the contrary, since except for one jocular couplet almost certainly his own Pope did not include any epigrams in that edition (*i.e.* the first of the "Variorum" *Dunciads*, published on 10 April 1729), nor in any of twelve or more issues which appeared during the succeeding seven months. Indeed, "The Second Edition, with some Additional Notes", published on 24 November 1729 (*i.e.* more than a year after Pope's letter), was the first in which more than one epigram was introduced. The following seven epigrams which appeared in *Dunciad* A are here printed together for convenience, though their dates of composition are uncertain, and though, as regards Pope's authorship, the same degree of probability may not attach to them all. The evidence for each is given in the footnotes, together with particulars about the text. It should be noted that the above bibliographical list does not mention all the intermediate issues of the *Dunciad* containing one or more of the epigrams, but only those which are important textually. (For the epigrams in later editions attributable to Pope, see under *Dunciad* in the index.)

I.

On a Translation of *ÆSCHYLUS*.

ALAS! poor *Æschylus*! unlucky Dog!
   Whom once a *Lobster* kill'd, and now a *Log*.

Title] *No title originally.*

II.

On *James Moore Smythe*.

M—RE always smiles whenever he recites;
   He smiles (you think) approving what he writes;
And yet in this no Vanity is shown;
A modest man may like what's not his own.

Title] *There is no title in the early texts.*
1 *M—re* ... smiles] *M—* ... laughs *1729*.
2 He ... writes.] He reads, and laughs, you think, at what he writes:
   1729.
3 And yet] But sure *1729*.

III.
On *Roome*.

YOU ask why *Roome* diverts you with his jokes,
  Yet, if he writes, is dull as other folks?
You wonder at it—This Sir is the case,
The jest is lost, unless he prints his Face.

Title] *There is no title in the early texts.*
1 You ... jokes,] Our laughter, *R—e,* whene'er he speaks, provokes;
  1729a. Roome] *R— 1729b.*
2 Yet, if ... is dull] But when ... he's dull *1729a.*
4 he prints] you print *1729a.*

IV.
On *Burnet* and *Ducket*.

BURNET and *Ducket*, friends in spite,
  Came hissing forth in verse;
Both were so forward, each would write,
  So dull, each hung an A——
Thus *Amphisbæna* (I have read)   5
  At either end assails;
None knows which leads, or which is led,
  For both Heads are but Tails.

Title] *None in Dunciad texts.* Epigram. *1729a. On* Homerides. *1737.*
1 *Burnet* and *Ducket,*] When, *D–ck–t B–rn–t, 1729a.*
4 A—] Arse. *1729a.*
5 *1729a reads:* So *Amphisbæna,* we have read, [with footnote] *A
  Serpent with two Heads.
7 or] nor *1729a.*

V.

On *Shakespeare* Restored.

'Tis generous, *Tibald*! in thee and thy brothers,
　To help us thus to read the works of others:
Never for this can just returns be shown;
For who will help us e'er to read thy own?

Title] *Title from 1737, none in 1729.*

VI.

On his Busto.

Well, Sir, suppose, the *Busto*'s a damn'd head,
　　Suppose, that *Pope*'s an Elf;
All he can say for 't is, he neither made
　　The *Busto* nor *Himself.*

Title] *No title in the early texts.*
1 Well . . . Busto's.] *Tis granted Sir; the Busto's* MS; *Well Sir,
　suppose the Busto 1735.*
2 Suppose . . . Elf;] *Pope is a little Elf,* MS; *Suppose the Man an
　Elf; 1735.*

VII.

On *Cibber.*

In merry old England it once was a rule,
　The King had his Poet, and also his Fool:
But now we're so frugal, I'd have you to know it,
That *Cibber* can serve both for Fool and for Poet.

Title] *No title in the early texts.*
4 *Cibber*] *C**r 1735 (fol. and 4to).*

I. This couplet occurs in a note on *Dunciad* A, I 210: "And last, his own cold Aeschylus took fire", as follows: "He [Theobald] had been (to use an expression of our Poet) *about Æschylus* for ten years, and had received Subscriptions for the same, but then went *about* other Books. The character of this tragic Poet is Fire and Boldness . . . but our Author supposes it to be very much cooled by the translation; Upon sight of a specimen of it, was made this Epigram, . . . [the couplet follows]. But this is a grievous error, for *Æschylus* was not slain by the fall of a Lobster on his head, but of a Tortoise, *teste* Val. Max. l. 9 cap. 12. SCRIBLERUS." This was the only epigram inserted in *The Dunciad, Variorum* published on 10 April 1729. And both it and its context are so inseparable, and so typical of Pope's pedant-mocking humour, there can be little doubt that he wrote both. It must, however, remain an attributed piece. The text is that of the *1729* quarto (with which *1741*, the last in Pope's lifetime, is in verbal agreement). It does not appear in *Dunciad* B.

II. This epigram was first printed with No. III in *The Flying-Post: Or, Weekly Medley*, for 12 April 1729, where they were prefaced with these words: "We insert the following Epigrams, not from any Pique against the Persons they may be levell'd at, but because we believe our Readers will be entertain'd with their Beauty." When, seven months later, Pope inserted them both in *Dunciad* A, this epigram was accompanied by a note (see Vol. V, p. 101*n*.) in explanation of "the phantom More" of the text, in the course of which, after attention had been drawn to Moore Smythe's recent plagiarism from Pope (see *ante*, p. 294), the epigram was introduced by the suspiciously noncommital statement: "The Plagiarisms of this person gave occasion to the following Epigram." The evidence for Pope's authorship may be summarized thus: (*a*) the existence, as early as 1715, of a couplet in his autograph which seems to foreshadow this epigram in reverse, as it were, and in vocabulary (see below, and *ante*, p. 235); (*b*) the revision of the epigram for the *Dunciad*; (*c*) its publication with Epigram No. III in the same two places, thus suggesting some connection between them, which, as their subjects differ, is probably that of authorship, especially as the other is likewise attributable to Pope; and, lastly, (*d*) Pope's antagonism to Moore Smythe on account of his plagiarisms was then at its height, and no one else is known to have nursed a similar grievance against the playwright at that time.

The text is that of *Dunciad* A, with collations from the first printing (*1729*).

1. *M—re*] Moore, that is James Moore Smythe (see Biog. App., Vol. IV); Warburton prints "More", *1751*.

3–4. Pope's earlier couplet (*Couplets on Wit*, VI, see p. 235) reads:

> For authors now are so conceited grown
> They praise no works but what are like their own.

But the last line of both is derived, more or less directly, from the prologue of Sir Samuel Tuke's play, *The Adventures of Five Hours*, 1663, line 8: "A Modest Man may praise what's not his own."

III. This epigram was first printed with No. II in *The Flying-Post: Or, Weekly*

Medley, for 12 April 1729. Its revision before inclusion in the *Dunciad* (A, III 146) suggests Pope's authorship. Furthermore, Savage seems to hint at Pope's responsibility in *An Author To be Lett . . . Numb. I.*, issued a week later (19 April 1729), as follows: "I have a Drollery in my Countenance; Egad! 'tis as *peculiar* a One as *R — — m*'s . . . Nay, the same Thing has been said of me, as was utter'd by a certain *Wit* (one very different from our Rank) on him, viz. that the *R — — g — —'s Misfortune is, he cannot print his Face to his Joke.*" In the *Dunciad* the epigram is introduced in a note on "Roome's funereal face" in this manner: "*Edward Roome*, Son of an Undertaker for Funerals . . . writ some of the papers call'd *Pasquin* [in which he had maliciously attacked Pope] . . . Of this Man was made the following Epigram." There was a late and unsupported ascription of this and the following epigram to Swift, by one "Ferdinando Foot" in *The Nut-Cracker*, 1751. The text follows that of *1729b* with collations from *1729a*. The full name is incorporated from *1741*.

1. *You ask why Roome* . . .] Cf. "You ask why Damon . . ." *Epigram on Cato* (see *ante*, p. 410).

IV. This epigram derives from the "Battle of the Iliad", 1715 (see *ante*, p. 144), and refers to the collaboration of Thomas Burnet and George Duckett in *Homerides*, etc. Pope counter-attacked several times, and if the *Sermon on Glass Bottles*, 1715, is his (see *Prose Works*, I, pp. lxxxiv-lxxxviii), the persistent enmity of these two people at last goaded him into repeating the then current charge of immorality against them—a charge which is substantiated in their *Letters*. Thus when Pope came to pay off old scores in the *Dunciad*, these two had eight lines to their discredit (A, III 173ff.).

The epigram was first printed anonymously in *The Evening Post* (26–8 June 1729). It was incorporated in *The Dunciad, Variorum* five months later, in the note (see Vol. V, p. 169) to the original passage, introduced with these words: "The Union of these two Authors gave occasion to this Epigram"—a guarded but characteristic statement not incompatible with Pope's authorship of it, as the notes to some of its fellow epigrams show. In addition the several corrections of text which appear only in the *Dunciad* version also suggest, as with Nos. II and III, Pope's revision of his own work. The epigram was suppressed in 1743. (For an unsupported attribution of this piece to Swift, see note to No. III *ante*.)

All the *Dunciad* versions agree verbally; the text follows that of *Dunciad* A with collations from *The Evening Post* (*1729a*) version.

V. This epigram forms part of Pope's retort upon Theobald's *Shakespeare restored: or, a Specimen of the Many Errors, as well Committed as Unamended, by Mr. Pope in his Late Edition of this Poet. Designed not only to correct the said Edition, but to restore the True Reading of Shakespeare in all the Editions ever yet publish'd. 1726.* It concludes a note on *Dunciad* A, I 153f.

> Old puns restore, lost blunders nicely seek
> And crucify poor Shakespear once a week,

which reads: "For some time, once a week or fortnight, he printed in *Mist*'s

Journal a single remark or poor conjecture on some *word* or *pointing* of *Shakespear*, either in his own name, or in letters to himself as from others without name. Upon these somebody made this Epigram . . ." Time, occasion, motive, and the parallel noted below, all suggest that "somebody" was Pope himself. The text is that of *Dunciad* A.

3. *just returns*] Pope uses this rather unusual phrase in the *Essay on Man*, III 143, and "returns" in several other places in the same sense.

VI. This epigram was introduced in a note to *Dunciad* A, II 134 thus: "The Gentlemen of the Dunciad, whose scurrilities were always Personal . . . went so far as to libel an eminent Sculptor for making our author's *Busto* in marble . . . which Rhimes had the undeserv'd honour to be answer'd in an *Impromptu* by the Earl of B——". "B——" may stand for Burlington (see Vol. V, p. 116), but it is not certain that he was alluded to; for Pope often used a temporary *nom de guerre* which might seem to suggest a certain individual, without directly implicating him. A different version of the epigram in Pope's autograph at Longleat and other alterations introduced in the *1735* text suggest that Pope himself was responsible for it. The "busto" in question seems to have been one made in 1725 by J. M. Rysbrack (1693–1770) for the Earl of Oxford. Public attention was called to it by Jonathan Smedley in an epigram "To Mr. Reisbank, on his Carving A. Pope's Busto" published in *Read's Weekly Journal* on 29 March 1729. The epigram was probably written two days later and revised for the *Dunciad Variorum* published on 26 November 1729. See Pope's *Correspondence*, ed. Sherburn, II 298, III 300; *Notes and Queries*, n.s., IV (1957), 465. The text is that of *Dunciad* A, with collations from the autograph (*MS*) and *The Works* (*1735*).

1. *Busto*] The sculptor of the bust was J. M. Rysbrack (1693–1770).

VII. In *Works* 1735, this epigram concludes a note on *Dunciad* A, III 319f:

> Beneath his reign, shall Eusden wear the bays,
> Cibber preside Lord-Chancellor of Plays,

which reads, "I have before observ'd something like Prophesy in our Author. Eusden, whom he here couples with Cibber, no sooner died but his place of Laureate was supply'd by Cibber, in the year 1730, on which was made the ensuing Epigram . . ." No earlier text survives than *1732* (see above), where the epigram was claimed as a reprint. Cibber reprinted it as a specimen of Pope's attacks on him in *A Letter from Mr. Cibber to Mr. Pope*, 1742 (p. 39); but though Pope was at pains to disprove some of Cibber's charges he never denied this particular accusation, but incorporated the epigram in the revised *Dunciad* (1743). The probabilities point to Pope's authorship.

The text is that of *1735*.

COUPLETS & VERSICLES
1721–1730
[See *ante*, p. 74.]

Contemporary transcripts: Longleat, Portland Papers, XIII [Nos. II, III]; BM
MS Harl. 7316 [Nos. III].

The Grub-street Journal. 19 November 1730. [No. v.]

A Collection of Pieces . . . publish'd on Occasion of the Dunciad . . . By Mr. Savage.
1732. [No. v.]

Memoirs of the Society of Grub-street. 1737. [No. v.]

The Works . . . In Prose. Vol. II. 1741. [Nos. III, IV.]

The Works . . . Vol. VII. Containing . . . Last Part of Letters. 1741. [Nos. III, IV.]

Dean Swift's Literary Correspondence . . . from 1714 to 1738. 1741. [Nos. III, IV.]

The Works . . . Vol. III. Part II. Containing the Dunciad, Book IV. 1742. [No. v.]

The Works . . . Vol. IV. Part III. Containing . . . Letters. 1742. [Nos. III, IV.]

The Works . . . Ed. Warburton. Vol. VI. 1751. [No. v]; and Vol. IX [Nos.
III, IV].

Letters . . . to a Lady. 1769. [No. I.]

Additions to the Works . . . 1776. [No. I.]

A Supplementary Volume to the Works . . . 1807. [No. I.]

The Works. Ed. Dyce. Vol. II. 1831. [No. I.]

The Works. Ed. Elwin and Courthope. Vol. VII. 1871. [No. II.]

I.
Verses to Mrs. Judith Cowper.

Tho' sprightly Sappho force our love and praise, ⎫
A softer wonder my pleas'd soul surveys,   ⎬
The mild Erinna, blushing in her bays.   ⎭
So while the sun's broad beam yet strikes the sight,
All mild appears the moon's more sober light,   5
Serene, in virgin majesty, she shines;
And, un-observed, the glaring sun declines.

4 while . . . yet strikes the sight] when . . . has tir'd the sight *1735.*
5 appears] ascends *1735.*
6 majesty] Modesty *1735.*
7 sun] Orb *1735.*

II.

Lines to *BOLINGBROKE*.

Wʜᴀᴛ pleasing Phrensy steals away my Soul?
      Thro' thy blest Shades (La Source) I seem to rove
I see thy fountains fall, thy waters roll
      And breath the Zephyrs that refresh thy Grove
I hear whatever can delight inspire   5
Villete's soft Voice and Sᵗ John's silver Lyre.

III.

LINES

In Conclusion of a Satire.

Bᴜᴛ what avails to lay down rules for sense?
      In ——'s Reign these fruitless lines were writ,
When Ambrose Philips was preferr'd for Wit!

IV.

Inscriptio.

Aɴᴅ thou! whose sense, whose humour, and whose rage,
      At once can teach, delight, and lash the age,
Whether thou choose Cervantes' serious air,
Or laugh and shake in Rab'lais' easy chair,
Praise courts, and monarchs, or extol mankind,   5
Or thy grieved country's copper chains unbind;
Attend whatever title please thine ear,
Dean, Drapier, Bickerstaff, or Gulliver.
From thy Bœotia, lo! the fog retires,
Yet grieve not thou at what our Isle acquires;   10
Here dulness reigns, with mighty wings outspread,
And brings the true Saturnian age of lead.

11*

V.

CANTICLE

A LL hail, arch-poet without peer!
    Vine, bay, or cabbage fit to wear,
And worthy of the *prince's ear.*

2 bay, or] Laurel, *1730.*
3 the] thy *1730.*

I. These Verses were first addressed by Pope to Judith Cowper in the exchange of compliments with which their correspondence began. In his second letter (18 October 1722), after expressing the wish of knowing her as a friend even more than as "a Kinswoman of Apollo", he praises her "writings", and then goes on to say: "I am willing to spare your modesty; and therefore, as to your writing, may perhaps never say more . . . than the few verses I send here; which . . . I made so long ago as the day you sate for your picture, and yet never till now durst confess to you." Whereupon he transcribes these lines, of which he thought well enough to keep a copy; for thirteen years later, in 1735, a revision (see collations) of the last four lines appeared in print for the first time in *Of the Characters of Women* (Vol. III II, p. 70; ll. 253–6) but now addressed to Martha Blount. The letter itself, with the original Verses, was not known till 1769, when with the rest of the Pope-Cowper correspondence it was published by Dodsley in *Letters . . . to a Lady*, from which the text is taken.

   3. *Erinna*] A Greek poetess, contemporary of Sappho, *c.* 600 B.C.

   4–7. *So . . . declines.*] First printed *1735,* see above.

II. Writing to Pope from France (18 February 1724), Bolingbroke tells him that his wife—"our Lady of La Source"—who was shortly to visit England, "neither sends nor receives any more messages". He then goes on to say that "she vows she will very shortly appear to you in a vision under the form of an old French woman." Pope's reply, dated 9 April 1724, ended thus: "You tell me . . . the Oracles of our Lady of La source are ceas'd and that She returns no more answers, I shall expect the favour She promises to a poor Hermit on the banks of the Thames. In the mean time I see Visions of her and of La source.

      ——*An me ludit amabilis*
       Insania? Audire et videor pios
        Errare per lucos, amœnæ
        Quos et aquæ subeunt et auræ."

[Whereupon the "Lines" follow, and in turn are followed by]

      "——*Seu voce nunc mavis acuta*
        Seu fidibus, citharave Phœbi.

I cannot subscribe myself better than as Horace did:

> *Vestris amicum fontibus et choris.*"

The text follows that of the Longleat manuscript.

2. *La Source*] Bolingbroke's residence in France near Orleans, the grounds of which contain the source of the river Loiret.

6. *Villete*] Bolingbroke's second wife, the Marquise de Villette.

Lyre] A pun—*Lyre/loire*—is intended. The two words were almost certainly homophones at this time; cf. Goldsmith's rhyme, *choir/Loire* in *The Traveller*, ll. 243–4.

III. Swift, writing to Pope from Ireland (29 September 1725), mentioned amongst other items of news Ambrose Philips's failure to obtain preferment there. In the course of his reply (15 October 1725), Pope wrote: "I'm sorry poor P. is not promoted in this age; for certainly if his reward be of the next, he is of all Poets the most miserable. I'm also sorry for another reason; if they don't promote him, they'll spoil the conclusion of one of my Satires, where having endeavour'd to correct the Taste of the town in wit and criticism, I end thus . . ." whereupon follow the above "Lines". No poem of Pope's as printed ends in this way; but the last line, practically unaltered, appeared in the first edition of the *Dunciad* (A, III 322) (see Vol. V). A variant of the last two lines appears in a contemporary manuscript in the British Museum (Harl. 7316), thus:

> This in the Days of good King George I writ,
> When Ambrose Philips had a place for Wit.
>
> > > A. Pope.

2. ——'s *Reign*] George's reign.

IV. On 22 October 1727, shortly before Pope decided to postpone the publication of the *Dunciad* until 1728, he wrote to Swift giving him some news of it, and ended the letter by saying: "Your name is in it . . . Adieu, and God bless you, and give you health and spirits.

> Whether thou chuse Cervantes' serious air,
> Or laugh and shake in Rablais' easy chair,
> Or in the graver Gown instruct mankind,
> Or silent, let thy morals tell thy mind.

These two verses are over and above what I've said of you in the Poem. Adieu." (The "two verses" are, of course, the last two lines which do not appear in the *Inscriptio* above or in the *Dunciad*.) Writing again some three months later (the actual date is uncertain) he says to Swift: "It grieves me to the soul that I cannot send you my *chef d'œuvre*, the poem on Dulness. . . I send you, however, what most nearly relates to yourself, the inscription to it." Whereupon follows *Inscriptio*, differing in many respects from the *Dunciad* versions (Vol. V, pp. 62f.). Pope "saved" the opening couplet and used it later in the epitaph on Gay (see *post*, p. 350).

V. This triplet is found in an anonymous article, entitled "Of the Poet Laureate" in *The Grub-street Journal* of 19 November 1730, and is reprinted in *Memoirs* (1737), signed with the letter "A" (see *post*, p. 325). Pope later included it in the "Appendix" to the *Dunciad* (1743) amongst other prose pieces of his, thereby acknowledging his authorship. The article describes the ceremonies which are said to have accompanied the appointment of the "archi-poeta" at Rome; in the course of which the triplet is introduced thus: "Next the public acclamation was expressed in a *canticle*, which is transmitted to us, as follows:

> *Salve, brassicea virens corona,*
> *Et lauro, archipoeta, pampinoque!*
> *Dignus principis auribus Leonis.*"

Whereupon the translation follows as above, the text of which is that of Pope's last revision (*1743*), with collations from the "Grub-street" version (*1730*), with which the *1732* and *1737* reprints agree.

PROLOGUE
TO
SOPHONISBA.
By a Friend.

WHEN learning, after the long *Gothic* night,
   Fair, o'er the western world, renew'd his light,
With arts arising *Sophonisba* rose:
The tragic muse, returning, wept her woes.
With her th' *Italian* scene first learnt to glow;   5
And the first tears for her were taught to flow.
Her charms the *Gallic* muses next inspir'd:
Corneille himself saw, wonder'd, and was fir'd.
   What foreign theatres with pride have shewn,
Britain, by juster title, makes her own.   10
When freedom is the cause, 'tis hers to fight;
And hers, when freedom is the theme, to write.
For this, a *British Author* bids again
The heroine rise, to grace the *British* scene.
Here, as in life, she breathes her genuine flame: 15

She asks what bosom has not felt the same?
Asks of the *British Youth*—Is silence there?
She dares to ask it of the *British Fair*.

 To night, our home-spun author would be true,
At once, to nature, history, and you.   20
Well-pleas'd to give our neighbours due applause,
He owns their learning, but disdains their laws.
Not to his patient touch, or happy flame,
'Tis to his *British* heart he trusts for fame.
If *France* excel him in one free-born thought, 25
The man, as well as poet, is in fault.

 [*Nature*! informer of the poet's art,
Whose force alone can raise or melt the heart,
Thou art his guide; each passion, every line,
Whate'er he draws to please, must all be thine. 30
Be thou his judge: in every candid breast,
Thy silent whisper is the sacred test.]

The Tragedy Of Sophonisba . . . By Mr. Thomson. 1730 (all issues, and later editions).

The Poems of Pope. Vol. II (in Johnson's *English Poets*, New Edition). 1790.

 The attribution to Pope of part of this Prologue rests upon Dr Johnson's remark in his life of Thomson (*Lives of the Poets*, ed. Hill, III 288): "I have been told by Savage that of the Prologue to *Sophonisba* the first part was written by Pope who could not be persuaded to finish it, and that the concluding lines were added by Mallet." Internal evidence corroborates Savage's assertion; for the *Prologue to Cato* (see *ante*, p. 96) begins similarly with the origins and functions of "the tragic muse"; explains the author's intentions, and points to his scorn of "French translations", and his resolve to write for "British ears" and "British hearts". The piece also contains echoes from Pope's other works (see footnotes). Thus, while there is nothing inherently improbable in the attribution, all the available evidence tends to confirm it. The invocation to "Nature", changing the tone and tempo of the piece, clearly betrays another hand, and perhaps marks the extent of Mallet's addition. It was presumably composed shortly before the first performance of the tragedy on 28 February 1730.

 The text follows that of the first printing.

 5. *first learnt to glow*] Cf. *Unfortunate Lady*, 45: "ne'er learn'd to glow".

 6. *tears . . . taught to flow*] Cf. *Eloisa*, 28: "Nor tears, for ages, taught to flow"; *Iliad*, IX 723: "Is it for him these tears are taught to flow".

 27–32. This concluding paragraph was presumably added by Mallet (see introductory note).

EPITAPH
On Sir GODFREY KNELLER,
In Westminster-Abby, 1723.

KNELLER, by Heav'n and not a Master taught,
Whose Art was Nature, and whose Pictures thought;
Now for two ages having snatch'd from fate
Whate'er was Beauteous, or whate'er was Great,
Lies crown'd with Princes Honours, Poets Lays,   5
Due to his Merit, and brave Thirst of Praise.
Living, great Nature fear'd he might outvie
Her works; and dying, fears herself may die.

3 When now two Ages, he had snatch'd [scratch'd *L*] from Fate
   1730, L, S.   4 or] and *S.*
5 Lies] Rests *1730, L, S, 1735a.* Honours] Honour *1730, S.*
7 might] would *S.*

Lapidary inscription in Westminster Abbey.
Contemporary transcript: Stowe MS 972.
The St. James's Evening Post. 21 April 1730.
The Grub-street Journal. 23 April 1730.
The Weekly Journal. 25 April 1730.
The Whitehall Evening-Post. 7–9 May 1730.
The London Evening-Post. 7–9 May 1730.
The Daily Post. 9 May 1730.
The Universal Spectator. 9 May 1730.
The Monthly Chronicle. No. xxix. [June 1730.]
The Works of Mr. Alexander Pope. Volume II. 1735 (folio and quarto).
The Works of Alexander Pope, Esq: Vol. II. 1735 (octavo).
The Works . . . Vol. II. Containing his Epistles and Satires. 1735 (and 1736).
Ethic Epistles, Satires, &c. . . . Written by Mr. Pope. 1735.
Ethic Epistles, to Henry St. John L. Bolingbroke. Written in the Year 1732. 1735.
The Works. Ed. Warburton. Vol. VI. 1751.
In a letter to Lord Strafford, dated 6 July [1725], Pope describes how Sir God-
frey sent for him just before he died, how the dying painter was troubled about
his burial-place, and how he swore he wouldn't be buried in Westminster Abbey,
because "they do bury fools there." "Then," Pope continues, "he s^d to me, My
good friend, where will you be buried? I said, Wherever I drop; very likely in
Twitnam. He reply'd, So will I; then proceeded to desire I w^d write his epitaph,
wch I promised him. It would be endless to tell y^r l^dship ye strange things he sug-

gested on that head: it must be in Latin, that all foreigners may read it: it must be in English too, &c. I desir'd him to be easy in all that matter, I w^d certainly do ye best I c^d." There was however much delay; and two years after Kneller's death (1723) the proposed location of his monument was the cause of a quarrel between Lady Kneller and Pope (see *ante*, p. 249). Indeed, her husband's epitaph was never put up in Twickenham church; and nothing more is heard of it until its first appearance in print in *The St. James's Evening Post*, 21 April 1730, with this introduction: "A curious Monument is putting up in Westminster-Abbey, ... in Memory of ... Sir Godfrey Kneller Bart. upon which the following Inscription (made by Mr. Pope) will be engraved, viz..." "I think it is the worst thing I ever wrote in my life," Pope confessed to Spence (p. 165) at some date between 1734 and 1736, and thereafter he consistently excluded it from every edition of his works.

The text is that of *Works*, Vol. II (quarto, 1735), corrected in one particular from the text of *Works*, Vol. II (octavo, 1735). Collations are given from the first printing (*1730*), the lapidary inscription (*L*), the Stowe transcript (*S*), the above-mentioned quarto (*1735a*), and Warburton's edition (*1751*).

2. *whose Pictures thought*] Cf. Pope's letter to Kneller (18 February 1718): "Dryden says he has seen a Fool think in y^r picture of him."

7–8. Imitated from the famous Epitaph on Raphael:

> ——*Raphael, timuit quo sospite, vinci*
> *Rerum magna parens, & moriente, mori.* [P. *1735, 51*].

EPITAPH

On the Monument of the Honble. ROBERT DIGBY, and of his Sister MARY, erected by their Father the Lord DIGBY, in the Church of Sherborne in Dorsetshire, 1727.

G o! fair Example of untainted youth,
    Of modest wisdom, and pacifick truth:

Title] *TSS read:* Epitaph on the Monument of the Honble Robert Digby, and of his Sister the Honble Mary Digby, in the Church of Sherborne in Dorset Shire, erected by their Father the Lord Digby.
Inscription reads: In Memory of Robert, Second Son, And Mary, Eldest Daughter of William, Lord Digby.
2 wisdom] Reason *Ins.*

Compos'd in suff'rings, and in joy sedate,
Good without noise, without pretension great.
Just of thy word, in ev'ry thought sincere,   5
Who knew no wish but what the world might hear:
Of softest manners, unaffected mind,
Lover of peace, and friend of human kind:
Go live! for heav'ns Eternal year is thine,
Go, and exalt thy Moral to Divine.   10
    And thou blest Maid! attendant on his doom,
Pensive hast follow'd to the silent tomb,
Steer'd the same course to the same quiet shore,
Not parted long, and now to part no more!
Go then, where only bliss sincere is known!   15
Go, where to love and to enjoy are one!
    Yet take these tears, Mortality's relief,
And till we share your joys, forgive our grief;
These little rites, a Stone, a Verse, receive,
'Tis all a Father, all a Friend can give!   20

3 joy] Joys *Ins.*
3f. *omm. in TSS and 1730. Transposed to follow l. 8. Ins. and 1735ab.*
  5 Just of thy] Go, just of *Ins.* in ev'ry] and in each *TSS and 1730.*
  7 softest] Gentlest *Ins.*   11 blest Maid!] too close *Ins.*
12 Pensive] Blest Maid; *Ins.*
13 Steer'd] Took *TSS and 1730.*   15f. *omm. Ins.*
16–17 *Between these lines TSS have a couplet:*
            Rejoyn Ye Kindred Souls, and flame on high,
            Through the long Instant of Eternity.
19 Stone, a Verse] Stone and Verse *TSS, Ins., 1730.*

Contemporary transcripts: Longleat, Portland Papers, XVII and XX (two copies); Welbeck Abbey, Harley Papers; BM MS Stowe 972; Bodleian MS Ballard 50; Bromley MS (on Robert only), Dobell.
    Inscription in Sherborne Abbey.
    Miscellaneous Poems, By Several Hands. D. Lewis. 1730 (published 5 May).
    The Grub-street Journal. No. 36. 2 July 1730.
    The Weekly Journal. 4 July 1730.
    Faithful Memoirs of the Grubstreet Society. 1732.
    The Works of Mr. Alexander Pope. Volume II. 1735 (folio and quarto).

The Works of Alexander Pope, Esq; Vol. II. 1735 (octavo).
The Works . . . Vol. II. Containing his Epistles and Satires. 1735 (and 1736).
Ethic Epistles, Satires, &c. . . . Written by Mr. Pope. 1735.
Ethic Epistles, to Henry St. John L. Bolingbroke. Written in the Year 1732. 1735.
Mr. Pope's Literary Correspondence. Vol. V. 1737 (on Robert only).
Memoirs of the Society of Grub-street. Vol. I. 1737.
The Works . . . Vol. II. Containing his Epistles, &c. 1739 (both editions).
The Works . . . Vol. II. Part I. Containing his Epistles, &c. 1740 (and 1743).
A Collection of Moral and Sacred Poems. J. Wesley. Vol. I. 1744.
The Works. Ed. Warburton. Vol. VI. 1751.

In a letter (Harley transcript, Welbeck Abbey) of 24 April 1730, Pope asks Samuel Wesley to deliver the following message to Lewis the publisher: "The epitaph he writes about may (I think) pass if he cancel only ye 2 lines (he will understand this) without altering the next page, I will be at that charge." Reference to Lewis's *Miscellaneous Poems*, where the epitaph was first published, shows that the epitaph is printed on pp. 124–5, and that the catchword, "Rejoin", on p. 124, does not recur at the top of p. 125, which further examination proves to be a cancel. In the three Harley transcripts, however, there is a couplet at this place beginning, "Rejoin . . ." which, as it does not appear in any printed copy, shows that the transcripts must have been made, more or less directly, from Pope's autograph, and that in all probability they antedate the printed versions.

Nevertheless it is probable that the epitaph had a still earlier form. Robert Digby, Pope's intimate friend and correspondent since 1717, died on 21 April 1726; and the poet's personal sorrow found voice in his letter of condolence (29 April) to Robert's brother, Edward. It is difficult to believe that Pope waited three years—until Mary had died of small-pox on 31 March 1729—before he was moved to write his friend's epitaph. That he did not wait is suggested both by the curious date, "1727", appended to the title in 1735, and by the discovery of two separate pieces of evidence which seem to prove that the epitaph first commemorated Robert alone, (1) an unrecorded printed text of ll. 1–10 as they appear later in the final version, with one word misprinted, and headed: "The honourable Robert Digby died in the year 1726 and is buried in the church of Sherburne in Dorsetshire, with the following Epitaph written by the Author." (2) a contemporary manuscript version, hitherto unknown, as follows:

> On the Honble Mr Rob. Digby who died in 1727.
> By Mr Pope.
>
> Go faire Example of untainted Youth,
> Of modest Sense, Integrity & Truth:
> Go just of Word, in every Thought sincere,
> Who knew no Wish, but what the World might hear.
> Of softest Manners, unaffected Mind,
> Lover of Peace, a Friend to Humane Kind:
> Compos'd in Sufferings, and in Joy sedate,
> Good without Noise, without Pretension Great.
> Go live! for Heaven's eternal Year is thine,

Go, and exalt thy Moral to Divine.
   Accept these Tears, Mortality's Relief,
Yet till we share thy Joys, forgive our Grief:
These little Rites, a Stone & Verse, receive;
'Tis all a Father, & a Friend can give!

It would therefore appear that the moving lines on Mary (ll. 11–16, plus the deleted couplet) were inserted in a revised version of Robert's epitaph, probably in 1729; that when Lewis asked Pope for contributions to his forthcoming miscellany, Pope included the joint Robert-Mary epitaph among the five pieces he sent him, but suddenly decided, after the book was printed, to delete the newly added couplet on "the long Instant of Eternity" (probably because the "eternal Year" had already been alluded to in the original "Robert" portion). The 1730 revision is taken as the date of the poem.

The *Works* in folio (*1735*) has been adopted for copy-text, but in the order of the couplets, about which Pope found some difficulty in satisfying himself, the final text of the *Works* in octavo (*1735*) has been followed.

Title: *1727*] As Mary died in 1729 (see below), the date may refer to a separate epitaph on Robert (see introductory note).

9. Cf. Dryden's *Ode to . . . Mrs. Anne Killigrew*, l. 15.

12. *Pensive hast follow'd*] The inscription reads: Robt dy'd Apr^l 21st An: Dom: 1726. Æt: 34. Mary dy'd Mar^h 31st An: Dom: 1729. Æt: 39.

EPIGRAM.

W HEN other Ladies to the Groves go down,
   Corinna still, and *Fulvia* stay in Town;
Those Ghosts of Beauty ling'ring here reside,
And haunt the Places where their Honour dy'd.

1 Ladies] Fair ones *MS.* Groves] Shades *MS, 1730.*
2 *Corinna* still, and *Fulvia*] Still Cloë, Flavia, Delia, *MS*; Still *Flavia, Chloris, Celia 1730.*
3 ling'ring] wandring *MS.* here reside] there abide *1730.*

Pope's autograph: BM MS Stowe 755.
Miscellaneous Poems, By Several Hands. Published by D. Lewis. 1730 (published 5 May 1730).
Miscellanies. The Third Volume. 1732 (and some, not all, later editions).
A Collection of Epigrams. Vol. II. 1737.
A Supplement to Dr. Swift's and Mr. Pope's Works. 1739.
Select Epigrams. Vol. II. 1797.

A Supplementary Volume to the Works of Alexander Pope, Esq. 1807.

The Works. Ed. Carruthers. Vol. IV. 1854.

Within three months of the anonymous publication of this epigram in Lewis's miscellany, Pope wrote to John Knight (30 July 1730): "I hope you both enjoy whatever is to be enjoyd in yᵉ Country. . . I am stuck at Twit'nam. . . So is Mrs. Patty Blount. . . Women seldom are planted in yᵉ Soil that wᵈ best agree with them, you see Carnations fading & dirty in Cheapside, wᶜʰ wᵈ blush & shine in yᵉ Country. Mrs. Cornish is (just now) going to some such soft Retreat, as Hampsted, or Richmᵈ, or Islington, having read the following Epigram"—whereupon these lines follow, with no allusion to source or authorship. Two years later he included the epigram (as usual without acknowledgement) in *Miscellanies. The Third Volume.* Seeing that the epigram had been progressively revised, Pope later incorporated its last two lines (after yet further revision) in his *Epistle to a Lady. Of the Characters of Women* (see Vol. III 11), there can be little doubt about its authorship, in spite of lack of acknowledgement. In the absence of any evidence of date of composition, it is tentatively assigned to 1730, the year of publication.

The text is that of *1732*, with collations from Pope's autograph (*MS*), and the first printing (*1730*).

3f. Cf. *Epistle to a Lady*, 1735 (ll. 241–2):

> Still round and round the Ghosts of Beauty glide,
> And haunt the places where their Honour dy'd.

EPITAPH.

Intended for Sir ISAAC NEWTON,

In Westminster-Abbey.

ISAACUS NEWTONIUS
Quem Immortalem,
Testantur Tempus, Natura, Cœlum:
Mortalem
Hoc Marmor fatetur.

Nature, and Nature's Laws lay hid in Night.
God said, *Let Newton be!* and All was *Light.*

1 NEWTONIUS:] NEWTON, *1730(a)*.

3 *1730(a) reads:* Cœli Natura, Tempus enarrant;

5 *1730(a) reads:* Hoc solum Marmor fatetur.

6 Nature, and Nature's] All Nature and her *1730(a)*; All Nature and its *1730(b)*, TS.

Contemporary transcript: BM MS Stowe 972.

The Present State of the Republick of Letters. For June, 1730. Vol. V. 1730.

The Grub-street Journal. No. 28. 16 July 1730.

The Works of Mr. Alexander Pope. Volume II. 1735. [In the quarto, but not the folio.]

The Works of Alexander Pope, Esq; Vol. II. 1735 (octavo).

The Works . . . Vol. II. Containing his Epistles and Satires. 1735 (and 1736).

Ethic Epistles, Satires, &c. . . . Written by Mr. Pope. 1735. [On "Errata" leaf, in some copies.]

Ethic Epistles, to Henry St. John L. Bolingbroke. Written in the Year 1732. 1735.

Memoirs of the Society of Grub-street. Vol. I. 1737.

The Works . . . Vol. II. Containing his Epistles, &c. 1739.

The Works . . . Vol. II. Part I. Containing his Epistles, &c. 1740 (and 1743).

The Gentleman's Magazine. October 1741.

The Works. Ed. Warburton. Vol. VI. 1751.

The text follows that of *1735* quarto, with collations from the two first printings, *1730a* and *1730b*, and from the transcript (*TS*).

EPITAPH

On Mr. ELIJAH FENTON,

At Easthamsted in Berks, 1730.

THIS modest Stone what few vain Marbles can
   May truly say, here lies an honest Man.
A Poet, blest beyond the Poet's fate,
Whom Heav'n kept sacred from the Proud and Great.
Foe to loud Praise, and Friend to learned Ease,   5
Content with Science in the Vale of Peace.
Calmly he look'd on either Life, and here
Saw nothing to regret, or there to fear;
From Nature's temp'rate feast rose satisfy'd,
Thank'd Heav'n that he had liv'd, and that he dy'd.   10

1 This] The *1730, TS*.   3 beyond the] beyond a *1730, TS*.
6 Vale] arms *1730, TS; and MS originally, but corrected by Lord Oxford to* vale.
8 or] Nor *1730, TS*.

Pope's autograph: Welbeck Abbey, Harley Papers.
Contemporary transcripts: BM MS Stowe 972; Downshire MSS, Reading.
The Daily Post-Boy. 22 October 1730.
The Whitehall Evening-Post. 20–22 October 1730.
The London Evening-Post. 20–22 October 1730.
Applebee's Original Weekly Journal. 24 October 1730.
The Grub-street Journal. No. 43. 29 October 1730.
The lapidary inscription at Easthampstead.
Faithful Memoirs of the Grubstreet Society. 1732.
The Works of Mr. Alexander Pope. Volume II. 1735 (folio and quarto).
The Works of Alexander Pope, Esq; Vol. II. 1735 (octavo).
The Works . . . Vol. II. Containing his Epistles and Satires. 1735 (and 1736).
Ethic Epistles, Satires, &c. . . . Written by Mr. Pope. 1735.
Ethic Epistles, to Henry St. John L. Bolingbroke. Written in the Year 1732. 1735.
Mr. Pope's Literary Correspondence. Vol. V. 1737.
The Works . . . Vol. II. Containing his Epistles, &c. 1739 (both editions).
The Works . . . Vol. II. Part I. Containing his Epistles, &c. 1740 (and 1743).
A Collection of Moral and Sacred Poems. J. Wesley. Vol. I. 1744.
The Agreeable Companion. 1745.
Joe Miller's Jests. 8th Edition. 1745 (and later editions).
The Works. Ed. Warburton. Vol. VI. 1751.

Pope wrote to Broome (29 August 1730) on Fenton's death: "I shall with pleasure take upon me to draw the amiable, quiet, deserving, unpretending, christian and philosophical character, in his epitaph. There truth may be spoken in a few words. As for flourish, and oratory, and poetry, I leave them to younger and more lively writers . . . who would rather show their own fine parts, than report the valuable ones of any other man." The epitaph first appeared anonymously in *The Daily Post-Boy* of 22 October 1730; was repeated in two evening papers of the same day, and subsequently in others (the question of the "first edition" being solved as it is in the case of the Harcourt epitaph; see *ante*, p. 243). Pope replied to Broome's later inquiry (14 December): "The epitaph on him I thought you must have seen, as they had got it into the public prints. However, such as it is, here take it. It is not good in any sense but as it is true, and really therefore exemplary to others." The copy he enclosed (as printed by EC, VIII 166) has five slight variants from the newspaper version.

The text follows that of *1735*, with which the lapidary inscription, the version sent to Broome, and subsequent printings, are in verbal agreement. Variant readings from the autograph (*MS*), the Stowe transcript (*TS*), and *The Daily Post-Boy* (*1730*) are recorded.

1–2. See Crashaw's Epitaph on Mr. Ashton, p. 122 of his Poems, to whom Mr. Pope forgot to acknowledge his Obligation for this Compliment paid Mr. Fenton . . .   The modest Front of this small Floor,
            Believe me Reader, can say more:
            Than many a braver Marble can
            Here lies a truly honest Man . . .   [*Curll, 1737*].

EPITAPH.

On General HENRY WITHERS,

In Westminster-Abby, 1729.

Here Withers rest! thou bravest, gentlest mind,
   Thy Country's friend, but more of Human kind.
Oh born to Arms! O Worth in Youth approv'd!
O soft Humanity, in Age belov'd!
For thee the hardy Vet'ran drops a tear,   5
And the gay Courtier feels the sigh sincere.
   Withers adieu! yet not with thee remove
Thy Martial spirit, or thy Social love!
Amidst corruption, luxury, and rage,
Still leave some ancient virtues to our age: 10
Nor let us say, (those English glories gone)
The last true Briton lies beneath this stone.

6 the sigh] his sigh *L*.

Contemporary transcripts: BM Cowper Papers, MS Add. 28101; and BM
MS Stowe 972.
   Lapidary inscription: Westminster Abbey.
   The Grub-street Journal. No. 50. 17 December 1730.
   Faithful Memoirs of the Grubstreet Society. 1732.
   The Works of Mr. Alexander Pope. Volume II. 1735 (folio and quarto).
   The Works of Alexander Pope, Esq; Vol. II. 1735 (octavo).
   The Works . . . Vol. II. Containing his Epistles and Satires. 1735 (and 1736).
   Ethic Epistles, Satires, &c. . . . Written by Mr. Pope. 1735.
   Ethic Epistles, to Henry St. John L. Bolingbroke. Written in the Year 1732. 1735.
   Memoirs of the Society of Grub-street. Vol. I. 1737.
   The Works . . . Vol. II. Containing his Epistles, &c. 1739.
   The Works . . . Vol. II. Part I. Containing his Epistles, &c. 1740 (and 1743).
   The Works. Ed. Warburton. Vol. VI. 1751.
When first printed, as also in the MSS mentioned above, these lines were pre-
ceded by a prose epitaph which appears on the monument and is believed to be
Pope's also:

   Henry Withers, Lieutenant General, descended from a military stock,
and bred in arms, in Britain, Dunkirk, and Tangier. Thro' the whole course of
the two last wars of England with France, he served in Ireland, in the Low
Countries, and in Germany; was present in every battle, and at every siege;

and distinguished in all by an activity, a valour, and zeal, which nature gave and honour improved. A love of glory and of his country, animated and raised him above that spirit which the trade of war inspires; a desire of acquiring riches and honours by the miseries of mankind. His temper was humane, his benevolence universal, and among all those ancient virtues, which he pre-served in practice and in credit, none was more remarkable than his hospi-tality. He died at the age of 78 years, on the 11th of November MDCCXXIX. To whom this Monument is erected by his Companion in the wars, and his friend thro' life, HENRY DISNEY.

Disney and Withers were both old friends of Pope.

The text follows that of *1735*, with a collation of the lapidary inscription (*L*).

To MR. *C.*

ST *JAMES'S* PLACE. *LONDON*, *October* 22.

Few words are best; I wish you well:
    Bethel, I'm told, will soon be here:
Some morning-walks along the Mall,
    And evening-friends will end the year.

If, in this interval, between   5
    The falling leaf and coming frost,
You please to see, on Twit'nam green,
    Your friend, your poet, and your host;

For three whole days you here may rest
    From office, business, news, and strife: 10
And (what most folks would think a jest)
    Want nothing else, except your wife.

The Edinburgh Magazine and Review. July 1774.
The Scots Magazine. July 1774.
The Weekly Magazine. 4 August 1774.
The London Chronicle. 8–10 September 1774.
The Weekly Miscellany. 26 September 1774.
The Monthly Miscellany. September 1774.
The Fugitive Miscellany . . . Part the Second. 1775.

The Flower-Piece. 1780.

A Select Collection of Poems. J. Nichols. Vol. IV. 1780.

The New Foundling Hospital for Wit. Vol. V. 1784 (and Vol. I. 1786).

The Poems of Pope. Vol. II (Johnson's *English Poets*, New Edition). 1790.

This poem, when first published, was accompanied by a letter from a certain "J. B.", who claimed to have "transcribed it from the original, in Pope's hand-writing". The attribution to Pope is corroborated by allusions to Bethel and Twickenham, and by the identification of "Mr. C." as William Cleland (1673–1741), a man of Scots descent, who (according to *The Daily Post*, 22 September 1741) "on Monday last died after a short illness, at his house in St. James's-place", having been "for many years . . . one of the Commissioners of the Land Tax". This is undoubtedly the Cleland of the *Dunciad* and the Timon-Chandos controversies (see Vol. III II, p. xxvii, and V, pp. xxv, 434), and of whose friendship with Pope the earliest documentary evidence seems to be the poet's letter to Lord Oxford (1 July 1728) in which Cleland is called "a friend of mine". Bethel's friendship with Cleland is corroborated by Pope's letter to Bethel containing news of him (9 August 1733); and Cleland's habit of taking "morning-walks along the Mall" is confirmed by Swift's letter to Pope (15 January 1731/2): "Pray tell me whether your Colonel Cleland be a tall Scots gentleman, walking perpetually in the Mall. . . As to his letter before the Dunciad I know not the secret. . ." The poem is tentatively dated 1730, in view of Swift's letter.

The text follows that of the first printing in every respect.

1. *Few words are best*] So, in a letter to Caryll about visiting him (27 August 1733) Pope writes: "Few words are best: you shall be troubled with me . . ."

2. *Bethel*] Hugh Bethel, see Biog. App., Vol. IV.

3. Cf. Swift's letter in introductory note.

10. *office*] Cleland was one of the Commissioners of the Land Tax.

EPITAPH.

On Mrs. CORBET,

Who dyed of a Cancer in her Breast.

HERE rests a Woman, good without pretence,
    Blest with plain Reason and with sober Sense;
No Conquests she, but o'er herself desir'd,
No Arts essay'd, but not to be admir'd.
Passion and Pride were to her soul unknown,   5
Convinc'd, that Virtue only is our own.

So unaffected, so compos'd a mind,
So firm yet soft, so strong yet so refin'd,
Heav'n, as its purest Gold, by Tortures try'd;
The Saint sustain'd it, but the Woman dy'd.   10

Title] *MS reads:* In Memory of Mrs Elisabeth Corbett who de-
parted this Life at Paris, March ye 1st 1724 [i.e., 1724/5], after a
long and painful Sickness, She was Daughter to Sr Uvedale Cor-
bett of Longnor in the County of Salop Bar^t by the right Honble
the Lady Mildred Cecill, who ordered this Monument to be
erected. [which practically coincides with the inscription on the
stone.]
    1730 reads: Epitaph on Mrs. Elizabeth Corbett.

Lapidary inscription: St Margaret's, Westminster.
Contemporary transcript: Welbeck Abbey, Harley Papers.
Miscellaneous Poems, By Several Hands. D. Lewis. 1730.
The Works of Mr. Alexander Pope. Volume II. 1735 (folio and quarto).
The Works of Alexander Pope, Esq; Vol. II. 1735 (octavo).
The Works . . . Vol. II. Containing his Epistles and Satires. 1735 (and 1736).
Ethic Epistles, Satires, &c. . . . Written by Mr. Pope. 1735.
Ethic Epistles, to Henry St. John L. Bolingbroke. Written in the Year 1732. 1735.
The Works . . . Vol. II. Containing his Epistles, &c. 1739 (both editions).
The Works . . . Vol. II. Part I. Containing his Epistles, &c. 1740 (and 1743).
A Collection of Moral and Sacred Poems. J. Wesley. Vol. I. 1744.
Poems . . . by . . . John Winstanley . . . with many Others, By Several Ingenious Hands.
Vol. II. 1751.
    The Works. Ed. Warburton. Vol. VI. 1751.
There can be little doubt about the identity of the lady commemorated. From
its first printing these lines were publicly associated with the name of Mrs
Corbett, whose death was thus announced in *The St. James's Evening Post* of 9–11
March 1725: "Mrs. Elizabeth Corbett, a Maiden Lady, Daughter of the Lady
Hotham, died lately in France; and her Corpse is to be brought to England."
Nevertheless, it is strange that no evidence has survived of Pope's acquaintance
with the deceased lady or her family, and that the cause of her death should be
stated in the later texts, but neither in the earlier texts nor in the inscription. For
these reasons C. W. Dilke argued with much plausibility (*The Athenaeum*, 22 and
29 July 1854) that the epitaph was probably originally written on a known friend
of Pope's, Mrs Cope, a cousin of John Caryll, in whose unhappy life Pope inter-
ested himself, contributing for some years towards her maintenance, and defray-
ing the expenses of her last illness in France, where she died of cancer in the breast
on 10 May 1728. Seeing that Lady Hotham herself died within two years of her
daughter, and was buried in the same grave, that at least one other epitaph of

Pope's was first written for a different person (see *ante*, p. 170), it is not impossible that these lines, which reveal a personal and even intimate knowledge of the deceased's character, were originally inspired by the death of Pope's friend, Mrs Cope, and were afterwards transferred to serve for Mrs Corbett shortly before their first appearance in print (5 May 1730) at the request of her brother, Sir Richard Corbett, by whom "this monument was finished". Evidence of any such transfer, however, is entirely lacking.

The text follows that of *1735*, there being no verbal variants except in the title.

EPIGRAMS.
from
The GRUB-STREET JOURNAL.
1730–1731.

The Evening Post. 26–28 August 1729. [No. I.]

The Grub-street Journal. 1730: 28 May [No. I]; 25 June [No. II]; 2 July [No. III]; 23 July [No. IV]; 12 November [No. V]; 19 November [No. VI].

The Grub-street Journal. 1731: 1 July [No. VII]; 2 December [No. VIII].

The Weekly Register. 5 December 1730. [No. VI.]

The Gentleman's Magazine. July 1731. [No. VII.]

The Windsor Medley. 1731. [No. VI.]

A Collection of Pieces . . . publish'd on Occasion of the Dunciad . . . By Mr. Savage. 1732. [Nos. I–V.]

Faithful Memoirs of the Grubstreet Society. 1732. [Nos. II–III, V–VIII.]

A Collection of Epigrams. Vol. II. 1737. [No. VII.]

Memoirs of the Society of Grub-street. 1737. [Nos. I–VIII.]

An Account of the Life of Mr. Richard Savage. By Samuel Johnson. 1744 (and later editions). [No. VII.]

The Works. Ed. Warburton. Vol. V. 1751. [No. VII.]

The Works. Ed. Bowles. Vol. IV. 1806. [No. VIII.]

The Works. Ed. Carruthers. New Edition. Vol. II. 1858. [Nos. II–VI.]

Many anonymous epigrams from *The Grub-street Journal* have been attributed to Pope, although he is not known to have acknowledged any. There can be no doubt (1) that the *Journal* was started largely in Pope's interest, and with his consent and support, to carry on the war against the "Dunces"; (2) that he contributed to it from time to time, *e.g.* several epitaphs (at least one first appeared there), and a nameless translation from Horace, *Sat.* I IV (p. 338). Moreover, when a selection of pieces in prose and verse from the first three years of the *Journal* was published in 1737 (there had been an earlier "unmarked" collection in 1732), the editors explained in the Preface how they had "done full justice to this Gentleman [Pope] and his particular friends, in relation to the few Pieces imagined to come from their hands, which are distinguished in this Collection by the letter A". The letters "B" and "M" were also introduced to denote the work of Bavius (J. Martyn) and Maevius (R. Russel), its two editors and chief writers. Carruthers included in his edition some twenty-six "Grub-street" epigrams, paying no apparent regard to their signature letters. Only some eight or ten of his selection have been generally accepted by later editors; but J. T. Hillhouse would add a few others on the grounds "that items marked 'A', dealing directly with Pope's own quarrels (especially those concerning Moore Smythe, Concanen, and perhaps the candidates for the laurel) and very like him in style, were *in general* from his hand." (*The Grub-street Journal*, 1928, p. 33.) That is almost certainly true; for only one of the "A" epigrams is definitely known to be *not* by Pope, namely, S. Wesley's "What makes you write at this odd Rate?"; and only one other has been disputed (see No. VII below). Thus, with Pope's more intimate friends *not* found among the "A" authors, and with Pope himself anonymously but indubitably writing exactly the same sort of thing at exactly the same time (*e.g.* the "Dunciad" epigrams, *ante*, p. 299), it is impossible to deny the extreme probability of his authorship of the most characteristic. The eight epigrams which follow (with a few elsewhere of later date) seem, on a fresh and independent examination, to demand inclusion in any edition which admits more than Pope's comparatively few formally acknowledged poems. The case for each epigram—apart from this general argument—is stated in the notes appended, together with details of text and date. (For the few later "Grub-street" epigrams, see *post*, p. 450.)

I.
On *J.M.S.* Gent.

To prove himself no Plagiary, Moore,
   Has writ such stuff, as none e'er writ before.
Thy prudence, Moore, is like that Irish Wit,
Who shew'd his breech, to prove 'twas not besh—

Title] *None originally; this is from 1737.*
1 To...Moore] *1729 reads:* To prove himself no Plagiary, a M—re
3 Moore] M—e *1737.*

II.
On Mr. *M—re*'s going to Law with Mr. *Gilliver*.
Inscrib'd to Attorney *Tibbald*.

O NCE in his Life M—RE judges right:
　　His Sword and Pen not worth a Straw,
An *Author* that cou'd never *write*,
A *Gentleman* that dares not *fight*,
　　Has but one way to teaze—by *Law*.   5

This suit dear TIBBALD kindly hatch;
　　Thus thou may'st help the sneaking Elf:
And sure a *Printer* is his Match,
　　Who's but a *Publisher* himself.

III.
On *J.M.S*. Gent.

A GOLD watch found on Cinder Whore,
　　Or a good verse on *J—my M—e*,
Proves but what either shou'd conceal,
Not that they're rich, but that they steal.

Title] *None originally, this is from Savage's "Collection", 1732.*

IV.
EPITAPH
On *JAMES MOORE SMYTHE*.

H ERE lyes what had nor *Birth*, nor *Shape*, nor *Fame*;
　　No *Gentleman!* no *man!* no-*thing!* no *name!*

Title] *None in the early texts.*

For *Jammie* ne'er grew *James*; and what they call
More, shrunk to *Smith*—and Smith's no name at all.
Yet dye thou can'st not, Phantom, oddly fated: 5
For how can no-thing be annihilated?
                Ex nihilo nihil fit.

V.
On the CANDIDATES for the LAUREL.

SHALL Royal praise be rhym'd by such a ribald,
   As fopling C——r, or Attorney T——d?
Let's rather wait one year for better luck;
One year may make a singing Swan of *Duck*.
Great G——! such servants since thou well can'st lack,   5
Oh! save the Salary, and drink the Sack!

VI.
On the Same.

BEHOLD! ambitious of the *British* bays,
   C——r and DUCK contend in rival lays:
But, gentle COLLEY, should thy verse prevail,
Thou hast no fence, alas! against his flail:
Wherefore thy claim resign, allow his right;   5
For DUCK can *thresh*, you know, as well as *write*.

Originally An Epigram.
C——r] CIBBER *1737*.

VII.
On *DENNIS*.

SHOU'D D——s print how once you robb'd your Brother,
  Traduc'd your Monarch, and debauch'd your Mother;
Say what revenge on D——s can be had;
Too dull for laughter, for reply too mad?
Of one so poor you cannot take the law;   5
On one so old your sword you scorn to draw.
   Uncag'd then let the harmless Monster rage,
Secure in dullness, madness, want, and age.

Title] *No title other than* "Epigram" *originally*.
1 Shou'd ... robb'd] Should Dennis publish, you had stabb'd *1751*.
2 Traduc'd ... and] Lampoon'd ... or *1751*.
3 Say what ... D—s] Say, what ... Dennis *1751*.

VIII.
Occasion'd by seeing some Sheets of Dr. B–TL–Y's Edition of MILTON's *Paradise Lost*.

DID MILTON's Prose, O CHARLES, thy Death defend?
  A furious Foe unconscious proves a Friend.
On MILTON's Verse does B—t—ly comment?—Know
A weak officious Friend becomes a Foe.
While he but sought his Author's Fame to further,   5
The murd'rous Critic has aveng'd thy Murder.

3 B–t–ly] BENTLEY *1737*.

I. This epigram was first published anonymously in *The Evening Post*, 26–28 August 1729, where it was introduced thus: "An Epigram Occasioned by some scurrilous Verses on Pope and Swift, privately handed about, and written by J—s M—re Sm—th." The "Verses", possibly never printed, have eluded identification. Early in 1730, Moore Smythe collaborated with Welsted in an attack on Pope entitled *One Epistle to Mr. Pope*, on the publication of which Pope wrote to Broome (2 May 1730) complaining about the lies of "these scoundrels" in "a thing just now published called an Epistle to me, by James Moore and others". On 28 May, the epigram, preceded by another likewise anonymous, was reprinted in *The Grub-street Journal* with the heading: "The Popeians have sent us the 2 following Epigrams". Lastly, in the *Memoirs* (1737), where it was similarly accompanied, it was signed with the letter "A" (see introductory note), the other piece being ascribed to "Mr. Th—n". The subject of the epigram is the earlier crime of Moore Smythe's plagiarism (see *ante*, p. 294). It is worth noting that Irish humour appealed to Pope; for besides the discussion of Irish bulls in a letter to Caryll, his prose works are not without quotations of "what the Irish man said" (see also note to Epigram IV, below). The text is that of *The Grub-street Journal*, with collations from the first printing (*1729*), and *Memoirs* (*1737*).

II. This piece, the second of the "A" epigrams (see introductory remarks), continues the attack on Moore Smythe; but, unlike the earlier piece, it has been accepted as Pope's by most editors since Carruthers. On its first printing in the *Journal* (25 June 1730), the epigram was preceded by the following paragraph:

> Whereas in the *Daily Post* and *Journal* of the 6th instant, the following Article was inserted, "Last Saturday Mr. *Gilliver* was served with an Information from the King's-bench, on account of the *Grubstreet Journal* of Thursday last:" This was a mistake, he being served only with a Rule, requiring him to shew cause why an Information should not be granted; which he will do next Term.

Gilliver was Pope's principal publisher, and Moore Smythe and Theobald among his chief abominations. The difficulty of naming any other writer of the period who stood in that relationship to those three persons adds to the credibility of this attribution.

The text is that of the first printing, *1730*, with which *1737* is in verbal agreement.

6. *Tibbald*] Lewis Theobald (see Biog. App., Vol. V).

8. *a Printer*] Lawton Gilliver (see above).

9. *a Publisher*] An allusion to Moore Smythe's plagiarism from Pope (see *ante*, p. 294).

III. Consensus of opinion, since Carruthers, gives this epigram to Pope. And seeing that on its first appearance in the *Journal*, and on its reprinting in the 1732 and 1737 "Grub-street" collections, it was immediately followed by Pope's anonymous epitaph on Robert and Mary Digby, and also that both pieces were signed "A" in *1737*, its attribution to Pope looks extremely convincing. But in addition to this evidence and the epigram's repetition of the old charge upon Moore Smythe of plagiarism, there is a striking prose echo (or anticipation) of this epigram in the preface to *An Author To be Lett . . . By Iscariot Hackney* (1729), which *C.B.E.L.* attributes to Savage and Pope: "Is the Poverty of *Moore*'s Genius an Excuse for filching *Pope*'s Lines ? And appears not the Theft in his Comedy as plain, as if a Cinder-Wench shou'd steal a Gold Watch, and afterwards wear it?" Transcripts of the epigram, without ascription, are to be found in two manuscripts, viz: BM MSS Stowe 972, and Add. 32463. The text follows that of the first printing *1730*, with which the "Grub-street" reprints, *1732* and *1737* are in verbal agreement.

   1. *Cinder Whore*] See p. 264, l. 2*n*.

   2. *J—my M—e*] Jemmy Moore [Smythe]. (See Biog. App., Vol. IV.)

IV. There are other indications of Pope's authorship of this piece in addition to the signature "A" appended to it on its reprinting from the *Journal* in the *Memoirs*, 1737 (see introductory note). The epitaph harks back to "the phantom More" of the *Dunciad* (Vol. V, p. 101), and repeats an old trick of Pope's, of composing mock epitaphs on living people. Furthermore, on 2 July 1730, *The Grub-street Journal* printed a letter purporting to be written by John Moore, the quack doctor, of "Worm Powder" fame (see *ante*, p. 161), to his pretended "nephew" James Moore (Smythe), urging him, amongst other things, to come to "my shop in Abchurch-lane" and be cured of his disease of writing and the vain pursuit of wit. This was followed on 23 July by James's reply in which the "prodigall Nephew" protests against being called an author; and, in obvious reference to his and Welsted's *One Epistle to Mr. Pope* (see Epigram 1*n*.), says: "It is true, I did go with some thing against P—PE, (or, rather, lyke a Puppy, *carried it to and fro in my mouth*) these two years and upwards: but,... as the *Irishman* [said] ... I got *nothing* by it, and had not got *that* neither, but for my good friend Mr. Welsted." The simile recalls Pope's lines in *Sandys' Ghost* (p. 171), in which another would-be poet is similarly described:

> *Rare Imp of* Phœbus, *hopeful Youth!*
> *Like Puppy tame that uses*
> *To fetch and carry, in his Mouth,*
> *The Works of all the Muses;*

And also the couplet in the *Epistle to Arbuthnot* (ll. 225–6):

> Nor like a Puppy daggled thro' the Town,
> To fetch and carry Sing-song up and down.

It adds greatly to the probability that the second letter, if not the first, was written by Pope. This second letter concludes with a comment, and the epitaph above, all obviously by the same hand, and all signed "A". The text follows the first printing *1730*, with which *1737* is in verbal agreement.

   5. *Phantom*] See above; and *Dunciad* A, II 46 (Vol. V).

V. On the death of the Poet Laureate, Eusden, on 27 September 1730, the names of possible successors were much canvassed in the papers. Pope's first contribution was apparently the epigram above, published on 12 November; and from that moment to the appointment of Cibber on 3 December, and thence onwards to the end of Pope's life, the Poet Laureate and his office were among the chief objects of his satire. Theobald and Cibber were his old foes;

but Stephen Duck, the "thresher poet", was just then being taken up by Queen Caroline and her court. Indeed, Swift wrote to Gay (19 November) that in Ireland it was rumoured that Duck was "absolutely to succeed Eusden in the laurel". Though Pope seems not to have had any personal quarrel with Duck, his appearance at such a time and in such a connection could not help but provoke his scorn. The epigram, which is signed "A" in the *Memoirs* 1737 (see introductory note), is almost certainly Pope's, and is now printed in full and correctly in his *Poetical Works* for the first time. The text is that of the first printing, *1730*, with which *1737* is in verbal agreement.

2. *C—r, . . . T—d*] Cibber, . . . Tibbald (Theobald), for whom see Biog. App., Vol. IV).

4. *Duck*] Stephen Duck (see above, and Biog. App., Vol. IV).

5. *G—*] George II (see Biog. App., Vol. IV).

VI. The second epigram on the "Candidates for the Laurel" has, since Carruthers, been generally regarded as Pope's. The piece, called simply "An Epigram", first appeared in the *Journal* on 19 November 1730, as a pendant to a "leading article" on the Poet Laureate, in which position it was subscribed "Bavius"—a signature possibly intended for the article as well. (In this early period of the *Journal*, "Bavius" was the pseudonym of more than one person; see *Memoirs*, 1737, p. xxix.) A fortnight later the epigram was reprinted alone and without a signature; on its next appearance (*1731*) it was headed: "An Epigram on Stephen Duck, by Mr P—" (presumably "Mr. Pope"); then "Bavius" was again its signature in the following year. In the 1737 *Memoirs*, the epigram was again printed in its original place at the foot of the article, with no signature, while the article was signed "A" (see introductory note); and lastly, the article alone, newly entitled "Of the Poet Laureate", was included in the "Appendix" to the *Dunciad* (1743) amongst other prose pieces of the author's, and was thereby tacitly acknowledged by Pope himself. The balance of probability is in favour of Pope's authorship.

The text is that of the first printing (*1730*), with which the reprints of *1732* and *1737* are in verbal agreement, except in the one particular noted.

2. *C—r and Duck*] Colley Cibber and Stephen Duck (see Biog. App., Vol. IV).

4. *fence . . . flail*] Swift in his "quibbling epigram" on Duck, written about the same time, also quotes from the proverb here alluded to: "No Fence against a Flayl" (*Works*, ii 1735).

VII. Originally published in *The Grub-street Journal* in 1731, and subscribed "A" in the 1737 *Memoirs* (see introductory note), this epigram is distinguished from the rest of these pieces by Warburton's attribution of it to Pope and his including it in the *Dunciad* in 1751, where it is inserted in a long "Remark" by Pope on the line: "And all the mighty Mad in Dennis rage" (i 106). In this note Pope accuses Dennis of having been concerned in an outrageous attack entitled, *A True Character of Mr. Pope and his Writings*, 1716 (see Dennis, *Crit. Works*, 1943, ii 103); and it was this attack, Warburton added, which had "provoked our incorrigible Poet to write the following Epigram: *Should Dennis pub-*

lish . . ." This assertion of Pope's authorship has been generally accepted, and is very probably true, corroborated as it is by the "A" signature, and by internal evidence noted below. Nevertheless, in his "Life" of Savage, Dr Johnson, writing of his friend's occasional "literary hypocrisy", reported (*Lives*, ed. Hill, II 362) that Savage "himself confessed that when he lived with great Familiarity with *Dennis*, he wrote an Epigram against him"; to which Johnson added a footnote, stating "This Epigram was, I believe, never published," whereupon he proceeded to quote at length Warburton's version, and *not 1731*. It seems, therefore, that Johnson either was misinformed, or had mistaken the particular epigram, since his statement about its non-publication cannot apply to this piece. Furthermore, after Dennis had abused Pope's person as well as poem in his *Reflections . . . upon . . . An Essay upon Criticism*, 1711, Pope had actually asked Cromwell (25 June 1711) this same question about revenge on this same person: "Give me your opinion in what manner such a critic ought to be answered"; and, in a letter to Caryll of the same date, had explored possible answers to that question, and concluded that although Dennis deserved to be cudgelled, his misfortunes would prevent it; and so Pope came at last to agree (2 August 1711) with Caryll's advice to let him alone—altogether a striking parallel to the theme of the epigram. Lastly, as Warburton's statement followed Johnson's in time, it should probably be regarded as an official correction of it; and if Warburton is right in asserting that the attack in *A True Character of Mr. Pope* provoked the epigram (perhaps the first sketch of it), such an early date of composition would only make it still more improbably Savage's.

The text is that of the first printing, with collations from Warburton's version (with which Johnson's is in verbal agreement).

VIII. The attribution to Pope of this epigram derives from Bowles, who claims to have "found [it] in his hand-writing". Carruthers also saw a copy (possibly the same) "in Pope's handwriting . . . among the Mapledurham MSS", and noted that the poet himself had made a slip in writing "Milton" for "Bentley" in the third line of his transcript. Although the existence of a poem in Pope's hand is not proof positive of his authorship of it, in a case like this, when the subject is one of his frequent butts, when the style is his and a line can be paralleled elsewhere in his work, his autograph must make the attribution a practical certainty. The reprint in *Memoirs* 1737 is not signed "A" (see introductory note), but the absence of that signature letter is discounted by the fact that several prose articles, of which there is good reason to believe Pope was the author, as well as Epigram VI above, were likewise left anonymous in *1737*. The text is that of the first printing, with collations from the *Memoirs* (*1737*).

1. *Milton's Prose*] In *Defensio pro populo Anglicano*, 1649, and *Defensio Secunda*, 1654 [Ward].

Charles] King Charles the First, executed 30 January 1649.

2. *A furious Foe . . . Friend.*] Cf. "He stood the furious Foe, the timid Friend." (*Ep. to Arbuthnot*, 343).

3. *B–t–ly*] Richard Bentley, the Cambridge scholar, for whose pedantic

methods of criticism Pope had had little use and less patience since early man-
hood (see Vol. IV, p. 344, and *Prose Works*, I, p. xxxf.).

LINES TO A FRIEND.
Written at his Mother's Bedside.

WHILE ev'ry Joy, successful Youth! is thine,
   Be no unpleasing Melancholy mine.
Me long, ah long! may these soft Cares engage;
To rock the Cradle of reposing Age,
With lenient Arts prolong a Parent's Breath,   5
Make Languor smile, and smooth the Bed of Death.
Me, when the Cares my better Years have shown
Another's Age, shall hasten on my own;
Shall some kind Hand, like *B****'s or thine,
Lead gently down, and favour the Decline?   10
In Wants, in Sickness, shall a *Friend* be nigh,
Explore my *Thought*, and watch my asking *Eye*?
Whether that Blessing be deny'd, or giv'n,
Thus far, is right; the rest belongs to Heav'n.

Lines.] *No title in 1751.* (*For subsequent use of these lines, see introductory
note.*)

A Collection of Letters . . . To the Late Aaron Hill, Esq; 1751.
The Life of Alexander Pope, Esq. By O. Ruffhead. 1769.
A Supplementary Volume to the Works of Alexander Pope, Esq. 1807.
   The history of these Lines, later to be used as the conclusion of *An Epistle to Dr.
Arbuthnot* (1734), is contained in a letter from Pope to Aaron Hill (3 September
1731), for which see Vol. IV, p. 127*n*. The identity of the "successful Youth" to
whom they are addressed is uncertain. William Murray (later Lord Mansfield)
has been frequently suggested; but Pope, who was forty-three, would have been
unlikely to call a barrister of twenty-six a "youth"; and as Murray was both
unfortunate in a love affair, and so poor that he talked of taking orders to be sure
of a livelihood, "successful" seems an inappropriate epithet. George Lyttelton
(later Lord Lyttelton) is a more credible choice. He was not more than twenty-

two at the time; and when at Eton (says Dr Johnson) had been "so much distinguished that his exercises were recommended as models to his school fellows", and had "retained the same reputation of superiority" at Christ Church. He had, however, left Oxford in 1728, after only two years, without a degree, and had immediately set out on the Grand Tour; two years later he had written *An Epistle to Mr. Pope from Rome*, 1730, and is thought to have been still abroad at the date of Pope's letter. Pope could still speak of him in 1738 as "the worthy Youth" and "young Lyttelton" (see Vol. IV, *Dia.* 1 48 and *Ep.* 1 i 29).

The text follows that of *1751*; but the title is an editorial addition.

9. *B * * * 's*] Bolingbroke's.

An Epistle to the Right Honourable Richard Earl of Burlington

[published 14 December 1731; vol. III ii, pp. 131–56]

EPITAPH

On CHARLES *Earl of* DORSET,

In the Church of Withyham *in* Sussex.

D ORSET, the Grace of Courts, the Muses Pride,
    Patron of Arts, and Judge of Nature, dy'd!
The Scourge of Pride, tho' sanctify'd or great,
Of Fops in Learning, and of Knaves in State:
Yet soft his Nature, tho' severe his Lay,   5
His Anger moral, and his Wisdom gay.
Blest Satyrist! who touch'd the Mean so true,
As show'd, Vice had his Hate and Pity too.
Blest Courtier! who could King and Country please,

Title] *1735a reads:* On . . . Dorset, In the Church of Knolle in Kent. *Corrected in the Errata (and all later editions) to:* On . . . Dorset, In the Church of Withyham in Sussex.

Yet sacred keep his Friendships, and his Ease.   10
Blest Peer! his great Forefathers ev'ry Grace
Reflecting, and reflected in his Race;
Where other Buckhursts, other Dorsets shine,
And Patriots still, or Poets, deck the Line.

The Works of Mr. Alexander Pope. Volume II. 1735 (folio and quarto).
The Works of Alexander Pope, Esq; Vol. II. 1735 (octavo).
Ethic Epistles, Satires, &c. With the Author's Notes. Written by Mr. Pope. 1735.
Ethic Epistles, to Henry St. John L. Bolingbroke. Written in the Year 1732. 1735.
The Works . . . Vol. II. Containing his Epistles and Satires. 1736.
The Works . . . Vol. II. Containing his Epistles, &c. 1739 (both editions).
The Works . . . Vol. II. Part I. Containing his Epistles, &c. 1740 (and 1743).
The Works. Ed. Warburton. Vol. VI. 1751.

Dorset died in 1706, but this poem was not published before 1735, when Pope
placed it second amongst the "Epitaphs" in the new volume of his *Works*, where
it followed the lines on Trumbull (died 1716). Four years later, the author moved
it to the first place in a sequence which for the most part successive editors have
since retained, though its order, following the dates neither of death nor of com-
position, has no apparent significance. Pope usually printed his epitaphs as
opportunity offered, one in *Works* (1717), three in *Miscellany Poems* (1726), six
more of various dates in 1730, and yet another in 1733. It is therefore difficult,
quite apart from questions of style, to believe this epitaph was the work of Pope's
youth—as might appear to be suggested by its position. Further corroboration is
found in a letter from Dorset's son, Lionel Sackville, first Duke of Dorset, to Pope's
friend and neighbour, the Countess of Suffolk (9 November 1731): "I will not
add to my impertinence by making you the messenger of my compliments to Mr.
Pope: when I see him I will make them myself, in the best manner I am able, and
at the same time I hope he will grant me a *free conference* [the technical name for a
personal discussion between the Lords and Commons] upon the subject matter of
the epitaph." (*Suffolk Corr.*, ii 33f.) There can be little doubt that the Duke was
referring to this poem, but his letter does not show what purpose he had in view.

The superscription of the epitaph on its first printing (*1735a*) ran: *On Charles
Earl of Dorset, In the Church of Knolle in Kent*, but was promptly corrected in the
Errata to read as above. Nevertheless, there is no church at Knole (only the
Duke's private chapel, containing no monuments or epitaphs), nor is this epitaph
at Withyham, either on Dorset's tomb or elsewhere in the church, and nothing
shows it was ever inscribed there. In accordance with the Duke's letter, the piece
is now tentatively dated 1731.

The text follows that of *1735*.

1. Charles Sackville, sixth Earl of Dorset (1638–1706). Pope told Spence
(pp. 136, 281) that he considered Dorset "the best of all those writers" (*i.e.* the
Restoration wits); his "things are all excellent in their way; for one should con-

sider his pieces as a sort of epigrams: wit was his talent.—He and Lord Rochester [who had "neither so much delicacy or exactness as Lord Dorset"] should be considered as holiday-writers; as gentlemen that diverted themselves now and then with poetry, rather than as poets." "This", adds Spence, "was said kindly of them; rather to excuse their defects, than to lessen their characters."

3–8. Dorset's reputation with his contemporaries was gained as much by his satires as by his lyrics (see Dryden *Essays*, ed. Ker, II 18–20). To which satires Pope refers in ll. 6–7 is not clear, though one "Fop in Learning" was doubtless Edward Howard, to whom Dorset addressed two verse epistles. For Pope's "imitations" of Dorset, see p. 48.

5. Cf. Rochester, *An Allusion to the Tenth Satire of the First Book of Horace*:
> For pointed satire I would Buckhurst [*i.e.* Dorset] choose,
> The best good man, with the worst-natur'd Muse.

11. *his great Forefathers*] particularly the first Earl, author of the Induction to *A Mirror for Magistrates*, and part-author of *Gorboduc* (acted, 1561), characterized by Pope (Spence, p. 21) as "the best English poet, between Chaucer's and Spenser's time".

On the Countess of B—— cutting Paper.

PALLAS grew vap'rish once and odd,
　　She would not do the least right thing,
Either for Goddess or for God,
　　Nor work, nor play, nor paint, nor sing.

Jove frown'd, and "Use (he cry'd) those Eyes　　　　　5
　　"So skilful and those Hands so taper;
"Do something exquisite, and wise—"
　　She bow'd, obey'd him, and cut Paper.

4 Nor] Not *L*.

5 Use, use (quoth Jove) those piercing eyes, *L*; Use, use (cry'd Jove) those skilfull Eyes, *C*[1].

6 So ... those] That head acute, and *L*; That Head so quick, those *C*[1].

7 exquisite] very fine *L*, *C*[1].

This vexing him who gave her Birth,
　　Thought by all Heav'n a burning Shame;　　10
What does she next, but bids on Earth
　　Her *B—l—n* do just the same.

Pallas, you give yourself strange Airs;
　　But sure you'll find it hard to spoil
The Sense and Taste of one that bears　　15
　　The Name of *Savil* and of *Boyle*.

Alas! one bad Example shown,
　　How quickly all the Sex pursue!
See Madam! see, the Arts o'erthrown,
　　Between *John Overton* and *You*.　　20

　9 vexing] ang'ring C^1. who] that L, C^2.
11 does she next,] sh^d she do; L.
12 *B–l–n*] *B—n* L; *Burlington* $C^{1.2}$.
13–16 *Pallas . . . Boyle.*] *Omm. L*, C^1.
15 The wit & sense of one who bears C^2.
17 Alas! one bad] And now, this great L; Ah Madam! this C^1;
　　Alas! one ill C^2.
18f. How . . . o'erthrown] L, C^1 *read:*
　　　　What earthly Good [thing C^1] will woman do?
　　　　Triumph! All Arts are overthrown,
19 see, the Arts] all the Arts C^2.
20 Between] Betwixt C^2.

Pope's autographs: Longleat, Portland Papers, XIII; Chatsworth, Devonshire MSS, 1st series, 143.70, 71.
　Miscellanies. The Third Volume. 1732 (and later editions).
　A Supplement to Dr. Swift's and Mr. Pope's Works. Dublin. 1739.
　Miscellanies. The Fourth Volume. Consisting of Verses . . . 1742 (and later editions).
　The Works. Ed. Roscoe. Vol. VI. 1824.
　The authorship of this poem is established by a letter from Pope to Lord Burlington (19 September 1732) recently discovered at Chatsworth. Pope writes: "I hope [Lady Burlington] will forgive a Crime I've committed tow^{ds} her, in putting into a Collection of Verses (wch I will soon trouble you with at Lanesborough) that little paper-thing ab^t her, with the addition only of one Stanza, to show I am as ready to commend as to blame her." "Cutting paper" was one of

the terms for a well-known accomplishment of eighteenth-century ladies, who used to cut out flowers, figures, and even landscapes in paper, sometimes of different colours. About 1737 Lady Andover was said to have "excelled in landscape and figures"; and the British Museum treasures in the Print Room the flower facsimiles in "paper Mosaiks" executed by Mrs Delany between 1774 and 1782. Pope accuses Lady Burlington of having set the fashion; and couples her with a print-seller, as the joint overthrowers of the Arts. The piece is provisionally dated 1732, the year of Pope's letter quoted above.

The text is that of the first printing, *1732*, with collations from the three autographs; Longleat, possibly the earliest (*L*), one at Chatsworth without the new stanza (*C*¹), and one with it (*C*²).

8. *cut Paper*] *i.e.* into shapes of flowers, etc. (see note above).

15–16. *Sense and Taste . . . Boyle.*] This coupling of sense and taste and Boyle recalls the couplet in the Epistle to Richard Boyle, her husband, *Of Taste*, which is mainly a panegyric of his sense and taste (Vol. III ii, p. 140).

> Something there is more needful than Expence,
> And something previous ev'n to Taste—'tis Sense.

Lady Burlington was a Savile.

20. *John Overton*] Doubtless a member of the family of print-sellers and engravers of that name, though hardly the original John, vendor of mezzotints, last heard of in 1708 at the age of sixty-eight. Henry Overton's name appears on an engraving of George I, reworked from a mezzotint (BM *Cat. of Engraved British Portraits*, ii 294). Cf. Gay, *Trivia*, ii 488: "The colour'd prints of *Overton* appear," and Swift, *Directions for a Birth-day Song* 1729, ll. 37f:

> As Overton has drawn his Sire
> Still seen or'e many an Alehouse fire.

HORACE, Satyr 4. Lib. 1. Paraphrased.
Inscribed to the Honorable Mr ——

¹· Absentem qui rodit Amicum ²· Qui non *defendit*, alio culpante:
³· Solutos Qui captat *Risus* hominum, *Famamque dicacis*: ⁴ Fingere
qui *Non Visa* potest: ⁵ *Commissa tacere* Qui nequit:—Hic Niger est:
　　　　　Hunc, tu Romane, caveto.

Title] *The Journal has the following heading:* "A paraphrase of four lines and a half of Horace, inscribed to the Honourable Mr. —— an imperfect copy of which was printed some time ago in *The Whitehall Evening Post*."

1. THE *Fop*, whose Pride affects a *Patron*'s name,
   Yet *absent*, wounds an author's honest fame:
2. That more abusive Fool, who calls me *Friend*,
   Yet wants the honour, injur'd to defend:
3. Who spreads a *Tale*, a *Libel* hands about,   5
   Enjoys the *Jest*, and copies *Scandal* out:
4. Who to the *Dean* and *Silver Bell* can swear,
   And sees at *C—n—ons* what was never there;
5. Who tells you all I *mean*, and all I *say*;
   And, if he *lyes* not, must at least *betray*:   10
   —Tis not the *sober Satyrist* you should dread,
   But such a *babling Coxcomb* in his stead.

Pope's autograph: Chatsworth MSS, 1st series, 143.67.
The London Evening Post. 22–25 January 1731–2.
The Grub-street Journal. No. 134. 27 July 1732.
This sketch of a Fop, later incorporated in the *Epistle to Dr. Arbuthnot*, 1734
[1735] (see Vol. IV, pp. 116–17), was first published as a separate poem, and
without attribution, in a newspaper about three years earlier. When reprinting
it in July 1732, *The Grub-street Journal* said that "an imperfect copy . . . was printed
some time ago in *The Whitehall Evening Post.*" A prolonged search has failed to
find it there; but the similarity in title between that paper and *The London Evening
Post* suggests that the *Journal* was mistaken in its reference.

The Paraphrase was occasioned by the gossip which immediately followed the
publication of Pope's epistle to Burlington, *Of Taste*, on 13 December 1731 (see
Vol. III II), gossip which, identifying the Duke of Chandos with "Timon" of the
poem, and the Duke's seat, Canons, with "Timon's villa", charged Pope with
ingratitude and treachery in satirizing one from whom he was (unwarrantably)
said to have received favours. This piece and the "Cleland" letter of *The Daily
Post-Boy* (22 December 1731) together constitute Pope's first prompt refutation
of the gossip.

The text follows that of the autograph MS. There are no verbal variants in the
newspaper texts.

Title.] The *Journal* has the following heading: "A paraphrase of four lines and
a half of Horace, inscribed to the Honourable Mr. —— an imperfect copy of
which was printed some time ago in *The Whitehall Evening Post.*"

7. *the Dean and Silver Bell*] Quoted from the description of "Timon's Villa" in
Of Taste (see Vol. III II):

> And now the Chapel's silver bell you hear. (l. 141)
> To rest, the Cushion and soft Dean invite,
> Who never mentions Hell to ears polite. (ll. 149–50)

8. *C–n–ns*] Canons, the Duke of Chandos's seat near Edgware (see introductory note).

Wrote by Mr. *P.* in a Volume of *Evelyn on Coins,* presented to a painter by a parson.

T–m *W*—*d* of *Ch–sw–c*, deep divine,
   To painter *K*—*t* presents his *coin*;
'Tis the first time I dare to say,
That *Churchman* e'er gave coin to *Lay*.

Title Wrote . . . parson.] *1753 reads:* By Mr. Pope. *The rest being relegated to a foot-note, thus:* Wrote in Evelyn's book of coins given by Mr. Wood to Kent: he had objected against the word *pio* in Mr. Pope's father's epitaph.
1 *T—m . . . Ch–sw–c*] Tom Wood of Chiswick *1753.*
2 *K—t* presents his] Kent gave all this *1753.*
3 time I dare] coin I'm bold *1753.*
4 That ever churchman gave to Lay. *1753. Churchman*] *1735 misprinted* Churchmen.

The Gentleman's Magazine. May 1735.
William Mason's transcript: R. G. Fitzgerald, Dayton, Ohio.
Notes and Queries. No. 73. 22 March 1851.
The Works. Ed. Carruthers. Vol. IV. 1854.
First published in Pope's lifetime under his initial, this epigram was never acknowledged by him, but has been accepted without question as authentic by every editor since Carruthers.

Thomas Wood was vicar of Chiswick from 1716 to 1732 according to the registers, which also record the burial of Pope's father there on 26 October 1717. At first sight, therefore, Mason's assertion on the back of a letter from Gray (4 July 1753), that the vicar "had objected against the word *pio* in Mr. Pope's father's epitaph", and so had provoked the epigram, appears credible. But the elder Pope's monument is in Twickenham Church (see Vol. IV, p. 125*n*.), not Chiswick, where there is no record of a monument or even of the grave itself. Whatever the grievance Pope may have felt against the Chiswick vicar (and it seems to have had something to do with money, and thus could have been connected with the elder Pope's burial), it is certain that all the *dramatis personae* of this mild reproof are quite consistent with Pope's authorship. Pope was still

friendly with Wood in 1732 (see *A Master Key to Popery*, Vol. III ii, p. 182);
"Painter Kent" was domiciled from about 1719 onwards, if not earlier, at Lord
Burlington's house at Chiswick, and became an intimate friend of the poet. Thus
at any time during a long period of friendship Pope could have seen the book,
Evelyn on Coins, in Kent's rooms, and scribbled in it this comment on a church-
man's parsimony. The epigram is tentatively dated 1732, the year of Wood's
death and of Pope's other reference to him.

  The text is that of the first printing, with collations from Mason's transcript
(*1753*).

  Title. *Evelyn on Coins*] Numismata. A Discourse of Medals, Antient and
Modern. By John Evelyn. 1697.

  1. *T–m W—d*] Thomas Wood, vicar of Chiswick, 1716–32 (see introductory
note above).

  2. *K—t*] William Kent, see Biog. App., Vol. IV.

  his coin] His copy of Evelyn's *Numismata*, which is profusely illustrated with
"life size" engravings of coins.

THE SIX MAIDENS.

A TOWER there is, where six Maidens do dwell;
  This Tow'r it belongs to the Dev'l of Hell;
And sure of all Devils this must be the best,
Who by six such fair Maidens at once is possest.

So bright are their beauties, so charming their eyes,   5
As in spite of his Fall, might make Lucifer rise;
But then they're so blithe and so buxome withall,
As, tho ten Devils rose, they could make them to fall.

Ah why, good Lord Grantham, were you so uncivil
To send at a dash all these Nymphs to the Devil?   10
And yet why, Madam Dives, at your lot should you stare?
'Tis known all the Dives's ever went there.

Title The Six Maidens.] *Suggested title; the MS has none.*
11 And yet] *written above* But *deleted.*

There, Mordaunt, Fitzwilliams, &c. remain;
(I promis'd I never would mention Miss Vane.)
Ev'n Cart'ret and Meadows, so pure of desires,   15
Are lump'd with the rest of these charming Hell fires.

O! sure to King George 'tis a dismal disaster,
To see his own Maids serve a new Lord and Master.
Yet this, like their old one, for nothing will spare,
And treateth them all, like a Prince of the Air.   20

Who climbs these High Seats oh his joy shall be great!
Tho strait be the passage, and narrow the Gate;
And who now of his Court, to this place would not go,
Prepard for the Devil and his Angells also?

19 this] *written above an undecipherable word.*
20 And] *written over* He.
21 climbs] *written above* reach *deleted.* these] *written over* that.
Seats] *written above* place *deleted.* his] *written above* their *deleted.*
23 now] *inserted between* who of this] *written over* the. would] *written above* will *deleted.*

Pope's autograph: Longleat, Portland Papers, XIII.
This poem was first printed in *New Light on Pope*, p. 276f. At the head of the manuscript, faintly written in pencil, are the words, "Believed to be Pope. J E J"; and the sheet is endorsed "From the Duchess of Portland's Papers.—Longleat." Since the manuscript reveals Pope in the act of composition, his authorship is virtually certain. Had the piece got abroad with Pope's name attached, the consequences might have been serious; for the persons lampooned, as well as the occasion and approximate date of the piece, are still easily recognizable. The thing is a squib on the Prince of Wales and his intrigues with the six maids of honour to Queen Caroline; corroboration and date being supplied by *The Pall Mall Miscellany*, published on 5 February 1732 (*The Daily Post-Boy*), in which is a poem entitled, *The Six wanton Maids; or, the Amours of P. Alexis. A new Ballad*, and concerned with the same six maids of honour.
    1. *A Tower*] Windsor Castle.
    9. *Lord Grantham*] Henry d'Auverquerque, Earl of Grantham (c. 1672–1754). Lord Chamberlain to Princess (later Queen) Caroline, 1716–37.
    11. *Madam Dives*] Charlotte Dives, or Dyve (1712–73). She was still a Maid of Honour in 1761, the year in which she married Samuel, Baron Masham (see H. Walpole to Conway, 14 July 1761, and G.E.C.).

13. *Mordaunt*] Anna Maria Mordaunt (d. 1771). Stephen Poyntz, the diplo-
matist (see D.N.B.), whom she married in 1733, died in 1750, "ruined in his
circumstances . . . by a simple wife, who had a devotion of marrying dozens of
her poor cousins at his expense" (H. Walpole to Mann, 19 December 1750).

Fitzwilliams] Mary, daughter of Viscount Fitzwilliams (1707–69), married
(1733) Henry Herbert, ninth Earl of Pembroke, and on his death (1751) "dis-
graced herself by marrying a Captain Barnard" (H. Walpole to Mann, 14 Octo-
ber 1751). Hervey (p. xxiii) comments on her manly appearance.

14. *Vane*] Anne Vane (1705–36). For her relations with the Prince of Wales
and Lord Hervey, see Hervey *Memoirs, passim.*

15. *Cart'ret*] The Hon. Bridget Carteret, niece of the first Lord Carteret, had
been a Maid of Honour since at least 1719 (*Suffolk*, I 40).

Meadows] Sister of Sir Sidney Meadows, had been a Maid of Honour since at
least 1720 (*Suffolk* I 60). She was already in 1729 "poor old M, who should now
take more care of herself" (*ibid.*, 334), yet was still, it seems, a Maid of Honour in
1761 (H. Walpole to Montagu, 10 July 1761). Her reputation was for gravity of
demeanour (see pp. 181, 201).

16. *Hell fires*] A term for reckless young people, derived from the Hell-fire
Club, 1720.

18. *New Lord and Master*] The Prince of Wales.

EPITAPH.

For Dr. FRANCIS ATTERBURY,

Bishop of Rochester,
Who died in Exile at Paris, in 1732.
[His only Daughter having expired in his arms, immediately after
she arrived in France to see him.]

DIALOGUE.

SHE. YES, we have liv'd—one pang, and then we part!
     May Heav'n, dear Father! now, have *all* thy Heart.
     Yet ah! how once we lov'd, remember still,
     Till you are Dust like me.

HE.

            Dear Shade! I will:
Then mix this Dust with thine—O spotless Ghost!   5

Title For] On *1751.* Paris, in 1732,] Paris, 1732, *1751.*

O more than Fortune, Friends, or Country lost!
Is there on earth one Care, one Wish beside?
Yes—*Save my Country, Heav'n,*
                                        —He said, and dy'd.

The Works of Mr. Alexander Pope. Volume II. 1735. (Epitaph originally included
in the quarto edition, but cancelled before publication, see below.)
   The Works . . . Ed. Warburton. Vol. VI. 1751.
   Francis Atterbury, Bishop of Rochester, died on 15 February 1731–2. Pope,
writing to Caryll (6 March 1732) told him of the death of "our poor friend
abroad", which, he said, "has suggested to me many reflections on human views
and infelicities". One result of those reflections is doubtless this epitaph on Atter-
bury and his daughter whose death (described in her father's letter to Pope,
20 November 1729) would inevitably be recalled at such a time. The epitaph did
not appear on the monument, nor was meant to; it was written on the poet's two
friends—and put on one side.
   The following year (1733) Pope wrote his first *Moral Essay* addressed to Lord
Cobham (see Vol. III II, p. 38), which he ended with the same thought, and
much the same words, as this epitaph:

                   And you! brave *Cobham*, to the latest breath
                   Shall feel your ruling passion strong in death:
                   Such in those moments as in all the past,
                   "Oh, save my Country, Heav'n!" shall be your last.

Conditions of publication (small pieces normally having to wait for an edition of
"collected poems", while major works, like this essay, were printed separately)
would seem to be responsible for the earlier printing of the later poem (published
16 January 1733–4). When preparing the "Second Volume" of his *Works* (1735)
for publication, Pope included the Atterbury lines on page 15 of the section
devoted to epitaphs, leaving the next page blank facing page 1 of *The Dunciad*;
and with this arrangement the quarto presumably went to press. On the eve of
publication, however, he cancelled the leaf (pp. 15–16) containing this epitaph,
thus leaving the couplet on Newton to conclude the section on page 14; following
which appears the "stub" (of the cancelled leaf) in all copies of the volume
examined. A copy of the cancelled leaf has survived, and has been inserted in
its original position in the British Museum quarto (see C. D. Sherborn, *Athenaeum*,
13 April 1907). The folio and quarto editions of the 1735 *Works* are ostensibly the
same book both in contents and arrangement; nevertheless the last epitaph in the
quarto (No. XI, on Newton) is absent from the folio where the "Epitaphs" section
ends with No. X on page 12. It seems that the folio also underwent some change
between printing and publication. The Atterbury epitaph seems originally to
have followed the Newton epitaph in the folio (in which case they *must* have
occupied the same leaf); thus when the Atterbury piece was excluded, the New-
ton couplet of necessity went with it. Some copies of the folio may show a stub at

that place; but it is not likely, as the leaf was probably a single leaf at the end of the section (or just possibly conjugate with some inessential preliminary matter of *The Dunciad* which immediately follows).

The reason for Pope's eleventh-hour change of mind seems to have been that, in a collection of little more than a score of pieces, he was in the act of printing two poems having the same ending. The epitaph remained unknown until Warburton incorporated it in the canon in 1751. See further, *New Light*, pp. 281–5, and V. A. Dearing, "The Prince of Wales's Set of Pope's Works", *Harvard Library Bulletin* (1950), Vol. IV, pp. 321–2, who describes a copy in which the epitaph is printed, not on a cancelled leaf, but on an additional leaf.

The text follows that of *1735*, with which *1751* agrees except for one word in the title.

1–4. Cf. Atterbury to Pope, 20 November 1729: ". . . she had her senses to the very last gasp, and exerted them to give me, in those few hours, greater marks of Duty and Love than she had done in all her life time, tho' she had never been wanting in either. The last words she said to me were the kindest of all; a reflection on the goodness of God, which had allow'd us in this manner to meet once more, before we parted for ever."

8. Cf. Atterbury to Pope, 23 November 1731: ". . . After all, I do and must love my country, with all its faults and blemishes . . . My last wish shall be like that of father Paul, *Esto perpetua!*"

POEMS
from
Miscellanies. The Third Volume. 1732.

The published correspondence of Pope and Swift shows that the final volume of their *Miscellanies* (which was edited by Pope and originally called "The Third") was mostly Swift's work: "almost six-sevenths of the whole verse part in the book," Swift says, was his (4 November 1732), and he later claimed a slightly higher proportion. Pope, in his foreword, says: "There are in this Volume, as in the former, one or two small pieces by other Hands,"—other, that is, than his and Swift's. Shortly before the book was published Gay wrote to Swift (24 July 1732) of a piece of news he had obviously only just heard: "Last post I had a letter from Mr. Pope, who informs me he hath heard from you and that he is preparing some scattered things of yours and his for the press. I believe I shall not see him till the winter. . ." As Gay makes no further allusion to Pope's forthcoming anthology, it is clear from these words that he had neither made, nor thought to make, any contribution to it. Indeed, apart from Swift and Pope, no author is known to have written any poem in the verse section; and the "one or two" other hands present in the volume were apparently limited to those stated elsewhere by Pope himself as having collaborated in the *Origine of Sciences* (and, maybe, some other of the prose items with which the book begins), namely Arbuthnot and Parnell. They may be ruled out as contributors of verse for reasons given in *New Light*, pp. 259f.

Pope's correspondence shows that he was intimately concerned with the edition of *Miscellanies. In Four Volumes* (published 3 July 1742) in which the original four *Miscellanies* were for the most part reprinted, with much rearrangement of matter, some revision of text, and "several additional pieces". The verse is collected in the fourth volume, in compiling which Pope suppressed one of his own pieces and included two others of his, one never before printed and the other dating only from the preceding year. And in this volume Swift's pieces are for the first time indicated by marking all the other poems with an asterisk. As in no case have these attributions been proved wrong, they may be taken as generally correct, though that is not to say that Swift may not have "collaborated" in a few of the starred pieces. Some light is therefore reflected back on those poems in the 1732 *Miscellanies* which reappeared in the 1742 edition (two of Swift's and one of Pope's were excluded). It thus becomes apparent that of the twenty-three pieces in the verse section of the 1732 volume, Swift wrote ten (most of them long poems). Of the rest (all short pieces), four are indubitably Pope's, and a fifth (*On a certain Lady at Court*) scarcely less certainly his; besides which there is also a long prose *Epitaph* (on Frances Chartres) which Pope said elsewhere was Arbuthnot's. Seven anonymous pieces remain, none of which is Swift's. Of these seven, four ("You beat your pate . . ."; "Sir, I admit . . ."; "Well, then poor G—"; and "Whence, deathless Kit-Cat . . .") are customarily attributed to Pope, though no evidence has ever been adduced for them; two others (*Verses to be placed under the Picture of England's Arch-Poet*, and *Epitaph of By-Words*) have with a similar lack of proof been sometimes given to Gay in the past, but are repudiated by Faber; and the remaining piece, a four-line *Epigram* ("Peter complains, that God . . ."), seems never to have been ascribed to anyone. Nevertheless, if the attributed four are still to be regarded as Pope's, the remaining three, in which his manner is even more discernible, should stand with them.

I.
EPITAPH [*of By-Words.*]

HERE lies a round Woman, who thought *mighty odd*
Every Word she e'er heard in this Church about God.
To convince her of *God* the good Dean did indeavour,
But still in her Heart she held *Nature* more *clever.*
Tho' he talk'd much of Virtue, her Head always run   5
Upon something or other, she found better *Fun.*
For the Dame, by her Skill in Affairs Astronomical,
Imagin'd, to live in the Clouds was but *comical.*

In this World, she despis'd every Soul she met here,
And now she's in t'other, she thinks it but *Queer*.   10

Contemporary transcript: BM MS Harl. 7316.

Miscellanies. The Third Volume. 1732 (and later editions).

A Supplement to Dr. Swift's and Mr. Pope's Works. Dublin. 1739.

Miscellanies. The Fourth Volume. Consisting of Verses . . . 1742 (and later editions).

Gay's *Poetical Works*, in Bell's edition of the British Poets, 1773–7 (and in a number of subsequent collections, such as "Johnson's", Anderson's, Cooke's, etc.).

This piece, occasionally credited to Gay, was marked with an asterisk in the four-volume *Miscellanies* (1742) to signify that it was not Swift's work. Gay's responsibility is however disputed by Faber (xxiv–xxv). Swift, Gay, Parnell, and Arbuthnot have been ruled out (see p. 346); yet someone in Pope's circle must have written it, and, considering the circumstances in which it was published, this elimination points strongly to Pope himself, whose manner when addressing Swift it closely resembles (see further, *New Light*, pp. 261f.). The piece is tentatively dated according to the year of its publication, 1732, for convenience of reference.

The text is that of the first printing.

1ff. With the exception of *God* and *Nature*, Pope had never used any of the italicized "by-words" in his poetry at the date of publication of this poem.

II.
EPIGRAM *from the* French.

SIR, I admit your gen'ral Rule
   That every Poet is a Fool:
But you yourself may serve to show it,
That every Fool is not a Poet.

Miscellanies. The Third Volume. 1732 (and later editions).

A Collection of Epigrams. Vol. II. 1737.

A Supplement to Dr. Swift's and Mr. Pope's Works. Dublin. 1739.

Miscellanies. The Fourth Volume. Consisting of Verses . . . 1742 (and later editions).

The Nut-Cracker. F. Foot. 1751.

A Select Collection of Epigrams. T. C. Rickman. 1796.

The Works. Ed. Roscoe. Vol. VI. 1824.

This epigram, marked by an asterisk in *Miscellanies* (1742) to indicate that it was not by Swift, has been ascribed to Pope without evidence or comment by several editors. The chief evidence for Pope's authorship has already been stated (p. 346); it remains to say that the epigram is distinctly in Pope's manner, and has never been attributed to any other person. The balance of probabilities seems

to favour Pope's authorship. There is no evidence of date; it is therefore provision-
ally placed according to year of publication.

The text is that of the first printing.

III.

Y OU beat your Pate, and fancy Wit will come:
  Knock as you please, there's no body at home.

Miscellanies. The Third Volume. 1732 (and later editions).
A Collection of Epigrams. Vol. II. 1737.
A Supplement to Dr. Swift's and Mr. Pope's Works. Dublin. 1739.
Miscellanies. The Fourth Volume. Consisting of Verses . . . 1742 (and later editions).
Joe Miller's Jests. 8th Edition. 1745 (and later editions).
The Agreeable Companion. 1745.
The Nut-Cracker. F. Foot. 1751.
The Sports of the Muses. Vol. II. 1752.
A Collection of Select Epigrams. J. Hackett. 1757.
The Festoon. 1766 (and later editions).
The Christmas Treat. 1767.
Select Epigrams. Vol. I. 1797.
The Works. Ed. Roscoe. Vol. IV. 1824.

This couplet has been accepted as Pope's by every editor of note since Roscoe,
but none has put forward any reason for the attribution. It was marked as *not* by
Swift in the 1742 *Miscellanies.* The epigram is like Pope; but there is nothing that
can be added to the evidence for his authorship given above (p. 346). The ascrib-
ed date is that of the year of publication. The text follows the first printing.

IV.
EPIGRAM.

P ETER complains, that God has given
  To his poor Babe a Life so short:
Consider *Peter*, he's in Heaven;
  'Tis good to have a Friend at Court.

Miscellanies. The Third Volume. 1732 (and later editions).
A Supplement to Dr. Swift's and Mr. Pope's Works. Dublin. 1739.
Miscellanies. The Fourth Volume. Consisting of Verses . . . 1742 (and later editions).

This Epigram, which seems never to have been attributed to, or claimed by,

anyone, was marked as *not* by Swift in *1742* (see p. 346). As the general arguments
for Pope's authorship (see p. 346) apply no less to this than to its fellow epigrams,
it too must be regarded as probably Pope's work. The date of the piece and the
identity of "Peter" are unknown. See further *New Light*, pp. 262ff.

The text is that of the first printing, with which *1742* agrees.

Of the Use of Riches,
An Epistle to the Right Honourable Allen
Lord Bathurst

[published 15 January 1732/3; vol. III ii, pp. 81–125]

The First Satire of the Second Book of Horace
Imitated

[published 15 February 1732/3; vol. IV, pp. 1–21]

EPITAPH.
On Mr. GAY.

In *Westminster-Abbey*, 1732.

O F Manners gentle, of Affections mild;
In Wit, a Man; Simplicity, a Child;

1–4 *L. TS and 1733 read:*
            A manly wit, a child's simplicity,
            The morals blameless, and the temper free,
            Words ever pleasing, yet sincerely true,
            Satyr still just, with humour ever new;
1 Of...mild] *W. TS reads:*
            Severe of Morals, of Affections mild,
    1735ab read: Severe of Morals, but of Nature mild;

With native Humour temp'ring virtuous Rage,
Form'd to delight at once and lash the age;
Above Temptation, in a low Estate,   5
And uncorrupted, ev'n among the Great;
A safe Companion, and an easy Friend,
Unblam'd thro' Life, lamented in thy End.
These are Thy Honours! not that here thy Bust
Is mix'd with Heroes, or with Kings thy dust;   10
But that the Worthy and the Good shall say,
Striking their pensive bosoms—*Here* lies GAY.

3f. *omm. in W. TS and 1735abcd.*
 6 And uncorrupted] Above corruption *W. TS.*
 8 Unblam'd] Belov'd *L. TS, 1733; both words as alternatives, W. TS.*
   thy End] the End *L. TS, W. TS.*
 9 These] Those *1733.*
12 pensive] aching *L. TS, 1733; both words as alternatives, W. TS.*
   bosoms] hearts *L. TS.*

(*a*) text; beginning, "*A manly wit . . .*"
Contemporary transcripts: Longleat, Portland Papers, and BM Cowper Papers, MS Add. 28101.
   The Gentleman's Magazine. June 1733.
   The London Magazine. July 1733.
   The Flowers of Parnassus. 1737.
   A Collection of Epigrams. Vol. II. 1737.

(*b*) text; beginning "*Severe of Morals . . .*"
Contemporary transcript: Welbeck Abbey, Harley Papers.
   The Works of Mr. Alexander Pope. Volume II. 1735 (folio and quarto).
   Ethic Epistles, Satires, &c. . . . Written by Mr. Pope. 1735.
   Read's Weekly Journal. 26 June 1736.
   The Whitehall Evening Post. 24–26 June 1736.
   The St. James's Evening Post. 24–26 June 1736.
   The London Evening-Post. 24–26 June 1736.
   The General Evening Post. 24–26 June 1736.
   The Gentleman's Magazine. June 1736 (published 1 July).
   Applebee's Original Weekly-Journal. 3 July 1736.
   The General Magazine. July 1736.

(c) text; beginning "*Of manners gentle . . .*"

The lapidary inscription in Westminster Abbey.

Contemporary transcript: Bodl. MS Ballard 50f, 104v.

The Works of Alexander Pope, Esq; Vol. II. 1735 (octavo).

The Works . . . Vol. II. Containing his Epistles and Satires. 1735 (and 1736).

Ethic Epistles, to Henry St. John L. Bolingbroke. Written in the Year 1732. 1735.

The London Evening-Post. 8–10 July 1736.

Fog's Weekly Journal. 17 July 1736.

Read's Weekly Journal. 17 July 1736.

The London Magazine. July 1736.

The Grub-street Journal. 5 May 1737.

The London Evening-Post. 3–5 May 1737.

The Universal Spectator. 7 May 1737.

A General Dictionary. P. Bayle. Vol. V. 1737.

The Works . . . Vol. II. Containing his Epistles, &c. 1739 (both editions).

The Works . . . Vol. II. Part I. Containing his Epistles, &c. 1740 (and 1743).

A Collection of Moral and Sacred Poems. J. Wesley. Vol. I. 1744.

Memoirs of . . . Alexander Pope, Esq. W. Ayre. Vol. II. 1745.

Art of Poetry made easy. 1746.

The London Magazine. (Dublin.) February 1750.

The Nut-Cracker. F. Foot. 1751.

The Works. Ed. Warburton. Vol. VI. 1751.

This epitaph appeared in three versions which overlapped considerably. Gay died on 4 December 1732; and on 16 February 1732-3, Pope wrote to Swift: "It is indeed impossible to speak on such a subject as the loss of Mr. Gay, to me an irreparable one. But I send you what I intend for the inscription on his tomb, which the Duke of Queensberry will set up at Westminster." On 31 March Swift replied: "I have not seen in so few lines more good sense, or more proper to the subject"; and suggested some slight alterations, most of which Pope adopted. It is doubtful whether a copy of the original draft survives; but a very early version —(a) text—is found in the Longleat transcript and the *1733* texts, beginning, "A manly wit, a child's simplicity". On 26 June 1736 *Read's Weekly Journal* (followed by five other papers), announced—"A curious Monument is now finished by Mr. Rysbrack, the famous Statuary, and will be put up in West-minster Abbey in a few Days, in Memory of the late celebrated Mr. Gay, on which is the following Epitaph . . ." This version—(b) text—begins, "Severe of Morals, but of Nature mild." *The London Evening Post*, 8–10 July 1736, inserted much the same paragraph, but concluded with a third version—(c) text—the first line of which reads, "Of Manners gentle, of Affections mild"; this is the first time ll. 3–4 were printed. Other papers followed suit. After another preliminary announcement in March 1737, four papers reported on 29 April:

Yesterday Evening a Monument, sacred to the Memory of Mr. John Gay, was open'd in the Poet's Corner of Westminster-Abbey, erected at the Expence of the Duke and Dutchess of Queensberry and Dover; an elegant Inscription is erected thereon, beginning with these Lines,

Life is a Jest, and all Things shew it,
I thought so once, but now I know it.

The following week the newspapers printed all the inscriptions on the monu-
ment, beginning with Gay's couplet on himself (quoted above), followed by
Pope's epitaph, "Of Manners gentle . . .", and ending with a prose epitaph pro-
bably Pope's work also. In addition to this quite unusual newspaper vogue—
partly accounted for by Gay's popularity—there were the magazines and the
ever-varying editions of Pope's *Works* printing concurrently one or other of the
three versions of the epitaph.

   The text follows that of *1735cd*, the (*c*) or final text, as amended for the last time
in *1736* by the addition of ll. 3–4; with collations from the (*a*) text—the Longleat
transcript (*L.TS*) and the *Gentleman's Magazine* (1733); and (*b*) text—the Welbeck
transcript (*W.TS*), and the *Works*, "Volume II" (*1735ab*).

An Essay on Man. Addressed to a Friend.
Part I

[published 20 February 1732/3; vol. III i, pp. 9–51]

An Essay on Man. In Epistles to a Friend.
Epistle II

[published 29 March 1732/3; vol. III i 53–90]

An Essay on Man. In Epistles to a Friend.
Epistle III

[published 8 May 1733; vol. III i 92–126]

The *CRUX-EASTON* Epigrams.

I.

On seeing the LADIES *at* Crux-Easton
Walk in the Woods *by the* Grotto.

Extempore by Mr. *Pope.*

Authors the world and their dull brains have trac'd,
    To fix the ground where paradise was plac'd.
Mind not their learned whims and idle talk,
Here, here's the place, where these bright angels walk.

Title Crux-Easton] *1750 misprints* Crux-Euston.

II.

Inscription *on a* Grotto of Shells at Crux-Easton
the Work of Nine young Ladies.

Here shunning idleness at once and praise,
    This radiant pile nine rural sisters raise;
The glitt'ring emblem of each spotless dame,
Clear as her soul, and shining as her frame;
Beauty which Nature only can impart,   5
And such a polish as disgraces Art;
But Fate dispos'd them in this humble sort,
And hid in desarts what wou'd charm a court.

Title] *MS and 1750 read:* An Inscription on a Grotto, the Work of
    Nine [Young *MS*] Ladys.
3 spotless] matchless *1750.*
4 Clear] Clean *1750.* shining] spotless *1750.*
5 Beauty] Beauties *MS, 1750.*
6 disgraces] disgraceth *MS, 1750.*

Orrery transcript: c. 1748: Harvard College Library. [No. ii.]
The Student. No. i. 31 January 1750. [Nos. i, ii.]
The Nut-Cracker. F. Foot. 1751. [Nos. i, ii.]
A Collection of Poems. R. Dodsley. Vol. VI. 1758 (and later editions). [No. ii.]
The Poetical Calendar. December 1763. [No. ii.]
The Festoon. 1766 (and later editions). [No. ii.]
The Christmas Treat. 1767. [No. ii.]
The Works. Ed. Warton. Vol. VIII, "Letters". 1797. [No. ii.]
The Works. Ed. Dyce. Vol. II. 1831. [No. ii.]
The Works. Ed. Carruthers. New Edition. Vol. II. 1858. [Nos. i, ii.]

These epigrams on the nine sisters of the Lisle family at Crux-Easton have been included in the canon without comment by all editors since Carruthers. A transcript of the longer poem, superscribed "By Mr. Pope", appears in a volume of papers belonging to Lord Orrery, who, as a friend of Pope, was in a better position than most to know the truth. As the transcript is thought to have been made not later than 1748, it would thus antedate the first printed copy, and be an independent witness. The authenticity of the epigrams is probable, but they must be classed amongst the attributed pieces.

The accomplishments and, more especially perhaps, the number of the Lisle sisters, seem to have attracted attention beyond their local "deserts" even before these tributes were known. The London periodical, *The Weekly Register* (5 February 1732) included a long poetical compliment addressed: *To Mrs.* —— *Who desir'd some Verses on Nine Maiden Ladies whom the Author had never seen*; which could hardly have referred to another family. The Misses Lisle, who, the *Inscription* says, had themselves made the grotto, used also, according to report (see EC, iv 458) "to amuse themselves by standing on niches in the Grotto as the Nine Muses; Pope being placed in the midst, as Apollo". As the shorter epigram is dated "August 25, 1733", that year is tentatively taken as the date for both pieces, which are not improbably owing to the same visit.

The text is that of the first printing for No. i and of Dodsley's *Collection* for No. ii with, for No. ii, collations from the transcript (*MS*) and *1750*.

The Impertinent, Or a Visit to the Court.
A Satyr.
The Fourth Satire of Dr. John Donne . . .
Versifyed.

[published 5 November 1733; vol. iv, pp. 23–49]

To the Earl of Burlington
asking who writ the Libels against him.

Y ou wonder Who this Thing has writ,
So full of Fibs, so void of Wit?
Lord! never ask who thus could serve ye?
Who can it be but Fibster H—y.

Title. Earl of Burlington] E. of B. *MS.*
1 wonder] ask me *erased, and* wonder *written in pencil above.*

Pope's autograph: Devonshire MSS, Chatsworth, 1st Series, 143.68.
The Grub-street Journal, No. 352. September 1736.
Lord Hervey's anonymous attack on Pope entitled *An Epistle to a Doctor of Divinity from a Nobleman at Hampton Court* was published (without Hervey's consent) in November 1733 (see Vol. IV, pp. xixf.). Pope was reported by Hervey to be "in a most violent fury". The preceding epigram, though not published till 1736, was probably written at this time. The text is that of the manuscript, which is verbally identical with the printed text.

PROLOGUE,
For the Benefit of Mr. DENNIS, 1733.

A s when that Hero, who in each Campaign
Had brav'd the *Goth,* and many a *Vandal* slain,
Lay Fortune-struck, a Spectacle of Woe!
Wept by each Friend, forgiv'n by ev'ry Foe:
Was there a gen'rous, a reflecting Mind,   5
But pities *Belisarius,* Old and Blind?
Was there a Chief, but melted at the Sight?
A common Soldier, but who clubb'd his *Mite?*
Such, such Emotions should in *Britons* rise,

Title] *1751 reads:* A Prologue By Mr. Pope, To a Play for Mr. Dennis's Benefit, in 1733, when he was old, blind, and in great Distress, a little before his Death.

When prest by Want and Weakness, Dennis lies;   10
Dennis, who long had warr'd with modern Huns,
Their Quibbles routed, and defy'd their Puns;
A desp'rate Bulwark, sturdy, firm, and fierce,
Against the Gothick Sons of frozen Verse;
How chang'd from him, who made the Boxes groan,   15
And shook the Stage with Thunders all his own!
Stood up to dash each vain Pretender's Hope,
Maul the French Tyrant, or pull down the Pope!
If there's a Briton, then, true bred and born,
Who holds Dragoons and Wooden-Shoes in scorn;   20
If there's a Critick of distinguish'd Rage;
If there's a Senior, who contemns this Age;
Let him to Night his just Assistance lend,
And be the Critick's, Briton's, Old-man's Friend.

The Publick Register: or, The Weekly Magazine. No. III. 17 January 1741.
The Works. Ed. Warburton. Vol. VI. 1751.

A performance of The Provoked Husband was given for Dennis's benefit by the King's Players at the Haymarket Theatre on 18 December 1733. The Daily Journal (18 December) announced that the play was to be performed with a new prologue, but all available evidence (see New Light, pp. 286–97) goes to show that if Pope's prologue was in fact spoken on this occasion, its authorship was not revealed. The version printed by Dodsley (and reprinted here) is likewise anonymous. The attribution of the piece to Pope was first made by Warburton, and has been accepted ever since, although there is no supporting evidence of earlier date. Warburton's text is verbally identical with Dodsley's.

6. Belisarius] A celebrated general under Justinian, and by him dishonourably accused of conspiracy against his life. Legend has it that he was condemned, deprived of his property, blinded, and reduced to beggary.

7. a Chief] The fine figure of the Commander in that capital Picture of Belisarius at Chiswick, supplied the Poet with this beautiful idea [Warburton].

16. Thunders all his own] Dennis was said to have invented an improved method of making stage-thunder for his play, Appius and Virginia, 1709. The play failed, but the thunder was a success, and was imitated by others. Hence Pope's joke here and elsewhere (see Prose Works, 1, p. xvii; and Dunciad A, II 218 and note).

18. French Tyrant] Dennis's hatred of the French is thought to derive from his visit to that country in 1680. He wrote a play against the French, Liberty Asserted, in 1704, which (so the tale went) so offended the French king "that he never would make Peace with England, unless the delivering up Mr. Dennis, was one of the Articles of it" (Life of Dennis, 1734). Pope teased Dennis about it, more than

once (see *Narrative of Dr. Norris* and *The Critical Specimen, Prose Works* I, pp. 16, 156–7, 168).

An Epistle to the Right Honourable Richard Lord Viscount Cobham

[published 16 January 1733/4; vol. III ii 13–38]

An Essay on Man. In Epistles to a Friend. Epistle IV

[published 24 January 1733/4; vol. III i 127–66]

To L^d. *Hervey & Lady Mary Wortley*

W HEN I but call a flagrant Whore unsound,
    Or have a Pimp or Flaterer in the Wind,
Sapho enrag'd crys out your Back is round,
    Adonis screams—Ah! Foe to all Mankind!

Thanks, dirty Pair! you teach me what to say,   5
    When you attack my Morals, Sense, or Truth,
I answer thus—poor Sapho you grow grey,
    And sweet Adonis—you have lost a Tooth.

Contemporary transcript: Holland House Papers.
Lord Hervey and his Friends. By the Earl of Ilchester. 1950.
References to Sappho and Lord Fanny in the first *Imitation of Horace* (February 1733) provoked Lord Hervey and Lady Mary Wortley Montagu to collaborate in *Verses Addressed to the Imitator of Horace*, published in March 1733 (see Vol. IV, pp. xvff.). A retort which Hervey attributed to Pope was sent by Hervey to Henry Fox with a letter dated 8 February 1733/4 (Ilchester, pp. 191f.). There is nothing improbable in the attribution, for the studied moderation of the second stanza was to be developed later in the year in *An Epistle to Dr. Arbuthnot*.
The text follows Hervey's transcript in all particulars.

[A CHARACTER]

*Mark by what wretched steps Great * * grows,* *291*
From dirt and sea-weed as proud Venice rose;
One equal course how Guilt and Greatness ran,
And all that rais'd the Hero sunk the Man.
Now Europe's Lawrels on his brows behold, *5*
But stain'd with Blood, or ill exchang'd for Gold.
What wonder tryumphs never turn'd his brain
Fill'd with mean fear to lose mean joy to gain.
Hence see him modest free from pride or shew
Some Vices were too high but none too low 10
Go then indulge thy age in Wealth and ease
Stretch'd on the spoils of plunder'd palaces
Alas what *wealth*, which no one act of fame
E'er taught to shine, or sanctified from shame
Alas what *ease* those furies of thy life 15
Ambition Av'rice and th' imperious Wife.
The trophy'd Arches, story'd Halls invade, *303*
And haunt his slumbers in the pompous Shade.
No joy no pleasure from successes past
Timid and therefore treacherous to the last 20
Hear him in accents of a pining Ghost
Sigh, with his Captive for his ofspring lost
Behold him loaded with unreverend years
Bath'd in unmeaning unrepentant tears
Dead, by regardless Vet'rans born on high 25
Dry pomps and Obsequies without a sigh.
Who now his fame or fortune shall prolong
In vain his consort bribes for venal song
No son nor Grandson shall the line sustain

Title] *None in the MS.*
1 *Great **] their glory E on M.*
3 *In each how guilt and greatness equal ran E on M.*
5 *his*] their *E on M.* 18 *his*] their *E on M.*

The husband toils the Adulterer sweats in vain: 30
In vain a nations zeal a senate's cares
"Madness and lust" (said God) "be you his heirs"
"O'er his vast heaps in drunkenness of pride
"Go wallow Harpyes and your prey divide"
Alas! not dazled with his Noontide ray,   35
Compute the Morn and Evening of his Day: *306*
The whole amount of that enormous Fame
A Tale! that blends the Glory with the Shame!

35 *his*] their *E on M.*   36 *of his*] to the *E on M.*
38 *the . . . the*] their . . . their *E on M.*

Pope's autograph: Yale University Library (Facsimile, EC III).

Pope told Spence (*Anecdotes*, p. 143; an. 1734–6) that he had omitted from the *Essay on Man* "a character (though I thought it one of the best I had ever written) of a very great man who had every thing from without to make him happy, and yet was very miserable; from the want of virtue in his own heart". "Though he did not say who this was," Spence comments, "it seemed to have been that of the Duke of Marlborough." Such a character was found amongst Warburton's papers, and now lies in the Yale University Library. It is a manuscript revision and expansion of *Essay*, IV 291–308 on a single leaf, pp. 69–70, of the quarto edition of the *Essay* (not the quarto edition of *Works*, 1735, as EC states), and was probably designed for the revised edition of *Essay* included in the quarto edition of *Works, Vol. II*. Spence records no reason for the suppression of the character. As it stands it is a type character. But since it can readily be interpreted as a character of Marlborough, Pope may have chosen to suppress it rather than risk offending the Duchess, who had recently made fellow cause with Walpole's political opponents. If this is the right reason, the lines must have been written soon after the publication of the whole *Essay* in quarto in May 1734.

Lines from the *Essay on Man* are printed in italic.

22. *his ofspring lost*] Marlborough's son died in 1703 at the age of seventeen.

25f. For an account of Marlborough's funeral on 9 August 1722, see J. Sutherland, *Background for Queen Anne* (London, 1939), pp. 204–24.

38. *Tale*] "Tally", as well as "story": cf. "compute", l. 36 [*Mack*].

The Second Satire of the Second Book of Horace
Paraphrased

[published 4 July 1734; vol. IV, pp. 54–69]

EPIGRAMS
Occasioned by *Cibber*'s Verses
in Praise of *Nash*.

I.

O NASH! more blest in ev'ry other thing,
　　But in thy Poet wretched as a King!
Thy Realm disarm'd of each offensive Tool,
Ah! leave not this, this Weapon to a Fool.
Thy happy Reign all other Discord quells;　　　　5
Oh doe but silence Cibber, and the Bells.
Apollo's genuine Sons thy fame shall raise
And all Mankind, but Cibber, sing thy praise.

II.

C IBBER! write all thy Verses upon Glasses,
　　The only way to save 'em from our A—s.

Pope's autograph: Longleat, Portland Papers, XII.
Contemporary transcript: BM Malet MSS.
Life and Times of Colley Cibber. By F. D. Senior. 1928.
New Light on Pope. By N. Ault. 1950.
Although the existence of these epigrams in Pope's handwriting does not con-
stitute proof of his authorship, the suspicion that he composed them is confirmed
by finding the witticism of the second also occurring in a letter from Pope to
Bethel of 28 September 1734. The text of Cibber's verses which follow is taken
from F. D. Senior, *Life and Times of Colley Cibber*, p. 123.

> Let Kings their power by lineal birth inherit,
> Nash holds his empire from his public spirit.
> If Populi with Dei Vox we join,
> This place at least he rules by right divine
> Learn Britons hence the needfull use of Kings,
> From Freedom bound general wellfare springs.

Both verses and epigrams are undated. They appear to have been written after
Cibber's retirement from the stage in the late 1730s, when much of his time was
passed at fashionable watering places, and are tentatively given the date (1734)
of Pope's letter to Bethel.

I. 1. Richard ("Beau") Nash (1674–1762), Arbiter Elegantiarum at Bath, c. 1705–c. 1745.

3. "... it was thought necessary to forbid the wearing of swords at Bath, as they often tore the ladies' clothes, and frighted them, by sometimes appearing upon trifling occasions." Goldsmith, *Life of Nash* (*Works*, ed. P. Cunningham, 1854, IV 55).

6. *the Bells*] "Upon a stranger's arrival at Bath he is welcomed by a peal of the Abbey bells", *ibid.*, p. 57.

II. Cf. Pope to Bethel, "Cibber is here [Bath] to celebrate her [a certain princess]; and he writes his verses now, in such a manner, that no body can use them as they were wont to do; for no body will, on certain occasions, use a pane of glass." Ruffhead, p. 390.

Sober Advice from Horace, To the Young Gentlemen about Town

[published 28 December 1734; vol. IV, pp. 73–89]

An Epistle from Mr Pope, to Dr Arbuthnot

[published 2 January 1734/5; vol. IV, pp. 95–127]

Of the Characters of Women: An Epistle to a Lady

[published 8 February 1734/5; vol. III ii 45–74]

The Second Satire of Dr. John Donne, Dean of St. Paul's, Versifyed

[revised version published April 1735; vol. IV, pp. 133–45]

EPITAPH.

On EDMUND *Duke of* BUCKINGHAM, *who died in the* Nineteenth *Year of his Age,* 1735.

IF modest Youth, with cool Reflection crown'd,
   And ev'ry opening Virtue blooming round,
Could save a Mother's justest Pride from fate,
Or add one Patriot to a sinking state;
This weeping marble had not ask'd thy Tear,   5
Or sadly told, how many Hopes lie here!
The living Virtue now had shone approv'd,
The Senate heard him, and his Country lov'd.
Yet softer Honours, and less noisy Fame
Attend the shade of gentle *Buckingham*:   10
In whom a Race, for Courage fam'd and Art,
Ends in the milder Merit of the Heart;
And Chiefs or Sages long to Britain giv'n,
Pays the last Tribute of a Saint to Heav'n.

3 Mother's] Parent's *1738a, 1740–51.*

The Works . . . Vol. II. Part II. Containing . . . Pieces . . . written since the former Volumes . . . 1738.
   The Works . . . Vol. II. Part I. Containing his Epistles, &c. 1740 (and 1743).
   The Works. Ed. Warburton. Vol. VI. 1751.
   For the relations of Pope with the Duchess of Buckingham see Vol. III ɪɪ, p. 59. On the young Duke's death in 1735, his mother asked Pope, with whom she had recently become reconciled, to write his epitaph. This seems not to have been printed till 1738 when it appeared in both issues of *Works Vol. II Part II* (whose publication seems to have been delayed until 1739). In the second of these Pope made a revision in l. 3, which appears to have escaped notice when the epitaph was reprinted in 1740 and subsequent years (see M. Mack, "Pope's Horatian Poems: Problems of Bibliography and Text", *Mod. Philology*, xLI, p. 39, *n.* 21). It is now restored to the text, which in other respects follows that of the first printing.
   Title: *Edmund*] Third but only surviving son of John Sheffield, first Duke of Buckingham and Normanby, and Katherine his wife, was born 3 January 1715–6. (For rejoicings on his seventh birthday, see *ante*, p. 155.) He died of consump-

tion at Rome, 30 October 1735, and was buried in Westminster Abbey, 31 January 1735–6 [GEC], but Pope's epitaph was not placed on his tomb.

EPIGRAM.

On One who made long Epitaphs.

FRIEND! for your Epitaphs I'm griev'd,
  Where still so much is said,
One half will never be believ'd,
  The other never read.

Title On . . . Epitaphs.] *MS reads:* To one who wrote Epitaphs.
1 for] in *MS.*
2 Where still so] So very *MS.*

Pope's autograph: BM MS Egerton 1947.
The Works of Alexander Pope, Esq; Vol. II. Part II containing . . . Pieces . . . written since the former Volumes . . . 1738.
The Works . . . Vol. II. Containing his Epistles, &c. 1739.
The Works . . . Vol. II. Part I. Containing his Epistles, &c. 1740 (and 1743).
The Works . . . Volume V. Containing the Dunciad. Ed. Warburton. 1751.
A Collection of Select Epigrams. J. Hackett. 1757.
The Festoon. 1766 (and later editions).
The Christmas Treat. 1767.
The County Magazine. November 1786.
The Poems of Pope. Vol. II (in Johnson's *English Poets*), 1790.
This epigram originally formed the postscript of a letter from Pope to Ralph Allen, dated "Twitnam. Apr. 30th". Warburton, who first printed the letter in 1751, omitted the postscript, but added "1736" to the date in accord with internal evidence. In the letter Pope, after advising his friend on some projected wall paintings in the hall of his house, went on to speak of wall decoration in churches, and deprecated the zeal of reformers who removed "*pictures* (that is to say, examples) out of churches", and yet suffered "*Epitaphs* (that is to say, Flatteries and False History) to be the Burden of church-walls, & ye Shame, as well as Derision, of all honest men."; and appended this epigram by way of postscript. In the *Dunciad* (A, 1 41) he had written "Sepulchral lyes our holy walls to grace", and had later added a note stating that that line "Is a just Satyr on the Flatteries and Falsehoods admitted to be inscribed on the walls of Churches in Epitaphs". —a sentiment which he seems to have had in mind when writing to Allen. In

13

1738 Pope included the epigram (one of the few he acknowledged) in his *Works*. Warburton, however, suppressed it both among the miscellaneous poems and in the Letters, but tacked it on to Pope's "Dunciad" note above quoted, with the addition of the words: "which occasioned the following Epigram". It is highly improbable that the first word, "Friend!" had any personal application when written; but some commentators have since conjectured that the epigram was aimed at "Dr. Freind, a celebrated composer of Latin epitaphs", and headmaster of Westminster School, 1711-33.

The text is that of *1738*. There are no variants except in the autograph (which was followed by Warburton in *1751*).

EPITAPH
On *JOHN KNIGHT*.

JOANNI KNIGHT
De *Goss-field* Com. *Essex*. Armig.
Qui obiit *Oct*. 2. 1733. Æt. 50.

ANNA CRAGGS,

JACOBI CRAGGS, Regi GEORGIO I A Secretis, Soror,

MEMORIÆ & AMORI SACRUM
Conjugi suo Charissimo H.S.P.

O FAIREST Pattern to a failing Age!
  Whose Publick Virtue knew no Party rage:
Whose Private Name all Titles recommend,
The pious Son, fond Husband, faithful Friend:
In Manners plain, in Sense alone refind,   5
Good without Show, and without weakness kind:
To Reason's equal dictates ever true,
Calm to resolve, and constant to pursue.
In Life, with ev'ry social Grace adorn'd,
In Death, by Friendship, Honour, Virtue; mourn'd. 10

The inscription in Gosfield Church.

The Daily Gazetteer. 17 July 1736.

The St. James's Evening Post. 15–17 July 1736.

The General Evening Post. 15–17 July 1736.

The London Evening-Post. 15–17 July 1736.

The Works. Ed. Elwin and Courthope. Correspondence. Vol. IV. 1886.

On 17 May 1736, Pope wrote to Mrs Knight, the sister of his dead friend Craggs,

> Madam, Though I forget all the town at this season, I would not have you think I forget your commissions; but (to put it upon a truer foot) I can't forget a person I so really loved and esteemed as the subject of the enclosed inscription. It is now as I think it ought to be, and the sooner it is engraved the better.

The enclosed inscription was probably the epitaph on her husband, John Knight, in Gosfield Church, about which two months later, four newspapers announce: "Yesterday a curious fine Monument was erected in the Church at Gossfield in the County of Essex, to the Memory of John Knight, Esq; and his Lady, on which is the following Inscription, viz . . .". George Vertue's diary at Welbeck contains a transcript of this epitaph, Latin and English, under the year 1739, with the comment:

> in the church of Gosfield—is a monument of Marble statues erected by Mrs. Knight, in memory of Mr. Knight and her self . . . at no small expence the work of M. Rysbrake—these lines by Mr. Pope. She soon married again . . . and since that has ordered it to be enclosed as it is with a wainscot screen to shutt up this Monument from her sight when she goes to church. tho' seldom.

Mrs Knight married Robert Nugent (see Vol. IV, pp. 289*n*., 319*n*.) on 23 March 1736–7, and thus provoked a couplet (II 108f.) in the *Epilogue to the Satires*, published the following year:

> Each Widow asks [Praise] for the Best of Men,
> For him she weeps, and him she weds agen.

The text is that of the actual inscription at Gosfield, from which the first printing (the *Daily Gazetteer*) derives.

2. Cf. *Imit. Hor., Ep.* II i 45, "In ev'ry publick Virtue we excell", and *Mor. Ess.*, III 151, "And nobly wishing Party-rage to cease."

BOUNCE to FOP.
AN HEROICK EPISTLE
From a DOG at TWICKENHAM
To a DOG at Court.

To thee, sweet *Fop*, these Lines I send,
  Who, tho' no Spaniel, am a Friend.
Tho, once my Tail in wanton play,
Now frisking this, and then that way,
Chanc'd, with a Touch of just the Tip,   5
To hurt your Lady-lap-dog-ship;
Yet thence to think I'd bite your Head off!
Sure *Bounce* is one you never read of.

  FOP! you can dance, and make a Leg,
Can fetch and carry, cringe and beg,   10
And (what's the Top of all your Tricks)
Can stoop to pick up *Strings* and *Sticks*.
We Country Dogs love nobler Sport,
And scorn the Pranks of Dogs at Court.
Fye, naughty Fop! where e'er you come   15
To f—t and p—ss about the Room,
To lay your Head in every Lap,
And, when they think not of you—snap!
The worst that Envy, or that Spite
E'er said of me, is, I can bite: 20
That sturdy Vagrants, Rogues in Rags,

Title An Heroick Epistle] An Epistle *TS, 1736, 1742.*
  3 *TSS read:* My Tail indeed 'twas but in play
  4 frisking . . . then] flurting . . . now *TSS.*
  5 Chanc'd] Did *TSS.*
  6 *TSS read:* Once chance to hurt your Lap dog ship
  7 Yet . . . I'd] But . . . I'le *TSS.*
15 Fop] thing *TSS.*   20 E'er said] Can say *TSS.*
21 sturdy Vagrants] Sturdy Beggars *TSS*; idle Gypsies *1736, 1742.*

Who poke at me, can make no Brags;
And that to towze such Things as *flutter*,
To honest *Bounce* is Bread and Butter.

While you, and every courtly Fop,   25
Fawn on the Devil for a Chop,
I've the Humanity to hate
A Butcher, tho' he brings me Meat;
And let me tell you, have a Nose,
(Whatever stinking Fops suppose)   30
That under Cloth of Gold or Tissue,
Can smell a Plaister, or an Issue.

Your pilf'ring Lord, with simple Pride,
May wear a Pick-lock at his Side;
My Master wants no Key of State,   35
For *Bounce* can keep his House and Gate.

When all such Dogs have had their Days,
As knavish *Pams*, and fawning *Trays*;
When pamper'd *Cupids*, bestly *Veni*'s,
And motly, squinting *Harvequini*'s,   40
Shall lick no more their Lady's Br—,
But die of Looseness, Claps, or Itch;
Fair *Thames* from either ecchoing Shoare
Shall hear, and dread my manly Roar.

22 Who] That *TSS*.
37–44, 49–56 *TSS transpose these paragraphs to read*: Before my . . . |
    See *Bounce* . . . | When all . . .
39f. The Motley Race of Hervey queenies
       And Courtly Vices, Beastly Venyes, *TS*.
40 Harvequini's] Harlequini's *1736 and 1742, with footnote*: "Alii
    legunt Harvequini's."
41f. *omm. TSS*.
43 from either ecchoing] shall hear from shoar to *TSS*.
44 Shall hear, and dread my] A hundred Bounces *TSS*.

See *Bounce*, like *Berecynthia*, crown'd   45
With thund'ring Offspring all around,
Beneath, beside me, and a top,
A hundred Sons! and not one *Fop*.

Before my Children set your Beef,
Not one true *Bounce* will be a Thief;   50
Not one without Permission feed,
(Tho' some of *J—*'s hungry Breed)
But whatsoe'er the Father's Race,
From me they suck a little Grace.
While your fine Whelps learn all to steal,   55
Bred up by Hand on Chick and Veal.

My Eldest-born resides not far,
Where shines great *Strafford*'s glittering Star:
My second (Child of Fortune!) waits
At *Burlington*'s Palladian Gates: 60
A third majestically stalks
(Happiest of Dogs!) in *Cobham*'s Walks:
One ushers Friends to *Bathurst*'s Door;
One fawns, at *Oxford*'s, on the Poor.

Nobles, whom Arms or Arts adorn,   65
Wait for my Infants yet unborn.

46 Offspring] Infants *TSS*.   47 me] her *TSS*.
49 Children] Puppyes *TSS*.
51 Not] Nor *TSS*.
52 some] come *TSS*. *J—*'s] I lays *TSS*; J—n's *1736, 1742*.
56 on] and *TSS*.   58 glittering] guilded *TSS*.
    Following l. 58, TSS read:
            To those high doors with equall grace
            He stands The Guardian of the Place
61-8 *omm. TSS. which read:*
            In whose Bright Palace every Guest,
            And every Dog's Supremely blest.

None but a Peer of Wit and Grace,
Can hope a Puppy of my Race.

And O! wou'd Fate the Bliss decree
To mine (a Bliss too great for me)   70
That two, my tallest Sons, might grace
Attending each with stately Pace,
Iülus' Side, as erst *Evander*'s,
To keep off Flatt'rers, Spies, and Panders,
To let no noble Slave come near,   75
And scare Lord *Fannys* from his Ear:
Then might a Royal Youth, and true,
Enjoy at least a Friend—or two:
A Treasure, which, of Royal kind,
Few but Himself deserve to find.   80

Then *Bounce* ('tis all that *Bounce* can crave)
Shall wag her Tail within the Grave.

And tho' no Doctors, Whig or Tory ones,
Except the Sect of *Pythagoreans*,
Have Immortality assign'd   85
To any Beast, but *Dryden*'s Hind:
Yet Master *Pope*, whom Truth and Sense
Shall call their Friend some Ages hence,

70 To Mine (I ask it not to Me) *TSS.*
72 Each walking with Majestick Pace *TSS.*
73 *Iülus'*] Iulus's *1736, 1742.*
74 Instead of Spyes, & Pimps, & Panders, *TSS.*
75f. *omm. TSS.*
77 Then might a Royal] That so a Noble *TSS.*
78 Enjoy] Might have *TSS.*
79f. *omm. TSS.*
83-94 *omm. 1736, 1742.*
87 *Pope*, whom Truth] P— Whom Witt *TSS.*
88 Have made Tremendous as a Prince *TSS.*

Tho' now on loftier Themes he sings
Than to bestow a Word on *Kings*,   90
Has sworn by *Sticks* (the Poet's Oath,
And Dread of Dogs and Poets both)
Man and his Works he'll soon renounce,
And roar in Numbers worthy *Bounce*.

89 on loftier Themes] of Mighty Peers *TSS*.
90 And now a word or two of Kings *TSS*.
91 *Sticks*] Styx *TSS*.
92 And] The *TSS*.
93f. His Lords and Laydes He'le renounce
      To sing Fidelity, and Bounce. *TSS*.

Contemporary transcripts: Longleat, Portland Papers, xx; Welbeck Abbey, Harley Papers; BM Stowe MSS 180, f. 216.

Bounce to Fop. An Heroick Epistle from a Dog at Twickenham to a Dog at Court. By Dr. S—T. Dublin, Printed, London, Reprinted for T. Cooper . . . 1736.

Bounce to Fop. An Heroick Epistle from A Dog at Twickenham to A Dog at Court. London: Printed. And Dublin Re-printed by George Faulkner . . . 1736.

The Gentleman's Magazine. May 1736.

The London Magazine. May 1736.

Miscellanies. The Third Volume. 1736 (and later editions).

Miscellanies. The Fourth Volume. Consisting of Verses . . . 1742 (and later editions).

Gay's *Miscellaneous Works*. J. Bell. Vol. IV. 1773.

The Works of the English Poets (Johnson's Edition). "The Poems of Gay". Vol. I. 1779.

The Works of the Rev. Dr. Jonathan Swift. T. Sheridan. Vol. XVII. 1784.

The Works of the Rev. Jonathan Swift, D.D. J. Nichols. Vol. XVII. 1801.

New Light on Pope. By N. Ault. 1950.

This poem has been erroneously attributed to Swift and Gay (see *New Light*, pp. 345f.).

The only contemporary association of Pope's name with its authorship is found in Lord Oxford's copy of the London folio, now in the Bodleian, on the title-page of which, after the words "By Dr. S—T", he has written "much altered by Mr. Pope"; but Oxford, by reason of his long friendship with both poets, should have been in a position to know.

In 1736 Pope had a much loved dog at Twickenham, called Bounce, a bitch, one of whose puppies was given to the Prince of Wales in that year (see poem on the subject, and note, p. 372). In 1742 she was reluctantly given to Lord and Lady Orrery, in whose care she died, only a few weeks before Pope himself, in 1744 (see poem on the subject, and note, p. 405). Fop's identity is only a little less certain. Swift, writing to Mrs Howard. on 9 July 1727, about people who curry favour with persons at court, says casually "... if they saw your dog, Fop, use me kindly ..."; and the same dog is probably alluded to in the line, "Fop is the delight of a lady", in *Molly Mog*, a poem written by Gay, Swift, and Pope (see *post*, p. 443), all of whom were friends of Mrs Howard; and as this dog was "a Dog at Court", and could have been alive in 1736, she was almost certainly the Fop of the epistle. Further confirmation is found in Walpole's statement: "Pope was a Friend of Lady Suffolk's [formerly Mrs. Howard] ... and wrote the Epitaph in her Garden on her Dog Fop, who was the Subject of an Epistle of Swift's call'd Bounce to Fop." The "Epitaph" is one of the lost pieces.

Two versions of the poem have survived, in the Welbeck transcript, and the *1736* folio. The folio text is mainly an expansion of that of the transcript, to judge by the inserted allusions to "Lord Fannys" who must be scared away from the Prince, and to Cobham, Bathurst, and Oxford, all close friends of Pope and proud owners of Bounce's puppies.

It appears probable that the poem originally dates from 1726 or 1727 when Swift was staying with Pope (and Bounce) at Twickenham, and when, on his visits to Mrs Howard, he met Fop as well. The poem would seem to have passed through three stages, the earliest being a Swift-Pope collaboration in a draft now vanished; the second, Pope's subsequent expansion of the joint draft as it has survived in the Welbeck transcript; the third, and final, stage being the text of the *1736* folio which is his expansion of the Welbeck version.

The text follows the London folio of 1736 with collations from the Stowe and Welbeck transcripts (*TSS*), and the *Miscellanies* of 1736 (*1736*) and 1742 (*1742*).

10. *fetch and carry*] Cf. *Ep. to Arbuthnot*, ll. 225f:

> Nor like a Puppy daggled thro' the Town,
> To fetch and carry Sing-song up and down.

12. For the image cf. "Voyage to Lilliput", chap. III § 4; *Ess. on Man*, IV 205; *Imit. Hor.*, *Ep.* I vi 14.

40. *Harlequini's*] A Harlequin is a small breed of spotted dog.

45-8. This imitation of Virgil, *Æneid*, VI 784ff. had been anticipated in *Dunciad* A, III 123-6.

52. Who *J—* was is unknown. Presumably he was the sire of one of Bounce's litters, and a ravenous feeder.

73. *Iülus*] Son of Æneas; reference to the Prince of Wales [P. *1736*].

as erst Evander's] Virg. Æn. VIII [P. *1736*] see ll. 461-2:

> Nec non et gemini custodes limine ab alto
> Praecedunt gressumque canes comitantur herilem.

76. Cf. *Ep. to Arbuthnot*, l. 319 and note.

81f. For similar phrasing see *New Light*, p. 347.

86. A Milk-white Hind, immortal and unchang'd. Ver. I. Of the *Hind* and *Panther*. [P. *1736*].

EPIGRAM.

Engraved on the Collar of a Dog which I gave to his Royal Highness.

I AM his Highness' Dog at *Kew*;
Pray tell me Sir, whose Dog are you?

The Works of Alexander Pope, Esq; Vol. II. Part II. Containing . . . Pieces . . . written since the former Volumes. 1738.

The Works . . . Vol. II. Containing his Epistles, &c. 1739.

The Works . . . Vol. II. Part I. Containing his Epistles, &c. 1740 (and 1743).

The Festoon. 1766 (and later editions).

The Christmas Treat. 1767.

Additions to the Works of Alexander Pope, Esq. Vol. I. 1776.

Correspondence between . . . Countess of Hartford . . . and . . . Countess of Pomfret . . . 1805.

The Works. Ed. Roscoe. Vol. III. 1824.

This couplet is best explained by a passage in a letter from George (later Lord) Lyttelton to Pope, dated "Bath, December 22nd, 1736" in which he says that he will curb his impatience to see Pope again "for a week or ten days longer, and then come to you in most outrageous spirits and overturn you like Bounce, when you let her loose after a regimen of physic and confinement. I am very glad that his Royal Highness has received two such honourable presents at a time, as a whelp of *hers* and the freedom of the city." It was doubtless for this "whelp" that Pope wrote the couplet.

The text is that of *1738*. There are no variants.

Possibly an adaptation of a passage in Sir W. Temple's "Heads Designed for an Essay on Conversation" (*Miscellanea*, Pt III; *Works*, Vol. II, Edinburgh, 1754, p. 473): "Mr. *Grantam*'s fool's reply to a great man that asked whose fool he was? I am Mr. *Grantam*'s fool: pray whose fool are you?"

Horace His Ode to Venus

[published 9 March 1736/7; vol. IV, pp. 150–3]

Part of the Ninth Ode of the Fourth Book of Horace

[vol. IV, p. 159]

The Second Epistle of the Second Book of Horace

[published 28 April 1737; vol. IV, pp. 164–187]

The First Epistle of the Second Book of Horace

[published 25 May 1737; vol. IV, pp. 191–231]

SONNET

Written upon Occasion of the Plague, and
found on a Glass-Window at Chalfont.

(*In Imitation of* MILTON.)

FAIR Mirrour of foul Times! whose fragile Sheene
 Shall as it blazeth, break; while Providence
 (Aye watching o'er his Saints with Eye unseen,)
  Spreads the red Rod of angry Pestilence,
  To sweep the wicked and their Counsels hence; 5

Yea all to break the Pride of lustful Kings,
 Who Heaven's Lore reject for brutish Sense;
As erst he scourg'd *Jessides*' Sin of yore
 For the fair *Hittite*, when on Seraph's Wings
 He sent him War, or Plague, or Famine sore. 10

Title Sonnet . . . Milton.] *None originally; this is taken from introductory
note, 1738.*

A Complete Collection of the . . . Works of John Milton. Vol. I. 1738.
The Poetical Calendar. August 1763.
The Life of Alexander Pope. By R. Carruthers. 1853 (and 1857).
The Works. Ed. Elwin and Courthope. Correspondence. Vol. IV. 1886.

These lines are found at the head of a letter from Pope to Richardson dated
18 July [1737] which reads:

> Dear Sir,—I have been in Oxfordshire and Buckinghamshire these ten days,
> and return to Twitnam by Thursday, when I hope to see you, and to fix a day
> after Sunday next, or on Friday or Saturday, if you can send me word to Lord
> Cornbury's. The above was given me by a gentleman as I travelled. I copied it
> for you. You'll tell me more of it perhaps than I can. Yours ever.

The piece was printed early in the following year in *The Works of John Milton*,
Vol. I, 1738 (p. xxxviii), where it is thus introduced by the editor (T. Birch):

> I have in my hands a Sonnet said to be written by *Milton* upon occasion of
> the Plague, and to have been lately found on a Glass-Window at *Chalfont*. It
> is as follows: [the poem is quoted in full]. But the obvious Mistake in this
> Sonnet, in representing the Pestilence as a Judgment upon *David* for his
> Adultery with *Bathsheba*, whereas it was on account of his numbring the
> People, renders it justly suspected not to be our Author's, who was too con-
> versant in Scripture to commit such an Error. For this and some other Reasons,
> which I might mention, I consider it only as a very happy Imitation of
> *Milton*'s Style and Manner. However I am inform'd by Mr. *George Vertue*, that
> he has seen a satirical Medal upon King *Charles* II . . . which corresponds
> extremely with the Sentiment in this Sonnet . . ."

Nevertheless a letter from George Vertue to Lord Oxford (24 February 1737-8)
shows how very nearly Birch was taken in by this pastiche, besides indicating its
authorship:

> Some time ago I related to your Lordship how some lines said to be writ by
> Milton on a glass window were sent to Mr. Richardson, and they are now
> printed in Milton's works now ready to be published. By a letter I saw last
> night in the hands of the Rev. Mr. Birch, the whole discovery is made that Mr.
> Pope and Lord Chesterfield (if I mistake not) had laid this bait for the Con-
> noisseur, who swallowed it, and entertained his intimates . . . many times con-
> cerning his knowledge of Milton's pen and style, which he pronounced he
> knew with the greatest certainty. I could wish your Honour had been in view
> of Richardson when this discovery was made a day or two ago only. In short,
> they are obliged to reprint the sheet in the book in a hurry, it being to be pub-
> lished next Monday. [Birch's letter was from Lyttelton; BM Add. MS 4312,
> f. 270.]
>
> (Hist. MSS Comm. Report—Portland MSS, Vol. VI, 1901, p. 66).

Pope was quite capable of perpetrating this hoax, but since he is not known to
have acknowledged it, the poem must be regarded as an attributed piece. It is
ascribed to 1737 on the evidence of Pope's letter.

The text is that of the first printing, *1738*.

Title: *the Plague*] The Plague of London, 1665, to escape which Milton went to live at Chalfont St Giles.

8. *Jessides*] David, son of Jesse.

9. *Hittite*] Bathsheba (see 2 Samuel XI 2ff.).

10. *War, or Plague, or Famine*] The choice of three punishments offered to David for his sin in numbering the people, *not* for his adultery with Bathsheba (2 Samuel, XXIV 12ff.).

The Sixth Epistle of the First Book of Horace Imitated

[published 23 January 1737/8; vol. IV, pp. 236–46]

An Imitation of the Sixth Satire of the Second Book of Horace

[published 1 March 1737/8; vol. IV, pp. 249–63]

The First Epistle of the First Book of Horace Imitated

[published 7 March 1737/8; vol. IV, pp. 278–93]

Epilogue to the Satires. Dialogue I

[published 16 May 1738; vol. IV, pp. 297–309]

Epilogue to the Satires. Dialogue II

[published 18 July 1738; vol. IV, pp. 313–27]

EPITAPH

For One who would not be buried in Westminster Abbey.

H EROES, and KINGS! your distance keep:
          In peace let one poor Poet sleep,
Who never flatter'd Folks like you:
Let Horace blush, and Virgil too.

*The Works of Alexander Pope, Esq; Vol. II. Part II. Containing . . . Pieces . . .
written since the former Volumes . . .* 1738.
The Works . . . Vol. II. Containing his Epistles, &c. 1739.
The Works . . . Vol. II. Part I. Containing his Epistles, &c. 1740 (and 1743).
The Works. Ed. Warburton. Vol. VI. 1751.

Published by Pope himself six years before his death, this epitaph was obviously
never meant to be taken too seriously; and moreover, was never allowed by the
poet to be a self-epitaph. Indeed, so far from wanting it to be used as his memorial,
he very definitely expressed his wishes in his last will, dated 12 December 1743,
as follows: "As to my body, my will is, that it be buried near the monument of my
dear parents at Twickenham, with the addition, after the words *filius fecit*—of
these only, *et sibi: Qui obiit anno 17— aetatis —*." Yet in spite of Pope's express
desire, Warburton, who must have known it, seven years later erected another
monument to the poet in Twickenham church, and on it (as Carruthers indig-
nantly remarked) had the bad taste to inscribe these lines. The date of composi-
tion being unknown the piece is provisionally ascribed to the year of publication.

The text is that of *1738*; there are no verbal variants.

The Seventh Epistle of the First Book of Horace
Imitated in the Manner of Dr. Swift

[published 1 May 1739; vol. IV, pp. 268–73]

CLOE:
A CHARACTER

"Yet Cloë sure was form'd without a Spot—"
    'Tis true, but something in her was *forgot.*
"With ev'ry pleasing, ev'ry prudent part,
"Say what can Cloë want?"—She wants a *Heart*:
She speaks, behaves, and acts just as she ought;   5
But never, never, reach'd one gen'rous Thought.
Virtue she finds too painful an endeavour,
Content to dwell in Decency for ever.
So very reasonable, so unmov'd,
As never yet to love, or to be lov'd.   10
She, while her Lover pants upon her breast,
Can mark the figures on an Indian Chest;
And when she sees her Friend in deep despair,
Observes how much a Chintz exceeds Mohair.
Forbid it Heav'n, a favour or a Debt   15
She e'er should cancel—but she may forget.
Safe is your secret still in Cloë's ear;
But none of Cloë's shall you ever hear.
Of all her Dears she never slander'd one,
But cares not if a thousand are undone.   20
Would Cloë know if you're alive or dead?
She bids her Footman put it in her head.
Cloë is prudent—would you too be wise?
Then never break your heart when Cloë dies.

The Works of Alexander Pope, Esq; Vol. II. Part II. Containing ... Pieces ... written since the former Volumes ... 1738.

    The Gentleman's Magazine. June 1739.

    The Works of Alexander Pope, Esq; Vol. II. Part I. 1740.

    The Works of Alexander Pope, Esq; Vol. II. Part I. 1743.

    For the history of these verses, which subsequently became ll. 157–80 of the second *Moral Essay*, see *New Light*, pp. 266–75, and Vol. III ii, pp. 42, 63.

On receiving from the Right Hon. the
LADY *FRANCES SHIRLEY*
A STANDISH AND TWO PENS

Y ES, I beheld th' Athenian Queen
    Descend in all her sober charms;
"And take (she said, and smil'd serene)
    "Take at this hand celestial arms:

"Secure the radiant weapons wield;   5
    "This golden lance shall guard Desert,
"And if a Vice dares keep the field,
    "This steel shall stab it to the heart."

Aw'd, on my bended knees I fell,
    Receiv'd the weapons of the sky;   10
And dipt them in the sable Well,
    The fount of Fame or Infamy.

"What *well?* what *weapon?* (Flavia cries)
    "A standish, steel and golden pen;
"It came from Bertrand's, not the skies;   15
    "I gave it you to write again.

"But, Friend, take heed whom you attack;
    "You'll bring a House (I mean of Peers)
"Red, Blue, and Green, nay white and black,
    "L . . . . . . and all about your ears.   20

"You'd write as smooth again on glass,
    "And run, on ivory, so glib,
"As not to stick at fool or ass,
    "Nor stop at Flattery or Fib.

> "*Athenian Queen!* and *sober charms!* 25
>   "I tell ye, fool, there's nothing in't:
> "'Tis Venus, Venus gives these arms;
>   "In Dryden's Virgil see the print.

> "Come, if you'll be a quiet soul,
>   "That dares tell neither Truth nor Lies, 30
> "I'll list you in the harmless roll
>   "Of those that sing of these poor eyes."

The Works. Ed. Warburton. Vol. IV. 1751.

Warburton, who is the sole authority for the text and genuineness of this poem, published it as an appendix to the *Epilogue to the Satires*, for which Pope had been threatened with prosecution in the House of Lords. "On which", Warburton continues, "with great resentment against his enemies, for not being willing to distinguish between

> *Grave Epistles bringing Vice to light,*

and licentious Libels, he began a *third Dialogue*, more severe and sublime than the first and second; which being no secret, matters were soon compromised. His enemies agreed to drop the prosecution, and he promised to leave the third Dialogue unfinished and suppressed. This affair occasioned this little beautiful poem, to which it alludes throughout, but more especially in the four last stanzas."

This circumstantial story is supported by external evidence of the threats both of prosecution and of a third dialogue (see Vol. IV, p. xl), and serves to authenticate the poem. Furthermore Lady Frances Shirley was Pope's neighbour at Twickenham, and was alive in 1751 to deny her gift, if denial had been required. The poem may therefore be accepted as Pope's work. It is tentatively dated 1739, the year when Pope was advised to read a warning into Paul Whitehead's summons before the House of Lords to answer for his *Manners. A Satire*, and when a letter to Martha Blount (*Correspondence*, ed. Sherburn, IV 212) shows that he was in touch with Lady Frances. See *Notes and Queries*, n.s., IV (1957) 465 *f.*

Title: *Lady Frances Shirley*] (*c.* 1706–78). One of twenty-seven legitimate children of Robert Shirley, Earl Ferrers (1650–1718), whose widow was Pope's neighbour at Twickenham. Her intimacy with Chesterfield, besides causing considerable speculation, evoked from him the famous song: "When Fanny, blooming fair, First caught my ravished sight," and caused him to procure her a government pension of £800 p.a. on his resignation from the office of Secretary of State in 1748. She became a convert to Methodism in 1749. (GEC *Orrery Papers*, 1903, ii 19. Walpole to Mann, 3 May 1749. Walpole to Mason, 16 July 1778.)

14. *standish*] an inkstand.

15. *Bertrand's*] A famous toy-shop at Bath [*1751*].

19. *Red, Blue, and Green*] The ribbons of the orders of the Bath, the Garter, and the Thistle respectively.

white and black] The spiritual Peers, who might have taken offence at *Epil. to Sat.*, II 70.

20. *L . . .*] Carruthers conjectures "Lambeth", and refers to the offence given by the allusion to Archbishop Wake in *Epil. to Sat.*, I 120.

23. *fool or ass*] The *Dunciad* [*1751*].

24. *Flattery or Fib*] The *Epistle to Dr Arbuthnot* [*1751*].

28. When she delivers Æneas a suit of heavenly armour [*1751*]. Dryden's *Virgil*, plate 79.

30. *i.e.*, If you have neither the courage to write *Satire*, nor the application to attempt an *Epic* poem.—He was then meditating on such a work [*1751*]. See p. 404.

On lying in the Earl of ROCHESTER's *Bed at* ATTERBURY.

WITH no poetick ardors fir'd,
    I press the bed where *Wilmot* lay:
That here he lov'd, or here expir'd,
    Begets no numbers grave or gay.

But 'neath thy roof, *Argyle*, are bred   5
    Such thoughts, as prompt the brave to lie,
Stretch'd forth in honour's nobler bed,
    Beneath a nobler roof, the sky.

Title On . . . Atterbury.] Verses left by Mr. *Pope*, upon his lying in the same Bed which Wilmot, Earl of *Rochester*, us'd at Atterbury, a Seat of the Duke of *Argyle*'s, in Oxfordshire, July 9, 1739 *GM*; Left by Mr Pope in a Window of the late Lᵈ Rochester's Bed Chamber at his Seat at Adderbury in Oxfordshire then in Possession of the Duke of Argyle, on occasion of his being lodg'd there *TS*.
1 ardors] ardor *GM*.   3 lov'd] liv'd *LM*.
5 'neath] in *GM*.   7 forth] out *GM*.

Such flames, as high in patriots burn,
   Yet stoop to bless a child or wife: 10
And such as wicked kings may mourn,
   When freedom is more dear than life.

9–12 *omm. TS.*

Contemporary transcripts: Longleat, Portland Papers, xiii and xviii; and BM Cowper Papers, MS Add. 28101.

The London Magazine. August 1739.
The Scots Magazine. August 1739.
The Gentleman's Magazine. September 1739.
A Collection of Original Poems. S. Derrick. 1755.
The Poetical Calendar. December 1763.
The Universal Museum. November 1770.
The New Foundling Hospital for Wit. Vol. VI. 1773 (and Vol. I. 1784).
Additions to the Works of Alexander Pope, Esq. Vol. I. 1776.
The Poems of Pope. Vol. I (in Johnson's *English Poets*) 1779.

These verses were first attributed to Pope in *The Gentleman's Magazine*, since when they have been admitted without question to the canon. But though they were never included in Pope's works in his life-time, nor were ever acknowledged by him, both the date and occasion of the poem strongly favour his authorship. In 1739 he went on one of his beloved "rambles" from house to house of his friends; and, writing on 4 July to Martha Blount from Stowe in Buckinghamshire, speaks with dread of his coming journey with Lyttelton "on the eighth or ninth" to Hagley in Worcestershire over "the worst of rugged roads". He then continues: "The Duke of Argyle was here yesterday, and assures me what Mr. Lyttelton talks of as one day's journey must be two, or an intolerable fatigue." Since one of the best roads from Stowe to Hagley passes through Atterbury (now Adderbury) where the Duke had a house, formerly the seat of Lord Rochester, it is not unlikely that the Duke succeeded in persuading Pope to take two days on the journey, and stay the night of "the ninth" at his house. Two other scraps of evidence corroborate Pope's authorship: first, its ascription to him in three contemporary manuscripts, each having some connection with his friends; and secondly, its lofty compliment to Argyle echoes Pope's warm approval of his recent secession from the ministerial party (see Vol. IV, pp. 318 and 349). Nevertheless as the piece lacks the final authority of Pope's acknowledgement, it must be listed among the attributed poems.

The text follows that of the first printing (with which the *Scots Magazine* agrees verbally), with collations from the *Gentleman's Magazine* (*GM*), and the Cowper transcript (*TS*). A printer's error has been corrected in l. 3.

Title: *Rochester*] John Wilmot, second Earl of Rochester (1647–80), the Restoration poet.

Atterbury] Now Adderbury, see introductory note.

5. *Argyle*] The original footnote ran: "Atterbury House formerly belonged to the witty Earl of Rochester, but is now a Country Seat belonging to his Grace the Duke of Argyle." For John Campbell, second Duke of Argyle, see Biog. App., Vol. IV.

VERSES *on a* GROTTO *by the River* Thames *at* Twickenham, *composed of Marbles, Spars, and Minerals.*

THOU who shalt stop, where *Thames'* translucent Wave
   Shines a broad Mirrour thro' the shadowy Cave;
Where lingering Drops from Mineral Roofs distill,
And pointed Crystals break the sparkling Rill,
Unpolish'd Gemms no Ray on Pride bestow,   5
And latent Metals innocently glow:
Approach. Great NATURE studiously behold!
And eye the Mine without a Wish for Gold.

Title] *No title* Ha, Bi; On the Grotto at Twickenham *Po, Ch, He, GMa, Ba*; Mr Pope on his Grotto *We, GMb*; Verses on a Grotto ... Minerals *GMc, 1745*; On his Grotto at Twickenham, Composed ... Minerals *1751*.

1 Thou ... shalt stop] You ... shall stop *Po, He, GMa, Ba, Ya* (*subsequently corrected by Pope to* Thou ... shalt stop), *Q, GMb, Wa*; O Thou who stop'st *We, Ad*.

2 shadowy] gloomy *We, Ad, Co*; watry *GMb*.

3 from] through *We, Ad.* Roofs] Rocks *Co.*

4 And pointed] And polished *Ha*; Unpolish'd *Bi*; And painted *GMa*; Whilst pointed *Co.* sparkling] glittering *Co.*

5–8 *These couplets reversed in* Co. *After line 6 Pope inserted in* Ya *a couplet also found here in* Q *and* Wa:
   Thou see'st [You see *Wa*] that Island's Wealth, where only free,
   Earth to her Entrails feels not Tyranny.

8 eye] view *corrected to* eye *in Ba.*

Approach: But aweful! Lo th' *Ægerian* Grott,
Where, nobly-pensive, ST. JOHN sate and thought; 10
Where *British* Sighs from dying WYNDHAM stole,
And the bright Flame was shot thro' MARCHMONT's Soul.
Let such, such only, tread this sacred Floor,
Who dare to love their Country, and be poor.

After line 8 GMb inserts:
>   The treasures of a land, where, only free,
>   Earth to her entrails feels not Tyranny.

9 Awful as Pluto's Grove or Numa's grot *Ha, Bi*; Artless & awfull,
   as th' Ægerian Grott *Po, Ch, He, GMa, Ba, Ya*; But enter awful
   the inspiring Grot *We, interlineated in Ba and Ya with* this *for*
   the, *Ad, Q* (this *for* the); Enter, but awful, the inspiring Grot
   Co.

10 Where] There *Ha*; Here *Bi, Po, Ch, He, GMa, Ba, Ya, Q.*

11 Here [There *Ha*] patriot sighs from Wyndham's bosom stole
   Ha, Bi; Here Wyndham, thy [this *Po*] last Sighs for Liberty *as
   l. 12, Po, Ch, He, GMa, Ba, Ya subsequently erased by Pope*; Here
   British groans from . . . stole *We*; Here British sighs . . . stole *Ba
   interlineated, Pope's correction in Ya, Q*; Here British sighs from
   Windham's bosom stole *Co*; To Wyndham's breast the patriot
   passion [passions *Wa*] stole *GMb, Wa.*

12 And shot the gen'rous flame thro' Marchmont's soul *Ha, Bi*;
   Here, stole the Honest Tear from Marchmont's Eye *as l. 11,
   Po, Ch, He, GMa, Ba, Ya subsequently erased by Pope.*

13 Let such, such only] Such only such shall *We, Ad, Co* [may];
   this sacred] this Poet's *Po, Ch, He, Ya subsequently erased by Pope*;
   the Poet's *GMa*; their Poet's *Ba*; the sacred *We, Ad, GMb.*

14 love] serve *We.*

Stage A.   Contemporary transcripts: BM MS Add. 35,586 (*Ha*).
Stage B.   Contemporary transcripts: Portland Papers, XVIII (*Po*); Chatsworth
             MS 143 (*Ch*); Alnwick MS 112 (*He*).
             Gentleman's Magazine, January 1741 (*GMa*).
Stage B2. Contemporary transcripts: Wellesley College MS (*We*); Bodleian MS
             Ballard 47 (*Ba*); BM MS Add. 4456 (*Ad*), 5832 (*Co*).
Stage C.   Contemporary transcript: Yale MS (*Ya*).
             Quarterly Review. Vol. 139, 1875 (*Q*).

Stage D.   *Gentleman's Magazine*. December 1741 (*GMb*).
            Warburton MS (*Wa*).
Stage E.   *Gentleman's Magazine*. October 1743 (*GMc*).
            A Plan of Mr. Pope's Garden . . . by J. Serle. 1745.
            Works. Ed. Warburton. Vol. VI. 1751.

These verses were written in the late summer of 1740, at some date subsequent to Sir William Wyndham's death on 17 July, and were subjected to frequent revision during the following autumn and winter. A version (Stage A) of the lines was sent by Pope to Bolingbroke appended to a letter dated 3 September 1740. The original letter no longer survives; but a transcript was made by Lord Hardwicke (BM MS Add. 35586, f. 298) and subsequently printed in *The Works of A. Pope . . . Supplement*, 1825, p. 64.

A revised version (Stage B) began circulating amongst Pope's friends during the next two months. One copy of it survives at Longleat (Portland Papers XVIII, f. 301); another in Lady Burlington's hand is at Chatsworth (MS 143, f. 75); and it was this version of which Lady Hartford obtained a copy to send to Lady Pomfret on 29 November 1740 (Alnwick MS 112, pp. 77f.), and which appeared in *The Gentleman's Magazine* in January 1741. There is still another version in the Yale University Library, in which Pope himself has corrected ll. 1, 9, 11, 12, and 13 and has inserted a new couplet after l. 8. This transcript (Stage C) is dated 6 February 1741, and is identical with the "amended version" sent by Pope to Dr Oliver (*Quarterly Review*, CXXXIX (1875), 384).

A Bodleian transcript (MS Ballard 47, f. 96) represents a closely related stage. The scribe has copied from a version of Stage B and has subsequently interlineated the revisions of ll. 9, 11, 12, and 13 from Stage C, but has not inserted the new couplet after l. 8. This stage is also represented by the Wellesley College transcript (see Helen Sard Hughes, "Mr Pope and his Grotto", *Mod. Phil.*, XXVIII (1930), 100–4), by another British Museum transcript (MS Add. 4456, f. 96), and, in more corrupt form, by a transcript in the hand of William Cole, the antiquary (MS Add. 5832, f. 127). It seems probable that these transcripts were made at a stage (Stage B2) intermediary between Stages B and C, before the new couplet was written.

This couplet appears in different forms and positions in the versions printed in *The Gentleman's Magazine* in December 1741 and in an autograph manuscript to which Warburton refers in the notes to his edition of 1751 (VI 77–8). These versions (Stage D) are alike in preserving the revisions of ll. 12 and 13 reached in Stage C, but they record fresh revisions of ll. 9 and 11.

After Stage D the new couplet was removed. At the final stage (Stage E), first printed in *The Gentleman's Magazine* in October 1743, Pope retained his last revision of l. 9, but reverted for l. 11 to the version of Stage C.

The text is taken from Serle's *Plan of Mr Pope's Garden* instead of *The Gentleman's Magazine*, which appears to have normalized Pope's "accidentals". Collations are given from all the versions listed above.

1f. The image of the mirror may have helped to recall Milton's phrasing, *Comus*, 861: "Under the glassie, cool, translucent Wave".

9. *Ægerian Grott*] Egeria was one of the goddesses of prophecy who instructed Numa Pompilius.

11. Sir William Wyndham, the leader of the Hanover Tories, died on 17 July 1740. See Biog. App., Vol. IV.

12. Hugh Hume, Lord Polwarth, a prominent member of the Whig opposition to Walpole's government, had succeeded to his father's title as Earl of March- mont on 27 February 1739/40. See Biog. App., Vol. IV. Pope implies that the three sections of the opposition were in consultation in his grotto.

14. Cf. *Æn.*, VIII 364; aude, hospes, contemnere opes; and Dryden's version, "Dare to be poor" [*Wakefield*].

EPIGRAM.
[On lopping Trees in his Garden.]

MY Ld. complains, that *P——* (stark mad with Gardens)
　　Has lopp'd three Trees, the Value of three Farthings:
But he's my Neighbour, cries the Peer polite,
And if he'll visit me, I'll wave my Right.
What? on Compulsion? and against my Will　　　　　5
A Lord's Acquaintance?—Let him file his *Bill.*

Title] *None in the early texts.*
1 Ld. . . . *P*—] Lord complains that Pope *1751*, *1805*.
2 lopp'd] cut *1805*.

　　The Publick Register: or, The Weekly Magazine. No. 1. 3 January 1741.
　　The Works of Alexander Pope, Esq. Volume V. Containing The Dunciad. Edited by W. Warburton. 1751.
　　The Festoon. 1766 (and later editions).
　　The Christmas Treat. 1767.
　　Select Epigrams. Vol. II. 1797.
　　Correspondence between . . . Countess of Hartford . . . and . . . Countess of Pomfret . . . 1738–41. Vol. II. 1805.
　　The Works. Ed. Carruthers. Vol. IV. 1854.

　　The new-found "first edition" of this epigram represents another of Pope's unchronicled kindnesses to Dodsley, to whose new (and short-lived) periodical he contributed some half dozen anonymous pieces, of which this was the first. Warburton later inserted it in his edition of the *Dunciad*, in a note on the line:

"A heavy Lord shall hang at ev'ry Wit" (IV, 132), with this preface: "Which every wit cannot so well shake off as the Author of the following Epigram". This roundabout attribution to Pope is corroborated in Shenstone's *Miscellany* (ed. I. A. Gordon, 1952, p. 48), and in the Hartford–Pomfret letters (*Correspondence*, 1805, ii 250), where the piece appears with this introduction or title:

> Epigram, By Mr. Pope, Who had cut down three walnut trees in a ground belonging to lady Ferrers (whom he makes a lord). These trees hindered his prospect of his garden.

Richard Graves likewise ascribed it to Pope in all editions of *The Festoon*, 1766. Nevertheless the epigram, though it echoes one of Pope's characteristic boasts, was never acknowledged by Pope, and must therefore remain an attributed piece. It was probably written in the latter half of 1740, a date with which the Hartford–Pomfret correspondence would seem to agree.

    The text is that of the first printing, with collations from Warburton's version (*1751*) and the *Correspondence* (*1805*).

    1. *My Ld.*] According to Warton the peer was Lord Radnor, Pope's neighbour at Twickenham; but see introductory note above.

One Thousand Seven Hundred and Forty

[vol. IV, pp. 332–7]

EPITAPH.
On Himself.

Under this Marble, or under this Sill,
  Or under this Turf, or e'en what they will;
Whatever an Heir, or a Friend in his stead,
Or any good Creature shall lay o'er my Head;
Lies He who ne'er car'd, and still cares not a Pin,   5
What they said, or may say of the Mortal within.
But who living and dying, serene still and free,
Trusts in God, that as well as he was, he shall be.

Title Epitaph. *1741*; Epitaph On Himself. *1744*; Another, on the Same. *1751* (*in which volume it follows:* Epitaph. For One who would not be buried in Westminster-Abbey). *Title omitted in MS.*

2 Or under] Under *1744.* e'en what they] just what you *1744.*

4 Creature . . . Head] Christian lays over my Head *MS*; Christian, may lay on his Head *1744.*

5 He] one *MS, 1744, 1751.* still] who *1744.*

7 *1744 reads:* Who living, or dying, still resign'd, and still free, serene] resign'd *MS.*

Contemporary transcripts: Longleat, Portland Papers, xviii; BM Cowper Papers, MS Add. 28101; Brotherton Library, Leeds; and Bodl. MS Ballard 50.

The Publick Register; or, Weekly Magazine, No. ii. 10 January 1741.

Dean Swift's Literary Correspondence . . . from 1714 to 1738. 1741.

The Norfolk Poetical Miscellany. Vol. II. 1744.

The London Magazine. February 1750.

The Works. Ed. Warburton. Vol. VI. 1751.

Although this epitaph was attributed to Pope more than once in his lifetime, he neither publicly acknowledged it nor included it in his *Works*; and its appearance in the canon is due to Warburton, who included it without comment. There cannot, however, be much question about its authenticity. Its first publication, hitherto unrecorded, provides another testimony to Pope's kindness for Dodsley the bookseller, in whose new magazine he allowed this poem to be printed, together with several other anonymous pieces which Warburton later claimed for Pope. Moreover in the Cowper family papers this piece appears with the title, "Mr. Pope's Epitaph on Himself"; and in *The Norfolk Poetical Miscellany.* edited by Ashley Cowper, as "Mr. P—'s Epitaph on Himself".

The text follows that of *1741*, with collations from the Portland Papers (*MS*), the Miscellany (*1744*), and Warburton's edition (*1751*).

Johnson (*Lives of the Poets*, ed. Hill, iii 272) detected Pope's source in Ariosto's *Ludovici Areost. Epit.*

Verbatim from BOILEAU,
Un jour, dit un Auteur, &c. EPISTLE II.

ONCE (says an Author, where, I need not say)
   Two Trav'lers found an Oyster in their Way;
Both fierce, both hungry, the Dispute grew strong,
While, Scale in Hand, Dame *Justice* past along.
Before her each with Clamour pleads the Laws,   5
Explain'd the Matter, and would win the Cause;
Dame *Justice*, weighing long the doubtful Right,
Takes, opens, swallows it, before their Sight.
The Cause of Strife remov'd so rarely well,
There, take (says *Justice*) take ye each a *Shell*.   10
We thrive at *Westminster* on Fools like you,
'Twas a fat Oyster——Live in Peace——Adieu.

The Publick Register: or, The Weekly Magazine. No. II. 10 January 1741.
The Works. Ed. Warburton. Vol. VI. 1751.

These verses, like the last, were first published anonymously in Dodsley's
Publick Register, and are ascribed to Pope on the sole authority of Warburton.
Though there is nothing improbable in the ascription, they remain merely an
attributed piece.

The text is taken from the first printing.

An imitation of the last 12 lines of *Épître* II:

> *Un jour, dit un auteur, n' importe en quel chapitre,*
> *Deux voyageurs à jeun rencontrèrent une huître.*
> *Tous deux la contestaient, lorsque dans leur chemin*
> *La Justice passa, la balance à la main.*
> *Devant elle à grand bruit ils expliquent la chose;*
> *Tous deux avec dépens veulent gagner leur cause.*
> *La Justice, pesant ce droit litigieux,*
> *Demande l'huitre, l'ouvre et l'avale à leurs yeux;*
> *Et par ce bel arrêt terminant la bataille:*
> *Tenez, voilà, dit-elle, à chacun une écaille.*
> *Des sottises d'autrui nous vivons au Palais.*
> *Messieurs, l'huître était bonne. Adieu. Vivez en paix.*

On the Benefactions in the late Frost, 1740.

Yes, 'tis the time! I cry'd, impose the chain!
　　Destin'd and due to wretches self-enslav'd!
But when I saw such Charity remain,
　　I half could wish this people might be sav'd.
Faith lost, and Hope, their Charity begins;　　　　5
　　And 'tis a wise design on pitying heav'n,
If this can cover multitudes of sins,
　　To take the only way to be forgiven.

4 might] should *H.*
5 their] our *H.*

The Gentleman's Magazine. March 1740.
Correspondence between . . . Countess of Hartford . . . and . . . Countess of Pomfret, Between . . . 1738 and 1741. Vol. I. 1805.
The Works. Ed. Carruthers. Vol. IV. 1854.

These verses were superinscribed "By an Eminent Hand" when first published in *The Gentleman's Magazine*, but at the end of the year they were ascribed in the index to Pope. The ascription is confirmed by Lady Hartford, who moved in circles close to the poet. On 20 February 1739–40 she wrote to Lady Pomfret: "the severity of the weather has occasioned greater sums of money to be given in charity, than ever was heard of before. Mr. Pope has written two stanzas on the occasion: which I must send you, because they are his; for they have no other merit to entitle them to be conveyed so far." Pope seems to have been inspired by observing the charities of Ralph Allen with whom he was staying at this time. See his account of them in a letter to Fortescue, 23 Jan. 1739–40 (*Correspondence* ed. Sherburn, IV 221).

The text is taken from *The Gentleman's Magazine*, with collations from Lady Hartford's version (*H*).

COUPLETS & VERSICLES
1731–1740
[see *ante*, p. 74.]

Pope's autograph: Chatsworth Papers [No. III] : BM MS Egerton 1950 [No. IV].

Contemporary transcript: Longleat, Portland Papers, XIX [No. IX].

Miscellaneous Works . . . of John Bancks. Vol. II. 1738. [No. V.]

The Life of Alexander Pope . . . By Owen Ruffhead. 1769. [No. VIII.]

The European Magazine. November 1787. [No. V.]

Anecdotes . . . Collected from the Conversation of Mr. Pope . . . and other eminent Persons. J. Spence. 1820. [No. VI.]

Letters to and from Henrietta, Countess of Suffolk . . . Vol. II. 1824. [No. I.]

The Works. Ed. Elwin and Courthope. Vol. VIII. 1872. [No. VII.]

The Works. Ed. Warton. Vol. IV. 1797. [Nos. II, III.]

I.
LINES FROM *HORACE*.

OUR ancient kings (and sure those kings were wise)
Judged for themselves, and saw with their own eyes.

II.
On Queen *Caroline*'s Death-bed.

HERE lies wrapt up in forty thousand towels
The only proof that C*** had bowels.

III.
On a Picture of Queen *Caroline*,
drawn by Lady *Burlington*.

ALAS! what room for Flattry, or for Pride!
She's dead!—but thus she lookd the hour she dy'd,
Peace, blubbring Bishop! peace thou flattring Dean!
This single Crayon, Madam, saints the Queen.

IV.
LINES
On Ministers

—But Ministers like Gladiators live;
Tis half their business, Blows to ward, or give,
The good their Virtue might effect, or sense,
Dies between Exigents, and self defence.

3 might] would *rejected MS reading.*
4 between ... and] under ... or *alternative MS reading.*

V.
COUPLET

MAY THESE put Money in your Purse,
For I assure you, I've read worse.
                                        A. P.

VI.
On Dr. *Alured Clarke*

LET Clarke make half his life the poor's support,
But let him give the other half to court.

VII.
COUPLET
From *HORACE.*

IN unambitious silence be my lot,
Yet ne'er a friend forgetting, till forgot.

VIII.
COUPLET.
On his GROTTO.

AND life itself can nothing more supply
    Than just to plan our projects, and to die.

IX.
LINES
To King GEORGE II.

O ALL-ACCOMPLISH'D Cæsar! on thy Shelf
    Is room for all Pope's Works—and Pope himself:

'Tis true, Great Bard, thou on my shelf shall lye
With Oxford, Cowper, Noble Strafford by:
But for thy Windsor, a New Fabric Raise   5
And There Triumphant Sing Thy Soverain's Praise.

I. The Hon. George Berkeley wrote to his future wife, the Countess of Suffolk, 27 June [1734]: "Pope diverted us with translating Horace: I am sorry for your sake I can remember but one couplet . . ." whereupon he proceeds to transcribe the above lines (*Suffolk*, II 79). Pope had evidently been showing his friends his *Sober Advice from Horace*, in which this couplet appears (ll. 112f.) as part of a version of Horace, *Sat.* I ii 86ff. (Vol. IV, pp. 84f.). The poem was published in the following December.

II. Pope's friendship for the Prince of Wales undoubtedly influenced his comments on the death of Queen Caroline. Regarding her alone he could write—as he did more than once—in praise of her courage and steadfastness during her last dreadful days in the surgeon's hands. But at the thought of her implacable hatred of her eldest son with whom, even on her deathbed, she refused to be reconciled (not to mention her reported refusal of the last sacrament) he was moved to make the well-known sarcastic reference to her death in the *Epilogues to the Satires. Dialogue I* (see Vol. IV, p. 304). This couplet derives from Warton (*Works*, Vol. IV, 1797, p. 308), who introduces it as follows: "At the same time [as that of the Queen's death] our Author himself wrote the following couplet on the same subject." The Queen died 20 November 1737, and the epigram, which is included as an attributed piece, is dated accordingly.

III. Pope's autograph MS of this epigram on Queen Caroline's death is preserved at Chatsworth in association with Lady Burlington's drawing. Warton (IV 329) printed another version of the second couplet:

> Peace! flattering Bishop, lying Dean!
> *This* portrait only saints the Queen!

"lying" is an alternative MS reading, with no indication of the poet's final choice. It was a dean who notoriously blubbered, namely John Gilbert, Dean of Exeter. He wept in the pulpit while preaching on the Queen at the King's command (25 December 1737). See Vol. IV, p. 322*n*. The epigram was presumably written not long after.

IV. These verses are taken from MS Egerton 1950. They are written in Pope's hand on the back of some notes about the *Essay on Criticism* and the *Essay on Man* (f. 86). Their subject suggests that they were drafted when Pope was at work on the later *Imitations of Horace*. They are tentatively dated 1738.

V. To the concluding lines of a poem entitled "The Author's Picture: A Fourth Epistle to Mr. Pope" which read:

> The most I seriously would hope,
> Is, just to read the Words, A. POPE,
> Writ, without Sneer, or Shew of Banter,
> Beneath your friendly *Imprimantur*.

the author, John Bancks, has appended a footnote stating:

> A copy of these Epistles having been sent to Mr. Pope, he was pleased to return them with Subscriptions for two Sets of the Author's Works, and the following Couplet . . .

The anecdote and couplet were reprinted in *The European Magazine*, November 1787.

VI. Spence (p. 211) reports Pope as saying that this couplet was in the manuscript for *Dunciad* IV. "But I believe I shall omit it; though, if rightly understood, it has more of commendation than satire in it.—The man will never be contented! He has already twice as much as I; for I am told he has a good thousand pound a year, and yet he is as eager for more preferment as ever he was." Warton, in a note on *Mor. Ess.*, IV 78, records a variant. "In Pope's MSS were two lines on Dr. *Alured Clarke*, Dean of Exeter, who must not be confounded with the *Rector of St. James's*:

> Let Clarke tire half his days the Poor's support,
> But let him pass the other half at Court.

for he was instrumental in building our two first county hospitals at Winchester and at Exeter." Alured Clarke (1696–1742) had been a prebendary of Winchester

(1723) and Westminster (1731) before being appointed Dean of Exeter (1741). Stephen Duck, the thresher poet, reports that Clarke had given him several testimonies of his bounty before recommending him to the attention of Queen Caroline. Clarke is glanced at in *Epil. to Sat.*, II 164, and perhaps in *Dunciad*, IV 97.

VII. Pope wrote to Lord Marchmont, 10 January 1739: "I am learning Horace's verse [*Epist.* I xi 9]—'Oblitusque meorum, obliviscendus et illis;' but I learn it (what I think the best way) backwards," and appended the couplet above. The phrasing recalls *Eloisa to Abelard*, 207-8:

> How happy is the blameless Vestal's lot!
> The world forgetting, by the world forgot.

See Vol. II, p. 315*n*.

VIII. From a letter of 17 June 1740 to Ralph Allen, quoted by Ruffhead (p. 199), in which Pope mourns that the lack of material has brought his "mine-adventure" (*i.e.* work on the grotto) to "a full stop at present". He adds, "However it is some satisfaction, that as far as I have gone, I am content; and that is all a mortal man can expect: for no man finishes any view he has, or any scheme he projects, but by halves—" whereupon follows the couplet. The couplet echoes *Essay on Man*, I 3f:

> Let us (since Life can little more supply
> Than just to look about us and to die) . . .

IX. These verses are taken from a contemporary transcript in the Portland Papers (Vol. IX) at Longleat, are endorsed in Oxford's hand "by Pope", and are subscribed "July 14, 1740. After 9 at night, dining with Lord and Lady Oxford that day". EC (VIII 320) glosses the last four lines: "the king answers that he permits the 'bard's' works to have a place in a library adorned with portraits of Oxford, Cowper, and Strafford—all politicians whom he honours more than authors,—but that he has no desire to see Pope in person, and his Windsor must be a second poetical fabric of his own raising, similar to the Windsor Forest in which he sang the praises of Queen Anne." Pope also wrote the first two lines in the scrap-book of Mrs Charles Caesar of Benington, *The Rothschild Library* (1954), item 564.

EPIGRAMS.

[On *Shakespear*'s Monument]

I.

AFTER an hundred and thirty years' nap,
Enter Shakespear, with a loud clap.

The Autobiography of Mary Granville, Mrs Delany. Vol. II. 1861.

II.

THUS Britain lov'd me; and preserv'd my Fame,
Clear from a *Barber*'s or a *Benson*'s Name.

2 Clear . . . *Barber*'s] Pure . . . Barber *1769.*

A Biographical History of England. By J. Granger. Vol. I. 1769.
The St. James's Chronicle. 30 September–3 October 1775.
Additions to the Works of Alexander Pope, Esq. Vol. I. 1776.
The Muse's Mirrour. Vol. I. 1778.
The Plays of William Shakespeare. Ed. S. Johnson and G. Steevens. Vol. I. 1778.
The Poems of Pope. Vol. II (in Johnson's *English Poets*). 1779.
In February 1740/1, the *Gentleman's Magazine* reported (p. 105) that

A fine Monument is erected in *Westminster-Abbey* to the Memory of *Shakespear*, by the Direction of the Earl of *Burlington*, Dr. *Mead*, Mr. *Pope*, and Mr. *Martin*. Mr *Fleetwood*, Master of *Drury-Lane* Theatre, and Mr. *Rich*, of that of *Covent-Garden*, gave each a Benefit, arising from one of his own plays towards it, and the Dean and Chapter made a present of the Ground. The Design, by Mr. *Kent*, was executed by Mr. *Scheemaker*.

The Poet is sculptured in the Dress of his Time, in white Marble, natural, free, and easy; above his Head is the following Inscription, in Capital Letters, raised in Gold, upon a Piece of curious dark coloured Marble.

GULIELMO SHAKESPEAR,
ANNO POST MORTEM CXXIV.
AMOR PUBLICUS POSUIT.

. . . It was reported, that Dr. *M* and Mr. *P* differed in their Opinion about the Words *Amor Publicus posuit*; but Mr. *P* insisting on them, the Dr., in a Letter to him, yielded the Point, concluding with

Omnia vincit Amor *et nos cedamus* Amori.

14

William Oldys is a further witness to Pope's interest in the project ([W. J. Thoms], *A Literary Antiquary*, 1862, p. 45).

Some difficulty seems to have arisen in choosing a suitable inscription for the scroll. When the statue was first erected, the scroll was blank, and it was not until May 1741 (*Gent. Mag.*, XI 276) that the lines from *The Tempest* ("The Cloud Capt Towers . . .") were inscribed upon it. Mrs Pendarves wrote to Mrs Dewes (21 December 1740) that many Latin inscriptions had been offered: "one was sent to Pope for his approbation; the sense of it meant that after many years neglect Shakespeare appeared with general aclamation. Mr Pope could not very well make out the author's meaning, and enclosed it to Dr. Mead with the following translation:" whereupon she quotes the first epigram printed above.

Granger (*Biog. Hist. Eng.* 1769, I 286) mentions that, in a print of the statue, "instead of 'The cloud-capt Towers,' &c. is the following inscription, on a scroll, to which he points with his finger." He then quotes a version of the second epigram. The only print of the statue in which this epigram is found is an engraving by James Hulett used as a frontispiece to *Poems on Several Occasions. By Shakespeare*, sold by A. Murden, R. Newton, and others. The book is undated; but from the evidence of the frontispiece, it would seem that it was published early in 1741. It is unlikely that Pope seriously intended the epigram for inscription on the scroll, but there is no reason to doubt its authenticity. The sentiment is characteristic of the poet who was proud to be "Un-plac'd, un-pension'd, no Man's Heir, or Slave", and the allusions to Barber and Benson (see below) offer confirmatory evidence of authorship. The text is taken from the engraving, with collations from *Additions* (*1776*) and Granger (*1769*).

That Pope was responsible for a third epigram is less probable. The following was published anonymously in the *London Evening Post*, 7–10 February 1740/1, and was ascribed to Pope in a rejoinder published in the *Daily Gazetteer* on 14 February.

> On this blank Scroll what I'd express,
> In vain must the Spectator guess:
> For though I earnest point below,
> No Meaning does the Tablet show.
> Some Thought express'd had sure been apter,
> Had so it pleas'd the *Dean* and *Chapter*;
> But why at last I nothing mean,
> Ask the wise *Chapter* and the *Dean*.

The bare assertion of a hostile journal (Vol. IV, p. 321*n*.) must not be allowed to weigh against stylistic evidence, which points away from Pope in every line.

II. 2. Alderman John Barber (1675–1740) erected a monument to Samuel Butler in Westminster Abbey. At the end of the Latin inscription appear the words:

> Hoc tandem, posito Marmore, curavit
> Johannes Barber, Civis Londinensis, 1721.

See Biog. App., Vol. V.

William Benson (1682–1754) succeeded Wren as Surveyor-General of Works. He erected a momument to Milton in Westminster Abbey in 1737. See *Dunciad*, IV 110–2, and Biog. App., Vol. V.

The New Dunciad
As it was Found in the Year 1741

[published 20 March 1741/2; vol. v, pp. 337–409]

EPIGRAM.
On CIBBER's *Declaration that he will have the Last Word with Mr. POPE.*

Q UOTH *Cibber* to *Pope*, tho' in Verse you foreclose,
    I'll have the last Word, for by G—d I'll write Prose.
    Poor *Colley*, thy Reas'ning is none of the strongest,
For know, the last Word is the Word that lasts longest.

1–3 Quoth . . . Reas'ning is . . .] *MS reads:*
       You will have the *last word*, after all y^t is past?
       And 'tis certain, dear Cibber, that you may *speak last*;
       But your reas'ning, God help you! is . . .

Pope's autograph: The Pierpont Morgan Library, New York.
The Summer Miscellany. 1742.
The Foundling Hospital for Wit. No. 1. 1743 (and 1763).
The Works of Alexander Pope, Esq. Volume V. Containing the Dunciad. Ed. War
burton. 1751.
The Sports of the Muses. Vol. II. 1752.
A Collection of Select Epigrams. J. Hackett. 1757.
The Festoon. 2nd Edition, 1767 (and later editions).
The earliest text of this epigram exists in the original autograph letter from Pope to Lord Orrery, dated 23 July 1742, where it is introduced in these words:

Cibber is printing a Letter to me, of ye expostulatory kind in prose. God knows when I shall read it when it is publish'd; & perhaps I may send to ask your

Account of it; yr Opinion whether or not to answer it, I need not ask. He swears he will have the *Last Word* with me, upon wch I've seen an Epigram. *You will have the* last word . . . [epigram quoted in full].

In reply, Orrery wrote (27 July): ". . . The epigram is excellent. This leads me to put you in mind of trying to collect your epigrams. . . Why will you let them be dispersed like Cybele's leaves, in air? Cibber cannot be properly answered than in the epigrammatical way."—Which shows that he knew or guessed the epigram was Pope's. A month or two later the piece appeared anonymously in print in *The Summer Miscellany*, which, according to the *London Magazine* for September 1742, was published during that month. Next, Warburton inserted it in the *Dunciad* (1751), appending it to Pope's note on the line: "Bays, form'd by nature Stage and Town to bless" (i 109), with this remark on Cibber: "And to shew his claim to what the Poet was so unwilling to allow him, of being *pert* as well as *dull*, he declares he will have the *last word*; which occasioned the following Epigram: *Quoth Cibber to Pope, . . .*" [quoted in full]. It would thus appear that the attribution of the epigram to Pope (which was in fact made a few years later by Richard Graves in the second edition of *The Festoon*, 1767), is probably correct; though, as Pope never admitted it, his authorship cannot be regarded as absolutely certain.

The text is that of the first printing (with which Warburton's version agrees), with collations from the autograph (*MS*).

1. *Cibber*] Colley Cibber, the actor-dramatist, see Biog. App., Vol. IV.

TOM SOUTHERNE's Birth-day Dinner at LD. *ORRERY*'s.

R ESIGN'D to live, prepar'd to die,
  With not one sin but poetry,
This day T OM's fair account has run
(Without a blot) to eighty one.
Kind *Boyle* before his poet lays   5
A table with a cloth of bays;
And *Ireland*, mother of sweet singers,
Presents her harp still to his fingers,
The feast, his towring genius marks
In yonder wildgoose, and the larks!   10
The mushrooms shew his wit was sudden!
And for his judgment lo a pudden!

Roast beef, tho' old, proclaims him stout,
And grace, altho' a bard, devout.
May Tom, whom heav'n sent down to raise   15
The price of prologues and of plays,
Be ev'ry birth-day more a winner,
Digest his thirty-thousandth dinner;
Walk to his grave without reproach,
And scorn a rascal and a coach!   20

13 old] cold *TS*.   18 his] this *TS*.
20 and] in *TS*.

Contemporary transcript: Longleat, Portland Papers, xviii.
The Gentleman's Magazine. February 1742.
The Works. Ed. Warburton. Vol. VI. 1751.
Although these verses are anonymous in the Portland Papers and in the
Gentleman's Magazine, both the friendship of Pope with Orrery and Southerne,
and stylistic evidence make Warburton's ascription highly probable.
The text follows that of the first printing, with which *1751* is in agreement.
4. *eighty one*] Southerne was eighty-two on 12 February 1741/2.
8. *harp*] "The Harp is generally wove upon the Irish Linen: such as table-cloths &c." *Gent. Mag.*

EPIGRAM
[On Bishop *HOUGH*.]

A bishop by his Neighbours hated
  Has Cause to wish himself translated.
But why shou'd *Hough* desire Translation,
Lov'd and esteem'd by all the Nation?
    Yet if it be the old Man's Case,   5
I'll lay my Life, I know the Place:
'Tis where God sent some that adore him,
And whither *Enoch* went before him.

Miscellanies. The Fourth Volume. Consisting of Verses . . . 1742 (and later editions).
Select Epigrams. Vol. I. 1797.

The Works. Ed. Roscoe. Vol. VI. 1824.

This anonymous epigram was marked with an asterisk in the Pope-Swift *Miscellanies*, on its first publication, to indicate that it is not the work of Swift. Although this need not be taken to imply that Pope was the author, it is a justifiable inference; for it was Pope's habit to use these collections for publishing his opuscula, and by 1742 other members of his circle who might have contributed were dead. Furthermore the sentiment of the epigram accords with Pope's opinion of Hough expressed a few years earlier (see *Epil. to Sat.*, II 240, and Biog. App., Vol. IV).

The text is that of the first printing.

EPITAPH
On Mr. *ROWE*.
In *Westminster-Abbey*.

THY Reliques, *Rowe*! to this sad Shrine we trust,
And near thy *Shakespear* place thy honour'd Bust,
Oh next him skill'd to draw the tender Tear,
For never Heart felt Passion more sincere:
To nobler Sentiment to fire the Brave,   5
For never *Briton* more disdain'd a Slave!
Peace to thy gentle Shade, and endless Rest,
Blest in thy Genius, in thy Love too blest;
And blest, that timely from Our Scene remov'd
Thy Soul enjoys that Liberty it lov'd.   10

To these, so mourn'd in Death, so lov'd in Life!
The childless Parent and the widow'd Wife
With tears inscribes this monumental Stone,
That holds their Ashes and expects her own.

Title] *1760 reads:* Intended for Mr. Rowe, in Westminster-Abbey.
5 Sentiment] sentiments *1743*.
10 that] the *1760*.

The lapidary inscription: Westminster Abbey.

Common Sense. 25 June 1743.

The Universal Spectator. 25 June 1743.

The London Magazine. June 1743.

Memoirs of . . . Alexander Pope, Esq. W. Ayre. Vol. I. 1745.

The Works. Ed. Warburton. Vol. VI. 1760.

Rowe died in 1718; and Pope at once wrote an epitaph of eight lines "Intended for Mr. Rowe, In Westminster-Abbey" (see *ante*, p. 208), which, though published in 1720 and included by him in his *Works*, was never put up in the Abbey. In 1743 a widely different version, expanded to ten lines plus a four-line pendant on Rowe's daughter, appeared anonymously in several papers with the announcement that this was the Inscription lately set up in Westminster Abbey to Rowe's memory.

Pope's authorship of this version has been denied (see A. Jackson, "Pope's Epitaphs on Nicholas Rowe," *Rev. of Eng. Stud.*, VII [1931], 76–9), but is nevertheless well founded (see *New Light*, pp. 149–55). Warburton, whose conservative treatment of the canon has not been seriously disputed, included the revised version in the 1760 edition of the *Works*; and it should also be noted that this version both reverts to an earlier text of the first version (l. 1), and echoes Pope's praise of Rowe in *Imit. Hor.* and Pope's epitaph on Trumbull.

The only authoritative text is that of the lapidary inscription which is therefore followed here, except that contractions have been expanded. Variants in the *London Magazine* (*1743*) and Warburton (*1760*) texts are recorded.

2. *thy Shakespear*] Rowe was the first editor of Shakespeare (1709).

4. Cf. *Imit. Hor.*, *Ep.* II i 86: "But, for the Passions, Southern sure and Rowe".

9f. Pope borrowed this couplet from the close of his epitaph on Trumbull (see p. 169).

11. *these*] *i.e.* Rowe and his daughter Charlotte Fane, whose death in 1739 at the age of twenty-two is recorded on the pedestal of Rowe's bust.

The Dunciad. In Four Books

[published 29 October 1743; vol. v, pp. 247–426]

EPIGRAM.

[*On Laureates.*]

WHEN Laureates make Odes, do you ask of what sort?
  Do you ask if they're good, or are evil?
You may judge—From the Devil they come to the Court,
  And go from the Court to the Devil.

Title] *No title originally.*

The Works of Alexander Pope, Esq; Vol. III. Part I. Containing the Dunciad. 1743.
The Works . . . Volume V. Containing the Dunciad. Ed. Warburton. 1751.
The Festoon. 2nd Edition. 1767 (and later editions).

This epigram seems to have been first printed in the octavo edition of the *Dunciad* in 1743, where Pope inserted it after the quarto had been published. It is found in the note to the line: "Back to the Devil the last ecchoes roll" (B,1 325), as follows: "The Devil Tavern in Fleet-street, where these [*i.e.* Cibber's] Odes are usually rehearsed before they are performed at Court. Upon which a Wit of those times made this epigram." Cibber had been made Poet Laureate in 1730: "those times", therefore, were not so very remote, even if the phrase was not whimsical in intention. The epigram was reprinted separately and attributed to Pope by Richard Graves in the second—and each successive—edition of *The Festoon*, 1767. Pope made a similar anonymous use of a number of his epigrams in the various editions of the *Dunciad* (see *ante*, p. 299); and there is no reason to suppose that this one is by another hand; nevertheless, in the absence of further contemporary evidence of his authorship, this piece should not be regarded as more than a probable attribution.

The text is that of the first printing, which agrees verbally with Warburton's edition.

VERSES

Upon the late D——ss of M——.

BUT what are these to great *Atossa*'s Mind,
  Scarce once herself, by Turns all Womankind?
Who with herself, and others from her Birth,
Finds all her Life one Warfare upon Earth;

Shines in exposing Knaves and painting Fools,   5
Yet is whate'er she hates or ridicules.
No Thought advances, but her eddy Brain
Whirls it about, and down it goes again.
Full sixty Years the World has been her Trade,
The wisest Fool much Time has ever made: 10
From Loveless Youth to unrespected Age,
No Passion gratify'd except her Rage;
So much the Fury still out-ran the Wit,
The Pleasure miss'd her, and the Scandal hit;
Who breaks with her, provokes Revenge from Hell,   15
But he's a bolder Man who dares be well;
Her ev'ry Turn with Violence pursu'd,
No more a Storm her Hate, than Gratitude:
To that each Passion turns or soon or late,
Love, if it make her yield, must make her hate.   20
Superior's Death! an Equal, what a Curse!
But an Inferior, not Dependant, worse.
Offend her, and she knows not to forgive,
Oblige her, and she'll hate you while you live.
But die, and she'll adore you—then the Bust   25
And Temple rise,—then fall again to Dust.
Last Night her Lord was all that's good and great;
A Knave this Morning, and his Will a Cheat.
Strange! by the Means defeated of the Ends.
By Spirit, robb'd of Power; by Warmth, of Friends;   30
By Wealth, of Followers; without one Distress,
Sick of herself thro' very Selfishness.
    Atossa's curs'd with ev'ry granted Prayer,
Childless with all her Children, wants an Heir:
To Heirs unknown, descends th' unnumber'd Store,   35
Or wanders, Heaven directed, to the Poor.

Contemporary transcript: Longleat, Portland Papers, XVIII.
Epistles to Several Persons. 1744.
Verses upon the late D—ss of M— By Mr. P—. 1746.
The Gentleman's Magazine. February 1746.

14*

The Harleian Miscellany. Vol. VIII. 1746.

The Foundling Hospital for Wit. No. III. 1746 (and 1763).

The insertion of the character of Atossa in the "death-bed edition" of the second Moral Essay, and the identity of the character, are exhaustively discussed in Vol. III II, pp. 39–42, 155–64. The character is reprinted here from the text as first and separately published early in February 1746 with the title *Verses Upon the Late D——ss of M——. By Mr. P——.* For the final note on this six-page leaflet, see Vol. III II, p. 162. See also V. A. Dearing, "The Prince of Wales's Set of Pope's Works", *Harvard Library Bulletin* (1950), Vol. IV, pp. 327–36.

Fragment of *Brutus*, an Epic

THE Patient Chief, who lab'ring long, arriv'd
    On Britains Shore and brought with fav'ring Gods
Arts Arms and Honour to her Ancient Sons:
Daughter of Memory! from elder Time
Recall; and me, with Britains Glory fir'd,   5
Me, far from meaner Care or meaner Song,
Snatch to thy Holy Hill of Spotless Bay,
My Countrys Poet, to record her Fame.

2 Shore] *replaces* Coast.

4 elder] *deleted in MS.*   from . . . Time] *replaces* instructive Muse.

8 *The fragment continues:*

            Say first wᵗ Cause? That Pow'r here
        Who decreed to restore . . . originall hight
        Who before Joves
        was conceiv'd by all men
            worship of one

Pope's autograph: BM MS Egerton 1950.

In 1743 Pope was meditating an epic poem on civil and ecclesiastical government, whose hero was to be "our Brutus from Troy". "Though there is none of it writ as yet", Pope said to Spence (pp. 288–9), "what I look upon as more than half the work is already done; for 'tis all exactly planned." The plan, which still exists (Egerton MS 1950), was summarized by Ruffhead (pp. 410–23), who concludes his account: "Our Author had actually begun this poem; and part of the manuscript, in *blank verse*, now lies before me. But various accidents concurred, to prevent his making any further progress in it." What Ruffhead had before him may well have been this fragment, which follows the "plan" in the manuscript. The lines are superscribed "in ye Character of a Legislator". Line 8 is the last completed verse, but a few more words have been jotted down. See H.-J. Zimmermann, "Bemerkungen Zum Manuskript und Text von Popes *Brutus*", *Archiv für das Studium der Neueren Sprachen und Literaturen*, 199 (1962) 100–6.

Lines on *BOUNCE*.

A H Bounce! ah gentle Beast! why wouldst thou dye,
  When thou had'st Meat enough, and Orrery?

Pope's autograph: The Pierpont Morgan Library, New York.
The Works. Ed. Elwin and Courthope. Correspondence. Vol. VIII. 1872.

These lines are printed from a letter written by Pope to Lord Orrery within a few weeks of the poet's death. Probably because of his own, or the dog's, increasing infirmities, he had given Bounce two years before into Lord Orrery's care, whose kindness to animals "and in particular to dogs" Pope praised in a letter to him (23 July 1742), in which he went on to say, "Yet I will not allow you should retard the satisfaction I was sure to receive in hearing of your own, till you could also acquaint me of Bounce's safe arrival in Somersetshire" (the Orrerys' house was at Marston). On 10 April 1744, after hearing from Orrery of the dog's death, he writes:

I dread to enquire into the particulars of ye Fate of Bounce. Perhaps you conceald them, as Heav'n often does Unhappy Events, in pity to the Survivors, or not to hasten on my End by Sorrow. I doubt not how much Bounce was lamented: They might say as the Athenians did to Arcite, in Chaucer,

> Ah Arcite! gentle Knight! why would'st thou die,
> When thou had'st Gold enough, and Emilye?

The couplet which follows was probably the last he ever wrote.
The text is that of the autograph letter.

IMPROMPTU

the stern Achilles
Stalked through a mead of daffodillies

This fragment from Spence's *Anecdotes* (p. 285) was overlooked in the first edition, where it should have appeared on p. 399. The impromptu forms the conclusion of Pope's reply to Spence's enquiry about Homer's asphodel: "Why believe, if one was to say the truth, 'twas nothing else but that poor yellow flower that grows about our orchards: and if so, the verse might·thus be translated in English:"

POEMS OF DOUBTFUL
AUTHORSHIP

The following poems of doubtful authorship have been attributed to Pope, but on evidence which appears less than decisive. They are placed here in chronological order of publication, except where the date of composition is clearly indicated. The text of those most plausibly attributed to Pope is printed, unless it is reasonably accessible in print elsewhere. The bibliographies make no pretence to completeness.

COUPLET.
On Sappho.

WHEN at Spring-garden Sappho deigns t'appear,
The Flow'rs march in her Van, Musk in her Rear.

Title] No title originally (see below).

This couplet, which Pope called a "compliment", is taken from a letter to
Cromwell, dated 7 May 1709, where it is thus introduced: "The Time now [is]
drawing nigh, when you use, with Sapho, to cross the water in an Ev'ning to
Spring Garden... I have been told of a very lucky Compliment of an Officer to
his Mistress in the same place, wch I cannot but set down, (and desire you at pre-
sent to take in good part instead of a Latine Quotation) that it may sometime or
other be improv'd by your Pronunciation, while you walk, Solus cum Sola, in
those Amourous Shades." Whereupon the couplet follows. The manner in which
the lines are introduced is so characteristic of Pope (who rarely quoted other peo-
ple's lines) that his authorship of them appears possible.

The text is that of the autograph MS (Bodleian MS Rawl. letters 90).

THE STORY OF ARETHUSA
Translated from the Fifth Book of Ovid's
Metamorphoses

Miscellaneous Poems and Translations. By Several Hands. 1712 (and 2nd Edition,
1714).

Tentatively attributed to Pope by N. Ault in *The Nineteenth Century and After*
(November 1934); see also *New Light*, pp. 38–48.

YARHELL'S-KITCHEN:
or, The Dogs of Egypt. An Heroic Poem.

Published anonymously in 1713, and variously attributed to William King, Gay, Pope (in the catalogue of Sion College Library), and Prior. See Faber, pp. xxxii–xxxiii.

EPIGRAM.
On "*CATO.*"

You ask why Damon does the College seek?
  Tis because Cato's not Rehearsd this week;
How long at Oxford then will Damon stay?
Damon returns not till they Cato Play:
Oldfield wants Damon—when will he be at her?   5
Oh, not till Oldfield shall be Cato's Daughter:
Why then if I can guess what may insue,
When Cato's clapp'd, Damon will be so too.

Caryll transcript: BM MS Add. 28618.

This epigram, which seems not to have been printed previously, is found in a letter (dated 30 April 1713) written by Pope to Caryll, in which, after describing the rapturous reception of Addison's tragedy on its first performance on 14 April, and its continued success with the town, he went on to say: "But of all the world none have been in so peculiar a manner enamour'd with Cato; as a young Gentleman of Oxford, who makes it the sole guide of all his Actions . . . he dates every thing from yᵉ first or third night &c. of Cato: he goes out of Town every day it is not play'd, & fell in love with Mrs Oldfield for no other reason than because she act'd Cato's Daughter! This has occasioned the following Epigram, which was dispers'd about yᵉ Coffee houses in holy week, & is much approv'd of by our Witts."

The epigram followed. It is introduced in the letter in the same equivocal way that Pope so frequently employed; it is one more witness of his dislike of the actress, Mrs Oldfield [see *New Light*, pp. 134f.]; it includes the pun on the word "clap" to which he seems to have been partial (see p. 201); and lastly he troubled to transcribe it (for his quotations of other people's verses in his letters are of the utmost rarity). Although this suggests that the epigram may have been written by Pope, the evidence is not strong enough for its inclusion in his works.

The text follows that of the transcript.

A Prophecy Of *Nostradamus*

WHEN as tway Sexes joint in one
    Shall in the Realme of Brute be shown,
Eke Factions shall unite (if I know)
To seke a Prince, Jure Divino:
Thilke Prodigy of common Gender   5
Is neither Sex, but a Pretender,
And so God shielde the Fayth's Defender.

These lines, which are extant in Pope's autograph at Mapledurham, were first printed in the two editions of the Letters, published on 12 May 1735, in modernized spelling. The autograph is an undated letter to the Misses Blount reporting an exhibition of a hermaphrodite in London, with a mock prophecy of its political significance: "Mr Poole looks upon it as a Prodigy portending some wonderful Revolution in the State, and to strengthen his Opinion produces the following Prophecy of Nostradamus, which he explains Politically." From certain indications in the letter, such as the mention of his one-time friend Cromwell (with whom relations were not yet entirely severed), a joke on an "hermaphroditical riding habit" (which was repeated—by Pope?—in, or from, *The Guardian* of 1 September 1713) and on the Pretender (which seems to anticipate the revolution of 1715) together suggest the latter part of 1713 as the probable date of the letter; and that would sufficiently agree with what appears to be a subsequent adaptation of this letter, dated 10 February 1714, which was sent to Miss Marriot —according to Dilke's transcript (EC, ix 473). The pretence that Benjamin Poole—the lawyer uncle of the Blount girls—was responsible for the Prophecy, looks like a piece of Pope's characteristic playfulness, as does also the absurd parenthetical rhyme, "if I know": he may perhaps have composed the verses.

The text follows the autograph.

LINES FROM *THE FAN*

The Fan. A Poem. In Three Books. By Mr. Gay. 1714.
Supplemental Volume to the Works of Alexander Pope, Esq. Ed. Dibdin. 1825.
Book III, ll. 11–20 attributed to Pope by Dibdin on stylistic evidence.

LINES FROM
THE SHEPHERD'S WEEK

The Shepherd's Week. In Six Pastorals. By Mr J. Gay. 1714 (and 2nd Edition, 1714).

Poems on Several Occasions. By J. Gay. 1720 (and later editions).

Memoirs of . . . Alexander Pope, Esq; W. Ayre. Vol. II. 1745.

Ll. 113–32 of the fifth Pastoral attributed to Pope by Ayre but without evidence.

UPON THE DUKE OF MARLBOROUGH'S
HOUSE AT WOODSTOCK

Contemporary transcript: Bodleian MS Ballard 47.

Original Poems and Translations. By Mr. Hill, Mr. Eusden, Mr. Broome, Dr. King, &c. 1714.

Miscellanea. The Second Volume. 1727 (published 1726).

First published anonymously in 1714 and 1726, this poem has since been attributed to several people. It was included in one of R. Guinnet's letters in *The Honourable Lovers*, 1732; anonymous again in *The British Magazine*, November 1749; ascribed to William King (died 1712) in the *Supplement to the Works of the Most celebrated Minor Poets*, Vol. III, 1750; anonymous once more in *The Nut-Cracker*. 1751; included as Pope's in the *Supplement to the Works of Alexander Pope, Esq.* 1757; anonymous in *The Complete London Jester*, 1765; given to Swift in *The Festoon*, 1766, by R. Graves, who corrected the attribution later, and gave it to Pope in the 2nd Edition, 1767 (and in later editions); printed as Swift's again in *The Christmas Treat*, 1767; definitely attributed to Pope in *Additions to the Works of Alexander Pope*, Vol. I. 1776; ascribed to Rev. Abel Evans by Nichols in his *Select Collection of Poems*, Vol. III, 1780; and restored again to Pope in Warton's edition of *The Works*, 1797. On the other hand, the manuscript versions encountered are mostly anonymous (*e.g.* BM MS Lansd. 852 and MS Bibl. Egerton 924, and Bodleian MS Ballard 47); but in the Cowper Papers (BM MS Add. 28101) it is assigned to "Ld Bolingbroke". Lastly, although Scott included it in Swift's *Works* in 1814, Williams preserves an open mind (p. 1150), and all the principal editors of Pope since Warton have printed it as Pope's without comment.

With no evidence adduced, attribution hitherto has seemed to depend on mere assertion. But there is one piece of evidence in Pope's favour which should be recorded, namely, his letter "To *** " (EC, x 264–5), in which he describes Blenheim with similar detail, and with exactly the same satirical intention and effect. In the 1757 *Supplement* the letter is immediately followed by this poem, as though it were a continuation, or had been enclosed with it.

EPIGRAM
On some snow melting in a lady's breast

Poetical Miscellanies . . . Publish'd by Mr. Steele. 1714 (and 1726; and 2nd Edition, 1727).
   A Collection of Epigrams. 1727.
   The County Magazine. December 1786.
   Attributed to Pope without evidence in the *County Magazine.*

ON MRS T—S

Poetical Miscellanies . . . Publish'd by Mr. Steele. 1714 (and 1726; and 2nd Edition, 1727).
   Miscellany Poems. Vol. I. 5th Edition. 1726 (and 1727).
   Miscellanies. The Last Volume. 1727 (and later editions).
   A Supplement to Dr. Swift's And Mr. Pope's Works. Dublin. 1739.
   Miscellanies. The Fourth Volume. Consisting of Verses . . . 1742 (and later editions).
   The Poems of Pope. Vol. II (Johnson's *English Poets*, New Edition). 1790.
   With author and subject both anonymous on its first publication, this epigram was not connected with Mrs Tofts, the opera singer, until Pope included it with a new title in *Miscellanies. The Last Volume*, 1727; and was not attributed to Pope before 1776, when Hawkins remarked that its author was "supposed to be Mr. Pope". Hawkins's supposition has since been accepted without question by all Pope's editors, except Warton and Bowles. The epigram has also been attributed, without evidence, to Swift in *The Festoon*, 1766. The evidence of Pope's authorship of the piece is of the slightest; it amounts to little more than the inclusion of the piece in Swift and Pope's *Miscellanies*, and Pope's knowledge that the anonymous subject of the epigram was Mrs Tofts.

LINES FROM *The Art of Sinking.*

I.
The Profound,
when it consists in the Thought.
Of a frighted Stag in full Chace, who—
Hears his own Feet, and thinks they sound like more;
And fears the hind Feet will o'ertake the fore.

II.

The Paranomasia, or Pun.

To see her Beauties no Man needs to stoop,
She has the whole *Horizon* for her *Hoop*.

III.

The Hyperbole.
Of a Lady at Dinner.

The silver Whiteness that adorns thy Neck,
Sullies the Plate, and makes the Napkin black.

IV.

Another.
The modest Request of two absent Lovers.

Ye Gods! annihilate but *Space* and *Time*,
And make two Lovers happy.

V.

The Vulgar.
Of Clouds big with Water compared to a Woman
in great Necessity.

Distended with the *Waters* in 'em pent,
The Clouds *hang deep* in Air, but *hang unrent*.

Miscellanies. The Last Volume. 1727 (and subsequent editions).
The Works . . . In Prose. Vol. II. 1741.
The Works. Ed. Warburton. Vol. VI. 1751.

In addition to the ludicrous poetical illustrations from various authors which Pope gibbeted in *The Art of Sinking*, and the lines he inserted from his own early poems signed "Anon." (see p. 20), he included five others without ascription or designation. These also are probably from his pen, or, possibly—seeing that the treatise was in part written at the time of the Scriblerus Club—the result of multiple suggestion or collaboration in which Gay, Swift, Parnell, or Arbuthnot may have assisted. As there is nothing to connect these lines with Pope's youthful poems, and as they do not look like his work in 1727, they are tentatively dated 1714, on 26 June of which year Arbuthnot wrote to Swift saying, "Pope has been collecting high flights of poetry, which are very good; they are to be solemn nonsense." For the concluding group of illustrations probably written by Pope for *The Art of Sinking* in 1727, see page 288.

The text is that of *1727*, except for II which first appears in *1736*, and may therefore be of later composition.

I. From chap. VII.　　　II. From chap. X.　　　III–V. From chap. XI.

ODE FOR MUSICK
ON THE LONGITUDE

Contemporary transcripts: Longleat, Portland Papers, xx; and BM MS
Harl. 7316.
  Miscellanies. The Last Volume. 1727 (and later editions).
  A Supplement to Dr. Swift's and Mr. Pope's Works. Dublin. 1739.
  Miscellanies. The Fourth Volume. Consisting of Verses . . . 1742 (and later editions).
  A New Method for discovering the Longitude both at Sea and Land by W. Whiston and
H. Ditton was published in July 1714, and a revised edition appeared in mid-
April 1715. In the latter month Gay and Pope wrote to Caryll [EC, vi 226]:
". . . Mr. Pope owes all his skill in astronomy . . . to him [Tidcombe] and Mr
Whiston, so celebrated of late for his discovery of the longitude in an extra-
ordinary copy of verses which you heard when you were last in town." These
scatological verses were attributed to Swift in *The Charmer*, to Pope in a copy of
Miscellanies 1727 at Welbeck belonging to Lord Oxford's daughter, and to
Parnell in a letter of 23 Dec. 1714 from Sir R. Cox to E. Southwell (BM Add.
38157), shown me by Mr C. Rawson. For a mistaken attribution to Gay by
Spence (p. 201) see J. M. Osborn, "'That on Whiston' by John Gay", *Papers
Bib. Soc. America*, LVI (1962), 73–8.

A PROLOGUE TO *LADY JANE GRAY*

  *The Tragedy of the Lady Jane Gray. As it is Acted at the Theatre-Royal in Drury-
Lane. By N. Rowe, Esq.* 1715 (and subsequent editions of Rowe's Works).
  See *New Light*, pp. 138–44.

THE RAMBLE
Between Belinda a Demy-Prude, and Cloe a
Court-Coquette

  State Poems. 1716.
  Court Poems, Part II. 1717.
  Pope's Miscellany. The Second Part. 1717.
  Court Poems In Two Parts Compleat. 1719.
  Attributed to Pope, but without much probability, by the implication of its
appearance in *Pope's Miscellany*.

THE BASSET-TABLE
An Eclogue

Court Poems. 1716 (and Dublin edition, 1716).
Pope's Miscellany. 1717 (and 2nd Edition, 1717).
Court Poems In Two Parts Compleat. 1719.
Court Poems. In Two Parts. By Mr. Pope, &c. 1726.
Miscellanea. The Second Volume. 1727.
Mr. Pope's Literary Correspondence. Vol. IV. 1736 (and 2nd Edition, 1736).
The Works. Ed. Warburton. Vol. VI. 1751.
Included in every edition since Warburton, but more probably the work of
Lady Mary Wortley Montagu. See *Notes & Queries*, 7 S. ix 225,515; 9 S. ii 141;
Sherburn, p. 204.

ROXANA
or, The Drawing-Room

Like *The Basset-Table, Roxana* was included in *Court Poems*, 1716, was attri-
buted there to Pope, and has since been included in many editions of his Works.
But it too is more probably the work of Lady Mary. See Sherburn, pp. 169, 204.

SONG
" 'Twas in this shade . . ."

See *P.O.M.*, pp. lxviii, 55.

UPON AURELIA'S SHOOTING AT
A DEER

See *P.O.M.*, pp. lx, 108. For this and the following four poems, see also Case,
pp. 308–10; Ault, pp. 182–3.

TO AURELIA
Addressed to the Ld L—n

See *P.O.M.*, pp. lxi, 109.

TO BRUNETTA

See *P.O.M.*, pp. lxii, 111.

THE KING'S BOX TO AURELIA

See *P.O.M.*, pp. lxiv, 115.

IN HER OWN ISLE THE GODDESS LAY

See *P.O.M.*, pp. lxv, 116.

PALÆMON
A Pastoral

See *P.O.M.*, pp. xlv, 84; Case, p. 313.

THREE TRANSLATIONS FROM
THE LATIN

These are *The Fourth Ode of Catullus. Paraphras'd in the manner of Cowley; Catullus. Ad Peninsulam Sirmionem; Lydia Imitated from the Lyric of Corn. Gallus.* See *P.O.M.*, pp. xxxiv–xxxvi, 66–70. Also ascribed to Pope by A. E. Case, *London Mercury* (October 1924), pp. 614–23.

FROM CLAUDIAN
On a Globe of Crystal containing Water in it

See *P.O.M.*, pp. xlviii, 82.

UPON THE PHENICIANS
INVENTORS OF LETTERS
From Brebœuf

See *P.O.M.*, pp. xlix, 83.

UPON CLEORA'S
MARRIAGE AND RETIREMENT

See *P.O.M.*, pp. lxiii, 113.

UPON THE LADY S—D
AFTER SHE WAS DEAD

See *P.O.M.*, pp. lxii, 112.

THE MONSTER OF RAGUSA
as it was seen in the Flying-Post, Feb. 1716
An excellent new Ballad

Poems on Several Occasions. [Edited by Pope.] 1717.
Miscellaneous Poems and Translations. 3rd Edition, 1720, and 4th Edition, 1722.
The Hive. 1724.
Miscellany Poems. 5th Edition. 1726 (reprinted 1727).

The Choice: Being a Collection Of Two Hundred and Fifty Celebrated Songs. 1729.
Miscellany Poems. 6th Edition. 1732.
Philomel . . . a Small Collection of Only the Best English Songs. 1744.
The Muses Banquet. Vol. I. 1752.
See *P.O.M.*, pp. xlvi, 92; Case, p. 313.

THE LOOKING-GLASS

Pope's Miscellany. 1717 (and 2nd Edition, 1717).
Court Poems In Two Parts Compleat. 1719.
Court Poems. In Two Parts. By Mr. Pope, &c. 1726.
Miscellanea. The Second Volume. 1727 (one variant omits this poem).
A Miscellany on Taste. By Mr. Pope, &c. 1732.
Mr. Pope's Literary Correspondence. Vol. II. 1735 (and 2nd Edition, 1735).
Mr. Pope's Literary Correspondence. Vol. IV. 2nd Edition, 1736.
Memoirs of . . . Pope. W. Ayre. Vol. II. 1745.
A Supplement to the Works . . . 1757.
Additions to the Works of Alexander Pope, Esq. Vol. I. 1776.
The Works. Ed. Warton. Vol. II. 1797.

The Looking-Glass was attributed to Pope by Curll in a number of his piratical publications; but it was neither acknowledged by the poet nor included by him anonymously in any of the various miscellanies he edited. The piece was first incorporated in the canon by Warton; but he gave no evidence, in which reticence he has been followed by his successors almost without exception. Bowles, however, supplied a footnote: "These lines were suppressed, as Pope afterwards received great civilities from Pulteney"; thus also taking Pope's responsibility for granted. "Unspeakable" though Curll may have been in some respects, it must be admitted, that, with the notorious exception of *Court Poems* (which he inflicted on Pope only after, and in revenge for, the emetic episode), whenever he definitely attributed a particular poem to Pope he has generally been proved right, when proof was possible. Nevertheless there is no evidence whatever for Pope's authorship of this piece except its general likeness to his style and the doubtful authority of Curll's word.

Not only has Pope had this poem ascribed to him, but he has also been accused of treachery in writing it. On 4 September 1724, Pulteney wrote to Pope inviting him to "spend a few days with Mrs. Pulteney and me"; and to this invitation Elwin and Courthope (x, 136) append the sneering annotation: "On whom Pope afterwards wrote some not very complimentary verses", and in proof of their statement refer to this poem, which had been published seven years earlier. As the poem was first published on 5 January 1716/17 (*The Daily Courant*), it must have been written not later than 1716; and as Pulteney's marriage to Anna Maria Gumley took place in December 1714, and some time must be allowed for it to affect her character, the year 1716 appears to be the probable date of composition.

TO PHOEBUS
Tibullus *Eleg.* iv. lib. iv.

See *P.O.M.*, pp. xlv, 49.

TO MR POPE
ON HIS TRANSLATION OF HOMER

See *P.O.M.*, pp. lxxvii, 40; Case, pp. 311–12.

ON A PICTURE
OF MRS CATHERINE L—

See *P.O.M.*, pp. lxvi, 117; Case, p. 308.

THE OLD GENTRY
Out of French

See *P.O.M.*, pp. liv, 40; Ault, pp. 185–7; Case, pp. 189–91.

ON THE RIVER DANUBE

The Early Career of Alexander Pope. By G. Sherburn. 1934.
See *P.O.M.*, pp. lii, 39.

THE PARSON'S DAUGHTER
A Tale for the Use of Pretty Girls
with Small Fortunes

Published by Curll in 1717, and included in *Pope's Miscellany The Second Part*, 1717, *Court Poems*, 1719, and *Mr. Pope's Literary Correspondence*, Vol. IV, 1736. It is ascribed to Pope by Griffith (I 1 61); but in two of his book advertisements of 1734 and 1735 Curll lists it as the work of Christopher Wyvill, and Jacob ascribes it to "Mr C. W." in *Poetical Register*, II 320.

DIANA's *Answer to* BRUTUS.

Brutus there lies beyond the *Gallick* Bounds
An Island which the Western Sea surrounds,
By Giants once possess'd; now few remain
To bar thy Entrance, or obstruct thy Reign.
To reach that happy Shore thy Sails employ: 5
There Fate decrees to raise a second *Troy*,
And found an Empire in thy Royal Line,
Which Time shall ne'er destroy, nor Bounds confine.

The British History. A. Thompson. 1718.
Attributed to Pope by G. Sherburn in *Manly Anniversary Studies*, 1923, pp. 174–6.

NEWS FROM COURT
A Ballad

To the Tune of, "To all you Ladies now at Land"

News From Court. A Ballad . . . By Mr. Pope. 1719.
The Court Miscellany. Number I. 1719.
An imitation of *The Court Ballad*, attributed to Pope on the broadsheet, and to "Mr Caley" in *The Court Miscellany*. No more was heard of it.

To His Grace the Duke of AR-
GYLE, upon reading the fol-
lowing short Preamble to the
Patent creating him Duke of
GREENWICH.

Cum viri illius, cui novos hisce literis patentibus Titulos decernimus, & egregia in nos Patriamque suam Merita, & illustre Genus, & Majorum res gestæ, Historiarum Monumentis celebratæ, satis inclaruerint, *quibus rationibus adducti sumus eum summo inter Proceres honore dignari,* nil opus est pluribus recensere.

M INDLESS of fate in these low vile abodes,
   TYRANTS have oft usurp'd the style of GODS:
But that the MORTAL might be thought DIVINE,
The HERALD strait new-modell'd *all his line;*
And venal PRIEST with well-dissembled lye,   5
Preambled to the crowd the *mimick* DEITY.
Not so great SATURN's son, imperial JOVE
HE reigns, unquestion'd, in his realms above:
No title from *descent* HE need infer,
His red right arm proclaims the THUNDERER.   10
   This, CAMPBELL, be thy pride, illustrious Peer!
Alike to shine distinguish'd in your sphere:
All *merit* but your *own* YOU may disdain,
And KINGS have been your ANCESTORS in vain.

Miscellaneous Poems and Translations. 3rd Edition. 1720 (and 4th Edition, 1722).
Miscellany Poems. Vol. II. 5th Edition. 1726 (and 1727; and 6th Edition, 1732).
The Poetical Calendar. December 1763.
The New Foundling Hospital for Wit . . . Part the Sixth. 1773 (and later editions).
The Works. Ed. Wakefield. [Vol. I.] 1794.

This poem, which Pope included anonymously in three successive editions of "Lintot's Miscellany", was first attributed to him in *The Poetical Calendar.* Though the poem has frequently been accepted as Pope's and is worthy of him, no evidence has been adduced and the attribution must therefore be regarded as doubtful. The poem cannot have been written before 27 April 1719, when Argyle was created Duke of Greenwich. For Pope's relations with Argyle, see Biog. App., Vol. IV.

The text is that of the first printing, which agrees verbally with Pope's last text (*1727*).

TO LADY MARY WORTLEY MONTAGU

Lady M. W. Montagu's autograph: Harrowby MS.
Scating: A Poem. By Mr. Addison. 1720.
A New Miscellany. A. H[ammond]. 1720.
Court Poems. In Two Parts. 1726.
Miscellanea. The Second Volume. 1727.
Miscellaneous Poems, By Several Hands. J. Ralph. 1729.
Mr. Pope's Literary Correspondence. Vol. II. 1735 (and 2nd Edition, 1735).
Memoirs of . . . Alexander Pope, Esq. W. Ayre. Vol. II. 1745.
A Supplement to the Works of Alexander Pope, Esq. 1757.
Additions to the Works of Alexander Pope, Esq. Vol. I. 1776.
The Poems of Pope. Vol. II in Johnson's *English Poets.* 1779 (and 1790).
The Poetical Works of Alexander Pope, in Anderson's *British Poets.* 1794.
The Works. Ed. Warton. Vol. II. 1797.

This poem ("In beauty or wit") was attributed to Pope on its first appearance in print and has frequently been accepted as his. But Lady Mary herself attributed it to "Judge Burnet", and in such a matter she is not likely to have been misinformed.

HAMAN and *MORDECAI.*

A MASQUE.
[Subsequently entitled "*Esther. An Oratorio*".]

The PERSONS represented.

Esther.	*Priest* of the *Israelites.*
Assuerus.	*Harbonah.*
First *Israelite.*	*Persian Officer.*
Haman.	Second *Israelite.*
Mordecai.	*Israelites.*
Israelite Boy.	*Officers.*

ACT I. SCENE I.
Haman, Harbonah, and Officers.

RECITATIVE.

Har.   'Tis greater far to spare than to destroy.

Ham.   I'll hear no more, it is decreed,
          All the *Jewish* race shall bleed.
             Hear and obey what *Haman*'s voice commands:
          Hath not the Lord of all the east
             Giv'n all his pow'r into my hands?   5
          Hear, all ye nations, far and wide,
             Which own our monarch's sway,
          Hear, and obey.

AIR.

          Pluck root and branch out of the land;   10
             Shall I the God of *Israel* fear?
          Let *Jewish* blood dye every hand;
             Nor age nor sex I'll spare:
          Raze, raze their temples to the ground,
          And let their place no more be found.   15

RECITATIVE.

Officer.   Our souls with ardour glow,
          To execute the blow.

CHORUS.

          Shall we the God of *Israel* fear?
          Nor age nor sex we'll spare.
          Pluck root and branch out of the land.   20
                           [Ex.

10 out of] from out *MS, TS; and in l. 20 also.*
13 I'll] I *MS, TS.*
19–20 *TS reverses order of these lines.*

Scene II.
Israelites.

RECITATIVE.

1st Is.   Now persecution shall lay by her iron rod,
Esther is queen, and *Esther* serves the living God.

AIR.

Tune your harps to chearful strains,
    Moulder idols into dust;
Great *Jehovah* lives and reigns,   25
    We in great *Jehovah* trust.

CHORUS.

Shall we of servitude complain,
The heavy yoke, and galling chain?

AIR.

Is. Boy.   Praise the Lord with chearful noise;
    Wake, my glory, wake, my lyre;   30
Praise the Lord, each mortal voice;
    Praise the Lord, ye heav'nly choir:
Zion now her head shall raise;
Tune your harps to songs of praise.

RECITATIVE.

2d. Is.   O God, who from the suckling's mouth,   35
    Ordainest early praise,
Of such as worship thee in truth,
    Accept the humble lays.

AIR.

2d. Is.   Sing songs of praise, bow down the knee,
    Our chains we slight,   40
    Our yoke is light,

Following l. 34] MS has another Air, which seems never to have been printed:

AIR.

Methinks I see each stately tow'r
Of Salem rise by Esther's pow'r;
She shall break the captive chain,
And Zion learn our songs again.

The worship of our God is free.
Zion again her head shall raise;
Tune all your harps to songs of praise.

CHORUS.

Shall we of servitude complain,   45
The heavy yoke, and galling chain?

SCENE III.
Enter the priest of the *Israelites.*

Priest.   How have our sins provok'd the Lord!
Wild persecution hath unsheath'd the sword,
Haman hath sent forth his decree,
     The sons of *Israel* all   50
     Shall in one ruin fall.
Methinks I hear the mother's groans,
While babes are dash'd against the stones;
I hear the infant's shriller screams,
     Stab'd at the mother's breast;   55
     Blood stains the murderer's vest,
And thro' the city flows in streams.

CHORUS.

Ye Sons of *Israel*, mourn,
Ye never to your country shall return.

AIR.

O *Jordan, Jordan,* sacred tide!   60
Shall we no more behold thee glide
     The fertile vales along,
As in our great fore-fathers days?
Shall not thy hills resound with praise,
     And learn our holy song?   65

CHORUS.

Ye Sons of *Israel*, mourn,
Ye never to your country shall return.

48 hath] has *MS.*

ACT II. SCENE I.
Esther, Mordecai, and *Israelites.*

RECITATIVE.

Esther.   Why sits that sorrow on thy brow?
          Why is thy reverend head
          With mournful ashes spread?   70
          Why is the humble sack-cloth worn?
          Speak, *Mordecai,* my kinsman, friend,
          Speak, and let *Esther* know
          Why all this solemn woe?

Mordecai. One fate involves us all,   75
               Haman's decree,
                 To strike at me,
           Hath said, that every *Jew* shall fall.
           Go stand before the king with weeping eye.

Est.   Who goes unsummon'd, by the law shall die.   80

AIR.

Mord.   Dread not, righteous queen, the danger,
           Love will pacify his anger;
               Fear is due to God alone:
           Follow great *Jehovah*'s calling;
           For thy kindred's safety falling,   85
               Death is better than a throne.

RECITATIVE.

Est.   I go before the king to stand:
           Stretch forth, O king, thy scepter'd hand.

AIR.

           Tears assist me, pity moving,
           Justice cruel fraud reproving;   90
               Hear, O God, thy servant's prayer:
           It is blood that must attone,
           Take, O take my life alone,
               And thy chosen people spare.

CHORUS.

           Save us, O Lord!   95
           And blunt the wrathful sword.
                                              [Ex.

80 law] Laws *MS, TS.*
92 It is] Is it *MS, TS.*

15

SCENE II.
Assuerus, Esther, and *Israelites.*

RECITATIVE.

Assuerus.	Who dares intrude into our presence, without our leave?	
	It is decreed,	
	He dies for this audacious deed.	
	Hah! *Esther* there!	100
	The law condemns, but love will spare.	

Esther.   My spirits sink, alas! I faint.

Assuerus.   Ye powers, what paleness spreads her beauteous face!
             Esther awake, thou fairest of thy race,
             Awake, and live, 'tis my command;   105
             Behold the golden sceptre in my hand,
             Sure sign of grace;
             The bloody stern decree,
             Was never meant, my queen, to strike at thee.

DUET.

Es.	Who calls my parting soul from death?	110
Ass.	Awake, my soul, my life, my breath.	
Esther.	Hear my suit, or else I die.	
Assuerus.	Ask, my queen; can I deny?	

AIR.

Assuerus.   O beauteous queen, unclose those eyes.
                My fairest shall not bleed;   115
             Hear love's soft voice, that bids thee rise,
                And bids thy suit succeed.
             Ask, and 'tis granted, from this hour;
             Who shares our heart shall share our pow'r.

RECITATIVE.

Esther.	If I find favour in thy sight,	120
	May the great monarch of the east	
	Honour my feast,	
	And deign to be his servant's guest;	
	The King and *Haman* I invite.	

97–109 and 114–19 are missing from *MS.*
105 Awake, and live] Esther, awake and live *TS.*

AIR.

Assuer. How can I stay when love invites? 125
I come, my queen, to chaste delights.
With joy, with pleasure, I obey,
To thee I give the day.

[Ex. Manent *Israelites*.

SCENE III.

RECITATIVE.

1st Israel. With inward joy his visage glows,
He to the queen's apartment goes: 130
Beauty has his fury charm'd,
And all his wrath disarm'd.

CHORUS.

Virtue, truth, and innocence
Shall ever be her sure defence:
She is heaven's peculiar care, 135
Propitious heav'n will hear our prayer.

ACT III.   SCENE I.
Priest of the *Israelites*.

AIR.

Priest. *Jehovah*, crown'd with glory bright,
Surrounded with eternal light,
Whose ministers are flames of fire,
Arise, and execute thine ire. 140

CHORUS.

He comes, he comes, to end our woes,
And pour his vengeance on our foes:
Earth trembles, lofty mountains nod:
Jacob, arise, to meet thy God.

[Ex.

136 our] her *MS, TS.*
141 He comes, he comes, to] He comes to *TS.*
144 to] *MS reads* and *first time, and* to *in the musical repetition.*

15*

SCENE II.

Assuerus, Haman, Esther, and *Israelites.*

RECITATIVE.

Assuer.   Now, O my queen! thy suit declare,   145
                Ask half my empire, it is thine.

Est.   O gracious king! my people spare,
                For in their lives you strike at mine;
              Reverse the dire decree,
              The blow is aim'd at *Mordecai* and me: 150
              And is the fate of *Mordecai* decreed,
                Who when the ruffian's sword
                Sought to destroy my royal lord,
              Brought forth to light the desp'rate deed?

Assuer.   Yes, yes, I own,   155
                To him alone,
                I owe my life and throne:
              Say then, my queen, who dares pursue
              The life to which reward is due?

Est.   'Tis *Haman*'s hate   160
                That sign'd his fate.

Assuer.   I swear by yon bright orb of light,
                That rules the day,
              That *Haman's* sight
                Shall never more behold the golden ray!   165

AIR.

Ham.   Turn not, O queen, thy face away,
                Behold me, prostrate, on the ground: [*kneels.*
              O speak! his growing fury stay,
                Let mercy in thy sight be found.

AIR.

Esther.   Flatt'ring tongue, no more I'll hear thee,   170
                Vain are all thy cruel wiles;

145 O my queen] O Queen *MS, TS.*
146 it is] and 'tis *MS, TS.*
162 orb] globe *MS, TS.*   163 That] Which *MS, TS.*
168 growing] *TS has* glowing *in the words,* growing *in the music.*
170 I'll] I *MS, TS.*

Bloody wretch, no more I fear thee,
  Vain thy frowns, and vain thy smiles:
Tyrant, when of power possess'd,
Now thou tremblest, when distress'd.   175

RECITATIVE.

Ass.   Guards, seize the traytor, bear him hence,
Death shall reward the dire offence:
To *Mordecai* be honour paid,
  The royal garment bring,
My diadem shall grace his head,   180
Let him in triumph thro' the streets be led,
  Who sav'd the king.

                [*Exeunt. Manet* Haman *guarded.*

AIR.

Ha.   How art thou fallen from thy height!
Tremble, ambition, at the sight:
  In power let mercy sway;   185
When adverse fortune be thy lot,
Lest thou by mercy be forgot,
  And perish in that day.

                [*Ex.*

SCENE III.

Enter *Israelites* with *Mordecai* in triumph.

GRAND CHORUS.

  The Lord our enemy has slain,
Ye sons of *Jacob*, sing a chearful strain.   190
  Sing songs of praise, bow down the knee,
  The worship of our God is free.
  The Lord our enemy has slain,
Ye sons of *Jacob*, sing a chearful strain.
For ever blessed be his holy name,   195
Let heaven and earth his praise proclaim.
  Let *Israel* songs of joy repeat;
    Sound, all ye tongues, *Jehovah*'s praise,

181 streets] Street *MS.*
186 be] is *MS, TS.*
195 his] thy *MS, TS, also in repetitions:* 201, 205, 211.
198 ye] the *TS.*

He plucks the mighty from his seat,
　　And cuts off half his days.   200
For ever blessed be his holy name,
Let heaven and earth his praise proclaim.
　　The Lord his people shall restore,
　　And we in *Salem* shall adore.
For ever blessed be his holy name,   205
Let heaven and earth his praise proclaim.
　　Mount *Lebanon* his firs resigns;
　　　Descend, ye cedars; haste, ye pines,
　　To build the temple of the Lord,
　　　For God his people hath restor'd: 210
For ever blessed be his holy name,
Let heaven and earth his praise proclaim.

210 hath] has *MS, TS.*

Handel's autograph: BM King's Music MSS.
Esther . . . Leipzig, 1882. (Words of masque from a contemporary transcript of Handel's autograph.)
The London Magazine. May 1732.
Esther, An Oratorio, As perform'd at the Castle Tavern . . . *Set to Musick by Mr. Handel.* 1748.
The Words of Such Pieces As are . . . *performed by The Academy of Ancient Music.* 1761 (and 2nd Edition, 1768).
[Note: None of the numerous editions of the expanded version is noted.]

The earliest association of Pope's name with Handel's oratorio *Esther* occurs in the diary of the first Earl of Egmont (then Viscount Perceval), 23 February 1731–2: "From dinner I went to the Music Club, where the King's Chapel boys acted the *History of Hester*, writ by Pope, and composed by Hendel. This oratoria or religious opera is exceeding fine, and the company were highly pleased, some of the parts being well performed." (*Hist. MSS. Comm.* 1920, p. 225.) This private production was followed within two months by the first public performance, announced as follows in *The Daily Journal* (19 April 1732):

Never Perform'd in Publick before,
At the Great Room in Villars-street York-Buildings, To-morrow being Thursday the 20th of this Instant April, will be perform'd, ESTHER an ORATORIO: or Sacred Drama. As it was compos'd originally for the most noble James Duke of Chandos, the Words by Mr. Pope, and the Musick by Mr. Handel. Tickets to be had at the Place of Performance at 5s each. To begin exactly at 7 o'clock.

This performance was apparently unauthorized by Handel, because on 19 April in the same issue of *The Daily Journal* is another announcement as follows:

By His Majesty's Command.
At the King's Theatre in the Hay-Market, on Tuesday the 2d Day of May, will be performed The Sacred Story of ESTHER: An Oratorio in English. Formerly composed by Mr. Handel, and now revised by him, with several Additions, and to be performed by a great Number of the best Voices and Instruments. N.B. There will be no Action on the Stage, but the House will be fitted up in a decent Manner, for the Audience. The Musick to be disposed after the Manner of the Coronation Service. Tickets will be delivered at the Office in the Opera House, at the usual Prices.

The words of the oratorio have survived in the two versions represented by these two performances: (*a*) the original "book" in six scenes as in Handel's autograph (or in three acts of three scenes each as the same matter was arranged in the oldest extant printed copy, 1732); and (*b*) the expanded version in three acts (totalling twelve scenes) whose oldest surviving book of words is probably that in the possession of Mr W. C. Smith of the British Museum with the following title-page:

Esther, An Oratorio; or; Sacred Drama. As it is Performed At the King's Theatre in the Hay-Market. The Musick formerly Composed by Mr. Handel, and now Revised by him, with several Additions. The Additional Words by Mr. Humphreys. London: . . . MDCCXXXII. [Price One Shilling.]

The foregoing quotations constitute the only contemporary documentary evidence as yet available bearing on the authorship of the libretto; but it is enough to enable the different writers' parts to be disentangled, and thus establish the original (or Pope's) text; though not enough to determine its early history. Tradition, however, is probably correct in placing the original composition at Cannons, about 1718–20, when Handel was Kappellmeister to the Duke of Chandos (in which period he also wrote the music of *Acis and Galatea* to Gay's words, as well as the famous twelve Anthems). Unfortunately the first leaf of Handel's autograph has been badly cropped, and the title is missing; but a contemporary transcript of the MS, now in Germany, is said by F. Chrysander to be entitled, *Haman and Mordecai. A Masque* (*Works of Handel*. Vols. XL, XLI. Leipzig, 1882). As there is no reason to suppose that Pope ever touched the libretto again, this title must be accepted for his share of *Esther*, not only to avoid possible future confusion, but also because it best agrees with the known facts, which seem to show that Pope wrote the words of a masque and not of an oratorio. Thus its contemporary "companion piece", *Acis and Galatea*, in which Pope also had some hand (see *ante*, p. 216), is likewise a masque; oratorios proper had not yet been evolved or spoken of by that name; and, on its first performance, "the King's Chapel boys *acted* the History of Hester," which itself was called a "religious opera" by way of explanation. Seeing that *Haman and Mordecai* was originally composed for the Duke, its first performance would naturally take place at Cannons, though no record of it seems to have survived; and the usual statement that it was first performed at the opening of the Duke's private chapel for divine service on 29 August 1720 has no foundation, the musical work on that occasion being "an anthem"—probably one of the famous twelve—according to a contemporary record in *The Weekly Journal* (3 September 1720); besides which a chapel is hardly the most likely place for the production of a masque.

Nothing is known of the place, time, or manner of the collaboration of Pope and Handel, but it is thought to have been the consequence of their meeting at the house of Lord Burlington, Pope's friend and neighbour at Chiswick, where, says the *Memoirs of . . . Handel*, 1760, between 1716 and 1718 "it frequently happened that he [Pope] and Handel were together at his [Burlington's] table." Pope's anonymity in the matter may possibly be explained by a consciousness of the relative poorness of his part of the work, which must have been done during the long continued stress and strain of the great *Iliad* translation; and when the expanded libretto with Humphreys' name attached became known as the official words of the oratorio, which happened so shortly after the first public performance of the original version, there would be still less inducement, or reason, for Pope to acknowledge it. Moreover, in most musical compositions the music is so much more important than the words, that it was the exception rather than the rule for the mere author's name to be recorded, and if recorded, then very often carelessly or wrongly. Thus in most editions of *Esther*, and in references to it, the words are anonymous; but an edition of 1742 gives the entire expanded version to Arbuthnot, and another, about 1780, gives it all to Humphreys; in the Preface to *Omnipotence, a sacred Oratorio*, 1774, Pope, Arbuthnot, and Gay are said to be responsible for the words of *Esther* and *Acis and Galatea*, and F. Chrysander editing *Esther* in 1882, for the great German edition of Handel's *Works*, sees Arbuthnot in the initiative and the design, and Pope "taking part in the poetical execution". The libretto itself probably owes more to Racine's *Esther* than to the Old Testament narrative, but even that debt is not large either in plot or dialogue; on the other hand so much use is made of biblical phraseology that it contains few verbal parallels to Pope's known verse; two or three examples of these, however, are cited in the footnotes. The probabilities on the whole seem to be in favour of Pope's authorship.

The text presents some difficulty: *Haman and Mordecai* was never printed as a masque; the autograph MS lacks several pages; and the German text of 1882, though based on the transcript of *c.* 1720 and verbally reliable, has obviously been modernized in spelling, punctuation, and typographical details. On the other hand, the oldest of the printed texts, while agreeing with the two former texts with only a few slight variants, was published after the piece had been renamed *Esther. An Oratorio*, and so in a measure has lost its old identity. The present text therefore follows that of 1732—with collations from the autograph (*MS*) and the printed transcript (*TS*)—but its late title is relegated to a footnote, and the original title is printed in its stead.

Title] *1732* reads, "*Esther:* An Oratorio; or Sacred Drama. As it is now acted at the Theatre-Royal in the *Hay-Market* with vast Applause. The Musick being composed by the Great Mr. *Handel*." If *The London Magazine* did not confuse the two versions of the oratorio, this would mean that performances of the original version were repeated and shortly followed that of the expanded version of 2 May, at the Theatre Royal (see introductory note); and subsequent performances are on record.

SCENE II.] The first part of this scene down to l. 26 is missing from *MS*.

21. *persecution . . . her iron rod*] This recalls "Th' Oppressor . . . his iron rod" in *Windsor Forest*, 74–5.

SCENE III.] *MS* and *TS* have no Priest in the cast; the direction is simply "Enter an Israelite".

63. *days?*] F. Chrysander says that the poet originally placed the note of interrogation at the end of l. 63; and that Handel changed it to the end of l. 62 for the sake of the music.

ACT II. SCENE I.] *MS*, which is not divided into acts, calls this *Scena 4*.

81–6. *Dread not . . . throne.*] Lost from *MS*.

SCENE II.] In *TS* this is Scene V; the beginning of the scene is lost from *MS*.

103. *paleness spreads her beauteous face*] cf. "paleness spreads o'er all her look," *Rape of the Lock*, III 80.

114. This "Air" was reprinted in *The British Musical Miscellany*, Vol. V. [1736].

120–4. Missing from *MS*, likewise 129–32.

125–8. Misplaced in *MS*. Scena IV (i.e. Act II. Sc. I.).

SCENE III.] *MS* and *TS* have no scene division at this place.

135. *heaven's peculiar care*] a favourite phrase of Pope's (see *P.O.M.*, pp. xlvi, lxxii).

ACT III. SCENE I.] *MS* and *TS* have no act or scene division in this place.

143–4. *Earth trembles . . . thy God.*] cf. Pope's *Iliad* XIII 29–31 (published 28 June 1718):

> Fierce as he past, the lofty Mountains nod,
> The Forests shake! Earth trembled as he trod,
> And felt the footsteps of th' immortal God.

and Chorus from *Acis and Galatea* (see p. 216).

SCENE II.] *MS* and *TS* call this "Scena VI".

177. *the dire offence*] cf. "What dire offence" *Rape of the Lock*, I i.

SCENE III.] *MS* and *TS* have no scene division in this place.

GRAND CHORUS.] This is divided into parts (not shown in *1732*) for the music, thus: 197. *Alto solo*; 201. *Chorus*; 203. Duet, Esther and Mordecai; 205. *Chorus*; 207. *Duet, Basso I. and II.*; 211. *Chorus*. MS, TS.

SONG.

WHEN thy Beauty appears
In its Graces and Airs,
All bright as an Angel new dropt from the Sky;
At distance I gaze, and am aw'd by my Fears,
So strangely you dazzle my Eye!   5

But when without Art,
Your kind Thoughts you impart,
When your Love runs in Blushes thro' ev'ry Vein;
When it darts from your Eyes, when it pants in your Heart,
Then I know you're a Woman again.   10

There's a Passion and Pride
In our Sex, (she reply'd,)
And thus (might I gratify both) I wou'd do:
Still an Angel appear to each Lover beside,
But still be a Woman to you.   15

Poems on Several Occasions. Written by Dr. Thomas Parnell . . . And Published by Mr. Pope. 1722 (and all later editions of Parnell's Poems).
The Hive . . . Volume the Second. 1724.
Miscellany Poems. Vol. II . . . The Fifth Edition. 1726 (and later editions).
The Musical Miscellany. Vol. IV. 1730.
The Merry Musician . . . Vol. III. [1731.]
The Tea-Table Miscellany. Vol. IV. [1737 not extant] 1740 (and later editions).
The Lark. Containing . . . English and Scotch Songs. 1740 (and 1742). [Numerous reprints of the song appeared after Pope's death in 1744.]
Letters to and from Henrietta, Countess of Suffolk. Vol. I. 1824.
"Mr Popes angell and woeman being both imaginary, and att his own disposall, he were to blame had he not made her kind; if it were in my power . . . my Angell & my Lady should be so too. However the little gentleman has brought Angell, woeman, man and Love together in a song, there was no expedient but that which he has taken to justifye the persuit of a She Angell . . . but methinks his song shows a way might make the persuit of the Heavenly creature neither fruitlesse nor rediculous . . . But seriously Madame was ever fate like mine . . ." Thus begins an undated autograph letter (BM MS Add. 22625) from Lord Peterborough to Mrs Howard, printed in the *Suffolk Correspondence* and headed with the present *Song*.

It is certain that Peterborough, who was an intimate friend of Pope's from about 1722 onwards, and with whom Pope lived from time to time, thought Pope was the author of this song; certain, too, that Mrs Howard, another great friend of Pope's, when replying to Peterborough's letter appeared to accept his statement about Pope's authorship of it without contradiction or remark. It is also certain that Pope, who edited Parnell's *Poems on Several Occasions* (dated 1722, though actually published on 7 December 1721), included this song without comment in that volume. As there is no evidence that the friendship of Peterborough with either Pope or Mrs Howard was in existence earlier than 1721, or even as early, there is no reason to suppose that he had obtained the song from Pope and sent it to Mrs Howard *before* it was published as Parnell's. It should follow, therefore, that the song was known to the world as Parnell's at the time that two of Pope's intimate friends speak of it in private as Pope's. Either Peterborough or Mrs Howard might separately have been mistaken about its author; but it is curious that they should both have made the same mistake. Simply to assert, as Aitken did (Parnell's *Poetical Works*, 1894) that Lord Peterborough was in error, leads nowhere: on the known facts it is impossible to prove, or disprove, his attribution of this song to Pope. It is not, however, usually realized how generous Pope was to his less gifted friends in the trouble he took to correct the poems they submitted to him—not infrequently with that idea in view. Besides his never-failing help to Gay, and his revision of Broome's poems (see his letter of 6 December 1715), there are his large additions to the work of Wycherley (see *ante*, p. 54). But the most significant evidence of all is Parnell's permission for Pope to correct his poems, which is implicit in Pope's reply to him on receipt of them: ". . . I scarce see anything to be altered in this whole piece [the MS of *Homer's Battle of the Frogs and Mice*, 1717]. In the poems you sent, I will take the liberty you allow me" (EC, VII 464); and his consequent corrections, some quite drastic, of five of them are on record in at least two editions of Parnell's *Works*. It is therefore conceivable that when preparing Parnell's poems for the press in 1721, he found this song among the papers, either in an unfinished state or in need of much revision, and had reacted in his customary manner, but to such effect that (as he probably later confided to Peterborough) the song when printed virtually lacked only his signature to become his own work. And when, lastly, the song itself is compared with Parnell's other songs and short poems, its obvious superiority in wit, neatness of versification, and brevity gives some support to Peterborough's attribution. The evidence, however, seems insufficient to permit the inclusion of the *Song* in the canon. The suggested date for Pope's handiwork is 1721, the actual year of publication.

The text follows that of the first printing in every respect.

15**

COSMELIA

Contemporary transcripts: Felbrigg Hall, Windham Papers; Longleat, Portland Papers, Vol. XIX; BM MS Harl. 7316; Taylor Papers, MSS Add. 37684; and Cowper Papers, MS Add. 28101.

Tunbrigialia. 1722.

The Hive. Vol. II. 1724.

Miscellany Poems. Vol. II. 5th Edition. 1726 (and 1727).

A Collection of Epigrams. 1727 (and 2nd Edition, 1735).

This extremely popular song ("Cosmelia's charms inspire my lays") is attributed to Pope in the Windham MS. The attribution is improbable. In a letter to Pitt of 2 August 1728 (EC, x 130) to which Pope added a postscript, Spence asked to be supplied with a more correct copy than he possessed, being "very much persuaded" that Pitt was the author. There seems no reason why Pope, had he written it, should not have told Spence. In fact he seems to have believed that the author was Pitt; see Vol. V, p. 102.

EPILOGUE TO *THE CAPTIVES*
Spoken by Mrs Oldfield

The Captives. A Tragedy. As it is Acted at the Theatre-Royal. 1724.

The attribution of this Epilogue to Pope is argued at length in *New Light*, pp. 207–14.

THE QUIDNUNCKI'S
A Tale Occasioned by the Death of the Duke Regent of France

Contemporary transcript: BM MS Add. 34109; Harley Papers, MS Lands. 852; P. J. Dobell, Bromley MS.

A Poem Address'd to the Quidnunc's at St. James's Coffee-House London. Occasion'd by the Death of the Duke of Orleans. 1724.

The Weekly Journal or Saturday's Post. 14 March 1724.

Miscellanies. The Last Volume. 1727 (and later editions).

A Supplement to Dr. Swift's and Mr. Pope's Works. Dublin. 1739.

Miscellanies. The Fourth Volume. Consisting of Verses ... 1742 (and later editions).
The Miscellaneous Works of Mr. John Gay. Vol. IV. 1773.
    Attributed to Pope in Add. transcript, and at various times to Swift and Gay,
but more probably the work of Arbuthnot. See Williams, III 1119.

Lady M. Wortley's Resolve
Imitated.

WHILST thirst of Conquest and desire of Fame
   In ev'ry Age, in ev'ry Mans the same,
Pleas'd with their Wit, of their own folly Proud
Their Wit still commonplace and talking Low'd
On ev'ry Fair bestowing some kind Glance   5
Constring good manners as some loose advance
Whilst thus the Fair is by pert Fops Persu'd
And each call'd willing who's not grossly Rude
Let this great maxim be my conducts Guide.
Never to blast the Fair, to please my Pride   10
And injure thousands tho' by all Denied.

3 their Wit] themselves
7 the Fair] the sex

    Contemporary transcripts: Felbrigg Hall, Windham Papers; and Longleat,
Portland Papers, Vol. XX.
    Lady Mary's *The Resolve* was first printed in *The Plain Dealer*, 1724. This reply
is attributed to Pope by Ashe Windham, whose relations were Pope's neighbours
at Twickenham. The attribution is not impossible, but it should be noted that
Windham was mistaken in attributing *Cosmelia* (p. 438) to Pope, and that in the
Portland transcript the verses are ascribed to "Sir W. Y." (i.e., Yonge). The text
follows the Felbrigg transcript, with collations from the Portland transcript.

SIGNORA DURASTANTI'S CANTATA

Contemporary transcript: BM MS Harl. 7316.
The Daily Journal. Wednesday, 18 March 1724.
The St. James's Evening Post. 17–19 March 1724.
The Weekly Journal. 21 March 1724.
Applebee's Original Weekly Journal. 21 March 1724.
The British Journal. 21 March 1724.
The Universal Journal. 25 March 1724.
The Hive. Vol. III. 1725.
Miscellaneous Poems, By several Hands. J. Ralph. 1729.
Additions to the Works of Alexander Pope, Esq. Vol. I. 1776.
The Works. Ed. Warton. Vol. II. 1797.

"On the 17th at Night Seignora Margaritta Durastanti, sang an English Cantata at the Opera House, it being then her Benefit Night, and she about to leave the Stage and Kingdom"—This report from *The Universal Journal* of Wednesday, 25 March 1724, though not actually the first to appear, is the fullest contemporary description extant of the occasion of this piece, but it should be supplemented with the heading of Lord Oxford's transcript of the cantata: "The following lines were sung by Durastanti when she took her leave of the English Stage. The words were in Haste put together by Mr. Pope at the earnest request of the Earl of Peterborow." So far as is known Pope never owned the piece; and it remained anonymous in every printed copy down to its first attribution to him in *The St James's Chronicle* in 1775, which has hitherto been thought its first printing also. The attribution remains a probability only, for it wholly depends on the Harleian transcript, which—however friendly Pope and Oxford were—lacks the ultimate sanction of the poet's acknowledgement or signature. Yet Pope's friendship with Peterborough was flourishing as early as the August of the previous year, 1723, when he wrote to Swift and mentioned that they were living together. And it would also seem quite in character for Peterborough (who later married another celebrated singer, Anastasia Robinson) to have interested himself so far as to persuade Pope to write a few lines for the occasion. Signora Durastanti had been brought to England by Handel in 1719, to sing in his operas.

THE NIGHTINGALE

Although this poem is ascribed to Pattison, who himself contributed the "Advertisement", in *A New Collection of Poems . . . By Mr. Prior, and Others*, 1725, and was claimed by him in his *Poetical Works*, 1728, it was ascribed to Pope, without evidence, in *The Bouquet*, Vol. II, 1792, and by E. Tomkins in *Poems on Various Subjects*, 1804.

On Miss HARVEY, *being a Day old.*
In Imitation of Mr. P——s.

LITTLE Girl, in Swaddling Cloathes,
Mother's Eyes, and Father's Nose;
Little Mouth, where, on a Row,
White and even Teeth will grow,
And the Dimple on the Chin,   5
Just beginning to begin;
And the Skin so fair and sleek;
And the Roses in the Cheek;
And the Neck, and Milk-white Breast,
Which hereafter shall be prest;   10
And the snowy Hand and Arm,
Which, as yet, can do no Harm;
And the Waste, so small and round,
Little Waste, with Roller bound;
And the taper Leg and Thigh,   15
And what is, and will be, by,
For which Thousand Swains will die.
   Keep her Heav'n from all Harms!
Give her all her Mother's Charms!
Give her all her Father's Wit!   20
Save her from Convulsion Fit!
May her Teeth, with Ease be bred!
May she keep her Maiden-head,
'Till she's in her Bridal Bed.
Then, may she be free from snarling;   25
May she be her Husband's Darling!
May her Days be Peace and Rest;
Like her happy Parents blest!
And may they, my Cares to drown,
Give the Poet Half a Crown.   30

Contemporary transcript: BM MS Add. 32463.

The Whitehall Evening-Post. 11–13 November 1725.

The Flower-Piece. 1731.

Another parody of Ambrose Philips's baby verse. It was published anonymously, and the scribe of MS Add. 32463 ventures no attribution. Swift wrote to Pope, 26 November 1725: "We have had a poem sent from London in imitation of his [A. Philips'] on Miss Carteret. It is on Miss Hervey, of a day old; and we say and think it is yours. I wish it were not, because I am against monopolies." Pope replied, 14 December: "Like the verses on Miss Hervey as well as you will, I am never the better for it; for they are none of mine, but I am much the happier for finding, a better thing than our wits, our judgements jump in the notion that all scribblers should be passed by in silence... So let Gildon and Philips rest in peace!" It is possible to interpret this repudiation equivocally.

An Extempory Distich: Written on a Glass by a Gentleman, who had borrow'd the Earl of C * * * * 's Pencil.

Accept a Miracle instead of Wit;
See two dull Lines by Stanhope's Pencil writ.

BM, Cowper Papers, MS Add. 28101.

The British Journal. 18 June 1726.

A Collection of Epigrams. 1727 (and 2nd Edition, 1735).

Anonymous when first published, and in many subsequent reprints, this distich was given to Pope in the 5th Edition of *Joe Miller's Jests*, 1742, in *The Agreeable Companion*, 1745, and *The Nut-Cracker*, 1751. H. Maty unhesitatingly gave it to Pope in his edition of *The Miscellaneous Works of . . . Chesterfield*, Vol. I, 1777, and Wakefield included it without comment in the canon. The epigram appears twice more as Pope's before the end of the eighteenth century, in *Select Epigrams*, Vol. I, 1797, and with a story of the occasion on which it was made, in Vol. XIII of *Interesting Anecdotes, Memoirs, . . . and Poetical Fragments.* In the Cowper family papers, however, it is entitled, "A Couplet-Extempore—by the Rev^d Mr. Ford at the request of Ld. Chesterfield who lent him his Pencil for that purpose". And in a late-dated "Supplement, 1758" in Spence's *Anecdotes*, 1820, the epigram is said to have been written by Edward Young.

The text follows that of *1726*.

MOLLY MOG
or the Fair Maid of the Inn
A Ballad

Ascribed at various times to Pope and Swift, but largely if not entirely the work of Gay. See Faber, p. 188; Williams, III 1129.

EPIGRAM
On *CELIA*.

D<small>ID</small> *Celia*'s person and her mind agree,
   What mortal could behold her, and be free?
But nature has, in pity to mankind,
Enrich'd the image, and defac'd the mind.

Title Epigram On Celia.] On the Dutchess of Queensberry. *MSS i and ii (with some variation of spelling)*. On the Duchess of Queens—y. *MS iii*; On the D<small>ss</small> of Q—nsb—y, *MS iv 1727 and 1735 omit title; and 1741 reads as printed above.*
1 mind] sense *MS iii.*
3 has] hath *MSS i and ii*; has, in pity] in compassion *MS iv.*
3–4 *1741 reads:*   But Nature, who has all Things well design'd,
            Enrich'd the Body, but deform'd the Mind.
4 and defac'd] but defac'd *MS ii*; but debas't *MS iii*; and deform'd *MS iv.*

Contemporary transcripts: (i) BM MS Stowe 970; (ii) Bodleian MS Ballard 50; (iii) Hist. MSS. Comm. Report 12; Ketton MSS; (iv) BM, Cowper Papers, MS Add. 28101.
A Collection of Epigrams. 1727 [Published 25 November 1726] (and 2nd Edition, 1735).
The attribution of this epigram to Pope depends in part on the witness of three contemporary manuscripts, and in part on the reply it provoked. One of the three manuscript attributions is especially important, namely that in the "Family Miscellany" of the Cowpers, with whom Pope had connections through his correspondence with Judith Cowper in 1722–3. As the *Letters . . . to a Lady* shows, he used occasionally to send unpublished verses to her. This may help to explain the presence in the "Miscellany" of some dozen of his acknowledged or attributed pieces, among which is this epigram inscribed "By A. Pope". All the manuscript versions of the piece, as well as the 1741 printed text, are accompanied by an "Answer" which, in the Stowe MS runs as follows:

A Reply upon Mr. Pope
By Lady Mary Wortley Montague
Had Pope a person equall to his Mind
How fatal wou'd he be to Womankind
But Nature which doth all things well ordain
Defac'd the Image and inrich'd the Brain.

In the other MSS and the 1741 text, however, the second epigram is simply called *The Answer* and, except in the Ketton MS, it begins: "Were Maro's person equal...". But whether Pope is named in the reply or not makes little difference, for the poet described could not easily be mistaken for anyone else; and there is consequently no doubt about the intention of the "answerer" to strike at Pope for having written the original epigram. Lastly, the attribution to Pope may seem to be supported by the idea embodied in the epigram, to which he returned again and again (see *ante*, p. 64) not without some similarity of language. The identification of Celia with the beautiful but somewhat eccentric Catherine Douglas, Duchess of Queensbury, "Prior's Kitty", which is made in all four MSS, may only reflect contemporary gossip (as the ascription of the *Reply* to Lady Mary W. Montagu in the Stowe MS almost certainly does). But if it is correct, the Duchess's real and continued kindness to Pope's best-loved friend, Gay, and Pope's own acquaintance with her, though never very intimate, together suggest that the epigram must have been written before these friendships had become established, i.e. at some date before 1725. It should however be remarked that in all the printed texts the Duchess is not even hinted at, much less named; and also that she was still Kitty Hyde, and still a child, when Pope first touched on this theme—that beauty without sense is worthless (see *ibid.*). The epigram is therefore tentatively dated 1726, in which year it was first printed.

The text follows that of the first printing, with collations from MSS i–iv (see above) and the last version printed in Pope's life-time (*1741*).

Mr. *P*— to Dr. *A*——*t*,
December 19. 1726.

WHILE you, Dear Sir, are clutching Fees,
　　I loll at *Twickenham* at my Ease,
Think little, mind not Right or Wrong,
Or carelessly indite a Song:
Both of us *Phoebus* Patronizes, 　　　　　5
He writes a Bill, or Song devizes;
Thus sometimes witty, sometimes wise is;
And tho' in this there's no great Wit,

By Penny-Post I send you it
Hoping in few Days near Cork-street   }   10
By Word of Mouth my Friend to greet,
And Chat of Trifles when we meet
When Conversation grows quite barren,
We'll talk of *Woman* turn'd to *Warren.*
Strange Metamorphose! strange and new!   15
But what a Knight says must be true,
He scorns like vulgar Folk to speak
He talks in *Latin* and in *Greek*
For Instance: (which you may rely on)
He calls a *Cond——m* a *Corion?*   20
Then wonders how (O Men's *Supina)*
Such things should come into *Vagina.*
You know *Vagina* means a Case,
It is dear Knight a tempting Place,
Where you have shewn great Inclination   25
To bring in Transubstantiation,
Tho' Doctors have no Faith they say,
We find that 'Pothecary may;
O wise, believing, learned Wight!
Apothecary, Doctor, Knight.   30

A——t.
But why of *M——m* this Chat,
Pert Monsieur too deserves a Pat.

P---e.
Of him but little shall be said,   }
I wish a Man so finely bred,
Would use his Heels, and not his Head.   35
Enough of this; now Moralize,
It is your Business to Advise.

A——t.
Hence learn the Ladies have a Place,
That makes the wisest Man an Ass,
Nay even Master *S——y,*   40
Surgeon, Anatomist miscarry,
And puts them to a greater Stand,
Than Fawkes with all his Slight of Hand:
Then change the Proverb, teach the Youth,
Seeing's not Faith, nor Feeling Truth.   45

P---e.
Thus will we then an Hour beguile
We'll prate, and gentle *G——y* shall smile.

Contemporary transcripts: BM MS Lansd. 852 and MS Add. 31152; and Longleat, Portland Papers, Vol. XX.

The Flying-Post: or Post-master. 5–7 January 1727.

This epistle was obviously inspired by *The Discovery* (see p. 259) which was to be published on the following day. It would therefore appear that the *Song* (mentioned in ll. 4–9) was sent with the epistle, either in the form of a transcript, or, more probably, an advance copy of the morrow's publication.

It is interesting to compare these lines to Arbuthnot with the two early rhymed epistles to Cromwell, especially the earlier (see *ante*, pp. 24, 39); and to note how the same high spirits called for the same technique—the acrobatic rhymes, the ridiculous puns, the mock pedantry, and the recurring triplets; and to remember that those two epistles had for the first time been published by Curll in Pope's letters to Cromwell only a few months earlier, 26 July (*The Post-Boy*), and had thus been recently recalled to Pope's memory. Indeed, when writing to Caryll on 5 December he went on to talk of the Cromwell letters after speaking of the rabbit-woman. The evidence, though not conclusive, may be thought to point to Pope's authorship.

The text follows the printed version.

EPIGRAM *PAPAL.*
On the Female Canticle.

As the three Children late in Council sate,
   And after many a long and warm Debate:
Well then! said *Ananias*, to his Brother,
Must this Song serve? Or, shall we look another?
In Troth, reply'd the gentle *Misael*,   5
My Lady has perform'd it pretty well;
Then let it stand; cry'd the bold *Azarias*,
But,—Gad! She'll get no Reputation by *Us*.

Contemporary transcript: Bodleian MS Rawl. letters 90.
Miscellanea. In Two Volumes. Vol. I. 1727 [1726].

The measure of Pope's responsibility for this epigram is uncertain. Although it is attributed to him by Curll in the table of contents of *Miscellanea*, the Bodleian MS itself is endorsed by Curll "This is Mr Cromwell's Handwriting." Though more than one contemporary paraphrase of the Song of the Three Children has survived, that which occasioned this epigram has not been discovered.

EPITAPH

"When purer Skies recal the kinder Ray ..."
"As she was once, few of her Sex you'll see ..."

Contemporary transcripts: B. Halliday; P. J. Dobell, Bromley MS.
The British Journal. No. 242. 6 May 1727.
Miscellaneous Poems on Several Occasions. By Mr. Dawson, &c. 1735 (omits ll. 7–10).
The Publick Register: or, The Weekly Magazine. No. V. 31 January 1741.

Anonymous on each appearance in print, this epitaph ("As she was once") is described in both manuscripts as "Mr. Pope's Epitaph on Mrs. Mary Digby", where it is accompanied (as in *The British Journal*) by an introductory poem, "To a young Lady, occasioned by a Request of some of her Friends who desired to see her Epitaph before she dy'd" ("When purer Skies"). No evidence for the attribution is offered; against it is the existence of an authentic epitaph on Mary Digby (p. 313), the unlikelihood of Pope writing two, and the existence of the poem in print two years before Mary's death.

BALLAD: "NELLY"

Miscellanies. The Last Volume. 1727 (and later editions).
The Choice. Vol. II. 1733.
The Vocal Miscellany. Vol. I. 2nd Edition. 1734 (and 3rd Edition, 1738).
A Supplement to Dr. Swift's and Mr. Pope's Works. Dublin. 1739.
Miscellanies. The Fourth Volume. Consisting of Verses ... 1742 (and later editions).

Attributed, without evidence or much probability, to Pope by Lady Oxford and her daughter in both copies of *Miscellanies* 1731 at Welbeck, this ballad is more likely to be the work of Arbuthnot or Gay. See Faber, pp. xxiv, 642; W. H. Irving, *John Gay*, 1940, p. 173.

EPIGRAM ON THE FEUDS BETWEEN HANDEL AND BONONCINI

First published anonymously in *Miscellanies. The Last Volume*, 1727. Though it is now generally given to John Byrom, it was included in Roscoe's edition of Pope and in several subsequent editions.

SONGS FROM
THE BEGGAR'S OPERA

Ayre (ii 115–16) asserts that much of the success of *The Beggar's Opera* "was owing to the Squibs that were thrown at the Court . . . many of which, of right appertain'd to Mr. *Pope*." In this he was anticipated by Broome writing to Fenton, 3 May 1728: "I doubt not . . . but those lines against courts and ministers are drawn, at least aggravated, by Mr. Pope, who delights to paint every man in the worst colours. He wounds from behind Gay, and like Teucer in Homer . . . shoots his arrows lurking under the shield of Ajax." Ayre continues, "The Song of *Peachum*, the Thief-catcher, ["Thro' all the Employments of Life"] . . . before it was alter'd by Mr. *Pope*, was not so sharp . . . and the Song of *Mackeath* after his being taken ["Since Laws were made"] was wholly added by Mr. *Pope*." These attributions were repeated by Warton (ix 99) and by Henry Angelo, *Reminiscences* (1828), p. 25, who asserts that the last two lines of Peachum's song "stood in Gay's manuscript"

> And there's many arrive to be Great,
> By a Trade not more honest than mine,

but were altered by Pope to read

> And the Statesman, because he's so great,
> Thinks his Trade is as honest as mine.

Pope, however, twice denied that he had any hand in it, except to "alter an expression here and there" (Spence, pp. 145, 159).

An Answer to What is Love

L OVE's no irregular desire,
    No sudden start or raging pain,
That in a moment turns to fire,
    And in a moment cools again.

Carruthers reports that he has found "the following in some of the Miscellanies ascribed to 'Mr. Pope'." It is ascribed to "Mr Harvey" in BM MS Stowe 972; but on its first appearance in print in Ralph's *Miscellaneous Poems*, 1729, and on the five subsequent appearances which have been traced, it was anonymous.

EPITAPH.

From the Latin in St. BOTOLPH'*S*, ALDERSGATE.

The Post-Boy. 30 January 1730.
The Universal Spectator. 31 January 1730.
The Grub-street Journal. (No. 5) 5 February 1730.
The Universal Spectator. 7 February 1730.
The Grub-street Journal. (No. 6) 12 February 1730.
Faithful Memoirs of the Grubstreet Society. 1732.
Memoirs of the Society of Grub-street. 1737.
The European Magazine. November 1787.
The occasion of these verses is told in the words of *The European Magazine.*

The Rev. Mr. Freeman, Curate of St. Botolph's, Aldersgate, having ob-
served the following lines upon a monument on the South side of the Chancel
there, which he could not find copied either in *Stow, Weever,* or *Le Neve,* was so
kind as to communicate them to us, as worthy the perusal of the learned part
of our readers.—But there is so much expressed in so few words, the Latin is so
concise, and the sense so full, that we beg to be excused attempting a trans-
lation of them in English. The verses are these:

> Hic conjuncta suo recubat Francisca marito;
> Et cinis est unus, qua fuit una caro.
> Huc cineres conferre suos soror Anna jubebat;
> Corpora sic uno pulvere trina jacent.
> Sic Opifex rerum Omnipotens; qui, trinus et unus,
> Pulvere ab hoc uno corpora trina dabit.

Upon reading this paragraph Mr. Pope immediately undertook the task,
and has literally rendered them as follows:

> Close to her husband, Frances, join'd once more,
> Lies here; *one* dust, which was *one* flesh before:
> Here, as injoin'd, her sister Anne's remains
> Were laid: *one* dust, *three* bodies thus contains.
> Th' Almighty Source of things, the immense *Three-One,*
> Will raise *three* bodies from this dust alone.

EPIGRAMS
from
THE GRUB-STREET JOURNAL.
1730–1731

The Grub-street Journal. 24 December 1730 [I, II]; 8 April 1731 [III].
The Windsor Medley. 3rd Edition. 1731 [II].
A Collection of Pieces . . . publish'd on Occasion of the Dunciad . . . By Mr. Savage. 1732 [I, II, III].
Faithful Memoirs of the Grub-street Society. 1732 [I, II, III].
Memoirs of the Society of Grub-street. 1737 [I, II, III].
Joe Miller's Jests. 5th Edition, 1742 (and later edd.) [II].
The Life of Alexander Pope. By R. Carruthers. 2nd Edition, 1857 [III].
The Poetical Works. Ed. Carruthers. 1858 [I, II].

I.
ANSWER to an EPIGRAM

printed in the *S. James's Evening-Post*, Sat. *Dec.* 12. and ending
Admire a VIRGIL, *and disdain a* POPE.

IF none must be admir'd but Poets born,
  Admire a HOMER, and a VIRGIL scorn;
Admire a HORACE, and contemn BOILEAU;
Admire a DRYDEN, and despise a ROWE.
But if on such as these with scorn we look;
What must be done to W—D, T—D, C—K?   5
Scorn were too little from each honest Briton;
These should be pump'd, duck'd pillory'd, pist, and sh— on.

II.
A Question by ANONYMOUS.

TELL, if you can, which did the worse,
  Caligula or Gr—n's Gr—ce?
That made a Consul of a Horse,
  And this a Laureate of an Ass.

III.

On Mr. JAMES MOORE's pretty Verses on the Birth-day of the Lord ANDOVER.

WHAT makes for once, Squire JEMMY's Muse so toward?
Mere joy to see a Cousin of NED HOWARD.

Title] *1731 and 1732 continue thus :* . . . Andover, printed in our last Journal.

I. *An Answer to an Epigram*] This epigram, signed "A", in the *Memoirs*, 1737, seems to have roused some protest on its original publication. Its last couplet was facetiously defended in the *Journal* (18 February 1731) in a letter signed "Bavius" which, even if not by Pope, as Carruthers averred, was almost certainly written with his collaboration (the signature "Bavius" is explained in the note to epigram VI, see p. 331). This letter, when first printed, ended by quoting—as a last excuse—from the "Longitude" piece, in the composition of which Pope's hand has been suspected (see p. 415). His authorship of the epigram is possible. The text follows that of its first printing, *1730*, with which the *1732* and *1737* "Grub-street" reprints verbally agree.

6. *W—d, T—d, C—k.*] Doubtless Welsted, Tibbald (Theobald), Cook, for whom see Biog. App., Vol. IV.

II. *A Question by Anonymous.*] The publication of this epigram within three weeks of Cibber's appointment as Poet Laureate on 3 December 1730, sufficiently indicates its subject. But the author cannot be identified with equal certainty. When, however, after several unascribed reprintings the epigram appeared in the 1737 *Memoirs*, it was signed "A" (see p. 325); and, since 1858, Carruthers's attribution of it to Pope has been generally accepted. The attribution is probably correct, supported as it is by the witness of date and occasion (see notes to Nos. V and VI, pp. 330, 331), and by Pope's well-known attitude towards Cibber's Laureateship. The text follows that of the first printing, *1730*, with which *1732* and *1737* are in verbal agreement.

2. *Gr—n's Gr—ce*] His Grace the Duke of Grafton, who as Lord Chamberlain, was responsible for Cibber's appointment.

III. *On Mr. James Moore's pretty Verses*] This couplet, subscribed "A" in the *Memoirs*, 1737 (see p. 325) concludes the attacks on Moore Smythe. It harks back to a short article which quoted some "pretty Verses" said to have been written by Moore Smythe, and by him "repeated the other day at an entertainment made on account of the Birth-day of the young Lord Andover, son to the Earl of Berkshire"—which article, because it and the couplet are printed together over the signature "A" in 1737 (thereby correcting their original, and separate, ascription to "Bavius": see note to No. VI, p. 331), has also been laid to Pope's credit. The "Ned Howard" of the epigram has been, not too convincingly, identified with the Hon. Edward Howard (fl. 1669), a Restoration playwright, whom Pope is supposed to have classified as an "Ostridge" in *The Art of Sinking* (chap. VI); but the significance of his cousinship with the young Lord Andover, and, therefore, the point of the epigram (possibly the charge of snobbery) has vanished. The text is that of the first printing, *1731*, with which the "Grub-street" reprints of *1732* and *1737* verbally agree.

DAWLEY Farm.

'Tis sung, that, exil'd by Tyrannick *Jove*,
    Apollo, from the starry Realms above,
To Silvan Shades, to Grots and Streams retir'd,
And that new Scene and that new State admir'd;
Admir'd, but found (with Pleasure and Surprize)   5
Himself the same on Earth as in the Skies;
A simple Majesty, and easy Grace
Compos'd his Steps, and lighten'd in his Face;
The wond'ring Swains and Nymphs, wheree'er he trod,
At Distance gaz'd, and recogniz'd the God;   10
Wheree'er he pass'd, the World his Infl'ence knew,
And Learning, Arts, and Wisdom, round him grew.
Still, tho' in silent Privacy, he gave
His wonted Aid; inspir'd the Wise and Brave;
Taught Patriots Policy; taught Poets Sense;   15
And bade all live, or die, in LIBERTY's Defence.
    Sure this is verify'd: What here we view
In B—GB—E, has made the Fiction true.
    See! Emblem of himself, his *Villa* stand!
Politely finish'd, regularly Grand!   20
Frugal of Ornament, but that the best,
And all with curious Negligence express'd.
No gaudy Colours stain the Rural Hall,
Blank Light and Shade discriminate the Wall:
Where thro' the Whole we see his lov'd Design,   25
To please with Mildness, without Glaring shine;
Himself neglects what must all others charm,
And what he built a Palace calls a *Farm*.
Here the proud Trophies, and the Spoils of War
Yield to the Scythe, the Harrow and the Car;   30
To whate'er Implement the Rustick wields,
Whate'er manures the Garden, or the Fields.
Contraste of Scenes! Behold a worthless Tool,

A dubb'd Plebeian, Fortune's Fav'rite Fool,
Laden with publick Plunder, loll in State, 35
'Midst dazling Gems, and Piles of massy Plate,
'Midst Arms, and Kings, and Gods and Heroes quaff,
His Wit all ending in an Ideot Laugh;
Whilst Noble *St. J*— in his sweet Recess,
(By those made greater who would make him less) 40
Sees, on the figur'd Wall, the Stacks of Corn
With Beauty more than theirs the Room adorn,
Young winged *Cupids* smiling guide the Plough,
And Peasants elegantly reap and sow.
The *Mantuan* Genius, thus, in rural Strains, 45
Adds Grace to Cotts, and Dignity to Swains,
Makes *Phœbus'* self partake the Farmer's Toil,
And all the Muses cultivate the Soil.
While free of Heart, and eloquent of Tongue,
His Speech, as tuneful as that Heav'nly Song, 50
Suspends in Rapture each attentive Guest;
Words more delicious than his gen'rous Feast;
Wit more inspiring than his flowing Bowl;
The Feast of Reason, and the Flow of Soul.
  O *Britain*!—But 'tis past—O lost to Fame! 55
The wond'rous Man, thy Glory, and thy Shame,
Conversing with the mighty Minds of old,
Names like his own, in Time's bright Lists inroll'd,
Here splendidly obscure, delighted lives,
And only for his wretched Country grieves. 60
While Thou, ingrate, infatuate, as thou art,
Of thy mad Conduct long shalt feel the Smart,
Long mourn the Folly which thy Weal destroys,
And rue the blest Retirement he enjoys.

Fog's Weekly Journal. No. 138. 26 June 1731.
The Gentleman's Magazine. June 1731 [published 3 July].
Select Letters taken from Fog's Weekly Journal. Vol. II. 1732.
Mr. Pope's Literary Correspondence. Vol. V. 1737.

This poem was originally introduced as follows:

To the Author of *Fog's* Journal.   *Oxford, June* 20.

SIR, I am one of those who, having lived a College Life, perhaps, will be
thought better acquainted with Books than with Men, yet I have pass'd some
Time lately in *London*, where I have convers'd indifferently with Men of all
Principles and Parties, and my own Temper of Mind made me pass rather for a
Looker-on than a Party in any of our political Disputes; but, however I made

this observation, that two or three Gentlemen, who are continually loaded with
Abuse by certain Writers, who stile themselves the well-affected, are the Per-
sons who have the warm Hearts of the People, the Persons with whose Praises
all Mouths are fill'd, and this I will venture to assert, that I never heard so
many kind Wishes poured out for the Prosperity of any Men, as for these, who
are so basely treated by these *reputed Hirelings*.

I will not tell you what Reflections this Observation rais'd in me;—perhaps
you wou'd not think it prudent to communicate them to the World, if I
shou'd; I will only inform you, that, in my Return to this Place, I pass'd within
a Mile of a fine Seat, which I was prevailed upon, by a Fellow Student, who
accompanied me, to go to see; I was so charm'd with the beautiful Simplicity
that appear'd in the House and Gardens, and so captivated with the good
Sense, and easy Politeness of its Owner, to whom I was introduced by my Com-
panion (who had the Honour of his Acquaintance) that it produced the fol-
lowing Lines, which are at your Service, if you think fit to publish them.

The attribution to Pope was first made in *The Hyp-Doctor* (9 November 1731):
"We are told, that Mr. *P—e* wrote the Poem call'd *The Dawley Farm*, and the
Norfolk Steward, besides several Letters in *Fog* and the *Craftsman* . . .". Griffith
(I 193), referring to this ascription, points to the general subject matter of the
poem, and to the presence of a couplet (ll. 53–4) the second line of which is
identical with *Imit. Hor.*, *Sat.* II i 128—"The Feast of Reason and the Flow of
Soul"— and continues: "Pope had taken James Moore Smythe so sharply to task
about a few borrowed verses in 1727–8 [see *ante*, p. 303] that he could hardly
hope to escape censure in 1733 if he appropriated another poet's line when both
poems are a compliment to the same famous man." Further confirmation of
Pope's authorship may be seen in the number of echoes of his work to be found in
these lines (examples of which are included in the footnotes); besides which there
are passages to be noted in his correspondence. Thus he wrote to Swift from
Dawley (28 June 1728): "I overheard [Bolingbroke] yesterday agree with a
painter for 200*l.* to paint his country-hall with trophies of rakes, spades, prongs,
&c., and other ornaments, merely to countenance his calling this place a farm,"
and to Bathurst (7 November 1728): "Lord Bolingbroke and I commemorated
you in our cups one day at Dawley,—farm I should say, and accordingly there
are all the insignia and instruments of husbandry painted now in the hall, that
one could wish to see in the fields of the most industrious farmer in christendom."
And it may further be noted, for what it is worth, that Curll included the poem
without comment in the final volume of *Mr. Pope's Literary Correspondence*, 1737. It
would also seem more than a coincidence that, in the covering letter (an obvious
fiction), the student's attitude to party politics is the same as that which Pope
declared his own to be,—which probably explains why such a panegyric of his
politically outlawed friend was printed anonymously. That the poem was
explosive matter is shown by an attack, on both the writer and the subject of it, in
The Weekly Register (10 July 1731), addressed *To the Author of a Poem intituled,
Dawley Farm, printed in Fog's Journal*. Similarly, when Pope transferred the couplet

praising Bolingbroke to the first *Imitation of Horace*, it immediately called forth the following attack in *The St. James's Evening Post* (1–3 March 1733):

To *Alexander Pope*, Esq.

When you, a Traitor to his Prince, commend,
To Virtue and her Friends you're not a Friend.
In this both Whig and Tory do agree,
A Truth so glaring all the World must see.
Christ was betray'd, and Man from Sin redeem'd;
Yet Judas ne'er by Christian was esteem'd;
Nor would a Jew prepare the Friendly Bowl,
To mingle with the Flow of such a Soul.

It is probable that the famous line, and therefore the poem originally containing it, were Pope's by creation and not by capture. The text follows that of the first printing.

[Thus Mr Ault. For evidence to the contrary, see Robert W. Rogers, *The Major Satires of Alexander Pope* (1955), p. 72. I am reluctant to credit Pope with such unpolished verse.]

9–12. *wheree'er . . . wheree'r*] Pope used this idea more than once; cf. *Summer*, 73–76: Where'er you walk, cool gales shall fan the glade . . .
Where'er you tread, the blushing flowers shall rise,
And all things flourish where you turn your eyes.

Where'er he passed, a purple stream pursued (*Iliad*, x 560).

He had been anticipated by Cowley (*The Spring*, 17):
Where'er you walked trees were as reverend made.

18. *B—gb—e*] Henry St John, Viscount Bolingbroke (see Biog. App., Vol. IV).

26. Cf. *Ep. to Jervas*, 66: "Soft without weakness, without glaring gay".

28. Cf. Pope's letter to Swift, 28 June 1728, quoted above.

53f. Cf. *Imit. Hor.*, *Sat.* II i 127–8:
There *St. John* mingles with my friendly Bowl,
The Feast of Reason and the Flow of Soul.

56. *thy Glory, and thy Shame*] Cf. "The glory of the Priesthood, and the shame" (*Ess. on Criticism*, 694); also: "A Tale, that blends their glory with their shame" (*Essay on Man*, IV 308).

TO MR POPE

The Grub-street Journal. No. 104. 30 December 1731.

This is a panegyric on Pope's poetry. An anonymous writer in *The Weekly Register*, 26 August 1732, affecting to believe that it was written by Pope himself, turned it into satire in some verses entitled "A proper Addition to some Verses in the *Grub-street Journal*, of *December* the 30th, 1731, written in Honour of Mr. *P—e*, by himself. By a Friend."

Translations
of
Atterbury's Lines on Himself.

> —*Hæc ego lusi*
> *Ad Sequanæ ripas, Thamesino a flumine longe,*
> *Jam senior, fractusque; sedet ipsâ morte meorum*
> *Quos colui, patriæque memor, nec degener usquam.*
>
> Atterbury.

Englished in blank verse:

> —Thus on the banks of Seine,
> Far from my native home, I pass my hours,
> Broken with years and pain; yet my firm heart
> Regards my friends and country e'en in death.

Also in couplets:

> Thus where the Seine through realms of slavery strays,
> With sportive verse I wing my tedious days,
> Far from Britannia's happy climate torn,
> Bow'd down with age, and with diseases worn;
> Yet e'en in death I act a steady part,
> And still my friends and country share my heart.

The Grub-street Journal. 22 June 1732.
Mr. Pope's Literary Correspondence. Vol. II. 1735 (and 2nd Edition, 1735).
A General Dictionary. P. Bayle. Vol. II. 1735.
Memoirs of the Society of Grub-street. Vol. II. 1737.
The Poetical Calendar. August 1763 [the blank verse lines only].
The Life of Alexander Pope. By R. Carruthers. 2nd Edition. 1857.

An article in *The Grub-street Journal* on Atterbury concludes: ". . . Let this last action of his [Atterbury's] life cast a veil upon his errors in sentiment or conduct, and induce us to think as favourably of them as we can; since it is a proof of his title, in some degree, at least, to the character he gave of himself in those lines prefixed to his Translation of Virgil's Georgics, which were lately published in most of the News Papers. With these I shall conclude my discourse; adding two translations, one literal in blank verse, and the other paraphrastical in rhime, communicated to our Society by one of our ingenious Correspondents." Taking Pope's relations both with Atterbury and the *Journal* into account, it is not unlikely that he was responsible for at least the paraphrastical translation.

PROLOGUE TO *ACHILLES*

Achilles. An Opera . . . Written by the late Mr. Gay. 1733.
See *New Light*, pp. 215–21.

A LOVE SONG
In the Modern Taste
1733

The Gentleman's Magazine. June 1733.
The Vocal Miscellany. Vol. II. 1734.
A Complete Collection of Old and New English and Scotch Songs. Vol. II. 1735.
Miscellanies, In Prose and Verse. Vol. V. 1735 (and 1745).
The Works of J.S. . . . Faulkner's Edition. Vol. II. 1735 (and 2nd Edition, 1737).
The British Musical Miscellany. Vol. VI. 1736.
The Works. Ed. Warburton. Vol. VI. 1751 (and included by every editor of Pope's works down to 1924).

In spite of being attributed to Swift on first publication and of appearing in an edition of his works which he partly overlooked, this poem has been accepted as Pope's by most editors since Warburton included it without evidence in the canon. Williams (II 660) accepts it as Swift's.

MEMORIÆ SACRUM
D.M.T. E.B. & L.P.

The Grub-street Journal. (No. 205) 29 November 1733.
The Grub-street Journal. By J. T. Hillhouse. 1928.

Attributed by Hillhouse (p. 138) without evidence to Pope. The epigram seems too crude in rhythm for Pope's work.

AN ODE FOR THE NEW YEAR

An Ode for the New Year. Written by Colley Cibber, Esq; Poet Laureat. [An undated quarto broadside, *c.* 1733; two issues with different ornaments.]
See *New Light*, pp. 315–22.

A LETTER
FROM THE WORLD TO COME

"Stript to the naked soul, escap'd from clay"

First printed in Aaron Hill's periodical *The Prompter*, VIII (1734), and reprinted in his *Works* (1753) iv 153. It is ascribed to Pope in *The Poetical Calendar*, December 1763 (p. 60), and with some show of circumstance by Ruffhead (p. 408), on whose authority, presumably, it was admitted to the canon by Warton.

WOMAN CONVINC'D

Being an Epistle supposed to be written by a certain great Poet, and inscrib'd to a very pretty Lady, [an intolerable Wit!] and which Epistle was, by her very great Lord, forbid to be printed; so that, had not this little, diminutive, Very Great Poet [luckily] preserv'd a Copy of this Epistle deliver'd in MS. the Publick had intirely lost the Benefit of reading so mere a Trifle.

The St. James's Register: or, Taste A-la-Mode. 1736.
There is no internal or external evidence to support the implied attribution to Pope.

THE FOURTH EPISTLE OF THE FIRST BOOK OF HORACE'S EPISTLES

A Modern Imitation. By A. P. of Twickenham, Esq.

This squib, purporting to be addressed by Pope to Bolingbroke, was published in April 1738. Though patently a reply by some government hack to Pope's *Imitation of the First Epistle of the First Book of Horace*, it imposed upon the editor of *Additions* 1776, and upon Anderson and Chalmers, who all included it in the canon.

ON AN OLD GATE
Brought from Chelsea to Chiswick

The Historical Manuscripts Commission. R. R. Hastings MSS. III. 1934.
The Edinburgh Magazine and Review. June 1775.
The Poems of Pope. Vol. II (in Johnson's *English Poets*). 1790.
First found as a postscript to a letter from William Kent to Selina, Countess of Huntingdon, 25 September 1739, and first attributed to Pope, without evidence, in *The Edinburgh Magazine*. It is not in Pope's manner, and it may be thought that, if it had been his, so close a friend as Kent would have known this and mentioned it to Lady Huntingdon.

THE GARDEN OF EDEN

A Collection of Original Poems. S. Derrick. 1755.
Attributed without evidence or much probability to Pope.

EPITAPH

S ᴇᴇ here, nice Death, to please his palate,
Takes a young Lettuce for a sallad.

This epitaph is recorded in his diary, 1 January 1760, by William Stukeley (1687–1765), a friend of Warburton, with the following preface: "A gentleman desir'd Mʳ Pope to give him an epitaph for his daʳ *Lætitia* of 3 years old. He gave him this." A variant, also ascribed to Pope, is printed in *The Fugitive Miscellany*, I, 1775, and *The Flower Piece*, 1780. The story is recorded too late and with too little circumstance for the ascription to be confidently accepted. See *New Light*, p. 336.

ODE ON SCIENCE

Published in Swift's *Works*, 1762, VIII 174, but disclaimed by Williams (III 1152). Roscoe (*Works*, 1824, III 338) thought that "to judge from the style, [it] is not unlikely to have been the work of Pope," an opinion which does not command assent.

LINES.

W ʜʏ shine thine Eyes, bright Maid, with rays severe?
Whence spring those sorrows, and why falls that tear?
O! let not headstrong Passion's giddy storm
Eclipse thy virtues, and thy charms deform!
Quick to thy ruffled breast, ah! call again   5
Reason's calm aid, and Pity's gentle train;
Then shall fair peace thy beating bosom guide,
Each tumult vanish, and each grief subside.
So when some lucid brook, with rushing force,
Pours through the craggy rocks its downward course,   10
A while disturb'd the frothy current flows,
Breaks on the stones, and murmurs as it goes;
But should it through the lowly valley stray,
In fainter sounds those murmurs die away;
Through the clear wave the scaly nations gleam,   15
And silver moon-beams glitter in the stream.

The Royal Magazine. June 1762.
The Scots Magazine. June 1762.
This poem was first printed with the following introduction:

SIR,—Looking over some papers lately, which formerly belonged to the celebrated Mr. Pope, I found the enclosed fragment in his hand-writing . . .

Nothing more has been discovered about the poem. The attribution is not impossible.

DIALOGUE ON A BIRTH-DAY
IN OCTOBER

The St. James's Magazine. February 1763.
A parody of Ambrose Philips's baby verse, ascribed to Pope, without evidence or probability, on first publication.

ON THE BRIDGE AT BLENHEIM

"The minnows as thro' this vast arch they pass . . ."

Contemporary transcripts: BM MS Lansd. 852; and MS Add. 28101.
The Festoon. 2nd Edition. 1767 (and later editions).
Select Epigrams. Vol. II. 1797.
Attributed to Pope without evidence by Richard Graves.

SONG

"Say Phoebe, why is gentle Love . . ."

The Scots Magazine. October 1769.
The New Foundling Hospital for Wit . . . Part the Fourth. 1771 (and later editions).
The Annual Register. Vol. XII.
Attributed to Pope on first publication and admitted to the canon without argument by Wakefield, but not reprinted by later editors.

FRIENDSHIP

"The world, my dear Myra, is full of deceit . . ."

The Modern Syren; or, Enchanting Songstress. 1781.
Attributed to Pope on first publication without evidence or probability.

EPIGRAM.

L o! Surrey's Lord, *that* Chappel quits,
   Where Priests dull Masses chant,
And in *St. Stephen's Chappel* sits,
   A zealous Protestant.

But since called up by Fate's Decree,   5
   The Upper House to enter,
A further Reformation see!
   His Grace becomes *Dissenter.**

* *This Word is supposed to allude to a Protest in the House of Lords, at the Head of
which is always placed the Word* Dissentient.

The St. James's Chronicle. (No. 4067) 24–27 March 1787.
The epigram is thus introduced:

Looking over some old Manuscripts, given me many Years ago, which were
said to be Fragments of the late Mr. Pope, I found the following Epigram,
which, perhaps, was prophetical, the Terms Prophet and Poet being among
the Ancients equivocal, and *Vates* signified in Latin, either a Poet or a Prophet.
Some of your Readers, versed in our History, may be able to tell us what these
Lines allude to . . .

CELIA

"Celia we know is sixty-five . . ."

The Works of Alexander Pope. (Aldine Edition). Ed. Dyce. Vol. III. 1831.
Attributed to Pope without evidence by Dyce and included in all subsequent
editions. No trace of the poem has been found in eighteenth-century books and
manuscripts.

ADDENDA

In the William Andrews Clark Memorial Library, University of California at Los Angeles, there is an undated "fair copy" manuscript of *On Silence* in Pope's hand. It is printed here for the first time by kind permission of the Director.

Upon Silence in Imitation of a Modern Poem on Nothing

Silence! thou primitive parent even to thought
Thy work er'e Nature was begun was wroght
Behind, and just behind; thy Elder Brother thought

(2)
Yet o're that mighty nothing thou didst reign
(Before rude Chaos broke thy easy chain)
And held'st o're chaos self a short liv'd Sway again.

(3)
Great breathing space! er'e time commenc'd with Earth,
Er'e fruitfull Thought conceivd Creations Birth
Or Midwife word gave aid and spake the Infant forth

(4)
Opposing Elements against thee joyn'd
And a long Race to break thy sway combin'd,
(Whom Elements compos'd) the Race of human kind

(5)
When thought thy captive offspring thou didst free
Whisper a soft Deserter stole from thee
And rebell Speech disturb'd thy Midnight Majesty

(6)
Then wanton Sence began abroad to go
And gawdy Science drest himself to shew
And wicked Witt arose thy most abusive foe.

(7)
But noisy witt deserts thee oft in vain
And in the wilds of speech he turns again
And seeks a surer state, and Courts thy gentler Reign

16 463

(8)

Opressed Sence, thou kindly dost set free,
Fatigu'd with argumentall Tyranny
And routed Reason finds a safe Retreat in thee

(9)

With thee in private Modest Dulness lyes
And in thy Bosom lurks in Thoughts disguise
Thou Varnisher of fools, and Cheat of all the Wise

(10)

Yet on both sides thy kindness is confest
Folly by thee lyes sleeping in the Breast
And 'tis in thee att last that Wisdom seeks for Rest

(11)

Thou Cloak of Vice that hid'st the Rascals name
Thou only Honor of the wishing Dame
Thy very want of Tongue makes thee a kind of Fame

(12)

But could'st thou seize some tongues that now are free
How Church and State would be oblig'd to thee
In Senate and att Bar how welcom woulds thou be

(13)

Yet speech thy Foe submissively withdraws
From Rights of Subjects and the Poor mans Cause
And Silence then in Pomp sits nodding ore the Laws

(14)

The Country's witt the Policy o'th Town
A Courtiers learning, Citts Religion
Are best by thee expressd and shine in thee alone

(15)

As Sleep and Night all disproportion quitt
So do'st thou equall sence, and art to witt
(What nothing is to man) both source and end of it.

(16)

Thou bashfull Goddes stop'st my weak essays
Thou fo[r]cest me too, and whilst my voice I raise
Thou fliest disturbd away and does avoid my Praise

ADDITIONAL NOTE TO *The Court Ballad*, p. 181, l. 24

The lady whose name is variously spelt Buckenburg, Pickenburg, and Pique-bourg was Sophie C. de Lippe, Countess of Bucquenbourg, as appears from a letter written by her to Craggs (preserved in the Tickell family papers) asking for an allocation of South Sea stock. Gay met her at the court of Hanover in August 1714 and recorded her kindness to him. She accompanied the Princess of Wales to England as lady-in-waiting. Perhaps it was owing to Gay's influence that her name appears amongst the subscribers to Pope's *Homer*. See *Letters of Swift to Ford*, ed. D. Nichol Smith (1935), p. 223.

ADDITIONAL NOTE TO *To Mr Addison, Occasioned by his Dialogues on Medals*, p. 206

A contemporary transcript of this poem, preserved in the Tickell family papers, may perhaps have been a copy of what Tickell, the editor of Addison's *Works* (1721), sent to press on Pope's behalf. It records variant, and presumably earlier, readings for ll. 69–71, as follows:

> Who sought nor public Praise, nor private end,
> Who broke no Promise, and who lost no Friend,
> Both by his Country, and his King approv'd.

Apart from l. 56 which in the transcript reads "And foreign Conquests stamp'd on foreign Gold", these are the only variants of substance between this version and *1721*. It would seem, however, that Pope made more extensive alterations in proof, since the pages on which the poem is printed in *1721* are cancels, and since a balance sheet (also preserved in the Tickell papers) shows that Tonson charged Tickell £3 4s. od. for "2 Cancell'd Leaves occasion'd by Mr Popes Alterations". Here at any rate is proof that Pope supervised the text of a poem appearing in a volume for which he was not otherwise responsible. I am indebted to Major-General Sir Eustace Tickell for a sight of these documents.

ADDITIONAL NOTE TO *Mrs M. B. on her Birth-day*, p. 244.

In "Two New Holographs of Pope's Birthday Lines to Martha Blount" (*Rev. of Eng. Stud.*, n.s., VIII (1957), 234–48), R. M. Schmitz published the text of the hitherto unknown autograph manuscript in the Pierpont Morgan Library. It appears to be the draft from which Pope made the fair copy sent to Martha Blount (Mapledurham MS). Another holograph is that contained in Pope's letter to Judith Cowper, 13 July 1723 (*Correspondence*, ed. Sherburn, ii 180) owned by Mr Arthur A. Houghton, Jr.

INDEX OF FIRST LINES

INDEX

Entries in italic type refer to passages in the notes. Poems attributed to Pope follow the canonical writings. P throughout signifies Pope.